# THE CONSTITUTION AND CRIMINAL JUDICIAL PROCESS

## Second Edition

**LAURIE KUBICEK**

PROFESSOR, DIVISION OF CRIMINAL JUSTICE
CALIFORNIA STATE UNIVERSITY, SACRAMENTO

WITH CONTRIBUTIONS FROM

**JENNIFER C. NOBLE**

ASSOCIATE PROFESSOR, DIVISION OF CRIMINAL JUSTICE
CALIFORNIA STATE UNIVERSITY, SACRAMENTO

WEST
ACADEMIC
PUBLISHING

© 2018 LEG, Inc. d/b/a West Academic
© 2022 LEG, Inc. d/b/a West Academic
     444 Cedar Street, Suite 700
     St. Paul, MN 55101
     1-877-888-1330

West, West Academic Publishing, and West Academic are trademarks of West Publishing Corporation, used under license.

Printed in the United States of America

**ISBN:** 978-1-63659-632-7

To my students, may this work inspire your passion for law and justice.

# Acknowledgments

No one can complete a project like this alone. The scope of this text necessitated the input and expertise of many and I am grateful to have found incredibly talented people willing to join me in the journey.

Thank you to my editor, Megan Putler and her conscientious and professional staff at West Academic.

I want to extend my deepest gratitude to my Sac State family. My colleagues are the hardest working people I know. They are exceptional teachers and scholars with a passion to bring out the best in every student. To my students, thank you for sharing your stories with me and investing your time and talent in each class.

I am so grateful for the opportunity to continue to work with Jennifer Noble in the development and writing of this second edition. It is better because of her contributions and the enthusiasm she continues to bring to this project.

Along the way I have leaned on many friends, family and colleagues for personal and professional support. I apologize that time and space does not allow the opportunity to say more about each of you.

I appreciate the permission to use copyrighted content (ABA Model Rules of Professional Conduct 3.8 and ABA Model Code of Judicial Conduct, Canons 1–4) provided by the American Bar Association and cited in chapters 4 and 6. © 2017 by the American Bar Association. Reprinted with permission. All rights reserved. This information or any portion thereof may not be copied or disseminated in any form or by any means or stored in an electronic database or retrieval system without the express written consent of the American Bar Association.

# Summary of Contents

# Table of Contents

# Table of Cases

# THE CONSTITUTION AND CRIMINAL JUDICIAL PROCESS

## Second Edition

# Introduction to the American Courts

This text examines the American criminal courts through the lens of the United States Constitution and explains how criminal cases make their way through the judicial system. This is often referred to as **judicial process**. The American courts resolve disputes involving every aspect of daily life. **Criminal law** involves the prosecution of individuals who are believed to have violated a criminal statute. **Civil law** is a broad category that includes areas such as family law, wills and trusts, contracts and torts. There is significant overlap in many of the principles of judicial process between civil and criminal law, but the focus of this text is the criminal courts. The American court system is part of the larger American system of criminal justice.

The **American criminal justice system** includes **law enforcement** and **correctional agencies** in addition to the courts. The American criminal justice system is a large and complex network of organizations existing at the federal, state and local levels. These organizations are sometimes dependent upon one another and at other times independent. There are differing perspectives that inform American criminal justice policy efforts and affect the American court system in important ways.

There are two primary theories of criminal justice in the United States: **crime control theory** and **due process theory**. Crime control theory focuses on increased police and prosecutorial powers employed to control crime and increase public safety. Due process theory focuses on the protection of individual rights and liberties and limited government power. Due process and crime control thinkers often agree on general goals and principles such as public safety, but they disagree about effective and appropriate ways to achieve those goals. An example of a crime control model policy would be "three strikes" sentencing statutes. An example of a due process model policy would be the implementation of drug treatment courts. These two theories are at the center of a great deal of debate regarding criminal justice policy in the United States.

Future chapters will discuss individual courtroom actors and their roles in the criminal judicial process. There are people who serve in a wide variety of roles, each with a unique purpose, ensuring that the courts function fairly and effectively. These actors compose the **courtroom work group**. Perceptions and understanding of these actors and their roles are often informed by television shows and Hollywood crime dramas featuring dynamic lawyers and judges. While the media sometimes portrays the courts accurately, the images they often portray are wildly fictional. It is important for students of criminology and criminal justice to have an accurate understanding of how American criminal courts function in reality. It is also important to remember that things do not always function in reality the way they are intended to function in theory.

There are detailed rules governing the structure and function of the American courts, but on any given day, courts may not be operating according to the rule of law. Some scholars refer to this phenomenon as the "law on the books" versus the "law in action." It is a valuable experience in studying the American criminal courts to include a personal visit to a local courthouse. Criminal court proceedings are public and may typically be observed so long as guests observe basic court rules (e.g., do not communicate with inmates, remove hats, silence cell phones, etc.). Exposure to the criminal courts in action can be exciting and profoundly educational.

## A.  BASIC PRINCIPLES OF COURT ORGANIZATION

The American court system is an organization of great size and breadth. In the United States there are parallel courts functioning at the local, state and federal levels. State courts serve the people of their respective communities by resolving disputes and ensuring justice. Disputes may arise between private parties or between the state and a criminal defendant. These disputes are resolved in proceedings in **trial courts**. Local or **municipal courts** are also trial courts, and they handle the lowest level of cases such as traffic and small claims matters. In addition to trial courts there are state **appellate courts**, which ensure that the law is applied correctly in the cases heard by the trial courts. In the state court systems these trial and appellate courts have a variety of names.

The federal court system has trial courts called **district courts**, and appellate courts called **circuit courts**, which are responsible for the same tasks as the state trial and appellate courts. In the federal court system, the **United States Supreme Court** is the **court of last resort**, the final forum to which a party may appeal a case. It is the highest court in the country. States also have courts of last resort, typically called supreme courts. All but two states have a single court of last resort; only Texas and Oklahoma have separate courts of last resort for civil and criminal cases.

Modern American courts are often required to do more than make decisions about the facts of a case or apply the law to the cases that come before them. They may be asked to collaborate with a wide range of public agencies in order to achieve justice for a diverse and evolving population. In many states and counties specialized or **collaborative courts** exist to ensure that defendants are offered mental health services, substance abuse treatment or other social services. These courts may provide defendants with access to services for homelessness or special programs for veterans. These specialized courts are discussed more fully in chapter 12.

## B. THE ACTORS IN THE JUDICIAL PROCESS

The key actors in the criminal judicial process are defendants, victims, witnesses, prosecutors, defense attorneys, judges and court staff. There may also be actors from outside agencies or organizations who play an important role in criminal cases. The **defendant** is the individual charged with committing a crime. While the defendant sits at the center of the court process, he or she has little power to affect or change their case. The crime may have caused harm to one or more individuals or **victims**. In American criminal judicial process, the role of victims is limited. They might provide statements and information to police prior to trial that results in the arrest of the defendant. They may be called to testify at the trial as a witness. While the prosecutor represents their interests, the prosecutor is not the attorney for the victims of crime in the same sense that the defense attorney represents the defendant individually. One of the most concrete ways that victims may participate in the trial process is by giving a victim impact statement at the sentencing of a convicted defendant. The victim is able to share how their life was affected by the crime in their own words.

The prosecutor is arguably the most powerful member of the courtroom work group. The **prosecutor** is a government attorney, who is employed to represent the people (the community at large) against the defendant charged with committing a crime. The prosecutor has the power to decide whether to charge the defendant and if so, what crimes to charge them with. Federal prosecutors are called United States Attorneys and work in a geographic region or district. State prosecutors, often called district attorneys, represent the government in state criminal cases.

**Defense attorneys** represent the defendant in criminal cases and provide advice and counsel about the charges they face in a criminal case. Criminal defense attorneys are obligated to provide their client with current, well-informed guidance about their case and to explain the risks and benefits of the decisions they make along the way. It is not their job or right to make decisions for the defendant, but rather to assist the defendant in navigating the complex criminal judicial process effectively. Defendants who have the financial resources to hire an attorney are represented by one of their choosing called private counsel. Those who are unable to afford an attorney also have the right to the assistance of counsel. This right is guaranteed by the Sixth Amendment to the U.S. Constitution. If a defendant cannot afford to hire their own attorney, the state is responsible for providing an attorney for them at no cost. **Indigent defendants**, those who are unable to pay for their own attorneys, are provided counsel in a variety of ways at the state and federal levels.

**Trial judges** preside over the trial much like a referee over a sporting event. Judges have the power to decide whether to release a defendant on bail, rule on motions and engage in sentencing. They sit above the rest of the courtroom and their position is referred to as "the bench." If a criminal defendant decides to forego a jury trial, the trial judge serves as the fact-finder in the case, making determinations about the guilt or innocence of the defendant based on all of the facts presented at trial. This is called a **bench trial**.

Trial judges and appellate judges have very different jobs. **Appellate judges** typically serve on a panel of three or more judges and they are called on to answer questions of law. When a trial has taken place (and even before or during a trial) parties to the case can raise issues on appeal, arguing that there was a mistake in the process or in the way the law was applied to them. Appellate courts review these appeals and issue written **opinions** explaining the answers to any questions raised in the appeal.

The **bailiff** is an officer assigned to keep order in the courtroom. The bailiff is a sworn police officer. Depending upon the jurisdiction, officers from law enforcement agencies may rotate through duty at the courts and jails. Bailiffs are assigned to protect court staff and help ensure that the parties who appear in court maintain a proper decorum.

The **court clerk** is an important administrative assistant to the judge. The clerk ensures that the judge's calendar is maintained and the procedures are followed during trials.

A **court reporter** or stenographer is charged with keeping a verbatim record of the proceedings that take place "on the record" in a trial or hearing. The court reporter's job is critical, as transcripts from trials can often play an important role in the appellate process.

**Judicial administrators** ensure that the courts can successfully and effectively engage in their daily responsibilities. The top-ranking employee of a court is the **court executive officer (CEO)**. The CEO reports to the judges and often works closely with the **presiding judge** (a leader among equals) to provide direction and leadership for the court in terms of the budget, staffing, court policies and procedures. The CEO also works with and manages an executive team. The executive team is usually made up of an assistant court executive officer, court operations officer, chief technology officer, chief financial officer, human resources manager and other division managers (ex: criminal division manager, civil division manager) who specialize in the different case type areas of the court.

There is a clear distinction between the lesser-known administrative functions of a court and highly visible courtroom/trial part of the court with actors such as the Judge, lawyers, and bailiffs. Judges apply the law and *administer justice* (trials) and court administrators *provide access to justice*.

# C. FOUNDATION OF THE AMERICAN JUDICIAL SYSTEM

The **United States Constitution** is the chartering document for our nation. It was drafted by a group of delegates at the Constitutional Convention and was signed in 1787. In March of 1789, after ratification by all thirteen original states, Congress convened for the first time operating under the Constitution. It is the highest law of the land in the United States of America. In the preamble to the Constitution the drafters explain their purpose in drafting the document:

> *We the People of the United States, in Order to form a more perfect Union, establish Justice, insure domestic Tranquility, provide for the common defence, promote the general Welfare, and secure the Blessings of Liberty to ourselves and our Posterity, do ordain and establish this Constitution for the United States of America.*[1]

In the first three articles, or sections, the Constitution outlines three branches of government: **legislative, executive and judicial**. The articulation of these three, in that specific order, is a statement on the values of the individuals who worked together to frame the government of the United States. A review of the

---

[1]    U.S. Const. preamble.

Constitution reveals something surprising to many new students of government: it is relatively brief. For such an important document, the Constitution may lack the kind of specificity one would expect from something so significant. The Constitution does not include highly detailed instructions or statements about how the government should be organized and operate. Instead, it paints with broad strokes, outlining the way the nation should be governed. That brevity has served the country well and allowed for a continual process of growth and evolution of a government that can meet the challenges of a dynamic nation.

In 1776 the Constitution's framers could not have anticipated the specific problems facing our nation in the 21st Century, but they provided a flexible framework for those following in their footsteps to answer difficult questions as society and American culture changed. The framers granted powers to each of the three branches of government that create **checks and balances** to ensure that one branch does not exert too much power over the others.

Article I explains the powers granted to the legislative branch or **Congress**. As former subjects of the King of England, the colonists placed self-governance above all else when it came to the organization of the United States. Avoiding the risk of abuse from centralized power was their top priority. They carefully constructed a government where the power is kept in check through balanced distribution, and they erred on the side of placing the most power in the hands of the people to govern themselves. Article I is first because in the distribution of power, the framers believed the voice of the people was the most important.

Congress is composed of two groups, the U.S. Senate and the U.S. House of Representatives. Each state elects two senators, so that each state has an equal voice in the Senate chamber. Members of the House of Representatives are apportioned based on population. As a result, states with larger populations have more members elected to the House of Representatives than less populous states. Small states like Vermont and Delaware have just one representative while California, a much larger state, has fifty-three. Members of both houses are elected to serve for a specific time period or **term**. Members of the House of Representatives serve two-year terms while senators are elected to six-year terms.

Article II explains the process for selection of the chief executive, the **president of the United States**, and the powers and responsibilities attached to the office. While the role of commander in chief is arguably the most important for an individual in U.S. government, Congress possesses powerful checks on the power of the president. The constitution grants to the president the role of commander in chief of the Armed Forces. It also confers the power to appoint, with the approval of the Senate, many important officials including: the justices of the United States Supreme Court, foreign ministers and consuls, ambassadors and other officials.

Article III provides specific detail regarding the construction of the U.S. Supreme Court as well as the process for selection of the justices who serve there. When Congress as a law-making body and the president as an administrator of the law are in conflict, the judicial branch exists to resolve those conflicts. The judicial branch is composed of trial and appellate courts and the U.S. Supreme Court.

The U.S. Supreme Court enjoys the power of judicial review. They are the final arbiters of questions of federal law. This was decided in the landmark case of *Marbury v. Madison (1803)*. **Judicial review** is the authority of the Supreme Court to review statutes and lower court decisions to ensure they meet the requirements of the U.S. Constitution. John Adams was near the end of his term as the second president of the United States. As he was completing his term he appointed numerous judges who were politically sympathetic to his federalist position, but he was unable to complete their appointments before leaving office. William Marbury was one of the men appointed to serve as a justice of the peace, but his commission was never delivered. Thomas Jefferson, the incoming president was unwilling to deliver it and as a result, Marbury joined with three others in the same situation and sued asking the Court to compel Jefferson to deliver their appointments.

Chief Justice John Marshall writing for a unanimous majority held that Section 3 of the Judiciary Act of 1789 was unconstitutional because it provided for the power to issue the requested writs of mandamus—a power which they held the Supreme Court does not have. The decision was a landmark case in its holding that the Supreme Court could invalidate an act of Congress, which established the doctrine of judicial review.[2]

Judicial review is arguably the single greatest check in the grand scheme of checks and balances in American government. Nine justices have the power to overrule the will of the people by invalidating an act of Congress if they determine that the Constitution and its principles have been violated. There is not a more important government body in the United States, and as a result, the significance of the presidential power of appointment of justices to the High Court cannot be overstated.

---

[2]   *Marbury v. Madison*, 5 U.S. 137 (1803).

The development of the other federal courts (both trial and appellate) is a power specifically given to Congress and over the years it has authorized an extensive system of federal courts through legislation. This system, along with the parallel state court systems, will be discussed at length in later chapters. They are separate and distinct judicial systems, the federal courts, and the courts of each state, and they operate to resolve cases and questions of law for their own individual jurisdiction.

## D. SOURCES OF LAW

There are four sources of law at both the state and federal levels: constitutions, **statutes**, judicial opinions and **administrative regulations**. The U.S. Constitution is the supreme law of the land and the state constitutions are the highest law in their respective states. Statutes or codes are rules of law passed by legislative bodies. Congress at the federal level, and state legislatures, create rules of law through the legislative process. This involves the introduction of bills that create or change some aspect of public policy. Bills are reviewed and voted on by committees and eventually the membership of the legislature. If approved, a bill is forwarded to the executive branch for signature and final approval. The president or a state governor must sign the bill in order for it to become law.

American law has English roots. In England, their court system evolved over hundreds of years. A process was established to allow judges to make legal rules on a case-by-case basis, referred to as **common law**. The common law process was brought to the colonies and became a part of American jurisprudence. An integral part of the common law system of justice is the **doctrine of stare decisis**. Translated literally from Latin this means: "let the decision stand." This doctrine dictates that when a court hears a case, and issues an opinion, that decision has the force of law for lower courts in future cases. The rules announced in these cases are **precedent** that lower courts are required to follow in future cases raising similar issues or questions.

Adherence to the doctrine of stare decisis is important because:

1.　It shows deference and respect to prior courts who have ruled on the issues.

2.　It helps to ensure consistent application of the law to different litigants.

3.　It provides notice to the public about how the law will be interpreted in future cases.

Administrative rules and regulations are sometimes overlooked as a source of law because the public is not aware of how they are developed or where to find them. Administrative regulations have the same force of law as a statute passed by the legislature because the grant of power to create them was given to the administrative agency by the legislature. For example, the Occupational Safety and Health Act of 1970 created the Occupational Safety and Health Administration (OSHA). The Act authorized the creation of OSHA and empowered the agency to create regulations that govern workplace safety. Once created, an agency is administered by the executive branch of government, but it's power to regulate comes from Congress. The rules and regulations passed by administrative agencies are law.

In legal research and writing the law is referred to as **primary authority**. The four sources of law are all primary authority. Case law is binding, or mandatory primary authority, when it comes from a court in the same jurisdiction or from a higher court than the one considering a case. This means that according to the doctrine of stare decisis it must be applied if a court is faced with a similar question. If a court from a jurisdiction outside the one hearing a case has issued an opinion on the same matter being considered, that law is called persuasive primary authority. It is still law, so it is primary, but because it is from a lower court or a different jurisdiction it is only persuasive.

For example, all of the state courts in Oregon are bound to follow decisions of the Oregon Supreme Court. Within the state of Oregon, those decisions are mandatory primary authority. Courts from outside of the jurisdiction are not bound to follow the Oregon Supreme Court's decision, but may choose to follow a case because it is persuasive primary authority. A decision from the U.S. Supreme Court is mandatory primary authority as applied to any other court in the country because the Supreme Court is the highest court in the land.

Any non-law legal resource, such as a legal dictionary or law journal article, is referred to as **secondary authority**. Secondary authority is never binding, and is always considered persuasive legal authority. Courts sometimes choose to utilize secondary sources to help them answer legal questions, but they are never bound by them or required to do so. On the other hand, courts must follow the law, and must determine what law applies to the issue raised in each case with which they are confronted. State courts must apply the law for the state where they are situated, and federal courts must apply federal law.

# E. CRIMINAL LAW

In studying criminal courts, it is useful to be reminded of the basic principles of American criminal law. A crime is composed of four **elements** and understanding this elemental structure of criminal law is important. In the American criminal courts, the prosecutor bears the **burden of proof** beyond a reasonable doubt for each element in order to convict the accused of the crime charged. The defendant in a criminal case is never responsible for proving his innocence.

The American criminal justice system is an **adversarial** one. This adversary system of justice in the United States has English common law roots. The American court system is modeled in many ways after the English courts familiar to the founders of the country. The adversary system in criminal courts is often described as a regulated storytelling contest. These stories are presented to an impartial decision-maker (judge or jury) and criminal liability is decided based on the credibility of the evidence.[3] Essentially the prosecutor and defendant "face off" against one another in court in order to determine which party wins the dispute. There are alternatives to an adversarial system of justice. In France and Germany, the courts employ an **inquisitorial system** of justice.

Key characteristics of the inquisitorial system include:

1.    The judge plays a leading role in defining issues and oversight of the collection of evidence.

2.    Trials may be held over a long period of time with significant breaks.

3.    The focus is on discovering the truth as opposed to the more effective presentation of evidence.

In the American criminal justice system, the elements of each individual crime charged against the defendant must be proved beyond a reasonable doubt. This standard of proof does not require the absence of all doubt, or absolute certainty on the part of the fact-finders. Instead, it requires that the evidence be sufficient to leave no other logical explanation than the defendant's guilt, overcoming the **presumption of innocence**. A legal presumption is a principle that operates as a "wall" or barrier requiring some evidence or action to overcome. The presumption of innocence is the most recognized legal presumption but there are others. The presumption of innocence is a rebuttable presumption because

---

[3]    Goodpaster, Gary, On the Theory of American Adversary Criminal Trial, 78 J. Crim. L. & Criminology 118 (1987–1988).

with sufficient evidence it can be overcome. In American criminal law every true crime consists of the following elements:

1.  **Actus reus**: the criminal act or omission.

2.  **Mens rea**: the guilty mind or unlawful intent.

    a.  **Specific intent** crimes are those whose mens rea by definition requires both the intent to do the act, and the intent to achieve some future consequence. A **general intent** crime requires only that the defendant intend to commit the act, even if they do not have in mind a particular result or hope for a specific outcome.

    b.  There must be **concurrence** between the criminal intent and the criminal act, a union or joint operation of act and intent or criminal negligence.

3.  **Causation**: the criminal act must be both the legal and factual cause of the injury.

    a.  Sine qua non or **cause-in-fact** is determined by applying the "but for" test to the criminal act (e.g., but for the defendant's unlawful act, would the harm or injury have occurred?).

    b.  **Proximate (legal) cause** is more difficult to evaluate but asks generally whether it is just or fair to hold the defendant responsible for the criminal act based on the relationship between their conduct and the resulting harm. Causation problems sometimes arise when there is an intervening act that raises questions about the defendant's moral culpability.

4.  **Resulting harm or injury**: this varies depending on the charged offense; it is the harm the criminal statute seeks to prevent.

## F.  LEARNING THE LAW

One of the most effective ways to learn the law is through **case briefing.** Case briefing is the process of reading and analyzing a judicial opinion issued by a court and preparing a written summary of the case. The court's opinion will typically include a brief summary of the facts of the case. The court's opinion also articulates the legal rules that apply to the type of case being heard. In case briefing this is called the rule. The analysis or application of the law to the facts is followed by the court's conclusion—or the result in the case.

Case briefing teaches the reader to identify the issue or question before the court in the case. This is called **issue spotting**. The reader must also determine what law (cases, codes, etc.) the court utilizes in addressing the issue, and explain the court's application of the law to the facts. This should be put into the writer's own words. Case briefing helps the reader achieve an understanding of why the law required the case to be resolved in the manner the court chose to resolve it and teaches important critical thinking and analytical reasoning skills in the process.

Briefing cases is an effective way to learn the substantive rules of law (what the law is) and more importantly to learn to think critically and reason analytically (why the law should apply the way it does). If a student has excellent critical thinking and analytical reasoning skills they can solve the legal problems they have read about, but can also apply their reasoning skills to solve unique problems in the future that involve different facts and circumstances.

This skill set is critical for students who will work in the American criminal justice system. Work in law enforcement demands the ability to solve problems analytically. Officers must evaluate facts and circumstances in a matter of seconds and make decisions about how to act. Their ability to do this in a well-reasoned manner is indispensable and often overlooked. Reading, critical thinking and analytical reasoning may be seen as a skill set for pre-law students, researchers or academics—but not for practitioners working in the field. Nothing could be further from the truth. A law enforcement officer's ability to exercise discretion through sound, well-reasoned conduct has the potential to impact policing in a positive way by avoiding rash, emotional judgments on the part of officers. The same logic applies when considering the importance of critical thinking skills to all of the other actors in the criminal justice system; from the attorneys and judges working in the courts, to officers working in corrections and law enforcement—there is tremendous value to be gained through improved critical thinking skills.

American law schools use case briefing to teach the law and train future attorneys to be better thinkers and problem-solvers. This undergraduate text utilizes court opinions for the same reason. Case briefing is an effective way to develop analytical reasoning and critical thinking skills; while enabling students to learn about American courts and the judicial process in a fun and engaging way. The components of a case brief are typically organized in an outline format for easy reading and review. While flexibility regarding format is encouraged, thorough case briefs should include the following components to be the most useful:

1.    Heading—identify the case by party names and citation.

2.    Facts—include only those facts that are significant to the specific legal issue (or question) being decided by the court.

3.    Procedural history—how the case made its way to the current level of review (for example: explain that the defendant was convicted, and appealed his conviction claiming there was a violation of his constitutional rights, the court of appeals affirmed, etc.)

4.    Issue—the legal question the court is faced with answering.

5.    Rule—the law (statutes, constitutional provisions, prior cases or administrative rules) that this court applied in answering the legal question(s) raised in this case. The ability to separate these legal rules from the court's analysis or application of them to the facts is of critical importance.

6.    Analysis—explain how the court applied the rule(s) to the specific facts in *this* case in solving the problem raised by the issue. Articulating the analysis demonstrates an understanding of why the court has reached the conclusion they have reached based on the applicable legal rules. It is important to understand the relationship between the rules of law and the court's analysis in order to utilize those rules in analyzing future legal questions.

7.    Conclusion—the specific outcome of the case. Did the court affirm, reverse or remand the case? If the court affirms the decision of the lower court this means that they agree with the decision and will not change the result. If the court reverses the decision of the lower court they disagree with the prior ruling and are changing the outcome of the case. If the court remands the case they are returning it to the lower court with instructions to reconsider the issues and typically the appellate court offers instructions or explanation that will guide the lower court in that process.

This text contains numerous court cases, presented at the end of the chapters, to be used as case briefing exercises. The cases have been carefully selected to supplement the material from each chapter. They represent important or **landmark decisions** by the U.S. Supreme Court resulting in changes to the law. These cases are edited to make reading, analyzing and briefing them more manageable. The full text opinions are longer and more challenging to read making these edited versions a helpful tool for learning the legal principles presented.

The remainder of this chapter is an edited opinion of the U.S. Supreme Court. The case, *Rochin v. California (1952),* deals with the topic of fundamental rights in the context of criminal investigation by law enforcement officers. This introduction to case briefing provides a well-structured judicial opinion that is conducive for students to try their hand at case briefing.

Read and brief *Rochin v. California* and consider the questions following
   the case:

---

# ROCHIN V. CALIFORNIA

Supreme Court of the United States
Argued Oct. 16, 1951
Decided Jan. 2, 1952
342 U.S. 165

**MR. JUSTICE FRANKFURTER delivered the opinion of the Court.**

Having "some information that [the petitioner here] was selling
narcotics," three deputy sheriffs of the County of Los Angeles, on the morning
of July 1, 1949, made for the two-story dwelling house in which Rochin lived
with his mother, common-law wife, brothers and sisters. Finding the outside
door open, they entered and then forced open the door to Rochin's room on
the second floor. Inside they found petitioner sitting partly dressed on the side
of the bed, upon which his wife was lying. On a "night stand" beside the bed
the deputies spied two capsules. When asked "Whose stuff is this?" Rochin
seized the capsules and put them in his mouth. A struggle ensued, in the course
of which the three officers "jumped upon him" and attempted to extract the
capsules. The force they applied proved unavailing against Rochin's resistance.
He was handcuffed and taken to a hospital. At the direction of one of the
officers a doctor forced an emetic solution through a tube into Rochin's
stomach against his will. This "stomach pumping" produced vomiting. In the
vomited matter were found two capsules which proved to contain morphine.

Rochin was brought to trial before a California Superior Court, sitting
without a jury, on the charge of possessing "a preparation of morphine" in
violation of the California Health and Safety Code, 1947, 11,500. Rochin was
convicted and sentenced to sixty days' imprisonment. The chief evidence
against him was the two capsules. They were admitted over petitioner's
objection, although the means of obtaining them was frankly set forth in the
testimony by one of the deputies, substantially as here narrated.

On appeal, the District Court of Appeal affirmed the conviction, despite
the finding that the officers "were guilty of unlawfully breaking into and
entering defendant's room and were guilty of unlawfully assaulting and
battering defendant while in the room," and "were guilty of unlawfully
assaulting, battering, torturing and falsely imprisoning the defendant at the
alleged hospital." . . . One of the three judges, while finding that "the record in
this case reveals a shocking series of violations of constitutional rights,"

concurred only because he felt bound by decisions of his Supreme Court. These, he asserted, "have been looked upon by law enforcement officers as an encouragement, if not an invitation, to the commission of such lawless acts." *Ibid.* The Supreme Court of California denied without opinion Rochin's petition for a hearing. Two justices dissented from this denial, and in doing so expressed themselves thus: ". . . a conviction which rests upon evidence of incriminating objects obtained from the body of the accused by physical abuse is as invalid as a conviction which rests upon a verbal confession extracted from him by such abuse. . . . Had the evidence forced from the defendant's lips consisted of an oral confession that he illegally possessed a drug . . . he would have the protection of the rule of law which excludes coerced confessions from evidence. But because the evidence forced from his lips consisted of real objects the People of this state are permitted to base a conviction upon it. [We] find no valid ground of distinction between a verbal confession extracted by physical abuse and a confession wrested from defendant's body by physical abuse." . . .

This Court granted certiorari, because a serious question is raised as to the limitations which the Due Process Clause of the Fourteenth Amendment imposes on the conduct of criminal proceedings by the States.

In our federal system the administration of criminal justice is predominantly committed to the care of the States. The power to define crimes belongs to Congress only as an appropriate means of carrying into execution its limited grant of legislative powers. U.S. Const., Art. I, 8, cl. 18. Broadly speaking, crimes in the United States are what the laws of the individual States make them, subject to the limitations of Art. I, 10, cl. 1, in the original Constitution, prohibiting bills of attainder and ex post facto laws, and of the Thirteenth and Fourteenth Amendments.

These limitations, in the main, concern not restrictions upon the powers of the States to define crime, except in the restricted area where federal authority has preempted the field, but restrictions upon the manner in which the States may enforce their penal codes. Accordingly, in reviewing a State criminal conviction under a claim of right guaranteed by the Due Process Clause of the Fourteenth Amendment, from which is derived the most far-reaching and most frequent federal basis of challenging State criminal justice, "we must be deeply mindful of the responsibilities of the States for the enforcement of criminal laws, and exercise with due humility our merely negative function in subjecting convictions from state courts to the very narrow scrutiny which the Due Process Clause of the Fourteenth Amendment authorizes." *Malinski v. New York*, 324 U.S. 401, 412, 418. Due process of law, "itself a historical product," *Jackman v. Rosenbaum Co.*, 260 U.S. 22, 31, is not to be turned into a destructive dogma against the States in the administration of their systems of criminal justice.

However, this Court too has its responsibility. Regard for the requirements of the Due Process Clause "inescapably imposes upon this Court an exercise of judgment upon the whole course of the proceedings [resulting in a conviction] in order to ascertain whether they offend those canons of decency and fairness which express the notions of justice of English-speaking peoples even toward those charged with the most heinous offenses." *Malinski v. New York*, supra, at 416–417. These standards of justice are not authoritatively formulated anywhere as though they were specifics. Due process of law is a summarized constitutional guarantee of respect for those personal immunities which, as Mr. Justice Cardozo twice wrote for the Court, are "so rooted in the traditions and conscience of our people as to be ranked as fundamental," *Snyder v. Massachusetts*, 291 U.S. 97, 105, or are "implicit in the concept of ordered liberty." *Palko v. Connecticut*, 302 U.S. 319, 325. 2 . . .

Applying these general considerations to the circumstances of the present case, we are compelled to conclude that the proceedings by which this conviction was obtained do more than offend some fastidious squeamishness or private sentimentalism about combatting crime too energetically. This is conduct that shocks the conscience. Illegally breaking into the privacy of the petitioner, the struggle to open his mouth and remove what was there, the forcible extraction of his stomach's contents—this course of proceeding by agents of government to obtain evidence is bound to offend even hardened sensibilities. They are methods too close to the rack and the screw to permit of constitutional differentiation.

It has long since ceased to be true that due process of law is heedless of the means by which otherwise relevant and credible evidence is obtained. This was not true even before the series of recent cases enforced the constitutional principle that the States may not base convictions upon confessions, however much verified, obtained by coercion. These decisions are not arbitrary exceptions to the comprehensive right of States to fashion their own rules of evidence for criminal trials. They are not sports in our constitutional law but applications of a general principle. They are only instances of the general requirement that States in their prosecutions respect certain decencies of civilized conduct. Due process of law, as a historic and generative principle, precludes defining, and thereby confining, these standards of conduct more precisely than to say that convictions cannot be brought about by methods that offend "a sense of justice." See Mr. Chief Justice Hughes, speaking for a unanimous Court in *Brown v. Mississippi*, 297 U.S. 278, 285–286. It would be a stultification of the responsibility which the course of constitutional history has cast upon this Court to hold that in order to convict a man the police cannot extract by force what is in his mind but can extract what is in his stomach.

To attempt in this case to distinguish what lawyers call "real evidence" from verbal evidence is to ignore the reasons for excluding coerced confessions. Use of involuntary verbal confessions in State criminal trials is constitutionally obnoxious not only because of their unreliability. They are inadmissible under the Due Process Clause even though statements contained in them may be independently established as true. Coerced confessions offend the community's sense of fair play and decency. So here, to sanction the brutal conduct which naturally enough was condemned by the court whose judgment is before us, would be to afford brutality the cloak of law. Nothing would be more calculated to discredit law and thereby to brutalize the temper of a society.

In deciding this case we do not heedlessly bring into question decisions in many States dealing with essentially different, even if related, problems. We therefore put to one side cases which have arisen in the State courts through use of modern methods and devices for discovering wrongdoers and bringing them to book. It does not fairly represent these decisions to suggest that they legalize force so brutal and so offensive to human dignity in securing evidence from a suspect as is revealed by this record. Indeed the California Supreme Court has not sanctioned this mode of securing a conviction. It merely exercised its discretion to decline a review of the conviction. All the California judges who have expressed themselves in this case have condemned the conduct in the strongest language.

We are not unmindful that hypothetical situations can be conjured up, shading imperceptibly from the circumstances of this case and by gradations producing practical differences despite seemingly logical extensions. But the Constitution is "intended to preserve practical and substantial rights, not to maintain theories." *Davis v. Mills*, 194 U.S. 451, 457.

On the facts of this case the conviction of the petitioner has been obtained by methods that offend the Due Process Clause. The judgment below must be

*Reversed.*

. . .

## MR. JUSTICE BLACK, concurring.

*Adamson v. California*, 332 U.S. 46, 68–123, sets out reasons for my belief that state as well as federal courts and law enforcement officers must obey the Fifth Amendment's command that "No person . . . shall be compelled [342 U.S. 165, 175] in any criminal case to be a witness against himself." I think a person is compelled to be a witness against himself not only when he is compelled to testify, but also when as here, incriminating evidence is forcibly taken from him by a contrivance of modern science. . . . California convicted this petitioner by using against him evidence obtained in this manner, and I agree with MR. JUSTICE DOUGLAS that the case should be reversed on this ground.

In the view of a majority of the Court, however, the Fifth Amendment imposes no restraint of any kind on the states. They nevertheless hold that California's use of this evidence violated the Due Process Clause of the Fourteenth Amendment. Since they hold as I do in this case, I regret my inability to accept their interpretation without protest. But I believe that faithful adherence to the specific guarantees in the Bill of Rights insures a more permanent protection of individual liberty than that which can be afforded by the nebulous standards stated by the majority.

What the majority hold is that the Due Process Clause empowers this Court to nullify any state law if its application "shocks the conscience," offends "a sense of justice" or runs counter to the "decencies of civilized conduct." The majority emphasize that these statements do not refer to their own consciences or to their senses of justice and decency. For we are told that "we may not draw on our merely personal and private notions"; our judgment must be grounded on "considerations deeply rooted in reason and in the compelling traditions of the legal profession." We are further admonished to measure the validity of state practices, not by our reason, or by the traditions of the legal profession, but by "the community's sense of fair play and decency"; by the "traditions and conscience of our people"; or by "those canons of decency and fairness which express the notions of justice of English-speaking peoples." These canons are made necessary, it is said, because of "interests of society pushing in opposite directions."

If the Due Process Clause does vest this Court with such unlimited power to invalidate laws, I am still in doubt as to why we should consider only the notions of English-speaking peoples to determine what are immutable and fundamental principles of justice. Moreover, one may well ask what avenues of investigation are open to discover "canons" of conduct so universally favored that this Court should write them into the Constitution? All we are told is that the discovery must be made by an "evaluation based on a disinterested inquiry pursued in the spirit of science, on a balanced order of facts."

Some constitutional provisions are stated in absolute and unqualified language such, for illustration, as the First Amendment stating that no law shall be passed prohibiting the free exercise of religion or abridging the freedom of speech or press. Other constitutional provisions do require courts to choose between competing policies, such as the Fourth Amendment which, by its terms, necessitates a judicial decision as to what is an "unreasonable" search or seizure. There is, however, no express constitutional language granting judicial power to invalidate every state law of every kind deemed "unreasonable" or contrary to the Court's notion of civilized decencies; yet the constitutional philosophy used by the majority has, in the past, been used to deny a state the right to fix the price of gasoline, *Williams v. Standard Oil Co.*, 278 U.S. 235; and even the right to prevent bakers from palming off smaller for larger loaves of bread, *Jay Burns Baking Co. v. Bryan*, 264 U.S. 504. These cases, and others show the extent to which the evanescent standards of the majority's philosophy have been used to nullify state legislative programs passed to suppress evil economic practices. What paralyzing role this same philosophy will play in the future economic affairs of this country is impossible to predict. Of even graver concern, however, is the use of the philosophy to nullify the Bill of Rights. I long ago concluded that the accordion-like qualities of this philosophy must inevitably imperil all the individual liberty safeguards specifically enumerated in the Bill of Rights. Reflection and recent decisions of this Court sanctioning abridgment of the freedom of speech and press have strengthened this conclusion.

. . .

### MR. JUSTICE DOUGLAS, concurring.

The evidence obtained from this accused's stomach would be admissible in the majority of states where the question has been raised. So far as the reported cases reveal, the only states which would probably exclude the evidence would be Arkansas, Iowa, Michigan, and Missouri. Yet the Court now says that the rule which the majority of the states have fashioned violates the "decencies of civilized conduct." To that I cannot agree. It is a rule formulated by responsible courts with judges as sensitive as we are to the proper standards for law administration.

As an original matter it might be debatable whether the provision in the Fifth Amendment that no person "shall be compelled in any criminal case to be a witness against himself" serves the ends of justice. Not all civilized legal procedures recognize it. But the choice was made by the Framers, a choice which sets a standard for legal trials in this country. The Framers made it a standard of due process for prosecutions by the Federal Government. If it is a requirement of due process for a trial in the federal courthouse, it is impossible for me to say it is not a requirement of due process for a trial in the state courthouse. That was the issue recently surveyed in *Adamson v. California*, 332 U.S. 46. The Court rejected the view that compelled testimony should be excluded and held in substance that the accused in a state trial can be forced to testify against himself. I disagree. Of course an accused can be compelled to be present at the trial, to stand, to sit, to turn this way or that, and to try on a cap or a coat. See *Holt v. United States*, 218 U.S. 245, 252–253. But I think that words taken from his lips, capsules taken from his stomach, blood taken from his veins are all inadmissible provided they are taken from him without his consent. They are inadmissible because of the command of the Fifth Amendment.

That is an unequivocal, definite and workable rule of evidence for state and federal courts. But we cannot in fairness free the state courts from that command and yet excoriate them for flouting the "decencies of civilized conduct" when they admit the evidence. That is to make the rule turn not on the Constitution but on the idiosyncrasies of the judges who sit here.

The damage of the view sponsored by the Court in this case may not be conspicuous here. But it is part of the same philosophy that produced *Betts v. Brady*, 316 U.S. 455, denying counsel to an accused in a state trial against the command of the Sixth Amendment, and *Wolf v. Colorado*, 338 U.S. 25, allowing evidence obtained as a result of a search and seizure that is illegal under the Fourth Amendment to be introduced in a state trial. It is part of the process of erosion of civil rights of the citizen in recent years. . .

# G. CASE BRIEFING WORKSHEET

I.   <u>Heading</u>—identify the case by party names and citation (include the date).

_____

II.  <u>Facts</u>—include only those facts that are significant to the specific legal issue being decided by the court.

_____

_____

_____

_____

_____

_____

_____

_____

_____

III. <u>Procedural History</u>—explain how the case made its way to the current level of review.

_____

_____

_____

IV.  <u>Issue</u>—the legal question the court is faced with answering that has been raised in the case.

_____

_____

_____

V.   <u>Rule</u>—what law (statutes, constitutional provisions, prior cases or administrative rules) did this court apply to enable them to solve the legal question(s) raised in this case?

_____

_____

_____

_____

_____

_____

_____

_____

_____

VI. <u>Analysis</u>—explain how the court applied the legal rule(s) to the facts in deciding the answer to the question posed by the issue in this case.

_____

_____

_____

_____

_____

_____

_____

_____

_____

_____

_____

_____

VII. <u>Conclusion</u>—did the court affirm, reverse, remand? This should be a very short statement of the outcome.

_____

_____

_____

**After preparing the case brief, consider the answers to the following questions:**

1.    Do you believe the fact that Rochin possessed narcotics justified the officer's entry into his home? The entry into his bedroom?

2.    The Court explains at the beginning of the opinion that they "must be deeply mindful of the responsibilities of the States for the enforcement of criminal laws, and exercise with due humility our merely negative function in subjecting convictions from state courts to the very narrow scrutiny which the Due Process Clause of the Fourteenth Amendment authorizes." Why is this principle of deference to the states so important?

3.    The Court explains that the Fourteenth Amendment's Due Process Clause protects *fundamental* rights. What language from the opinion helps you understand what fundamental means in this context?

4.    Identify some of the prior cases the Court referred to in making their decision in *Rochin*. How does the Court discuss those prior decisions?

5.    Do you agree that the officer's conduct in this case "shocked the conscience"?

## Chapter 1 Key Terms for Review

- **Judicial process**: the way that cases make their way through the court system.

- **Criminal law**: substantive law proscribing or requiring conduct, the violation of which is subject to criminal legal sanctions.

- **Civil law**: substantive law that governs disputes between private parties in areas such as personal injury, family law, wills and trusts, and contracts.

- **American criminal justice system**: composed of organizations and agencies representing law enforcement, corrections and the courts, at the federal, state and local levels.

- **Law enforcement**: agencies composed of sworn officers who enforce the law through investigation and arrest.

- **Correctional agencies**: organizations which provide both institutional and out-of-custody supervision of convicted offenders as well as programs and treatment.

- **Crime control theory of criminal justice**: theory and public policy focused on increased police and prosecutorial powers in order to achieve the primary goals of public safety and punishment of offenders.

- **Due process theory of criminal justice**: theory and public policy focused on individual rights and liberties and limits on government power in order to achieve the primary goals of offender rehabilitation and fundamental fairness.

- **Courtroom workgroup**: the actors involved in criminal court process including the judge, prosecutor, defense attorney and court staff.

- **Trial courts**: conduct adversarial trials where evidence is presented by both parties to a fact finder (the jury, or a judge in a bench trial) in order to resolve a legal dispute.

- **Municipal courts**: lower-level trial courts responsible for minor criminal violations and civil matters.

- **Appellate courts**: review the decisions of trial courts to resolve disputes about whether the law was followed and applied correctly in a prior case.

- **District courts**: federal trial courts.

- **Circuit courts of appeal**: federal intermediate appellate courts.

- **Court of last resort**: the highest court for a particular jurisdiction.

- **United States Supreme Court**: the highest court in the United States and the final arbiter of questions of federal law and the Constitution.

- **Collaborative courts**: specialized courts tasked with a specific caseload in partnership with outside agencies in order to address a social problem. Examples are drug courts, domestic violence courts and mental health courts.

- **Defendant**: an individual charged with a crime.

- **Victim**: an individual who was injured or harmed by the commission of a crime.

- **Prosecutor**: an attorney who represents the government in criminal cases.

- **Defense attorney**: an attorney who represents the criminal defendant in criminal cases.

- **Indigent defendants**: defendants who are unable to pay for their own attorney and are appointed an attorney at the government's expense to represent them in a criminal trial.

- **Trial judge**: presides over a trial much like a referee. In criminal court has the power to rule on motions, decide whether to grant bail and conduct sentencing of convicted offenders.

- **Bench trial**: a trial before a judge sitting as the fact-finder in the place of a jury.

- **Appellate judges**: typically serve on panels of three or more to review cases on appeal. They review written arguments and briefs and conduct questioning and oral argument by attorneys in criminal appeals.

- **Judicial opinions**: the decisions made by appellate judges are written and published as opinions. These opinions or cases are law.

- **Bailiff**: an officer assigned to maintain order in the courtroom.

- **Court clerk**: administrative assistant to the judge.

- **Court reporter**: also called a stenographer is charged with keeping a verbatim record of court proceedings.

- **Judicial administrators**: provide access to justice by ensuring the effective operation of the courts from an administrative and staffing perspective.

- **Presiding judge**: the chief judicial officer for a particular court.

- **United States Constitution**: the chartering document for the United States, providing the framework of government, and the supreme law of the land.

- **Legislative branch**: composed of the Senate and House of Representatives, Congress is the legislative or rule-making body for the federal government. Representatives from individual states serve in Congress as representatives of the people who elect them.

- **Executive branch**: composed of the president of the United States and administrative agencies over which the president has control. The president is the chief executive and the commander in chief of the Armed Forces in the United States.

- **Judicial branch**: is composed of the U.S. Supreme Court and the lower federal courts.

- *Marbury v. Madison (1803):* landmark Supreme Court decision establishing the Supreme Court's power of judicial review.

- **Judicial review**: the power to review and strike down, if necessary, acts of Congress.

- **Statutes**: rules of law which have been codified or considered and approved by the legislature. Federal statutes are promulgated by Congress, and state statutes by each of the state legislatures.

- **Administrative regulations**: rules of law which are promulgated by administrative agencies, with power granted to them by the legislature.

- **Common law**: the process of allowing judges to make legal rules on a case-by-case basis.

- **Doctrine of stare decisis**: Individual disputes and legal problems are considered, and the decision made in the instant case is made applicable to future cases as rules of law which must be followed.

- **Precedent**: rules announced in court opinions made applicable to future cases through the doctrine of stare decisis.

- **Primary authority**: law is primary authority—constitutions, judicial opinions, codes or statutes, and administrative rules or regulations. Primary authority is binding, or mandatory, when it comes from a higher court or within the same geographic jurisdiction.

- **Secondary authority**: non-law legal resources such as legal dictionaries, treatises or law journal articles used in legal research.

- **Elements of crime**: the elements of a true crime are the required components which must be proved in order to convict a criminal defendant.

- **Burden of proof**: the burden of proof or persuasion requires the prosecutor (in criminal trials) prove the elements of the crime(s) charged beyond a reasonable doubt in order to convict the defendant.

- **Adversarial system of justice**: is a contest between the two parties—prosecution and defense—to convince the fact-finder of the truth in the case.

- **Inquisitorial system of justice**: system used in other countries where the fact-finding responsibility is placed largely on the judge, and discovering truth takes priority over the effective presentation of evidence.

- **Presumption of innocence**: criminal defendants in American courts are presumed innocent until the prosecutor has carried the burden of proof beyond a reasonable doubt.

- **Actus reus**: the criminal act or omission, an element of any true crime.

- **Mens rea**: the guilty mind, an element of any true crime.

- **Causation**: a connection between the defendant's criminal act and the resulting harm or injury, an element of any true crime.

- **Cause-in-fact**: determined by applying the "but for" test to the criminal act (e.g., but for the defendant's unlawful act, would the harm or injury have occurred?).

- **Proximate cause**: determines whether it is fair to hold the defendant responsible for the criminal act based on the relationship between their conduct and the resulting harm.

- **Injury or harm**: it is the injury the criminal statute seeks to prevent; proof of injury is an element of any true crime.

- **Case briefing**: the process of reading and analyzing a judicial opinion and preparing a summary of the case.

- **Issue spotting**: identifying the legal issue in a set of facts or judicial opinion.

- **Landmark decisions**: opinions written by the Supreme Court of such legal significance that they change public policy as a result.

# Federal and State Courts

## A. FEDERAL COURTS

The federal courts make up a large and complex organization with branches throughout the United States and American territories. The federal courts are authorized and governed by Congress. The grant of power to establish the federal courts was given to Congress in Article III of the U.S. Constitution. Article III provides a skeletal framework for the federal courts leaving the details of their development to Congress' discretion:

> SECTION 1, The judicial Power of the United States, shall be vested in one supreme Court, and in such inferior Courts as the Congress may from time to time ordain and establish. The Judges, both of the supreme and inferior Courts, shall hold their Offices during good Behaviour, and shall, at stated Times, receive for their Services, a Compensation, which shall not be diminished during their Continuance in Office.

> SECTION 2, The judicial Power shall extend to all Cases, in Law and Equity, arising under this Constitution, the Laws of the United States, and Treaties made, or which shall be made, under their Authority;—to all Cases affecting Ambassadors, other public Ministers and Consuls;— to all Cases of admiralty and maritime Jurisdiction;—[*to Controversies to which the United States shall be a Party;—to Controversies between two or more States;—between a State and Citizens of another State;—between Citizens of the same State claiming Lands under Grants of different States, and between a State, or the State, or the Citizens thereof, and foreign States, Citizens or Subjects.*][1]

---

[1] A section of Article III was changed by the 11th Amendment in 1789: *"Amendment XI The judicial power of the United States shall not be construed to extend to any suit in law or equity, commenced or prosecuted against one of the United States by citizens of another state, or by citizens or subjects of any foreign state."*

In all Cases affecting Ambassadors, other public Ministers and Consuls, and those in which a State shall be Party, the supreme Court shall have original Jurisdiction. In all the other Cases before mentioned, the supreme Court shall have appellate Jurisdiction, both as to Law and Fact, with such Exceptions, and under such Regulations as the Congress shall make.

The Trial of all Crimes, except in Cases of Impeachment; shall be by Jury; and such Trial shall be held in the State where the said Crimes shall have been committed; but when not committed within any State, the Trial shall be at such Place or Places as the Congress may by Law have directed.

SECTION 3, Treason against the United States, shall consist only in levying War against them, or in adhering to their Enemies, giving them Aid and Comfort. No Person shall be convicted of Treason unless on the Testimony of two Witnesses to the same overt Act, or on Confession in open Court.

The Congress shall have Power to declare the Punishment of Treason, but no Attainder of Treason shall work Corruption of Blood, or Forfeiture except during the Life of the Person attainted.

## i.   The United States Supreme Court

The brief guidelines for the development of the federal courts provided by Article III have allowed for the growth of the federal court system to correspond to the growth of the nation. The framers of the U.S. Constitution did not micromanage the specific details for development of the judicial branch. The one court specifically created by Article III is the **United States Supreme Court** and it is the highest court in the nation. It is composed of nine judges, called justices, eight associates and one chief justice. These justices are appointed by the president and confirmed by the U.S. Senate. U.S. Supreme Court justices serve life terms. Their caseload consists almost exclusively of appeals from the federal circuit courts.

The number of cases filed in the Supreme Court averaged between 7,000 and 8,000 cases for many years but has fallen in recent years. The total number of cases filed in 2019 was 5,411.[2] The vast majority of cases in the Supreme Court are appeals. Only a fraction involve **original jurisdiction**, meaning they originated or began in the Supreme Court. Original jurisdiction in the Supreme

---

[2]   https://www.supremecourt.gov/publicinfo/year-end/2020year-endreport.pdf.

Court is rare. Examples of cases where the Supreme Court has original jurisdiction are suits between two or more states or cases involving public ambassadors and other public ministers. In 2015 the state of Kansas sued the states of Nebraska and Colorado over water rights connected to the Republican River Contract and the U.S. Supreme Court heard the case under their original jurisdiction.[3] A **writ of certiorari** is a request for the Supreme Court to review a case on appeal. The Supreme Court is not required to grant every petition for a writ of certiorari. The justices review petitions and if four of the nine agree to hear the appeal the writ of certiorari is granted. This is referred to as the **rule of four**. If the Supreme Court issues the writ of certiorari the parties submit written briefs and may also argue their position during oral argument.

The justices ask the attorneys questions during oral argument, and after it is complete, they take time to consider the case and prepare a written decision called an **opinion**. One justice will author the opinion for the majority of the Court, and often other justices write separately to **concur** (agree) or **dissent** (disagree) with the majority opinion. These opinions are published for lower courts faced with similar questions to follow in future cases. In reaching a decision, the Supreme Court may **affirm** and agree with the lower court, or **reverse** the prior decision and disagree with the lower court. In some cases the Court will **reverse and remand** the decision, meaning they disagree with the lower court and the case is sent back for review in light of the Supreme Court's opinion and instructions.

The vast majority of petitions to the Supreme Court are not granted. Of the thousands of cases filed for review, the Court heard oral argument in just 73 cases and issued written opinions in 53 cases in 2019. Unfortunately for the majority of petitioners, they are denied review, their case ends and the appellate court's decision is the final ruling in the case. The U.S. Supreme Court convenes annually, with each term beginning the first Monday in October and ends in the summer, typically in late June.

## ii. Federal Circuit Courts of Appeal

There are thirteen federal intermediate appellate courts called **circuit courts**. The circuit courts are established by Congress and are outlined geographically. There are eleven numbered circuit courts and one for the District of Columbia. There is one with nationwide jurisdiction called the **Court of Appeals for the Federal Circuit**, which hears specialized cases, such as patent law matters and appeals from the U.S. Court of Federal Claims and the U.S. Court of International

---

[3]   *Kansas v. Nebraska and Colorado*, 574 U.S. 445 (2015).

Trade. Beyond the federal circuit, additional specialized courts have been established to deal with specific matters including the United States Court of Appeals for Veteran's Claims and the United States Court of Appeals for the Armed Forces.[4]

Each circuit court has multiple judges, ranging from six on the First Circuit to twenty-nine on the Ninth Circuit. These judges typically work in panels of three. Parties may appeal to the circuit courts once the district court has finalized a decision (some issues can be appealed before a final decision by making an "interlocutory appeal").[5] In rare circumstances a case may be heard **en banc**, meaning that all of the judges for the circuit will hear the case. The majority of cases brought before the federal courts of appeal are civil filings, 15,112 in 2020. In 2020 there were 10,425 appeals in criminal cases and 12,388 prisoner petitions brought before the federal circuit courts of appeal.[6]

The **Federal Judicial Center** (FJC) is the research and education agency of the judicial branch of the U.S. Government. Its responsibility is to support the efficient, effective administration of justice and judicial independence. It is a separate agency within the judicial branch designed to encourage critical and careful examination of ways to improve judicial administration. The written history of the development of the Federal Circuit Courts of Appeal explains:

> *In 1866 Congress reorganized the states into nine circuits and established the geographical outline that has remained unchanged except for the inclusion of new states within existing circuits and the division of two circuits. In 1929, Congress divided the Eighth Circuit to create a Tenth Circuit, and in 1980 an Eleventh Circuit was established to include three states formerly part of the Fifth Circuit. The act establishing the circuit courts of appeals in 1891 gave the circuits a new jurisdictional role at the same time that reliance on the existing circuit organization gave the judiciary's principal appellate courts a regional identity. (The Federal Circuit, established in 1982, is the only circuit defined exclusively by its jurisdiction.) . . . The circuit judicial councils established in 1939 exercise administrative authority over all the federal courts within a circuit, and the circuit judicial conferences provide a forum for judges and lawyers to discuss the administration of federal justice within a circuit.[7]*

---

[4]  United States Department of Justice, https://www.justice.gov/usao/justice-101/federal-courts.

[5]  *Id.*

[6]  https://www.uscourts.gov/statistics-reports/federal-judicial-caseload-statistics-2020.

[7]  Federal Judicial Council, http://www.fjc.gov/history/home.nsf/page/admin_02.html.

Map of the Federal Circuit Courts of Appeal (figure 2.1):

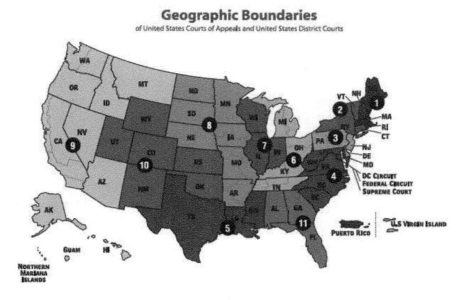

## iii. Federal Trial Courts

The federal trial courts are called district courts. There are 94 federal districts with at least one in each state. Four territories also have U.S. District Courts: Puerto Rico, the Virgin Islands, Guam, and the Northern Mariana Islands. For each judicial district there is also a bankruptcy court as a unit of the district court. There are also two special district courts, the Court of International Trade and the Court of U.S. Claims.

The federal trial courts, like the state trial courts, are charged with deciding questions of fact in both civil and criminal cases. They hear evidence in criminal cases and decide the guilt or innocence of the defendant. In jury trials the jurors are responsible for deciding whether the defendant is guilty. In a case where the defendant has waived his right to a jury trial, the district court judge would rule on the whether the facts and evidence prove the defendant is guilty of the crimes charged. This is called a **bench trial**.

In the federal trial courts a single district court judge presides over cases. They are often called **Article III judges** because they are appointed through the process articulated in Article III. The president nominates these judges and the Senate must vote to approve the nominations. Once approved, these judges serve life terms. District court judges preside over all aspects of a trial in federal court. As of 2021, there were 167 approved Article III judgeships for the regional courts of appeal, with additional positions for specialized federal courts, and 673 approved District Court judgeships.[8] In addition to Article III Judges, there are federal **magistrate judges**. According to the Federal Judicial Center, magistrate judges serve as judicial officers of the U.S. district courts and exercise the jurisdiction delegated to them by law and assigned by the district judges. Magistrate judges may be authorized by the district court judges to preside in almost every type of federal trial proceeding *except* for felony cases. They often prepare recommendations for the district court judges to follow and can be tasked with completing the majority of tasks required for misdemeanor trials. There are approximately 600 authorized magistrate judgeships in the United States.[9]

Congress has the power to determine the specific organization and structure of the federal courts. The **Judiciary Act of 1789** was the first and arguably most important step in that development. While additional changes have been made to the Act in the years that followed, its basic principles—a federal judiciary composed of district courts and circuit courts to enforce federal law alongside the constitutionally created Supreme Court—are still intact. For further reading, a detailed study of the history of the federal judiciary, *Creating the Federal Judicial System*, 3rd Edition, is available from the Federal Judicial Center. It was published to celebrate the bicentennial of the federal courts in 1989 and continues to be updated for students and judicial officers.[10] It is an excellent resource that provides a detailed summary of the evolution of the federal judiciary.

### iv. Federal Criminal Jurisdiction

As a matter of constitutional law when a case raises a **federal question** the federal courts have **jurisdiction**. Jurisdiction is the authority to hear the case. Violations of federal criminal statutes result in federal jurisdiction because they are federal questions. While there are many federal criminal statutes, state criminal laws far outnumber federal ones. The **Reserve Powers Clause** in the Tenth Amendment dictates that the power to make law in areas not specifically given to the federal government belongs to the states.[11] The framers intended to limit the federal government from overstepping its bounds and legislating in areas of state sovereignty.

---

[8]   https://www.uscourts.gov/sites/default/files/allauth.pdf.

[9]   http://www.fjc.gov/history/home.nsf/page/judges_magistrate.html; https://www.fedbar.org/wp-content/uploads/2019/10/FBA-White-Paper-2016-pdf-2.pdf.

[10]   Harrison, C. and Wheeler, R., *Creating the Federal Judiciary*, 3rd Ed., Federal Judicial Center, 2005.

[11]   U.S. Const. amend X, "The powers not delegated to the United States by the Constitution, nor prohibited by it to the States, are reserved to the States respectively, or to the people."

The federal government's jurisdiction over crimes began only with acts of treason and crimes against the government, but has been extended over the years with the expansion of federal government power. After the Civil War, Congress began to pass legislation that criminalized conduct outside the scope of crimes against the government. It amended the Postal Code to regulate the passage of obscene material through the U.S. Mail Service,[12] made it unlawful to transport a woman across state lines for immoral purposes[13] and, possibly the pinnacle of this movement in federal power, made it illegal to sell, purchase or use alcohol. The Commerce Clause in the U.S. Constitution empowers the federal government to regulate *interstate* commerce. Congress has used its enumerated power in the **Interstate Commerce Clause** as the foundation for a wide range of other criminal statutes. Because of this, many federal criminal statutes govern gun, narcotics or human trafficking across state lines.

The Supreme Court has at times allowed for the expansion of federal judicial power without restraint, but in recent years has employed the Tenth Amendment to restrict Congress' power to enact criminal codes. In *United States v. Lopez (1995)* the Supreme Court held that federal gun regulations were unconstitutional because they encroached on an area of state regulatory power under the Tenth Amendment. A federal civil remedy for gender-motivated violence was struck down for the same reason in *United States v. Morrison (2000)*.

The **Administrative Office of the United States Courts** (AOUSC) is a federal administrative agency tasked with providing support to the federal courts. It supports efforts relating to legislation, financing, technology and other areas. It develops the budget for the federal court for submission to Congress. Its primary responsibility is to provide staff and counsel to the Judicial Conference and its committees. The **Judicial Conference** is the national policy making body for the federal courts.

The AOUSC reports the caseload of the federal district and circuit courts each year. These reports provide statistical data and year-to-year comparisons regarding the caseload of the federal courts. The federal courts hear civil and criminal cases, bankruptcy, prisoner petitions and other special filings and appeals. In reports for the year ending March, 2021 the AOUSC reported that there were 286,289 civil filings and 64,868 criminal filings in the federal district courts. During

---

[12]   The Post Office Code of 1872.

[13]   36 Stat. 825 (1910).

the same period, the U.S. Bankruptcy Courts had 764,282 filings and the federal courts had 126,875 former inmates in post-conviction supervision.[14]

## v.  Steps in a Federal Criminal Trial

In the federal court system there are clearly articulated rules governing each step a criminal defendant will go through from arrest to sentencing. These steps in a federal prosecution may vary *significantly* from the processes employed by individual states. It is important to note that terms such as arraignment or initial appearance may mean something different in a state criminal trial than they do in the federal courts. When observing a criminal trial locally make note of what takes place during the arraignment or preliminary hearing as it might differ a great deal from the experience of a defendant in federal court.

## vi.  Federal Criminal Prosecutions Step-by-Step

**1.  Complaint and Arrest Warrant**: Law enforcement obtains a *warrant for arrest* of the alleged offender. The warrant is based on an *indictment* or a *complaint* filed with the U.S. District Court. An *affidavit*, signed by a law enforcement officer, usually accompanies the complaint. The affidavit explains the crime committed as well as the role of the accused in that crime. The affidavit is used to establish *probable cause* that the accused committed the crime.

**2.  Initial Appearance**: As soon as practical after arrest, the alleged offender must be granted an *initial appearance* before a magistrate judge. The magistrate judge advises the accused of his or her rights and determines if he or she has the financial ability to hire an attorney or if a public defender must be appointed. The magistrate judge also sets release conditions, including any *bond*. At the same time, a federal prosecutor, known as an *assistant United States Attorney*, may ask that the defendant be detained.

**3.  Detention Hearing**: If the alleged offender is detained, a *detention hearing* must be held within three working days. At that hearing, the magistrate judge considers evidence about the accused's *risk of flight* or *danger to the community* and decides whether the accused should be released prior to trial.

**4.  Preliminary Hearing**: Within 10 days of arrest on a complaint, the accused has the right to a *preliminary hearing*, during which an assistant U.S. attorney may offer testimony to establish probable cause, and the defense attorney may provide evidence on behalf of the accused. If the magistrate judge finds sufficient

---

[14]   https://www.uscourts.gov/statistics-reports/federal-judicial-caseload-statistics-2020-tables.

probable cause as to the commission of the crime as well as the accused's role in it, the accused is bound over for further proceedings by a grand jury. (Note, if the grand jury returns an indictment against an alleged offender before arrest is made, a preliminary hearing is not necessary).

5.     **Grand Jury**: The final decision to prosecute a federal criminal case rests with a *grand jury*. A federal grand jury is comprised of 23 randomly selected citizens from across the judicial district. Those selected to serve on the grand jury do so for a few days each month for approximately one year.

6.     **Indictment Sought**: Instead of filing a complaint, or after filing a complaint, assistant U.S. attorneys appear before the grand jury to establish probable cause that a particular person committed a federal *felony*. They do this by calling witnesses and presenting evidence obtained with *grand jury subpoenas*. Defense attorneys are not allowed to appear before the grand jury; the accused does not need to testify before the grand jury; and the work of the grand jury is to be kept secret.

7.     **Indictment Returned**: If the grand jury decides the evidence presented establishes probable cause, it issues an *indictment* against the accused. At least 16 of the 23 members of the grand jury must be present to conduct business, and at least 12 jurors must vote to indict. The Indictment is called a *true bill*. If the grand jury does not find sufficient probable cause, it returns a *no bill*. In a misdemeanor case, or in a felony case where the accused has waived indictment and has agreed, instead, to plead guilty, no case is presented to the grand jury. In those instances, an *information*, which is a document outlining probable cause, is filed with the U.S. District Court.

8.     **Arraignment**: Within 10 days from the time an indictment or information has been filed and arrest has been made, an *arraignment* must take place before a magistrate judge. The accused, now called the *defendant*, is read the charges against him or her and advised of his or her rights and enters a *plea of guilty* or *not guilty*. The Federal Speedy Trial Act dictates the defendant has right to trial within 70 days from his or her initial appearance in U.S. District Court.

9.     **Plea Agreement**: Defendants are presumed innocent until they admit guilt or are proven guilty. If a defendant pleads not guilty, a trial takes place unless a *plea agreement* can be reached between the assistant U.S. attorney and the defense attorney on behalf of the defendant. A U.S. District Court judge must approve the terms of the plea agreement.

10.    **Trial**: A trial is heard before a jury of citizens selected at random from across the judicial district and overseen by a U.S. District Court judge. At trial, the

assistant U.S. attorney must—and the defense attorneys may—call witnesses and present evidence. The government has the burden of proving the elements of the offense beyond a reasonable doubt. Afterward, the jury must unanimously decide the *verdict*. If the defendant is found not guilty, he or she is released. If he or she is *convicted*, however, the pre-sentencing process begins.

**11.  Pre-Sentencing**: After the entry of a guilty plea or the unanimous finding of guilt by a jury following trial, the U.S. Probation Office collects information about the defendant and crime victims and supplies it, along with a recommendation for sentence, to the U.S. District Court judge as part of a pre-sentence investigation report.

**12.  Sentencing**: Approximately eight weeks after the entry of a guilty plea or a jury finding of guilt, the U.S. District Court judge imposes the sentence. The sentence may include incarceration in a federal prison; a term of *supervised release* (formerly called *probation*); the imposition of a monetary fine; and/or an *order of restitution* directing the defendant to pay the crime victims money lost or expenses incurred due to the offense.

**13.  Appeal**: The defendant may *appeal* either the finding of guilt or the sentence or both. To do so, he or she must file with the sentencing court a *Notice of appeal* within 10 days from the sentencing or *judgment*. If the defendant pled guilty, generally only the sentence may be appealed.[15]

## vii. The Relationship Between State and Federal Courts

Like the federal government, each state is also governed by a constitution. Much like the U.S. Constitution, this founding document articulates key organizational principles and is the highest law in the state. Because each state is unique in terms of history, culture and population, it is important that states are governed independently. This independence is balanced by state subordination to the federal constitution. Article VI of the U.S. Constitution contains a Supremacy Clause, which reads:

> *This Constitution, and the laws of the United States which shall be made in pursuance thereof; and all treaties made, or which shall be made, under the authority of the United States, shall be the supreme law of the land; and the judges in every state shall be bound thereby, anything in the Constitution or laws of any State to the contrary notwithstanding.*

---

[15]  https://www.justice.gov/usao-mn/criminal-procedures.

It might be easiest to understand these basic principles of federalism by visualizing a set of train tracks. One track represents the federal judicial system and the other track represents the state courts. On them both, working in tandem, runs the "engine" of the American courts. Because Americans enjoy dual citizenship of both the federal government and their home state, they are provided access to both the state and federal court systems to resolve legal disputes. They are also subject to the criminal judicial process of both the state and federal government if accused of a crime.

# B. STATE COURTS

State courts have jurisdiction over cases that arise under state law. State courts are governed by rules of criminal and civil procedure, which detail the steps required for cases as they progress through the courts. **Procedural law** provides rules for the process by which a case is brought in the courts, and the manner in which an individual is treated throughout the course of a judicial proceeding. Requirements such as notice prior to hearings or timelines for filing documents in a case are procedural law. Those rules are different for each state, and potentially differ among jurisdictions within a state.

Each of the fifty states has their own statutes and codes that deal with the **substantive law** of property, contracts, crimes, domestic relations and many others. Substantive criminal law deals with whether conduct is prohibited or required. Commission of a crime may involve action that is unlawful or the failure to act when a legal duty exists to do so. For example, the penal code makes it unlawful to kill another human being (prohibiting specific actions) and makes it unlawful to neglect or fail to care for a child (a criminal omission or failure to act).

## i.   State Trial Courts

State courts are responsible for civil and criminal trials involving state law. The state courts are independent and the organization of each state court system is unique. The majority of states have **trial courts of limited jurisdiction** and **trial courts of general jurisdiction,** each of which handle a different caseload. Nine states have only trial courts of general jurisdiction (CA, DC, ID, IL, IA, ME, MN, PR and VT.)[16] State trial courts of limited jurisdiction have specific subject matter responsibilities such as domestic violence, juvenile matters, city ordinance violations and family court matters. Trial courts of general jurisdiction are typically

---

[16] LaFountain, R., Lews, K., Schauffler, R., Strickland, S., and Holt, K., eds., Court Statistics Project DataViewer, www.courtstatistics.org.

responsible for all other more serious civil and criminal cases outside the jurisdiction of the lower or specialized courts.

It is important to remember that because each state's judiciary is independent, the rules and processes they employ all share similarities but also significant differences. In one state an initial appearance may refer to a hearing that mirrors the federal initial appearance: the defendant may be read their rights, a bail decision may be made and counsel appointed if they are indigent. The defendant in that scenario was not read charges at the initial appearance and would return to court on a future date to have charges read at an arraignment. In other states the arraignment takes the place of the initial appearance. In true "one stop" fashion in some state at arraignments for crimes like driving under the influence, an observer might see the rights of defendants read to a group of "out of custody" defendants as they sit in the courtroom gallery. As each person is called to the podium they would be read the charges, assigned indigent defense counsel if necessary and may even return later that same day to enter a plea and be sentenced.

State court systems vary widely in structure and organization. It is useful to consider some examples: California superior courts are responsible for all trial matters from small claims to felony criminal trials, while New York's courts are organized into 10 separate sections, each handling specific types of disputes. See figures 2.2 and 2.3 for charts outlining the organization of the state courts in California and New York. Compare the two systems and note the similarities and differences between them.

New York Criminal Court Structure (figure 2.2):[17]

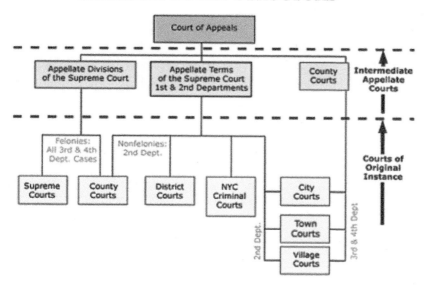

California Court Structure (figure 2.3):

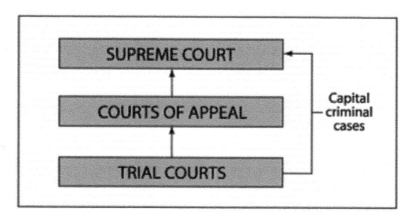

The caseload of state courts also varies widely among states. California courts serve the most populous state in the country (39.5 million people) and handled 5.9 million total filings in 2019.[18] In contrast, Alaska reported just 23,402 total case filings for 2019.[19] In 2018 the total caseload of state courts nationally was 83.5

[17]   https://www.nycourts.gov/courts/structure.shtml.

[18]   https://www.courts.ca.gov/documents/2020-Court-Statistics-Report.pdf.

[19]   http://courts.alaska.gov/admin/docs/fy19.pdf.

million. The caseload of the state trial courts is a striking contrast to the 1.1 million total cases filed in the federal district courts in 2020.[20]

## ii.   State Appellate Courts

The state appellate courts are responsible for answering questions of law. They evaluate claims brought by parties whose cases have been heard and decided by the trial courts, and determine whether the law has been correctly applied. Appeals are typically brought upon a final decision by the trial court, but can sometimes be brought when a final decision has not been reached; this is called an interlocutory appeal. Appellate courts function differently than trial courts in that they are not charged with evaluating facts and evidence in order to determine which party should prevail. Instead, they consider questions of law raised by the parties to the case, and determine whether there were errors made during the trial. In reaching a decision, state appellate courts affirm, reverse, or reverse and remand in the same fashion as the federal appellate courts.

If errors were made, they must decide the nature of the error. It may be a **harmless error** that did not impact the outcome of the case, or a **reversible error**, which is prejudicial and requires reversal of the decision. There are circumstances when the law was not interpreted or applied correctly by the trial court, but that mistake did not affect the outcome of the case. In these circumstances the court of appeal will deem the error harmless and the outcome of the original trial is upheld regardless of the mistake. In other circumstances, errors in interpretation or application of the law are so significant that the outcome of the trial cannot be trusted to be fair. These errors are reversible and cases must be sent back to the lower court for reconsideration, or dismissed altogether.

Appellate courts operate much differently than trial courts and because they are not often featured on television programs or in movies, most people are unfamiliar with their processes. When a party wishes to appeal, they file their intent to do so with the appropriate appellate court, which has jurisdiction over their case. They will follow a timeline for submitting written briefs to the court and their opposing party, and the opponent will have the opportunity to respond. The case is later scheduled for oral argument, which takes place before a panel of judges. Rather than calling witnesses and bringing physical evidence to share with the appellate judges, the parties will argue the merits of their case before the panel, answering their questions, in an effort to sway their decision to their client's favor.

---

[20]  For the year ending March 31, 2021: https://www.uscourts.gov/statistics-reports/federal-judicial-caseload-statistics-2020-tables.

These oral arguments are much briefer than most people imagine, and the attorneys must be excellent at speaking and answering questions on their feet as the judges typically do not allow for prepared speech-making. Instead judges interrupt the attorneys with questions that illuminate the strengths and weaknesses of their position on the issues in question.

The majority of states (41) have **intermediate courts of appeal** and all of the states have a **court of last resort**.[21] The court of last resort is typically referred to as the supreme court. In states where they are utilized, intermediate appellate courts are the first state courts to review questions on appeal, where the majority of appeals receive a final decision. They are typically organized geographically throughout the state where they are situated. Litigants can appeal again, to the state supreme court if they are unhappy with the outcome in the intermediate appellate court. The supreme court of the state is its highest court and has the authority to issue the final ruling in a case interpreting state law. The states of Oklahoma and Texas are unique, in that they have two supreme courts, one that hears civil appeals and the other criminal appeals.

State supreme courts may have original jurisdiction over certain matters, such as habeas corpus petitions in death penalty cases. Original jurisdiction means that the case originates, or begins, in the court where the case is brought. When a case originates in the state supreme court, it presents a unique situation where the justices must serve as fact-finders because no trial court has reviewed the case, leaving them to wear two hats in one case: that of trial court and appellate court.

In the majority of criminal cases, a decision by the state supreme court marks the end of the appellate road for the defendant. It is a common misconception that a case can automatically be appealed in federal court after a defendant loses the appeal in state court. In order for the federal court to have jurisdiction, the defendant must raise a federal question. One effective way to do so is for a defendant to utilize a **writ of habeas corpus**, or a habeas petition. Habeas corpus is Latin, translated literally "you have the body." A habeas petition is a civil action brought by an inmate alleging that their detention is unlawful. Usually the warden of the institution where the inmate (or mental patient) is incarcerated is named as the opposing party to the lawsuit. Habeas petitions can also be used to examine extradition processes, bail questions and the jurisdiction of the court.

---

[21] Delaware, Maine, Montana, New Hampshire, Rhode Island, South Dakota, Vermont, West Virginia and Wyoming do not have intermediate courts of appeal.

Read and brief *United States v. Lopez* and consider the questions following the case:

---

## UNITED STATES V. LOPEZ

Supreme Court of the United States
Argued Nov. 8, 1994
Decided April 26, 1995
514 U.S. 549

### Opinion

### CHIEF JUSTICE REHNQUIST delivered the opinion of the Court.

In the Gun-Free School Zones Act of 1990, Congress made it a federal offense "for any individual knowingly to possess a firearm at a place that the individual knows, or has reasonable cause to believe, is a school zone." 18 U.S.C. § 922(q)(1)(A) (1988 ed., Supp. V). The Act neither regulates a commercial activity nor contains a requirement that the possession be connected in any way to interstate commerce. We hold that the Act exceeds the authority of Congress "[t]o regulate Commerce . . . among the several States. . . ." U.S. Const., Art. I, § 8, cl. 3.

On March 10, 1992, respondent, who was then a 12th-grade student, arrived at Edison High School in San Antonio, Texas, carrying a concealed .38-caliber handgun and five bullets. Acting upon an anonymous tip, school authorities confronted respondent, who admitted that he was carrying the weapon. He was arrested and charged under Texas law with firearm possession on school premises. See Tex. Penal Code Ann. § 46.03(a)(1) (Supp.1994). The next day, the state charges were dismissed after federal agents charged respondent by complaint with violating the Gun-Free School Zones Act of 1990. 18 U.S.C. § 922(q)(1)(A) (1988 ed., Supp. V).[1]

A federal grand jury indicted respondent on one count of knowing possession of a firearm at a school zone, in violation of § 922(q). Respondent moved to dismiss his federal indictment on the ground that § 922(q) "is unconstitutional as it is beyond the power of Congress to legislate control over our public schools." The District Court denied the motion, concluding that § 922(q) "is a constitutional exercise of Congress' well-defined power to regulate activities in and affecting commerce, and the 'business' of elementary, middle and high schools . . . affects interstate commerce." App. to Pet. for Cert. 55a. Respondent waived his right to a jury trial. The District Court conducted

---

[1] The term "school zone" is defined as "in, or on the grounds of, a public, parochial or private school" or "within a distance of 1,000 feet from the grounds of a public, parochial or private school." § 921(a)(25).

a bench trial, found him guilty of violating § 922(q), and sentenced him to six months' imprisonment and two years' supervised release.

On appeal, respondent challenged his conviction based on his claim that § 922(q) exceeded Congress' power to legislate under the Commerce Clause. The Court of Appeals for the Fifth Circuit agreed and reversed respondent's conviction. It held that, in light of what it characterized as insufficient congressional findings and legislative history, "section 922(q), in the full reach of its terms, is invalid as beyond the power of Congress under the Commerce Clause." 2 F.3d 1342, 1367–1368 (1993). Because of the importance of the issue, we granted certiorari, 511 U.S. 1029 (1994), and we now affirm.

We start with first principles. The Constitution creates a Federal Government of enumerated powers. See Art. I, § 8. As James Madison wrote: "The powers delegated by the proposed Constitution to the federal government are few and defined. Those which are to remain in the State governments are numerous and indefinite." The Federalist No. 45, pp. 292–293 (C. Rossiter ed. 1961). This constitutionally mandated division of authority "was adopted by the Framers to ensure protection of our fundamental liberties." *Gregory v. Ashcroft*, 501 U.S. 452, 458 (1991) (internal quotation marks omitted). "Just as the separation and independence of the coordinate branches of the Federal Government serve to prevent the accumulation of excessive power in any one branch, a healthy balance of power between the States and the Federal Government will reduce the risk of tyranny and abuse from either front." *Ibid.*

The Constitution delegates to Congress the power "[t]o regulate Commerce with foreign Nations, and among the several States, and with the Indian Tribes." Art. I, § 8, cl. 3. . .

But even these modern-era precedents which have expanded congressional power under the Commerce Clause confirm that this power is subject to outer limits. In *Jones & Laughlin Steel*, the Court warned that the scope of the interstate commerce power "must be considered in the light of our dual system of government and may not be extended so as to embrace effects upon interstate commerce so indirect and remote that to embrace them, in view of our complex society, would effectually obliterate the distinction between what is national and what is local and create a completely centralized government." 301 U.S., at 37; see also *Darby, supra,* 312 U.S., at 119–120 (Congress may regulate intrastate activity that has a "substantial effect" on interstate commerce); *Wickard, supra,* at 125 (Congress may regulate activity that "exerts a substantial economic effect on interstate commerce"). Since that time, the

Court has heeded that warning and undertaken to decide whether a rational basis existed for concluding that a regulated activity sufficiently affected interstate commerce. . . .

Consistent with this structure, we have identified three broad categories of activity that Congress may regulate under its commerce power. *Perez, supra,* at 150; First, Congress may regulate the use of the channels of interstate commerce. See, e.g., *Darby,* 312 U.S., at 114; *Heart of Atlanta Motel, supra,* at 256 (" '[T]he authority of Congress to keep the channels of interstate commerce free from immoral and injurious uses has been frequently sustained, and is no longer open to question.' " (quoting *Caminetti v. United States,* 242 U.S. 470 (1917)). Second, Congress is empowered to regulate and protect the instrumentalities of interstate commerce, or persons or things in interstate commerce, even though the threat may come only from intrastate activities. See, e.g., *Shreveport Rate Cases,* 234 U.S. 342 (1914); (upholding amendments to Safety Appliance Act as applied to vehicles used in intrastate commerce); *Perez, supra,* at 150, 91 S.Ct., at 1359 ("[F]or example, the destruction of an aircraft (18 U.S.C. § 32), or . . . thefts from interstate shipments (18 U.S.C. § 659)"). Finally, Congress' commerce authority includes the power to regulate those activities having a substantial relation to interstate commerce, *Jones & Laughlin Steel,* 301 U.S., at 37, *i.e.,* those activities that substantially affect interstate commerce, *Wirtz, supra,* at 196, n. 27.

Within this final category, admittedly, our case law has not been clear whether an activity must "affect" or "substantially affect" interstate commerce in order to be within Congress' power to regulate it under the Commerce Clause. Compare *Preseault v. ICC,* 494 U.S. 1, 17 (1990), with *Wirtz, supra,* at 196, n. 27 (the Court has never declared that "Congress may use a relatively trivial impact on commerce as an excuse for broad general regulation of state or private activities"). We conclude, consistent with the great weight of our case law, that the proper test requires an analysis of whether the regulated activity "substantially affects" interstate commerce.

We now turn to consider the power of Congress, in the light of this framework, to enact § 922(q). The first two categories of authority may be quickly disposed of: § 922(q) is not a regulation of the use of the channels of interstate commerce, nor is it an attempt to prohibit the interstate transportation of a commodity through the channels of commerce; nor can § 922(q) be justified as a regulation by which Congress has sought to protect an instrumentality of interstate commerce or a thing in interstate commerce.

Thus, if § 922(q) is to be sustained, it must be under the third category as a regulation of an activity that substantially affects interstate commerce.

First, we have upheld a wide variety of congressional Acts regulating intrastate economic activity where we have concluded that the activity substantially affected interstate commerce. Examples include the regulation of intrastate coal mining; *Hodel, supra,* intrastate extortionate credit transactions, *Perez, supra,* restaurants utilizing substantial interstate supplies, *McClung, supra,* inns and hotels catering to interstate guests, *Heart of Atlanta Motel, supra,* and production and consumption of homegrown wheat, *Wickard v. Filburn,* 317 U.S. 111 (1942). These examples are by no means exhaustive, but the pattern is clear. Where economic activity substantially affects interstate commerce, legislation regulating that activity will be sustained.

Even *Wickard,* which is perhaps the most far reaching example of Commerce Clause authority over intrastate activity, involved economic activity in a way that the possession of a gun in a school zone does not. Roscoe Filburn operated a small farm in Ohio, on which, in the year involved, he raised 23 acres of wheat. It was his practice to sow winter wheat in the fall, and after harvesting it in July to sell a portion of the crop, to feed part of it to poultry and livestock on the farm, to use some in making flour for home consumption, and to keep the remainder for seeding future crops. The Secretary of Agriculture assessed a penalty against him under the Agricultural Adjustment Act of 1938 because he harvested about 12 acres more wheat than his allotment under the Act permitted. The Act was designed to regulate the volume of wheat moving in interstate and foreign commerce in order to avoid surpluses and shortages, and concomitant fluctuation in wheat prices, which had previously obtained. The Court said, in an opinion sustaining the application of the Act to Filburn's activity:

> "One of the primary purposes of the Act in question was to increase the market price of wheat and to that end to limit the volume thereof that could affect the market. It can hardly be denied that a factor of such volume and variability as home-consumed wheat would have a substantial influence on price and market conditions. This may arise because being in marketable condition such wheat overhangs the market and, if induced by rising prices, tends to flow into the market and check price increases. But if we assume that it is never marketed, it supplies a need of the man who grew it which would otherwise be reflected by purchases in the open market. Home-grown wheat in this sense competes with wheat in commerce." 317 U.S., at 128.

Section 922(q) is a criminal statute that by its terms has nothing to do with "commerce" or any sort of economic enterprise, however broadly one might define those terms.[3] Section 922(q) is not an essential part of a larger regulation of economic activity, in which the regulatory scheme could be undercut unless the intrastate activity were regulated. It cannot, therefore, be sustained under our cases upholding regulations of activities that arise out of or are connected with a commercial transaction, which viewed in the aggregate, substantially affects interstate commerce.

. . .

The Government argues that possession of a firearm in a school zone may result in violent crime and that violent crime can be expected to affect the functioning of the national economy in two ways. First, the costs of violent crime are substantial, and, through the mechanism of insurance, those costs are spread throughout the population. See *United States v. Evans,* 928 F.2d 858, 862 (CA9 1991). Second, violent crime reduces the willingness of individuals to travel to areas within the country that are perceived to be unsafe. Cf. *Heart of Atlanta Motel,* 379 U.S., at 253. The Government also argues that the presence of guns in schools poses a substantial threat to the educational process by threatening the learning environment. A handicapped educational process, in turn, will result in a less productive citizenry. That, in turn, would have an adverse effect on the Nation's economic well-being. As a result, the Government argues that Congress could rationally have concluded that § 922(q) substantially affects interstate commerce.

We pause to consider the implications of the Government's arguments. The Government admits, under its "costs of crime" reasoning, that Congress could regulate not only all violent crime, but all activities that might lead to violent crime, regardless of how tenuously they relate to interstate commerce. See Tr. of Oral Arg. 8–9. Similarly, under the Government's "national productivity" reasoning, Congress could regulate any activity that it found was related to the economic productivity of individual citizens: family law (including marriage, divorce, and child custody), for example. Under the theories that the Government presents in support of § 922(q), it is difficult to perceive any limitation on federal power, even in areas such as criminal law enforcement or education where States historically have been sovereign. Thus,

---

[3]    Under our federal system, the " 'States possess primary authority for defining and enforcing the criminal law' ". . .

if we were to accept the Government's arguments, we are hard pressed to posit any activity by an individual that Congress is without power to regulate.

Although Justice BREYER argues that acceptance of the Government's rationales would not authorize a general federal police power, he is unable to identify any activity that the States may regulate but Congress may not. Justice BREYER posits that there might be some limitations on Congress' commerce power, such as family law or certain aspects of education. *Post,* at 1661–1662. These suggested limitations, when viewed in light of the dissent's expansive analysis, are devoid of substance.

Justice BREYER focuses, for the most part, on the threat that firearm possession in and near schools poses to the educational process and the potential economic consequences flowing from that threat. *Post,* at 1659–1662. Specifically, the dissent reasons that (1) gun-related violence is a serious problem; (2) that problem, in turn, has an adverse effect on classroom learning; and (3) that adverse effect on classroom learning, in turn, represents a substantial threat to trade and commerce. *Post,* at 1661. This analysis would be equally applicable, if not more so, to subjects such as family law and direct regulation of education.

For instance, if Congress can, pursuant to its Commerce Clause power, regulate activities that adversely affect the learning environment, then, *a fortiori,* it also can regulate the educational process directly. Congress could determine that a school's curriculum has a "significant" effect on the extent of classroom learning. As a result, Congress could mandate a federal curriculum for local elementary and secondary schools because what is taught in local schools has a significant "effect on classroom learning," cf. *post,* at 1661, and that, in turn, has a substantial effect on interstate commerce.

Justice BREYER rejects our reading of precedent and argues that "Congress . . . could rationally conclude that schools fall on the commercial side of the line." *Post,* at 1664. Again, Justice BREYER's rationale lacks any real limits because, depending on the level of generality, any activity can be looked upon as commercial. Under the dissent's rationale, Congress could just as easily look at child rearing as "fall[ing] on the commercial side of the line" because it provides a "valuable service—namely, to equip [children] with the skills they need to survive in life and, more specifically, in the workplace." *Ibid.* . . .

The possession of a gun in a local school zone is in no sense an economic activity that might, through repetition elsewhere, substantially affect any sort of interstate commerce. Respondent was a local student at a local school; there is no indication that he had recently moved in interstate commerce, and there is no requirement that his possession of the firearm have any concrete tie to interstate commerce.

To uphold the Government's contentions here, we would have to pile inference upon inference in a manner that would bid fair to convert congressional authority under the Commerce Clause to a general police power of the sort retained by the States. Admittedly, some of our prior cases have taken long steps down that road, giving great deference to congressional action. See *supra,* at 1629. The broad language in these opinions has suggested the possibility of additional expansion, but we decline here to proceed any further. To do so would require us to conclude that the Constitution's enumeration of powers does not presuppose something not enumerated, cf. *Gibbons v. Ogden, supra,* at 195, and that there never will be a distinction between what is truly national and what is truly local, cf. This we are unwilling to do.

For the foregoing reasons the judgment of the Court of Appeals is

*Affirmed.*

**JUSTICE KENNEDY, with whom JUSTICE O'CONNOR joins, concurring.**

The history of the judicial struggle to interpret the Commerce Clause during the transition from the economic system the Founders knew to the single, national market still emergent in our own era counsels great restraint before the Court determines that the Clause is insufficient to support an exercise of the national power. That history gives me some pause about today's decision, but I join the Court's opinion with these observations on what I conceive to be its necessary though limited holding.

. . .

**JUSTICE THOMAS, concurring.**

The Court today properly concludes that the Commerce Clause does not grant Congress the authority to prohibit gun possession within 1,000 feet of a school, as it attempted to do in the Gun-Free School Zones Act of 1990, Pub.L. 101–647, 104 Stat. 4844. Although I join the majority, I write separately to observe that our case law has drifted far from the original understanding of the Commerce Clause. In a future case, we ought to temper our Commerce Clause jurisprudence in a manner that both makes sense of our more recent case law and is more faithful to the original understanding of that Clause.

. . .

**JUSTICE STEVENS, dissenting.**

The welfare of our future "Commerce with foreign Nations, and among the several States," U.S. Const., Art. I, § 8, cl. 3, is vitally dependent on the character of the education of our children. I therefore agree entirely with Justice BREYER's explanation of why Congress has ample power to prohibit the possession of firearms in or near schools—just as it may protect the school environment from harms posed by controlled substances such as asbestos or alcohol. I also agree with Justice SOUTER's exposition of the radical character of the Court's holding and its kinship with the discredited, pre-Depression version of substantive due process. I believe, however, that the Court's extraordinary decision merits this additional comment.

Guns are both articles of commerce and articles that can be used to restrain commerce. Their possession is the consequence, either directly or indirectly, of commercial activity. In my judgment, Congress' power to regulate commerce in firearms includes the power to prohibit possession of guns at any location because of their potentially harmful use; it necessarily follows that Congress may also prohibit their possession in particular markets. The market for the possession of handguns by school-age children is, distressingly, substantial. Whether or not the national interest in eliminating that market would have justified federal legislation in 1789, it surely does today.

**JUSTICE SOUTER, dissenting.**

. . . A look at history's sequence will serve to show how today's decision tugs the Court off course, leading it to suggest opportunities for further developments that would be at odds with the rule of restraint to which the Court still wisely states adherence. . . .To be sure, the occasion for today's decision reflects the century's end, not its beginning. But if it seems anomalous that the Congress of the United States has taken to regulating school yards, the Act in question is still probably no more remarkable than state regulation of bake shops 90 years ago. In any event, there is no reason to hope that the Court's qualification of rational basis review will be any more successful than the efforts at substantive economic review made by our predecessors as the century began. Taking the Court's opinion on its own terms, Justice BREYER has explained both the hopeless porosity of "commercial" character as a ground of Commerce Clause distinction in America's highly connected economy, and the inconsistency of this categorization with our rational basis precedents from the last 50 years.

. . .

I respectfully dissent.

**JUSTICE BREYER, with whom JUSTICE STEVENS, JUSTICE SOUTER, and JUSTICE GINSBURG join, dissenting.**

The issue in this case is whether the Commerce Clause authorizes Congress to enact a statute that makes it a crime to possess a gun in, or near, a school. 18 U.S.C. § 922(q)(1)(A) (1988 ed., Supp. V). In my view, the statute falls well within the scope of the commerce power as this Court has understood that power over the last half century.

I

In reaching this conclusion, I apply three basic principles of Commerce Clause interpretation. First, the power to "regulate Commerce . . . among the several States," U.S. Const., Art. I, § 8, cl. 3, encompasses the power to regulate local activities insofar as they significantly affect interstate commerce. . . . As the majority points out, *ante,* at 1630, the Court, in describing how much of an effect the Clause requires, sometimes has used the word "substantial" and sometimes has not. . . . And, as the majority also recognizes in quoting Justice Cardozo, the question of degree (how *much* effect) requires an estimate of the "size" of the effect that no verbal formulation can capture with precision. See *ante,* at 1633. I use the word "significant" because the word "substantial" implies a somewhat narrower power than recent precedent suggests. . . .But to speak of "substantial effect" rather than "significant effect" would make no difference in this case.

Second, in determining whether a local activity will likely have a significant effect upon interstate commerce, a court must consider, not the effect of an individual act (a single instance of gun possession), but rather the cumulative effect of all similar instances (*i.e.,* the effect of all guns possessed in or near schools). . . .

Third, the Constitution requires us to judge the connection between a regulated activity and interstate commerce, not directly, but at one remove. Courts must give Congress a degree of leeway in determining the existence of a significant factual connection between the regulated activity and interstate commerce—both because the Constitution delegates the commerce power directly to Congress and because the determination requires an empirical judgment of a kind that a legislature is more likely than a court to make with accuracy. The traditional words "rational basis" capture this leeway. See *Hodel, supra,* 452 U.S., at 276–277. Thus, the specific question before us, as the Court recognizes, is not whether the "regulated activity sufficiently affected interstate commerce," but, rather, whether Congress could have had "*a rational basis*" for so concluding. *Ante,* at 1629 (emphasis added).

. . .

Respectfully, I dissent. . . .

**After preparing the case brief, consider the answers to the following questions:**

1.  What was the purpose of the Gun-Free School Zones Act of 1990?

2.  Why did the framers create a federal government of enumerated powers?

3.  How did the dissent argue that the Act's regulation of guns in schools "substantially affected" interstate commerce?

4.  What was the Court's rationale for holding that the Act was beyond the scope of Congress' power?

## Chapter 2 Key Terms for Review

- **United States Supreme Court**: the highest court in the United States and the final arbiter of questions of federal law and the Constitution.

- **Original jurisdiction**: when a court has the authority to hear a case it is permitted to originate or begin in that court. For the U.S. Supreme Court original jurisdiction is limited to a narrow class of cases—the vast majority involve appellate review.

- **Writ of certiorari**: a request submitted to the U.S. Supreme Court to review a case on appeal.

- **Rule of four**: four of the justices of the U.S. Supreme Court must agree to grant a writ of certiorari in order for a case to be reviewed.

- **Opinion**: the written decision of an appellate court after reviewing a case.

- **Concur**: to agree with another justice in the decision of a case, but write separately to explain the rationale for the decision.

- **Dissent**: to disagree with the majority of the court in a case and write separately to explain the reasons for the dissent.

- **Affirm**: to uphold the decision of the lower court leaving it unchanged.

- **Reverse**: to reverse or undo the decision of the lower court and changing the outcome of the case.

- **Reverse and remand**: to reverse the decision of the lower court and send it back down for reconsideration based on specific instructions in the opinion.

- **Circuit courts of appeal**: the federal intermediate appellate courts. There are eleven numbered circuit courts, and a separate one for the District of Columbia, and the court of appeals for the Federal Circuit.

- **En banc**: when an appellate court sits to hear a case with all of its judges or justices rather than a panel.

- **Federal Judicial Center**: the research and education agency of the judicial branch of the U.S. Government.

- **Bench trial**: when a judge sits as the fact-finder in a trial rather than a jury.

- **Article III Judges**: judges who appointed by the president with approval by the Senate according to the rules articulated in Article III of the U.S. Constitution.

- **Magistrate judges**: federal judges serving as officers of the U.S. District Courts (trial courts) to assist federal judges in managing the caseload of the federal courts. They may be delegated to oversee every type of federal trial proceeding except for felony cases.

- **Judiciary Act of 1789**: Congress' first legislative act establishing the federal courts. The Act created a federal judiciary composed of district courts and circuit courts to enforce the law alongside the U.S. Supreme Court.

- **Federal question jurisdiction**: when a federal court has authority to hear a case because the issue presented arises under the Constitution and laws of the United States (federal law).

- **Reserve Powers Clause**: the Tenth Amendment requires that any powers not specifically granted to the federal government in the Constitution belong to the states.

- **Interstate Commerce Clause**: authorizes Congress to pass laws that regulate commerce (the sale of goods) between states.

- **Administrative Office of the United States Courts**: federal administrative agency tasked with providing support to the federal courts relating to legislation, finance/budget, technology and other areas.

- **Judicial Conference**: the national policy-making body for the federal courts.

- **Procedural law**: governs the process by which a case progresses through the courts and sets requirements for the treatment of defendants in the judicial system.

- **Substantive law**: governs whether specific conduct is prohibited or required.

- **Trial court of limited jurisdiction**: tasked with a specific caseload, typically limited to minor criminal offenses or civil matters. The vast majority of states have trial courts of limited jurisdiction.

- **Trial courts of general jurisdiction**: trial courts which are responsible for more serious civil and criminal cases. Nine states have only trial courts of general jurisdiction.

- **Harmless error**: when an error is made during a trial that did not affect the outcome of the case.

- **Reversible error**: also called prejudicial error, takes place when an error is made during a trial, and if corrected there is a reasonable probability of a different result in the case.

- **Intermediate courts of appeal**: review the decisions of trial courts, and are used in the majority of states.

- **Court of last resort**: the highest court in a jurisdiction. The U.S. Supreme Court in the federal system and the state supreme courts in each state. Two states, Oklahoma and Texas have separate civil and criminal courts of last resort.

- **Writ of habeas corpus**: a petition from an inmate in federal court challenging their confinement as unlawful.

# Fundamental Rights and Selective Incorporation

The first ten amendments to the U.S. Constitution are referred to as the **Bill of Rights**. They represent critical values held by the framers of the Constitution. The body of the U.S. Constitution is brief by design. It articulates a narrow range of specific powers granted to the new federal government, organized into three branches: legislative, executive and judicial. James Madison, often referred to the as the "Father of the Constitution," believed the Bill of Rights was unnecessary. He argued the Constitution was already clear: the new federal government could exercise only those powers it was expressly provided in the Constitution. Some of the other framers feared that if certain fundamental rights were not articulated, it would be too easy for the new government to take them away. Two factions developed among the framers: the Federalists along with James Madison, and the anti-Federalists led by Thomas Jefferson. After much debate, the Bill of Rights was ratified along with the Constitution in 1789.

The First Amendment recognizes that freedom of religion, both in terms of beliefs and practices, is a right of the highest order, along with freedom of speech, the press and the freedom to assemble together. While these certainly might have been "understood" at the time of the drafting of the Constitution to be true, the inclusion of these rights and their position at the top of the Bill of Rights speaks to the framers commitment to protecting them at all cost. It was, after all, for the sake of free exercise of religion that so many lost their lives in pursuit of liberty during the Revolutionary War. This new government did not provide justice for all. The framers inability to agree to abolish slavery as they crafted the Bill of Rights is arguably the greatest failure of the Constitutional Convention. Their failure to do so put the country's future and the dream of democracy and self-governance at grave risk.

Further study of the Bill of Rights reveals the framers' concern for justice in the treatment of those accused of crimes and defendants in criminal court. The Fourth, Fifth, Sixth and Eighth Amendments speak specifically to the rights of the accused. These amendments ensure that the federal government cannot violate the right to freedom from unreasonable search and seizure, the right to have notice of criminal charges and an opportunity for a hearing, the right to the assistance of counsel in one's defense, and protection against excessive bail and cruel and unusual punishment. These provisions of the federal Constitution apply only to federal government action, and over time, serious concerns arose about the way defendants were being treated in state courts.

State courts are bound to follow state constitutions and laws. They are not obligated, in most cases, to abide by federal law, unless there is a conflict invoking the **Supremacy Clause**. The Supremacy Clause dictates that where there is a conflict between state and federal law, the federal rule prevails. Substantive criminal law is primarily an area of state jurisdiction and control. The vast majority of criminal trials take place in state courts. The important provisions of the Bill of Rights, set out to protect the accused from abuse by government actors in the investigation and prosecution of crime, did not always apply to defendants in state court. As a result those protections were not enjoyed in the vast majority of criminal cases.

The U.S. Supreme Court wrestled with the question of whether the Bill of Rights should apply to state court defendants for decades before making many of them applicable in state criminal proceedings. The Court could have applied the Bill of Rights to state criminal cases all at once, a theory called *total incorporation*. While this approach would have been clearer the Court declined to do so, instead deciding that each individual provision in the Bill of Rights must be evaluated independently to decide whether it is *fundamental*.

Justice Cardozo authored the Court's opinion in *Palko v. Connecticut (1937)*, establishing that rather than total incorporation, the Bill of Rights would be applied to the states on a case-by-case basis through **selective incorporation**. According to *Palko* the critical question regarding incorporation was whether the right in question is **fundamental**. The Court explained that the answer can be determined by asking whether the right at issue was "implicit in the concept of ordered liberty?" Could a well-organized and free society be envisioned without it? If not, the right is fundamental and must be provided to defendants in state criminal cases.

# A. INCORPORATION IN THE WARREN COURT ERA

In *Palko*, the Court held that the protection against **double jeopardy**, being tried twice for the same offense, did not extend to state courts. It was *not* fundamental. Over 30 years later, the Court revisited the issue in *Benton v. Maryland (1969)*. They reversed the decision in *Palko* and incorporated the Fifth Amendment's double jeopardy clause. The *Benton* Court wrote:

> . . .*Recently, however, this Court has 'increasingly looked to the specific guarantees of the (Bill of Rights) to determine whether a state criminal trial was conducted with due process of law.'* . . . *In an increasing number of cases, the Court 'has rejected the notion that the Fourteenth Amendment applies to the States only a 'watered-down, subjective version of the individual guarantees of the Bill of Rights* * * *.".* . . . *Only last Term we found that the right to trial by jury in criminal cases was 'fundamental to the American scheme of justice,' and held that the Sixth Amendment right to a jury trial was applicable to the States through the Fourteenth Amendment. For the same reasons, we today find that the double jeopardy prohibition of the Fifth Amendment represents a fundamental ideal in our constitutional heritage, and that it should apply to the States through the Fourteenth Amendment.*[1]

*Benton v. Maryland (1969)* is the landmark case that incorporated the Fifth Amendment's Double Jeopardy Clause making it applicable to criminal defendants in state court. While *Benton* was a great victory, it was meaningless to Frank Palko, his friends, loved ones, and those who advocated on his behalf. It came too late for Palko who was executed on April 12, 1938, in a Connecticut electric chair. The protection against double jeopardy found in the Fifth Amendment was applied to the states through the **Due Process Clause of the Fourteenth Amendment**. The Fourteenth Amendment provides "no state shall. . . deprive any person of life, liberty or property, without due process of law."[2] It is the critical phrase "no state shall" that is the foundation on which the doctrine of incorporation rests. The federal government and federal courts must respect and abide by the Bill of Rights under the Fifth Amendment's Due Process Clause and the Fourteenth Amendment's "no state shall" language is the legal mechanism that provides these constitutional protections against the violation of fundamental rights at the hand of state governments.

*Benton* took place during what is often referred to as the **Due Process Revolution**, under Chief Justice Earl Warren. Warren was appointed as Chief

---

[1] *Benton v. Maryland*, 395 U.S. 784 (1969).

[2] U.S. Const. amend XIV.

Justice by President Dwight Eisenhower in October 1953 and served until his retirement in June 1969. Warren led the U.S. Supreme Court through the culmination of the American Civil Rights Movement, and the Due Process Revolution was certainly intertwined with the extraordinary events taking place in American social and political culture at the time. The chart below connects the provisions of the Bill of Rights and the landmark Supreme Court decisions, which incorporated them. Note the date of each decision and the impact of the Warren Court Era on the incorporation of the Bill of Rights.

Selective Incorporation of Fundamental Rights by the United States Supreme Court (figure 3.1):

| | |
|---|---|
| Freedom of Speech | • *Gitlow v. New York (1925)* |
| Freedom of the Press | • *Near v. Minnesota (1931)* |
| Right to Counsel in Capital Cases | • *Powell v. Alabama (1932)* |
| Freedom of Assembly | • *DeJonge v. Oregon (1937)* |
| Free Exercise of Religion | • *Cantwell v. Connecticut (1940)* |
| No Established National Religion | • *Everson v. Board of Education (1947)* |
| Right to Public Trial | • *In re Oliver (1948)* |
| Ban on Unreasonable Search and Seizure | • *Wolf v. Colorado (1949)* |
| Exclusionary Rule Banning Illegally Obtained Evidence From Trials | • *Mapp v. Ohio (1961)* |
| No Cruel and Unusual Punishment | • *Robinson v. California (1962)* |
| Right to Counsel in Felony Cases | • *Gideon v. Wainwright (1963)* |
| No Self-Incrimination | • *Malloy v. Hogan (1964)* |
| Right to Confront Adverse Witnesses | • *Pointer v. Texas (1965)* |
| Right to an Impartial Jury | • *Parker v. Gladden (1966)* |
| Right to Obtain Defense Witnesses | • *Washington v. Texas (1967)* |
| Right to a Speedy Trial | • *Klopfer v. North Carolina (1967)* |
| Protection Against Double Jeopardy | • *Benton v. Maryland (1968)* |
| Right to a Jury Trial in Non-Death Penalty Cases | • *Duncan v. Louisiana (1968)* |
| Right to Counsel for Imprisonable Misdemeanors | • *Argersinger v. Hamlin (1972)* |

| Right to Notice of Accusation | • *Rabe v. Washington (1972)* |
|---|---|
| Right to Keep and Bear Arms | • *McDonald v. Chicago (2010)* |

**Read and brief each of the following cases relating to the Fifth Amendment protection against double jeopardy and consider the questions following each case:**

1. *Palko v. Connecticut*: double jeopardy.

2. *Benton v. Maryland*: incorporation and double jeopardy as a fundamental right.

---

## PALKO V. CONNECTICUT

Supreme Court of the United States
Argued Nov. 12, 1937
Decided Dec. 6, 1937
302 U.S. 319

### OPINION

### MR. JUSTICE CARDOZO delivered the opinion of the Court.

A statute of Connecticut permitting appeals in criminal cases to be taken by the state is challenged by appellant as an infringement of the Fourteenth Amendment of the Constitution of the United States. Whether the challenge should be upheld is now to be determined.

Appellant was indicted in Fairfield County, Connecticut, for the crime of murder in the first degree. A jury found him guilty of murder in the second degree, and he was sentenced to confinement in the state prison for life. Thereafter the State of Connecticut, with the permission of the judge presiding at the trial, gave notice of appeal to the Supreme Court of Errors. This it did pursuant to an act adopted in 1886 which is printed in the margin.[1] Public Acts, 1886, p. 560; now § 6494 of the General Statutes. Upon such appeal, the Supreme Court of Errors reversed the judgment and ordered a new trial. *State v. Palko*, 121 Conn. 669, 186 Atl. 657. It found that there had been error of law to the prejudice of the state (1) in excluding testimony as to a confession by defendant; (2) in excluding testimony upon cross-examination of defendant to

---

[1] "Sec. 6494. Appeals by the state in criminal cases. Appeals from the rulings and decisions of the superior court or of any criminal court of common pleas, upon all questions of law arising on the trial of criminal cases, may be taken by the state, with the permission of the presiding judge, to the supreme court of errors, in the same manner and to the same effect as if made by the accused."

A statute of Vermont (G. L. 2598) was given the same effect and upheld as constitutional in *State* v. *Felch*, 92 Vt. 477, 105 Atl. 23.

Other statutes, conferring a right of appeal more or less limited in scope, are collected in the American Law Institute Code of Criminal Procedure, June 15, 1930, p. 1203.

impeach his credibility, and (3) in the instructions to the jury as to the difference between first and second degree murder.

Pursuant to the mandate of the Supreme Court of Errors, defendant was brought to trial again. Before a jury was impaneled and also at later stages of the case he made the objection that the effect of the new trial was to place him twice in jeopardy for the same offense, and in so doing to violate the Fourteenth Amendment of the Constitution of the United States. Upon the overruling of the objection the trial proceeded. The jury returned a verdict of murder in the first degree, and the court sentenced the defendant to the punishment of death. The Supreme Court of Errors affirmed the judgment of conviction, 122 Conn. 529; 191 Atl. 320, adhering to a decision announced in 1894, *State v. Lee*, 65 Conn. 265; 30 Atl. 1110, which upheld the challenged statute. Cf. *State v. Muolo*, 118 Conn. 373; 172 Atl. 875. The case is here upon appeal. 28 U.S.C. § 344.

*1.    The execution of the sentence will not deprive appellant of his life without the process of law assured to him by the Fourteenth Amendment of the Federal Constitution.*

The argument for appellant is that whatever is forbidden by the Fifth Amendment is forbidden by the Fourteenth also. The Fifth Amendment, which is not directed to the states, but solely to the federal government, creates immunity from double jeopardy. No person shall be "subject for the same offense to be twice put in jeopardy of life or limb." The Fourteenth Amendment ordains, "nor shall any State deprive any person of life, liberty, or property, without due process of law." To retry a defendant, though under one indictment and only one, subjects him, it is said, to double jeopardy in violation of the Fifth Amendment, if the prosecution is one on behalf of the United States. From this the consequence is said to follow that there is a denial of life or liberty without due process of law, if the prosecution is one on behalf of the People of a State. Thirty-five years ago a like argument was made to this court in *Dreyer v. Illinois*, 187 U.S. 71, 85, and was passed without consideration of its merits as unnecessary to a decision. The question is now here.

We do not find it profitable to mark the precise limits of the prohibition of double jeopardy in federal prosecutions. The subject was much considered in *Kepner v. United States*, 195 U.S. 100, decided in 1904 by a closely divided court. The view was there expressed for a majority of the court that the prohibition was not confined to jeopardy in a new and independent case. It forbade jeopardy in the same case if the new trial was at the instance of the government and not upon defendant's motion. Cf. *Trono v. United States*, 199 U.S. 521. All this may be assumed for the purpose of the case at hand, though the dissenting opinions (195 U.S. 100, 134, 137) show how much was to be said in favor of a different ruling. Right-minded men, as we learn from those opinions, could reasonably, even if mistakenly, believe that a second trial was lawful in prosecutions subject to the Fifth Amendment, if it was all in the same case. Even more plainly, right-minded men could reasonably believe that in espousing that conclusion they were not favoring a practice repugnant to the conscience of mankind. Is double jeopardy in such circumstances, if double jeopardy it must be called, a denial of due process forbidden to the states? The tyranny of labels, *Snyder v. Massachusetts*, 291 U.S. 97, 114, must not lead us to leap to a conclusion that a word which in one set of facts may stand for oppression or enormity is of like effect in every other.

We have said that in appellant's view the Fourteenth Amendment is to be taken as embodying the prohibitions of the Fifth. His thesis is even broader. Whatever would be a violation of the original bill of rights (Amendments I to VIII) if done by the federal government is now equally unlawful by force of the Fourteenth Amendment if done by a state. There is no such general rule.

The Fifth Amendment provides, among other things, that no person shall be held to answer for a capital or otherwise infamous crime unless on presentment or indictment of a grand jury. This court has held that, in prosecutions by a state, presentment or indictment by a grand jury may give way to informations at the instance of a public officer. *Hurtado v. California*, 110 U.S. 516. . . . The Fifth Amendment provides also that no person shall be compelled in any criminal case to be a witness against himself. This court has said that, in prosecutions by a state, the exemption will fail if the state elects to end it. *Twining v. New Jersey*, 211 U.S. 78, 106, 111, 112. Cf. . . . The Sixth Amendment calls for a jury trial in criminal cases and the Seventh for a jury trial in civil cases at common law where the value in controversy shall exceed twenty dollars. This court has ruled that consistently with those amendments trial by jury may be modified by a state or abolished altogether. . . . As to the Fourth Amendment, one should refer to *Weeks v. United States*, 232 U.S. 383, 398, and as to other provisions of the Sixth, to *West v. Louisiana*, 194 U.S. 258.

On the other hand, the due process clause of the Fourteenth Amendment may make it unlawful for a state to abridge by its statutes the freedom of speech which the First Amendment safeguards against encroachment by the Congress, . . .; or the like freedom of the press, . . .; or the free exercise of religion, . . .; or the right of peaceable assembly, without which speech would be unduly trammeled, . . .; or the right of one accused of crime to the benefit of counsel, *Powell v. Alabama*, 287 U.S. 45. In these and other situations immunities that are valid as against the federal government by force of the specific pledges of particular amendments[2] have been found to be implicit in the concept of ordered liberty, and thus, through the Fourteenth Amendment, become valid as against the states.

The line of division may seem to be wavering and broken if there is a hasty catalogue of the cases on the one side and the other. Reflection and analysis will induce a different view. There emerges the perception of a rationalizing principle which gives to discrete instances a proper order and coherence. The right to trial by jury and the immunity from prosecution except as the result of an indictment may have value and importance. Even so, they are not of the very essence of a scheme of ordered liberty. To abolish them is not to violate a "principle of justice so rooted in the traditions and conscience of our people as to be ranked as fundamental." *Snyder v. Massachusetts, supra*, p. 105; *Brown v. Mississippi, supra*, p. 285; *Hebert v. Louisiana*, 272 U.S. 312, 316. Few would be so narrow or provincial as to maintain that a fair and enlightened system of justice would be impossible without them. What is true of jury trials and indictments is true also, as the cases show, of the immunity from compulsory self-incrimination. *Twining v. New Jersey, supra*. This too might be lost, and justice still be done. Indeed, today as in the past there are students of our penal system who look upon the immunity as a mischief rather than a benefit, and who would limit its scope, or destroy it altogether.[3] No doubt there would remain the need to give protection against torture, physical or mental. *Brown v. Mississippi, supra*. Justice, however, would not perish if the accused were subject to a duty to respond to orderly inquiry. The exclusion of these immunities and privileges from the privileges and immunities protected against the action of the states has not been arbitrary or casual. It has been dictated by a study and appreciation of the meaning, the essential implications, of liberty itself.

---

[2]   First Amendment: "Congress shall make no law respecting an establishment of religion, or prohibiting the free exercise thereof; or abridging the freedom of speech, or of the press; or the right of the people peaceably to assemble, and to petition the Government for a redress of grievances."

Sixth Amendment: "In all criminal prosecutions, the accused shall enjoy the right . . . to have the assistance of counsel for his defence."

[3]   See, e.g., Bentham, Rationale of Judicial Evidence, Book IX, Pt. 4, c. III; Glueck, Crime and Justice, p. 94; cf. Wigmore, Evidence, vol. 4, § 2251.

Compulsory self-incrimination is part of the established procedure in the law of Continental Europe. Wigmore, supra, p. 824; Garner, Criminal Procedure in France, 25 Yale L. J. 255, 260; Sherman, Roman Law in the Modern World, vol. 2, pp. 493, 494; Stumberg, Guide to the Law and Legal Literature of France, p. 184. Double jeopardy too is not everywhere forbidden. Radin, Anglo American Legal History, p. 228.

We reach a different plane of social and moral values when we pass to the privileges and immunities that have been taken over from the earlier articles of the federal bill of rights and brought within the Fourteenth Amendment by a process of absorption. These in their origin were effective against the federal government alone. If the Fourteenth Amendment has absorbed them, the process of absorption has had its source in the belief that neither liberty nor justice would exist if they were sacrificed. *Twining v. New Jersey, supra*, p. 99.[4] This is true, for illustration, of freedom of thought, and speech. Of that freedom one may say that it is the matrix, the indispensable condition, of nearly every other form of freedom. With rare aberrations a pervasive recognition of that truth can be traced in our history, political and legal. So it has come about that the domain of liberty, withdrawn by the Fourteenth Amendment from encroachment by the states, has been enlarged by latter-day judgments to include liberty of the mind as well as liberty of action.[5] The extension became, indeed, a logical imperative when once it was recognized, as long ago it was, that liberty is something more than exemption from physical restraint, and that even in the field of substantive rights and duties the legislative judgment, if oppressive and arbitrary, may be overridden by the courts. Cf. *Near v. Minnesota ex rel. Olson, supra; De Jonge v. Oregon, supra.* Fundamental too in the concept of due process, and so in that of liberty, is the thought that condemnation shall be rendered only after trial. *Scott v. McNeal*, 154 U.S. 34; *Blackmer v. United States*, 284 U.S. 421. The hearing, moreover, must be a real one, not a sham or a pretense. *Moore v. Dempsey*, 261 U.S. 86; *Mooney v. Holohan*, 294 U.S. 103. For that reason, ignorant defendants in a capital case were held to have been condemned unlawfully when in truth, though not in form, they were refused the aid of counsel. *Powell v. Alabama, supra*, pp. 67, 68. The decision did not turn upon the fact that the benefit of counsel would have been guaranteed to the defendants by the provisions of the Sixth Amendment if they had been prosecuted in a federal court. The decision turned upon the fact that in the particular situation laid before us in the evidence the benefit of counsel was essential to the substance of a hearing.

Our survey of the cases serves, we think, to justify the statement that the dividing line between them, if not unfaltering throughout its course, has been true for the most part to a unifying principle. On which side of the line the case

---

[4]   "It is possible that some of the personal rights safeguarded by the first eight Amendments against National action may also be safeguarded against state action, because a denial of them would be a denial of due process of law. *Chicago, Burlington & Quincy Railroad v. Chicago*, 166 U.S. 226. If this is so, it is not because those rights are enumerated in the first eight Amendments, but because they are of such a nature that they are included in the conception of due process of law."

made out by the appellant has appropriate location must be the next inquiry and the final one. Is that kind of double jeopardy to which the statute has subjected him a hardship so acute and shocking that our polity will not endure it? Does it violate those "fundamental principles of liberty and justice which lie at the base of all our civil and political institutions"? *Hebert v. Louisiana, supra.* The answer surely must be "no." What the answer would have to be if the state were permitted after a trial free from error to try the accused over again or to bring another case against him, we have no occasion to consider. We deal with the statute before us and no other. The state is not attempting to wear the accused out by a multitude of cases with accumulated trials. It asks no more than this, that the case against him shall go on until there shall be a trial free from the corrosion of substantial legal error. *State v. Felch,* 92 Vt. 477, 105 Atl. 23; *State v. Lee, supra.* This is not cruelty at all, nor even vexation in any immoderate degree. If the trial had been infected with error adverse to the accused, there might have been review at his instance, and as often as necessary to purge the vicious taint. A reciprocal privilege, subject at all times to the discretion of the presiding judge, *State v. Carabetta,* 106 Conn. 114, 137 Atl. 394, has now been granted to the state. There is here no seismic innovation. The edifice of justice stands, its symmetry, to many, greater than before.

2.    *The conviction of appellant is not in derogation of any privileges or immunities that belong to him as a citizen of the United States.*

There is argument in his behalf that the privileges and immunities clause of the Fourteenth Amendment as well as the due process clause has been flouted by the judgment.

*Maxwell v. Dow, supra,* p. 584, gives all the answer that is necessary.

The judgment is affirmed.

**MR. JUSTICE BUTLER dissents.**

## After preparing the case brief, consider the answers to the following questions:

1.    What is double jeopardy?

2.    Should double jeopardy attach to a case once it has been tried in every situation or are there circumstances in which courts should be able to retry a defendant?

---

[5]    The cases are brought together in Warren, The New Liberty under the 14th Amendment, 39 Harv. L. Rev. 431.

3.    Could the Court have adopted a general rule that anything forbidden by the Bill of Rights is also forbidden by the states? Would that have been a better result?

4.    The Court makes their holding on the basis that this case is really about having a trial free of error, not about placing Palko twice in jeopardy. Is this persuasive?

# BENTON V. MARYLAND

Supreme Court of the United States
Reargued March 24, 1969
Decided June 23, 1969
395 U.S. 784

## Opinion

### MR. JUSTICE MARSHALL, delivered the opinion of the Court.

In August 1965, petitioner was tried in a Maryland state court on charges of burglary and larceny. The jury found petitioner not guilty of larceny but convicted him on the burglary count. He was sentenced to 10 years in prison. Shortly after his notice of appeal was filed in the Maryland Court on Appeals, that court handed down its decision in the case of *Schowgurow v. State*, 240 Md. 121, 213 A.2d 475 (1965). In Schowgurow the Maryland Court of Appeals struck down a section of the state constitution which required jurors to swear their belief in the existence of God. As a result of this decision, petitioner's case was remanded to the trial court. Because both the grand and petit juries in petitioner's case had been selected under the invalid constitutional provision, petitioner was given the option of demanding re-indictment and retrial.

He chose to have his conviction set aside, and a new indictment and new trial followed. At this second trial, petitioner was again charged with both larceny and burglary. Petitioner objected to retrial on the larceny count, arguing that because the first jury had found him not guilty of larceny, retrial would violate the constitutional prohibition against subjecting persons to double jeopardy for the same offense. The trial judge denied petitioner's motion to dismiss the larceny charge, and petitioner was tried for both larceny and burglary. This time the jury found petitioner guilty of both offenses, and the judge sentenced him to 15 years on the burglary count and 5 years for larceny, the sentences to run concurrently. On appeal to the newly created Maryland Court of Special Appeals, petitioner's double jeopardy claim was rejected on the merits. The Court of Appeals denied discretionary review.

On the last day of last Term, we granted certiorari but limited the writ to the consideration of two issues:

'(1) Is the double jeopardy clause of the Fifth Amendment applicable to the States through the Fourteenth Amendment?

'(2) If so, was the petitioner 'twice put in jeopardy' in this case?'

. . .

On the merits, we hold that the Double Jeopardy Clause of the Fifth Amendment is applicable to the States through the Fourteenth Amendment, and we reverse petitioner's conviction for larceny.

. . .

## II.

While Maryland apparently agrees that there is no jurisdictional bar to consideration of petitioner's larceny conviction, it argues that the possibility of collateral consequences is so remote in this case that any double jeopardy violation should be treated as a species of 'harmless error.' The Solicitor General, while not commenting at length on the facts of this particular case, suggests that we treat the concurrent sentence doctrine as a principle of judicial efficiency which permits judges to avoid decision of issues which have no appreciable impact on the rights of any party. Both Maryland and the Solicitor General argue that the defendant should bear the burden of convincing the appellate court of the need to review all his concurrent sentences. Petitioner, on the other hand, sees in Sibron a command that federal appellate courts treat all errors which may possibly affect a defendant's rights, and he argues that the concurrent sentence rule therefore has no continuing validity, even as a rule of convenience.

Because of the special circumstances in this case, we find it unnecessary to resolve this dispute. For even if the concurrent sentence doctrine survives as a rule of judicial convenience, we find good reason not to apply it here. On direct appeal from petitioner's conviction, the Maryland Court of Special Appeals did in fact rule on his double jeopardy challenge to the larceny count. It is unclear whether Maryland courts always consider all challenges raised on direct appeal, notwithstanding the existence of concurrent sentences, but at least in this case the State decided not to apply the concurrent sentence rule. This may well indicate that the State has some interest in keeping the larceny conviction alive; if, as Maryland argues here, the larceny conviction is of no importance to either party, one wonders why the state courts found it necessary to pass on it. Since the future importance of the conviction may well turn on issues of state law about which we are not well informed, we propose, on direct appeal from the Maryland courts, to accept their judgment on this question. Since they decided this federal constitutional question, we see no reason why we should not do so as well. Moreover, the status of petitioner's burglary conviction and the eventual length of his sentence are both still in some doubt. Should any attack on the burglary conviction be successful, or should the length of the burglary sentence be reduced to less than five years, petitioner would then clearly have a right to have his larceny conviction reviewed. As we said in *Sibron v. New York*, supra, at 56–57, it is certainly preferable to have that review now on direct appeal, rather than later. For these reasons, and because there is no jurisdictional bar, we find it appropriate to reach the questions specified in our original writ of certiorari.

III.

In 1937, this Court decided the landmark case of *Palko v. Connecticut*, 302 U.S. 319. Palko, although indicted for first-degree murder, had been convicted of murder in the second degree after a jury trial in a Connecticut state court. The State appealed and won a new trial. Palko argued that the Fourteenth Amendment incorporated, as against the States, the Fifth Amendment requirement that no person 'be subject for the same offense to be twice put in jeopardy of life or limb.' The Court disagreed. Federal double jeopardy standards were not applicable against the States. Only when a kind of jeopardy subjected a defendant to 'a hardship so acute and shocking that our polity will not endure it,' id., at 328, 58 S.Ct., at 153, did the Fourteenth Amendment apply. The order for a new trial was affirmed. In subsequent appeals from state courts, the Court continued to apply this lesser Palko standard. See, e.g., *Brock v. North Carolina*, 344 U.S. 424 (1953).

Recently, however, this Court has 'increasingly looked to the specific guarantees of the (Bill of Rights) to determine whether a state criminal trial was conducted with due process of law.' *Washington v. Texas*, 388 U.S. 14, 18 (1967). In an increasing number of cases, the Court 'has rejected the notion that the Fourteenth Amendment applies to the States only a 'watered-down, subjective version of the individual guarantees of the Bill of Rights * * *.'' *Malloy v. Hogan*, 378 U.S. 1, 10–11 (1964). Only last Term we found that the right to trial by jury in criminal cases was 'fundamental to the American scheme of justice,' *Duncan v. Louisiana*, 391 U.S. 145, 149 (1968), and held that the Sixth Amendment right to a jury trial was applicable to the States through the Fourteenth Amendment. For the same reasons, we today find that the double jeopardy prohibition of the Fifth Amendment represents a fundamental ideal in our constitutional heritage, and that it should apply to the States through the Fourteenth Amendment. Insofar as it is inconsistent with this holding, *Palko v. Connecticut* is overruled.

*Palko* represented an approach to basic constitutional rights which this Court's recent decisions have rejected. It was cut of the same cloth as *Betts v. Brady*, 316 U.S. 455 (1942), the case which held that a criminal defendant's right to counsel was to be determined by deciding in each case whether the denial of that right was 'shocking to the universal sense of justice.' Id., at 462. It relied upon *Twining v. New Jersey*, 211 U.S. 78 (1908), which held that the right against compulsory self-incrimination was not an element of Fourteenth Amendment due process. *Betts* was overruled by *Gideon v. Wainwright*, 372 U.S. 335 (1963); *Twining*, by *Malloy v. Hogan* (1964). Our recent cases have thoroughly rejected the *Palko* notion that basic constitutional rights can be denied by the States as long as the totality of the circumstances does not disclose a denial of 'fundamental fairness.' Once it is decided that a particular Bill of Rights guarantee is 'fundamental to the American scheme of justice,' *Duncan v. Louisiana*, supra, at 149, the same constitutional standards apply against both the State and Federal Governments. *Palko*'s roots had thus been cut away years ago. We today only recognize the inevitable.

The fundamental nature of the guarantee against double jeopardy can hardly be doubted. Its origins can be traced to Greek and Roman times, and it became established in the common law of England long before this Nation's independence. See *Bartkus v. Illinois*, 359 U.S. 121, 151–155 (1959) (Black, J., dissenting). As with many other elements of the common law, it was carried into the jurisprudence of this Country through the medium of Blackstone, who codified the doctrine in his Commentaries. '(T)he plea of autrefoits acquit, or a former acquittal,' he wrote, 'is grounded on this universal maxim of the common law of England, that no man is to be brought into jeopardy of his life more than once for the same offence.' Today, every State incorporates some form of the prohibition in its constitution or common law. As this Court put it in *Green v. United States*, 355 U.S. 184, 187–188 (1957), '(t)he underlying idea, one that is deeply ingrained in at least the Anglo-American system of jurisprudence, is that the State with all its resources and power should not be allowed to make repeated attempts to convict an individual for an alleged offense, thereby subjecting him to embarrassment, expense and ordeal and compelling him to live in a continuing state of anxiety and insecurity, as well as enhancing the possibility that even though innocent he may be found guilty.' This underlying notion has from the very beginning been part of our constitutional tradition. Like the right to trial by jury, it is clearly 'fundamental to the American scheme of justice.' The validity of petitioner's larceny conviction must be judged, not by the watered-down standard enunciated in Palko, but under this Court's interpretations of the Fifth Amendment double jeopardy provision.

IV.

It is clear that petitioner's larceny conviction cannot stand once federal double jeopardy standards are applied. Petitioner was acquitted of larceny in his first trial. Because he decided to appeal his burglary conviction, he is forced to suffer retrial on the larceny count as well. As this Court held in *Green v. United States*, supra, at 193–194, 78 S.Ct., at 227, '(c)onditioning an appeal of one offense on a coerced surrender of a valid plea of former jeopardy on another offense exacts a forfeiture in plain conflict with the constitutional bar against double jeopardy.'

. . . case is totally indistinguishable. Petitioner was acquitted of larceny. He has, under Green, a valid double jeopardy plea which he cannot be forced to waive. Yet Maryland wants the earlier acquittal set aside, over petitioner's objections, because of a defect in the indictment. This it cannot do. Petitioner's larceny conviction cannot stand.

V.

. . . Accordingly, we think it 'just under the circumstances,' 28 U.S.C. s 2106, to vacate the judgment below and remand for consideration of this question. The judgment is vacated and the case is remanded for further proceedings not inconsistent with this opinion.

It is so ordered.

Judgment vacated and case remanded.

**MR. JUSTICE WHITE, concurring.**

While I agree with the Court's extension of the prohibition against double jeopardy to the States, and with the Court's conclusion that the concurrent sentence rule constitutes no jurisdictional bar, additional comment on the wisdom and effects of applying a concurrent sentence rule seems appropriate.

. . .

**MR. JUSTICE HARLAN, whom MR. JUSTICE STEWART joins, dissenting.**

One of the bedrock rules that has governed, and should continue to govern, the adjudicative processes of this Court is that the decision of constitutional questions in the disposition of cases should be avoided whenever fairly possible. Today the Court turns its back on that sound principle by refusing, for the flimsiest of reasons, to apply the 'concurrent sentence doctrine' so as not to be required to decide the far-reaching question whether the Double Jeopardy Clause of the Fifth Amendment is 'incorporated' into the

Due Process Clause of the Fourteenth, thereby making the former applicable lock, stock, and barrel to the States. Indeed, it is quite manifest that the Court has actually been at pains to 'reach out' to decide that very important constitutional issue. . . .In the present case, the State did not appeal, and the defect in the composition of the grand jury could not have affected petitioner's subsequent acquittal at trial. Society's legitimate interest in punishing wrongdoers could have been fully vindicated by retrying petitioner on the burglary count alone, that being the offense of which he was previously convicted. The State had no more interest in compelling petitioner to stand trial again for larceny, of which he had been acquitted, than in retrying any other person declared innocent after an error-free trial. He retrial on the larceny count therefore, in my opinion, denied due process, and on that ground reversal would be called for under *Palko*.

**After preparing the case brief, consider the answers to the following questions:**

1.   How was the Court's reasoning in *Benton* different than their reasoning in *Palko*?

2.   How did their shift in focus from 'error free trials' to double jeopardy impact the outcome?

3.   Is the protection against double jeopardy a right you believe is "implicit in the concept of ordered liberty"? Explain why.

## Chapter 3 Key Terms for Review

- **Bill of Rights**: the first ten amendments to the U.S. Constitution. They contain a list of important rights and freedoms for criminal defendants and suspects in criminal investigations.

- **Supremacy Clause**: dictates that the U.S. Constitution is the supreme law of the land and when there is conflict between federal and state law, the federal rule prevails.

- **Selective incorporation**: the process of applying the rights found in the Bill of Rights to state criminal proceedings on a case-by-case basis.

- **Fundamental right**: a right of such significance that it is "implicit in the concept of ordered liberty." A free and democratic society cannot be envisioned without it.

- **Double jeopardy**: when a defendant is put on trial twice for the same offense, they are placed in double jeopardy; the U.S. Constitution forbids double jeopardy in federal criminal trials and the right has been extended to state criminal trials.

- **Due Process Clause of the Fourteenth Amendment**: "no state shall. . .deprive any person of life, liberty or property without due process of law." This clause is the vehicle for the application of fundamental rights from the Bill of Rights to state criminal proceedings.

- **Due Process Revolution**: under Chief Justice Earl Warren the U.S. Supreme Court applied the majority of defendant's rights found in the Bill of Rights to state criminal proceedings.

# The Role and Duties of Prosecutors, Prosecutorial Ethics, Misconduct and Immunity from Civil Liability

## A. THE ROLE OF PROSECUTORS

**Prosecutors** are attorneys who represent the people of a community in a criminal case against a defendant accused of committing a crime. Prosecutors do not represent a client in the same way defense attorneys do. They do not answer personally to each individual member of the community; instead, they work as representatives on their behalf. Prosecutors in federal court are called **United States Attorneys**. They represent the people of the United States in trials of federal criminal defendants. State prosecutors, sometimes called district attorneys, city attorney, commonwealth's attorney, county attorney or county prosecutor, represent the people of their respective states and counties in a criminal prosecution in state court.

Federal and state prosecutors work closely with law enforcement agencies. They are dependent upon the investigative work of law enforcement personnel to assist them in deciding whether probable cause exists to charge a suspect with a crime. In turn, the work of prosecutors in successfully seeing criminal defendants convicted and sentenced is of the utmost importance to law enforcement. As a result they have a mutually dependent relationship. A good working relationship between law enforcement agencies and prosecutors benefits both groups and helps to achieve their mutual goal of public safety.

Acting on behalf of the people prosecutors play a critical role in ensuring justice for victims of crime and protecting the community. It is common for prosecutors to establish victim support services or work in tandem with private agencies who do so. Prosecutors may provide victim-witness assistance programs, such as victim advocates to help victims navigate the trial process and coordinate restitution efforts on their behalf. Private groups also raise awareness and support for the victim's rights movement. Organizations such as Mothers Against Drunk Driving (M.A.D.D.) have become household names. M.A.D.D. is one of the largest victim's rights organizations in the world and has at least one office in every state and extensive educational programs throughout the country. Other victim's rights organizations provide support to victims of domestic violence, engage in victim-offender mediation and reconciliation, and provide counseling services to crime victims. In 2004 Congress passed the **Crime Victims' Rights Act**.[1] This legislation represents a significant achievement on behalf of crime victims. It provides support for victims during the criminal trial process as well as post-trial rights including notice prior to the release of offenders.

Prosecutors are arguably the most powerful of the courtroom actors. **Prosecutorial discretion** is the power to make independent decisions. The power to charge defendants is a significant source of prosecutorial discretion. The prosecutor determines whether probable cause exists to charge the defendant and then chooses the appropriate charges to bring against them (or refers the case to a grand jury to make that decision). The vast majority of criminal cases are brought by way of a prosecutor's **information**. The information is a document accusing the defendant of a crime(s). In the majority of criminal cases it is the prosecutor who hails the defendant into court signaling the start of the criminal judicial process. There are three other methods of charging: an **arrest warrant** (issued by a judicial officer), an **indictment** by a grand jury, and the filing of a **complaint** by an individual (either the victim or arresting police officer provide a sworn statement). Once the defendant has been arraigned and made aware of the charges, and employed or been appointed counsel, the next step in a case is often plea negotiations.

## i.   Plea Bargains

The vast majority of criminal charges are resolved by way of a **plea bargain**. Research estimates that between 85% and 95% of cases end in a guilty plea.[2] This is an agreement between the defendant and the prosecutor under which the defendant pleads guilty to committing the crime(s) charged in exchange for a benefit from the government. The terms of the agreement vary widely from case to case, taking into account factors such as the specific crimes charged and their seriousness, the number of criminal acts alleged against the defendant, and the defendant's criminal history. Once the charges are filed, the prosecutor will

---

[1]     18 U.S.C. § 3771 (2004).

[2]     Hashimoto, Erica, *Toward Ethical Plea Bargaining*, Cardozo Law Review 30: 949–963, 2008.

communicate to defense counsel whether they would like to make a plea bargain available to the defendant and offer the terms of the deal. The defense attorney explains those terms to the defendant and communicates his or her decision to the prosecutor in response. This negotiation may have several steps as the attorneys advocate for what they believe is the most appropriate resolution of the case.

The Supreme Court held that a plea agreement is more than an admission of guilt and also represents a waiver of fundamental constitutional rights in *Boykin v. Alabama (1969)*.[3] In order to ensure the waiver of these rights is intelligent and voluntary courts utilize a **Boykin form**. This signed form explains the rights the defendant is waiving by entering into the plea agreement.

To accept a plea agreement the defendant must voluntarily waive their rights to:

1. A trial by jury.

2. Confront and cross-examine witnesses.

3. Compel witnesses to attend and testify.

4. Testify on their behalf.

5. The privilege against self-incrimination.

6. The presumption that they are innocent until proven guilty beyond a reasonable doubt and the right to appeal their conviction.

In the process of plea bargaining prosecutors are in a position of power. They come to the bargaining table with very little to lose and the power to offer the defendant significant benefits in exchange for an admission of guilt. A plea bargain can take one of three forms: a charge bargain, a count bargain or a sentence bargain. A **charge bargain** offers a reduced or lesser charge in exchange for an admission of guilt; **count bargain** offers fewer counts in exchange for an admission of guilt; and a **sentence bargain** offers a reduced sentence for the same. Defendants have a constitutional right to counsel in this process.[4] If counsel provides ineffective advice that leads to the rejection of a plea agreement, the defendant is entitled to a hearing to determine whether the principles for effective assistance of counsel were violated under *Strickland v. Washington (1984)*.[5] The

---

[3]   395 US 238 (1969).

[4]   *Lafler v. Cooper*, 566 U.S. 156 (2012) and *Missouri v. Frye*, 566 U.S. 134 (2012).

[5]   466 U.S. 668 (1984).

defendant must prove there was a reasonable probability of a different result in the plea bargaining process if the attorney had offered competent advice.

Judges must ratify or approve the plea bargain before it is accepted as a final disposition. The judge must determine that the defendant is competent to enter the plea, that it is voluntary, and ensure that the defendant understands the impact of his or her decision to enter the guilty plea. The judge may require the defendant to allocute or admit the factual basis for the plea. This is done in an **allocution hearing** in many jurisdictions. Under some circumstances the judge may accept it even if the defendant denies culpability (factual guilt). In *North Carolina v. Alford (1970)*, the Supreme Court held that where strong evidence of actual guilt substantially negated defendant's claim of innocence and provided strong factual basis for the guilty plea, the trial court could accept the plea despite defendant's claim of innocence.[6] It was important to the High Court in that case that Alford was represented by competent counsel and was making a well-reasoned decision. The **Alford plea** is not accepted in every state (Indiana, Michigan and New Jersey forbid them) and they are only conservatively allowed in the federal system.

Prosecutors are bound to honor the terms of a plea agreement once the guilty plea has been accepted and ratified by the court.[7] Prosecutors are permitted to threaten more serious charges against the defendant if they refuse to accept a plea agreement. In *Bordenkircher v. Hayes (1978)*[8] the Supreme Court held that this is not a vindictive exercise of the prosecutor's discretion in charging and not a violation of the defendant's due process rights.

## ii.   Prosecutorial Duty to Disclose Evidence

**Discovery** involves sharing information between the parties in a case prior to trial. Discovery in civil cases is often extensive and can be a lengthy process of interviewing (deposing) witnesses and sharing documents between parties. In criminal cases discovery involves the **duty to disclose of evidence** and is almost exclusively the duty of the prosecutor. The defendant enjoys the Fifth Amendment privilege against self-incrimination and as a result is not obligated to disclose evidence to the prosecutor that would incriminate him. Defendants have a duty to disclose an alibi defense. This preserves judicial resources by preventing an unnecessary trial and alerts police that the suspect in custody could not have committed the crime charged.

---

6    *North Carolina v. Alford*, 400 U.S. 25 (1970).

7    *Santobello v. N.Y.*, 404 U.S. 257 (1971).

8    434 U.S. 357 (1978).

The prosecutor has a duty to disclose **exculpatory evidence** to the defendant. Exculpatory evidence is information that tends to prove the defendant's innocence. In *Brady v. Maryland (1963)* the Supreme Court held that a defendant's right to due process of law is violated when a prosecutor fails to disclose exculpatory evidence.[9] Under Brady, evidence is material and must be disclosed if there is a "reasonable probability that, had the evidence been disclosed, the result of the proceeding would have been different."[10]

In the cases regarding prosecutorial disclosure that followed *Brady* the Supreme Court refined the *Brady* rule narrowing its application. In *U.S. v. Agurs (1976)* they held that exculpatory evidence only required disclosure if the withheld evidence would have been persuasive and created a reasonable doubt about the defendant's guilt.[11] The Court addressed the issue again in *Kyles v. Whitley (1995)* and held that in determining whether the evidence would have created a reasonable doubt about guilt, reviewing courts should consider the entire body of evidence in the case against the defendant.[12] In *Kyles* the Court explained that "*a "reasonable probability" means that the likelihood of a different result is great enough to undermine confidence in the outcome of the trial.*"

In *Smith v. Cain (2012)* the Supreme Court held that the duty to disclose exculpatory evidence turns on whether it is **material**.[13] They held that evidence is material when there is a reasonable probability that the outcome would have been different. It need not be demonstrated that a different verdict would have been reached, only that the likelihood of a different result is great enough to undermine confidence in the outcome of the trial.

Prosecutors also have a duty to disclose **prior inconsistent statements** made by witnesses.[14] Knowing about prior statements made by witnesses allows the defendant to uncover inconsistencies to impeach witnesses. **Impeachment** is the process of showing that a witness is not trustworthy and their testimony should not be believed. Under *United States v. Bagley (1985)* prior inconsistencies in the testimony of witnesses are subject to disclosure under the Brady evidence rules.[15] Unlike the Brady evidence rules, the prosecutor doesn't have a duty to automatically disclose prior inconsistent statements; instead the burden is on

---

[9]   373 U.S. 83 (1963).

[10]  *Id.*

[11]  427 U.S. 97 (1976).

[12]  514 U.S. 419 (1995).

[13]  565 U.S. 73 (2012).

[14]  *Jencks v. United States,* 353 U.S. 657 (1957).

[15]  473 U.S. 667 (1985).

defense counsel to request the information.[16] In federal court both sides must disclose, at the request of the opposing party, prior written statements by a witness after the witness testifies on direct examination.[17]

# B. PROSECUTORIAL ETHICS AND MISCONDUCT

Prosecutors are respected members of the legal profession. The U.S. Supreme Court has held that despite an occasional misstep, the excellence of their work justifies the presumption that "they have properly discharged their official duties."[18] Prosecutors are entitled to the benefit of the doubt and it should be presumed that in the absence of evidence to the contrary, they are acting in good faith in discharging the duties of the office. In the vast majority of cases prosecutors are well regarded by the communities they serve. They advocate for victims of crime and are tasked with ensuring that criminals receive the punishment they deserve. Prosecutors, like all attorneys, are bound to follow the ethical rules and guidelines set out by the American Bar Association (ABA), their state bar association and any federal or state statutes in the jurisdiction where they are licensed to practice. In addition to the ABA Rules, each state has a series of rules governing the conduct of attorneys.

The American Bar Association maintains a series of rules for attorneys to follow and has specific guidelines for prosecutors. Rule 3.8 of the **ABA Model Rules of Professional Conduct** explains the role and responsibilities of a prosecutor:

*Advocate*

**Rule 3.8 Special Responsibilities Of A Prosecutor**

The prosecutor in a criminal case shall:

> (a)   refrain from prosecuting a charge that the prosecutor knows is not supported by probable cause;
>
> (b)   make reasonable efforts to assure that the accused has been advised of the right to, and the procedure for obtaining, counsel and has been given reasonable opportunity to obtain counsel;

---

[16]   18 U.S.C. § 3500.

[17]   *Id.*

[18]   *United States v. Chemical Foundation, Inc.*, 272 U.S. 1, 14–15 (Justice Stevens, dissenting in *U.S. v. Armstrong*).

(c)   not seek to obtain from an unrepresented accused a waiver of important pretrial rights, such as the right to a preliminary hearing;

(d)   make timely disclosure to the defense of all evidence or information known to the prosecutor that tends to negate the guilt of the accused or mitigates the offense, and, in connection with sentencing, disclose to the defense and to the tribunal all unprivileged mitigating information known to the prosecutor, except when the prosecutor is relieved of this responsibility by a protective order of the tribunal. . .

(f)   except for statements that are necessary to inform the public of the nature and extent of the prosecutor's action and that serve a legitimate law enforcement purpose, refrain from making extrajudicial comments that have a substantial likelihood of heightening public condemnation of the accused . . .

(g)   When a prosecutor knows of new, credible and material evidence creating a reasonable likelihood that a convicted defendant did not commit an offense of which the defendant was convicted, the prosecutor shall:

(1)   promptly disclose that evidence to an appropriate court or authority, and

(2)   if the conviction was obtained in the prosecutor's jurisdiction,

(i)   promptly disclose that evidence to the defendant unless a court authorizes delay, and

(ii)   undertake further investigation, or make reasonable efforts to cause an investigation, to determine whether the defendant was convicted of an offense that the defendant did not commit.

(h)   When a prosecutor knows of clear and convincing evidence establishing that a defendant in the prosecutor's jurisdiction was convicted of an offense that the defendant did not commit, the prosecutor shall seek to remedy the conviction.[19]

Prosecutorial discretion is an issue of concern because their power is broad and largely unchecked. Prosecutors enjoy the discretion to charge defendants with crime, make plea offers to a defendant, or make a sentencing recommendation to the court. The decision to charge a defendant is very significant because it hails

---

[19]   ABA Model Rules of Professional Conduct, Rule 3.8.

them into court signaling the start of the formal court process. Because of the lack of accountability for prosecutors in this area there is an inherent risk of **prosecutorial misconduct**. If a prosecutor acts unethically criminal defendants and the community the prosecutor has a duty to serve suffer.

There are many cases that could illustrate the problem of prosecutorial misconduct, but a recent and troubling example is the Duke Lacrosse case. The local prosecutor, Mike Nifong, brought charges against four members of the Duke University lacrosse team in 2006 after receiving reports of a sexual assault at a team party. The team had hired two strippers, both African-American women, to dance at a party held off campus. One of the women made a police report the next day alleging that three of the men had raped and sodomized her in the bathroom at the party.

Even though the entire team (with the exception of one African-American athlete) submitted to DNA testing, and those test results provided clear evidence that none of the players on the team had sexual contact with the alleged victim, Nifong continued with a grand jury proceeding to charge two of the players and an indictment was issued. A third athlete was later charged in the scandal. In November 2006 Mike Nifong ran for and was re-elected district attorney in Durham County, North Carolina. His election turned on successfully securing the votes of the African-American community in the county and his handling of the Duke Lacrosse case had been a source of significant support from African-American voters.

Just over a month after he was elected, on Dec. 15, 2006, a lab technician from the DNA crime lab testified that he had "doctored" the DNA reports in cooperation with and at Nifong's request. As a result of the revelation Nifong reduced the charges against the students. On Dec. 22, 2006, the North Carolina Bar Association launched an investigation into Nifong's conduct and by April 2007 all charges against the students had been dropped. In addition allegations had been levied against Nifong for overreaching, withholding evidence and lying to the court. Nifong's misconduct resulted in his disbarment on July 16, 2007, after the bar disciplinary committee found him guilty of 27 of the 32 ethics violations with which he was charged. After the hearings, the head of the disciplinary panel of the North Carolina State Bar reviewing the case, Lane Williamson, called it a fiasco involving:

*"dishonesty, fraud, deceit and misrepresentation." Williamson further stated, "At the time he was facing a primary, and yes, he was politically naive, but we can draw no other conclusion that those initial statements he made were to further his political*

*ambitions." In the end, the panel concluded, "there is no discipline short of disbarment
appropriate in this case given the magnitude of the offenses found."*

Another example of prosecutorial misconduct involves the prosecution of
famous comedian, Bill Cosby. In June, 2021 Bill Cosby was released from prison
after the high court of Pennsylvania overturned his conviction based on
prosecutorial misconduct. His success on appeal turned on an informal promise
made by then-prosecutor Bruce Castor in 2005. Cosby faced allegations of sexual
misconduct and a civil suit by Andrea Constand. Castor was the acting prosecutor
at the time and explains that he believed any criminal case against Cosby was weak
based on evidence that Constand had stayed in a relationship with the actor for a
year after the alleged assault. As a result, the prosecutor promised not to prosecute
Cosby criminally with the hope that he would answer questions freely in the civil
case, allowing Constand to recover damages. The strategy worked and Cosby
made incriminating statements which he and his lawyer claim he would have never
made in the absence of the non-prosecution agreement.

In 2015 Cosby was arrested and Castor's successor Kevin Steele chose to
prosecute him claiming that Castor's non-prosecution agreement did not apply to
him. After all, the agreement was informal and the only mention of it was in a
press release from 2005. The court held, "denying the defendant the benefit of
that decision is an affront to fundamental fairness, particularly when it results in a
criminal prosecution that was foregone for more than a decade" with regard to
Cosby's decision to waive his right to remain silent under the belief that he was
immune from prosecution.[20]

In another high-profile case, then-District Attorney Jackie Johnson was
indicted on charges in September, 2021. Johnson is accused of violating her oath
of office and hindering law enforcement in the investigation into Ahmaud
Arbery's death. Arbery, a black man was shot and killed by three white men while
out jogging in Brunswick, Georgia. The case sparked national protests. The three
defendants were tried and convicted for Arbery's murder in late 2021 and on
January 7, 2022 the killers were sentenced to life in prison – two without the
possibility of parole.

# C. PROSECUTORIAL IMMUNITY

Prosecutorial ethics is an issue of the utmost importance and the power to
discipline attorneys goes beyond bar association misconduct hearings. If a
prosecutor engages in criminal conduct they may face charges for their actions. In

---

[20]  *Commonwealth v. Cosby*, 252 A.3d 1092 (2021).

Nifong's case he was held in contempt of court and served one day in jail for the offense. If they violate an individual's civil rights by their actions prosecutors may be subject to civil liability as well. Immunity is protection against being held liable in a civil suit for errors or misconduct. Prosecutors enjoy **absolute immunity** for their conduct during their preparation for and conducting a criminal trial.[21] Absolute immunity turns on whether the prosecutor was engaged in their core prosecutorial duties or functions. If so, while they are subject to discipline and even potentially criminal charges; they enjoy absolute immunity from civil liability—even though their conduct is unethical.

In contrast, prosecutors enjoy only **qualified immunity** for conduct that is outside the scope of those core prosecutorial functions. In Nifong's case he was also sued civilly by the victims of his unethical prosecution and in a settlement agreement issued in 2014, he was required to pay $1,000 to the North Carolina Innocence Inquiry Commission, a non-profit organization which assists defendants with appeals. The City of Durham also made a $50,000 donation to the Commission in order to settle the long-running suit. The athletes did not receive any money in the settlement, but it is estimated that Duke University paid $50 million in settlements to the athletes to resolve cases against it in 2007 (the actual settlement terms were not disclosed).

---

[21]  *Imbler v. Pachtman*, 424 U.S. 409 (1976).

Read and brief each of the following cases relating to the role and responsibilities of prosecutors and consider the questions following each case:

1.   *United States v. Armstrong*: prosecutorial misconduct (selective prosecution)

2.   *Buckley v. Fitzsimmons*: prosecutorial misconduct and immunity from civil liability

3.   *Santobello v. New York*: prosecutorial duty to honor plea agreements

4.   *United States v. Agurs*: prosecutorial duty to disclose exculpatory evidence

5.   *Smith v. Cain*: materiality of exculpatory evidence

---

## UNITED STATES V. ARMSTRONG

Supreme Court of the United States
Argued Feb. 26, 1996
Decided May 13, 1996
517 U.S. 456

### OPINION

**CHIEF JUSTICE REHNQUIST delivered the opinion of the Court.**

In this case, we consider the showing necessary for a defendant to be entitled to discovery on a claim that the prosecuting attorney singled him out for prosecution on the basis of his race. We conclude that respondents failed to satisfy the threshold showing: They failed to show that the Government declined to prosecute similarly situated suspects of other races.

In April 1992, respondents were indicted in the United States District Court for the Central District of California on charges of conspiring to possess with intent to distribute more than 50 grams of cocaine base (crack) and conspiring to distribute the same, in violation of 21 U.S.C. §§ 841 and 846 (1988 ed. and Supp. IV), and federal firearms offenses. For three months prior to the indictment, agents of the Federal Bureau of Alcohol, Tobacco, and Firearms and the Narcotics Division of the Inglewood, California, Police Department had infiltrated a suspected crack distribution ring by using three confidential informants. On seven separate occasions during this period, the informants had bought a total of 124.3 grams of crack from respondents and witnessed respondents arraying firearms during the sales. The agents searched the hotel room in which the sales were transacted, arrested respondents

Armstrong and Hampton in the room, and found more crack and a loaded gun. The agents later arrested the other respondents as part of the ring.

In response to the indictment, respondents filed a motion for discovery or for dismissal of the indictment, alleging that they were selected for federal prosecution because they are black. In support of their motion, they offered only an affidavit by a "Paralegal Specialist," employed by the Office of the Federal Public Defender representing one of the respondents. The only allegation in the affidavit was that, in every one of the 24 § 841 or § 846 cases closed by the office during 1991, the defendant was black. Accompanying the affidavit was a "study" listing the 24 defendants, their race, whether they were prosecuted for dealing cocaine as well as crack, and the status of each case.[1]

The Government opposed the discovery motion, arguing, among other things, that there was no evidence or allegation "that the Government has acted unfairly or has prosecuted non-black defendants or failed to prosecute them." App. 150. The District Court granted the motion. It ordered the Government (1) to provide a list of all cases from the last three years in which the Government charged both cocaine and firearms offenses, (2) to identify the race of the defendants in those cases, (3) to identify what levels of law enforcement were involved in the investigations of those cases, and (4) to explain its criteria for deciding to prosecute those defendants for federal cocaine offenses. *Id.*, at 161–162.

The Government moved for reconsideration of the District Court's discovery order. With this motion it submitted affidavits and other evidence to explain why it had chosen to prosecute respondents and why respondents' study did not support the inference that the Government was singling out blacks for cocaine prosecution. The federal and local agents participating in the case alleged in affidavits that race played no role in their investigation. An Assistant United States Attorney explained in an affidavit that the decision to prosecute met the general criteria for prosecution, because

> "There was over 100 grams of cocaine base involved, over twice the threshold necessary for a ten year mandatory minimum sentence; there were multiple sales involving multiple defendants, thereby indicating a fairly substantial crack cocaine ring; . . . there were

---

[1]    Other defendants had introduced this study in support of similar discovery motions in at least two other Central District cocaine prosecutions. App. 83. Both motions were denied. One District Judge explained from the bench that the 23-person sample before him was "statistically insignificant," and that the evidence did not indicate, "whether there is a bias in the distribution of crime that says black people use crack cocaine, Hispanic people use powdered cocaine, Caucasian people use whatever it is they use." *Id.*, at 119, 120.

multiple federal firearms violations intertwined with the narcotics trafficking; the overall evidence in the case was extremely strong, including audio and videotapes of defendants; . . . and several of the defendants had criminal histories including narcotics and firearms violations." *Id.*, at 81.

The Government also submitted sections of a published 1989 Drug Enforcement Administration report which concluded that "large-scale, interstate trafficking networks controlled by Jamaicans, Haitians and Black street gangs dominate the manufacture and distribution of crack." J. Featherly & E. Hill, Crack Cocaine Overview 1989; App. 103.

In response, one of respondents' attorneys submitted an affidavit alleging that an intake coordinator at a drug treatment center had told her that there are "an equal number of Caucasian users and dealers to minority users and dealers." *Id.*, at 138. Respondents also submitted an affidavit from a criminal defense attorney alleging that in his experience many nonblacks are prosecuted in state court for crack offenses, *id.*, at 141, and a newspaper article reporting that federal "crack criminals . . . are being punished far more severely than if they had been caught with powder cocaine, and almost every single one of them is black," Newton, Harsher Crack Sentences Criticized as Racial Inequity, Los Angeles Times, Nov. 23, 1992, p. 1; App. 208–210.

The District Court denied the motion for reconsideration. When the Government indicated it would not comply with the court's discovery order, the court dismissed the case. . .

A divided three-judge panel of the Court of Appeals for the Ninth Circuit reversed, holding that, because of the proof requirements for a selective-prosecution claim, defendants must "provide a colorable basis for believing that 'others similarly situated have not been prosecuted'" to obtain discovery. . .

The Court of Appeals voted to rehear the case en banc, and the en banc panel affirmed the District Court's order of dismissal, holding that "a defendant is not required to demonstrate that the government has failed to prosecute others who are similarly situated." 48 F.3d 1508, 1516 (1995) (emphasis deleted). We granted certiorari to determine the appropriate standard for discovery for a selective-prosecution claim. 516 U.S. 942 (1995). . .

In *Wade v. United States*, 504 U.S. 181 (1992), we considered whether a federal court may review a Government decision not to file a motion to reduce a defendant's sentence for substantial assistance to the prosecution, to determine whether the Government based its decision on the defendant's race or religion. In holding that such a decision was reviewable, we assumed that discovery would be available if the defendant could make the appropriate threshold showing, although we concluded that the defendant in that case did not make such a showing. See *id.*, at 186. We proceed on a like assumption here.

A selective-prosecution claim is not a defense on the merits to the criminal charge itself, but an independent assertion that the prosecutor has brought the charge for reasons forbidden by the Constitution. Our cases delineating the necessary elements to prove a claim of selective prosecution have taken great pains to explain that the standard is a demanding one. These cases afford a "background presumption," cf. *United States v. Mezzanatto*, 513 U.S. 196, 203 (1995), that the showing necessary to obtain discovery should itself be a significant barrier to the litigation of insubstantial claims.

. . .In the ordinary case, "so long as the prosecutor has probable cause to believe that the accused committed an offense defined by statute, the decision whether or not to prosecute, and what charge to file or bring before a grand jury, generally rests entirely in his discretion." *Bordenkircher v. Hayes*, 434 U.S. 357, 364 (1978).

Of course, a prosecutor's discretion is "subject to constitutional constraints." *United States v. Batchelder*, 442 U.S. 114, 125 (1979). One of these constraints, imposed by the equal protection component of the Due Process Clause of the Fifth Amendment, *Bolling v. Sharpe*, 347 U.S. 497, 500 (1954), is that the decision whether to prosecute may not be based on "an unjustifiable standard such as race, religion, or other arbitrary classification," *Oyler v. Boles*, 368 U.S. 448, 456 (1962). A defendant may demonstrate that the administration of a criminal law is "directed so exclusively against a particular class of persons . . . with a mind so unequal and oppressive" that the system of prosecution amounts to "a practical denial" of equal protection of the law. *Yick Wo v. Hopkins*, 118 U.S. 356, 373 (1886).

In order to dispel the presumption that a prosecutor has not violated equal protection, a criminal defendant must present "clear evidence to the contrary." *Chemical Foundation, supra,* at 14–15. We explained in *Wayte* why courts are "properly hesitant to examine the decision whether to prosecute." 470 U.S. at 608. Judicial deference to the decisions of these executive officers rests in part on an assessment of the relative competence of prosecutors and courts. "Such factors as the strength of the case, the prosecution's general deterrence value, the Government's enforcement priorities, and the case's relationship to the

Government's overall enforcement plan are not readily susceptible to the kind of analysis the courts are competent to undertake." *Id.*, at 607. It also stems from a concern not to unnecessarily impair the performance of a core executive constitutional function. "Examining the basis of a prosecution delays the criminal proceeding, threatens to chill law enforcement by subjecting the prosecutor's motives and decision-making to outside inquiry, and may undermine prosecutorial effectiveness by revealing the Government's enforcement policy." *Ibid.*

The requirements for a selective-prosecution claim draw on "ordinary equal protection standards." *Id.*, at 608. The claimant must demonstrate that the federal prosecutorial policy "had a discriminatory effect and that it was motivated by a discriminatory purpose." *Ibid.*; accord, *Oyler, supra*, at 456. To establish a discriminatory effect in a race case, the claimant must show that similarly situated individuals of a different race were not prosecuted. This requirement has been established in our case law since *Ah Sin v. Wittman*, 198 U.S. 500 (1905). . .

The similarly situated requirement does not make a selective-prosecution claim impossible to prove. Twenty years before *Ah Sin*, we invalidated an ordinance, also adopted by San Francisco, that prohibited the operation of laundries in wooden buildings. *Yick Wo*, 118 U.S. at 374. The plaintiff in error successfully demonstrated that the ordinance was applied against Chinese nationals but not against other laundry-shop operators. The authorities had denied the applications of 200 Chinese subjects for permits to operate shops in wooden buildings, but granted the applications of 80 individuals who were not Chinese subjects to operate laundries in wooden buildings "under similar conditions." *Ibid.* We explained in *Ah Sin* why the similarly situated requirement is necessary:

> "No latitude of intention should be indulged in a case like this. There should be certainty to every intent. Plaintiff in error seeks to set aside a criminal law of the State, not on the ground that it is unconstitutional on its face, not that it is discriminatory in tendency and ultimate actual operation as the ordinance was which was passed on in the *Yick Wo case*, but that it was made so by the manner of its administration. This is a matter of proof, and *no fact should be omitted to make it out completely*, when the power of a Federal court is invoked to interfere with the course of criminal justice of a State." 198 U.S. at 508 (emphasis added).

Although *Ah Sin* involved federal review of a state conviction, we think a similar rule applies where the power of a federal court is invoked to challenge an exercise of one of the core powers of the Executive Branch of the Federal Government, the power to prosecute. . .

Having reviewed the requirements to prove a selective-prosecution claim, we turn to the showing necessary to obtain discovery in support of such a claim. If discovery is ordered, the Government must assemble from its own files documents which might corroborate or refute the defendant's claim. Discovery thus imposes many of the costs present when the Government must respond to a prima facie case of selective prosecution. It will divert prosecutors' resources and may disclose the Government's prosecutorial strategy. The justifications for a rigorous standard for the elements of a selective-prosecution claim thus require a correspondingly rigorous standard for discovery in aid of such a claim.

The parties, and the Courts of Appeals which have considered the requisite showing to establish entitlement to discovery, describe this showing with a variety of phrases, like "colorable basis," "substantial threshold showing," Tr. of Oral Arg. 5, "substantial and concrete basis," or "reasonable likelihood," Brief for Respondents Martin et al. 30. However, the many labels for this showing conceal the degree of consensus about the evidence necessary to meet it. The Courts of Appeals "require some evidence tending to show the existence of the essential elements of the defense," discriminatory effect and discriminatory intent. *United States v. Berrios*, 501 F.2d 1207, 1211 (CA2 1974).

In this case we consider what evidence constitutes "some evidence tending to show the existence" of the discriminatory effect element. The Court of Appeals held that a defendant may establish a colorable basis for discriminatory effect without evidence that the Government has failed to prosecute others who are similarly situated to the defendant. 48 F.3d at 1516. We think it was mistaken in this view. The vast majority of the Courts of Appeals require the defendant to produce some evidence that similarly situated defendants of other races could have been prosecuted, but were not, and this requirement is consistent with our equal protection case law. . . . As the three-judge panel explained, " 'selective prosecution' implies that a selection has taken place." 21 F.3d at 1436.[3]

---

[3]    We reserve the question whether a defendant must satisfy the similarly situated requirement in a case "involving direct admissions by [prosecutors] of discriminatory purpose." Brief for United States 15.

The Court of Appeals reached its decision in part because it started "with the presumption that people of *all* races commit *all* types of crimes—not with the premise that any type of crime is the exclusive province of any particular racial or ethnic group." 48 F.3d at 1516–1517. It cited no authority for this proposition, which seems contradicted by the most recent statistics of the United States Sentencing Commission. Those statistics show: More than 90% of the persons sentenced in 1994 for crack cocaine trafficking were black, United States Sentencing Comm'n, 1994 Annual Report 107 (Table 45); 93.4% of convicted LSD dealers were white, *ibid.*; and 91% of those convicted for pornography or prostitution were white, *id.*, at 41 (Table 13). Presumptions at war with presumably reliable statistics have no proper place in the analysis of this issue.

The Court of Appeals also expressed concern about the "evidentiary obstacles defendants face." 48 F.3d at 1514. But all of its sister Circuits that have confronted the issue have required that defendants produce some evidence of differential treatment of similarly situated members of other races or protected classes. In the present case, if the claim of selective prosecution were well founded, it should not have been an insuperable task to prove that persons of other races were being treated differently than respondents. For instance, respondents could have investigated whether similarly situated persons of other races were prosecuted by the State of California and were known to federal law enforcement officers, but were not prosecuted in federal court. We think the required threshold—a credible showing of different treatment of similarly situated persons—adequately balances the Government's interest in vigorous prosecution and the defendant's interest in avoiding selective prosecution.

In the case before us, respondents' "study" did not constitute "some evidence tending to show the existence of the essential elements of" a selective-prosecution claim. *Berrios, supra*, at 1211. The study failed to identify individuals who were not black and could have been prosecuted for the offenses for which respondents were charged, but were not so prosecuted. This omission was not remedied by respondents' evidence in opposition to the Government's motion for reconsideration. The newspaper article, which discussed the discriminatory effect of federal drug sentencing laws, was not relevant to an allegation of discrimination in decisions to prosecute. Respondents' affidavits, which recounted one attorney's conversation with a drug treatment center employee and the experience of another attorney defending drug prosecutions in state court, recounted hearsay and reported personal conclusions based on anecdotal evidence. The judgment of the Court of Appeals is therefore reversed, and the case is remanded for proceedings consistent with this opinion.

*It is so ordered. . . .*

**After preparing the case brief, consider the answers to the following questions:**

1.    What type of claim is selective prosecution?

2.    What are the "ordinary Equal Protection Standards" the Court discusses?

3.    What test does the Court require defendants to employ in proving they were singled out for prosecution based on race? How is the test for *discovery* in the context of selective prosecution different?

4.    What kinds of evidence might have been more convincing to the Court in supporting the defendant's discovery request in this case?

# BUCKLEY V. FITZSIMMONS

Supreme Court of the United States
Argued Feb. 22, 1993
Decided June 24, 1993
509 U.S. 259

## Opinion

### JUSTICE STEVENS delivered the opinion of the Court.

In an action brought under 42 U.S.C. § 1983, petitioner seeks damages from respondent prosecutors for allegedly fabricating evidence during the preliminary investigation of a crime and making false statements at a press conference announcing the return of an indictment. The questions presented are whether respondents are absolutely immune from liability on either or both of these claims.

As the case comes to us, we have no occasion to consider whether some or all of respondents' conduct may be protected by qualified immunity. Moreover, we make two important assumptions about the case: first, that petitioner's allegations are entirely true; and, second, that they allege constitutional violations for which § 1983 provides a remedy. Our statement of facts is therefore derived entirely from petitioner's complaint and is limited to matters relevant to respondents' claim to absolute immunity.

I

Petitioner commenced this action on March 4, 1988, following his release from jail in Du Page County, Illinois. He had been incarcerated there for three years on charges growing out of the highly publicized murder of Jeanine Nicarico, an 11-year-old child, on February 25, 1983. The complaint named 17 defendants, including Du Page County, its sheriff and seven of his assistants, two expert witnesses and the estate of a third, and the five respondents.

Respondent Fitzsimmons was the duly elected Du Page County State's Attorney from the time of the Nicarico murder through December 1984, when he was succeeded by respondent Ryan, who had defeated him in a Republican primary election on March 21, 1984. Respondent Knight was an assistant state's attorney under Fitzsimmons and served as a special prosecutor in the Nicarico case under Ryan. Respondents Kilander (who came into office with Ryan) and King were assistant prosecutors, also assigned to the case.

The theory of petitioner's case is that in order to obtain an indictment in a case that had engendered "extensive publicity" and "intense emotions in the community," the prosecutors fabricated false evidence, and that in order to gain votes, Fitzsimmons made false statements about petitioner in a press conference announcing his arrest and indictment 12 days before the primary election. Petitioner claims that respondents' misconduct created a "highly prejudicial and inflamed atmosphere" that seriously impaired the fairness of the judicial proceedings against an innocent man and caused him to suffer a serious loss of freedom, mental anguish, and humiliation.

The fabricated evidence related to a bootprint on the door of the Nicarico home apparently left by the killer when he kicked in the door. After three separate studies by experts from the Du Page County Crime Lab, the Illinois Department of Law Enforcement, and the Kansas Bureau of Identification, all of whom were unable to make a reliable connection between the print and a pair of boots that petitioner had voluntarily supplied, respondents obtained a "positive identification" from one Louise Robbins, an anthropologist in North Carolina who was allegedly well known for her willingness to fabricate unreliable expert testimony. Her opinion was obtained during the early stages of the investigation, which was being conducted under the joint supervision and direction of the sheriff and respondent Fitzsimmons, whose police officers and assistant prosecutors were performing essentially the same investigatory functions.

Thereafter, having failed to obtain sufficient evidence to support petitioner's (or anyone else's) arrest, respondents convened a special grand jury for the sole purpose of investigating the Nicarico case. After an 8-month investigation, during which the grand jury heard the testimony of over 100 witnesses, including the bootprint experts, it was still unable to return an indictment. On January 27, 1984, respondent Fitzsimmons admitted in a public statement that there was insufficient evidence to indict anyone for the rape and murder of Jeanine Nicarico. Although no additional evidence was obtained in the interim, the indictment was returned in March, when Fitzsimmons held the defamatory press conference so shortly before the primary election. Petitioner was then arrested, and because he was unable to meet the bond (set at $3 million), he was held in jail.

Petitioner's trial began 10 months later, in January 1985. The principal evidence against him was provided by Robbins, the North Carolina anthropologist. Because the jury was unable to reach a verdict on the charges against petitioner, the trial judge declared a mistrial. Petitioner remained in prison for two more years, during which a third party confessed to the crime and the prosecutors prepared for petitioner's retrial. After Robbins died, however, all charges against him were dropped. He was released, and filed this action.

II

We are not concerned with petitioner's actions against the police officers (who have asserted the defense of qualified immunity), against the expert witnesses (whose trial testimony was granted absolute immunity by the District Court, App. 53–57), and against Du Page County (whose motion to dismiss on other grounds was granted in part, *id.,* at 57–61). At issue here is only the action against the prosecutors, who moved to dismiss based on their claim to absolute immunity. The District Court held that respondents were entitled to absolute immunity for all claims except the claim against Fitzsimmons based on his press conference. *Id.,* at 53. With respect to the claim based on the alleged fabrication of evidence, the District Court framed the question as whether the effort "to obtain definitive boot evidence linking [petitioner to the crime] was in the nature of acquisition of evidence or in the nature of evaluation of evidence for the purpose of initiating the criminal process." *Id.,* at 45. The Court concluded that it "appears" that it was more evaluative than acquisitive.

Both petitioner and Fitzsimmons appealed, and a divided panel of the Court of Appeals for the Seventh Circuit ruled that the prosecutors had absolute immunity on both claims. *Buckley v. Fitzsimmons,* 919 F.2d 1230 (1990). In the Court of Appeals' view, "damages remedies are unnecessary," *id.,* at 1240, when "[c]ourts can curtail the costs of prosecutorial blunders . . . by cutting short the prosecution or mitigating its effects," *id.,* at 1241. Thus, when "out-of-court acts cause injury only to the extent a case proceeds" in court, *id.,* at 1242, the prosecutor is entitled to absolute immunity and "the defendant must look to the court in which the case pends to protect his interests," *id.,* at 1241. By contrast, if "a constitutional wrong is complete before the case begins," the prosecutor is entitled only to qualified immunity. *Id.,* at 1241–1242. Applying this unprecedented theory to petitioner's allegations, the Court of Appeals concluded that neither the press conference nor the fabricated evidence caused any constitutional injury independent of the indictment and trial. *Id.,* at 1243, 1244.

Judge Fairchild dissented in part. He agreed with the District Court that Fitzsimmons was entitled only to qualified immunity for his press statements. He noted that the majority had failed to examine the particular function that Fitzsimmons was performing, and concluded that conducting a press conference was not among "the functions that entitle judges and prosecutors in the judicial branch to absolute immunity." *Id.,* at 1246 (opinion dissenting in part and concurring in part). Responding directly to the majority's reasoning, he wrote: "It is true that procedures afforded in our system of justice give a defendant a good chance to avoid such results of prejudicial publicity as excessive bail, difficulty or inability of selecting an impartial jury, and the like. These procedures reduce the cost of impropriety by a prosecutor, but I do not find that the courts have recognized their availability as a sufficient reason for conferring immunity." *Ibid.*

We granted Buckley's petition for certiorari, vacated the judgment, and remanded the case for further proceedings in light of our intervening decision in *Burns v. Reed,* 500 U.S. 478 (1991)... On remand, the same panel, again divided, reaffirmed its initial decision, with one modification not relevant here. 952 F.2d 965 (CA7 1992) *(per curiam).* The Court of Appeals held that "[n]othing in *Burns* undermine[d]" its initial holding that prosecutors are absolutely immune for "normal preparatory steps"; unlike the activities at issue in *Burns,* "[t]alking with (willing) experts is trial preparation." 952 F.2d, at 966–967. In similar fashion, the court adhered to its conclusion that Fitzsimmons was entitled to absolute immunity for conducting the press conference. The court recognized that the press conference bore some similarities to the conduct in *Burns* (advising the police as to the propriety of an arrest). It did not take place in court, and it was not part of the prosecutor's trial preparation. 952 F.2d, at 967. The difference, according to the court, is that "[a]n arrest causes injury whether or not a prosecution ensues," whereas the only constitutional injury caused by the press conference depends on judicial action. *Ibid.* . . .

We granted certiorari for a second time, limited to issues relating to prosecutorial immunity. . . We now reverse.

III

The principles applied to determine the scope of immunity for state officials sued under Rev.Stat. § 1979, as amended, 42 U.S.C. § 1983 are by now familiar. Section 1983, on its face admits of no defense of official immunity. It subjects to liability "[e]very person" who, acting under color of state law, commits the prohibited acts. In *Tenney v. Brandhove,* 341 U.S. 367, 376 (1951), however, we held that Congress did not intend § 1983 to abrogate immunities "well grounded in history and reason." Certain immunities were so well established in 1871, when § 1983 was enacted, that "we presume that Congress would have specifically so provided had it wished to abolish" them. *Pierson v. Ray,* 386 U.S. 547, 554–555 (1967) . . .

We have recognized, however, that some officials perform "special functions" which, because of their similarity to functions that would have been immune when Congress enacted § 1983, deserve absolute protection from damages liability. *Id.,* at 508, 98 S.Ct., at 2911. "[T]he official seeking absolute immunity bears the burden of showing that such immunity is justified for the function in question." *Burns v. Reed,* 500 U.S., at 486; *Antoine v. Byers & Anderson, Inc.,* 508 U.S. 429, 432, and n. 4 (1993). Even when we can identify a common-law tradition of absolute immunity for a given function, we have considered "whether § 1983's history or purposes nonetheless counsel against recognizing the same immunity in § 1983 actions." *Tower v. Glover,* 467 U.S., at 920. Not surprisingly, we have been "quite sparing" in recognizing absolute immunity for state actors in this context. *Forrester v. White,* 484 U.S. 219, 224 (1988).

In determining whether particular actions of government officials fit within a common-law tradition of absolute immunity, or only the more general standard of qualified immunity, we have applied a "functional approach," see, e.g., *Burns,* 500 U.S., at 486, 111 S.Ct., at 1939, which looks to "the nature of the function performed, not the identity of the actor who performed it," *Forrester v. White,* 484 U.S., at 229, 108 S.Ct., at 545. We have twice applied this approach in determining whether the functions of contemporary prosecutors are entitled to absolute immunity.

In *Imbler v. Pachtman,* 424 U.S. 409 (1976), we held that a state prosecutor had absolute immunity for the initiation and pursuit of a criminal prosecution, including presentation of the state's case at trial. Noting that our earlier cases had been "predicated upon a considered inquiry into the immunity historically accorded the relevant official at common law and the interests behind it," *id.,* at 421, 96 S.Ct., at 990, we focused on the functions of the prosecutor that had most often invited common-law tort actions. We concluded that the common-law rule of immunity for prosecutors was "well settled" and that "the same considerations of public policy that underlie the common-law rule likewise countenance absolute immunity under § 1983." Those considerations supported a rule of absolute immunity for conduct of prosecutors that was "intimately associated with the judicial phase of the criminal process." *Id.,* at 430, 96 S.Ct., at 995. In concluding that "in initiating a prosecution and in presenting the State's case, the prosecutor is immune from a civil suit for damages under § 1983," we did not attempt to describe the line between a prosecutor's acts in preparing for those functions, some of which would be absolutely immune, and his acts of investigation or "administration," which would not. *Id.,* at 431, and n. 33, 96 S.Ct., at 995, and n. 33.

We applied the *Imbler* analysis two Terms ago in *Burns v. Reed,* 500 U.S. 478, 111 S.Ct. 1934, 114 L.Ed.2d 547 (1991). There the § 1983 suit challenged two acts by a prosecutor: (1) giving legal advice to the police on the propriety of hypnotizing a suspect and on whether probable cause existed to arrest that suspect, and (2) participating in a probable-cause hearing. We held that only the latter was entitled to absolute immunity. Immunity for that action under § 1983 accorded with the common-law absolute immunity of prosecutors and other attorneys for eliciting false or defamatory testimony from witnesses or for making false or defamatory statements during, and related to, judicial proceedings. . . . Under that analysis, appearing before a judge and presenting evidence in support of a motion for a search warrant involved the prosecutor's " 'role as advocate for the State.' " . . . Because issuance of a search warrant is a judicial act, appearance at the probable-cause hearing was " 'intimately associated with the judicial phase of the criminal process,' " *Burns,* 500 U.S., at 492, 111 S.Ct., at 1942, quoting *Imbler,* 424 U.S., at 430, 96 S.Ct., at 995.

We further decided, however, that prosecutors are not entitled to absolute immunity for their actions in giving legal advice to the police. We were unable to identify any historical or common-law support for absolute immunity in the performance of this function. . . . We also noted that any threat to the judicial process from "the harassment and intimidation associated with litigation" based on advice to the police was insufficient to overcome the "[a]bsen[ce] [of] a tradition of immunity comparable to the common-law immunity from malicious prosecution, which formed the basis for the decision in *Imbler.*" . . .

## IV

In this case the Court of Appeals held that respondents are entitled to absolute immunity because the injuries suffered by petitioner occurred during criminal proceedings. That holding is contrary to the approach we have consistently followed since *Imbler.* As we have noted, the *Imbler* approach focuses on the conduct for which immunity is claimed, not on the harm that the conduct may have caused or the question whether it was lawful. The location of the injury may be relevant to the question whether a complaint has adequately alleged a cause of action for damages (a question that this case does not present, see *supra,* at 2609). It is irrelevant, however, to the question whether the conduct of a prosecutor is protected by absolute immunity. Accordingly, although the Court of Appeals' reasoning may be relevant to the proper resolution of issues that are not before us, it does not provide an acceptable basis for concluding that either the preindictment fabrication of evidence or the postindictment press conference was a function protected by absolute immunity. We therefore turn to consider each of respondents' claims of absolute immunity.

A

We first address petitioner's argument that the prosecutors are not entitled to absolute immunity for the claim that they conspired to manufacture false evidence that would link his boot with the bootprint the murderer left on the front door. To obtain this false evidence, petitioner submits, the prosecutors shopped for experts until they found one who would provide the opinion they sought. App. 7–9. At the time of this witness shopping the assistant prosecutors were working hand in hand with the sheriff's detectives under the joint supervision of the sheriff and state's attorney Fitzsimmons.

Petitioner argues that *Imbler*'s protection for a prosecutor's conduct "in initiating a prosecution and in presenting the State's case,". . . extends only to the act of initiation itself and to conduct occurring in the courtroom. This extreme position is plainly foreclosed by our opinion in *Imbler* itself. We expressly stated that "the duties of the prosecutor in his role as advocate for the State involve actions preliminary to the initiation of a prosecution and actions apart from the courtroom," and are nonetheless entitled to absolute immunity. . . . We noted in particular that an out-of-court "effort to control the presentation of [a] witness' testimony" was entitled to absolute immunity because it was "fairly within [the prosecutor's] function as an advocate." . . . To be sure, *Burns* made explicit the point we had reserved in *Imbler*. . . . A prosecutor's administrative duties and those investigatory functions that do not relate to an advocate's preparation for the initiation of a prosecution or for judicial proceedings are not entitled to absolute immunity. . . .We have not retreated, however, from the principle that acts undertaken by a prosecutor in preparing for the initiation of judicial proceedings or for trial, and which occur in the course of his role as an advocate for the State, are entitled to the protections of absolute immunity. Those acts must include the professional evaluation of the evidence assembled by the police and appropriate preparation for its presentation at trial or before a grand jury after a decision to seek an indictment has been made.

On the other hand, as the function test of *Imbler* recognizes, the actions of a prosecutor are not absolutely immune merely because they are performed by a prosecutor. Qualified immunity " 'represents the norm' " for executive officers, *Malley v. Briggs,* 475 U.S., at 340, quoting *Harlow v. Fitzgerald,* 457 U.S., at 807, so when a prosecutor "functions as an administrator rather than as an officer of the court" he is entitled only to qualified immunity. . . . There is a difference between the advocate's role in evaluating evidence and interviewing witnesses as he prepares for trial, on the one hand, and the detective's role in searching for the clues and corroboration that might give him probable cause to recommend that a suspect be arrested, on the other hand. When a prosecutor performs the investigative functions normally performed by a detective or police officer, it is "neither appropriate nor justifiable that, for the same act, immunity should protect the one and not the other." *Hampton v. Chicago,* 484 F.2d 602, 608 (CA7 1973) internal quotation marks omitted), cert. denied, 415 U.S. 917 (1974). Thus, if a prosecutor plans and executes a raid on a suspected weapons cache, he "has no greater claim to complete immunity than activities of police officers allegedly acting under his direction." 484 F.2d, at 608–609.

The question, then, is whether the prosecutors have carried their burden of establishing that they were functioning as "advocates" when they were endeavoring to determine whether the bootprint at the scene of the crime had been made by petitioner's foot. A careful examination of the allegations concerning the conduct of the prosecutors during the period before they convened a special grand jury to investigate the crime provides the answer. . . . The prosecutors do not contend that they had probable cause to arrest petitioner or to initiate judicial proceedings during that period. Their mission at that time was entirely investigative in character. A prosecutor neither is, nor should consider himself to be, an advocate before he has probable cause to have anyone arrested.

It was well after the alleged fabrication of false evidence concerning the bootprint that a special grand jury was empaneled. And when it finally was convened, its immediate purpose was to conduct a more thorough investigation of the crime—not to return an indictment against a suspect whom there was already probable cause to arrest. Buckley was not arrested, in fact, until 10 months after the grand jury had been convened and had finally indicted him. Under these circumstances, the prosecutors' conduct occurred well before they could properly claim to be acting as advocates. Respondents have not cited any authority that supports an argument that a prosecutor's fabrication of false evidence during the preliminary investigation of an unsolved crime was immune from liability at common law, either in 1871 or at any date before the enactment of § 1983. It therefore remains protected only by qualified immunity.

After *Burns,* it would be anomalous, to say the least, to grant prosecutors only qualified immunity when offering legal advice to police about an unarrested suspect, but then to endow them with absolute immunity when conducting investigative work themselves in order to decide whether a suspect may be arrested. That the prosecutors later called a grand jury to consider the evidence this work produced does not retroactively transform that work from the administrative into the prosecutorial. A prosecutor may not shield his investigative work with the aegis of absolute immunity merely because, after a suspect is eventually arrested, indicted, and tried, that work may be retrospectively described as "preparation" for a possible trial; every prosecutor might then shield himself from liability for any constitutional wrong against innocent citizens by ensuring that they go to trial. When the functions of prosecutors and detectives are the same, as they were here, the immunity that protects them is also the same.

B

We next consider petitioner's claims regarding Fitzsimmons' statements to the press. Petitioner alleged that, during the prosecutor's public announcement of the indictment, Fitzsimmons made false assertions that numerous pieces of evidence, including the bootprint evidence, tied Buckley to a burglary ring that committed the Nicarico murder. App. 12. Petitioner also alleged that Fitzsimmons released mug shots of him to the media, "which were prominently and repeatedly displayed on television and in the newspapers." *Ibid.* Petitioner's legal theory is that "[t]hese false and prejudicial statements inflamed the populace of DuPage County against" him, *ibid.;* see also *id.,* at 14, thereby defaming him, resulting in deprivation of his right to a fair trial, and causing the jury to deadlock rather than acquit, *id.,* at 19.

Fitzsimmons' statements to the media are not entitled to absolute immunity. Fitzsimmons does not suggest that in 1871 there existed a common-law immunity for a prosecutor's, or attorney's, out-of-court statement to the press. The Court of Appeals agreed that no such historical precedent exists. . . . Indeed, while prosecutors, like all attorneys, were entitled to absolute immunity from defamation liability for statements made during the course of judicial proceedings and relevant to them, . . .most statements made out of court received only good-faith immunity. The common-law rule was that "[t]he speech of a counsel is privileged by the occasion on which it is spoken. . . ." . . .

The functional approach of *Imbler,* which conforms to the common-law theory, leads us to the same conclusion. Comments to the media have no functional tie to the judicial process just because they are made by a prosecutor. At the press conference, Fitzsimmons did not act in " 'his role as advocate for the State,' " *Burns v. Reed,* 500 U.S., at 491, quoting *Imbler v. Pachtman,* 424 U.S., at 431, n. 33. The conduct of a press conference does not involve the initiation of a prosecution, the presentation of the state's case in court, or actions preparatory for these functions. Statements to the press may be an integral part of a prosecutor's job, see National District Attorneys Assn., National Prosecution Standards 107, 110 (2d ed. 1991), and they may serve a vital public function. But in these respects a prosecutor is in no different position than other executive officials who deal with the press, and, as noted above, *supra*, at 2612–2613, 2617, qualified immunity is the norm for them.

Fitzsimmons argues nonetheless that policy considerations support extending absolute immunity to press statements. . . . we see little reason to suppose that qualified immunity would provide adequate protection to prosecutors in their provision of legal advice to the police. . .yet would fail to provide sufficient protection in the present context.

V

. . . As to the two challenged rulings on absolute immunity, however, the judgment of the United States Court of Appeals for the Seventh Circuit is reversed, and the case is remanded for further proceedings consistent with this opinion.

*It is so ordered.* . . .

### After preparing the case brief, consider the answers to the following questions:

1.   Explain the difference between qualified and absolute immunity?

2.   What types of prosecutorial conduct or activities are protected by absolute immunity under *Imbler v. Pachtman*?

3.   Explain the difference between the lower court's holding that immunity depends on harm to the defendant, and the Supreme Court's opinion in that immunity turns upon the conduct or tasks in which the prosecutor is engaged.

4.   Is the Court's holding that statements to the press lack a connection or tie to the judicial process convincing? Explain.

## SANTOBELLO V. NEW YORK

Supreme Court of the United States
Argued Nov. 15, 1971
Decided Dec. 20, 1971
404 U.S. 257

### OPINION

### MR. CHIEF JUSTICE BURGER delivered the opinion of the Court.

We granted certiorari in this case to determine whether the State's failure to keep a commitment concerning the sentence recommendation on a guilty plea required a new trial.

The facts are not in dispute. The State of New York indicted petitioner in 1969 on two felony counts, Promoting Gambling in the First Degree, and Possession of Gambling Records in the First Degree, N.Y. Penal Law, McKinney's Consol. Laws, c. 40, §§ 225.10, 225.20. Petitioner first entered a plea of not guilty to both counts. After negotiations, the Assistant District Attorney in charge of the case agreed to permit petitioner to plead guilty to a lesser-included offense, Possession of Gambling Records in the Second Degree, N.Y. Penal Law § 225.15, conviction of which would carry a maximum prison sentence of one year. The prosecutor agreed to make no recommendation as to the sentence.

On June 16, 1969, petitioner accordingly withdrew his plea of not guilty and entered a plea of guilty to the lesser charge. Petitioner represented to the sentencing judge that the plea was voluntary and that the facts of the case, as described by the Assistant District Attorney, were true. The court accepted the plea and set a date for sentencing. A series of delays followed, owing primarily to the absence of a pre-sentence report, so that by September 23, 1969, petitioner had still not been sentenced. By that date petitioner acquired new defense counsel.

Petitioner's new counsel moved immediately to withdraw the guilty plea. In an accompanying affidavit, petitioner alleged that he did not know at the time of his plea that crucial evidence against him had been obtained as a result of an illegal search. The accuracy of this affidavit is subject to challenge since petitioner had filed and withdrawn a motion to suppress, before pleading guilty. In addition to his motion to withdraw his guilty plea, petitioner renewed the motion to suppress and filed a motion to inspect the grand jury minutes.

These three motions in turn caused further delay until November 26, 1969, when the court denied all three and set January 9, 1970, as the date for sentencing. On January 9 petitioner appeared before a different judge, the judge who had presided over the case to this juncture having retired. Petitioner renewed his motions, and the court again rejected them. The court then turned to consideration of the sentence.

At this appearance, another prosecutor had replaced the prosecutor who had negotiated the plea. The new prosecutor recommended the maximum one-year sentence. In making this recommendation, he cited petitioner's criminal record and alleged links with organized crime. Defense counsel immediately objected on the ground that the State had promised petitioner before the plea was entered that there would be no sentence recommendation by the prosecution. He sought to adjourn the sentence hearing in order to have time to prepare proof of the first prosecutor's promise. The second prosecutor, apparently ignorant of his colleague's commitment, argued that there was nothing in the record to support petitioner's claim of a promise, but the State, in subsequent proceedings, has not contested that such a promise was made.

The sentencing judge ended discussion, with the following statement, quoting extensively from the pre-sentence report:

'Mr. Aronstein (Defense Counsel), I am not at all influenced by what the District Attorney says, so that there is no need to adjourn the sentence, and there is no need to have any testimony. It doesn't make a particle of difference what the District Attorney says he will do, or what he doesn't do.

'I have here, Mr. Aronstein, a probation report. I have here a history of a long, long serious criminal record. I have here a picture of the life history of this man. . . .

'He is unamenable to supervision in the community. He is a professional criminal.' This is in quotes. 'And a recidivist. Institutionalization—'; that means, in plain language, just putting him away, 'is the only means of halting his anti-social activities,' and protecting you, your family, me, my family, protecting society. 'Institutionalization.' Plain language, put him behind bars.

'Under the plea, I can only send him to the New York City Correctional Institution for men for one year, which I am hereby doing.'

The judge then imposed the maximum sentence of one year.

Petitioner sought and obtained a certificate of reasonable doubt and was admitted to bail pending an appeal. The Supreme Court of the State of New York, Appellate Division, First Department, unanimously affirmed petitioner's conviction, . . . and petitioner was denied leave to appeal to the New York

Court of Appeals. Petitioner then sought certiorari in this Court. Mr. Justice Harlan granted bail pending our disposition of the case.

This record represents another example of an unfortunate lapse in orderly prosecutorial procedures, in part, no doubt, because of the enormous increase in the workload of the often understaffed prosecutor's offices. The heavy workload may well explain these episodes, but it does not excuse them. The disposition of criminal charges by agreement between the prosecutor and the accused, sometimes loosely called 'plea bargaining,' is an essential component of the administration of justice. Properly administered, it is to be encouraged. If every criminal charge were subjected to a full-scale trial, the States and the Federal Government would need to multiply by many times the number of judges and court facilities.

Disposition of charges after plea discussions is not only an essential part of the process but a highly desirable part for many reasons. It leads to prompt and largely final disposition of most criminal cases; it avoids much of the corrosive impact of enforced idleness during pre-trial confinement for those who are denied release pending trial; it protects the public from those accused persons who are prone to continue criminal conduct even while on pretrial release; and, by shortening the time between charge and disposition, it enhances whatever may be the rehabilitative prospects of the guilty when they are ultimately imprisoned. See *Brady v. United States,* 397 U.S. 742, 751–752 (1970).

However, all of these considerations presuppose fairness in securing agreement between an accused and a prosecutor. It is now clear, for example, that the accused pleading guilty must be counseled, absent a waiver. *Moore v. Michigan,* 355 U.S. 155 (1957). Fed. Rule Crim.Proc. 11, governing pleas in federal courts, now makes clear that the sentencing judge must develop, on the record, the factual basis for the plea, as, for example, by having the accused describe the conduct that gave rise to the charge. The plea must, of course, be voluntary and knowing and if it was induced by promises, the essence of those promises must in some way be made known. There is, of course, no absolute right to have a guilty plea accepted. *Lynch v. Overholser,* 369 U.S. 705, 719 (1962); Fed. Rule Crim.Proc. 11. A court may reject a plea in exercise of sound judicial discretion.

This phase of the process of criminal justice, and the adjudicative element inherent in accepting a plea of guilty, must be attended by safeguards to insure the defendant what is reasonably due in the circumstances. Those circumstances will vary, but a constant factor is that when a plea rests in any significant degree on a promise or agreement of the prosecutor, so that it can be said to be part of the inducement or consideration, such promise must be fulfilled.

On this record, petitioner 'bargained' and negotiated for a particular plea in order to secure dismissal of more serious charges, but also on condition that no sentence recommendation would be made by the prosecutor. It is now conceded that the promise to abstain from a recommendation was made, and at this stage the prosecution is not in a good position to argue that its inadvertent breach of agreement is immaterial. The staff lawyers in a prosecutor's office have the burden of 'letting the left hand know what the right hand is doing' or has done. That the breach of agreement was inadvertent does not lessen its impact.

. . .we conclude that the interests of justice and appropriate recognition of the duties of the prosecution in relation to promises made in the negotiation of pleas of guilty will be best served by remanding the case to the state courts for further consideration. The ultimate relief to which petitioner is entitled we leave to the discretion of the state court, which is in a better position to decide whether the circumstances of this case require only that there be specific performance of the agreement on the plea, in which case petitioner should be resentenced by a different judge, or whether, in the view of the state court, the circumstances require granting the relief sought by petitioner, i.e., the opportunity to withdraw his plea of guilty. We emphasize that this is in no sense to question the fairness of the sentencing judge; the fault here rests on the prosecutor, not on the sentencing judge.

**The judgment is vacated and the case is remanded for reconsideration not inconsistent with this opinion. . . .**

**MR. JUSTICE MARSHALL, with whom MR. JUSTICE BRENNAN and MR. JUSTICE STEWART join, concurring in part and dissenting in part.**

I agree with much of the majority's opinion, but conclude that petitioner must be permitted to withdraw his guilty plea. This is the relief petitioner requested and, on the facts set out by the majority, it is a form of relief to which he is entitled.

There is no need to belabor the fact that the Constitution guarantees to all criminal defendants the right to a trial by judge or jury, or, put another way, the 'right not to plead guilty,' *United States v. Jackson*, 390 U.S. 570, 581 (1968). This and other federal rights may be waived through a guilty plea, but such waivers are not lightly presumed and, in fact, are viewed with the 'utmost solicitude.' *Boykin v. Alabama*, 395 U.S. 238, 243 (1969). Given this, I believe that where the defendant presents a reason for vacating his plea and the government has not relied on the plea to its disadvantage, the plea may be vacated and the right to trial regained at least where the motion to vacate is made prior to sentence and judgment. In other words, in such circumstances I would not deem the earlier plea to have irrevocably waived the defendant's federal constitutional right to a trial. . . .

**After preparing the case brief, consider the answers to the following questions:**

1. Define a plea bargain and explain how each party might benefit.

2. Why is it important for plea agreements to be resolved promptly after they are reached?

3. Did the Court adequately recognize the challenges facing prosecutors as they balanced their needs against the rights of defendants in the plea bargaining process?

4. Should the breach of an agreement be treated differently if it was intentional versus inadvertent? Why?

# UNITED STATES V. AGURS

Supreme Court of the United States
Argued April 28, 1976
Decided June 24, 1976
427 U.S. 97

## Opinion

### MR. JUSTICE STEVENS delivered the opinion of the Court.

After a brief interlude in an inexpensive motel room, respondent repeatedly stabbed James Sewell, causing his death. She was convicted of second-degree murder. The question before us is whether the prosecutor's failure to provide defense counsel with certain background information about Sewell, which would have tended to support the argument that respondent acted in self-defense, deprived her of a fair trial under the rule of *Brady v. Maryland,* 373 U.S. 83 (1963).

The answer to the question depends on (1) a review of the facts, (2) the significance of the failure of defense counsel to request the material, and (3) the standard by which the prosecution's failure to volunteer exculpatory material should be judged.

I

At about 4:30 p. m. on September 24, 1971, respondent, who had been there before, and Sewell, registered in a motel as man and wife. They were assigned a room without a bath. Sewell was wearing a bowie knife in a sheath, and carried another knife in his pocket. Less than two hours earlier, according to the testimony of his estranged wife, he had had $360 in cash on his person. About 15 minutes later three motel employees heard respondent screaming for help. A forced entry into their room disclosed Sewell on top of respondent struggling for possession of the bowie knife. She was holding the knife; his bleeding hand grasped the blade; according to one witness he was trying to jam the blade into her chest. The employees separated the two and summoned the authorities. Respondent departed without comment before they arrived. Sewell was dead on arrival at the hospital.

Circumstantial evidence indicated that the parties had completed an act of intercourse, that Sewell had then gone to the bathroom down the hall, and that the struggle occurred upon his return. The contents of his pockets were in disarray on the dresser and no money was found; the jury may have inferred that respondent took Sewell's money and that the fight started when Sewell re-entered the room and saw what she was doing. On the following morning respondent surrendered to the police. She was given a physical examination which revealed no cuts or bruises of any kind, except needle marks on her upper arm. An autopsy of Sewell disclosed that he had several deep stab wounds in his chest and abdomen, and a number of slashes on his arms and hands, characterized by the pathologist as "defensive wounds."

Respondent offered no evidence. Her sole defense was the argument made by her attorney that Sewell had initially attacked her with the knife, and that her actions had all been directed toward saving her own life. The support for this self-defense theory was based on the fact that she had screamed for help. Sewell was on top of her when help arrived, and his possession of two knives indicated that he was a violence-prone person. It took the jury about 25 minutes to elect a foreman and return a verdict.

Three months later defense counsel filed a motion for a new trial asserting that he had discovered (1) that Sewell had a prior criminal record that would have further evidenced his violent character; (2) that the prosecutor had failed to disclose this information to the defense; and (3) that a recent opinion of the United States Court of Appeals for the District of Columbia Circuit made it clear that such evidence was admissible even if not known to the defendant. . . . The District Court denied the motion. . . . The Court of Appeals reversed. The court found no lack of diligence on the part of the defense and no misconduct by the prosecutor in this case. It held, however, that the evidence was material, and that its nondisclosure required a new trial because the jury might have returned a different verdict if the evidence had been received.

The decision of the Court of Appeals represents a significant departure from this Court's prior holding; because we believe that that court has incorrectly interpreted the constitutional requirement of due process, we reverse.

II

The rule of *Brady v. Maryland*, 373 U.S. 83, arguably applies in three quite different situations. Each involves the discovery, after trial of information which had been known to the prosecution but unknown to the defense.

In the first situation, typified by *Mooney v. Holohan*, 294 U.S. 103, the undisclosed evidence demonstrates that the prosecution's case includes perjured testimony and that the prosecution knew, or should have known, of the perjury. . . .

The second situation, illustrated by the Brady case itself, is characterized by a pretrial request for specific evidence. In that case defense counsel had requested the extrajudicial statements made by Brady's accomplice, one Boblit. This Court held that the suppression of one of Boblit's statements deprived Brady of due process, noting specifically that the statement had been requested and that it was "material." A fair analysis of the holding in Brady indicates that implicit in the requirement of materiality is a concern that the suppressed evidence might have affected the outcome of the trial. . . . The test of materiality in a case like Brady in which specific information has been requested by the defense is not necessarily the same as in a case in which no such request has been made. Indeed, this Court has not yet decided whether the prosecutor has any obligation to provide defense counsel with exculpatory information when no request has been made. Before addressing that question, a brief comment on the function of the request is appropriate. In Brady the request was specific. It gave the prosecutor notice of exactly what the defense desired. . . . In many cases, however, exculpatory information in the possession of the prosecutor may be unknown to defense counsel. In such a situation he may make no request at all, or possibly ask for "all Brady material" or for "anything exculpatory." Such a request really gives the prosecutor no better notice than if no request is made. If there is a duty to respond to a general request of that kind, it must derive from the obviously exculpatory character of certain evidence in the hands of the prosecutor. . . .

The third situation in which the Brady rule arguably applies, typified by this case, therefore embraces the case in which only a general request for "Brady material" has been made.

We now consider whether the prosecutor has any constitutional duty to volunteer exculpatory matter to the defense, and if so, what standard of materiality gives rise to that duty.

## III

We are not considering the scope of discovery authorized by the Federal Rules of Criminal Procedure, or the wisdom of amending those Rules to enlarge the defendant's discovery rights. We are dealing with the defendant's right to a fair trial mandated by the Due Process Clause of the Fifth Amendment to the Constitution. Our construction of that Clause will apply equally to the comparable Clause in the Fourteenth Amendment applicable to trials in state courts. . . .

The Court of Appeals appears to have assumed that the prosecutor has a constitutional obligation to disclose any information that might affect the jury's verdict. That statement of a constitutional standard of materiality approaches the "sporting theory of justice" which the Court expressly rejected in Brady. For a jury's appraisal of a case "might" be affected by an improper or trivial consideration as well as by evidence giving rise to a legitimate doubt on the issue of guilt. If everything that might influence a jury must be disclosed, the only way a prosecutor could discharge his constitutional duty would be to allow complete discovery of his files as a matter of routine practice.

Whether or not procedural rules authorizing such broad discovery might be desirable, the Constitution surely does not demand that much. While expressing the opinion that representatives of the State may not "suppress substantial material evidence," former Chief Justice Traynor of the California Supreme Court has pointed out that "they are under no duty to report sua sponte to the defendant all that they learn about the case and about their witnesses." *In re Imbler*, 60 Cal.2d 554, 569 (1963). And this Court recently noted that there is "no constitutional requirement that the prosecution make a complete and detailed accounting to the defense of all police investigatory work on a case." *Moore v. Illinois*, 408 U.S. 786, 795. The mere possibility that an item of undisclosed information might have helped the defense, or might have affected the outcome of the trial, does not establish "materiality" in the constitutional sense.

. . .since we have rejected the suggestion that the prosecutor has a constitutional duty routinely to deliver his entire file to defense counsel, we cannot consistently treat every nondisclosure as though it were error. It necessarily follows that the judge should not order a new trial every time he is unable to characterize a nondisclosure as harmless under the customary harmless-error standard. Under that standard when error is present in the record, the reviewing judge must set aside the verdict and judgment unless his "conviction is sure that the error did not influence the jury, or had but very slight effect." *Kotteakos v. United States*, 328 U.S. 750, 764. Unless every nondisclosure is regarded as automatic error, the constitutional standard of materiality must impose a higher burden on the defendant.

The proper standard of materiality must reflect our overriding concern with the justice of the finding of guilt. Such a finding is permissible only if supported by evidence establishing guilt beyond a reasonable doubt. It necessarily follows that if the omitted evidence creates a reasonable doubt that did not otherwise exist, constitutional error has been committed. This means that the omission must be evaluated in the context of the entire record. If there is no reasonable doubt about guilt whether or not the additional evince is considered, there is no justification for a new trial. On the other hand, if the verdict is already of questionable validity, additional evidence of relatively minor importance might be sufficient to create a reasonable doubt.

This statement of the standard of materiality describes the test which courts appear to have applied in actual cases although the standard has been phrased in different language. It is also the standard which the trial judge applied in this case. He evaluated the significance of Sewell's prior criminal record in the context of the full trial which he recalled in detail. Stressing in particular the incongruity of a claim that Sewell was the aggressor with the evidence of his multiple wounds and respondent's unscathed condition, the trial judge indicated his unqualified opinion that respondent was guilty. He noted that Sewell's prior record did not contradict any evidence offered by the prosecutor, and was largely cumulative of the evidence that Sewell was wearing a bowie knife in a sheath and carrying a second knife in his pocket when he registered at the motel.

Since the arrest record was not requested and did not even arguably give rise to any inference of perjury, since after considering it in the context of the entire record the trial judge remained convinced of respondent's guilt beyond a reasonable doubt, and since we are satisfied that his firsthand appraisal of the record was thorough and entirely reasonable, we hold that the prosecutor's failure to tender Sewell's record to the defense did not deprive respondent of a fair trial as guaranteed by the Due Process Clause of the Fifth Amendment. Accordingly, the judgment of the Court of Appeals is *Reversed.*

**MR. JUSTICE MARSHALL, with whom MR. JUSTICE BRENNAN joins, dissenting.**

The Court today holds that the prosecutor's constitutional duty to provide exculpatory evidence to the defense is not limited to cases in which the defense makes a request for such evidence. But once having recognized the existence of a duty to volunteer exculpatory evidence, the Court so narrowly defines the category of "material" evidence embraced by the duty as to deprive it of all meaningful content. . .

Under today's ruling, if the prosecution has not made knowing use of perjury, and if the defense has not made a specific request for an item of information, the defendant is entitled to a new trial only if the withheld evidence actually creates a reasonable doubt as to guilt in the judge's mind.

With all respect, this rule is completely at odds with the overriding interest in assuring that evidence tending to show innocence is brought to the jury's attention. The rule creates little, if any, incentive for the prosecutor conscientiously to determine whether his files contain evidence helpful to the defense. Indeed, the rule reinforces the natural tendency of the prosecutor to overlook evidence favorable to the defense, and creates an incentive for the prosecutor to resolve close questions of disclosure in favor of concealment.

More fundamentally, the Court's rule usurps the function of the jury as the trier of fact in a criminal case. The Court's rule explicitly establishes the judge as the trier of fact with respect to evidence withheld by the prosecution. The defendant's fate is sealed so long as the evidence does not create a reasonable doubt as to guilt in the judge's mind, regardless of whether the evidence is such that reasonable men could disagree as to its import regardless, in other words, of how "close" the case may be.

The Court asserts that this harsh standard of materiality is the standard that "courts appear to have applied in actual cases although the standard has been phrased in different language." Ante, at 2402 (footnote omitted). There is no basis for this assertion. None of the cases cited by the Court in support of its statement suggests that a judgment of conviction should be sustained so long as the judge remains convinced beyond a reasonable doubt of the defendant's guilt. The prevailing view in the federal courts of the standard of materiality for cases involving neither a specific request for information nor other indications of deliberate misconduct a standard with which the cases cited by the Court are fully consistent is quite different. It is essentially the following: If there is a significant chance that the withheld evidence, developed by skilled counsel, would have induced a reasonable doubt in the minds of enough jurors to avoid a conviction, then the judgment of conviction must be set aside. This standard, unlike the Court's, reflects a recognition that the determination must be in terms of the impact of an item of evidence on the jury, and that this determination cannot always be made with certainty. . .

This case, however, does not involve deliberate prosecutorial misconduct. Leaving open the question whether a different rule might appropriately be applied in cases involving deliberate misconduct, I would hold that the defendant in this case and the burden of demonstrating that there is a significant chance that the withheld evidence, developed by skilled counsel, would have induced a reasonable doubt in the minds of enough jurors to avoid a conviction. This is essentially the standard applied by the Court of Appeals, and I would affirm its judgment.

**After preparing the case brief, consider the answers to the following questions:**

1.    What are the three situations in which prosecutors have a duty to disclose evidence under *Brady*?

2.    Explain what the Court meant by a "sporting theory of justice" which was rejected in *Brady*.

3.    What rule must courts follow in making determinations of materiality of evidence after this case?

4.    Does the Court's holding allow for trial judges to usurp the jury's role as the trier of fact by deciding whether Brady evidence would raise a reasonable doubt?

## SMITH V. CAIN

Supreme Court of the United States
Argued Nov. 8, 2011
Decided Jan. 10, 2012
565 U.S. 73

### OPINION

### CHIEF JUSTICE ROBERTS delivered the opinion of the Court.

The State of Louisiana charged petitioner Juan Smith with killing five people during an armed robbery. At Smith's trial a single witness, Larry Boatner, linked Smith to the crime. Boatner testified that he was socializing at a friend's house when Smith and two other gunmen entered the home, demanded money and drugs, and shortly thereafter began shooting, resulting in the death of five of Boatner's friends. In court Boatner identified Smith as the first gunman to come through the door. He claimed that he had been face to face with Smith during the initial moments of the robbery. No other witnesses and no physical evidence implicated Smith in the crime.

The jury convicted Smith of five counts of first-degree murder. The Louisiana Court of Appeal affirmed Smith's conviction. The Louisiana Supreme Court denied review, as did this Court.

Smith then sought postconviction relief in the state courts. As part of his effort, Smith obtained files from the police investigation of his case, including those of the lead investigator, Detective John Ronquillo. Ronquillo's notes contain statements by Boatner that conflict with his testimony identifying Smith as a perpetrator. The notes from the night of the murder state that Boatner "could not . . . supply a description of the perpetrators other then [*sic*] they were black males." App. 252–253. Ronquillo also made a handwritten account of a conversation he had with Boatner five days after the crime, in which Boatner said he "could not ID anyone because [he] couldn't see faces" and "would not know them if [he] saw them." *Id.*, at 308. And Ronquillo's typewritten report of that conversation states that Boatner told Ronquillo he "could not identify any of the perpetrators of the murder." *Id.*, at 259–260.

Smith requested that his conviction be vacated, arguing, *inter alia,* that the prosecution's failure to disclose Ronquillo's notes violated this Court's decision in *Brady v. Maryland,* 373 U.S. 83 (1963). The state trial court rejected Smith's *Brady* claim, and the Louisiana Court of Appeal and Louisiana Supreme Court denied review. We granted certiorari, and now reverse.

Under *Brady,* the State violates a defendant's right to due process if it withholds evidence that is favorable to the defense and material to the defendant's guilt or punishment. The State does not dispute that Boatner's statements in Ronquillo's notes were favorable to Smith and that those statements were not disclosed to him. The sole question before us is thus whether Boatner's statements were material to the determination of Smith's guilt. We have explained that "evidence is 'material' within the meaning of *Brady* when there is a reasonable probability that, had the evidence been disclosed, the result of the proceeding would have been different." *Cone v. Bell,* 556 U.S. 449, 469–470 (2009). A reasonable probability does not mean that the defendant "would more likely than not have received a different verdict with the evidence," only that the likelihood of a different result is great enough to "undermine[ ] confidence in the outcome of the trial." *Kyles v. Whitley,* 514 U.S. 419, 434 (1995) (internal quotation marks omitted).

We have observed that evidence impeaching an eyewitness may not be material if the State's other evidence is strong enough to sustain confidence in the verdict. See *United States v. Agurs,* 427 U.S. 97, 112–113, and n. 21 (1976).

That is not the case here. Boatner's testimony was the *only* evidence linking Smith to the crime. And Boatner's undisclosed statements directly contradict his testimony: Boatner told the jury that he had "[n]o doubt" that Smith was the gunman he stood "face to face" with on the night of the crime, but Ronquillo's notes show Boatner saying that he "could not ID anyone because [he] couldn't see faces" and "would not know them if [he] saw them." App. 196, 200, 308. Boatner's undisclosed statements were plainly material.

The State and the dissent advance various reasons why the jury might have discounted Boatner's undisclosed statements. They stress, for example, that Boatner made other remarks on the night of the murder indicating that he could identify the first gunman to enter the house, but not the others. That merely leaves us to speculate about which of Boatner's contradictory declarations the jury would have believed. The State also contends that Boatner's statements made five days after the crime can be explained by fear of retaliation. Smith responds that the record contains no evidence of any such fear. Again, the State's argument offers a reason that the jury *could* have disbelieved Boatner's undisclosed statements, but gives us no confidence that it *would* have done so.

The police files that Smith obtained in state postconviction proceedings contain other evidence that Smith contends is both favorable to him and material to the verdict. Because we hold that Boatner's undisclosed statements alone suffice to undermine confidence in Smith's conviction, we have no need to consider his arguments that the other undisclosed evidence also requires reversal under *Brady*.

The judgment of the Orleans Parish Criminal District Court of Louisiana is reversed, and the case is remanded for further proceedings not inconsistent with this opinion.

*It is so ordered.*

**JUSTICE THOMAS, dissenting.**

The Court holds that Juan Smith is entitled to a new murder trial because the State, in violation of *Brady v. Maryland,* 373 U.S. 83 (1963), did not disclose that the eyewitness who identified Smith at trial stated shortly after the murders that he could not identify any of the perpetrators. I respectfully dissent. In my view, Smith has not shown a "reasonable probability" that the jury would have been persuaded by the undisclosed evidence. *United States v. Bagley,* 473 U.S. 667, 682 (1985) (opinion of Blackmun, J.). That materiality determination must be made "in the context of the entire record," *United States v. Agurs,* 427 U.S. 97, 112 (1976), and "turns on the cumulative effect of all such evidence suppressed by the government," *Kyles v. Whitley,* 514 U.S. 419, 421 (1995). Applying these principles, I would affirm the judgment of the Louisiana trial court. . .

Like the postconviction court below, I conclude that Smith is not entitled to a new trial under *Brady.* In my view, Smith has not established a reasonable probability that the cumulative effect of this evidence would have caused the jury to change its verdict.

II

A

Smith first identifies two undisclosed statements by Boatner, which the Court concludes are "plainly material." *Ante,* at 630. First, a note by Ronquillo, documenting a conversation he had with Boatner at the scene, states that Boatner "could not . . . supply a description of the perpetrators other than that they were black males." 5 Record 809. Second, a handwritten note by Ronquillo, documenting a phone conversation he had with Boatner on March 6, five days after the murders, states that "Boatner . . . could not ID anyone because couldn't see faces . . . glanced at 1st one—saw man—through door— can't tell if had—faces covered didn't see anyone . . . Could not ID—would not know them if—I saw them." 13 *id.,* at 2515. Ronquillo's typed summary of this note states that Boatner advised him that he "could not identify any perpetrators of the murder." 5 *id.,* at 817.

Smith is correct that these undisclosed statements could have been used to impeach Boatner and Ronquillo during cross-examination. But the statements are not material for purposes of *Brady* because they cannot "reasonably be taken to put the whole case in such a different light as to undermine confidence in the verdict." *Kyles,* 514 U.S., at 435, 115 S.Ct. 1555. When weighed against the substantial evidence that Boatner had opportunities to view the first perpetrator, offered consistent descriptions of him on multiple occasions, and even identified him as Smith, the undisclosed statements do not warrant a new trial. The evidence showed that, notwithstanding Ronquillo's on-scene note, Boatner offered a description of the perpetrator at the scene. Officer Narcisse testified that Boatner provided him with a description of the perpetrator that Boatner saw. Narcisse's testimony thus corroborated Boatner's trial testimony that he saw the first man and described him to police. Narcisse's testimony also mitigated the impeachment value of Ronquillo's on-scene note by indicating that, although Boatner may have provided no detailed description to Ronquillo at the scene, Boatner had described the first man to another officer.

. . . Moreover, the description Boatner provided was consistent with Smith's appearance. The Court completely ignores Boatner's station house statement, but our cases instruct us to evaluate "the net effect of the evidence withheld by the State" in assessing materiality. See *Kyles, supra,* at 421–422, 115 S.Ct. 1555.

The evidence not only shows that Boatner described the first perpetrator twice in the immediate aftermath of the crime, but also that Boatner described him again three weeks later when he viewed a photograph array and eliminated a similar-looking individual. The evidence before the jury further indicated that, several months after the crime, Boatner confidently identified Smith in an array, after evincing a discriminating, careful eye over a 4-month investigative period. What is more, the reliability of Boatner's out-of-court identification was extensively tested during cross-examination at Smith's trial. In particular, Boatner was asked whether the fact that he saw Smith's picture in a newspaper article naming Smith as a suspect had tainted his identification. Boatner did not waiver, responding, "I picked out the person I seen come in that house that held a gun to my head and under my chin and the person that was there when all my friends died." Tr. 190 (Dec. 5, 1995). That Boatner credibly rejected defense counsel's "suggestion" theory is supported by the fact that Boatner did *not* identify cosuspect Robert Trackling—whose photograph was included in a separate array shown to Boatner on the same day that Boatner identified Smith—even though Trackling's picture was next to Smith's in the same newspaper article. 5 Record 833, 835. . .

Of course, had the jury been presented with Ronquillo's notes of Boatner's on-scene and March 6 statements, it might have believed that Boatner could not identify any of the perpetrators, but a *possibility* of a different verdict is insufficient to establish a *Brady* violation. . . .

Instead of requiring Smith to show a reasonable probability that Boatner's undisclosed statements would have caused the jury to acquit, the Court improperly requires the *State* to show that the jury would have given Boatner's undisclosed statements no weight. . . .

The question presented here is not whether a prudent prosecutor should have disclosed the information that Smith identifies. Rather, the question is whether the cumulative effect of the disclosed and undisclosed evidence in Smith's case "put[s] the whole case in such a different light as to undermine confidence in the verdict." *Kyles,* 514 U.S., at 435, 115 S.Ct. 1555. . . .

Because what remains is evidence of such minimal impeachment and exculpatory value as to be immaterial in light of the whole record, I must dissent from the Court's holding that the State violated *Brady.*

### After preparing the case brief, consider the answers to the following questions:

1. Identify the rule employed by the Court in this case for determining whether a Brady violation has taken place.

2. What does the Court say is required to demonstrate a "reasonable probability" of a different result in the trial?

3. How would the Court's analysis have changed if there had been other eyewitnesses to testify to the defendant's presence at the scene of the crime?

4. The majority sees this evidence as the only evidence connecting the defendant to the crime, thus making it material; the dissenters argue that the evidence in this case would have minimal exculpatory value in light of the whole record. Which position is more convincing?

## Chapter 4 Key Terms for Review

- **Prosecutor**: attorney who represents the people of the community in a criminal case against a defendant accused of committing a crime.

- **United States Attorney**: the appointed federal prosecutor who oversees a specific federal district; assistant United States Attorneys work as prosecutors in federal court within the various federal districts.

- **Crime Victims' Rights Act**: 2004 legislation that provides support for crime victims during trials as well as post-trial rights including notice prior to release of offenders.

- **Prosecutorial discretion**: the power to make independent decisions regarding criminal prosecutions, including the power to decide whether to charge a defendant, and if so, what charges to file.

- **Information**: the charging document filed by a prosecutor against a defendant in a criminal case.

- **Arrest warrant**: a charging document filed by a judicial officer upon a finding of probable cause that the suspect has committed a crime.

- **Indictment**: a charging document presented by a grand jury after a finding of probable cause.

- **Complaint**: a charging document filed by an individual (either the victim or a police officer) upon a sworn statement alleging probable cause that the accused has committed a crime.

- **Plea bargain**: a negotiated guilty plea where the defendant agrees to waive significant rights (including the right to a trial) and plead guilty in exchange for agreed-upon benefits.

- **Boykin form**: a signed form acknowledging that a defendant entering a plea agreement understands and voluntarily waives his rights.

- **Charge bargain**: a guilty plea accepted in exchange for a lesser charge.

- **Count bargain**: a guilty plea accepted in exchange for fewer criminal counts.

- **Sentence bargain**: a guilty plea accepted in exchange for a lighter sentence.

- **Allocution hearing**: a hearing where the court requires a defendant to admit the factual basis for his guilty plea.

- **Alford plea**: when a defendant pleads guilty as part of a plea bargain but maintains his innocence. *North Carolina v. Alford (1970).*

- **Discovery**: sharing information between the prosecution and defense prior to trial.

- **Duty to disclose evidence**: the responsibility to provide certain evidence to the opposing party; in criminal cases often refers to the prosecutor's duty to disclose exculpatory evidence to the defense under *Brady v. Maryland (1963).*

- **Exculpatory evidence**: evidence that tends to prove the defendant's innocence.

- **Material evidence**: in the context of *Brady v. Maryland*, evidence is material and must be disclosed to the defense when there is a reasonable probability that the outcome would have been different if the evidence had been produced.

- **Prior inconsistent statement**: prior statements by witnesses which differ from the witnesses later statements or testimony in court must be disclosed to the defense and can be used to impeach or discredit a witness.

- **Impeachment of a witness**: process of showing that the witness is not trustworthy because of their inconsistent statements or testimony about the facts of the case.

- **ABA Model Rules of Professional Conduct**: professional guidelines which attorneys are bound to follow in the practice of law.

- **Prosecutorial misconduct**: unethical conduct on the part of prosecutors which can happen intentionally or inadvertently.

- **Absolute immunity**: provides complete protection against civil liability in the event of wrongdoing or misconduct.

- **Qualified immunity**: provides protection against civil liability for misconduct under specific circumstances.

# The Right to Counsel and Defense Attorneys

Every day, in every court system across the country, someone is accused of committing a crime. Sometimes, it's a minor violation of the law. Other times, it's a heinous, violent act. But no matter the crime, someone will stand next to the accused as the charges are read. **Defense counsel** is an attorney either retained privately by the defendant or appointed to represent them by the court. That attorney will be there each time the defendant appears in court until the end of the criminal prosecution—and even beyond that if there is an appeal. This chapter examines the evolution of the right to counsel, how it has been shaped since the Supreme Court's decision in *Gideon v. Wainwright (1963)*,[1] and other Sixth Amendment guarantees, such as the right to effective assistance of counsel and the right of self-representation.

## A. THE RIGHT TO COUNSEL

The Sixth Amendment of the Constitution provides that "In all criminal prosecutions, the accused shall enjoy the right . . . to have the Assistance of Counsel for his defence."[2] For many years, this was interpreted as permitting a defendant to bring a lawyer to assist him in a criminal proceeding, if he could afford to do so. Those too poor to pay a lawyer had to represent themselves.

That began to change in the 1930s with the Supreme Court's decision on *Powell v. Alabama (1932)*. Nine African-American youths were arrested and charged with a capital crime—the rape of two white women.[3] The "Scottsboro Boys", as they were known in the press, were not told that they had a right to counsel. As required under Alabama law, they were assigned lawyers, but not until the day of

---

[1] 372 U.S. 335.

[2] U.S. Const. amend. VI.

[3] *Powell v. Alabama*, 287 U.S. 45 (1932).

trial. The trials each lasted one day and all were convicted. They appealed to the Supreme Court, arguing that they were denied due process of law because they were not given reasonable time and opportunity to secure counsel for their defense. The Supreme Court held 7–2 that the defendants were deprived of due process under the Fourteenth Amendment, citing the defendants' age, ignorance, and the hostile environment in which the trials were held. The court stated that:

> *Even the intelligent and educated layman has small and sometimes no skill in the science of law. If charged with crime, he is incapable, generally, of determining for himself whether the indictment is good or bad. He is unfamiliar with the rules of evidence. Left without the aid of counsel he may be put on trial without a proper charge, and convicted upon incompetent evidence, or evidence irrelevant to the issue or otherwise inadmissible. He lacks both the skill and knowledge adequately to prepare his defense, even though he have a perfect one. He requires the guiding hand of counsel at every step in the proceedings against him. Without it, though he be not guilty, he faces the danger of conviction because he does not know how to establish his innocence. If that be true of men of intelligence, how much more true is it of the ignorant and illiterate, or those of feeble intellect.*[4]

The case established a **right to appointed counsel** for indigent defendants in state death penalty cases, or in cases where the denial of counsel would offend all notions of due process. But it did not go further than that.

A few years later, the Supreme Court expanded the right to counsel to indigent criminal defendants in federal court, holding that a person who cannot afford to defend himself against the government is at a significant disadvantage.[5] In *Johnson v. Zerbst (1938)*, the Court again recognized the disparity between criminal defendants and prosecutors that was so starkly represented in *Powell*. This time, the court relied on the Sixth Amendment to establish a right to counsel for federal criminal defendants. As the Sixth Amendment had not yet been incorporated under the Fourteenth Amendment to apply to the states, this holding only applied to federal courts.

That changed in 1963, when the Supreme Court decided the landmark case of ***Gideon v. Wainwright***.[6] Clarence Earl Gideon was arrested for breaking into a pool hall in Florida. He asked the court to appoint counsel to represent him, and the court refused because Gideon was not charged with a capital offense. Gideon went to trial, where he represented himself, and was found guilty and sentenced

---

4    *Powell*, 287 U.S. at 69.

5    *Johnson v. Zerbst*, 304 U.S. 458 (1938).

6    *Gideon v. Wainwright*, 372 U.S. 335 (1963).

to five years in state prison. While in prison, Gideon appealed his conviction on the grounds that the trial court's refusal to appoint counsel to represent him violated his Sixth Amendment rights. The appeal eventually reached the U.S. Supreme Court, which agreed to hear the case.[7]

This time, Gideon did not go into battle alone. The Court assigned attorney Abe Fortas to represent Gideon. A prominent litigator, Fortas would later be appointed to the Supreme Court by President Lyndon Johnson. Gideon also had the support of 23 state attorneys general, who joined in an amici brief on Gideon's behalf and urged the Court to protect defendants' rights. At this time, 35 states already required courts to appoint counsel in all felony cases.[8] But other states were leery of a federal constitutional requirement that might impinge on states' rights.

The issue before the Court was whether the Sixth Amendment right to counsel for indigent defendants applied to the states, as it did to the federal courts. Only 20 years prior, the Court had declined to extend the Sixth Amendment right to counsel to states, in a case that was quite similar to the facts in Gideon's case.[9] In *Betts v. Brady (1942)*, the defendant argued that he had a Sixth Amendment right to have appointed counsel and asked the Supreme Court to extend *Zerbst* to the states. The Court declined to do so, finding that Mr. Betts was a man of ordinary intelligence who could defend himself against the charges, and that the Sixth Amendment right to counsel did not apply to the states.

But with *Gideon*, the Court came to the opposite conclusion. In a unanimous decision, the Supreme Court held that indigent defendants charged with a felony in state court must be provided counsel at the government's expense.

*[I]n our adversary system of criminal justice, any person haled into court, who is too poor to hire a lawyer, cannot be assured a fair trial unless counsel is provided for him. This seems to us to be an obvious truth. Governments, both state and federal, quite properly spend vast sums of money to establish machinery to try defendants accused of crime. Lawyers to prosecute are everywhere deemed essential to protect the public's interest in an orderly society. Similarly, there are few defendants charged with crime. . .who fail to hire the best lawyers they can get to prepare and present their defenses. That government hires lawyers to prosecute and defendants who have the*

---

[7]   A copy of Clarence Gideon's handwritten petition for writ of certiorari is available online at the National Archives at https://research.archives.gov/id/597554.

[8]   Green, B., *Gideon's* Amici, 122 Yale L.J. 2336, 2341 (2013).

[9]   *Betts v. Brady*, 316 U.S. 455 (1942).

*money hire lawyers to defend are the strongest indications of the wide-spread believe that lawyers in criminal courts are necessities, not luxuries.*[10]

The Sixth Amendment right to counsel was a **fundamental right**, essential to a fair trial, the Supreme Court held, and was therefore incorporated into the Fourteenth Amendment's due process clause and applied to the states. The decision changed the criminal justice system in the United States in a fundamental way. It laid the groundwork for further protections—including the right to conflict-free and competent counsel, the right to hire counsel of one's choosing, protection of the attorney-client relationship, and the right to assistance of counsel in an appeal. Most immediately, though, it required states to create systems to provide lawyers to indigent defendants, and a way to pay for that.

## B. SHAPING THE RIGHT TO COUNSEL

*Gideon* created an obligation for states to provide counsel for indigent defendants in felony cases, but it left many questions unanswered, such as when the right to counsel arises and who can assert that right. Over the next two decades, the Supreme Court would continue to shape the edges of the right to counsel.

A misdemeanor charge can also carry a term of incarceration of up to one year in jail. Did that potential loss of liberty trigger the right to counsel guarantee of the Sixth Amendment? The Court would take that case up first in *Argersinger v. Hamlin* in 1972.

The defendant in *Argersinger* was charged with a misdemeanor and asked the trial court to appoint a lawyer to represent him. The court refused, stating that the law only required appointed counsel in felony cases. The defendant was convicted, sentenced to a term of 90 days in jail, and appealed. The rule created by the Supreme Court said that no defendant could be sentenced to a term of imprisonment unless he had been represented by counsel at trial. This was a difficult rule to implement—the judge, who would have no facts about the case at this early stage of the case, would have to make a determination at that stage as to whether the defendant would face potential prison time. If no counsel were assigned, that foreclosed the possibility of a jail sentence if the defendant were ultimately convicted.

Later, in *Scott v. Illinois (1979)*, the Supreme Court clarified that the penalty of incarceration was the bright-line test as to whether the defendant was entitled to

---

[10]  *Gideon*, 372 U.S. at 344.

court-appointed counsel.[11] This rule was affirmed again in *Alabama v. Shelton (2002)*, which held that a defendant who violated a term of probation could not be sentenced to jail if he was not represented by an attorney at the original trial.[12]

## C. CRITICAL STAGES

The right to have appointed counsel is triggered at the initiation of the adversarial proceeding, typically at an initial appearance or at an arraignment. This includes any method of initiating the adversarial proceedings—whether by formal charge, preliminary hearing, indictment, information, or arraignment.[13] After that, the accused has the right to counsel at all "critical stages" in the criminal proceedings.

A **critical stage** is any point in the proceedings where a defendant's rights may be affected.[14] These include post-indictment lineups, court appearances, plea bargaining, trial, sentencing, and at post-conviction probation or parole violation hearings, if there is a risk that the defendant could be incarcerated.[15] As defendants have a right to appeal a conviction, they also have a right to appointed counsel on a first appeal.[16] Because there is no right to subsequent appeals or habeas corpus petitions, there is also no right to assistance of counsel for those proceedings.

## D. EFFECTIVE ASSISTANCE OF COUNSEL

Merely assigning an attorney to represent a defendant is not enough. "The Sixth Amendment recognizes the right to the assistance of counsel because it envisions counsel's playing a role that is critical to the ability of the adversarial system to produce just results."[17] The Supreme Court has recognized that "a fair trial is one in which evidence subject to adversarial testing is presented to an impartial tribunal" which requires "counsel's skill and knowledge" to ensure that the defendant can thoroughly test the evidence against him. The Supreme Court set forth the standard for determining whether defense counsel was effective in

---

[11]   *Scott v. Illinois*, 440 U.S. 367 (1979).

[12]   *Alabama v. Shelton*, 535 U.S. 654 (2002).

[13]   *Rothgery v. Gillespie County, Tex.*, 554 U.S. 191 (2009).

[14]   *Mempa v. Rhay*, 389 U.S. 128 (1967).

[15]   *Gilbert v. California*, 388 U.S. 263 (1967) (post-indictment lineups); *Rothgery*, 554 U.S. 191 (2009) (first appearance); *Missouri v. Frye*, 566 U.S. 133 (2012) (plea bargaining); *Gideon v. Wainwright*, 372 U.S. 335 (1963) (trial); *McConnell v. Rhay*, 393 U.S. 2 (1968) (sentencing); *Mempa v. Rhay*, 389 U.S. 128 (1967) (post-conviction proceedings).

[16]   *Douglas v. California*, 372 U.S. 353 (1963).

[17]   *Strickland v. Washington*, 466 U.S. 668 (1984).

1984, in the case of *Strickland v. Washington*. The two-pronged test for **ineffective assistance of counsel** asks:

1.  Was defense counsel's performance deficient?

2.  Did the attorney's deficient performance prejudice the defendant?

To merit a reversal for ineffective assistance of counsel, the defendant must meet both requirements. The first part examines the trial attorney's conduct and requires evidence that the defense lawyer "made errors so serious that counsel was not functioning as 'counsel' guaranteed the defendant by the Sixth Amendment." Defense attorneys have many duties in representing a criminal defendant, including a duty of loyalty, a duty to avoid conflicts of interest, to advocate for the defendant, and to consult with the defendant and keep him informed of developments in the case. The overarching obligation on counsel is to "bring to bear such skill and knowledge as will render the trial a reliable adversarial testing process."

But the Court declined to make a checklist for what defense counsel must do. Rather, the test looks at whether what the defense attorney did was reasonable considering all the circumstances. This is a highly deferential test, and if there is any tactical or strategic reason for counsel's actions, the test presumes that the attorney exercises his or her professional judgment.

The second prong of the *Strickland* test looks at whether the attorney's error was prejudicial to the defendant. Even if counsel made an error that is professionally unreasonable, it may not warrant setting aside a guilty verdict if the error did not affect the outcome. In the face of overwhelming evidence of guilt, a court may find that the attorney's error was not the sole source of the conviction. Therefore, the second part of the test requires the defendant to show that there is a "reasonable probability that, but for counsel's unprofessional errors, the result of the proceeding would have been different. . ." and this probability is "sufficient to undermine confidence in the outcome."

The two parts of the *Strickland* test create a high bar for ineffective assistance of counsel claims and as a result, few appeals are overturned on these grounds. If there is an indication that the defense attorney's poor investigation, lackluster cross-examination, or other sub-par performance was done for a reason, the appellate court will chalk that up to strategy. And even if there is not a justification for defense counsel's conduct, if there is other evidence of the defendant's guilt, it is difficult to show that the attorney's failures prejudiced the defendant.

The right to effective assistance of counsel extends beyond trial to all stages of representation. Most recently, the Supreme Court has heard cases involving plea bargains and legal advice regarding immigration consequences. In *Padilla v. Kentucky (2010)*, the defendant had been a lawful permanent resident of the United States for more than 40 years when he was arrested on a drug-distribution charge.[18] His attorney advised him to not worry about the immigration consequences of a guilty plea, as he had been in the country for a long time. Relying on his lawyer's advice, Padilla pleaded guilty. This triggered mandatory deportation proceedings against him.

On appeal, the Supreme Court agreed with Padilla that a defense attorney must inform a non-citizen client whether a plea or conviction carries a risk of immigration consequences. Deportation is a civil proceeding, not a criminal sanction, but it is closely connected to criminal law as certain convictions make removal nearly an automatic result for many noncitizen offenders.

In 2012, the Supreme Court decided a pair of cases that addressed the right to effective assistance of counsel in plea negotiations. The vast majority of criminal cases are resolved by guilty pleas and the decisions in *Missouri v. Frye (2012)* and *Lafler v. Cooper (2012)* underscore the importance in defense counsel's advocacy and advice in that part of the process. In *Frye*, the defendant was charged with driving on a revoked license—for the fourth time.[19] Because of his record, he was charged with a felony that carried up to a four-year prison term. The prosecutor sent a letter to Frye's attorney, offering a plea bargain that would reduce the charge to a misdemeanor with a 90-day jail sentence. Frye was not informed of the offer and later pleaded guilty with no plea agreement. He was sentenced to three years in prison. On appeal, he argued that his attorney's failure to inform him of the early plea offer denied him effective assistance of counsel.

The Supreme Court held that defense counsel has a duty to communicate formal plea offers from the prosecutor, and Frye's attorney's failure to do so fell short of the standard for effective assistance of counsel. The companion case decided on the same day as *Frye* concerned an attorney's advice to reject a favorable plea agreement. Blaine Lafler was charged with several criminal counts, including with assault with intent to murder, for shooting and wounding a woman.[20] The prosecutor twice offered to dismiss two of the charges and recommend a sentence of 51 to 85 months in exchange for a guilty plea. Lafler indicated to the court that he wanted to accept the offer. But he later rejected it

---

[18]   *Padilla v. Kentucky*, 559 U.S. 356 (2010).

[19]   *Missouri v. Frye*, 566 U.S. 133 (2012).

[20]   *Lafler v. Cooper*, 566 U.S. 156 (2012).

on the advice of his attorney, who convinced him that the prosecutor could not prove intent to murder.

At trial, Lafler was convicted on all counts and was sentenced to 185 to 360 months. On appeal, all of the parties agreed that the defense lawyer's advice was deficient. The issue before the Supreme Court was whether the attorney's advice prejudiced the defendant. On this point, Lafler showed that he would have taken the plea deal if not for his attorney's advice—and the lost opportunity resulted in a sentence that was more than three times greater than he would have received under the plea offer.

In all three cases—*Padilla, Frye,* and *Lafler*—the Supreme Court stressed that the Sixth Amendment is not solely concerned with a defendant's right to a fair trial. Rather, it seeks to protect a properly functioning adversarial system, which includes effective assistance of counsel in all parts of the criminal proceedings.

## E. THE RIGHT OF SELF-REPRESENTATION

A defendant can also waive her right to counsel and represent herself and proceed **pro se**—on his or her own behalf. With some limitations, a trial court must permit a defendant to act as his or her own attorney. In *Faretta v. California (1975)*, the defendant was granted the right to represent himself at trial.[21] Following a hearing where he quizzed Faretta about criminal procedure and jury selection, the judge overturned his decision and reappointed the public defender to represent Faretta. He was found guilty at trial. On appeal, the Supreme Court held that the Sixth Amendment right to counsel grants the **right of self-representation**, also.

> *The Sixth Amendment does not provide merely that a defense shall be made for the accused; it grants to the accused personally the right to make his defense. It is the accused, not counsel, who must be 'informed of the nature and cause of the accusation,' who must be 'confronted with the witnesses against him,' and who must be accorded 'compulsory process for obtaining witnesses in his favor.' Although not stated in the Amendment in so many words the right to self-representation—to make one's own defense personally—is thus necessarily implied by the structure of the Amendment. The right to defend is given directly to the accused; for it is he who suffers the consequences if the defense fails.*

To waive the right to counsel, the defendant must "knowingly and intelligently" decline the benefits of having an attorney's assistance. This means he must be advised of the dangers and disadvantages of self-representation. The

---

[21]  *Faretta v. California*, 422 U.S. 806 (1975).

court will often appoint **standby** or **advisory counsel,** who are available to assist the defendant with legal research and advice, but the pro se defendant is in charge of the case. While the Court has ruled that any defendant who is competent to stand trial may waive the right to counsel, more recently the justices have wrestled with whether there should be a higher bar than mere competency to permit a defendant to represent himself. Two cases taken up by the Supreme Court show the tension between those ideas.[22]

The first case came to the court in 1993. Richard Allan Moran shot and killed two people in the robbery of a Las Vegas bar. Nine days later, he shot his former wife and attempted to kill himself. He was charged with three counts of murder. Two court-ordered psychiatric evaluations found him competent to stand trial, as he had the ability to aid his counsel and understood the charges against him. Moran then sought to fire his appointed counsel and change his plea to guilty. The judge advised Moran of the risk of self-representation, and then found that the defendant was aware that he was waiving his right to counsel and accepted the guilty plea. Moran was later sentenced to death.

Moran appealed from death row, arguing that he had been "mentally incompetent to represent himself." The Ninth Circuit Court of Appeals agreed, reversing the conviction, and holding that the Due Process Clause required the trial court to hold an evidentiary hearing to determine Moran's competency before accepting his guilty plea. The appellate court found that competency to waive a constitutional right "requires a higher level of mental functioning than that required to stand trial." The Supreme Court disagreed, rejecting the idea that there is a higher standard of competency for the decision to waive counsel. To determine whether a defendant can stand trial, the court must examine whether he has "sufficient present ability to consult with his lawyer with a reasonable degree of rational understanding" and has "a rational as well as factual understanding of the proceedings against him."

When a defendant pleads guilty, as Moran did, he waives certain constitutional rights—the right to a jury trial, the right to testify in his own defense (or to not take the stand), and the right to confront witnesses against him, among others. The Supreme Court reasoned that "there is no reason to believe that the decision to waive counsel requires an appreciably higher level of mental functioning than the decision to waive other constitutional rights."

In 2008, the Supreme Court heard a similar case. Ahmad Edwards was charged with attempted murder and other crimes for a shooting during his attempt

---

[22] *Godinez v. Moran,* 509 U.S. 389 (1993); *Indiana v. Edwards,* 554 U.S. 164 (2008).

to steal a pair of shoes. He underwent three competency proceedings, and twice sought to represent himself at trial. The judge denied Edwards' request to fire his lawyers, even though he had been found competent to stand trial. Edwards was convicted. He appealed, arguing that his Sixth Amendment right of self-representation was violated. Both Edward and Moran were "borderline competent criminal defendants" who sought to represent themselves, but the two cases differed because Edward wanted to represent himself at trial, where Moran wanted to plead guilty. This time, the Supreme Court held that courts can insist on representation for defendants who are competent to stand trial, but who suffer from severe mental illness such that they would not be able to conduct trial proceedings by themselves.

## F.  DEFENDER SYSTEMS

The decision in *Gideon* caused a major shift in criminal justice as all states were now required to provide attorneys to poor defendants. States were free to come up with their own way to meet the constitutional requirement, and three types of public defense systems were developed. **Public defenders** are salaried government employees. They oversee a staff of lawyers, paralegals, investigators, and others whose sole job is to represent defendants who cannot afford to retain lawyers. **Appointed counsel** are private attorneys who are assigned to represent defendants for an hourly rate, usually at a rate far lower than what a retained attorney would charge for legal services. The rate per case is usually capped, depending on the type of case. The courts keep a roster of attorneys, who have generally been screened for their experience, and then assigns the cases to lawyers depending on availability and expertise.

Some jurisdictions may also use a **contract system**, where law firms bid for the contract to provide indigent defense for a period of time. The county pays a set amount for the attorneys to handle all of the indigent defense cases. Jurisdictions may have a combination of these systems, as well. A public defender's office might not be able to take all defendants, due to workload issues or because of a legal conflict. For instance, an attorney can only represent one defendant in a case where multiple people are charged in the same indictment. Otherwise, there is a risk that defendants would have conflicting defenses. In cases with multiple defendants, that means only one person can be assigned an attorney from the public defender's office. The others are generally assigned to private attorneys on a "conflict" panel who are paid under contract or as appointed counsel.

**Conflict counsel** can also take over a case if the public defender's office has represented a victim or witness in a case. Attorneys have a duty of confidentiality to their clients, which continues after the case is over. As such, the lawyers in the public defender's office may have information about a witness or victim that they would not otherwise know except for the past relationship.

This is similar to the structure of the federal public defense system. The Federal Public Defenders' offices in each U.S. judicial district have a staff of attorneys, paralegals, investigators and clerical assistants to handle the majority of indigent defendants. And each district is supplemented with a panel of attorneys who are authorized under the Criminal Justice Act.[23] These private attorneys are paid a rate that is set by Congress to represent indigent criminal defendants. Having a panel of attorneys available when the need arises is more flexible than hiring more federal employees for the Federal Defenders' offices, and helps protect each defendant's right to conflict-free representation.

A minority of defendants hire their own attorneys with the vast majority seeking court-appointed counsel. Approximately 75% of state prison inmates were represented by appointed counsel. In larger cities—where 82% of defendants request appointed counsel.[24] There is virtually no difference in outcome between defendants who have private, retained counsel and those represented by public defenders, according to a 2014 study.[25] That study did find that defendants represented by assigned counsel, rather than a public defender, fared worse when it came to conviction and sentencing outcomes.

## G. THE ROLE OF DEFENSE COUNSEL

The defendant stands at the center of the criminal court proceedings. They are the reason why everyone else is there and are the focus of the evidence presented. Yet the defendant actually has a limited number of decisions for which he or she is responsible in the court proceedings. The defendant has the sole authority to make certain decisions, including whether to plead guilty or not guilty, whether to accept or reject a plea agreement, whether to waive a jury trial, whether to testify at trial, or conversely, whether to not take the stand. At sentencing, the defendant has the right to make a statement to the court, a process called allocution.

---

[23]  18 U.S.C. § 3006A.

[24]  Bureau of Justice Statistics, 2012. *Indigent Defense Systems.*

[25]  Cohen, T. H. (2014). Who is better at defending criminals? Does type of defense attorney matter in terms of producing favorable case outcomes. *Criminal Justice Policy Review*, 25(1), 29–58.

All other decisions about the defense strategy are left to the defendant's attorney. These include what motions to file, which witnesses to call and how to question them, whether to hire an expert witness, whether to give an opening statement or closing argument, and other tactical decisions. This can lead to conflict between counsel and client when there is a disagreement about how best to defend a case, such as what sort of defense to present or whether there are grounds to file a motion to suppress evidence.

When a defendant has retained his or her own counsel, an interpersonal conflict may lead the defendant to seek a new attorney. In the case of *United States v. Gonzalez-Lopez (2006)*, the defendant, charged in federal court in Missouri, was initially represented by an attorney hired by his family.[26] After the arraignment, he hired a new attorney from California. The trial court denied the new attorney's petition to represent Gonzalez-Lopez and refused to allow him to assist at trial. Gonzalez-Lopez was convicted and appealed on the grounds that the court denied his Sixth Amendment right to hire counsel of his choosing.

The Supreme Court agreed, holding that a defendant has the right to hire the attorney of his choosing. Further, Gonzalez-Lopez did not have to show that the attorney who represented him was ineffective at trial. "Deprivation of the right is 'complete' when the defendant is erroneously prevented from being represented by the lawyer he wants, regardless of the quality of the representation he received."

Denying the defendant his choice of counsel is a **structural error** because it bears on every aspect of the defense.

> *Different attorneys will pursue different strategies with regard to investigation and discovery, development of the theory of defense, selection of the jury, presentation of the witnesses, and style of witness examination and jury argument. And the choice of attorney will affect whether and on what terms the defendant cooperates with the prosecution, plea bargains, or decides instead to go to trial. In light of these myriad aspects of representation, the erroneous denial of counsel bears directly on the "framework within which the trial proceeds,". . . or indeed on whether it proceeds at all.*

While a defendant with the funds to hire a lawyer has the constitutional right to choose his counsel, when the defendant has an *appointed* attorney, courts treat the relationship quite differently.

A defendant who has court-appointed counsel does not have the right to choose the attorney assigned to his or her case. Standards vary for how appointed

---

[26]   *United States v. Gonzalez-Lopez*, 548 U.S. 140 (2006).

counsel are removed from a case, but that generally must be approved by the court. For example, in federal court, a defendant who seeks a new appointed lawyer must make a timely request, and then show that there is an extensive, irreconcilable conflict that resulted in a complete breakdown in communication that substantially interferes with the attorney-client relationship.[27] Absent that showing, the defendant and attorney must continue to work together.

## H. DEFENSE COUNSEL ETHICS

In most cases, a defendant first meets his or her attorney in court. Defendants have little reason to trust the stranger assigned to represent them. Defendants may be suspicious of court-appointed lawyers because they are employees of the same government that employs the police officers and prosecutors. This is a big hurdle for defense lawyers because a large part of their job is to counsel their clients. It is critical for defense attorneys to respect their clients, working to develop trust so that defendants enjoy the benefit of their advice during the criminal trial process.

One way the system fosters trust between attorneys and clients is by having a code of **legal ethics** to protect the relationship from interference. Legal ethics are rules governing the professional and sometimes personal behavior of licensed attorneys. Lawyers must avoid conflicts of interest, keep the client informed of developments in the case, and be a zealous advocate for the client's interests. They must also not assist their client in conduct that the attorney knows is criminal or fraudulent. Attorneys are required to keep client communications confidential and cannot typically be forced to disclose information provided by clients.

Most communication between the client and lawyer is covered by the **duty of confidentiality**, but there is a crime-fraud exception. This applies in cases where the client asks for assistance to carry out a continuing or future crime. In those situations, the attorney is not bound to keep the information confidential. A state may have permissive rules for revealing confidential information about a client's intention to commit future crimes. Or a state may even require disclosure if the lawyer "has confidential information clearly establishing that a client is likely to commit a criminal or fraudulent act that is likely to result in death or substantial bodily harm to a person."[28]

---

[27]   *United States v. Prime*, 431 F.3d 1147 (9th Cir. 2005).

[28]   See *Henderson v. State*, 962 S.W.2d 554, 554 (Tex. Crim. Appl. 1997) (citing Tex. Disc. R. Prof. Conduct 105(c)(7), and 105(e)).

The ethical duties of defense attorneys may conflict with each other. Take the following hypothetical situation as an example.

> *The client kidnaps a victim and places the victim, securely bound and gagged, in an old, abandoned warehouse. When the victim is discovered to be missing, the client is arrested for kidnapping. The client tells the attorney representing her on the kidnapping charge the location of the victim—a fact that only the client, and now her attorney, knows. That communication is not only an admission that the client did in fact kidnap the victim, but it also connects client to the crime by showing her knowledge of the victim's location. The communication is clearly relevant to the attorney's representation of the client for the kidnapping already committed and is therefore privileged so long as the client intended the information to be confidential. If the client does not seek the attorney's help in perpetuating the kidnapping but merely conveys the details of the continuing crime, then the crime-fraud exception is inapplicable, and in fact, no exception to the privilege applies. But, if the attorney fails to convey the information given by his client to the authorities, the victim will eventually die. . . . The attorney in this hypothetical is caught in an apparent conflict between the attorney-client privilege and the ethical rule requiring disclosure.*[29]

In the above conflict, "privilege must yield to some extent."[30]

All attorneys are also officers of the court and have a **duty of candor** to the tribunal. This rule means they cannot knowingly mislead the court, obstruct access to witnesses or evidence, or present false evidence or testimony. This presents another type of conflict that may arise when a client intends to commit perjury at trial. See *Nix v. Whiteside (1986)*.

The legal profession is both held up as an honorable profession, and is also widely distrusted, even reviled, for the perception that attorneys will act outside the bounds of propriety to win a case. In truth, it is a profession that takes ethics and integrity seriously—arguably more so than many other professions. Each state regulates the practice of law and enacts its own code of ethics. Most states have adopted the American Bar Association's **Model Rules of Professional Conduct**, at least in substance if not structure. Law students are typically required to take courses in professional responsibility to graduate. In order to be admitted to practice, applicants must also pass the Multi-State Professional Responsibility Exam, a national examination on legal ethics and the legal obligations of attorneys.

---

[29] This hypothetical was used to illustrate the ethical dilemma faced by attorneys in the case of *Henderson v. State*, 962 S.W.2d 554 (Tex. Crim. Appl. 1997).

[30] *Id.* at 555.

The idea of beginning legal training with an emphasis on ethics came about after the Watergate scandal that led to the resignation of President Richard Nixon. Of the dozens of individuals ensnared by the scandal, more than 20 were lawyers—including several high-ranking justice department attorneys. John Dean, former White House counsel for Nixon, summed up the idea as:

> *Lawyers can do a great deal of harm in the world, and it is important that law schools not unleash on the world lawyers who are armed with legal knowledge, but lack the judgment to keep their skills and conduct in perspective.*[31]

The education does not end in law school, either. Attorneys must take **continuing legal education** courses to keep their law licenses, and a certain number of hours are required to be on the subject of ethics. Lawyers who violate their state bar's rules can be disciplined, fined, suspended, or even disbarred.

Despite this focus on ethics and professional responsibility, the adversarial system of justice can leave an impression of zealous advocates who go too far or who bend the rules to help their clients. There are plenty of lawyer jokes that promote this reputation.[32] But at the heart of the practice of law is the belief that everyone deserves a fair system of justice and is entitled to legal representation, no matter how heinous the accusation.

---

[31]   Clark, K., *The Legacy of Watergate for Legal Ethics Instruction*, 51 Hastings L.J. 673 1999–2000.

[32]   How many lawyer jokes are there? Three. The rest are true stories.

Read and brief each of the following cases relating to the role of defense attorneys and defendant's right to the assistance of counsel and consider the questions following each case:

1. *Gideon v. Wainwright*: Appointed Counsel for Indigent Defendants

2. *Missouri v. Frye*: Effective Assistance of Counsel in Plea Negotiations

3. *Indiana v. Edward*: Competence in Self-Representation

4. *Nix v. Whiteside*: Effective Assistance of Counsel and Attorney Ethics

5. *Padilla v. Kentucky*: Effective Assistance of Counsel and Immigration Consequences

6. *Garza v. Idaho*: Ineffective Assistance of Counsel

---

## GIDEON V. WAINWRIGHT

Supreme Court of the United States
Argued Jan. 15, 1963
Decided March 18, 1963
372 U.S. 335

### OPINION

### MR. JUSTICE BLACK delivered the opinion of the Court.

Petitioner was charged in a Florida state court with having broken and entered a poolroom with intent to commit a misdemeanor. This offense is a felony under Florida law. Appearing in court without funds and without a lawyer, petitioner asked the court to appoint counsel for him, whereupon the following colloquy took place:

> 'The COURT: Mr. Gideon, I am sorry, but I cannot appoint Counsel to represent you in this case. Under the laws of the State of Florida, the only time the Court can appoint Counsel to represent a Defendant is when that person is charged with a capital offense. I am sorry, but I will have to deny your request to appoint Counsel to defend you in this case.
>
> 'The DEFENDANT: The United States Supreme Court says I am entitled to be represented by Counsel.'

Put to trial before a jury, Gideon conducted his defense about as well as could be expected from a layman. He made an opening statement to the jury, cross-examined the State's witnesses, presented witnesses in his own defense, declined to testify himself, and made a short argument 'emphasizing his innocence to the charge contained in the Information filed in this case.' The jury returned a verdict of guilty, and petitioner was sentenced to serve five years in the state prison. Later, petitioner filed in the Florida Supreme Court this habeas corpus petition attacking his conviction and sentence on the ground that the trial court's refusal to appoint counsel for him denied him rights 'guaranteed by the Constitution and the Bill of Rights by the United States Government.' Treating the petition for habeas corpus as properly before it, the State Supreme Court, 'upon consideration thereof' but without an opinion, denied all relief. Since 1942, when *Betts v. Brady* was decided by a divided Court, the problem of a defendant's federal constitutional right to counsel in a state court has been a continuing source of controversy and litigation in both state and federal courts. To give this problem another review here, we granted certiorari. Since Gideon was proceeding in forma pauperis, we appointed counsel to represent him and requested both sides to discuss in their briefs and oral arguments the following: 'Should this Court's holding in *Betts v. Brady. . .*be reconsidered?'

## I.

The facts upon which Betts claimed that he had been unconstitutionally denied the right to have counsel appointed to assist him are strikingly like the facts upon which Gideon here bases his federal constitutional claim. Betts was indicted for robbery in a Maryland state court. On arraignment, he told the trial judge of his lack of funds to hire a lawyer and asked the court to appoint one for him. Betts was advised that it was not the practice in that county to appoint counsel for indigent defendants except in murder and rape cases. He then pleaded not guilty, had witnesses summoned, cross-examined the State's witnesses, examined his own, and chose not to testify himself. He was found guilty by the judge, sitting without a jury, and sentenced to eight years in prison. Like Gideon, Betts sought release by habeas corpus, alleging that he had been denied the right to assistance of counsel in violation of the Fourteenth Amendment. Betts was denied any relief, and on review this Court affirmed. It was held that a refusal to appoint counsel for an indigent defendant charged with a felony did not necessarily violate the Due Process Clause of the Fourteenth Amendment, which for reasons given the Court deemed to be the only applicable federal constitutional provision. The Court said:

> Asserted denial (of due process) is to be tested by an appraisal of the
> totality of facts in a given case. That which may, in one setting,

constitute a denial of fundamental fairness, shocking to the universal sense of justice, may, in other circumstances, and in the light of other considerations, fall short of such denial.'

Treating due process as 'a concept less rigid and more fluid than those envisaged in other specific and particular provisions of the Bill of Rights,' the Court held that refusal to appoint counsel under the particular facts and circumstances in the Betts case was not so 'offensive to the common and fundamental ideas of fairness' as to amount to a denial of due process. Since the facts and circumstances of the two cases are so nearly indistinguishable, we think the *Betts v. Brady* holding if left standing would require us to reject Gideon's claim that the Constitution guarantees him the assistance of counsel. Upon full reconsideration we conclude that *Betts v. Brady* should be overruled.

## II.

The Sixth Amendment provides, 'In all criminal prosecutions, the accused shall enjoy the right. . .to have the Assistance of Counsel for his defence.' We have construed this to mean that in federal courts counsel must be provided for defendants unable to employ counsel unless the right is competently and intelligently waived. *Betts* argued that this right is extended to indigent defendants in state courts by the Fourteenth Amendment. In response the Court stated that, while the Sixth Amendment laid down 'no rule for the conduct of the states, the question recurs whether the constraint laid by the amendment upon the national courts expresses a rule so fundamental and essential to a fair trial, and so, to due process of law, that it is made obligatory upon the states by the Fourteenth Amendment.' In order to decide whether the Sixth Amendment's guarantee of counsel is of this fundamental nature, the Court in *Betts* set out and considered '(r)elevant data on the subject. . .afforded by constitutional and statutory provisions subsisting in the colonies and the states prior to the inclusion of the Bill of Rights in the national Constitution, and in the constitutional, legislative, and judicial history of the states to the present date.' On the basis of this historical data the Court concluded that 'appointment of counsel is not a fundamental right, essential to a fair trial.' It was for this reason the *Betts* Court refused to accept the contention that the Sixth Amendment's guarantee of counsel for indigent federal defendants was extended to or, in the words of that Court, 'made obligatory upon the states by the Fourteenth Amendment'. Plainly, had the Court concluded that appointment of counsel for an indigent criminal defendant was 'a fundamental right, essential to a fair trial,' it would have held that the Fourteenth

Amendment requires appointment of counsel in a state court, just as the Sixth Amendment requires in a federal court.

We think the Court in *Betts* had ample precedent for acknowledging that those guarantees of the Bill of Rights which are fundamental safeguards of liberty immune from federal abridgment are equally protected against state invasion by the Due Process Clause of the Fourteenth Amendment. This same principle was recognized, explained, and applied in *Powell v. Alabama*, 287 U.S. 45 (1932), a case upholding the right of counsel, where the Court held that despite sweeping language to the contrary in *Hurtado v. California*, 110 U.S. 516 (1884), the Fourteenth Amendment 'embraced' those "fundamental principles of liberty and justice which lie at the base of all our civil and political institutions," even though they had been 'specifically dealt with in another part of the Federal Constitution.' In many cases other than *Powell* and *Betts*, this Court has looked to the fundamental nature of original Bill of Rights guarantees to decide whether the Fourteenth Amendment makes them obligatory on the States. Explicitly recognized to be of this 'fundamental nature' and therefore made immune from state invasion by the Fourteenth, or some part of it, are the First Amendment's freedoms of speech, press, religion, assembly, association, and petition for redress of grievances. For the same reason, though not always in precisely the same terminology, the Court has made obligatory on the States the Fifth Amendment's command that private property shall not be taken for public use without just compensation, the Fourth Amendment's prohibition of unreasonable searches and seizures, and the Eighth's ban on cruel and unusual punishment. On the other hand, this Court in *Palko v. Connecticut*, 302 U.S. 319 (1937), refused to hold that the Fourteenth Amendment made the double jeopardy provision of the Fifth Amendment obligatory on the States. In so refusing, however, the Court, speaking through Mr. Justice Cardozo, was careful to emphasize that 'immunities that are valid as against the federal government by force of the specific pledges of particular amendments have been found to be implicit in the concept of ordered liberty, and thus, through the Fourteenth Amendment, become valid as against the states' and that guarantees 'in their origin. . .effective against the federal government alone' had by prior cases 'been taken over from the earlier articles of the Federal Bill of Rights and brought within the Fourteenth Amendment by a process of absorption.

We accept *Betts v. Brady*'s assumption, based as it was on our prior cases, that a provision of the Bill of Rights which is 'fundamental and essential to a fair trial' is made obligatory upon the States by the Fourteenth Amendment.

We think the Court in Betts was wrong, however, in concluding that the Sixth Amendment's guarantee of counsel is not one of these fundamental rights. Ten years before *Betts v. Brady*, this Court, after full consideration of all the historical data examined in *Betts*, had unequivocally declared that 'the right to the aid of counsel is of this fundamental character.' *Powell*, 287 U.S. at 68. While the Court at the close of its *Powell* opinion did by its language, as this Court frequently does, limit its holding to the particular facts and circumstances of that case, its conclusions about the fundamental nature of the right to counsel are unmistakable. Several years later, in 1936, the Court reemphasized what it had said about the fundamental nature of the right to counsel in this language:

> 'We concluded that certain fundamental rights, safeguarded by the first eight amendments against federal action, were also safeguarded against state action by the due process of law clause of the Fourteenth Amendment, and among them the fundamental right of the accused to the aid of counsel in a criminal prosecution.'

And again in 1938 this Court said:

> '(The assistance of counsel) is one of the safeguards of the Sixth Amendment deemed necessary to insure fundamental human rights of life and liberty. . . .The Sixth Amendment stands as a constant admonition that if the constitutional safeguards it provides be lost, justice will not 'still be done.'

In light of these and many other prior decisions of this Court, it is not surprising that the *Betts* Court, when faced with the contention that 'one charged with crime, who is unable to obtain counsel, must be furnished counsel by the state,' conceded that '(e)xpressions in the opinions of this court lend color to the argument. . .' The fact is that in deciding as it did—that 'appointment of counsel is not a fundamental right, essential to a fair trial'— the Court in *Betts v. Brady* made an abrupt break with its own well-considered precedents. In returning to these old precedents, sounder we believe than the new, we but restore constitutional principles established to achieve a fair system of justice. Not only these precedents but also reason and reflection require us to recognize that in our adversary system of criminal justice, any person haled into court, who is too poor to hire a lawyer, cannot be assured a fair trial unless counsel is provided for him. This seems to us to be an obvious truth. Governments, both state and federal, quite properly spend vast sums of money to establish machinery to try defendants accused of crime. Lawyers to prosecute are everywhere deemed essential to protect the public's interest in an orderly society. Similarly, there are few defendants charged with crime, few indeed, who fail to hire the best lawyers they can get to prepare and present their defenses. That government hires lawyers to prosecute and defendants who have the money hire lawyers to defend are the strongest indications of the wide—spread belief that lawyers in criminal courts are necessities, not luxuries. The right of one charged with crime to counsel may not be deemed fundamental and essential to fair trials in some countries, but it is in ours. From the very beginning, our state and national constitutions and laws have laid great emphasis on procedural and substantive safeguards designed to assure fair trials before impartial tribunals in which every defendant stands equal before the law. This noble ideal cannot be realized if the poor man charged with crime has to face his accusers without a lawyer to assist him. A defendant's need for a lawyer is nowhere better stated than in the moving words of Mr. Justice Sutherland in *Powell v. Alabama*:

> 'The right to be heard would be, in many cases, of little avail if it did not comprehend the right to be heard by counsel. Even the intelligent and educated layman has small and sometimes no skill in the science of law. If charged with crime, he is incapable, generally, of determining for himself whether the indictment is good or bad. He is unfamiliar with the rules of evidence. Left without the aid of counsel he may be put on trial without a proper charge, and convicted upon incompetent evidence, or evidence irrelevant to the issue or otherwise inadmissible. He lacks both the skill and knowledge adequately to prepare his defense, even though he have a perfect one. He requires the guiding hand of counsel at every step in the proceedings against him. Without it, though he be not guilty, he faces the danger of conviction because he does not know how to establish his innocence.'

The Court in *Betts v. Brady* departed from the sound wisdom upon which the Court's holding in *Powell v. Alabama* rested. Florida, supported by two other States, has asked that *Betts v. Brady* be left intact. Twenty-two States, as friends of the Court, argue that *Betts* was 'an anachronism when handed down' and that it should now be overruled. We agree.

The judgment is reversed and the cause is remanded to the Supreme Court of Florida for further action not inconsistent with this opinion.

**Reversed. . . .**

**After preparing the case brief, consider the answers to the following questions:**

1.     What characteristics of counsel make their advice fundamental in a criminal trial?

2.     What other important facts did the Court point to in arguing that counsel for indigent defendants was a fundamental right?

3.     Would a case-by-case approach to right to counsel decisions have been sufficient and a more cost-effective approach to the problem of indigent defense? Why or why not?

## MISSOURI V. FRYE

Supreme Court of the United States
Argued Oct. 31, 2011
Decided March 21, 2012
566 U.S. 134

### OPINION

### JUSTICE KENNEDY delivered the opinion of the Court.

The Sixth Amendment, applicable to the States by the terms of the Fourteenth Amendment, provides that the accused shall have the assistance of counsel in all criminal prosecutions. The right to counsel is the right to effective assistance of counsel. See *Strickland v. Washington,* 466 U.S. 668 (1984). This case arises in the context of claimed ineffective assistance that led to the lapse of a prosecution offer of a plea bargain, a proposal that offered terms more lenient than the terms of the guilty plea entered later. The initial question is whether the constitutional right to counsel extends to the negotiation and consideration of plea offers that lapse or are rejected. If there is a right to effective assistance with respect to those offers, a further question is what a defendant must demonstrate in order to show that prejudice resulted from counsel's deficient performance. Other questions relating to ineffective assistance with respect to plea offers, including the question of proper remedies, are considered in a second case decided today. See *Lafler v. Cooper.*

I

In August 2007, respondent Galin Frye was charged with driving with a revoked license. Frye had been convicted for that offense on three other occasions, so the State of Missouri charged him with a class D felony, which carries a maximum term of imprisonment of four years.

On November 15, the prosecutor sent a letter to Frye's counsel offering a choice of two plea bargains. The prosecutor first offered to recommend a 3-year sentence if there was a guilty plea to the felony charge, without a recommendation regarding probation but with a recommendation that Frye serve 10 days in jail as so-called "shock" time. The second offer was to reduce the charge to a misdemeanor and, if Frye pleaded guilty to it, to recommend a 90-day sentence. The misdemeanor charge of driving with a revoked license carries a maximum term of imprisonment of one year. The letter stated both offers would expire on December 28. Frye's attorney did not advise Frye that the offers had been made. The offers expired.

Frye's preliminary hearing was scheduled for January 4, 2008. On December 30, 2007, less than a week before the hearing, Frye was again arrested for driving with a revoked license. At the January 4 hearing, Frye waived his right to a preliminary hearing on the charge arising from the August 2007 arrest. He pleaded not guilty at a subsequent arraignment but then changed his plea to guilty. There was no underlying plea agreement. The state trial court accepted Frye's guilty plea. The prosecutor recommended a 3-year sentence, made no recommendation regarding probation, and requested 10 days shock time in jail. The trial judge sentenced Frye to three years in prison.

Frye filed for postconviction relief in state court. He alleged his counsel's failure to inform him of the prosecution's plea offer denied him the effective assistance of counsel. At an evidentiary hearing, Frye testified he would have entered a guilty plea to the misdemeanor had he known about the offer.

A state court denied the postconviction motion, but the Missouri Court of Appeals reversed. It determined that Frye met both of the requirements for showing a Sixth Amendment violation under *Strickland*. First, the court determined Frye's counsel's performance was deficient because the "record is void of any evidence of any effort by trial counsel to communicate the Offer to Frye during the Offer window." The court next concluded Frye had shown his counsel's deficient performance caused him prejudice because "Frye pled guilty to a felony instead of a misdemeanor and was subject to a maximum sentence of four years instead of one year."

To implement a remedy for the violation, the court deemed Frye's guilty plea withdrawn and remanded to allow Frye either to insist on a trial or to plead guilty to any offense the prosecutor deemed it appropriate to charge. This Court granted certiorari.

II

A

It is well settled that the right to the effective assistance of counsel applies to certain steps before trial. The "Sixth Amendment guarantees a defendant the right to have counsel present at all 'critical' stages of the criminal proceedings." Critical stages include arraignments, postindictment interrogations, postindictment lineups, and the entry of a guilty plea.

With respect to the right to effective counsel in plea negotiations, a proper beginning point is to discuss two cases from this Court considering the role of counsel in advising a client about a plea offer and an ensuing guilty plea: *Hill v. Lockhart*, 474 U.S. 52 (1985); and *Padilla v. Kentucky*, 559 U.S. 356 (2010).

*Hill* established that claims of ineffective assistance of counsel in the plea bargain context are governed by the two-part test set forth in *Strickland*. As noted above, in Frye's case, the Missouri Court of Appeals, applying the two part test of *Strickland*, determined first that defense counsel had been ineffective and second that there was resulting prejudice.

In *Hill*, the decision turned on the second part of the *Strickland* test. There, a defendant who had entered a guilty plea claimed his counsel had misinformed him of the amount of time he would have to serve before he became eligible for parole. But the defendant had not alleged that, even if adequate advice and assistance had been given, he would have elected to plead not guilty and proceed to trial. Thus, the Court found that no prejudice from the inadequate advice had been shown or alleged.

In *Padilla*, the Court again discussed the duties of counsel in advising a client with respect to a plea offer that leads to a guilty plea. *Padilla* held that a guilty plea, based on a plea offer, should be set aside because counsel misinformed the defendant of the immigration consequences of the conviction. The Court made clear that "the negotiation of a plea bargain is a critical phase of litigation for purposes of the Sixth Amendment right to effective assistance of counsel." It also rejected the argument made by petitioner in this case that a knowing and voluntary plea supersedes errors by defense counsel.

In the case now before the Court the State, as petitioner, points out that the legal question presented is different from that in *Hill* and *Padilla*. In those cases the claim was that the prisoner's plea of guilty was invalid because counsel had provided incorrect advice pertinent to the plea. In the instant case, by contrast, the guilty plea that was accepted, and the plea proceedings concerning it in court, were all based on accurate advice and information from counsel. The challenge is not to the advice pertaining to the plea that was accepted but rather to the course of legal representation that preceded it with respect to other potential pleas and plea offers.

To give further support to its contention that the instant case is in a category different from what the Court considered in *Hill* and *Padilla*, the State urges that there is no right to a plea offer or a plea bargain in any event. It claims Frye therefore was not deprived of any legal benefit to which he was entitled. Under this view, any wrongful or mistaken action of counsel with respect to earlier plea offers is beside the point.

The State is correct to point out that *Hill* and *Padilla* concerned whether there was ineffective assistance leading to acceptance of a plea offer, a process involving a formal court appearance with the defendant and all counsel present. Before a guilty plea is entered the defendant's understanding of the plea and its consequences can be established on the record. This affords the State substantial protection against later claims that the plea was the result of inadequate advice. At the plea entry proceedings the trial court and all counsel have the opportunity to establish on the record that the defendant understands the process that led to any offer, the advantages and disadvantages of accepting it, and the sentencing consequences or possibilities that will ensue once a conviction is entered based upon the plea. *Hill* and *Padilla* both illustrate that, nevertheless, there may be instances when claims of ineffective assistance can arise after the conviction is entered. Still, the State, and the trial court itself, have had a substantial opportunity to guard against this contingency by establishing at the plea entry proceeding that the defendant has been given proper advice or, if the advice received appears to have been inadequate, to remedy that deficiency before the plea is accepted and the conviction entered.

When a plea offer has lapsed or been rejected, however, no formal court proceedings are involved. This underscores that the plea-bargaining process is often in flux, with no clear standards or timelines and with no judicial supervision of the discussions between prosecution and defense. Indeed, discussions between client and defense counsel are privileged. So the prosecution has little or no notice if something may be amiss and perhaps no capacity to intervene in any event. And, as noted, the State insists there is no right to receive a plea offer. For all these reasons, the State contends, it is unfair to subject it to the consequences of defense counsel's inadequacies, especially when the opportunities for a full and fair trial, or, as here, for a later guilty plea albeit on less favorable terms, are preserved.

The State's contentions are neither illogical nor without some persuasive force, yet they do not suffice to overcome a simple reality. Approximately 97% of federal convictions and 94% of state convictions are the result of guilty pleas. The reality is that plea bargains have become so central to the administration of the criminal justice system that defense counsel have responsibilities in the plea bargain process, responsibilities that must be met to render the adequate assistance of counsel that the Sixth Amendment requires in the criminal process at critical stages. Because ours "is for the most part a system of pleas, not a system of trials," it is insufficient simply to point to the guarantee of a fair trial as a backstop that inoculates any errors in the pretrial process. "To a large extent . . . horse trading [between prosecutor and defense counsel] determines who goes to jail and for how long. That is what plea bargaining is. It is not some adjunct to the criminal justice system; it *is* the criminal justice system." Scott & Stuntz, Plea Bargaining as Contract, 101 Yale L. J. 1909, 1912 (1992). See also Barkow, Separation of Powers and the Criminal Law, 58 Stan. L.Rev. 989, 1034 (2006) ("[Defendants] who do take their case to trial and lose receive longer sentences than even Congress or the prosecutor might think appropriate, because the longer sentences exist on the books largely for bargaining purposes. This often results in individuals who accept a plea bargain receiving shorter sentences than other individuals who are less morally culpable but take a chance and go to trial."). In today's criminal justice system, therefore, the negotiation of a plea bargain, rather than the unfolding of a trial, is almost always the critical point for a defendant.

To note the prevalence of plea bargaining is not to criticize it. The potential to conserve valuable prosecutorial resources and for defendants to admit their crimes and receive more favorable terms at sentencing means that a plea agreement can benefit both parties. In order that these benefits can be realized, however, criminal defendants require effective counsel during plea negotiations. "Anything less . . . might deny a defendant 'effective representation by counsel at the only stage when legal aid and advice would help him.' "

B

The inquiry then becomes how to define the duty and responsibilities of defense counsel in the plea bargain process. This is a difficult question. "The art of negotiation is at least as nuanced as the art of trial advocacy and it presents questions farther removed from immediate judicial supervision." Bargaining is, by its nature, defined to a substantial degree by personal style. The alternative courses and tactics in negotiation are so individual that it may be neither prudent nor practicable to try to elaborate or define detailed standards for the proper discharge of defense counsel's participation in the process.

This case presents neither the necessity nor the occasion to define the duties of defense counsel in those respects, however. Here the question is whether defense counsel has the duty to communicate the terms of a formal offer to accept a plea on terms and conditions that may result in a lesser sentence, a conviction on lesser charges, or both.

This Court now holds that, as a general rule, defense counsel has the duty to communicate formal offers from the prosecution to accept a plea on terms and conditions that may be favorable to the accused. Any exceptions to that rule need not be explored here, for the offer was a formal one with a fixed expiration date. When defense counsel allowed the offer to expire without advising the defendant or allowing him to consider it, defense counsel did not render the effective assistance the Constitution requires.

Though the standard for counsel's performance is not determined solely by reference to codified standards of professional practice, these standards can be important guides. The American Bar Association recommends defense counsel "promptly communicate and explain to the defendant all plea offers made by the prosecuting attorney," . . .and this standard has been adopted by numerous state and federal courts over the last 30 years. The standard for prompt communication and consultation is also set out in state bar professional standards for attorneys.

The prosecution and the trial courts may adopt some measures to help ensure against late, frivolous, or fabricated claims after a later, less advantageous plea offer has been accepted or after a trial leading to conviction with resulting harsh consequences. First, the fact of a formal offer means that its terms and its processing can be documented so that what took place in the negotiation process becomes more clear if some later inquiry turns on the conduct of earlier pretrial negotiations. Second, States may elect to follow rules that all offers must be in writing, again to ensure against later misunderstandings or fabricated charges. Third, formal offers can be made part of the record at any subsequent plea proceeding or before a trial on the merits, all to ensure that a defendant has been fully advised before those further proceedings commence. At least one State often follows a similar procedure before trial. . .

Here defense counsel did not communicate the formal offers to the defendant. As a result of that deficient performance, the offers lapsed. Under *Strickland,* the question then becomes what, if any, prejudice resulted from the breach of duty.

C

To show prejudice from ineffective assistance of counsel where a plea offer has lapsed or been rejected because of counsel's deficient performance, defendants must demonstrate a reasonable probability they would have accepted the earlier plea offer had they been afforded effective assistance of counsel. Defendants must also demonstrate a reasonable probability the plea would have been entered without the prosecution canceling it or the trial court refusing to accept it, if they had the authority to exercise that discretion under state law. To establish prejudice in this instance, it is necessary to show a reasonable probability that the end result of the criminal process would have been more favorable by reason of a plea to a lesser charge or a sentence of less prison time.

This application of *Strickland* to the instances of an uncommunicated, lapsed plea does nothing to alter the standard laid out in *Hill*. In cases where a defendant complains that ineffective assistance led him to accept a plea offer as opposed to proceeding to trial, the defendant will have to show "a reasonable probability that, but for counsel's errors, he would not have pleaded guilty and would have insisted on going to trial." *Hill* was correctly decided and applies in the context in which it arose. *Hill* does not, however, provide the sole means for demonstrating prejudice arising from the deficient performance of counsel during plea negotiations. Unlike the defendant in *Hill*, Frye argues that with effective assistance he would have accepted an earlier plea offer (limiting his sentence to one year in prison) as opposed to entering an open plea (exposing him to a maximum sentence of four years' imprisonment). In a case, such as this, where a defendant pleads guilty to less favorable terms and claims that ineffective assistance of counsel caused him to miss out on a more favorable earlier plea offer, *Strickland*'s inquiry into whether "the result of the proceeding would have been different," requires looking not at whether the defendant would have proceeded to trial absent ineffective assistance but whether he would have accepted the offer to plead pursuant to the terms earlier proposed.

In order to complete a showing of *Strickland* prejudice, defendants who have shown a reasonable probability they would have accepted the earlier plea offer must also show that, if the prosecution had the discretion to cancel it or if the trial court had the discretion to refuse to accept it, there is a reasonable probability neither the prosecution nor the trial court would have prevented the offer from being accepted or implemented. This further showing is of particular importance because a defendant has no right to be offered a plea, . . . nor a federal right that the judge accept it. In at least some States, including Missouri, it appears the prosecution has some discretion to cancel a plea agreement to which the defendant has agreed. The Federal Rules, some state rules including in Missouri, and this Court's precedents give trial courts some leeway to accept or reject plea agreements. It can be assumed that in most jurisdictions prosecutors and judges are familiar with the boundaries of acceptable plea bargains and sentences. So in most instances it should not be difficult to make an objective assessment as to whether or not a particular fact or intervening circumstance would suffice, in the normal course, to cause prosecutorial withdrawal or judicial nonapproval of a plea bargain. The determination that there is or is not a reasonable probability that the outcome of the proceeding would have been different absent counsel's errors can be conducted within that framework.

### III

These standards must be applied to the instant case. As regards the deficient performance prong of *Strickland,* the Court of Appeals found the "record is void of *any* evidence of *any* effort by trial counsel to communicate the [formal] Offer to Frye during the Offer window, let alone any evidence that Frye's conduct interfered with trial counsel's ability to do so." On this record, it is evident that Frye's attorney did not make a meaningful attempt to inform the defendant of a written plea offer before the offer expired. The Missouri Court of Appeals was correct that "counsel's representation fell below an objective standard of reasonableness."

The Court of Appeals erred, however, in articulating the precise standard for prejudice in this context. As noted, a defendant in Frye's position must show not only a reasonable probability that he would have accepted the lapsed plea but also a reasonable probability that the prosecution would have adhered to the agreement and that it would have been accepted by the trial court. Frye can show he would have accepted the offer, but there is strong reason to doubt the prosecution and the trial court would have permitted the plea bargain to become final.

There appears to be a reasonable probability Frye would have accepted the prosecutor's original offer of a plea bargain if the offer had been communicated to him, because he pleaded guilty to a more serious charge, with no promise of a sentencing recommendation from the prosecutor. . . . The Court of Appeals did not err in finding Frye's acceptance of the less favorable plea offer indicated that he would have accepted the earlier (and more favorable) offer had he been apprised of it; and there is no need to address here the showings that might be required in other cases.

The Court of Appeals failed, however, to require Frye to show that the first plea offer, if accepted by Frye, would have been adhered to by the prosecution and accepted by the trial court. Whether the prosecution and trial court are required to do so is a matter of state law, and it is not the place of this

Court to settle those matters. The Court has established the minimum requirements of the Sixth Amendment as interpreted in *Strickland,* and States have the discretion to add procedural protections under state law if they choose. A State may choose to preclude the prosecution from withdrawing a plea offer once it has been accepted or perhaps to preclude a trial court from rejecting a plea bargain. In Missouri, it appears "a plea offer once accepted by the defendant can be withdrawn without recourse" by the prosecution. The extent of the trial court's discretion in Missouri to reject a plea agreement appears to be in some doubt.

We remand for the Missouri Court of Appeals to consider these state-law questions, because they bear on the federal question of *Strickland* prejudice. If, as the Missouri court stated here, the prosecutor could have canceled the plea agreement, and if Frye fails to show a reasonable probability the prosecutor would have adhered to the agreement, there is no *Strickland* prejudice. Likewise, if the trial court could have refused to accept the plea agreement, and if Frye fails to show a reasonable probability the trial court would have accepted the plea, there is no *Strickland* prejudice. In this case, given Frye's new offense for driving without a license on December 30, 2007, there is reason to doubt that the prosecution would have adhered to the agreement or that the trial court would have accepted it at the January 4, 2008, hearing, unless they were required by state law to do so.

It is appropriate to allow the Missouri Court of Appeals to address this question in the first instance. The judgment of the Missouri Court of Appeals is vacated, and the case is remanded for further proceedings not inconsistent with this opinion.

### *It is so ordered.*

**JUSTICE SCALIA, with whom THE CHIEF JUSTICE, JUSTICE THOMAS, and JUSTICE ALITO join, dissenting.**

This is a companion case to *Lafler v. Cooper.* The principal difference between the cases is that the fairness of the defendant's conviction in *Lafler* was established by a full trial and jury verdict, whereas Frye's conviction here was established by his own admission of guilt, received by the court after the usual colloquy that assured it was voluntary and truthful. In *Lafler* all that could be said (and as I discuss there it was quite enough) is that the *fairness* of the conviction was clear, though a unanimous jury finding beyond a reasonable doubt can sometimes be wrong. Here it can be said not only that the process was fair, but that the defendant acknowledged the correctness of his conviction. Thus, as far as the reasons for my dissent are concerned, this is an *a fortiori* case. I will not repeat here the constitutional points that I discuss at length in *Lafler,* but I will briefly apply those points to the facts here and comment upon a few statements in the Court's analysis.

Galin Frye's attorney failed to inform him about a plea offer, and Frye ultimately pleaded guilty without the benefit of a deal. Counsel's mistake did not deprive Frye of any substantive or procedural right; only of the opportunity to accept a plea bargain to which he had no entitlement in the first place. So little entitlement that, had he known of and accepted the bargain, the prosecution would have been able to withdraw it right up to the point that his guilty plea pursuant to the bargain was accepted.

The Court acknowledges, moreover, that Frye's conviction was untainted by attorney error: "[T]he guilty plea that was accepted, and the plea proceedings concerning it in court, were all based on accurate advice and information from counsel." Given the "ultimate focus" of our ineffective-assistance cases on "the fundamental fairness of the proceeding whose result is being challenged," that should be the end of the matter. Instead, here, as in *Lafler,* the Court mechanically applies an outcome-based test for prejudice, and mistakes the possibility of a different result for constitutional injustice. As I explain in *Lafler* (dissenting opinion), that approach is contrary to our precedents on the right to effective counsel, and for good reason.

The Court announces its holding that "as a general rule, defense counsel has the duty to communicate formal offers from the prosecution" as though that resolves a disputed point; in reality, however, neither the State nor the Solicitor General argued that counsel's performance here was adequate. The only issue was whether the inadequacy deprived Frye of his constitutional right to a fair trial. In other cases, however, it will not be so clear that counsel's plea-bargaining skills, which must now meet a constitutional minimum, are adequate. "[H]ow to define the duty and responsibilities of defense counsel in the plea bargain process," the Court acknowledges, "is a difficult question," since "[b]argaining is, by its nature, defined to a substantial degree by personal style." Indeed. What if an attorney's "personal style" is to establish a reputation as a hard bargainer by, for example, advising clients to proceed to trial rather than accept anything but the most favorable plea offers? It seems inconceivable that a lawyer could compromise his client's *constitutional rights* so that he can secure better deals for other clients in the future; does a hard-bargaining "personal style" now violate the Sixth Amendment? The Court ignores such difficulties, however, since "[t]his case presents neither the necessity nor the occasion to define the duties of defense counsel in those respects." Perhaps not. But it does present the necessity of confronting the serious difficulties that will be created by constitutionalization of the plea-bargaining process. It will not do simply to announce that they will be solved in the sweet by-and-by.

While the inadequacy of counsel's performance in this case is clear enough, whether it was prejudicial (in the sense that the Court's new version of *Strickland* requires) is not. The Court's description of how that question is to be answered on remand is alone enough to show how unwise it is to constitutionalize the plea-bargaining process. Prejudice is to be determined, the Court tells us, by a process of retrospective crystal-ball gazing posing as legal analysis. First of all, of course, we must estimate whether the defendant *would have accepted* the earlier plea bargain. Here that seems an easy question, but as the Court acknowledges, it will not always be. Next, since Missouri, like other States, permits accepted plea offers to be withdrawn by the prosecution (a reality which alone should suffice, one would think, to demonstrate that Frye had no entitlement to the plea bargain), we must estimate whether the prosecution *would have withdrawn* the plea offer. And finally, we must estimate whether the trial court *would have approved* the plea agreement. These last two estimations may seem easy in the present case, since Frye committed a new infraction before the hearing at which the agreement would have been presented; but they assuredly will not be easy in the mine run of cases.

The Court says "[i]t can be assumed that in most jurisdictions prosecutors and judges are familiar with the boundaries of acceptable plea bargains and sentences." Assuredly it can, just as it can be assumed that the sun rises in the west; but I know of no basis for the assumption. Virtually no cases deal with the standards for a prosecutor's withdrawal from a plea agreement beyond stating the general rule that a prosecutor may withdraw any time prior to, but not after, the entry of a guilty plea or other action constituting detrimental reliance on the defendant's part. And cases addressing trial courts' authority to accept or reject plea agreements almost universally observe that a trial court enjoys broad discretion in this regard. Of course after today's opinions there will be cases galore, so the Court's *assumption* would better be cast as an optimistic *prediction* of the certainty that will emerge, many years hence, from our newly created constitutional field of plea-bargaining law. Whatever the "boundaries" ultimately devised (if that were possible), a vast amount of discretion will still remain, and it is extraordinary to make a defendant's constitutional rights depend upon a series of retrospective mind-readings as to how that discretion, in prosecutors and trial judges, *would have been* exercised.

The plea-bargaining process is a subject worthy of regulation, since it is the means by which most criminal convictions are obtained. It happens not to be, however, a subject covered by the Sixth Amendment, which is concerned not with the fairness of bargaining but with the fairness of conviction. "The Constitution . . . is not an all-purpose tool for judicial construction of a perfect world; and when we ignore its text in order to make it that, we often find ourselves swinging a sledge where a tack hammer is needed." In this case and its companion, the Court's sledge may require the reversal of perfectly valid, eminently just, convictions. A legislature could solve the problems presented by these cases in a much more precise and efficient manner. It might begin, for example, by penalizing the attorneys who made such grievous errors. That type of sub-constitutional remedy is not available to the Court, which is limited to penalizing (almost) everyone else by reversing valid convictions or sentences. Because that result is inconsistent with the Sixth Amendment and decades of our precedent, I respectfully dissent.

## After preparing the case brief, consider the answers to the following questions:

1. Describe the 2-prong test for determining whether defense counsel has provided effective assistance.

2. Do you agree with the Court that failure to communicate the plea offers to the defendant rendered his counsel deficient? Explain.

3. Why should plea bargains be covered by the guarantee of effective assistance of counsel?

4. Consider the dissenting opinion of Justice Scalia. He argues that in the end, the Sixth Amendment is concerned with fairness of convictions—and since this defendant admitted his guilt, and did so to an even more serious charge—his conviction is fair. Is this argument convincing?

## INDIANA V. EDWARDS

Supreme Court of the United States
Argued March 26, 2008
Decided June 19, 2008
554 U.S. 164

### OPINION

### JUSTICE BREYER delivered the opinion of the Court.

This case focuses upon a criminal defendant whom a state court found mentally competent to stand trial if represented by counsel but not mentally competent to conduct that trial himself. We must decide whether in these circumstances the Constitution prohibits a State from insisting that the defendant proceed to trial with counsel, the State thereby denying the defendant the right to represent himself. See U.S. Const., Amdt. 6; *Faretta v. California,* 422 U.S. 806 (1975). We conclude that the Constitution does not forbid a State so to insist.

I.

In July 1999, Ahmad Edwards, the respondent, tried to steal a pair of shoes from an Indiana department store. After he was discovered, he drew a gun, fired at a store security officer, and wounded a bystander. He was caught and then charged with attempted murder, battery with a deadly weapon, criminal recklessness, and theft. His mental condition subsequently became the subject of three competency proceedings and two self-representation requests, mostly before the same trial judge:

1.  *First Competency Hearing: August 2000.* Five months after Edwards' arrest, his court-appointed counsel asked for a psychiatric evaluation. After hearing psychiatrist and neuropsychologist witnesses (in February 2000 and again in August 2000), the court found Edwards incompetent to stand trial, and committed him . . . for evaluation and treatment.

2.  *Second Competency Hearing: March 2002.* Seven months after his commitment, doctors found that Edwards' condition had improved to the point where he could stand trial. Several months later, however, but still before trial, Edwards' counsel asked for another psychiatric evaluation. In March 2002, the judge held a competency hearing. . .and (in April) found that Edwards, while "suffer[ing] from mental illness," was "competent to assist his attorneys in his defense and stand trial for the charged crimes."

3.    *Third Competency Hearing: April 2003.* Seven months later but still before trial, Edwards' counsel sought yet another psychiatric evaluation of his client. . . Edwards' counsel presented further psychiatric and neuropsychological evidence showing that Edwards was suffering from serious thinking difficulties and delusions. A testifying psychiatrist reported that Edwards could understand the charges against him, but he was "unable to cooperate with his attorney in his defense because of his schizophrenic illness"; "[h]is delusions and his marked difficulties in thinking make it impossible for him to cooperate with his attorney." In November 2003, the court concluded that Edwards was not then competent to stand trial and ordered his recommitment to the state hospital.

4.    *First Self-Representation Request and First Trial: June 2005.* About eight months after his commitment, the hospital reported that Edwards' condition had again improved to the point that he had again become competent to stand trial. And almost one year after that, Edwards' trial began. Just before trial, Edwards asked to represent himself. He also asked for a continuance, which, he said, he needed in order to proceed *pro se.* The court refused the continuance. Edwards then proceeded to trial represented by counsel. The jury convicted him of criminal recklessness and theft but failed to reach a verdict on the charges of attempted murder and battery.

5.    *Second Self-Representation Request and Second Trial: December 2005.* The State decided to retry Edwards on the attempted murder and battery charges. Just before the retrial, Edwards again asked the court to permit him to represent himself. Referring to the lengthy record of psychiatric reports, the trial court noted that Edwards still suffered from schizophrenia and concluded that "[w]ith these findings, he's competent to stand trial but I'm not going to find he's competent to defend himself." The court denied Edwards' self-representation request. Edwards was represented by appointed counsel at his retrial. The jury convicted Edwards on both of the remaining counts.

Edwards subsequently appealed to Indiana's intermediate appellate court. He argued that the trial court's refusal to permit him to represent himself at his retrial deprived him of his constitutional right of self-representation. The court agreed and ordered a new trial. The matter then went to the Indiana Supreme Court. That court found that "[t]he record in this case presents a substantial basis to agree with the trial court," but it nonetheless affirmed the intermediate appellate court on the belief that this Court's precedents, namely, *Faretta,* and *Godinez v. Moran,* required the State to allow Edwards to represent himself. At

Indiana's request, we agreed to consider whether the Constitution required the trial court to allow Edwards to represent himself at trial.

## II.

Our examination of this Court's precedents convinces us that those precedents frame the question presented, but they do not answer it. The two cases that set forth the Constitution's "mental competence" standard, *Dusky v. United States,* and *Drope v. Missouri,* specify that the Constitution does not permit trial of an individual who lacks "mental competency." *Dusky* defines the competency standard as including both (1) "whether" the defendant has "a rational as well as factual understanding of the proceedings against him" and (2) whether the defendant "has sufficient present ability *to consult with his lawyer with a reasonable degree of rational understanding.*" *Drope* repeats that standard, stating that it "has long been accepted that a person whose mental condition is such that he lacks the capacity to understand the nature and object of the proceedings against him, *to consult with counsel, and to assist in preparing his defense* may not be subjected to a trial." (emphasis added). Neither case considered the mental competency issue presented here, namely, the relation of the mental competence standard to the right of self-representation.

The Court's foundational "self-representation" case, *Faretta,* held that the Sixth and Fourteenth Amendments include a "constitutional right to proceed *without* counsel when" a criminal defendant "voluntarily and intelligently elects to do so." The Court implied that right from: (1) a "nearly universal conviction," made manifest in state law, that "forcing a lawyer upon an unwilling defendant is contrary to his basic right to defend himself if he truly wants to do so"; (2) Sixth Amendment language granting rights to the "accused"; (3) Sixth Amendment structure indicating that the rights it sets forth, related to the "fair administration of American justice," are "persona[l]" to the accused; (4) the absence of historical examples of *forced* representation; and (5) " 'respect for the individual,' " quoting *Illinois v. Allen,* 397 U.S. 337 (1970) (Brennan, J., concurring) (a knowing and intelligent waiver of counsel "must be honored out of 'that respect for the individual which is the lifeblood of the law' ").

*Faretta* does not answer the question before us both because it did not consider the problem of mental competency (cf. 422 U.S., at 835 (Faretta was "literate, competent, and understanding")), and because *Faretta* itself and later cases have made clear that the right of self-representation is not absolute, see *Martinez v. Court of Appeal of Cal., Fourth Appellate Dist.* (no right of self-representation on direct appeal in a criminal case); *McKaskle v. Wiggins* (appointment of standby counsel over self-represented defendant's objection is permissible); *Faretta* (no right "to abuse the dignity of the courtroom"); (no right to avoid compliance with "relevant rules of procedural and substantive law"); (no right to "engag[e] in serious and obstructionist misconduct"). The question here concerns a mental-illness-related limitation on the scope of the self-representation right.

The sole case in which this Court considered mental competence and self-representation together, *Godinez,* presents a question closer to that at issue here. The case focused upon a borderline-competent criminal defendant who had asked a state trial court to permit him to represent himself and to change his pleas from not guilty to guilty. The state trial court had found that the defendant met *Dusky's* mental competence standard, that he "knowingly and intelligently" waived his right to assistance of counsel, and that he "freely and voluntarily" chose to plead guilty. And the state trial court had consequently granted the defendant's self-representation and change-of-plea requests. A federal appeals court, however, had vacated the defendant's guilty pleas on the ground that the Constitution required the trial court to ask a further question, namely, whether the defendant was competent to waive his constitutional right to counsel. Competence to make that latter decision, the appeals court said, required the defendant to satisfy a higher mental competency standard than the standard set forth in *Dusky. Dusky's* more general standard sought only to determine whether a defendant represented by counsel was competent to stand trial, not whether he was competent to waive his right to counsel.

This Court, reversing the Court of Appeals, "reject[ed] the notion that competence to plead guilty or to waive the right to counsel must be measured by a standard that is higher than (or even different from) the *Dusky* standard." The decision to plead guilty, we said, "is no more complicated than the sum total of decisions that a [represented] defendant may be called upon to make during the course of a trial." Hence "there is no reason to believe that the decision to waive counsel requires an appreciably higher level of mental functioning than the decision to waive other constitutional rights." And even assuming that self-representation might pose special trial-related difficulties, "the competence that is required of a defendant seeking to waive his right to counsel is the competence to *waive the right,* not the competence to represent himself." For this reason, we concluded, "the defendant's 'technical legal knowledge' is 'not relevant' to the determination."

We concede that *Godinez* bears certain similarities with the present case. Both involve mental competence and self-representation. Both involve a defendant who wants to represent himself. Both involve a mental condition that falls in a gray area between *Dusky's* minimal constitutional requirement that measures a defendant's ability to stand trial and a somewhat higher standard that measures mental fitness for another legal purpose.

We nonetheless conclude that *Godinez* does not answer the question before us now. In part that is because the Court of Appeals' higher standard at issue in *Godinez* differs in a critical way from the higher standard at issue here. In *Godinez*, the higher standard sought to measure the defendant's ability to proceed on his own to enter a guilty plea; here the higher standard seeks to measure the defendant's ability to conduct trial proceedings. To put the matter more specifically, the *Godinez* defendant sought only to change his pleas to guilty, he did not seek to conduct trial proceedings, and his ability to conduct a defense at trial was expressly not at issue. Thus we emphasized in *Godinez* that we needed to consider only the defendant's "competence to *waive the right*." And we further emphasized that we need *not* consider the defendant's "technical legal knowledge" about how to proceed at trial. We found our holding consistent with this Court's earlier statement in *Massey v. Moore,* that "[o]ne might not be insane in the sense of being incapable of standing trial and yet lack the capacity to stand trial without benefit of counsel." In this case, the very matters that we did not consider in *Godinez* are directly before us.

For another thing, *Godinez* involved a State that sought to *permit* a gray-area defendant to represent himself. *Godinez's* constitutional holding is that a State may do so. But that holding simply does not tell a State whether it may *deny* a gray-area defendant the right to represent himself—the matter at issue here. . . . The upshot is that, in our view, the question before us is an open one.

III.

We now turn to the question presented. We assume that a criminal defendant has sufficient mental competence to stand trial . . . and that the defendant insists on representing himself during that trial. We ask whether the Constitution permits a State to limit that defendant's self-representation right by insisting upon representation by counsel at trial—on the ground that the defendant lacks the mental capacity to conduct his trial defense unless represented.

Several considerations taken together lead us to conclude that the answer to this question is yes. First, the Court's precedent, while not answering the question, points slightly in the direction of our affirmative answer. *Godinez*, as we have just said, simply leaves the question open. But the Court's "mental competency" cases set forth a standard that focuses directly upon a defendant's "present ability to consult with his lawyer"; a "capacity . . . to consult with counsel," and an ability "to assist [counsel] in preparing his defense." "It has long been accepted that a person whose mental condition is such that he lacks the capacity to understand the nature and object of the proceedings against him, *to consult with counsel,* and to assist in preparing his defense may not be subjected to a trial." These standards assume representation by counsel and emphasize the importance of counsel. They thus suggest. . . that an instance in which a defendant who would choose to forgo counsel at trial presents a very different set of circumstances, which in our view, calls for a different standard.

At the same time *Faretta,* the foundational self-representation case, rested its conclusion in part upon pre-existing state law set forth in cases all of which are consistent with, and at least two of which expressly adopt, a competency limitation on the self-representation right.

Second, the nature of the problem before us cautions against the use of a single mental competency standard for deciding both (1) whether a defendant who is represented by counsel can proceed to trial and (2) whether a defendant who goes to trial must be permitted to represent himself. Mental illness itself is not a unitary concept. It varies in degree. It can vary over time. It interferes with an individual's functioning at different times in different ways. The history of this case illustrates the complexity of the problem. In certain instances an individual may well be able to satisfy *Dusky*'s mental competence standard, for he will be able to work with counsel at trial, yet at the same time he may be unable to carry out the basic tasks needed to present his own defense without the help of counsel.

The American Psychiatric Association (APA) tells us (without dispute) in its *amicus* brief filed in support of neither party that "[d]isorganized thinking, deficits in sustaining attention and concentration, impaired expressive abilities, anxiety, and other common symptoms of severe mental illnesses can impair the defendant's ability to play the significantly expanded role required for self-representation even if he can play the lesser role of represented defendant." . . .

Third, in our view, a right of self-representation at trial will not "affirm the dignity" of a defendant who lacks the mental capacity to conduct his defense without the assistance of counsel. To the contrary, given that defendant's uncertain mental state, the spectacle that could well result from his self-representation at trial is at least as likely to prove humiliating as ennobling. Moreover, insofar as a defendant's lack of capacity threatens an improper conviction or sentence, self-representation in that exceptional context undercuts the most basic of the Constitution's criminal law objectives, providing a fair trial. . . .

Further, proceedings must not only be fair, they must "appear fair to all who observe them." An *amicus* brief reports one psychiatrist's reaction to having observed a patient (a patient who had satisfied *Dusky*) try to conduct his own defense: "[H]ow in the world can our legal system allow an insane man to defend himself?" See *Massey* ("No trial can be fair that leaves the defense to a man who is insane, unaided by counsel, and who by reason of his mental condition stands helpless and alone before the court"). The application of *Dusky*'s basic mental competence standard can help in part to avoid this result. But given the different capacities needed to proceed to trial without counsel, there is little reason to believe that *Dusky* alone is sufficient. At the same time, the trial judge. . .who presided over one of Edwards' competency hearings and his two trials, will often prove best able to make more fine-tuned mental capacity decisions, tailored to the individualized circumstances of a particular defendant.

We consequently conclude that the Constitution permits judges to take realistic account of the particular defendant's mental capacities by asking whether a defendant who seeks to conduct his own defense at trial is mentally competent to do so. That is to say, the Constitution permits States to insist upon representation by counsel for those competent enough to stand trial under *Dusky* but who still suffer from severe mental illness to the point where they are not competent to conduct trial proceedings by themselves.

IV.

. . .Indiana has also asked us to overrule *Faretta*. We decline to do so. We recognize that judges have sometimes expressed concern that *Faretta*, contrary to its intent, has led to trials that are unfair. But recent empirical research suggests that such instances are not common. See, *e.g.*, Hashimoto, Defending the Right of Self-Representation: An Empirical Look at the Pro Se Felony Defendant, 85 N.C.L.Rev. 423 (2007) (noting that of the small number of defendants who chose to proceed *pro se*—"roughly 0.3% to 0.5%" of the total, state felony defendants in particular "appear to have achieved higher felony acquittal rates than their represented counterparts in that they were less likely to have been convicted of felonies"). At the same time, instances in which the trial's fairness is in doubt may well be concentrated in the 20% or so of self-representation cases where the mental competence of the defendant is also at issue. See *id.* (about 20% of federal *pro se* felony defendants ordered to undergo competency evaluations). If so, today's opinion, assuring trial judges the authority to deal appropriately with cases in the latter category, may well alleviate those fair trial concerns.

For these reasons, the judgment of the Supreme Court of Indiana is vacated, and the case is remanded for further proceedings not inconsistent with this opinion.

*So ordered.*

**JUSTICE SCALIA, with whom JUSTICE THOMAS joins, dissenting.**

The Constitution guarantees a defendant who knowingly and voluntarily waives the right to counsel the right to proceed *pro se* at his trial. A mentally ill defendant who knowingly and voluntarily elects to proceed *pro se* instead of through counsel receives a fair trial that comports with the Fourteenth Amendment. The Court today concludes that a State may nonetheless strip a mentally ill defendant of the right to represent himself when that would be fairer. In my view the Constitution does not permit a State to substitute its own perception of fairness for the defendant's right to make his own case before the jury—a specific right long understood as essential to a fair trial.

I.

Ahmad Edwards suffers from schizophrenia, an illness that has manifested itself in different ways over time, depending on how and whether Edwards was treated as well as on other factors that appear harder to identify. In the years between 2000 and 2003—years in which Edwards was apparently not treated with the antipsychotic medications and other drugs that are commonly prescribed for his illness—Edwards was repeatedly declared incompetent to stand trial. Even during this period, however, his mental state seems to have fluctuated. For instance, one psychiatrist in March 2001 described Edwards in a competency report as "free of psychosis, depression, mania, and confusion," "alert, oriented, [and] appropriate," apparently "able to think clearly" and apparently "psychiatrically normal."

Edwards seems to have been treated with antipsychotic medication for the first time in 2004. He was found competent to stand trial the same year. The psychiatrist making the recommendation described Edwards' thought processes as "coherent" and wrote that he "communicate[d] very well," that his speech was "easy to understand," that he displayed "good communications skills, cooperative attitude, average intelligence, and good cognitive functioning," that he could "appraise the roles of the participants in the courtroom proceedings," and that he had the capacity to challenge prosecution witnesses realistically and to testify relevantly.

. . . Edwards sought to act as his own lawyer. He filed a number of incoherent written pleadings with the judge on which the Court places emphasis, but he also filed several intelligible pleadings, such as a motion to dismiss counsel, a motion to dismiss charges under the Indiana speedy trial provision, and a motion seeking a trial transcript.

Edwards made arguments in the courtroom that were more coherent than his written pleadings. In seeking to represent himself at his first trial, Edwards complained in detail that the attorney representing him had not spent adequate time preparing and was not sharing legal materials for use in his defense. The trial judge concluded that Edwards had knowingly and voluntarily waived his right to counsel and proceeded to quiz Edwards about matters of state law. Edwards correctly answered questions about the meaning of *voir dire* and how it operated, and described the basic framework for admitting videotape evidence to trial, though he was unable to answer other questions, including questions about the topics covered by state evidentiary rules that the judge identified only by number. He persisted in his request to represent himself, but the judge denied the request because Edwards acknowledged he would need a continuance. Represented by counsel, he was convicted of criminal recklessness and theft, but the jury deadlocked on charges of attempted murder and battery.

At his second trial, Edwards again asked the judge to be allowed to proceed *pro se*. He explained that he and his attorney disagreed about which defense to present to the attempted murder charge. Edwards' counsel favored lack of intent to kill; Edwards, self-defense. As the defendant put it: "My objection is me and my attorney actually had discussed a defense, I think prosecution had mentioned that, and we are in disagreement with it. He has a defense and I have a defense that I would like to represent or present to the Judge."

The court again rejected Edwards' request to proceed *pro se,* and this time it did not have the justification that Edwards had sought a continuance. The court did not dispute that Edwards knowingly and intelligently waived his right to counsel, but stated it was "going to carve out a third exception" to the right of self-representation, and—without explaining precisely what abilities Edwards lacked—stated Edwards was "competent to stand trial but I'm not going to find he's competent to defend himself." Edwards sought—by a request through counsel and by raising an objection in open court—to address the judge on the matter, but the judge refused, stating that the issue had already been decided. Edwards' court-appointed attorney pursued the defense the attorney judged best—lack of intent, not self-defense—and Edwards was convicted of both attempted murder and battery. The Supreme Court of Indiana held that he was entitled to a new trial because he had been denied the right to represent himself. The State of Indiana sought certiorari, which we granted.

## II.

### A.

The Constitution guarantees to every criminal defendant the "right to proceed *without* counsel when he voluntarily and intelligently elects to do so." The right reflects "a nearly universal conviction, on the part of our people as well as our courts, that forcing a lawyer upon an unwilling defendant is contrary to his basic right to defend himself if he truly wants to do so." *Faretta's* discussion of the history of the right, includes the observation that "[i]n the long history of British criminal jurisprudence, there was only one tribunal that ever adopted a practice of forcing counsel upon an unwilling defendant in a criminal proceeding. The tribunal was the Star Chamber." *Faretta* described the right to proceed *pro se* as a premise of the Sixth Amendment, which confers the tools for a defense on the "accused," and describes the role of the attorney as one of "assistance." The right of self-representation could also be seen as a part of the traditional meaning of the Due Process Clause. Whichever provision provides its source, it means that a State simply may not force a lawyer upon a criminal defendant who wishes to conduct his own defense.

Exercising the right of self-representation requires waiving the right to counsel. A defendant may represent himself only when he "knowingly and intelligently" waives the lawyer's assistance that is guaranteed by the Sixth Amendment. He must "be made aware of the dangers and disadvantages of self-representation," and the record must "establish that 'he knows what he is doing and his choice is made with eyes open.'" This limitation may be relevant to many mentally ill defendants, but there is no dispute that Edwards was not one of them. Edwards was warned extensively of the risks of proceeding *pro se*. The trial judge found that Edwards had "knowingly and voluntarily" waived his right to counsel at his first trial and at his second trial the judge denied him the right to represent himself only by "carv[ing] out" a new "exception" to the right beyond the standard of knowing and voluntary waiver.

When a defendant appreciates the risks of forgoing counsel and chooses to do so voluntarily, the Constitution protects his ability to present his own defense even when that harms his case. In fact waiving counsel "usually" does so. We have nonetheless said that the defendant's "choice must be honored out of 'that respect for the individual which is the lifeblood of the law.' " What the Constitution requires is not that a State's case be subject to the most rigorous adversarial testing possible—after all, it permits a defendant to eliminate *all* adversarial testing by pleading guilty. What the Constitution requires is that a defendant be given the right to challenge the State's case against him using the arguments *he* sees fit.

In *Godinez*, we held that the Due Process Clause posed no barrier to permitting a defendant who suffered from mental illness both to waive his right to counsel and to plead guilty, so long as he was competent to stand trial and knowingly and voluntarily waived trial and the counsel right. It was "never the rule at common law" that a defendant could be competent to stand trial and yet incompetent to either exercise or give up some of the rights provided for his defense. We rejected the invitation to craft a higher competency standard for waiving counsel than for standing trial. That proposal, we said, was built on the "flawed premise" that a defendant's "competence to represent himself" was the relevant measure: "[T]he competence that is required of a defendant seeking to waive his right to counsel is the competence to *waive the right*, not the competence to represent himself." We grounded this on *Faretta*'s candid acknowledgment that the Sixth Amendment protected the defendant's right to conduct a defense to his disadvantage.

### B.

The Court is correct that this case presents a variation on *Godinez*. It presents the question not whether another constitutional requirement (in *Godinez*, the proposed higher degree of competence required for a waiver) limits a defendant's constitutional right to elect self-representation, but whether a State's view of fairness (or of other values) permits it to strip the defendant of this right. But that makes the question before us an easier one. While one constitutional requirement must yield to another in case of conflict, nothing permits a State, because of *its* view of what is fair, to deny a constitutional protection. Although "the purpose of the rights set forth in [the Sixth] Amendment is to ensure a fair trial," it "does not follow that the rights can be disregarded so long as the trial is, on the whole, fair." Thus, although the Confrontation Clause aims to produce fairness by ensuring the reliability of testimony, States may not provide for unconfronted testimony to be used at trial so long as it is reliable. *Crawford v. Washington*, 541 U.S. 36 (2004). . . .

Until today, the right of self-representation has been accorded the same respect as other constitutional guarantees. The only circumstance in which we have permitted the State to deprive a defendant of this trial right is the one under which we have allowed the State to deny *other* such rights: when it is necessary to enable the trial to proceed in an orderly fashion. That overriding necessity, we have said, justifies forfeiture of even the Sixth Amendment right to be present at trial—if, after being threatened with removal, a defendant "insists on conducting himself in a manner so disorderly, disruptive, and disrespectful of the court that his trial cannot be carried on with him in the courtroom." *Illinois v. Allen,* 397 U.S. 337 (1970). A *pro se* defendant may not "abuse the dignity of the courtroom," nor may he fail to "comply with relevant rules of procedural and substantive law," and a court may "terminate" the self-representation of a defendant who "deliberately engages in serious and obstructionist misconduct." This ground for terminating self-representation is unavailable here, however, because Edwards was not even allowed to begin to represent himself, and because he was respectful and compliant and did not provide a basis to conclude a trial could not have gone forward had he been allowed to press his own claims.

Beyond this circumstance, we have never constrained the ability of a defendant to retain "actual control over the case he chooses to present to the jury"—what we have termed "the core of the *Faretta* right." Thus, while *Faretta* recognized that the right of self-representation does not bar the court from appointing standby counsel, we explained in *Wiggins* that "[t]he *pro se* defendant must be allowed to control the organization and content of his own defense, to make motions, to argue points of law, to participate in *voir dire,* to question witnesses, and to address the court and the jury at appropriate points in the trial." . . .

As I have explained, I would not adopt an approach to the right of self-representation that we have squarely rejected for other rights—allowing courts to disregard the right when doing so serves the purposes for which the right was intended. But if I were to adopt such an approach, I would remain in dissent, because I believe the Court's assessment of the purposes of the right of self-representation is inaccurate to boot. While there is little doubt that preserving individual "dignity" (to which the Court refers), is paramount among those purposes, there is equally little doubt that the loss of "dignity" the right is designed to prevent is *not* the defendant's making a fool of himself by presenting an amateurish or even incoherent defense. Rather, the dignity at issue is the supreme human dignity of being master of one's fate rather than a ward of the State—the dignity of individual choice. . . . In sum, if the Court is to honor the particular conception of "dignity" that underlies the self-representation right, it should respect the autonomy of the individual by honoring his choices knowingly and voluntarily made.

A further purpose that the Court finds is advanced by denial of the right of self-representation is the purpose of ensuring that trials "appear fair to all who observe them." To my knowledge we have never denied a defendant a right simply on the ground that it would make his trial appear less "fair" to outside observers, and I would not inaugurate that principle here. But were I to do so, I would not apply it to deny a defendant the right to represent himself when he knowingly and voluntarily waives counsel. When Edwards stood to say that "I have a defense that I would like to represent or present to the Judge," it seems to me the epitome of both actual and apparent unfairness for the judge to say, I have heard "your desire to proceed by yourself and I've denied your request, so your attorney will speak for you from now on."

### III.

It may be that the Court permits a State to deprive mentally ill defendants of a historic component of a fair trial because it is suspicious of the constitutional footing of the right of self-representation itself. The right is not explicitly set forth in the text of the Sixth Amendment, and some Members of this Court have expressed skepticism about *Faretta*'s holding.

While the Sixth Amendment makes no mention of the right to forgo counsel, it provides the defendant, and not his lawyer, the right to call witnesses in his defense and to confront witnesses against him, and counsel is permitted to assist in "*his* defence." Our trial system, however, allows the attorney representing a defendant "full authority to manage the conduct of the trial"—an authority without which "[t]he adversary process could not function effectively." We have held that "the client must accept the consequences of the lawyer's decision to forgo cross-examination, to decide not to put certain witnesses on the stand, or to decide not to disclose the identity of certain witnesses in advance of trial." Thus, in order for the defendant's right to call his own witnesses, to cross-examine witnesses, and to put on a defense to be anything more than "a tenuous and unacceptable legal fiction," a defendant must have consented to the representation of counsel. Otherwise, "the defense presented is not the defense guaranteed him by the Constitution, for, in a very real sense, it is not *his* defense."

The facts of this case illustrate this point with the utmost clarity. Edwards wished to take a self-defense case to the jury. His counsel preferred a defense that focused on lack of intent. Having been denied the right to conduct his own defense, Edwards was convicted without having had the opportunity to present to the jury the grounds he believed supported his innocence. I do not doubt that he likely would have been convicted anyway. But to hold that a defendant may be deprived of the right to make legal arguments for acquittal simply because a state-selected agent has made different arguments on his behalf is, as Justice Frankfurter wrote. . .to "imprison a man in his privileges and call it the Constitution." In singling out mentally ill defendants for this treatment, the Court's opinion does not even have the questionable virtue of being politically correct. At a time when all society is trying to mainstream the mentally impaired, the Court permits them to be deprived of a basic constitutional right—for their own good.

Today's holding is extraordinarily vague. The Court does not accept Indiana's position that self-representation can be denied " 'where the defendant cannot communicate coherently with the court or a jury.' " It does not even hold that Edwards was properly denied his right to represent himself. It holds only that lack of mental competence can under some circumstances form a basis for denying the right to proceed *pro se*. We will presumably give some meaning to this holding in the future, but the indeterminacy makes a bad holding worse. Once the right of self-representation for the mentally ill is a sometime thing, trial judges will have every incentive to make their lives easier—to avoid the painful necessity of deciphering occasional pleadings of the sort contained in the Appendix to today's opinion—by appointing knowledgeable and literate counsel.

Because I think a defendant who is competent to stand trial, and who is capable of knowing and voluntary waiver of assistance of counsel, has a constitutional right to conduct his own defense, I respectfully dissent.

## After preparing the case brief, consider the answers to the following questions:

1.   What is the constitutional foundation for the right of self-representation?

2.   What must be true in order for a defendant to waive his right to be represented by counsel?

3.   Should all criminal defendants have the right to be "master of their own fate" as the dissent argues? Do you agree?

## NIX V. WHITESIDE

Supreme Court of the United States
Argued Nov. 5, 1985
Decided Feb. 26, 1986
475 U.S. 157

**OPINION**

**CHIEF JUSTICE BURGER delivered the opinion of the Court.**

We granted certiorari to decide whether the Sixth Amendment right of a criminal defendant to assistance of counsel is violated when an attorney refuses to cooperate with the defendant in presenting perjured testimony at his trial.[1]

### I

### A

Whiteside was convicted of second-degree murder by a jury verdict which was affirmed by the Iowa courts. The killing took place on February 8, 1977, in Cedar Rapids, Iowa. Whiteside and two others went to one Calvin Love's apartment late that night, seeking marihuana. Love was in bed when Whiteside and his companions arrived; an argument between Whiteside and Love over the marihuana ensued. At one point, Love directed his girlfriend to get his "piece," and at another point got up, then returned to his bed. According to Whiteside's testimony, Love then started to reach under his pillow and moved toward Whiteside. Whiteside stabbed Love in the chest, inflicting a fatal wound.

Whiteside was charged with murder, and when counsel was appointed he objected to the lawyer initially appointed, claiming that he felt uncomfortable with a lawyer who had formerly been a prosecutor. Gary L. Robinson was then appointed and immediately began an investigation. Whiteside gave him a statement that he had stabbed Love as the latter "was pulling a pistol from underneath the pillow on the bed." Upon questioning by Robinson, however, Whiteside indicated that he had not actually seen a gun, but that he was convinced that Love had a gun. No pistol was found on the premises; shortly after the police search following the stabbing, which had revealed no weapon, the victim's family had removed all of the victim's possessions from the apartment. Robinson interviewed Whiteside's companions who were present

---

[1] Although courts universally condemn an attorney's assisting in presenting perjury, Courts of Appeals have taken varying approaches on how to deal with a client's insistence on presenting perjured testimony. The Seventh Circuit, for example, has held that an attorney's refusal to call the defendant as a witness did not render the conviction constitutionally infirm where the refusal to call the defendant was based on the attorney's belief that the defendant would commit perjury. The Third Circuit found a violation of the Sixth Amendment where the attorney could not state any basis for her belief that defendant's proposed alibi testimony was perjured.

during the stabbing, and none had seen a gun during the incident. Robinson advised Whiteside that the existence of a gun was not necessary to establish the claim of self-defense, and that only a reasonable belief that the victim had a gun nearby was necessary even though no gun was actually present.

Until shortly before trial, Whiteside consistently stated to Robinson that he had not actually seen a gun, but that he was convinced that Love had a gun in his hand. About a week before trial, during preparation for direct examination, Whiteside for the first time told Robinson and his associate Donna Paulsen that he had seen something "metallic" in Love's hand. When asked about this, Whiteside responded:

> "[I]n Howard Cook's case there was a gun. If I don't say I saw a gun, I'm dead."

Robinson told Whiteside that such testimony would be perjury and repeated that it was not necessary to prove that a gun was available but only that Whiteside reasonably believed that he was in danger. On Whiteside's insisting that he would testify that he saw "something metallic" Robinson told him, according to Robinson's testimony:

> "[W]e could not allow him to [testify falsely] because that would be perjury, and as officers of the court we would be suborning perjury if we allowed him to do it; . . . I advised him that if he did do that it would be my duty to advise the Court of what he was doing and that I felt he was committing perjury; also, that I probably would be allowed to attempt to impeach that particular testimony."

Robinson also indicated he would seek to withdraw from the representation if Whiteside insisted on committing perjury.

Whiteside testified in his own defense at trial and stated that he "knew" that Love had a gun and that he believed Love was reaching for a gun and he had acted swiftly in self-defense. On cross-examination, he admitted that he had not actually seen a gun in Love's hand. Robinson presented evidence that Love had been seen with a sawed-off shotgun on other occasions, that the police search of the apartment may have been careless, and that the victim's family had removed everything from the apartment shortly after the crime. Robinson presented this evidence to show a basis for Whiteside's asserted fear that Love had a gun.

The jury returned a verdict of second-degree murder, and Whiteside moved for a new trial, claiming that he had been deprived of a fair trial by Robinson's admonitions not to state that he saw a gun or "something metallic."

The trial court held a hearing, heard testimony by Whiteside and Robinson, and denied the motion. The trial court made specific findings that the facts were as related by Robinson.

The Supreme Court of Iowa affirmed respondent's conviction. That court held that the right to have counsel present all appropriate defenses does not extend to using perjury, and that an attorney's duty to a client does not extend to assisting a client in committing perjury. Relying on. . .the Iowa Code of Professional Responsibility for Lawyers, which expressly prohibits an attorney from using perjured testimony, and Iowa Code § 721.2. . .which criminalizes subornation of perjury, the Iowa court concluded that not only were Robinson's actions permissible, but were required. The court commended "both Mr. Robinson and Ms. Paulsen for the high ethical manner in which this matter was handled."

Whiteside then petitioned for a writ of habeas corpus. . . In that petition Whiteside alleged that he had been denied effective assistance of counsel and of his right to present a defense by Robinson's refusal to allow him to testify as he had proposed. The District Court denied the writ. Accepting the state trial court's factual finding that Whiteside's intended testimony would have been perjurious, it concluded that there could be no grounds for habeas relief since there is no constitutional right to present a perjured defense.

The United States Court of Appeals for the Eighth Circuit reversed and directed that the writ of habeas corpus be granted. The Court of Appeals accepted the findings of the trial judge, affirmed by the Iowa Supreme Court, that trial counsel believed with good cause that Whiteside would testify falsely and acknowledged that under *Harris v. New York,* 401 U.S. 222 (1971), a criminal defendant's privilege to testify in his own behalf does not include a right to commit perjury. Nevertheless, the court reasoned that an intent to commit perjury, communicated to counsel, does not alter a defendant's right to effective assistance of counsel and that Robinson's admonition to Whiteside that he would inform the court of Whiteside's perjury constituted a threat to violate the attorney's duty to preserve client confidences. According to the Court of Appeals, this threatened violation of client confidences breached the standards of effective representation set down in *Strickland v. Washington.* The court also concluded that *Strickland's* prejudice requirement was satisfied by an implication of prejudice from the conflict between Robinson's duty of loyalty to his client and his ethical duties. A petition for rehearing en banc was denied. . . We granted certiorari, and we reverse.

## II

### A

The right of an accused to testify in his defense is of relatively recent origin. Until the latter part of the preceding century, criminal defendants in this country, as at common law, were considered to be disqualified from giving sworn testimony at their own trial by reason of their interest as a party to the case. Iowa was among the states that adhered to this rule of disqualification.

By the end of the 19th century, however, the disqualification was finally abolished by statute in most states and in the federal courts. Although this Court has never explicitly held that a criminal defendant has a due process right to testify in his own behalf, cases in several Circuits have so held, and the right has long been assumed. We have also suggested that such a right exists as a corollary to the Fifth Amendment privilege against compelled testimony.

### B

In *Strickland v. Washington,* we held that to obtain relief by way of federal habeas corpus on a claim of a deprivation of effective assistance of counsel under the Sixth Amendment, the movant must establish both serious attorney error and prejudice. To show such error, it must be established that the assistance rendered by counsel was constitutionally deficient in that "counsel made errors so serious that counsel was not functioning as 'counsel' guaranteed the defendant by the Sixth Amendment." To show prejudice, it must be established that the claimed lapses in counsel's performance rendered the trial unfair so as to "undermine confidence in the outcome" of the trial.

In *Strickland,* we acknowledged that the Sixth Amendment does not require any particular response by counsel to a problem that may arise. Rather, the Sixth Amendment inquiry is into whether the attorney's conduct was "reasonably effective." To counteract the natural tendency to fault an unsuccessful defense, a court reviewing a claim of ineffective assistance must "indulge a strong presumption that counsel's conduct falls within the wide range of reasonable professional assistance." In giving shape to the perimeters of this range of reasonable professional assistance, *Strickland* mandates that

> "[p]revailing norms of practice as reflected in American Bar Association Standards and the like, . . . are guides to determining what is reasonable, but they are only guides."

Under the *Strickland* standard, breach of an ethical standard does not necessarily make out a denial of the Sixth Amendment guarantee of assistance of counsel.

When examining attorney conduct, a court must be careful not to narrow the wide range of conduct acceptable under the Sixth Amendment so restrictively as to constitutionalize particular standards of professional conduct and thereby intrude into the state's proper authority to define and apply the standards of professional conduct applicable to those it admits to practice in its courts. In some future case challenging attorney conduct in the course of a state-court trial, we may need to define with greater precision the weight to be given to recognized canons of ethics, the standards established by the state in statutes or professional codes, and the Sixth Amendment, in defining the proper scope and limits on that conduct. Here we need not face that question, since virtually all of the sources speak with one voice.

## C

We turn next to the question presented: the definition of the range of "reasonable professional" responses to a criminal defendant client who informs counsel that he will perjure himself on the stand. We must determine whether, in this setting, Robinson's conduct fell within the wide range of professional responses to threatened client perjury acceptable under the Sixth Amendment.

In *Strickland,* we recognized counsel's duty of loyalty and his "overarching duty to advocate the defendant's cause." Plainly, that duty is limited to legitimate, lawful conduct compatible with the very nature of a trial as a search for truth. Although counsel must take all reasonable lawful means to attain the objectives of the client, counsel is precluded from taking steps or in any way assisting the client in presenting false evidence or otherwise violating the law. This principle has consistently been recognized in most unequivocal terms by expositors of the norms of professional conduct since the first Canons of Professional Ethics were adopted by the American Bar Association in 1908. . . .

These principles have been carried through to contemporary codifications of an attorney's professional responsibility. Disciplinary Rule 7–102 of the Model Code of Professional Responsibility (1980), entitled "Representing a Client Within the Bounds of the Law," provides:

"(A) In his representation of a client, a lawyer shall not:

. . .

"(4) Knowingly use perjured testimony or false evidence.

. . .

"(7) Counsel or assist his client in conduct that the lawyer knows to be illegal or fraudulent."

This provision has been adopted by Iowa, and is binding on all lawyers who appear in its courts. See Iowa Code of Professional Responsibility for Lawyers (1985). The more recent Model Rules of Professional Conduct (1983) similarly admonish attorneys to obey all laws in the course of representing a client:

> "*RULE 1.2*   Scope of Representation
>
> "(d) A lawyer shall not counsel a client to engage, or assist a client, in conduct that the lawyer knows is criminal or fraudulent. . . ."

Both the Model Code of Professional Responsibility and the Model Rules of Professional Conduct also adopt the specific exception from the attorney-client privilege for disclosure of perjury that his client intends to commit or has committed. DR 4–101(C)(3) (intention of client to commit a crime); Rule 3.3 (lawyer has duty to disclose falsity of evidence even if disclosure compromises client confidences). Indeed, both the Model Code and the Model Rules do not merely *authorize* disclosure by counsel of client perjury; they *require* such disclosure.

These standards confirm that the legal profession has accepted that an attorney's ethical duty to advance the interests of his client is limited by an equally solemn duty to comply with the law and standards of professional conduct; it specifically ensures that the client may not use false evidence. This special duty of an attorney to prevent and disclose frauds upon the court derives from the recognition that perjury is as much a crime as tampering with witnesses or jurors by way of promises and threats, and undermines the administration of justice.

The offense of perjury was a crime recognized at common law, and has been made a felony in most states by statute, including Iowa. An attorney who aids false testimony by questioning a witness when perjurious responses can be anticipated risks prosecution for subornation of perjury. . .

It is universally agreed that at a minimum the attorney's first duty when confronted with a proposal for perjurious testimony is to attempt to dissuade the client from the unlawful course of conduct. A statement directly in point is found in the commentary to the Model Rules of Professional Conduct under the heading "False Evidence":

> "When false evidence is offered by the client, however, a conflict may arise between the lawyer's duty to keep the client's revelations

confidential and the duty of candor to the court. Upon ascertaining that material evidence is false, the lawyer *should seek to persuade the client that the evidence should not be offered* or, if it has been offered, that its false character should immediately be disclosed."

The commentary thus also suggests that an attorney's revelation of his client's perjury to the court is a professionally responsible and acceptable response to the conduct of a client who has actually given perjured testimony. Similarly, the Model Rules and the commentary, as well as the Code of Professional Responsibility adopted in Iowa, expressly permit withdrawal from representation as an appropriate response of an attorney when the client threatens to commit perjury. Withdrawal of counsel when this situation arises at trial gives rise to many difficult questions including possible mistrial and claims of double jeopardy.[6]

The essence of the brief *amicus* of the American Bar Association reviewing practices long accepted by ethical lawyers is that under no circumstance may a lawyer either advocate or passively tolerate a client's giving false testimony. This, of course, is consistent with the governance of trial conduct in what we have long called "a search for truth." The suggestion sometimes made that "a lawyer must believe his client, not judge him" in no sense means a lawyer can honorably be a party to or in any way give aid to presenting known perjury.

### D

Considering Robinson's representation of respondent in light of these accepted norms of professional conduct, we discern no failure to adhere to reasonable professional standards that would in any sense make out a deprivation of the Sixth Amendment right to counsel. Whether Robinson's conduct is seen as a successful attempt to dissuade his client from committing the crime of perjury, or whether seen as a "threat" to withdraw from representation and disclose the illegal scheme, Robinson's representation of

---

[6] In the evolution of the contemporary standards promulgated by the American Bar Association, an early draft reflects a compromise suggesting that when the disclosure of intended perjury is made during the course of trial, when withdrawal of counsel would raise difficult questions of a mistrial holding, counsel had the option to let the defendant take the stand but decline to affirmatively assist the presentation of perjury by traditional direct examination. Instead, counsel would stand mute while the defendant undertook to present the false version in narrative form in his own words unaided by any direct examination. This conduct was thought to be a signal at least to the presiding judge that the attorney considered the testimony to be false and was seeking to disassociate himself from that course. Additionally, counsel would not be permitted to discuss the known false testimony in closing arguments.

Most courts treating the subject rejected this approach and insisted on a more rigorous standard. The Eighth Circuit in this case and the Ninth Circuit have expressed approval of the "free narrative" standards. The Rule finally promulgated in the current Model Rules of Professional Conduct rejects any participation or passive role whatever by counsel in allowing perjury to be presented without challenge.

Whiteside falls well within accepted standards of professional conduct and the range of reasonable professional conduct acceptable under *Strickland*.

The Court of Appeals assumed for the purpose of the decision that Whiteside would have given false testimony had counsel not intervened; its opinion denying a rehearing en banc states:

> "[W]e presume that appellant would have testified falsely.
>
> ". . . Counsel's actions prevented [Whiteside] from testifying falsely. We hold that counsel's action deprived appellant of due process and effective assistance of counsel.
>
> . . .
>
> "Counsel's actions also impermissibly compromised appellant's right to testify in his own defense by conditioning continued representation by counsel and confidentiality upon appellant's restricted testimony."

While purporting to follow Iowa's highest court "on all questions of state law," the Court of Appeals reached its conclusions on the basis of federal constitutional due process and right to counsel.

The Court of Appeals' holding that Robinson's "action deprived [Whiteside] of due process and effective assistance of counsel" is not supported by the record since Robinson's action, at most, deprived Whiteside of his contemplated perjury. Nothing counsel did in any way undermined Whiteside's claim that he believed the victim was reaching for a gun. Similarly, the record gives no support for holding that Robinson's action "also impermissibly compromised [Whiteside's] right to testify in his own defense by conditioning continued representation . . . and confidentiality upon [Whiteside's] *restricted* testimony." The record in fact shows the contrary: (a) that Whiteside did testify, and (b) he was "restricted" or restrained only from testifying falsely and was aided by Robinson in developing the basis for the fear that Love was reaching for a gun. Robinson divulged no client communications until he was compelled to do so in response to Whiteside's post-trial challenge to the quality of his performance. We see this as a case in which the attorney successfully dissuaded the client from committing the crime of perjury.

Paradoxically, even while accepting the conclusion of the Iowa trial court that Whiteside's proposed testimony would have been a criminal act, the Court of Appeals held that Robinson's efforts to persuade Whiteside not to commit that crime were improper, *first*, as forcing an impermissible choice between the right to counsel and the right to testify; and, *second*, as compromising client confidences because of Robinson's threat to disclose the contemplated perjury.[7]

Whatever the scope of a constitutional right to testify, it is elementary that such a right does not extend to testifying *falsely*. In *Harris v. New York,* we assumed the right of an accused to testify "in his own defense, or to refuse to do so" and went on to hold:

> "[T]hat privilege cannot be construed to include the right to commit perjury. Having voluntarily taken the stand, petitioner was under an obligation to speak truthfully. . . ."

In *Harris* we held the defendant could be impeached by prior contrary statements which had been ruled inadmissible under *Miranda v. Arizona. Harris* and other cases make it crystal clear that there is no right whatever—constitutional or otherwise—for a defendant to use false evidence.

The paucity of authority on the subject of any such "right" may be explained by the fact that such a notion has never been responsibly advanced; the right to counsel includes no right to have a lawyer who will cooperate with planned perjury. A lawyer who would so cooperate would be at risk of prosecution for suborning perjury, and disciplinary proceedings, including suspension or disbarment.

Robinson's admonitions to his client can in no sense be said to have forced respondent into an *impermissible* choice between his right to counsel and his right to testify as he proposed for there was no *permissible* choice to testify falsely. For defense counsel to take steps to persuade a criminal defendant to testify truthfully, or to withdraw, deprives the defendant of neither his right to counsel nor the right to testify truthfully. In *United States v. Havens,* we made clear that "when defendants testify, they must testify truthfully or suffer the consequences." When an accused proposes to resort to perjury or to produce false evidence, one consequence is the risk of withdrawal of counsel.

On this record, the accused enjoyed continued representation within the bounds of reasonable professional conduct and did in fact exercise his right to testify; at most he was denied the right to have the assistance of counsel in the presentation of false testimony. Similarly, we can discern no breach of

---

[7] The Court of Appeals also determined that Robinson's efforts to persuade Whiteside to testify truthfully constituted an impermissible threat to testify against his own client. We find no support for a threat to testify against Whiteside while he was acting as counsel. The record reflects testimony by Robinson that he had admonished Whiteside that if he withdrew he "probably would be allowed to attempt to impeach that particular testimony," if Whiteside testified falsely. The trial court accepted this version of the conversation as true.

professional duty in Robinson's admonition to respondent that he would disclose respondent's perjury to the court. The crime of perjury in this setting is indistinguishable in substance from the crime of threatening or tampering with a witness or a juror. A defendant who informed his counsel that he was arranging to bribe or threaten witnesses or members of the jury would have no "right" to insist on counsel's assistance or silence. Counsel would not be limited to advising against that conduct. An attorney's duty of confidentiality, which totally covers the client's admission of guilt, does not extend to a client's announced plans to engage in future criminal conduct. In short, the responsibility of an ethical lawyer, as an officer of the court and a key component of a system of justice, dedicated to a search for truth, is essentially the same whether the client announces an intention to bribe or threaten witnesses or jurors or to commit or procure perjury. No system of justice worthy of the name can tolerate a lesser standard.

The rule adopted by the Court of Appeals, which seemingly would require an attorney to remain silent while his client committed perjury, is wholly incompatible with the established standards of ethical conduct and the laws of Iowa and contrary to professional standards promulgated by that State. The position advocated by petitioner, on the contrary, is wholly consistent with the Iowa standards of professional conduct and law, with the overwhelming majority of courts, and with codes of professional ethics. Since there has been no breach of any recognized professional duty, it follows that there can be no deprivation of the right to assistance of counsel under the *Strickland* standard.

E

We hold that, as a matter of law, counsel's conduct complained of here cannot establish the prejudice required for relief under the second strand of the *Strickland* inquiry. Although a defendant need not establish that the attorney's deficient performance more likely than not altered the outcome in order to establish prejudice under *Strickland,* a defendant must show that "there is a reasonable probability that, but for counsel's unprofessional errors, the result of the proceeding would have been different." According to *Strickland,* "[a] reasonable probability is a probability sufficient to undermine confidence in the outcome." The *Strickland* Court noted that the "benchmark" of an ineffective-assistance claim is the fairness of the adversary proceeding, and that in judging prejudice and the likelihood of a different outcome, "[a] defendant has no entitlement to the luck of a lawless decisionmaker."

Whether he was persuaded or compelled to desist from perjury, Whiteside has no valid claim that confidence in the result of his trial has been diminished by his desisting from the contemplated perjury. Even if we were to assume that the jury might have believed his perjury, it does not follow that Whiteside was prejudiced.

In his attempt to evade the prejudice requirement of *Strickland*, Whiteside relies on cases involving conflicting loyalties of counsel. In *Cuyler v. Sullivan*, we held that a defendant could obtain relief without pointing to a specific prejudicial default on the part of his counsel, provided it is established that the attorney was "actively represent[ing] conflicting interests."

Here, there was indeed a "conflict," but of a quite different kind; it was one imposed on the attorney by the client's proposal to commit the crime of fabricating testimony without which, as he put it, "I'm dead." This is not remotely the kind of conflict of interests dealt with in *Cuyler v. Sullivan*. Even in that case we did not suggest that all multiple representations necessarily resulted in an active conflict rendering the representation constitutionally infirm. If a "conflict" between a client's proposal and counsel's ethical obligation gives rise to a presumption that counsel's assistance was prejudicially ineffective, every guilty criminal's conviction would be suspect if the defendant had sought to obtain an acquittal by illegal means. Can anyone doubt what practices and problems would be spawned by such a rule and what volumes of litigation it would generate?

Whiteside's attorney treated Whiteside's proposed perjury in accord with professional standards, and since Whiteside's truthful testimony could not have prejudiced the result of his trial, the Court of Appeals was in error to direct the issuance of a writ of habeas corpus and must be reversed.

*Reversed. . . .*

**After preparing the case brief, consider the answers to the following questions:**

1. What is the attorney's duty of confidentiality to a client?

2. Why is it important for attorneys to keep client communication confidential?

3. What is required for a defendant to demonstrate ineffective assistance of counsel?

4. Do you agree with the Court's decision that the attorney was not unreasonable or ineffective in this case?

## PADILLA V. KENTUCKY

Supreme Court of the United States
Argued Oct. 13, 2009
Decided March 31, 2010
559 U.S. 356

### JUSTICE STEVENS delivered the opinion of the Court.

Petitioner Jose Padilla, a native of Honduras, has been a lawful permanent resident of the United States for more than 40 years. Padilla served this Nation with honor as a member of the U.S. Armed Forces during the Vietnam War. He now faces deportation after pleading guilty to the transportation of a large amount of marijuana in his tractor-trailer in the Commonwealth of Kentucky.

In this postconviction proceeding, Padilla claims that his counsel not only failed to advise him of this consequence prior to his entering the plea, but also told him that he " 'did not have to worry about immigration status since he had been in the country so long.' " Padilla relied on his counsel's erroneous advice when he pleaded guilty to the drug charges that made his deportation virtually mandatory. He alleges that he would have insisted on going to trial if he had not received incorrect advice from his attorney.

Assuming the truth of his allegations, the Supreme Court of Kentucky denied Padilla postconviction relief without the benefit of an evidentiary hearing. The court held that the Sixth Amendment's guarantee of effective assistance of counsel does not protect a criminal defendant from erroneous advice about deportation because it is merely a "collateral" consequence of his conviction. In its view, neither counsel's failure to advise petitioner about the possibility of removal, nor counsel's incorrect advice, could provide a basis for relief.

We granted certiorari to decide whether, as a matter of federal law, Padilla's counsel had an obligation to advise him that the offense to which he was pleading guilty would result in his removal from this country. We agree with Padilla that constitutionally competent counsel would have advised him that his conviction for drug distribution made him subject to automatic deportation. Whether he is entitled to relief depends on whether he has been prejudiced, a matter that we do not address.

## I

The landscape of federal immigration law has changed dramatically over the last 90 years. While once there was only a narrow class of deportable offenses and judges wielded broad discretionary authority to prevent deportation, immigration reforms over time have expanded the class of deportable offenses and limited the authority of judges to alleviate the harsh consequences of deportation. The "drastic measure" of deportation or removal is now virtually inevitable for a vast number of noncitizens convicted of crimes.

The Nation's first 100 years was "a period of unimpeded immigration." An early effort to empower the President to order the deportation of those immigrants he "judge[d] dangerous to the peace and safety of the United States," was short lived and unpopular. It was not until 1875 that Congress first passed a statute barring convicts and prostitutes from entering the country. In 1891, Congress added to the list of excludable persons those "who have been convicted of a felony or other infamous crime or misdemeanor involving moral turpitude."

The Immigration Act of 1917 (1917 Act) brought "radical changes" to our law. For the first time in our history, Congress made classes of noncitizens deportable based on conduct committed on American soil. Section 19 of the 1917 Act authorized the deportation of "any alien who is hereafter sentenced to imprisonment for a term of one year or more because of conviction in this country of a crime involving moral turpitude, committed within five years after the entry of the alien to the United States . . . ." And § 19 also rendered deportable noncitizen recidivists who commit two or more crimes of moral turpitude at any time after entry. Congress did not, however, define the term "moral turpitude."

While the 1917 Act was "radical" because it authorized deportation as a consequence of certain convictions, the Act also included a critically important procedural protection to minimize the risk of unjust deportation: At the time of sentencing or within 30 days thereafter, the sentencing judge in both state and federal prosecutions had the power to make a recommendation "that such alien shall not be deported." This procedure, known as a judicial recommendation against deportation, or JRAD, had the effect of binding the Executive to prevent deportation; the statute was "consistently . . . interpreted as giving the sentencing judge conclusive authority to decide whether a particular conviction should be disregarded as a basis for deportation." Thus, from 1917 forward, there was no such creature as an automatically deportable offense. Even as the class of deportable offenses expanded, judges retained discretion to ameliorate unjust results on a case-by-case basis.

Although narcotics offenses—such as the offense at issue in this case—provided a distinct basis for deportation as early as 1922, the JRAD procedure was generally available to avoid deportation in narcotics convictions. Except for "technical, inadvertent and insignificant violations of the laws relating to narcotics," it appears that courts treated narcotics offenses as crimes involving moral turpitude for purposes of the 1917 Act's broad JRAD provision.

In light of both the steady expansion of deportable offenses and the significant ameliorative effect of a JRAD, it is unsurprising that, in the wake of *Strickland v. Washington,* 466 U.S. 668 (1984), the Second Circuit held that the Sixth Amendment right to effective assistance of counsel applies to a JRAD request or lack thereof. In its view, seeking a JRAD was "part of the sentencing" process, even if deportation itself is a civil action. Under the Second Circuit's reasoning, the impact of a conviction on a noncitizen's ability to remain in the country was a central issue to be resolved during the sentencing process—not merely a collateral matter outside the scope of counsel's duty to provide effective representation.

However, the JRAD procedure is no longer part of our law. Congress first circumscribed the JRAD provision in the 1952 Immigration and Nationality Act (INA), and in 1990 Congress entirely eliminated it. In 1996, Congress also eliminated the Attorney General's authority to grant discretionary relief from deportation, an authority that had been exercised to prevent the deportation of over 10,000 noncitizens during the 5-year period prior to 1996. Under contemporary law, if a noncitizen has committed a removable offense after the 1996 effective date of these amendments, his removal is practically inevitable but for the possible exercise of limited remnants of equitable discretion vested in the Attorney General to cancel removal for noncitizens convicted of particular classes of offenses. Subject to limited exceptions, this discretionary relief is not available for an offense related to trafficking in a controlled substance.

These changes to our immigration law have dramatically raised the stakes of a noncitizen's criminal conviction. The importance of accurate legal advice for noncitizens accused of crimes has never been more important. These changes confirm our view that, as a matter of federal law, deportation is an integral part—indeed, sometimes the most important part—of the penalty that may be imposed on noncitizen defendants who plead guilty to specified crimes.

## II

Before deciding whether to plead guilty, a defendant is entitled to "the effective assistance of competent counsel." The Supreme Court of Kentucky rejected Padilla's ineffectiveness claim on the ground that the advice he sought about the risk of deportation concerned only collateral matters, *i.e.,* those matters not within the sentencing authority of the state trial court. In its view, "collateral consequences are outside the scope of representation required by the Sixth Amendment," and, therefore, the "failure of defense counsel to advise the defendant of possible deportation consequences is not cognizable as a claim for ineffective assistance of counsel." The Kentucky high court is far from alone in this view.

We, however, have never applied a distinction between direct and collateral consequences to define the scope of constitutionally "reasonable professional assistance" required under *Strickland.* Whether that distinction is appropriate is a question we need not consider in this case because of the unique nature of deportation.

We have long recognized that deportation is a particularly severe "penalty," but it is not, in a strict sense, a criminal sanction. Although removal proceedings are civil in nature, deportation is nevertheless intimately related to the criminal process. Our law has enmeshed criminal convictions and the penalty of deportation for nearly a century. And, importantly, recent changes in our immigration law have made removal nearly an automatic result for a broad class of noncitizen offenders. Thus, we find it "most difficult" to divorce the penalty from the conviction in the deportation context. Moreover, we are quite confident that noncitizen defendants facing a risk of deportation for a particular offense find it even more difficult.

Deportation as a consequence of a criminal conviction is, because of its close connection to the criminal process, uniquely difficult to classify as either a direct or a collateral consequence. The collateral versus direct distinction is thus ill suited to evaluating a *Strickland* claim concerning the specific risk of deportation. We conclude that advice regarding deportation is not categorically removed from the ambit of the Sixth Amendment right to counsel. *Strickland* applies to Padilla's claim.

## III

Under *Strickland,* we first determine whether counsel's representation "fell below an objective standard of reasonableness." Then we ask whether "there is a reasonable probability that, but for counsel's unprofessional errors, the result of the proceeding would have been different." The first prong—constitutional deficiency—is necessarily linked to the practice and expectations of the legal community: "The proper measure of attorney performance remains simply reasonableness under prevailing professional norms." We long have recognized that "[p]revailing norms of practice as reflected in American Bar Association standards and the like . . . are guides to determining what is reasonable . . . ." Although they are "only guides," and not "inexorable commands," these standards may be valuable measures of the prevailing professional norms of effective representation, especially as these standards have been adapted to deal with the intersection of modern criminal prosecutions and immigration law.

The weight of prevailing professional norms supports the view that counsel must advise her client regarding the risk of deportation. "[A]uthorities of every stripe—including the American Bar Association, criminal defense and public defender organizations, authoritative treatises, and state and city bar publications—universally require defense attorneys to advise as to the risk of deportation consequences for non-citizen clients . . . ."

We too have previously recognized that " '[p]reserving the client's right to remain in the United States may be more important to the client than any potential jail sentence.' " Likewise, we have recognized that "preserving the possibility of" discretionary relief from deportation under § 212(c) of the 1952 INA, repealed by Congress in 1996, "would have been one of the principal benefits sought by defendants deciding whether to accept a plea offer or instead to proceed to trial." We expected that counsel who were unaware of the discretionary relief measures would "follo[w] the advice of numerous practice guides" to advise themselves of the importance of this particular form of discretionary relief.

In the instant case, the terms of the relevant immigration statute are succinct, clear, and explicit in defining the removal consequence for Padilla's conviction. See 8 U.S.C. § 1227(a)(2)(B)(i) ("Any alien who at any time after admission has been convicted of a violation of (or a conspiracy or attempt to violate) any law or regulation of a State, the United States or a foreign country relating to a controlled substance. . ., other than a single offense involving possession for one's own use of 30 grams or less of marijuana, is deportable"). Padilla's counsel could have easily determined that his plea would make him eligible for deportation simply from reading the text of the statute, which addresses not some broad classification of crimes but specifically commands removal for all controlled substances convictions except for the most trivial of marijuana possession offenses. Instead, Padilla's counsel provided him false assurance that his conviction would not result in his removal from this country. This is not a hard case in which to find deficiency: The consequences of Padilla's plea could easily be determined from reading the removal statute, his deportation was presumptively mandatory, and his counsel's advice was incorrect.

Immigration law can be complex, and it is a legal specialty of its own. Some members of the bar who represent clients facing criminal charges, in either state or federal court or both, may not be well versed in it. There will, therefore, undoubtedly be numerous situations in which the deportation consequences of a particular plea are unclear or uncertain. The duty of the private practitioner in such cases is more limited. When the law is not succinct and straightforward (as it is in many of the scenarios posited by Justice ALITO), a criminal defense attorney need do no more than advise a noncitizen client that pending criminal charges may carry a risk of adverse immigration consequences. But when the deportation consequence is truly clear, as it was in this case, the duty to give correct advice is equally clear.

Accepting his allegations as true, Padilla has sufficiently alleged constitutional deficiency to satisfy the first prong of *Strickland.* Whether Padilla is entitled to relief on his claim will depend on whether he can satisfy *Strickland*'s second prong, prejudice, a matter we leave to the Kentucky courts to consider in the first instance.

## IV

The Solicitor General has urged us to conclude that *Strickland* applies to Padilla's claim only to the extent that he has alleged affirmative misadvice. In the United States' view, "counsel is not constitutionally required to provide advice on matters that will not be decided in the criminal case . . .," though counsel is required to provide accurate advice if she chooses to discusses these matters.

Respondent and Padilla both find the Solicitor General's proposed rule unpersuasive, although it has support among the lower courts. Kentucky describes these decisions isolating an affirmative misadvice claim as "result-driven, incestuous . . . [, and] completely lacking in legal or rational bases." We do not share that view, but we agree that there is no relevant difference "between an act of commission and an act of omission" in this context.

A holding limited to affirmative misadvice would invite two absurd results. First, it would give counsel an incentive to remain silent on matters of great importance, even when answers are readily available. Silence under these circumstances would be fundamentally at odds with the critical obligation of counsel to advise the client of "the advantages and disadvantages of a plea agreement." When attorneys know that their clients face possible exile from this country and separation from their families, they should not be encouraged to say nothing at all. Second, it would deny a class of clients least able to represent themselves the most rudimentary advice on deportation even when it is readily available. It is quintessentially the duty of counsel to provide her client with available advice about an issue like deportation and the failure to do so "clearly satisfies the first prong of the *Strickland* analysis."

We have given serious consideration to the concerns that the Solicitor General, respondent, and *amici* have stressed regarding the importance of protecting the finality of convictions obtained through guilty pleas. We confronted a similar "floodgates" concern in *Hill*, but nevertheless applied *Strickland* to a claim that counsel had failed to advise the client regarding his parole eligibility before he pleaded guilty.

A flood did not follow in that decision's wake. Surmounting *Strickland*'s high bar is never an easy task. Moreover, to obtain relief on this type of claim, a petitioner must convince the court that a decision to reject the plea bargain would have been rational under the circumstances. There is no reason to doubt that lower courts—now quite experienced with applying *Strickland*—can effectively and efficiently use its framework to separate specious claims from those with substantial merit.

It seems unlikely that our decision today will have a significant effect on those convictions already obtained as the result of plea bargains. For at least the past 15 years, professional norms have generally imposed an obligation on counsel to provide advice on the deportation consequences of a client's plea. We should, therefore, presume that counsel satisfied their obligation to render competent advice at the time their clients considered pleading guilty.

Likewise, although we must be especially careful about recognizing new grounds for attacking the validity of guilty pleas, in the 25 years since we first applied *Strickland* to claims of ineffective assistance at the plea stage, practice has shown that pleas are less frequently the subject of collateral challenges than convictions obtained after a trial. Pleas account for nearly 95% of all criminal convictions. But they account for only approximately 30% of the habeas petitions filed. The nature of relief secured by a successful collateral challenge to a guilty plea—an opportunity to withdraw the plea and proceed to trial— imposes its own significant limiting principle: Those who collaterally attack their guilty pleas lose the benefit of the bargain obtained as a result of the plea. Thus, a different calculus informs whether it is wise to challenge a guilty plea in a habeas proceeding because, ultimately, the challenge may result in a *less favorable* outcome for the defendant, whereas a collateral challenge to a conviction obtained after a jury trial has no similar downside potential.

Finally, informed consideration of possible deportation can only benefit both the State and noncitizen defendants during the plea-bargaining process. By bringing deportation consequences into this process, the defense and prosecution may well be able to reach agreements that better satisfy the interests of both parties. As in this case, a criminal episode may provide the basis for multiple charges, of which only a subset mandate deportation following conviction. Counsel who possess the most rudimentary understanding of the deportation consequences of a particular criminal offense may be able to plea bargain creatively with the prosecutor in order to craft a conviction and sentence that reduce the likelihood of deportation, as by avoiding a conviction for an offense that automatically triggers the removal consequence. At the same time, the threat of deportation may provide the defendant with a powerful incentive to plead guilty to an offense that does not mandate that penalty in exchange for a dismissal of a charge that does.

In sum, we have long recognized that the negotiation of a plea bargain is a critical phase of litigation for purposes of the Sixth Amendment right to effective assistance of counsel. The severity of deportation—"the equivalent of banishment or exile,"—only underscores how critical it is for counsel to inform her noncitizen client that he faces a risk of deportation.

V

It is our responsibility under the Constitution to ensure that no criminal defendant—whether a citizen or not—is left to the "mercies of incompetent counsel." To satisfy this responsibility, we now hold that counsel must inform her client whether his plea carries a risk of deportation. Our longstanding Sixth Amendment precedents, the seriousness of deportation as a consequence of a criminal plea, and the concomitant impact of deportation on families living lawfully in this country demand no less.

Taking as true the basis for his motion for postconviction relief, we have little difficulty concluding that Padilla has sufficiently alleged that his counsel was constitutionally deficient. Whether Padilla is entitled to relief will depend on whether he can demonstrate prejudice as a result thereof, a question we do not reach because it was not passed on below.

The judgment of the Supreme Court of Kentucky is reversed, and the case is remanded for further proceedings not inconsistent with this opinion.

*It is so ordered.*

\* \* \*

**JUSTICE ALITO, with whom THE CHIEF JUSTICE joins, concurring in the judgment.**

I concur in the judgment because a criminal defense attorney fails to provide effective assistance within the meaning of *Strickland v. Washington,* if the attorney misleads a noncitizen client regarding the removal consequences of a conviction. In my view, such an attorney must (1) refrain from unreasonably providing incorrect advice and (2) advise the defendant that a criminal conviction may have adverse immigration consequences and that, if the alien wants advice on this issue, the alien should consult an immigration attorney. I do not agree with the Court that the attorney must attempt to explain what those consequences may be. As the Court concedes, "[i]mmigration law can be complex"; "it is a legal specialty of its own"; and "[s]ome members of the bar who represent clients facing criminal charges, in either state or federal court or both, may not be well versed in it." The Court nevertheless holds that a criminal defense attorney must provide advice in this specialized area in those cases in which the law is "succinct and straightforward"—but not, perhaps, in other situations. This vague, halfway test will lead to much confusion and needless litigation. . . .

In sum, a criminal defense attorney should not be required to provide advice on immigration law, a complex specialty that generally lies outside the scope of a criminal defense attorney's expertise. On the other hand, any competent criminal defense attorney should appreciate the extraordinary importance that the risk of removal might have in the client's determination whether to enter a guilty plea. Accordingly, unreasonable and incorrect information concerning the risk of removal can give rise to an ineffectiveness claim. In addition, silence alone is not enough to satisfy counsel's duty to assist the client. Instead, an alien defendant's Sixth Amendment right to counsel is satisfied if defense counsel advises the client that a conviction may have immigration consequences, that immigration law is a specialized field, that the attorney is not an immigration lawyer, and that the client should consult an immigration specialist if the client wants advice on that subject.

**JUSTICE SCALIA, with whom JUSTICE THOMAS joins, dissenting.**

In the best of all possible worlds, criminal defendants contemplating a guilty plea ought to be advised of all serious collateral consequences of conviction, and surely ought not to be misadvised. The Constitution, however, is not an all-purpose tool for judicial construction of a perfect world; and when we ignore its text in order to make it that, we often find ourselves swinging a sledge where a tack hammer is needed.

The Sixth Amendment guarantees the accused a lawyer "for his defence" against a "criminal prosecutio[n]"—not for sound advice about the collateral consequences of conviction. For that reason, . . . I dissent from the Court's conclusion that the Sixth Amendment requires counsel to provide accurate advice concerning the potential removal consequences of a guilty plea. For the same reasons, but unlike the concurrence, I do not believe that affirmative misadvice about those consequences renders an attorney's assistance in defending against the prosecution constitutionally inadequate; or that the Sixth Amendment requires counsel to warn immigrant defendants that a conviction may render them removable. Statutory provisions can remedy these concerns in a more targeted fashion, and without producing permanent, and legislatively irreparable, overkill. . . .

**After preparing the case brief, consider the answers to the following questions:**

1. What is required for a defendant to demonstrate ineffective assistance of counsel?

2. Which aspect of the *Strickland* test includes advising a defendant regarding immigration status?

3. Why does the Court characterize risks to immigration status as a collateral rather than direct consequence of the defendant's guilty plea?

4. What are some possible risks associated with having criminal defense attorneys advise defendants on immigration status?

## GARZA V. IDAHO

Supreme Court of the United States
Argued Oct. 30, 2018
Decided Feb. 27, 2019
139 S.Ct. 738

### Opinion

### JUSTICE SOTOMAYOR delivered the opinion of the Court.

In *Roe v. Flores-Ortega*, 528 U.S. 470 (2000), this Court held that when an attorney's deficient performance costs a defendant an appeal that the defendant would have otherwise pursued, prejudice to the defendant should be presumed "with no further showing from the defendant of the merits of his underlying claims." *Id.,* at 484, 120 S.Ct. 1029. This case asks whether that rule applies even when the defendant has, in the course of pleading guilty, signed what is often called an "appeal waiver"—that is, an agreement forgoing certain, but not all, possible appellate claims. We hold that the presumption of prejudice recognized in *Flores-Ortega* applies regardless of whether the defendant has signed an appeal waiver.

I

In early 2015, petitioner Gilberto Garza, Jr., signed two plea agreements, each arising from criminal charges brought by the State of Idaho. Each agreement included a clause stating that Garza "waive[d] his right to appeal." App. to Pet. for Cert. 44a, 49a. The Idaho trial court accepted the agreements and sentenced Garza to terms of prison in accordance with the agreements.

Shortly after sentencing, Garza told his trial counsel that he wished to appeal. In the days that followed, he would later attest, Garza "continuously reminded" his attorney of this directive "via phone calls and letters," Record 210, and Garza's trial counsel acknowledged in his own affidavit that Garza had "told me he wanted to appeal the sentence(s) of the court," *id.,* at 151. Garza's trial counsel, however, did not file a notice of appeal. Instead, counsel "informed Mr. Garza that an appeal was problematic because he waived his right to appeal." *Ibid.* The period of time for Garza's appeal to be preserved came and went with no notice having been filed on Garza's behalf.

Roughly four months after sentencing, Garza sought postconviction relief in Idaho state court. As relevant here, Garza alleged that his trial counsel rendered ineffective assistance by failing to file notices of appeal despite Garza's requests. The Idaho trial court denied relief, and both the Idaho Court of Appeals and the Idaho Supreme Court affirmed that decision. See 162 Idaho 791, 793 (2017). The Idaho Supreme Court ruled that Garza, given the appeal waivers, needed to show both deficient performance and resulting prejudice; it concluded that he could not. See *id.*, at 798, 405 P.3d at 583.

In ruling that Garza needed to show prejudice, the Idaho Supreme Court acknowledged that it was aligning itself with the minority position among courts. For example, 8 of the 10 Federal Courts of Appeals to have considered the question have applied *Flores-Ortega*'s presumption of prejudice even when a defendant has signed an appeal waiver. 162 Idaho, at 795, 405 P.3d at 580.

We granted certiorari to resolve the split of authority. 585 U.S. ___, 138 S.Ct. 2649, 201 L.Ed.2d 1048 (2018). We now reverse.

II

A

The Sixth Amendment guarantees criminal defendants "the right . . . to have the Assistance of Counsel for [their] defence." The right to counsel includes " 'the right to the effective assistance of counsel.' " *Strickland v. Washington*, 466 U.S. 668, 686 (1984) (quoting *McMann v. Richardson*, 397 U.S. 759, 771 (1970)). Under *Strickland*, a defendant who claims ineffective assistance of counsel must prove (1) "that counsel's representation fell below an objective standard of reasonableness," and (2) that any such deficiency was "prejudicial to the defense."

"In certain Sixth Amendment contexts," however, "prejudice is presumed." *Ibid.* For example, no showing of prejudice is necessary "if the accused is denied counsel at a critical stage of his trial," *United States v. Cronic*, 466 U.S. 648, 659 (1984), or left "entirely without the assistance of counsel on appeal," *Penson v. Ohio*, 488 U.S. 75, 88 (1988). Similarly, prejudice is presumed "if counsel entirely fails to subject the prosecution's case to meaningful adversarial testing." *Cronic*, 466 U.S. at 659, 104 S.Ct. 2039. And, most relevant here, prejudice is presumed "when counsel's constitutionally deficient performance deprives a defendant of an appeal that he otherwise would have taken." *Flores-Ortega*, 528 U.S. at 484, 120 S.Ct. 1029. We hold today that this final presumption applies even when the defendant has signed an appeal waiver.

B

It is helpful, in analyzing Garza's case, to first address two procedural devices on which the case hinges: appeal waivers and notices of appeal.

1

We begin with the term "appeal waivers." While the term is useful shorthand for clauses like those in Garza's plea agreements, it can misleadingly suggest a monolithic end to all appellate rights. In fact, however, no appeal waiver serves as an absolute bar to all appellate claims.

As courts widely agree, "[a] valid and enforceable appeal waiver . . . only precludes challenges that fall within its scope." *United States v. Hardman*, 778 F.3d 896, 899 (CA11 2014); see also *ibid.*, n. 2 . . . That an appeal waiver does not bar claims outside its scope follows from the fact that, "[a]lthough the analogy may not hold in all respects, plea bargains are essentially contracts." *Puckett v. United States*, 556 U.S. 129, 137 (2009).

As with any type of contract, the language of appeal waivers can vary widely, with some waiver clauses leaving many types of claims unwaived. Additionally, even a waived appellate claim can still go forward if the prosecution forfeits or waives the waiver. *E.g., United States v. Story*, 439 F.3d 226, 231 (CA5 2006). Accordingly, a defendant who has signed an appeal waiver does not, in directing counsel to file a notice of appeal, necessarily undertake a quixotic or frivolous quest.

Separately, all jurisdictions appear to treat at least some claims as unwaiveable. Most fundamentally, courts agree that defendants retain the right to challenge whether the waiver itself is valid and enforceable—for example, on the grounds that it was unknowing or involuntary. Consequently, while signing an appeal waiver means giving up some, many, or even most appellate claims, some claims nevertheless remain.

2

It is also important to consider what it means—and does not mean—for trial counsel to file a notice of appeal.

"Filing such a notice is a purely ministerial task that imposes no great burden on counsel." *Flores-Ortega*, 528 U.S. at 474, 120 S.Ct. 1029. It typically takes place during a compressed window: 42 days in Idaho, for example, and just 14 days in federal court. See Idaho Rule App. Proc. 14(a) (2017); Fed. Rule App. Proc. 4(b)(1)(A). By the time this window has closed, the defendant likely will not yet have important documents from the trial court, such as transcripts of key proceedings, see, *e.g.,* Idaho Rules App. Proc. 19 and 25; Fed. Rule App. Proc. 10(b), and may well be in custody, making communication with counsel difficult, see *Peguero v. United States*, 526 U.S. 23, 26 (1999). And because some defendants receive new counsel for their appeals, the lawyer responsible for deciding which appellate claims to raise may not yet even be involved in the case.

Filing requirements reflect that claims are, accordingly, likely to be ill defined or unknown at this stage. In the federal system, for example, a notice of appeal need only identify who is appealing; what "judgment, order, or part thereof" is being appealed; and "the court to which the appeal is taken." Fed. Rule App. Proc. 3(c)(1). Generally speaking, state requirements are similarly nonsubstantive.

A notice of appeal also fits within a broader division of labor between defendants and their attorneys. While "the accused has the ultimate authority" to decide whether to "take an appeal," the choice of what specific arguments to make within that appeal belongs to appellate counsel. *Jones v. Barnes*, 463 U.S. 745, 751 (1983); see also *McCoy v. Louisiana*, 138 S.Ct. 1500, 1507 (2018). In other words, filing a notice of appeal is, generally speaking, a simple, nonsubstantive act that is within the defendant's prerogative.

C

With that context in mind, we turn to the precise legal issues here. As an initial matter, we note that Garza's attorney rendered deficient performance by not filing the notice of appeal in light of Garza's clear requests. As this Court explained in *Flores-Ortega*:

> "We have long held that a lawyer who disregards specific instructions from the defendant to file a notice of appeal acts in a manner that is professionally unreasonable. This is so because a defendant who instructs counsel to initiate an appeal reasonably relies upon counsel to file the necessary notice. Counsel's failure to do so cannot be considered a strategic decision; filing a notice of appeal is a purely ministerial task, and the failure to file reflects inattention to the defendant's wishes." 528 U.S. at 477, 120 S.Ct. 1029 (citations omitted); see also *id.*, at 478, 120 S.Ct. 1029.

Idaho maintains that the risk of breaching the defendant's plea agreement renders counsel's choice to override the defendant's instructions a strategic one. See *Strickland*, 466 U.S. at 690–691, 104 S.Ct. 2052 ("[S]trategic choices made after thorough investigation of law and facts relevant to plausible options are virtually unchallengeable . . ."). That is not so. While we do not address what constitutes a defendant's breach of an appeal waiver or any responsibility counsel may have to discuss the potential consequences of such a breach, it should be clear from the foregoing that simply filing a notice of appeal does not necessarily breach a plea agreement, given the possibility that the defendant will end up raising claims beyond the waiver's scope. And in any event, the bare decision whether to appeal is ultimately the defendant's, not counsel's, to make. Where, as here, a defendant has expressly requested an appeal, counsel performs deficiently by disregarding the defendant's instructions.

D

We now address the crux of this case: whether *Flores-Ortega*'s presumption of prejudice applies despite an appeal waiver. The holding, principles, and facts of *Flores-Ortega* show why that presumption applies equally here.

With regard to prejudice, *Flores-Ortega* held that, to succeed in an ineffective-assistance claim in this context, a defendant need make only one showing: "that, but for counsel's deficient failure to consult with him about an appeal, he would have timely appealed." So long as a defendant can show that "counsel's constitutionally deficient performance deprive[d him] of an appeal that he otherwise would have taken," courts are to "presum[e] prejudice with no further showing from the defendant of the merits of his underlying claims." *Ibid.* Because there is no dispute here that Garza wished to appeal, direct application of *Flores-Ortega*'s language resolves this case.

*Flores-Ortega*'s reasoning shows why an appeal waiver does not complicate this straightforward application. That case, like this one, involves a lawyer who forfeited an appellate proceeding by failing to file a notice of appeal. As the Court explained, given that past precedents call for a presumption of prejudice whenever " 'the accused is denied counsel at a critical stage,' " it makes even greater sense to presume prejudice when counsel's deficiency forfeits an "appellate proceeding altogether." After all, there is no disciplined way to "accord any 'presumption of reliability'. . . to judicial proceedings that never took place."

That rationale applies just as well here because, as discussed, Garza retained a right to appeal at least some issues despite the waivers he signed. In other words, Garza had a right to a proceeding, and he was denied that proceeding altogether as a result of counsel's deficient performance.

. . .

Instead, we reaffirm that, "when counsel's constitutionally deficient performance deprives a defendant of an appeal that he otherwise would have taken, the defendant has made out a successful ineffective assistance of counsel claim entitling him to an appeal," with no need for a "further showing" of his claims' merit, regardless of whether the defendant has signed an appeal waiver.

III

*Flores-Ortega* states, in one sentence, that the loss of the "entire [appellate] proceeding itself, which a defendant wanted at the time and to which he had a right, . . . demands a presumption of prejudice." *Id.,* at 483, 120 S.Ct. 1029. Idaho and the U.S. Government, participating as an *amicus* on Idaho's behalf, seize on this language, asserting that Garza never "had a right" to his appeal and thus that any deficient performance by counsel could not have caused the loss of any such appeal. See Brief for Respondent 11, 23–26; Brief for United States as *Amicus Curiae* 7, 13, 21–22. These arguments miss the point. Garza did retain a right to his appeal; he simply had fewer possible claims than some other appellants. Especially because so much is unknown at the notice-of-appeal stage, it is wholly speculative to say that counsel's deficiency forfeits no proceeding to which a defendant like Garza has a right.

. . .

This Court has already rejected attempts to condition the restoration of a defendant's appellate rights forfeited by ineffective counsel on proof that the defendant's appeal had merit. In *Flores-Ortega,* the Court explained that prejudice should be presumed "with no further showing from the defendant of the merits of his underlying claims.". . .

Moreover, while it is the defendant's prerogative whether to appeal, it is not the defendant's role to decide what arguments to press. See *Barnes,* 463 U.S. at 751, 754, 103 S.Ct. 3308. That makes it especially improper to impose that role upon the defendant simply because his opportunity to appeal was relinquished by deficient counsel. "Those whose right to appeal has been frustrated should be treated exactly like any other appellants; they should not be given an additional hurdle to clear just because their rights were violated at some earlier stage in the proceedings." *Rodriquez,* 395 U.S. at 330, 89 S.Ct. 1715. We accordingly decline to place a pleading barrier between a defendant and an opportunity to appeal that he never should have lost.

Meanwhile, the Government's assumption that unwaived claims can reliably be distinguished from waived claims through case-by-case postconviction review is dubious. There is no right to counsel in postconviction proceedings, see *Pennsylvania v. Finley,* 481 U.S. 551, 555 (1987), and most applicants proceed *pro se.* That means that the Government effectively puts its faith in asking "an indigent, perhaps *pro se,* defendant to demonstrate that his hypothetical appeal might have had merit before any advocate has ever reviewed the record in his case in search of potentially meritorious grounds for appeal," We have already explained why this would be "unfair" and ill advised. Compounding the trouble, defendants would be asked to make these showings in the face of the heightened standards and related hurdles that attend many postconviction proceedings. See, *e.g.,* 28 U.S.C. §§ 2254, 2255; see also Brief for Idaho Association of Criminal Defense Lawyers et al. as *Amici Curiae* 22–25.

. . .

The more administrable and workable rule, rather, is the one compelled by our precedent: When counsel's deficient performance forfeits an appeal that a defendant otherwise would have taken, the defendant gets a new opportunity to appeal. That is the rule already in use in 8 of the 10 Federal Circuits to have considered the question, and neither Idaho nor its *amici* have pointed us to any evidence that it has proved unmanageable there. That rule does no more than restore the status quo that existed before counsel's deficient performance forfeited the appeal, and it allows an appellate court to consider the appeal as that court otherwise would have done—on direct review, and assisted by counsel's briefing.

IV

We hold today that the presumption of prejudice recognized in *Flores-Ortega* applies regardless of whether a defendant has signed an appeal waiver. This ruling follows squarely from *Flores-Ortega* and from the fact that even the broadest appeal waiver does not deprive a defendant of all appellate claims. Accordingly where, as here, an attorney performed deficiently in failing to file a notice of appeal despite the defendant's express instructions, prejudice is presumed "with no further showing from the defendant of the merits of his underlying claims." See *Flores-Ortega*, 528 U.S. at 484, 120 S.Ct. 1029.

The judgment of the Supreme Court of Idaho is therefore reversed, and the case is remanded for further proceedings not inconsistent with this opinion.

*It is so ordered.*

## After preparing the case brief, consider the answers to the following questions:

1.    What test for proving ineffective assistance of counsel was announced in *Strickland v. Washington*?

2.    In this case, the state argued that counsel's failure to file a petition for the appeal was strategic. If the Court had agreed, how would that have changed the outcome?

3.    What rule does the Court announce in this case for situations where counsel's deficient performance causes the defendant to forfeit an appeal?

## Chapter 5 Key Terms for Review

- **Defense counsel**: an attorney retained or appointed to represent the accused in a criminal trial.

- **Right to appointed counsel**: the Sixth Amendment guarantees the assistance of counsel in criminal cases and if defendants are unable to pay to retain counsel, the court must appoint counsel for them at state expense.

- *Gideon v. Wainwright (1963)*: landmark U.S. Supreme Court decision which incorporated the right to counsel. The Court held the right to counsel is fundamental, requiring appointed counsel for indigent defendants in all state felony cases.

- **Fundamental right**: a right of such significance that it is "implicit in the concept of ordered liberty." A free and democratic society cannot be envisioned without it.

- **Critical stage**: any stage in the criminal judicial process where substantial rights are at issue and there is potential prejudice to the defendant. For example, the appointment of counsel for indigent defendants is required, because proceeding without an attorney risks prejudice to the defendant.

- **Ineffective assistance of counsel**: when defense counsel's performance was deficient and that deficiency resulted in prejudice to the defendant. See *Strickland v. Washington (1984)*.

- **Pro se**: when a defendant chooses to represent him or herself in a criminal trial.

- **Right of self-representation**: the right to proceed without counsel and represent oneself in a criminal trial (guaranteed by the Sixth Amendment). See *Faretta v. California (1975)*.

- **Standby or advisory counsel**: shadow counsel for a pro se defendant who is available to assist them if necessary as they prepare or present their case.

- **Public defenders**: indigent defense attorneys who are salaried government employees.

- **Appointed counsel**: private attorneys who are assigned to represent indigent defendants at an hourly rate.

- **Contract system**: a system for indigent defense where a law firm bids for the contract to provide indigent defense for a period of time.

- **Conflict counsel**: counsel who is available to take over representing a defendant if a conflict of interest is presented such as prior representation of a victim in the case.

- **Structural error**: when a court's error impacts every aspect of the defense. Denial of the defendant's counsel of choice is a structural error.

- **Legal ethics**: rules governing the professional and sometimes personal behavior of licensed attorneys.

- **Duty of confidentiality**: the majority of communication between an attorney and her client is privileged. The attorney has a duty to keep the information confidential.

- **Duty of candor**: attorneys have a duty to be truthful to the court and may not knowingly mislead it, obstruct access to witnesses or evidence, or present false evidence or testimony.

- **Model rules of professional conduct**: the American Bar Association rules governing attorney behavior and ethics.

- **Continuing legal education**: attorneys are required to maintain currency in the field and practice of law by regularly taking continuing legal education courses.

# Judges

## A. THE ROLE OF JUDGES

Judges are the most recognizable of the courtroom actors. Judges are seated on the bench higher than the rest of the people in the court. They wear a black robe and hold a gavel to call the proceedings to order. Their role and position command respect. There are judges who serve in the federal courts and those who serve in state and local courts. There are both trial and appellate judges in both the federal and state courts. The most revered judges in the United States are the **United States Supreme Court Justices**, who are appointed by the president of the United States with the advice and consent (approval) of the U.S. Senate.

## B. TRIAL JUDGES AT WORK

**Trial judges** are responsible for presiding over civil and criminal trials. In local and state court systems they may have different titles such as municipal court judge, county court judge, and justice of the peace. These lower court judges typically handle misdemeanors, traffic, and small claims cases. General trial court judges handle more serious civil and criminal cases in state court. Federal trial court judges are called **district court judges** or Article III Judges and they are assisted by federal **magistrate judges**.

If the trial is a bench trial, one being conducted without a jury, the judge also serves as the fact-finder in the case; requiring them to make decisions about the truthfulness of evidence and claims brought by the litigants. The daily responsibilities of trial judges vary depending upon their calendar assignment. If the judge is assigned to a calendar for civil trials, a single case may run for weeks or even months, and the courtroom action might be fairly slow and quiet. If a judge is assigned to a criminal arraignments calendar, the action might be very fast-paced. Trial judges who do motion hearings or oversee jury trials function much like a referee. They listen to the proceedings unfold, and when necessary interject to rule motions or offer insight or instructions to witnesses or jurors.

Trial judges handling an arraignment calendar for a large county might handle 30 cases in a single morning or afternoon session, and in each case, they may interact with the defendant for just a few moments. The judge reads an explanation of the charges the defendant is facing, explains the defendant's rights, and then in most cases assigns the defendant counsel with any further action to take place at a later time. The repetition of these hearings can be extremely boring, and presents a challenge for many judges, many of whom left high-powered legal positions to serve as judges. The role might lack the kind of intellectual challenge and excitement they were accustomed to in their law practice. While there are many perks to serving as a judge, not the least of which are the respect and honor bestowed upon them by the community, there are also negative aspects to the job.

**Administrative law judges**, adjudicators and hearing officers serve in a similar role as trial judges but in a different capacity. They are typically employed by local, state and federal administrative agencies to hear and resolve disputes. The specific nature of these positions and their assignments vary a great deal from jurisdiction to jurisdiction making it very difficult to generalize about their roles. These are a uniquely important group of judicial officers whose work is not the subject of television or movies, and as a result, they are lesser known than their more traditional judicial counterparts. One example would be an administrative law judge employed by a state office of administrative hearings.

## C. APPELLATE JUDGES AT WORK

Appellate judges preside over appellate proceedings, which operate very differently from trials. Appellate judges work in panels or groups, and they do not hear evidence or witness testimony, instead they hear arguments regarding issues the parties allege occurred in the courts below. Decisions are made by a majority vote. The **majority opinion** is a written decision issued by the court. Other justices who agreed with the outcome of the case may write separate **concurring opinions**. Those who voted against the outcome may write a **dissenting opinion**, but it has no force of law. It is merely an expression of their disagreement with the court's decision. Sometimes judicial opinions are splintered where a majority of the members of the court vote for a specific result, but do not agree with each other about the rationale for the decision. When this happens it is referred to as a **plurality opinion**.

Appellate attorneys function much differently than trial lawyers. Appellate attorneys engage in a great deal of legal research, write lengthy briefs and submit them to the court in advance, and then engage in oral argument before the appellate court to try to convince them of the merits of their client's position. Appellate attorneys must be able to pivot quickly from one topic to the next during oral argument as the judges ask them questions and demand explanation for the position they have argued in their briefs. They do not know what questions to expect and can easily get caught off-guard if they are unprepared.

In appellate proceedings, the judges are responsible to review and analyze the briefs, listen to the oral arguments, and issue a decision or opinion. This opinion is written and explains the court's holding in the case. The opinion is law, because in the United States we abide by the **Doctrine of Stare Decisis** or precedent. This means that when a court issues an opinion in a case, when cases arise in the future in the same jurisdiction and with regard to the same or similar issues, the prior case and it's reasoning should be followed. *Stare decisis* is Latin for "let the decision stand." This principle ensures justice by providing for notice to future litigants about what to expect in a similar situation and consistent legal decision-making. It also demonstrates deference and respect for the judicial decisions handed down from prior courts.

# D. JUSTICES OF THE UNITED STATES SUPREME COURT

The United State Supreme Court is an institution of great importance in the United States of America and the justices of the High Court hold positions of high regard. The Judiciary Act of 1789 was the first piece of legislation passed by the newly formed Congress of the United States. The Judiciary Act established the parameters for the Supreme Court. In 1790 the Court assembled for the first time in New York (then the nation's Capital). The Court moved again twice, once to Philadelphia in 1790 and then to its permanent home in Washington, D.C. in 1800. For the first 101 years, the justices of the Court were required to **ride circuit** between the 13 judicial districts, in 3 regions around the country. This meant that the justices travelled around the country and were required to hold circuit court twice a year in each district. This was an extraordinary challenge in an era when travel was cumbersome and often dangerous.

Justices of the High Court are appointed by the President of the United States and approved by the United States Senate. The number of justices on the Court has varied over the years, but was set to 9 in 1869. They serve during "good

Behaviour" which has translated into lifetime appointments. Justices of the Court have traditionally served lengthy terms. The longest-serving justice was William O. Douglas (36 years) and the average tenure for a justice of the Court is 16 years. Continuity of membership is meaningful and has allowed for consistency in constitutional interpretation. It provides protection for the justices to decide cases in accordance with their interpretation of the Constitution. It was the intention of the Framers to preserve judicial independence and protect the justices against undue political influence. The Court maintains many traditions dating back to the early years of its existence. Attorneys appearing before the Court are expected to be dressed in formal attire, and there are white quill pens positioned on the counsel desks, just as they were when the Court first began hearing cases.

Justices of the Supreme Court take an oath to uphold the United States Constitution: "I, _____, do solemnly swear (or affirm) that I will support and defend the Constitution of the United States against all enemies, foreign and domestic; that I will bear true faith and allegiance to the same; that I take this obligation freely, without any mental reservation or purpose of evasion; and that I will well and faithfully discharge the duties of the office on which I am about to enter. So help me God." In addition, justices are required to take a second oath, a "Judicial Oath" as well. According to the Official website of the United States Supreme Court, the origin of the second oath is found in the Judiciary Act of 1789, which reads "the justices of the Supreme Court, and the district judges, before they proceed to execute the duties of their respective offices" to take a second oath or affirmation. From 1789 to 1990, the original text used for this oath (1 Stat. 76 § 8) was:

> *"I, _____, do solemnly swear or affirm that I will administer justice without respect to persons, and do equal right to the poor and to the rich, and that I will faithfully and impartially discharge and perform all the duties incumbent upon me as _____, according to the best of my abilities and understanding, agreeably to the constitution and laws of the United States. So help me God."*

In December 1990, this oath was updated, and the new version found at 28 U.S.C. § 453, reads:

> *"I, _____, do solemnly swear (or affirm) that I will administer justice without respect to persons, and do equal right to the poor and to the rich, and that I will faithfully and impartially discharge and perform all the duties incumbent upon me as*

_____ *under the Constitution and laws of the United States. So help me God.*"[1]

The justices of the United States Supreme Court are not political figures, but they are appointed by political figures. While there are protections in place to insulate the justices from political influence, the process of their appointment and approval is undoubtedly wrought with politics. Recent appointments have played out in the media and the Senate's confirmation hearings have proven to be contentious. This has been true regardless of the political affiliation of the appointing President. Senate confirmation hearings, now televised, are often ruthless and function much like an inquisition. Nominees must be willing to face formidable criticism of their life's work as attorneys and judges, and about any aspect of their personal lives.

Over the years there have been battles about whether an outgoing president should have the right to nominate justices. In 2016 President Barack Obama nominated Merrick Garland to fill the vacancy left by Justice Antonin Scalia's death. The Senate, then held by a Republican majority, refused to 'advise and consent' to Garland's nomination. In fact, no hearing was held to even consider his nomination. Democrats were powerless to compel a hearing or floor vote. Just a few years later, at the end of Donald Trump's presidency, his appointment of Amy Coney Barrett upon the death of Ruth Bader Ginsburg has been argued as an act of great hypocrisy: Republicans refused Garland's nomination, then pushed through Coney's nomination in the waning months of Trump's presidency. These were obviously political battles; but arguably either political party would act selfishly in the same circumstances. In 1992 George W. Bush was in office, he was "advised" by then Senate Judiciary Committee Chair Joe Biden to withhold any nominations until the end of the 'political season.' This inference that no approval would be given to a Bush nominee if named has been referred to as the 'Biden Rule' by conservatives.

# E. JUDICIAL ETHICS

The **ABA Model Code of Judicial Conduct** provides ethical rules for judges to follow. Judges who violate these rules can be disciplined by the ABA and like attorneys who engage in misconduct, may face a variety of criminal and civil sanctions in addition to bar association discipline. There are four "canons" or rules for judicial conduct:

---

[1] Supreme Court of the United States, History and Traditions, https://www.supremecourt.gov/about/historyandtraditions.aspx.

*CANON 1*

*A judge shall uphold and promote the independence, integrity, and impartiality of the judiciary, and shall avoid impropriety and the appearance of impropriety.*

*CANON 2*

*A judge shall perform the duties of judicial office impartially, competently, and diligently.*

*CANON 3*

*A judge shall conduct the judge's personal and extrajudicial activities to minimize the risk of conflict with the obligations of judicial office.*

*CANON 4*

*A judge or candidate for judicial office shall not engage in political or campaign activity that is inconsistent with the independence, integrity, or impartiality of the judiciary.*

The preamble to the Model Rules of Judicial Conduct explain the need for and purpose of the rules:

*"An independent, fair and impartial judiciary is indispensable to our system of justice. The United States legal system is based upon the principle that an independent, impartial, and competent judiciary, composed of men and women of integrity, will interpret and apply the law that governs our society. Thus, the judiciary plays a central role in preserving the principles of justice and the rule of law. Inherent in all the Rules contained in this Code are the precepts that judges, individually and collectively, must respect and honor the judicial office as a public trust and strive to maintain and enhance confidence in the legal system. . . ."*

## F.  SELECTION OF JUDGES

Judges in the United States acquire their positions through election, legislative appointment, executive appointment or a combination of these processes. Elections may be partisan or non-partisan depending upon the jurisdiction. This process varies from state to state. Only two states utilize legislative appointment, Virginia and South Carolina. The other states vary widely.

In California, Superior court judges are chosen in nonpartisan elections for six-year terms. The governor fills vacancies on the superior court by appointment. As with appellate court appointments, prospective nominees must first be investigated by the Commission on Judicial Nominees Evaluation. In California, the vast majority of superior court judges initially reach the bench via gubernatorial appointment, and once on the bench, incumbents are rarely challenged for reelection. In contrast, in Illinois, the judiciary is composed of the supreme court, the appellate court, and the circuit court (trial courts). Illinois judges are initially chosen in partisan elections. Judges run in uncontested, nonpartisan retention elections to serve additional terms. Judges of the state's supreme court and appellate court serve ten-year terms; circuit court judges serve six-year terms.

In Missouri, the judiciary consists of a supreme court, a court of appeals, and a circuit court (trial court). In 1940, Missouri became the first state to adopt **merit selection** of judges. The Nonpartisan Selection of Judges Court Plan, which has come to be known as the **Missouri Plan**, has served as a model for the 34 other states that use merit selection to fill some or all judicial vacancies. This plan utilizes an appointment process, where judges serve a short term after being selected by a non-partisan commission. At the end of their initial term, the public votes upon these judges for retention. Prior to the adoption of the Missouri Plan, political machines controlled judicial selection in Missouri and party bosses who sought to unseat judges who issued unfavorable rulings.

There is debate about which form of judicial selection is best, but the trend is definitely toward merit selection in some form. Proponents of election argue that it is critical to allow the public to have a voice in the selection of judges by directly electing them. The arguments in favor of merit selection are that it removes politics from the process of selecting judges. They point to the fact that voters are traditionally ill-informed when it comes to judicial elections, often with no idea who the candidates are other than the title listed on the ballot. Opponents of elections also argue that they are inherently political affairs, even when they are non-partisan. They assert that merit selection offers the benefits of well-informed appointment processes in combination with allowing voters to have a voice in the process through a vote for retention judges.

Article III of the Constitution dictates that federal judges and the U.S. Supreme Court justices are appointed by the president with the approval of the U.S. Senate. Article III judges and U.S. Supreme Court justices enjoy lifetime appointments (assuming good behavior). These lifetime appointments ensure judicial independence by protecting the judges from political repercussions from their decisions. These judges do not have to fear the impact of negative public opinion and have the freedom to engage in judicial decision-making that reflects their interpretation of the law regardless of the popularity of those opinions.

Federal magistrate judges serve shorter terms. The full-time magistrate judges serve 8-year terms and part-time magistrates are appointed to 4-year terms. These magistrates may be reappointed. They are appointed by majority vote of the active district judges of the court to exercise jurisdiction over matters assigned by statute as well as those delegated by the district judges. The number of magistrate judge positions is determined by the Judicial Conference of the United States, based on recommendations of the respective district courts, the judicial councils of the circuits, and the Director of the Administrative Office of the U.S. Courts.[2]

---

[2]   http://www.uscourts.gov/faqs-federal-judges.

**Read and brief** *Forrester v. White* **and consider the questions following the case:**

---

### FORRESTER V. WHITE

Supreme Court of the United States
Argued Nov. 2, 1987
Decided Jan. 12, 1988
484 U.S. 219

#### OPINION

#### JUSTICE O'CONNOR delivered the opinion of the Court.

This case requires us to decide whether a state-court judge has absolute immunity from a suit for damages under 42 U.S.C. § 1983 for his decision to dismiss a subordinate court employee. The employee, who had been a probation officer, alleged that she was demoted and discharged on account of her sex, in violation of the Equal Protection Clause of the Fourteenth Amendment. We conclude that the judge's decisions were not judicial acts for which he should be held absolutely immune.

I

Respondent Howard Lee White served as Circuit Judge of the Seventh Judicial Circuit of the State of Illinois and Presiding Judge of the Circuit Court in Jersey County. Under Illinois law, Judge White had the authority to hire adult probation officers, who were removable in his discretion. Ill.Rev.Stat., ch. 38, ¶ 204–1 (1979). In addition, as designee of the Chief Judge of the Seventh Judicial Circuit, Judge White had the authority to appoint juvenile probation officers to serve at his pleasure. Ill.Rev.Stat., ch. 37, ¶ 706–5 (1979).

In April 1977, Judge White hired petitioner Cynthia A. Forrester as an adult and juvenile probation officer. Forrester prepared presentence reports for Judge White in adult offender cases, and recommendations for disposition and placement in juvenile cases. She also supervised persons on probation and recommended revocation when necessary. In July 1979, Judge White appointed Forrester as Project Supervisor of the Jersey County Juvenile Court Intake and Referral Services Project, a position that carried increased supervisory responsibilities. Judge White demoted Forrester to a nonsupervisory position in the summer of 1980. He discharged her on October 1, 1980.

Forrester filed this lawsuit in the United States District Court for the Southern District of Illinois in July 1982. She alleged violations of Title VII of the Civil Rights Act of 1964, 78 Stat. 253, as amended, 42 U.S.C. § 2000e *et seq.,* and § 1 of the Civil Rights Act of 1871, Rev.Stat. § 1979, as amended, 42 U.S.C. § 1983. A jury found that Judge White had discriminated against Forrester on account of her sex, in violation of the Equal Protection Clause of the Fourteenth Amendment. The jury awarded her $81,818.80 in compensatory damages under § 1983. Forrester's other claims were dismissed in the course of the lawsuit.

After Judge White's motion for judgment notwithstanding the verdict was denied, he moved for a new trial. The District Court granted this motion, holding that the jury verdict was against the weight of the evidence. Judge White then moved for summary judgment on the ground that he was entitled to "judicial immunity" from a civil damages suit. This motion, too, was granted. Forrester appealed.

A divided panel of the Court of Appeals for the Seventh Circuit affirmed the grant of summary judgment. The majority reasoned that judges are immune for activities implicating the substance of their decisions in the cases before them, although they are not shielded "from the trials of life generally." 792 F.2d 647, 652 (1986). Some members of a judge's staff aid in the performance of adjudicative functions, and the threat of suits by such persons could make a judge reluctant to replace them even after losing confidence in their work. This could distort the judge's decision-making and thereby indirectly affect the rights of litigants. Here, Forrester performed functions that were "inextricably tied to discretionary decisions that have consistently been considered judicial acts." *Id.,* at 657. Unless Judge White felt free to replace Forrester, the majority thought, the quality of his own decisions might decline. The Court of Appeals therefore held that Judge White was absolutely immune from Forrester's civil damages suit. In view of this holding, the court found it unnecessary to decide whether the District Court had erred in granting Judge White's motion for a new trial.

In dissent, Judge Posner argued that judicial immunity should protect only adjudicative functions, and that employment decisions are administrative functions for which judges should not be given absolute immunity.

In *Goodwin v. Circuit Court of St. Louis County, Mo.,* 729 F.2d 541, 549, cert. denied, 469 U.S. 828, 105 S.Ct. 112, 83 L.Ed.2d 55 (1984), the United States Court of Appeals for the Eighth Circuit held that a judge was not immune from civil damages for his decision to demote a hearing officer. We granted certiorari to resolve the conflict.

## II

Suits for monetary damages are meant to compensate the victims of wrongful actions and to discourage conduct that may result in liability. Special problems arise, however, when government officials are exposed to liability for damages. To the extent that the threat of liability encourages these officials to carry out their duties in a lawful and appropriate manner, and to pay their victims when they do not, it accomplishes exactly what it should. By its nature, however, the threat of liability can create perverse incentives that operate to *inhibit* officials in the proper performance of their duties. In many contexts, government officials are expected to make decisions that are impartial or imaginative, and that above all are informed by considerations other than the personal interests of the decision-maker. Because government officials are engaged by definition in governing, their decisions will often have adverse effects on other persons. When officials are threatened with personal liability for acts taken pursuant to their official duties, they may well be induced to act with an excess of caution or otherwise to skew their decisions in ways that result in less than full fidelity to the objective and independent criteria that ought to guide their conduct. In this way, exposing government officials to the same legal hazards faced by other citizens may detract from the rule of law instead of contributing to it.

Such considerations have led to the creation of various forms of immunity from suit for certain government officials. Aware of the salutary effects that the threat of liability can have, however, as well as the undeniable tension between official immunities and the ideal of the rule of law, this Court has been cautious in recognizing claims that government officials should be free of the obligation to answer for their acts in court. Running through our cases, with fair consistency, is a "functional" approach to immunity questions other than those that have been decided by express constitutional or statutory enactment. Under that approach, we examine the nature of the functions with which a particular official or class of officials has been lawfully entrusted, and we seek to evaluate the effect that exposure to particular forms of liability would likely have on the appropriate exercise of those functions. Officials who seek exemption from personal liability have the burden of showing that such an exemption is justified by overriding considerations of public policy, and the Court has recognized a category of "qualified" immunity that avoids unnecessarily extending the scope of the traditional concept of absolute immunity. . .

This Court has generally been quite sparing in its recognition of claims to absolute official immunity. One species of such legal protection is beyond challenge: the legislative immunity created by the Speech or Debate Clause, U.S. Const., Art. I, § 6, cl. 1. Even here, however, the Court has been careful not to extend the scope of the protection further than its purposes require. See, *e.g., Gravel v. United States,* 408 U.S. 606, 622–627 (1972); . . . Furthermore, on facts analogous to those in the case before us, the Court indicated that a United States Congressman would not be entitled to absolute immunity, in a sex-discrimination suit filed by a personal aide whom he had fired, unless such immunity was afforded by the Speech or Debate Clause. *Davis v. Passman,* 442 U.S. 228, 246 (1979) (reserving question of qualified immunity).

Among executive officials, the President of the United States is absolutely immune from damages liability arising from official acts. *Nixon v. Fitzgerald,* 457 U.S. 731 (1982). This immunity, however, is based on the President's "unique position in the constitutional scheme,". . .

III

As a class, judges have long enjoyed a comparatively sweeping form of immunity, though one not perfectly well-defined. Judicial immunity apparently originated, in medieval times, as a device for discouraging collateral attacks and thereby helping to establish appellate procedures as the standard system for correcting judicial error. See Block, *Stump v. Sparkman* and the History of Judicial Immunity, 1980 Duke L.J. 879. More recently, this Court found that judicial immunity was "the settled doctrine of the English courts for many centuries, and has never been denied, that we are aware of, in the courts of this country." *Bradley v. Fisher,* 13 Wall. 335, 347, 20 L.Ed. 646 (1872). Besides protecting the finality of judgments or discouraging inappropriate collateral attacks, the *Bradley* Court concluded, judicial immunity also protected judicial independence by insulating judges from vexatious actions prosecuted by disgruntled litigants. *Id.,* at 348.

In the years since *Bradley* was decided, this Court has not been quick to find that federal legislation was meant to diminish the traditional common-law protections extended to the judicial process. . . .

One can reasonably wonder whether judges, who have been primarily responsible for developing the law of official immunities, are not inevitably more sensitive to the ill effects that vexatious lawsuits can have on the judicial function than they are to similar dangers in other contexts. Cf. *id.,* at 528, n., 98 S.Ct., at 2921, n. (REHNQUIST, J., concurring in part and dissenting in part). Although Congress has not undertaken to cut back the judicial immunities recognized by this Court, we should be at least as cautious in extending those immunities as we have been when dealing with officials whose peculiar problems we know less well than our own. At the same time, we cannot pretend that we are writing on a clean slate or that we should ignore compelling reasons that may well justify broader protections for judges than for some other officials.

The purposes served by judicial immunity from liability in damages have been variously described. In *Bradley v. Fisher, supra,* at 348, and again in *Pierson v. Ray, supra,* at 554, the Court emphasized that the nature of the adjudicative function requires a judge frequently to disappoint some of the most intense and ungovernable desires that people can have. . . . If judges were personally liable for erroneous decisions, the resulting avalanche of suits, most of them frivolous but vexatious, would provide powerful incentives for judges to avoid rendering decisions likely to provoke such suits. *Id.,* at 660–661. The resulting timidity would be hard to detect or control, and it would manifestly detract from independent and impartial adjudication. Nor are suits against judges the only available means through which litigants can protect themselves from the consequences of judicial error. Most judicial mistakes or wrongs are open to correction through ordinary mechanisms of review, which are largely free of the harmful side-effects inevitably associated with exposing judges to personal liability. . .

This Court has never undertaken to articulate a precise and general definition of the class of acts entitled to immunity. The decided cases, however, suggest an intelligible distinction between judicial acts and the administrative, legislative, or executive functions that judges may on occasion be assigned by law to perform. Thus, for example, the informal and *ex parte* nature of a proceeding has not been thought to imply that an act otherwise within a judge's lawful jurisdiction was deprived of its judicial character. See *Stump v. Sparkman,* 435 U.S. 349, 363, n. 12 (1978). Similarly, acting to disbar an attorney as a sanction for contempt of court, by invoking a power "possessed by all courts which have authority to admit attorneys to practice," does not become less judicial by virtue of an allegation of malice or corruption of motive. *Bradley v. Fisher,* 13 Wall., at 354. As the *Bradley* Court noted: "Against the consequences of [judges'] erroneous or irregular action, from whatever motives proceeding, the law has provided for private parties numerous remedies, and to those remedies they must, in such cases, resort." *Ibid.*

Administrative decisions, even though they may be essential to the very functioning of the courts, have not similarly been regarded as judicial acts. In *Ex parte Virginia,* 100 U.S. (10 Otto) 339, 25 L.Ed. 676 (1880), for example, this Court declined to extend immunity to a county judge who had been charged in a criminal indictment with discriminating on the basis of race in selecting trial jurors for the county's courts. The Court reasoned:

> "Whether the act done by him was judicial or not is to be determined by its character, and not by the character of the agent. Whether he was a county judge or not is of no importance. The duty of selecting jurors might as well have been committed to a private person as to one holding the office of a judge. . . . That the jurors are selected for a court makes no difference. So are court-criers, tipstaves, sheriffs, &c. Is their election or their appointment a judicial act?"

*Id.,* at 348.

Although this case involved a criminal charge against a judge, the reach of the Court's analysis was not in any obvious way confined by that circumstance. . .

## IV

In the case before us, we think it clear that Judge White was acting in an administrative capacity when he demoted and discharged Forrester. Those acts—like many others involved in supervising court employees and overseeing the efficient operation of a court—may have been quite important in providing the necessary conditions of a sound adjudicative system. The decisions at issue, however, were not themselves judicial or adjudicative. As Judge Posner pointed out below, a judge who hires or fires a probation officer cannot meaningfully be distinguished from a district attorney who hires and fires assistant district attorneys, or indeed from any other Executive Branch official who is responsible for making such employment decisions. Such decisions, like personnel decisions made by judges, are often crucial to the efficient operation of public institutions (some of which are at least as important as the courts), yet no one suggests that they give rise to absolute immunity from liability in damages under § 1983.

The majority below thought that the threat of vexatious lawsuits by disgruntled ex-employees could interfere with the quality of a judge's decisions:

> "The evil to be avoided is the following: A judge loses confidence in his probation officer, but hesitates to fire him because

of the threat of litigation. He then retains the officer, in which case the parties appearing before the court are the victims, because the quality of the judge's decision-making will decline."

792 F.2d, at 658.

There is considerable force in this analysis, but it in no way serves to distinguish judges from other public officials who hire and fire subordinates. Indeed, to the extent that a judge is less free than most Executive Branch officials to delegate decision-making authority to subordinates, there may be somewhat less reason to cloak judges with absolute immunity from such suits than there would be to protect such other officials. This does not imply that qualified immunity, like that available to Executive Branch officials who make similar discretionary decisions, is unavailable to judges for their employment decisions. . . . Absolute immunity, however, is "strong medicine, justified only when the danger of [officials' being] deflect[ed from the effective performance of their duties] is very great." 792 F.2d, at 660 (Posner, J., dissenting). The danger here is not great enough. Nor do we think it significant that, under Illinois law, only a judge can hire or fire probation officers. To conclude that, because a judge acts within the scope of his authority, such employment decisions are brought within the court's "jurisdiction," or converted into "judicial acts," would lift form above substance. Under Virginia law, only that State's judges could promulgate and enforce a Bar Code, but we nonetheless concluded that neither function was judicial in nature. See *Supreme Court of Virginia v. Consumers Union, supra.*

We conclude that Judge White was not entitled to absolute immunity for his decisions to demote and discharge Forrester. In so holding, we do not decide whether Judge White is entitled to a new trial, or whether he may be able to claim a qualified immunity for the acts complained of in Forrester's suit. The judgment of the Court of Appeals is reversed, and the case is remanded for further proceedings consistent with this opinion.

**It is so ordered.**

## After preparing the case brief, consider the answers to the following questions:

1. What is absolute immunity from civil liability?

2. What arguments in favor of immunity for judges does the Court recognize in this case?

3.    Why is the distinction between judicial and administrative action by judges important?

4.    Do you agree with the Court's decision? Explain.

## Chapter 6 Key Terms for Review

- **United States Supreme Court Justices**: the judges who sit on the United States Supreme Court, appointed by the president with the approval of the Senate to life terms.

- **Trial judges**: preside over civil and criminal trials.

- **District court judge**: also called Article III Judges, federal judges serving in the federal trial courts (district courts).

- **Magistrate judge**: serves the federal district court, appointed to a term of years and selected by the judges in the federal judicial district. Magistrate judges assist with the heavy caseload of the federal courts by presiding over preliminary and less serious matters delegated to them by the district court judges.

- **Administrative law judge**: a hearing officer who serves in a quasi-judicial role to oversee administrative hearings.

- **Majority opinion**: the majority opinion represents the winning side of an appellate argument, written by one or more judges and it is law.

- **Concurring opinion**: a separate opinion written by a judge who agrees with the outcome or decision, but might explain a separate or different rationale for their vote

- **Dissenting opinion**: written by judges who disagree with the outcome of a case and write to express the reasons for their disagreement. It is not law.

- **Plurality opinion**: where the majority of judges agree with the result in the case, but do not agree on a single rationale they write separately explaining their view, creating a splintered or plurality opinion. This has weaker precedential value than a majority opinion.

- **Doctrine of *stare decisis*** court opinions are precedent for future cases involving the same or similar issues and future or lower courts are bound by prior decisions.

- **Ride circuit**: the requirement that early United States Supreme Court justices travel around the country to hold circuit court twice a year in each of the judicial districts.

- **ABA Model Code of Judicial Conduct**: ethical rules governing the conduct of judges.

- **Merit selection of judges**: The Nonpartisan Selection of Judges Court Plan or "Missouri Plan" began in 1940 and now employed in 34 states selects judges in a hybrid model, first by appointing them to a probationary term, and then confirmation in a non-partisan public election.

# Pre-Trial Criminal Judicial Process

Arrest marks an individual's entry into the criminal justice system. Police, often referred to as gatekeepers, bring suspects into the system. For a suspect being taken into custody booking is the first step in the pre-trial process. Basic identifying information is collected, including fingerprints, and the suspect is placed in police custody at a police station or jail. The next steps in the suspect's journey will turn on whether they are charged with a felony or misdemeanor, and whether they will be charged in federal or state court.

The steps in the pre-trial process are:

1. Crime: a violation of the criminal law is committed

2. Arrest: the suspect is taken into physical custody

3. Initial appearance: the suspect is brought before a judge for the first time (note: in some jurisdictions this is combined with other pre-trial steps such as the preliminary hearing or arraignment)

4. Bail: pre-trial release is offered if the defendant qualifies

5. Preliminary hearing: a probable cause hearing is held if necessary

6. Grand jury: a grand jury is convened to determine probable cause if necessary

7. Arraignment: the defendant is formally charged and must enter a plea

# A. PRE-TRIAL JUDICIAL PROCESS IN FEDERAL COURT

## i. Initial Appearance

Defendants must be brought before a magistrate *without unnecessary delay* after they are arrested for an **initial appearance**. The initial appearance must take place within a reasonable time in light of all the facts and circumstances of the case.[1] There is no specific time frame or set number of days, but this typically takes place within a few days. The initial appearance in federal court is an opportunity for the suspect to be informed of the charges against them and the penalties for the charges. The judge also informs the suspect of her right to a trial by jury and the right to counsel, including the right to appointed counsel for indigent defendants. The magistrate judge also sets release conditions, including any bond.

## ii. Bail Rights and Procedures

Decisions about bail may be made at the initial appearance, otherwise a bail hearing will be scheduled soon afterwards. The magistrate evaluates whether there is a risk that the defendant will not return for trial. If so, the defendant is considered a **flight risk**, and will not be released. The judge might also deny pretrial release if the defendant poses a threat to the safety of others.[2] Defendants may be released on their own recognizance (ROR) and no fees are charged, or they may be required to pay or post a bond in order to be released on bail. While the judge exercises a great deal of discretion in evaluating whether to grant the defendant release prior to trial, the **Eighth Amendment** prohibits excessive bail or fines: "*Excessive bail shall not be required, nor excessive fines imposed, nor cruel and unusual punishments inflicted.*"[3] This language has roots in English common law. The 1689 English Bill of Rights contained similar language and the provision, "that excessive bail ought not to be required, nor excessive fines imposed, nor cruel and unusual punishments inflicted." The principle supports the presumption of innocence, favoring pre-trial release for defendants not yet convicted of a crime.

The primary purpose of bail is to ensure that the defendant returns to court when required. Bail is an agreement between the defendant and the court, and if the defendant does not honor the agreement and appear when required, a warrant will be issued for their arrest and any bail paid is forfeited. Bail also serves practical

---

[1]  Fed. R. Crim. P. 5.

[2]  *United States v. Salerno*, 481 U.S. 739 (1987).

[3]  U.S. Const. amend VIII.

purposes in a modern context. It frees space in jails and prisons for inmates who pose the highest risk or threat to public safety. Bail also saves valuable financial resources necessary for the housing and care of other inmates who cannot be released. Bail serves to ensure that a defendant maintains community and family support where it exists, and is free to actively assist in the preparation of his own defense of the charges against him.

The Supreme Court considered the question of excessive bail in *Stack v. Boyle (1951)*.[4] In this landmark case the Court held that *bail is excessive when it is set above an amount reasonably calculated to ensure the defendant's return for trial.* The Bail Reform Act of 1984 permits detention of certain defendants prior to trial if they pose a risk to public safety. In *United States v. Salerno (1987)*[5] the U.S. Supreme Court upheld the constitutionality of the Bail Reform Act of 1984 and held that pre-trial detention for the purpose of public safety, even in the absence of flight risk is lawful.

## iii. The Right to Indictment by a Grand Jury

In federal felony cases it is not the prosecutor who will decide whether probable cause exists and a suspect should face felony charges. There is a **right to indictment by a grand jury** for felony offenses. This right to a grand jury indictment is found in the Fifth Amendment to the United States Constitution:

> *No person shall be held to answer for a capital, or otherwise infamous crime, unless on a presentment or indictment of a Grand Jury. . .*[6]

Rule 6 of the Federal Rules of Criminal Procedure governs federal grand juries. It dictates that they be composed of between 16 and 23 members, that their proceedings are secret, and that at least 12 members of the grand jury agree to issue the indictment charging the defendant. The federal prosecutor presents evidence of possible charges to the grand jury. The rules of evidence typical in criminal trials do not apply providing the grand jury very broad investigative powers. The Constitution does not provide for the right to indictment by a grand jury for misdemeanor charges.

## iv. Arraignment

The purpose of arraignment is to provide the defendant with formal notice of the charges against her and to ask her to enter a plea. The defendant may plead

---

4   *Stack v. Boyle*, 342 U.S. 1 (1951).

5   *United States v. Salerno*, 481 U.S. 739 (1987).

6   U.S. Const. amend. V.

guilty, not guilty, *nolo contendere* (no contest), or may remain silent—or stand mute. Standing mute means the defendant refuses to enter a plea and the court will enter a "not guilty" plea on the defendant's behalf. A "guilty" plea by the defendant admits wrongdoing and accepts the proscribed punishment, typically as negotiated in the plea-bargaining process. A "not guilty" plea denies guilt and moves the case forward to prepare for trial. When a defendant pleads "no contest" they deny factual guilt, but accept the punishment. This plea operates the same way a guilty plea would for the purposes of sentencing without an admission of guilt by the defendant. It can be argued that little of significance takes place at the arraignment, and while this may be true in the federal court, at times it is much different in state courts.

### v.  Preliminary Hearing

The **preliminary hearing** provides a judicial determination of probable cause to support the charges brought against the defendant. In situations where an indictment was issued by a grand jury prior to arrest, a preliminary hearing is unnecessary because the requirement for a hearing to determine probable cause has already been met. Within 10 days of arrest on a complaint, the accused has the right to a preliminary hearing, during which the prosecutor may offer testimony to establish probable cause, and the defense attorney may provide evidence on behalf of the accused. If the magistrate judge overseeing the hearing finds sufficient probable cause as to the commission of the crime as well as the accused's role in it, the accused is **bound over** for further proceedings by a grand jury.

## B.  PRE-TRIAL JUDICIAL PROCESS IN STATE COURT

### i.  Initial Appearance and Arraignment

Pre-trial judicial process in state courts is not uniform among the states nor is it identical to the federal system. In the majority of jurisdictions, at a felony arraignment the judge informs the defendant of the charges against him and the penalties for the charges. The defendant is advised of their rights including the right to a preliminary (probable cause) hearing, jury trial, and the assistance of counsel. If requested the court determines whether the defendant qualifies for appointed counsel based on his income. The case will be set for a preliminary hearing if one is needed and the judge may evaluate and set bail for the defendant.

No plea is entered at the felony arraignment. It is possible that a defendant may choose to enter a plea at their arraignment in a misdemeanor case.

## ii. Bail Issues

In misdemeanor cases, where the offenses are minor, defendants can be released after being arrested and booked based on a **bail schedule**. The bail schedule is a list of minor offenses and the bail amounts charged for the violation of each. In these cases, the **out-of-custody** defendant will return to court for an arraignment where he is informed of his rights, the charges against him, and may even enter a plea and submit to sentencing the same day.

Some defendants are **released on their own recognizance (ROR),** and are not required to pay a bail amount for their pre-trial release. These defendants promise to return to court when summoned and are offered release ROR because they have low risk of failing to appear. Others are required to pay bail or post a bond in exchange for their pre-trial release. The **bail bonds system** attempts to make bail affordable for defendants who are unable to pay the full amount of the bail required by the court. A **bail bondsman** posts a bond, or guarantee of payment, on the defendant's behalf in exchange for a fee. The fee is typically 10% of the bail amount. Bail bondsmen ensure that their clients return for hearings because they have a vested interest: their money is at risk if the defendants fail to appear.

There is significant debate regarding the quality and effectiveness of the cash bail and bail bonds systems. Many reformers point to evidence that high bail amounts are consciously used by judges to unlawfully detain defendants in cases where the defendant poses no risk of flight or threat to public safety. Reformers are working on the legislative front to change public policy regarding when bail can be denied and the factors judges must consider in making bail decisions. In 2017 New Jersey made sweeping bail reforms—essentially eliminating cash bail. The new system is a risk-assessment considering 9 specific facts from the defendant's criminal history. Evaluation of the likelihood the defendant will return to court when required and the risk of new offenses while awaiting trial are key considerations. New Jersey's new "Public Safety Assessment" tool helps judges to predict defendant's potential success on pre-trial release. Assessment of the New Jersey reform thus far has indicated that the reforms have been successful.[7]

In 2018 California passed legislation to eliminate cash bail entirely—but it was quickly reversed when the voters approved a proposition reinstituting cash

---

[7]   https://www.njcourts.gov/courts/assets/criminal/cjrreport2018.pdf?c=xNT.

bail. While the state continues to work toward bail reform, they responded to the COVID-19 pandemic by issuing emergency zero-bail policies. These pandemic-related policies in California have not been as successful as the thoughtfully crafted New Jersey reforms. In many cases, arrestees in California received no assessment of any kind by a judge, and in September, 2021 a Sacramento woman was brutally murdered by a parolee who had been re-arrested and then immediately released under the zero-bail policy without appearing before a judge.[8] California's state Supreme Court held that defendants cannot be held without bail simply because of their financial inability to pay. This development will certainly drive California, like many other states, to evaluate and test new bail reforms in the years ahead.

Other reformers are actively working to support defendants while bail systems are still in place. Non-profit organizations have established bail funds in major cities like Brooklyn, Seattle, Nashville and Boston. These funds provide money to pay bail for defendants who are poor and unable to post bond on their own. Because the money is returned when defendants successfully complete the judicial process and make all of their appearances, the funds can be used over and over to support additional defendants.

The Bronx Freedom Fund was one example, that was born out of the public defender's office. Between 2007 and 2020 they provided cash bail resources to indigent defendants. The fund is no longer necessary in the wake of New York bail reforms. Their website explains:

> *Founded in 2007, The Bronx Freedom Fund was the first of its kind effort to disrupt the injustice of cash bail in New York City by posting bail for thousands of low-income New Yorkers incarcerated before trial. Through its decade-long effort to transform pretrial justice in New York, The Bronx Freedom Fund reunited thousands of families separated by bail, while pioneering the revolving bail fund model as a tool in the fight against mass incarceration and the criminalization of race and poverty.*

> *On January 1, 2020, after more than a decade, The Bronx Freedom Fund stopped posting bails in light of **long overdue reforms** that ended cash bail for the majority of cases where charitable bail funds can provide assistance under state law. From the bottom of our hearts, we thank the thousands of people who powered the Freedom Fund over the years.[9]*

---

8   https://www.sacbee.com/news/local/crime/article254050703.html.

9   http://www.thebronxfreedomfund.org/.

### iii. The Use of Grand Juries

In *Hurtado v. California (1884)*[10] the Supreme Court held that the right to indictment by a grand jury does not apply in state criminal prosecutions. This is as practical as it is theoretical in light of the extraordinary number of criminal cases processed by the state courts. If required even just in felony prosecutions, grand jury proceedings would be an unworkable burden on state courts. That does not mean state courts never use grand juries. According to the American Bar Association about half of all states employ grand juries in some fashion.

The grand jury must decide if probable cause exists to believe the defendant has engaged in the crimes alleged. As in the federal system, state prosecutors present evidence to the grand jury in order to convince them that probable cause exists to move forward with charges against the defendant. If the grand jury issues an indictment, it is called a true bill and the prosecutor is responsible for filing charges against the defendant based on their decision. If no probable cause is found by the grand jury they return no bill.

In states where indictment is an option there are a variety of reasons why a prosecutor would refer the case to a grand jury. The case may be politically charged or the defendant a high-profile person. Prosecutors may face political backlash whether they choose to charge or not to charge, so sending the case to a grand jury may help insulate them. In the shooting death of Michael Brown in Ferguson, Missouri, the prosecutor referred the case to a grand jury. The extremely high-profile nature of the case against the local police officer that killed Brown made the case a good candidate for grand jury review. Grand juries must be composed of people from the county they serve and must reflect the county's population demographics.

There was criticism of the Ferguson grand jury because it was composed of only 25% African-American jurors, while the population of the city of Ferguson is 90% African-American. The make-up of St. Louis County, where Ferguson is located, is 24% African-American and 68% Caucasian so the grand jury met the requirement for representation in the county. Unique about the Ferguson case was the fact that the prosecutor presented all of the evidence in the case to the grand jury, rather than only the minimum amount believed sufficient to prove probable cause. This decision was made in order to minimize skepticism if the grand jury failed to indict the officer because they considered all of the evidence

---

[10]   110 U.S. 516 (1884).

in the case. In the end, the grand jury's failure to indict still gave rise to significant public outcry, and was a catalyst for the *Black Lives Matter* movement.

Another high-profile case taken to a grand jury involved NASCAR driver Tony Stewart. On August 6, 2014, Kevin Ward, Jr. was killed in an accident at Canandaigua (N.Y.) Motorsports Park. Ward exited his car in the incident approaching Stewart's car on the track, apparently angry because of something that occurred during the race. Ward's family, in a wrongful death lawsuit, claimed that Stewart saw Ward and revved his engine just before impact.[11] Stewart claimed that he did not see Ward on the track until immediately prior to impact. The two charges the grand jury considered were second-degree manslaughter and criminally negligent homicide. In New York state it takes 12 of 23 votes from the grand jury to return charges. They delivered their verdict in less than an hour declining to indict Stewart on either charge.

### iv.  Preliminary Hearings

Like other pretrial procedures, the preliminary hearing process varies from state to state. Typically, at the preliminary hearing a judge will hear the evidence from the prosecutor, offered to establish probable cause to charge the defendant. The defendant is present and in some states has a right to call his own witnesses and cross-examine prosecution witnesses. Police officers are often key witnesses in preliminary hearings because they investigated the crime and were the ones who observed the facts and circumstances that establish probable cause. If the judge decides that probable cause exists to charge the defendant, the defendant is bound over and the case is set for trial. If the judge determines that probable cause is lacking, the case is dismissed and the defendant is released from custody.

In *Coleman v. Alabama (1970)* the U.S. Supreme Court considered whether the preliminary hearing is a **critical stage** in the criminal trial process for the purposes of the Sixth Amendment right to counsel.[12] In determining whether a particular step in criminal judicial process is a critical stage requiring the assistance of counsel, courts are to consider "whether potential substantial prejudice to defendant's rights inheres in the . . . confrontation and the ability of counsel to help avoid that prejudice."[13] The Court held that the preliminary hearing is in fact a critical stage and appointed counsel is required by the Constitution.

---

[11]   As of the date of this publication, the Ward family's wrongful death lawsuit against Stewart was in the process of settlement negotiations in advance of trial.

[12]   *Coleman v. Alabama*, 399 U.S. 1 (1970).

[13]   *United States v. Wade*, 388 U.S. 218, at 227 (1967).

The Supreme Court recognized a distinction between the preliminary hearings considered in *Coleman*, and those being held to validate pre-trial detention after a police determination of probable cause as the foundation for an arrest. When police officers make an arrest based upon their observations and determination of probable cause without a warrant, a suspect must be brought before a judge as soon as possible to ensure there is probable cause to support their detention. In contrast, when an arrest warrant is issued prior to arrest, the defendant has the benefit of a judicial determination of probable cause, and a preliminary hearing is not required.

In *Gerstein v. Pugh (1975)*,[14] the Supreme Court considered these post arrest preliminary hearings and held that suspects have a constitutional right to a prompt judicial determination of probable cause. The Court recognized the wide variance among the states in pre-trial procedures and concluded that a full adversary hearing is not required to fulfill the constitutional requirement. Instead, they held that states satisfy the requirement so long as a *reliable* determination or probable cause is made in a *prompt* manner:

> *Although we conclude that the Constitution does not require an adversary determination of probable cause, we recognize that state systems of criminal procedure vary widely. There is no single preferred pretrial procedure, and the nature of the probable cause determination usually will be shaped to accord with a State's pretrial procedure viewed as a whole. While we limit our holding to the precise requirement of the Fourth Amendment, we recognize the desirability of flexibility and experimentation by the States. It may be found desirable, for example, to make the probable cause determination at the suspect's first appearance before a judicial officer. . . or the determination may be incorporated into the procedure for setting bail or fixing other conditions of pretrial release. In some States, existing procedures may satisfy the requirement of the Fourth Amendment. Others may require only minor adjustment, such as acceleration of existing preliminary hearings. Current proposals for criminal procedure reform suggest other ways of testing probable cause for detention. Whatever procedure a State may adopt, it must provide a fair and reliable determination of probable cause as a condition for any significant pretrial restraint of liberty, and this determination must be made by a judicial officer either before or promptly after arrest.*[15]

In *County of Riverside v. McLaughlin (1991)*, the U.S. Supreme Court considered the meaning of "prompt" in the context of *Gerstein* and the Fourth Amendment

---

[14]  *Gerstein v. Pugh*, 420 U.S. 103 (1975).

[15]  *Id.* at 123.

probable cause hearing requirement. They held that in order to satisfy the constitutional requirement from *Gerstein* the hearing must be held within 48 hours of arrest, or sooner, if practicable.[16]

# C. ISSUES AFFECTING PRE-TRIAL JUDICIAL PROCESS

## i.    Assembly Line Justice

These first steps leading up to a trial may seem routine and often give rise to criticism of the American courts as engaging in "assembly line justice." **Assembly line justice** occurs when the criminal courts function so that individuals lose their identity and are treated as objects, rather than people. The criminal arraignment is a stage in the pre-trial process where this phenomenon is readily apparent. On a typical day in most large counties the arraignment calendar will progress by calling defendants to the center aisle of the courtroom by last name, often having read them their constitutional rights as a group, and then spending just 3–5 minutes per person. The judge explains what charges they face and typically assigns counsel to work with the defendant. In some courts or specific calendars the defendant might even enter a plea at that time (with little information and even less understanding of the proceeding in which they are taking part). In more serious felony cases, it is unlikely to see a defendant enter a plea at this stage. He will typically be informed of the charges against him, be read his rights and asked if he has counsel or needs to have counsel appointed for him. If a defendant is indigent or too poor to pay for his own attorney, the court will appoint an attorney to represent him.

In *Argersinger v. Hamlin (1972)*, the U.S. Supreme Court explained the problem of assembly line justice:

> *Wherever the visitor looks at the system, he finds great numbers of defendants being processed by harassed and overworked officials. Police have more cases than they can investigate. Prosecutors walk into courtrooms to try simple cases as they take their initial looks at the files. Defense lawyers appear having had no more than time for hasty conversations with their clients. Judges face long calendars with the certain knowledge that their calendars tomorrow and the next day will be, if anything longer, and so there is no choice but to dispose of the cases. Suddenly it becomes clear that for most defendants in the criminal process, there is scant regard for them as individuals. They are numbers on dockets, faceless ones to be processed and sent on their way. The*

---

[16]    *County of Riverside v. McLaughlin*, 500 U.S. 44 (1991).

*gap between the theory and the reality is enormous. Very little such observation of the administration of criminal justice in operation is required to reach the conclusion that it suffers from basic ills.*[17]

## ii.  The Right to a Speedy Trial

The Sixth Amendment to the U.S. Constitution **speedy trial clause** which provides: "In all criminal prosecutions, the accused shall enjoy the right to a speedy and public trial. . ."[18] What does it mean for a court to abide by this requirement of a "speedy" trial? Both state and federal courts must provide for a speedy trial, and every state has a "speedy trial act" that provides standards the courts should follow with regard to the timeline for disposition of cases. The federal statute is the Speedy Trial Act of 1974, and is set forth in 18 U.S.C. §§ 3161–3174. The Act establishes time limits for completing the various stages of a federal criminal prosecution. The information or indictment must be filed within 30 days from the date of arrest or service of the summons. Trial must commence within 70 days from the date the information or indictment was filed, or from the date the defendant appears before an officer of the court in which the charge is pending, whichever is later. The Speedy Trial Act is inapplicable to juvenile delinquency proceedings, which have their own speedy trial provision.

Trial courts are overwhelmed with caseloads and under-resourced. The result is that cases take a long time to reach final disposition. In 2011 the National Center for State Courts published revised Model Time Standards for State Trial Courts. The lengthy report compares the time standards set by the American Bar Association (ABA), the conference Of State Court Administrators (COSCA) and the newly articulated Model Standards. Unlike the ABA guidelines, the Model Time Standards acknowledge the complexity of a certain (very small) number of felony cases which are so complex the trials cannot be completed within one year. They recommend that 98% of all felony cases be completed within 365 days. Many less serious felonies (75%) should be completed within 180 days.

For misdemeanor cases a similar model is employed: they recommend that 98% be completed within 180 days, and that 75% be completed within 60 days. The reality is that often these timelines go unheeded. In many states it could take years for a complex case to reach completion. Sometimes this is the result of decisions made by the defendant, the choice to "waive time" can be strategic, and

---

[17]  *Argersinger v. Hamlin*, 407 U.S. 25, 35 (1972).

[18]  U.S. Const. amend VI.

the delay tactical. In other cases the delay is the fault of lacking or mismanaged judicial resources.

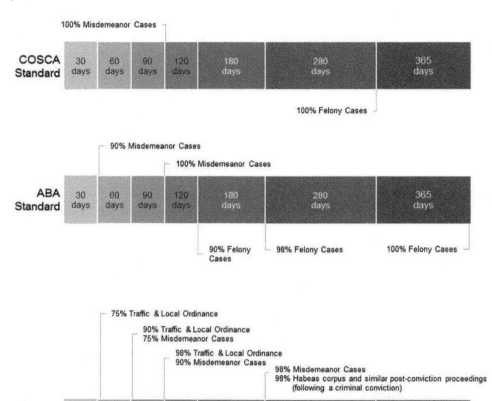

Model Time Standards, National Center For State Trial Courts, http://ncsc.contentdm.oclc.org/cdm/ref/collection/ctadmin/id/1836 (figure 7.1).

The test for evaluating violations of the right to a speedy trial is a **four-prong balancing test** announced by the Supreme Court in the landmark case of *Barker v. Wingo (1972).*[19] In *Barker* two men, Willie Barker and Silas Manning, were accused of the brutal murder of an elderly couple.[20] The state prosecuted Manning first because they believed the case against him was stronger and they intended to use his conviction in their case against Barker. The prosecution of Manning did not go smoothly and took nearly five years. During this time Willie Barker was

---

[19]  407 U.S. 514 (1972).

[20]  *Id.*

awaiting trial, and for the majority of the time was free on bail. When the prosecutor was finally able to convict Manning and move forward in the case against Barker, he objected on the grounds that they had violated his right to a speedy trial. In affirming his conviction the Court utilized a balancing test rather than a bright-line rule for deciding speedy trial questions.

Pre-trial judicial processes are sometimes boring or routine and can appear inconsequential. For defendants and their families experiencing the criminal justice system as outsiders, who are unfamiliar with the courts and the rules that govern them, each step in the process is profoundly important. A judge who takes care to explain a defendant's rights and charges in a meaningful way at arraignment has a positive impact on that defendant, his family, and the observers in court. Public confidence in the judicial system is important and is built upon taking care to follow the rules in place to ensure fairness for each individual served by the courts.

### iii. Case Attrition

What will happen to a felony defendant after arrest? The disposition of a case from arrest to sentencing might seem like a mechanical process where each case is treated the same way: initial appearance, arraignment, bail and on to trial. **Case attrition** is the failure of arrests to come to trial. In the United States less than half of all arrests result in conviction.[21] Researchers have endeavored to identify the reasons for attrition.

Once an arrest is made the case is affected as members of the courtroom work group exercise discretion. They make legal judgments such as evaluating the quality of the evidence available to the prosecutor or considering public policy objectives of local officials when deciding how to proceed with a case. These factors impact the importance of prosecuting an individual case and may result in dismissal of charges, the offer a plea bargain or pre-trial release. The **Bureau of Justice Statistics** collects and analyzes crime data. Their research on case attrition in large urban counties shows that of 100 felony defendants whose cases are arraigned in state courts, nearly 1/3 are dismissed or diverted to other programs such as drug treatment. Of the remaining 2/3 over 94% enter a guilty plea. The remaining 5%–6% move forward and a trial is held. In those cases 3 out of every 4 result in a guilty verdict. The reality for defendants is that once a case has progressed to the point of charging, the likelihood of acquittal is very slim.

---

[21]   Abrahamse, A., Petersilia, J. and Wilson, J., *Police Performance and Case Attrition*, for the National Institute of Justice, Rand, 1987.

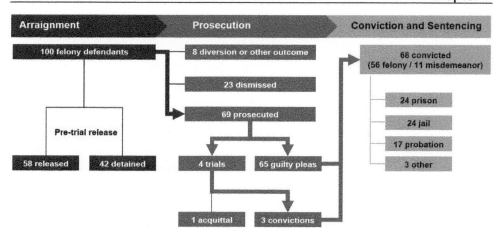

Bureau of Justice Statistics, 2010. *Felony Defendants in Large Urban Counties*, 2006. Washington DC: Department of Justice. (figure 7.2).

**Read and brief each of the following cases relating to pre-trial criminal judicial process and consider the questions following each case:**

1.  *Stack v. Boyle*: constitutional requirements for bail

2.  *United States v. Salerno*: preventive detention

3.  *Coleman v. Alabama*: preliminary hearings

4.  *Barker v. Wingo*: the right to a speedy trial

---

## STACK V. BOYLE

Supreme Court of the United States
Argued Oct. 18, 1951
Decided Nov. 5, 1951
342 U.S. 1

### OPINION

### MR. CHIEF JUSTICE VINSON delivered the opinion of the Court.

Indictments have been returned in the Southern District of California charging the twelve petitioners with conspiring to violate the Smith Act, 18 U.S.C. (Supp. IV) §§ 371, 2385. Upon their arrest, bail was fixed for each petitioner in the widely varying amounts of $ 2,500, $ 7,500, $ 75,000 and $ 100,000. On motion of petitioner Schneiderman following arrest in the Southern District of New York, his bail was reduced to $ 50,000 before his removal to California. On motion of the Government to increase bail in the case of other petitioners, and after several intermediate procedural steps not material to the issues presented here, bail was fixed in the District Court for the Southern District of California in the uniform amount of $ 50,000 for each petitioner.

Petitioners moved to reduce bail on the ground that bail as fixed was excessive under the Eighth Amendment.[1] In support of their motion, petitioners submitted statements as to their financial resources, family relationships, health, prior criminal records, and other information. The only evidence offered by the Government was a certified record showing that four persons previously convicted under the Smith Act in the Southern District of New York had forfeited bail. No evidence was produced relating those four persons to the petitioners in this case. At a hearing on the motion, petitioners

---

[1]  "Excessive bail shall not be required, nor excessive fines imposed, nor cruel and unusual punishments inflicted." U.S. Const., Amend. VIII.

were examined by the District Judge and cross-examined by an attorney for the Government. Petitioners' factual statements stand uncontroverted.

After their motion to reduce bail was denied, petitioners filed applications for habeas corpus in the same District Court. Upon consideration of the record on the motion to reduce bail, the writs were denied. The Court of Appeals for the Ninth Circuit affirmed. Prior to filing their petition for certiorari in this Court, petitioners filed with MR. JUSTICE DOUGLAS an application for bail and an alternative application for habeas corpus seeking interim relief. Both applications were referred to the Court and the matter was set down for argument on specific questions covering the issues raised by this case.

Relief in this type of case must be speedy if it is to be effective. The petition for certiorari and the full record are now before the Court and, since the questions presented by the petition have been fully briefed and argued, we consider it appropriate to dispose of the petition for certiorari at this time. Accordingly, the petition for certiorari is granted for review of questions important to the administration of criminal justice.[2]

*First.* From the passage of the Judiciary Act of 1789, 1 Stat. 73, 91, to the present Federal Rules of Criminal Procedure, Rule 46(a)(1), federal law has unequivocally provided that a person arrested for a non-capital offense *shall* be admitted to bail. This traditional right to freedom before conviction permits the unhampered preparation of a defense, and serves to prevent the infliction of punishment prior to conviction. See *Hudson v. Parker*, 156 U.S. 277, 285 (1895). Unless this right to bail before trial is preserved, the presumption of innocence, secured only after centuries of struggle, would lose its meaning.

The right to release before trial is conditioned upon the accused's giving adequate assurance that he will stand trial and submit to sentence if found guilty. *Ex parte Milburn*, 9 Pet. 704, 710 (1835). Like the ancient practice of securing the oaths of responsible persons to stand as sureties for the accused, the modern practice of requiring a bail bond or the deposit of a sum of money subject to forfeiture serves as additional assurance of the presence of an accused. Bail set at a figure higher than an amount reasonably calculated to fulfill this purpose is "excessive" under the Eighth Amendment. See *United States v. Motlow*, 10 F.2d 657 (1926, opinion by Mr. Justice Butler as Circuit Justice of the Seventh Circuit).

---

[2]    In view of our action in granting and making final disposition of the petition for certiorari, we have no occasion to determine the power of a single Justice or Circuit Justice to fix bail pending disposition of a petition for certiorari in a case of this kind.

Since the function of bail is limited, the fixing of bail for any individual defendant must be based upon standards relevant to the purpose of assuring the presence of that defendant. The traditional standards as expressed in the Federal Rules of Criminal Procedure are to be applied in each case to each defendant. In this case petitioners are charged with offenses under the Smith Act and, if found guilty, their convictions are subject to review with the scrupulous care demanded by our Constitution. *Dennis v. United States*, 341 U.S. 494, 516 (1951).

Upon final judgment of conviction, petitioners face imprisonment of not more than five years and a fine of not more than $ 10,000. It is not denied that bail for each petitioner has been fixed in a sum much higher than that usually imposed for offenses with like penalties and yet there has been no factual showing to justify such action in this case. The Government asks the courts to depart from the norm by assuming, without the introduction of evidence, that each petitioner is a pawn in a conspiracy and will, in obedience to a superior, flee the jurisdiction. To infer from the fact of indictment alone a need for bail in an unusually high amount is an arbitrary act. Such conduct would inject into our own system of government the very principles of totalitarianism which Congress was seeking to guard against in passing the statute under which petitioners have been indicted.

> Rule 46(c). "AMOUNT. If the defendant is admitted to bail, the amount thereof shall be such as in the judgment of the commissioner or court or judge or justice will insure the presence of the defendant, having regard to the nature and circumstances of the offense charged, the weight of the evidence against him, the financial ability of the defendant to give bail and the character of the defendant."

If bail in an amount greater than that usually fixed for serious charges of crimes is required in the case of any of the petitioners, that is a matter to which evidence should be directed in a hearing so that the constitutional rights of each petitioner may be preserved. In the absence of such a showing, we are of the opinion that the fixing of bail before trial in these cases cannot be squared with the statutory and constitutional standards for admission to bail.

. . .

The Court concludes that bail has not been fixed by proper methods in this case and that petitioners' remedy is by motion to reduce bail, with right of appeal to the Court of Appeals. Accordingly, the judgment of the Court of Appeals is vacated and the case is remanded to the District Court with directions to vacate its order denying petitioners' applications for writs of habeas corpus and to dismiss the applications without prejudice. Petitioners may move for reduction of bail in the criminal proceeding so that a hearing may be held for the purpose of fixing reasonable bail for each petitioner.

**It is so ordered. . . .**

**After preparing the case brief, consider the answers to the following questions:**

1.    What is the primary purpose of bail according to the Court?

2.    According to the Court, why is pre-trial release important for defendants? What risks are inherent with being in custody prior to trial?

3.    Do you agree with the Court that the bail amounts in this case were excessive? Explain.

# UNITED STATES V. SALERNO

Supreme Court of the United States
Argued Jan. 21, 1987
Decided May 26, 1987
481 U.S. 739

## OPINION

### CHIEF JUSTICE REHNQUIST delivered the opinion of the Court.

The Bail Reform Act of 1984 (Act) allows a federal court to detain an arrestee pending trial if the Government demonstrates by clear and convincing evidence after an adversary hearing that no release conditions "will reasonably assure . . . the safety of any other person and the community." The United States Court of Appeals for the Second Circuit struck down this provision of the Act as facially unconstitutional, because, in that court's words, this type of pretrial detention violates "substantive due process." We granted certiorari because of a conflict among the Courts of Appeals regarding the validity of the Act.

We hold that, as against the facial attack mounted by these respondents, the Act fully comports with constitutional requirements. We therefore reverse.

I

Responding to "the alarming problem of crimes committed by persons on release," Congress formulated the *Bail Reform Act of 1984*, 18 U.S.C. § 3141 *et seq.* (1982 ed., Supp. III), as the solution to a bail crisis in the federal courts. The Act represents the National Legislature's considered response to numerous perceived deficiencies in the federal bail process. By providing for sweeping changes in both the way federal courts consider bail applications and the circumstances under which bail is granted, Congress hoped to "give the courts adequate authority to make release decisions that give appropriate recognition to the danger a person may pose to others if released."

To this end, § 3141(a) of the Act requires a judicial officer to determine whether an arrestee shall be detained. Section 3142(e) provides that "[i]f, after a hearing pursuant to the provisions of subsection (f), the judicial officer finds that no condition or combination of conditions will reasonably assure the appearance of the person as required and the safety of any other person and the community, he shall order the detention of the person prior to trial." Section 3142(f) provides the arrestee with a number of procedural safeguards. He may request the presence of counsel at the detention hearing, he may testify and present witnesses in his behalf, as well as proffer evidence, and he may cross-examine other witnesses appearing at the hearing. If the judicial officer finds that no conditions of pretrial release can reasonably assure the safety of other persons and the community, he must state his findings of fact in writing, § 3142(i), and support his conclusion with "clear and convincing evidence," § 3142(f).

The judicial officer is not given unbridled discretion in making the detention determination. Congress has specified the considerations relevant to that decision. These factors include the nature and seriousness of the charges, the substantiality of the Government's evidence against the arrestee, the arrestee's background and characteristics, and the nature and seriousness of the danger posed by the suspect's release. § 3142(g). Should a judicial officer order detention, the detainee is entitled to expedited appellate review of the detention order. §§ 3145(b), (c).

Respondents Anthony Salerno and Vincent Cafaro were arrested on March 21, 1986, after being charged in a 29-count indictment alleging various Racketeer Influenced and Corrupt Organizations Act (RICO) violations, mail and wire fraud offenses, extortion, and various criminal gambling violations. The RICO counts alleged 35 acts of racketeering activity, including fraud, extortion, gambling, and conspiracy to commit murder. At respondents' arraignment, the Government moved to have Salerno and Cafaro detained pursuant to § 3142(e), on the ground that no condition of release would assure the safety of the community or any person. The District Court held a hearing at which the Government made a detailed proffer of evidence. The Government's case showed that Salerno was the "boss" of the Genovese crime family of La Cosa Nostra and that Cafaro was a "captain" in the Genovese family. According to the Government's proffer, based in large part on conversations intercepted by a court-ordered wiretap, the two respondents had participated in wide-ranging conspiracies to aid their illegitimate enterprises through violent means. The Government also offered the testimony of two of its trial witnesses, who would assert that Salerno personally participated in two murder conspiracies. Salerno opposed the motion for detention, challenging the credibility of the Government's witnesses. He offered the testimony of several character witnesses as well as a letter from his doctor stating that he was suffering from a serious medical condition. Cafaro presented no evidence at the hearing, but instead characterized the wiretap conversations as merely "tough talk."

The District Court granted the Government's detention motion, concluding that the Government had established by clear and convincing evidence that no condition or combination of conditions of release would ensure the safety of the community or any person:

> "The activities of a criminal organization such as the Genovese Family do not cease with the arrest of its principals and their release on even the most stringent of bail conditions. The illegal businesses, in place for many years, require constant attention and protection, or they will fail. Under these circumstances, this court recognizes a strong incentive on the part of its leadership to continue business as usual. When business as usual involves threats, beatings, and murder, the present danger such people pose in the community is self-evident."

Respondents appealed, contending that to the extent that the Bail Reform Act permits pretrial detention on the ground that the arrestee is likely to commit future crimes, it is unconstitutional on its face. Over a dissent, the United States Court of Appeals for the Second Circuit agreed. . . . The dissenting judge concluded that on its face, the Bail Reform Act adequately balanced the Federal Government's compelling interests in public safety against the detainee's liberty interests.

II

A facial challenge to a legislative Act is, of course, the most difficult challenge to mount successfully, since the challenger must establish that no set of circumstances exists under which the Act would be valid. The fact that the Bail Reform Act might operate unconstitutionally under some conceivable set of circumstances is insufficient to render it wholly invalid, since we have not recognized an "overbreadth" doctrine outside the limited context of the First Amendment. *Schall v. Martin, supra,* at 269, n. 18. We think respondents have failed to shoulder their heavy burden to demonstrate that the Act is "facially" unconstitutional.

Respondents present two grounds for invalidating the Bail Reform Act's provisions permitting pretrial detention on the basis of future dangerousness. First, they rely upon the Court of Appeals' conclusion that the Act exceeds the limitations placed upon the Federal Government by the Due Process Clause of the Fifth Amendment. Second, they contend that the Act contravenes the Eighth Amendment's proscription against excessive bail. We treat these contentions in turn. . .

B

Respondents also contend that the Bail Reform Act violates the Excessive Bail Clause of the Eighth Amendment. The Court of Appeals did not address this issue because it found that the Act violates the Due Process Clause. We think that the Act survives a challenge founded upon the Eighth Amendment.

The Eighth Amendment addresses pretrial release by providing merely that "[e]xcessive bail shall not be required." This Clause, of course, says nothing about whether bail shall be available at all. Respondents nevertheless contend that this Clause grants them a right to bail calculated solely upon considerations of flight. They rely on *Stack v. Boyle,* 342 U.S. 1, 5, 72 S.Ct. 1, 3, 96 L.Ed. 3 (1951), in which the Court stated that "[b]ail set at a figure higher than an amount reasonably calculated [to ensure the defendant's presence at trial] is 'excessive' under the Eighth Amendment." In respondents' view, since the Bail Reform Act allows a court essentially to set bail at an infinite amount for reasons not related to the risk of flight, it violates the Excessive Bail Clause. Respondents concede that the right to bail they have discovered in the Eighth Amendment is not absolute. A court may, for example, refuse bail in capital cases. And, as the Court of Appeals noted and respondents admit, a court may refuse bail when the defendant presents a threat to the judicial process by intimidating witnesses. Brief for Respondents 21–22. Respondents characterize these exceptions as consistent with what they claim to be the sole purpose of bail—to ensure the integrity of the judicial process.

While we agree that a primary function of bail is to safeguard the courts' role in adjudicating the guilt or innocence of defendants, we reject the proposition that the Eighth Amendment categorically prohibits the government from pursuing other admittedly compelling interests through regulation of pretrial release. The above-quoted *dictum* in *Stack v. Boyle* is far too slender a reed on which to rest this argument. The Court in *Stack* had no occasion to consider whether the Excessive Bail Clause requires courts to admit all defendants to bail, because the statute before the Court in that case in fact allowed the defendants to be bailed. Thus, the Court had to determine only whether bail, admittedly available in that case, was excessive if set at a sum greater than that necessary to ensure the arrestees' presence at trial. . .

Nothing in the text of the Bail Clause limits permissible Government considerations solely to questions of flight. The only arguable substantive limitation of the Bail Clause is that the Government's proposed conditions of release or detention not be "excessive" in light of the perceived evil. Of course, to determine whether the Government's response is excessive, we must compare that response against the interest the Government seeks to protect by means of that response. Thus, when the Government has admitted that its only interest is in preventing flight, bail must be set by a court at a sum designed to ensure that goal, and no more. *Stack v. Boyle, supra.* We believe that when Congress has mandated detention on the basis of a compelling interest other than prevention of flight, as it has here, the Eighth Amendment does not require release on bail.

### III

In our society liberty is the norm, and detention prior to trial or without trial is the carefully limited exception. We hold that the provisions for pretrial detention in the Bail Reform Act of 1984 fall within that carefully limited exception. The Act authorizes the detention prior to trial of arrestees charged with serious felonies who are found after an adversary hearing to pose a threat to the safety of individuals or to the community which no condition of release can dispel. The numerous procedural safeguards detailed above must attend this adversary hearing. We are unwilling to say that this congressional determination, based as it is upon that primary concern of every government— a concern for the safety and indeed the lives of its citizens—on its face violates either the Due Process Clause of the Fifth Amendment or the Excessive Bail Clause of the Eighth Amendment.

The judgment of the Court of Appeals is therefore

**Reversed.**

JUSTICE MARSHALL, with whom JUSTICE BRENNAN joins, **dissenting.**

This case brings before the Court for the first time a statute in which Congress declares that a person innocent of any crime may be jailed indefinitely, pending the trial of allegations which are legally presumed to be untrue, if the Government shows to the satisfaction of a judge that the accused is likely to commit crimes, unrelated to the pending charges, at any time in the future. Such statutes, consistent with the usages of tyranny and the excesses of what bitter experience teaches us to call the police state, have long been thought incompatible with the fundamental human rights protected by our Constitution. Today a majority of this Court holds otherwise. Its decision disregards basic principles of justice established centuries ago and enshrined beyond the reach of governmental interference in the Bill of Rights. . .

## II

The majority approaches respondents' challenge to the Act by dividing the discussion into two sections, one concerned with the substantive guarantees implicit in the Due Process Clause, and the other concerned with the protection afforded by the Excessive Bail Clause of the Eighth Amendment. . . .

The logic of the majority's Eighth Amendment analysis is equally unsatisfactory. The Eighth Amendment, as the majority notes, states that "[e]xcessive bail shall not be required." The majority then declares, as if it were undeniable, that: "[t]his Clause, of course, says nothing about whether bail shall be available at all." *Ante,* at 2104. If excessive bail is imposed the defendant stays in jail. The same result is achieved if bail is denied altogether. Whether the magistrate sets bail at $1 million or refuses to set bail at all, the consequences are indistinguishable. It would be mere sophistry to suggest that the Eighth Amendment protects against the former decision, and not the latter. Indeed, such a result would lead to the conclusion that there was no need for Congress to pass a preventive detention measure of any kind; every federal magistrate and district judge could simply refuse, despite the absence of any evidence of risk of flight or danger to the community, to set bail. This would be entirely constitutional, since, according to the majority, the Eighth Amendment "says nothing about whether bail shall be available at all."

But perhaps, the majority says, this manifest absurdity can be avoided. Perhaps the Bail Clause is addressed only to the Judiciary. "[W]e need not decide today," the majority says, "whether the Excessive Bail Clause speaks at all to Congress' power to define the classes of criminal arrestees who shall be admitted to bail." *Ante,* at 2105. The majority is correct that this question need not be decided today; it was decided long ago. Federal and state statutes which purport to accomplish what the Eighth Amendment forbids, such as imposing cruel and unusual punishments, may not stand. See, *e.g., Trop v. Dulles,* 356 U.S. 86, 78 S.Ct. 590, 2 L.Ed.2d 630 (1958); *Furman v. Georgia,* 408 U.S. 238, 92 S.Ct. 2726, 33 L.Ed.2d 346 (1972). The text of the Amendment, which provides simply that "[e]xcessive bail shall not be required, nor excessive fines imposed, nor cruel and unusual punishments inflicted," provides absolutely no support for the majority's speculation that both courts and Congress are forbidden to inflict cruel and unusual punishments, while only the courts are forbidden to require excessive bail.

The majority's attempts to deny the relevance of the Bail Clause to this case are unavailing, but the majority is nonetheless correct that the prohibition of excessive bail means that in order "to determine whether the Government's response is excessive, we must compare that response against the interest the Government seeks to protect by means of that response." *Ante,* at 2105. The majority concedes, as it must, that "when the Government has admitted that its only interest is in preventing flight, bail must be set by a court at a sum designed to ensure that goal, and no more." *Ibid.* But, the majority says, "when Congress has mandated detention on the basis of a compelling interest other than prevention of flight, as it has here, the Eighth Amendment does not require release on bail." *Ante,* at 2105. This conclusion follows only if the "compelling" interest upon which Congress acted is an interest which the Constitution permits Congress to further through the denial of bail. The majority does not ask, as a result of its disingenuous division of the analysis, if there are any substantive limits contained in both the Eighth Amendment and the Due Process Clause which render this system of preventive detention unconstitutional. The majority does not ask because the answer is apparent and, to the majority, inconvenient.

### III

The essence of this case may be found, ironically enough, in a provision of the Act to which the majority does not refer. Title 18 U.S.C. § 3142(j) (1982 ed., Supp. III) provides that "[n]othing in this section shall be construed as modifying or limiting the presumption of innocence." But the very pith and purpose of this statute is an abhorrent limitation of the presumption of innocence. The majority's untenable conclusion that the present Act is constitutional arises from a specious denial of the role of the Bail Clause and the Due Process Clause in protecting the invaluable guarantee afforded by the presumption of innocence. . .

I dissent. . . .

**After preparing the case brief, consider the answers to the following questions:**

1. What is a "facial challenge" to a statute?

2. On what grounds did Salerno argue that the Bail Reform Act of 1984 was unconstitutional?

3. What factors are judges to consider when deciding whether to allow a defendant to be released prior to trial?

4.   Are you convinced by Justice Marshall's argument that the presumption of innocence should prevent pretrial detention in this case? Why?

# COLEMAN V. ALABAMA

Supreme Court of the United States
Argued Nov. 18, 1969
Decided June 22, 1970
399 U.S. 1

## OPINION

**MR. JUSTICE BRENNAN announced the judgment of the Court and delivered the following opinion.**

Petitioners were convicted in an Alabama Circuit Court of assault with intent to murder in the shooting of one Reynolds after he and his wife parked their car on an Alabama highway to change a flat tire. The Alabama Court of Appeals affirmed, and the Alabama Supreme Court denied review. We granted certiorari. We vacate and remand.

Petitioners make two claims in this Court. First, they argue that they were subjected to a station-house lineup in circumstances so unduly prejudicial and conducive to irreparable misidentification as fatally to taint Reynolds' in-court identifications of them at the trial. Second, they argue that the preliminary hearing prior to their indictment was a "critical stage" of the prosecution and that Alabama's failure to provide them with appointed counsel at the hearing therefore unconstitutionally denied them the assistance of counsel. . .

### II[2]

This Court has held that a person accused of crime "requires the guiding hand of counsel at every step in the proceedings against him," *Powell v. Alabama*, 287 U.S. 45, 69 (1932), and that that constitutional principle is not limited to the presence of counsel at trial. "It is central to that principle that in addition to counsel's presence at trial, the accused is guaranteed that he need not stand alone against the State at any stage of the prosecution, formal or informal, in court or out, where counsel's absence might derogate from the accused's right to a fair trial." *United States v. Wade, supra*, at 226. Accordingly, "the principle of *Powell v. Alabama* and succeeding cases requires that we scrutinize *any* pretrial confrontation of the accused to determine whether the presence of his counsel is necessary to preserve the defendant's basic right to a fair trial as affected by his right meaningfully to cross-examine the witnesses against him and to have effective assistance of counsel at the trial itself. It calls upon us to analyze whether potential substantial prejudice to defendant's rights inheres in the

---

[2]    MR. JUSTICE DOUGLAS, MR. JUSTICE WHITE, and MR. JUSTICE MARSHALL join this Part II.

particular confrontation and the ability of counsel to help avoid that prejudice." *Id.*, at 227. Applying this test, the Court has held that "critical stages" include the pretrial type of arraignment where certain rights may be sacrificed or lost, *Hamilton v. Alabama*, 368 U.S. 52, 54 (1961). . .where the Court held that the privilege against compulsory self-incrimination includes a right to counsel at a pretrial custodial interrogation. See also *Massiah v. United States*, 377 U.S. 201 (1964).

The preliminary hearing is not a required step in an Alabama prosecution. The prosecutor may seek an indictment directly from the grand jury without a preliminary hearing. *Ex parte Campbell*, 278 Ala. 114, 176 So. 2d 242 (1965). The opinion of the Alabama Court of Appeals in this case instructs us that under Alabama law the sole purposes of a preliminary hearing are to determine whether there is sufficient evidence against the accused to warrant presenting his case to the grand jury, and, if so, to fix bail if the offense is bailable. 44 Ala. App., at 433, 211 So. 2d, at 920. See Ala. Code, Tit. 15, §§ 139, 140, 151.[3] The court continued:

> "At the preliminary hearing . . . the accused is not required to advance any defenses, and failure to do so does not preclude him from availing himself of every defense he may have upon the trial of the case. Also *Pointer v. State of Texas* [380 U.S. 400 (1965)] bars the admission of testimony given at a pre-trial proceeding where the accused did not have the benefit of cross-examination by and through counsel. Thus, nothing occurring at the preliminary hearing in absence of counsel can substantially prejudice the rights of the accused on trial." 44 Ala. App., at 433, 211 So. 2d, at 921.

This Court is of course bound by this construction of the governing Alabama law, *Kingsley International Pictures Corp. v. Regents*, 360 U.S. 684, 688 (1959). . . However, from the fact that in cases where the accused has no lawyer at the hearing the Alabama courts prohibit the State's use at trial of anything that occurred at the hearing, it does not follow that the Alabama preliminary

---

[3] A textbook, Criminal Procedure in Alabama, by M. Clinton McGee (University of Alabama Press 1954), p. 41, states:

> "A preliminary hearing or examination is not a trial in its ordinary sense nor is it a final determination of guilt. It is a proceeding whereby an accused is discharged or held to answer, as the facts warrant. It seeks to determine whether there is probable cause for believing that a crime has been committed and whether the accused is probably guilty, in order that he may be informed of the nature of such charge and to allow the state to take the necessary steps to bring him to trial. Such hearing also serves to perpetuate evidence and to keep the necessary witnesses within the control of the state. It also safeguards the accused against groundless and vindictive prosecutions, and avoids for both the accused and the state the expense and inconvenience of a public trial."

hearing is not a "critical stage" of the State's criminal process. The determination whether the hearing is a "critical stage" requiring the provision of counsel depends, as noted, upon an analysis "whether potential substantial prejudice to defendant's rights inheres in the . . . confrontation and the ability of counsel to help avoid that prejudice." *United States v. Wade, supra,* at 227. Plainly the guiding hand of counsel at the preliminary hearing is essential to protect the indigent accused against an erroneous or improper prosecution. First, the lawyer's skilled examination and cross-examination of witnesses may expose fatal weaknesses in the State's case that may lead the magistrate to refuse to bind the accused over. Second, in any event, the skilled interrogation of witnesses by an experienced lawyer can fashion a vital impeachment tool for use in cross-examination of the State's witnesses at the trial, or preserve testimony favorable to the accused of a witness who does not appear at the trial. Third, trained counsel can more effectively discover the case the State has against his client and make possible the preparation of a proper defense to meet that case at the trial. Fourth, counsel can also be influential at the preliminary hearing in making effective arguments for the accused on such matters as the necessity for an early psychiatric examination or bail.

The inability of the indigent accused on his own to realize these advantages of a lawyer's assistance compels the conclusion that the Alabama preliminary hearing is a "critical stage" of the State's criminal process at which the accused is "as much entitled to such aid [of counsel] . . . as at the trial itself." *Powell v. Alabama, supra,* at 57.

III

**MR. JUSTICE BLACK, MR. JUSTICE DOUGLAS, MR. JUSTICE WHITE, and MR. JUSTICE MARSHALL join this Part III.**

There remains, then, the question of the relief to which petitioners are entitled. The trial transcript indicates that the prohibition against use by the State at trial of anything that occurred at the preliminary hearing was scrupulously observed.[5] Cf. *White v. Maryland, supra.* But on the record it cannot

---

[5]     The trial judge held a hearing two months before the trial on motions on behalf of petitioners to suppress "any evidence or discovery whatsoever obtained . . . on the preliminary hearing . . . and further any statements relating to any identification . . . during any line-up. . . ." The State conceded that the motion should be granted as to any statements of either petitioner taken by the police upon their arrests, and written and oral confessions made by them were therefore not offered at the trial. At an early stage of the hearing on the motions, the trial judge said:

> "It has been my consistent ruling, and I don't know of any law to the contrary, that, on the basis of what happened at the preliminary hearing, that if a lawyer was not representing the defendant that anything that may have occurred at that preliminary which might work against the defendant,

be said whether or not petitioners were otherwise prejudiced by the absence of counsel at the preliminary hearing. That inquiry in the first instance should more properly be made by the Alabama courts. The test to be applied is whether the denial of counsel at the preliminary hearing was harmless error under *Chapman v. California*, 386 U.S. 18 (1967). See *United States v. Wade, supra*, at 242.

We accordingly vacate the petitioners' convictions and remand the case to the Alabama courts for such proceedings not inconsistent with this opinion as they may deem appropriate to determine whether such denial of counsel was harmless error, see *Gilbert v. California, supra*, at 272, and therefore whether the convictions should be reinstated or a new trial ordered.

**It is so ordered.**

**MR. JUSTICE BLACKMUN took no part in the consideration or decision of this case. . .**

**MR. JUSTICE DOUGLAS, concurring.**

While I have joined MR. JUSTICE BRENNAN's opinion, I add a word as to why I think that a strict construction of the Constitution requires the result reached.

The critical words are: "In all criminal prosecutions, the accused shall enjoy the right . . . to have the Assistance of Counsel for his defence." As MR. JUSTICE BLACK states, a preliminary hearing is "a definite part or stage of a criminal prosecution in Alabama." A "criminal prosecution" certainly does not start only when the trial starts. If the commencement of the trial were the start of the "criminal prosecution" in the constitutional sense, then indigents would likely go to trial without effective representation by counsel. . . .

If we are to adhere to the mandate of the Constitution and not give it merely that meaning which appeals to the personal tastes of those who from time to time sit here, we should read its terms in light of the realities of what "criminal prosecutions" truly mean. . .

---

whether it be anything he said there, assuming he might have taken the stand, anything of that nature, would, on the trial of the case on the merits, be inadmissible.

"I wouldn't anticipate the State offering anything like that, but that has been my ruling on that ever since we changed some of our ways of doing things.

"It wouldn't be material from the standpoint that a man down there, when not represented by counsel on the preliminary, made some statement, said, 'I am guilty.' You know, a lot of times he might say, 'I am guilty.'

"That that would not be admissible if he weren't represented by counsel, and that sort of thing."

**MR. JUSTICE STEWART,** with whom **THE CHIEF JUSTICE** joins, **dissenting.**

On a July night in 1966 Casey Reynolds and his wife stopped their car on Green Springs Highway in Birmingham, Alabama, in order to change a flat tire. They were soon accosted by three men whose evident purpose was armed robbery and rape. The assailants shot Reynolds twice before they were frightened away by the lights of a passing automobile. Some two months later the petitioners were arrested, and later identified by Reynolds as two of the three men who had assaulted him and his wife.

A few days later the petitioners were granted a preliminary hearing before a county judge. At this hearing the petitioners were neither required nor permitted to enter any plea. The sole purpose of such a hearing in Alabama is to determine whether there is sufficient evidence against the accused to warrant presenting the case to a grand jury, and, if so, to fix bail if the offense is bailable.[1] At the conclusion of the hearing the petitioners were bound over to the grand jury, and their bond was set at $ 10,000. No record or transcript of any kind was made of the hearing.

Less than a month later the grand jury returned an indictment against the petitioners, charging them with assault to commit murder. Promptly after their indictment, a lawyer was appointed to represent them. At their arraignment two weeks later, where they were represented by their appointed counsel, they entered a plea of not guilty. Cf. *Hamilton v. Alabama*, 368 U.S. 52. Some months later they were brought to trial, again represented by appointed counsel. Cf. *Gideon v. Wainwright*, 372 U.S. 335. The jury found them guilty as charged, and they were sentenced to the penitentiary.

If at the trial the prosecution had used any incriminating statements made by the petitioners at the preliminary hearing, the convictions before us would quite properly have to be set aside. *White v. Maryland*, 373 U.S. 59. But that did not happen in this case. Or if the prosecution had used the statement of any other witness at the preliminary hearing against the petitioners at their trial, we would likewise quite properly have to set aside these convictions. *Pointer v. Texas*, 380 U.S. 400. But that did not happen in this case either. For, as the prevailing opinion today perforce concedes, "the prohibition against use by the State at trial of anything that occurred at the preliminary hearing was scrupulously observed."

---

[1]   Ala. Code, Tit. 15, §§ 133–140 (1958).

Nevertheless, the Court sets aside the convictions because, it says, counsel should have been provided for the petitioners at the preliminary hearing. None of the cases relied upon in that opinion points to any such result. Even the *Miranda* decision does not require counsel to be present at "pretrial custodial interrogation." That case simply held that the constitutional guarantee against compulsory self-incrimination prohibits the introduction at the *trial* of statements made by the defendant during custodial interrogation if the *Miranda* "guidelines" were not followed. 384 U.S. 436. See also *United States v. Wade*, 388 U.S. 218; *Gilbert v. California*, 388 U.S. 263. And I repeat that in this case no evidence of anything said or done at the preliminary hearing was introduced at the petitioners' trial.

But the prevailing opinion holds today that the Constitution required Alabama to provide a lawyer for the petitioners at their preliminary hearing, not so much, it seems, to assure a fair trial as to assure a fair preliminary hearing. A lawyer at the preliminary hearing, the opinion says, might have led the magistrate to "refuse to bind the accused over." Or a lawyer might have made "effective arguments for the accused on such matters as the necessity for an early psychiatric examination or bail."

If *those* are the reasons a lawyer must be provided, then the most elementary logic requires that a new preliminary hearing must now be held, with counsel made available to the petitioners. In order to provide such relief, it would, of course, be necessary not only to set aside these convictions, but also to set aside the grand jury indictments, and the magistrate's orders fixing bail and binding over the petitioners. Since the petitioners have now been found by a jury in a constitutional trial[2] to be guilty beyond a reasonable doubt, the prevailing opinion understandably boggles at these logical consequences of the reasoning therein. It refrains, in short, from now turning back the clock by ordering a new preliminary hearing to determine all over again whether there is sufficient evidence against the accused to present their case to a grand jury. Instead, the Court sets aside these convictions and remands the case for determination "whether the convictions should be reinstated or a new trial ordered," and this action seems to me even more quixotic.

The petitioners have simply not alleged that anything that happened at the preliminary hearing turned out in this case to be critical to the fairness of their *trial*. They have not alleged that they were affirmatively prejudiced at the trial by anything that occurred at the preliminary hearing. They have not pointed to

---

2   I agree with the result reached in Part I of the prevailing opinion.

any affirmative advantage they would have enjoyed at the trial if they had had a lawyer at their preliminary hearing.

No record or transcript of any kind was made of the preliminary hearing. Therefore, if the burden on remand is on the petitioners to show that they were prejudiced, it is clear that that burden cannot be met, and the remand is a futile gesture. If, on the other hand, the burden is on the State to disprove beyond a reasonable doubt any and all speculative advantages that the petitioners might conceivably have enjoyed if counsel had been present at their preliminary hearing, then obviously that burden cannot be met either, and the Court should simply reverse these convictions. All I can say is that if the Alabama courts can figure out what they are supposed to do with this case now that it has been remanded to them, their perceptiveness will far exceed mine.

The record before us makes clear that no evidence of what occurred at the preliminary hearing was used against the petitioners at their now completed trial. I would hold, therefore, that the absence of counsel at the preliminary hearing deprived the petitioners of no constitutional rights. Accordingly, I would affirm these convictions.

**After preparing the case brief, consider the answers to the following questions:**

1. What is a "critical stage"? How does the Court explain that a critical stage can be identified?

2. What are some of the important tasks that attorneys might perform during, or in preparation for, a preliminary hearing?

3. No transcript was kept in the Alabama preliminary hearings in this case and the testimony was not used against the defendants. Why was the Court still convinced they were a critical stage?

## BARKER V. WINGO

Supreme Court of the United States
Argued April 11, 1972
Decided June 22, 1972
407 U.S. 514

### OPINION

### MR. JUSTICE POWELL delivered the opinion of the Court.

Although a speedy trial is guaranteed the accused by the Sixth Amendment to the Constitution,[1] this Court has dealt with that right on infrequent occasions. . . . The Court's opinion in *Klopfer v. North Carolina*, 386 U.S. 213 (1967), established that the right to a speedy trial is "fundamental" and is imposed by the Due Process Clause of the Fourteenth Amendment on the States.[2] . . . in none of these cases have we attempted to set out the criteria by which the speedy trial right is to be judged. . . . This case compels us to make such an attempt.

I

On July 20, 1958, in Christian County, Kentucky, an elderly couple was beaten to death by intruders wielding an iron tire tool. Two suspects, Silas Manning and Willie Barker, the petitioner, were arrested shortly thereafter. The grand jury indicted them on September 15. Counsel was appointed on September 17, and Barker's trial was set for October 21. The Commonwealth had a stronger case against Manning, and it believed that Barker could not be convicted unless Manning testified against him. Manning was naturally unwilling to incriminate himself. Accordingly, on October 23, the day Silas Manning was brought to trial, the Commonwealth sought and obtained the first of what was to be a series of 16 continuances of Barker's trial.[3] Barker made no objection. By first convicting Manning, the Commonwealth would remove possible problems of self-incrimination and would be able to assure his testimony against Barker.

---

[1]   The Sixth Amendment provides:

"In all criminal prosecutions, the accused shall enjoy the right to a speedy and public trial, by an impartial jury of the State and district wherein the crime shall have been committed, which district shall have been previously ascertained by law, and to be informed of the nature and cause of the accusation; to be confronted with the witnesses against him; to have compulsory process for obtaining witnesses in his favor, and to have the Assistance of Counsel for his defence."

[2]   "We hold here that the right to a speedy trial is as fundamental as any of the rights secured by the Sixth Amendment." 386 U.S., at 223.

[3]   There is no explanation in the record why, although Barker's initial trial was set for October 21, no continuance was sought until October 23, two days after the trial should have begun.

The Commonwealth encountered more than a few difficulties in its prosecution of Manning. The first trial ended in a hung jury. A second trial resulted in a conviction, but the Kentucky Court of Appeals reversed because of the admission of evidence obtained by an illegal search. *Manning v. Commonwealth*, 328 S. W. 2d 421 (1959). At his third trial, Manning was again convicted, and the Court of Appeals again reversed because the trial court had not granted a change of venue. *Manning v. Commonwealth*, 346 S. W. 2d 755 (1961). A fourth trial resulted in a hung jury. Finally, after five trials, Manning was convicted, in March 1962, of murdering one victim, and after a sixth trial, in December 1962, he was convicted of murdering the other.[4]

The Christian County Circuit Court holds three terms each year—in February, June, and September. Barker's initial trial was to take place in the September term of 1958. The first continuance postponed it until the February 1959 term. The second continuance was granted for one month only. Every term thereafter for as long as the Manning prosecutions were in process, the Commonwealth routinely moved to continue Barker's case to the next term. When the case was continued from the June 1959 term until the following September, Barker, having spent 10 months in jail, obtained his release by posting a $ 5,000 bond. He thereafter remained free in the community until his trial. Barker made no objection, through his counsel, to the first 11 continuances.

When on February 12, 1962, the Commonwealth moved for the twelfth time to continue the case until the following term, Barker's counsel filed a motion to dismiss the indictment. The motion to dismiss was denied two weeks later, and the Commonwealth's motion for a continuance was granted. The Commonwealth was granted further continuances in June 1962 and September 1962, to which Barker did not object.

In February 1963, the first term of court following Manning's final conviction, the Commonwealth moved to set Barker's trial for March 19. But on the day scheduled for trial, it again moved for a continuance until the June term. It gave as its reason the illness of the ex-sheriff who was the chief investigating officer in the case. To this continuance, Barker objected unsuccessfully.

The witness was still unable to testify in June, and the trial, which had been set for June 19, was continued again until the September term over Barker's objection. This time the court announced that the case would be dismissed for

---

[4] Apparently Manning chose not to appeal these final two convictions.

lack of prosecution if it were not tried during the next term. The final trial date was set for October 9, 1963. On that date, Barker again moved to dismiss the indictment, and this time specified that his right to a speedy trial had been violated.[5] The motion was denied; the trial commenced with Manning as the chief prosecution witness; Barker was convicted and given a life sentence.

Barker appealed his conviction to the Kentucky Court of Appeals, relying in part on his speedy trial claim. The court affirmed. *Barker v. Commonwealth*, 385 S. W. 2d 671 (1964). In February 1970 Barker petitioned for habeas corpus in the United States District Court for the Western District of Kentucky. Although the District Court rejected the petition without holding a hearing, the Court granted petitioner leave to appeal *in forma pauperis* and a certificate of probable cause to appeal. On appeal, the Court of Appeals for the Sixth Circuit affirmed the District Court. 442 F.2d 1141 (1971). It ruled that Barker had waived his speedy trial claim for the entire period before February 1963, the date on which the court believed he had first objected to the delay by filing a motion to dismiss. In this belief the court was mistaken, for the record reveals that the motion was filed in February 1962. The Commonwealth so conceded at oral argument before this Court. The court held further that the remaining period after the date on which Barker first raised his claim and before his trial— which it thought was only eight months but which was actually 20 months— was not unduly long. In addition, the court held that Barker had shown no resulting prejudice, and that the illness of the ex-sheriff was a valid justification for the delay. We granted Barker's petition for certiorari. 404 U.S. 1037 (1972).

II

The right to a speedy trial is generically different from any of the other rights enshrined in the Constitution for the protection of the accused. In addition to the general concern that all accused persons be treated according to decent and fair procedures, there is a societal interest in providing a speedy trial which exists separate from, and at times in opposition to, the interests of the accused. The inability of courts to provide a prompt trial has contributed to a large backlog of cases in urban courts which, among other things, enables defendants to negotiate more effectively for pleas of guilty to lesser offenses and otherwise manipulate the system.[7] In addition, persons released on bond

---

[5]   The written motion Barker filed alleged that he had objected to every continuance since February 1959. The record does not reflect any objections until the motion to dismiss, filed in February 1962, and the objections to the continuances sought by the Commonwealth in March 1963 and June 1963.

[7]   Report of the President's Commission on Crime in the District of Columbia 256 (1966).

for lengthy periods awaiting trial have an opportunity to commit other crimes.[8] It must be of little comfort to the residents of Christian County, Kentucky, to know that Barker was at large on bail for over four years while accused of a vicious and brutal murder of which he was ultimately convicted. Moreover, the longer an accused is free awaiting trial, the more tempting becomes his opportunity to jump bail and escape.[9] Finally, delay between arrest and punishment may have a detrimental effect on rehabilitation.[10]

If an accused cannot make bail, he is generally confined, as was Barker for 10 months, in a local jail. This contributes to the overcrowding and generally deplorable state of those institutions. Lengthy exposure to these conditions "has a destructive effect on human character and makes the rehabilitation of the individual offender much more difficult." At times the result may even be violent rioting. Finally, lengthy pretrial detention is costly. The cost of maintaining a prisoner in jail varies from $ 3 to $ 9 per day, and this amounts to millions across the Nation. In addition, society loses wages which might have been earned, and it must often support families of incarcerated breadwinners. . .

A second difference between the right to speedy trial and the accused's other constitutional rights is that deprivation of the right may work to the accused's advantage. Delay is not an uncommon defense tactic. As the time between the commission of the crime and trial lengthens, witnesses may become unavailable or their memories may fade. If the witnesses support the prosecution, its case will be weakened, sometimes seriously so. And it is the prosecution which carries the burden of proof. Thus, unlike the right to counsel or the right to be free from compelled self-incrimination, deprivation of the right to speedy trial does not *per se* prejudice the accused's ability to defend himself.

Finally, and perhaps most importantly, the right to speedy trial is a more vague concept than other procedural rights. It is, for example, impossible to determine with precision when the right has been denied. We cannot definitely say how long is too long in a system where justice is supposed to be swift but

---

[8]   In Washington, D. C., in 1968, 70.1% of the persons arrested for robbery and released prior to trial were re-arrested while on bail. Mitchell, Bail Reform and the Constitutionality of Pretrial Detention, 55 Va. L. Rev. 1223, 1236 (1969), citing Report of the Judicial Council Committee to Study the Operation of the Bail Reform Act in the District of Columbia 20–21 (1969).

[9]   The number of these offenses has been increasing. See Annual Report of the Director of the Administrative Office of the United States Courts, 1971, p. 321.

[10]   "(I)t is desirable that punishment should follow offence as closely as possible; for its impression upon the minds of men is weakened by distance, and, besides, distance adds to the uncertainty of punishment, by affording new chances of escape." J. Bentham, The Theory of Legislation 326 (Ogden ed. 1931).

deliberate.[15] As a consequence, there is no fixed point in the criminal process when the State can put the defendant to the choice of either exercising or waiving the right to a speedy trial. If, for example, the State moves for a 60-day continuance, granting that continuance is not a violation of the right to speedy trial unless the circumstances of the case are such that further delay would endanger the values the right protects. It is impossible to do more than generalize about when those circumstances exist. There is nothing comparable to the point in the process when a defendant exercises or waives his right to counsel or his right to a jury trial. Thus, as we recognized in *Beavers v. Haubert, supra*, any inquiry into a speedy trial claim necessitates a functional analysis of the right in the particular context of the case:

> "The right of a speedy trial is necessarily relative. It is consistent with delays and depends upon circumstances. It secures rights to a defendant. It does not preclude the rights of public justice." 198 U.S., at 87.

The amorphous quality of the right also leads to the unsatisfactorily severe remedy of dismissal of the indictment when the right has been deprived. This is indeed a serious consequence because it means that a defendant who may be guilty of a serious crime will go free, without having been tried. Such a remedy is more serious than an exclusionary rule or a reversal for a new trial,[16] but it is the only possible remedy.

### III

Perhaps because the speedy trial right is so slippery, two rigid approaches are urged upon us as ways of eliminating some of the uncertainty which courts experience in protecting the right. The first suggestion is that we hold that the Constitution requires a criminal defendant to be offered a trial within a specified time period. The result of such a ruling would have the virtue of clarifying when the right is infringed and of simplifying courts' application of it. . . .

But such a result would require this Court to engage in legislative or rulemaking activity, rather than in the adjudicative process to which we should confine our efforts. We do not establish procedural rules for the States, except

---

[15] "(I)n large measure because of the many procedural safeguards provided an accused, the ordinary procedures for criminal prosecution are designed to move at a deliberate pace. A requirement of unreasonable speed would have a deleterious effect both upon the rights of the accused and upon the ability of society to protect itself." *United States v. Ewell*, 383 U.S. 116, 120 (1966).

[16] Mr. Justice White noted in his opinion for the Court in *Ewell, supra*, at 121, that overzealous application of this remedy would infringe "the societal interest in trying people accused of crime, rather than granting them immunization because of legal error. . . ."

when mandated by the Constitution. We find no constitutional basis for holding that the speedy trial right can be quantified into a specified number of days or months. The States, of course, are free to prescribe a reasonable period consistent with constitutional standards, but our approach must be less precise.

The second suggested alternative would restrict consideration of the right to those cases in which the accused has demanded a speedy trial. Most States have recognized what is loosely referred to as the "demand rule," although eight States reject it. It is not clear, however, precisely what is meant by that term. Although every federal court of appeals that has considered the question has endorsed some kind of demand rule, some have regarded the rule within the concept of waiver, whereas others have viewed it as a factor to be weighed in assessing whether there has been a deprivation of the speedy trial right. We shall refer to the former approach as the demand-waiver doctrine. The demand-waiver doctrine provides that a defendant waives any consideration of his right to speedy trial for any period prior to which he has not demanded a trial. Under this rigid approach, a prior demand is a necessary condition to the consideration of the speedy trial right. This essentially was the approach the Sixth Circuit took below. . .

Such an approach, by presuming waiver of a fundamental right from inaction, is inconsistent with this Court's pronouncements on waiver of constitutional rights. The Court has defined waiver as "an intentional relinquishment or abandonment of a known right or privilege." *Johnson v. Zerbst*, 304 U.S. 458, 464 (1938). Courts should "indulge every reasonable presumption against waiver," *Aetna Ins. Co. v. Kennedy*, 301 U.S. 389, 393 (1937), and they should "not presume acquiescence in the loss of fundamental rights," *Ohio Bell Tel. Co. v. Public Utilities Comm'n*, 301 U.S. 292, 307 (1937).

. . .

It is also noteworthy that such a rigid view of the demand-waiver rule places defense counsel in an awkward position. Unless he demands a trial early and often, he is in danger of frustrating his client's right. If counsel is willing to tolerate some delay because he finds it reasonable and helpful in preparing his own case, he may be unable to obtain a speedy trial for his client at the end of that time. Since under the demand-waiver rule no time runs until the demand is made, the government will have whatever time is otherwise reasonable to bring the defendant to trial after a demand has been made. . .

We reject, therefore, the rule that a defendant who fails to demand a speedy trial forever waives his right. This does not mean, however, that the defendant has no responsibility to assert his right. We think the better rule is that the defendant's assertion of or failure to assert his right to a speedy trial is one of the factors to be considered in an inquiry into the deprivation of the right. Such a formulation avoids the rigidities of the demand-waiver rule and the resulting possible unfairness in its application. It allows the trial court to exercise a judicial discretion based on the circumstances, including due consideration of any applicable formal procedural rule. It would permit, for example, a court to attach a different weight to a situation in which the defendant knowingly fails to object from a situation in which his attorney acquiesces in long delay without adequately informing his client, or from a situation in which no counsel is appointed. It would also allow a court to weigh the frequency and force of the objections as opposed to attaching significant weight to a purely *pro forma* objection. . .

But the rule we announce today, which comports with constitutional principles, places the primary burden on the courts and the prosecutors to assure that cases are brought to trial. We hardly need add that if delay is attributable to the defendant, then his waiver may be given effect under standard waiver doctrine, the demand rule aside.

We, therefore, reject both of the inflexible approaches—the fixed-time period because it goes further than the Constitution requires; the demand-waiver rule because it is insensitive to a right which we have deemed fundamental. The approach we accept is a balancing test, in which the conduct of both the prosecution and the defendant are weighed. . .

IV

A balancing test necessarily compels courts to approach speedy trial cases on an *ad hoc* basis. We can do little more than identify some of the factors which courts should assess in determining whether a particular defendant has been deprived of his right. Though some might express them in different ways, we identify four such factors: Length of delay, the reason for the delay, the defendant's assertion of his right, and prejudice to the defendant.[30]

---

[30] See, e.g., *United States v. Simmons*, 338 F.2d 804, 807 (CA2 1964), cert. denied, 380 U.S. 983 (1965); Note, The Right to a Speedy Trial, 20 Stan. L. Rev. 476, 478 n. 15 (1968).

In his concurring opinion in *Dickey*, MR. JUSTICE BRENNAN identified three factors for consideration: the source of the delay, the reasons for it, and whether the delay prejudiced the interests protected by the right. 398 U.S., at 48. He included consideration of the defendant's failure to assert his right in the cause-of-delay category, and he thought the length of delay was relevant primarily to the reasons for delay and its prejudicial effects. *Id.*, n. 12. In essence, however, there is little difference between his approach and the one we adopt today. See also Note, The Right to a Speedy Trial, *supra*, for another slightly different approach.

The length of the delay is to some extent a triggering mechanism. Until there is some delay which is presumptively prejudicial, there is no necessity for inquiry into the other factors that go into the balance. Nevertheless, because of the imprecision of the right to speedy trial, the length of delay that will provoke such an inquiry is necessarily dependent upon the peculiar circumstances of the case.[31] To take but one example, the delay that can be tolerated for an ordinary street crime is considerably less than for a serious, complex conspiracy charge.

Closely related to length of delay is the reason the government assigns to justify the delay. Here, too, different weights should be assigned to different reasons. A deliberate attempt to delay the trial in order to hamper the defense should be weighted heavily against the government.[32] A more neutral reason such as negligence or overcrowded courts should be weighted less heavily but nevertheless should be considered since the ultimate responsibility for such circumstances must rest with the government rather than with the defendant. Finally, a valid reason, such as a missing witness, should serve to justify appropriate delay.

We have already discussed the third factor, the defendant's responsibility to assert his right. Whether and how a defendant asserts his right is closely related to the other factors we have mentioned. The strength of his efforts will be affected by the length of the delay, to some extent by the reason for the delay, and most particularly by the personal prejudice, which is not always readily identifiable, that he experiences. The more serious the deprivation, the more likely a defendant is to complain. The defendant's assertion of his speedy trial right, then, is entitled to strong evidentiary weight in determining whether the defendant is being deprived of the right. We emphasize that failure to assert the right will make it difficult for a defendant to prove that he was denied a speedy trial.

A fourth factor is prejudice to the defendant. Prejudice, of course, should be assessed in the light of the interests of defendants which the speedy trial right was designed to protect. This Court has identified three such interests: (i) to prevent oppressive pretrial incarceration; (ii) to minimize anxiety and concern of the accused; and (iii) to limit the possibility that the defense will be

---

[31] For example, the First Circuit thought a delay of nine months overly long, absent a good reason, in a case that depended on eyewitness testimony. *United States v. Butler*, 426 F.2d 1275, 1277 (1970).

[32] We have indicated on previous occasions that it is improper for the prosecution intentionally to delay "to gain some tactical advantage over [defendants] or to harass them." *United States v. Marion*, 404 U.S. 307, 325 (1971). See *Pollard v. United States*, 352 U.S. 354, 361 (1957).

impaired.[33] Of these, the most serious is the last, because the inability of a defendant adequately to prepare his case skews the fairness of the entire system. If witnesses die or disappear during a delay, the prejudice is obvious. There is also prejudice if defense witnesses are unable to recall accurately events of the distant past. Loss of memory, however, is not always reflected in the record because what has been forgotten can rarely be shown.

We have discussed previously the societal disadvantages of lengthy pretrial incarceration, but obviously the disadvantages for the accused who cannot obtain his release are even more serious. The time spent in jail awaiting trial has a detrimental impact on the individual. It often means loss of a job; it disrupts family life; and it enforces idleness. Most jails offer little or no recreational or rehabilitative programs.[34] The time spent in jail is simply dead time. Moreover, if a defendant is locked up, he is hindered in his ability to gather evidence, contact witnesses, or otherwise prepare his defense.[35] Imposing those consequences on anyone who has not yet been convicted is serious. It is especially unfortunate to impose them on those persons who are ultimately found to be innocent. Finally, even if an accused is not incarcerated prior to trial, he is still disadvantaged by restraints on his liberty and by living under a cloud of anxiety, suspicion, and often hostility. See cases cited in n. 33, *supra.*

We regard none of the four factors identified above as either a necessary or sufficient condition to the finding of a deprivation of the right of speedy trial. Rather, they are related factors and must be considered together with such other circumstances as may be relevant. In sum, these factors have no talismanic qualities; courts must still engage in a difficult and sensitive balancing process. But, because we are dealing with a fundamental right of the accused, this process must be carried out with full recognition that the accused's interest in a speedy trial is specifically affirmed in the Constitution. . .

V

The difficulty of the task of balancing these factors is illustrated by this case, which we consider to be close. It is clear that the length of delay between

---

[33]  *United States v. Ewell,* 383 U.S., at 120; *Smith v. Hooey,* 393 U.S. 374, 377–378 (1969). In *Klopfer v. North Carolina,* 386 U.S. 213, 221–222 (1967), we indicated that a defendant awaiting trial on bond might be subjected to public scorn, deprived of employment, and chilled in the exercise of his right to speak for, associate with, and participate in unpopular political causes.

[34]  See To Establish Justice, To Insure Domestic Tranquility, Final Report of the National Commission on the Causes and Prevention of Violence 152 (1969).

[35]  There is statistical evidence that persons who are detained between arrest and trial are more likely to receive prison sentences than those who obtain pretrial release, although other factors bear upon this correlation. See Wald, Pretrial Detention and Ultimate Freedom: A Statistical Study, 39 N. Y. U. L. Rev. 631 (1964).

arrest and trial—well over five years—was extraordinary. Only seven months of that period can be attributed to a strong excuse, the illness of the ex-sheriff who was in charge of the investigation. Perhaps some delay would have been permissible under ordinary circumstances, so that Manning could be utilized as a witness in Barker's trial, but more than four years was too long a period, particularly since a good part of that period was attributable to the Commonwealth's failure or inability to try Manning under circumstances that comported with due process.

Two counterbalancing factors, however, outweigh these deficiencies. The first is that prejudice was minimal. Of course, Barker was prejudiced to some extent by living for over four years under a cloud of suspicion and anxiety. Moreover, although he was released on bond for most of the period, he did spend 10 months in jail before trial. But there is no claim that any of Barker's witnesses died or otherwise became unavailable owing to the delay. The trial transcript indicates only two very minor lapses of memory—one on the part of a prosecution witness—which were in no way significant to the outcome.

More important than the absence of serious prejudice, is the fact that Barker did not want a speedy trial. Counsel was appointed for Barker immediately after his indictment and represented him throughout the period. No question is raised as to the competency of such counsel. Despite the fact that counsel had notice of the motions for continuances, the record shows no action whatever taken between October 21, 1958, and February 12, 1962, that could be construed as the assertion of the speedy trial right. On the latter date, in response to another motion for continuance, Barker moved to dismiss the indictment. The record does not show on what ground this motion was based, although it is clear that no alternative motion was made for an immediate trial. Instead the record strongly suggests that while he hoped to take advantage of the delay in which he had acquiesced, and thereby obtain a dismissal of the charges, he definitely did not want to be tried. Counsel conceded as much at oral argument:

> "Your honor, I would concede that Willie Mae Barker probably—I don't know this for a fact—probably did not want to be tried. I don't think any man wants to be tried. And I don't consider this a liability on his behalf. I don't blame him." Tr. of Oral Arg. 39.

The probable reason for Barker's attitude was that he was gambling on Manning's acquittal. The evidence was not very strong against Manning, as the reversals and hung juries suggest, and Barker undoubtedly thought that if Manning were acquitted, he would never be tried. Counsel also conceded this:

> "Now, it's true that the reason for this delay was the Commonwealth of Kentucky's desire to secure the testimony of the accomplice, Silas Manning. And it's true that if Silas Manning were never convicted, Willie Mae Barker would never have been convicted. We concede this." . . .[39]

That Barker was gambling on Manning's acquittal is also suggested by his failure, following the *pro forma* motion to dismiss filed in February 1962, to object to the Commonwealth's next two motions for continuances. Indeed, it was not until March 1963, after Manning's convictions were final, that Barker, having lost his gamble, began to object to further continuances. At that time, the Commonwealth's excuse was the illness of the ex-sheriff, which Barker has conceded justified the further delay.[40]

We do not hold that there may never be a situation in which an indictment may be dismissed on speedy trial grounds where the defendant has failed to object to continuances. There may be a situation in which the defendant was represented by incompetent counsel, was severely prejudiced, or even cases in which the continuances were granted *ex parte*. But barring extraordinary circumstances, we would be reluctant indeed to rule that a defendant was denied this constitutional right on a record that strongly indicates, as does this one, that the defendant did not want a speedy trial. We hold, therefore, that Barker was not deprived of his due process right to a speedy trial.

The judgment of the Court of Appeals is

**Affirmed. . . .**

---

[39]  Hindsight is, of course, 20/20, but we cannot help noting that if Barker had moved immediately and persistently for a speedy trial following indictment, and if he had been successful, he would have undoubtedly been acquitted since Manning's testimony was crucial to the Commonwealth's case. It could not have been anticipated at the outset, however, that Manning would have been tried six times over a four-year period. Thus, the decision to gamble on Manning's acquittal may have been a prudent choice at the time it was made.

[40]  At oral argument, counsel for Barker stated:

"That was after the sheriff, the material witness, was ill; the man who had arrested the petitioner, yes. And the Sixth Circuit held that this was a sufficient reason for delay, and we don't deny this. We concede that this was sufficient for the delay from March 1963 to October, but it does not explain the delays prior to that." Tr. of Oral Arg. 19–20.

**After preparing the case brief, consider the answers to the following questions:**

1. Apart from the 4-Prong Balancing Test, what alternatives did the Court consider for evaluating speedy trial claims?

2. Describe each of the factors from the 4-Prong Balancing Test.

3. Do you agree with the Court's discussion and application of the test in this case? Why?

4. What facts were the most important in convincing the Court that Barker's right was not violated?

5. Imagine if the facts were slightly different (e.g., if the length of delay had only been 3 years, or if Manning had been convicted at the first trial). How would those different facts affect the analysis?

## Chapter 7 Key Terms for Review

- **Initial appearance**: the defendant's first appearance before a judge after arrest.

- **Flight risk**: a defendant who may not return for trial if released.

- **Eighth Amendment**: prohibits excessive bail and cruel or unusual punishment of offenders.

- **Right to indictment by a grand jury**: the Fifth Amendment guarantees to defendants in federal felony cases the right to a probable cause determination by a grand jury.

- **Guilty plea**: defendant admits guilt and submits to punishment.

- **Not guilty plea**: the defendant denies guilt and the case moves forward to prepare for trial.

- *Nolo contendere* **(no contest) plea**: the defendant does not admit guilt, but submits to punishment—this operates the same as a guilty plea and concludes the prosecution of the case and the defendant is sentenced.

- **Standing mute**: the defendant remains silent at the point of plea and a "not guilty" plea is entered on their behalf.

- **Preliminary hearing**: a hearing to determine whether probable cause exists to charge the defendant with a crime.

- **Bound over**: sending a defendant forward to trial after finding probable cause in a preliminary hearing.

- **Bail schedule**: a list of minor offenses and the bail amounts for each allowing a defendant to pay the bail amount and be released without a bail hearing.

- **Out-of-custody defendant**: a defendant who has been released from custody prior to trial either on bail or on their own recognizance.

- **Released on their own recognizance (ROR)**: pre-trial release allowed without a fee upon a defendant's promise to return to court when summoned.

- **Bail bonds system**: allows defendants to post a bond guaranteeing the full amount of their bail (typically 10%).

- **Bail bondsman**: an individual who provides bail bonds to defendants for a fee.

- **Critical stage**: any stage in the criminal judicial process where substantial rights are at issue and there is potential prejudice to the defendant requiring the appointment of counsel for indigent defendants. The preliminary hearing is a critical stage. *Coleman v. Alabama (1970)*.

- **Assembly line justice**: the functioning of the criminal courts so that individuals lose their identity and are treated as objects rather than people.

- **Speedy trial clause**: the Sixth Amendment guarantees the accused a speedy and public trial.

- **Four-prong balancing test**: test used to determine whether a defendant has suffered a violation of his right to a speedy trial. Considers the length of delay, reasons for delay, whether the defendant asserted his right and whether his case was prejudiced by the delay. *Barker v. Wingo (1972)*.

- **Case attrition**: the failure of arrests to result in conviction.

- **Bureau of Justice Statistics**: federal agency that collects and analyzes crime data.

# The Fourth Amendment and Judicial Process

Search and seizure in criminal justice is most commonly associated with the actions of police officers. While it is the police who are responsible for conducting investigations, searching for and seizing evidence of crimes, the product of their work is critically important to the courts. Courts are tasked with determining whether evidence collected by police is admissible in a trial against a defendant. The Fourth Amendment provides:

> *The right of the people to be secure in their persons, houses, papers, and effects, against unreasonable searches and seizures, shall not be violated, and no warrants shall issue, but upon probable cause, supported by oath or affirmation, and particularly describing the place to be searched, and the persons or things to be seized.*[1]

This Fourth Amendment language is dense with meaning. Throughout American history the Supreme Court has examined and explained in great detail how the Fourth Amendment should be interpreted. The Fourth Amendment deals with a variety of issues, some raised by its plain language: probable cause, warrants, searches and seizures. Other more nuanced and complex issues have arisen as a result of Fourth Amendment violations. In the daily operation of the courts it is important that these constitutional protections are understood and abided by to ensure fairness in criminal trials.

The threshold question when addressing Fourth Amendment issues is whether government action was involved. If a government official or actor does not conduct the search or seize the evidence in question, the Fourth Amendment does not apply. Warrants are documents that provide judicial authorization for a government search or seizure. The Constitution favors the use of warrants for search and seizure because they offer assurance of probable cause. A **search** is

---

[1]   U.S. Const. amend. IV.

any governmental intrusion upon a person's reasonable expectation of privacy.[2] **Seizure** is defined as a governmental exercise of control over a person or thing.

## A.  THE WARRANT REQUIREMENT

A **search warrant** is a document explaining why **probable cause** exists to believe specific contraband, or evidence of a crime exists and details about the location to be searched for the evidence. Probable cause is the reasonable basis for believing that a crime may have been committed (for arrest) or that evidence of a crime or contraband is in a specific location (for a search). An **arrest warrant** describes a person suspected of a crime, authorizing law enforcement personnel to take the suspect into physical custody. In both cases, the warrant must be supported by a sworn statement (oath or affidavit) and must be issued by a judicial officer (neutral or detached magistrate). In *Coolidge v. New Hampshire (1971)* the Supreme Court held that the attorney general, even though a sworn justice of the peace, could not serve as a neutral or detached magistrate.[3]

In most cases, warrants are issued to law enforcement, supported by a sworn affidavit attesting to facts and evidence acquired through an investigation. If after evaluating the facts, the judge determines that probable cause exists, they will issue the warrant. The warrant must specifically describe the places to be searched and persons or things to be seized. The warrant also specifies the nature of the search or seizure to be conducted. This fulfills the Fourth Amendment's **particularity requirement**.

Warrants must be executed within a reasonable time frame or they may be deemed "stale" and officers would be required to secure a new one. **Stale search warrants** arise in two situations: (1) the government waited an extended period of time between the information provided and the execution of the warrant; and (2) the information supporting the search warrant was too old to provide "present" probable cause.[4]

The framers were diligent to ensure against **general warrants**, a source of significant injustice under the King of England. General warrants were issued allowing for a sort of free-for-all or fishing-expedition to be conducted against individuals with no basis in suspicion or fact. This is contrary to the American presumption of innocence, one of our most cherished principles of justice.

---

[2]   *Katz v. United States*, 389 U.S. 347 (1967).

[3]   403 U.S. 443 (1971).

[4]   *United States v. McCall*, 740 F.2d 1331 (4th Cir. 1984).

# B. EXCLUSION OF EVIDENCE

The exclusion of evidence is intricately connected with the Fourth Amendment, but is not found in the Constitution or the Fourth Amendment. The reason for this is that the exclusionary rule is a judicially created remedy for the violation of Fourth Amendment rights, crafted to deter future police misconduct. This important distinction is often ignored. The protections afforded by the Fourth Amendment exist to place restraints on law enforcement and government actors. They demand that searches and seizures be grounded in evidence (probable cause). Warrants must be specific and when necessary, searches be conducted in a reasonable fashion.

The **exclusionary rule** was first announced in *Boyd v. United States (1886)*.[5] Justice Bradley writing for the majority announced that the defendant was not required to produce his books and papers because they might incriminate him. Rather than finding footing in the Fifth Amendment's privilege against self-incrimination, he argued that the Fourth Amendment's protection against unreasonable searches and seizure was applicable. While his colleagues on the Court agreed with the outcome, they disagreed with its constitutional root. They specifically argued it was the Fifth Amendment that protected the defendant against being compelled to testify against himself.

It was not until 1914 that the Court utilized the Fourth Amendment as the foundation for the exclusionary rule again, in *Weeks v. United States*.[6] *Weeks* announced that in federal criminal proceedings, evidence secured through an unlawful search was inadmissible against the defendant. The force of the remedy has been a source of controversy. The result of the exclusionary rule is that evidence which is typically true and accurate, and which reveals important information about a criminal act must be hidden from the jurors in the case against the defendant. It is excluded not because the nature of the evidence is bad, or would lead to injustice, but because the nature of its collection would do so. It is a harsh penalty intended to motivate law enforcement to conduct their work within the framework of the Constitution.

The Court finally incorporated the exclusionary rule, making it applicable in state felony cases, in 1961 in the landmark case of *Mapp v. Ohio*.[7] *Mapp* is one of the most celebrated of the Warren Court era. Defendants now enjoy the protection of the exclusionary rule in state prosecutions.

---

[5]   116 U.S. 616 (1886).

[6]   232 U.S. 383 (1914).

[7]   367 U.S. 643 (1961).

The exclusionary rule applies to evidence seized during the course of an unlawful search. The search may have been conducted without a warrant where one was required, or it may have been pursuant to a warrant, which was incomplete or unlawful. It is possible that the unlawful search did not produce a piece of evidence directly, but because of something discovered through an unlawful search other **derivative evidence** was discovered as a result of the search. This evidence is referred to as **fruit of the poisonous tree** and it is subject to the exclusionary rule if the initial search was unconstitutional.[8]

## C. EXCEPTIONS TO THE WARRANT REQUIREMENT AND EXCLUSIONARY RULE

Almost immediately after the Court's decision in *Mapp* a long line of cases challenging its application began. The Court has been further developed the framework within which the exclusionary rule operates. When it was announced, the exclusionary rule seemed to be a complete bar to evidence seized unlawfully. The reality though, is that the Court has recognized numerous exceptions to the warrant requirement and to the exclusion of related evidence.

**Consent** is the most common exception to the warrant requirement. If a suspect consents to a search, the evidence is admissible—even if a warrant was necessary, their consent overrides the warrant requirement. Consent must be freely and voluntarily given.

A limited stop and frisk for weapons, or **Terry Stop**, is another exception to the warrant requirement. In *Terry v. Ohio (1961)* the Court held that officers do not need a warrant to stop and frisk the outer clothing of a suspect for weapons.[9] The officer must possess reasonable, articulable suspicion that the suspect poses a threat to the safety of the officer or the public.

The **automobile exception** to the warrant requirement allows for the search of automobiles based on probable cause that evidence of a crime will likely be found inside.[10] The automobile exception is based on the mobility of vehicles and the lesser expectation of privacy of the people inside. **Hot pursuit** is another exception to the warrant requirement which allows police to enter private property in the immediate pursuit of a fleeing felon.[11] The rule does not automatically allow

---

[8]   *Wong Sun v. United States*, 371 U.S. 471 (1963).

[9]   392 U.S. 1 (1969).

[10]  *Carroll v. United States*, 267 U.S. 132 (1925).

[11]  *United States v. Santana*, 427 U.S. 38 (1976).

police to pursue a misdemeanor suspect onto private property. In 2021 the Supreme Court held that:

> *The flight of a suspected misdemeanant does not always justify a warrantless entry into a home. An officer must consider all the circumstances in a pursuit case to determine whether there is a law enforcement emergency. On many occasions, the officer will have good reason to enter—to prevent imminent harms of violence, destruction of evidence or escape from the home. But when the officer has time to get a warrant, he must do so—even though the misdemeanant fled.[12]*

**Plain view** is another very common exception to the warrant requirement. Evidence obtained without a warrant is admissible if it is left in plain view.[13] The officer must observe the plain view evidence from a lawful vantage point, and he may not manipulate or touch it in order to determine its character as contraband—it must be readily identifiable from his observation. Another exception to the warrant requirement is a **search incident to a lawful arrest**. The Court held in *Chimel v. California (1969)*[14] that officers may search the area within a suspect's "wingspan" or arms-reach without a warrant, incident to a lawful arrest.

In 2016 in *Utah v. Strieff*, the Supreme Court examined the admissibility of evidence tainted by its connection with an unlawful search.[15] In *Strieff* the Court held that the taint of the original illegality had dissipated (or resolved) as the result of **attenuation**. The attenuation doctrine examines the illegality by considering three factors: (1) temporal proximity, or the time between the unconstitutional conduct and the discovery of evidence to determine how closely the discovery of evidence followed the unconstitutional search; (2) the presence of intervening circumstances; and (3) particularly significant, the court examines the purpose and flagrancy of the official misconduct. These factors must be balanced to determine whether attenuation has occurred. If there was a sufficient break between the police misconduct and the discovery of the evidence, it is admissible.

In *Strieff* the officer made an unlawful stop of a suspect walking outside of a convenience store. The officer admitted that he lacked even reasonable suspicion to validate the stop. Once stopped, the officer asked the suspect for identification and detained him while he ran a warrant check. The officer arrested the suspect based on outstanding warrants and then conducted a search incident to arrest. Strieff challenged the admission of evidence found during the search incident to

---

[12]  *Lange v. California*, 141 S.Ct. 617 (2021).
[13]  *Coolidge v. New Hampshire*, 403 U.S. 443 (1971).
[14]  395 U.S. 752 (1969).
[15]  579 U.S. 232 (2016).

arrest based on the fruit of the poisonous tree doctrine. He argued that the unlawful stop tainted the evidence making it inadmissible. In admitting the evidence, the Supreme Court held that the discovery of the lawful outstanding warrant after the illegal stop was an intervening circumstance which broke the causal chain between the stop and the lawful search incident to arrest.

Taken together, these many exceptions have significantly reduced the force of the exclusionary rule. While the Constitution demands reasonableness from police when conducting searches, the exceptions to the warrant requirement reduce the effectiveness of the exclusionary rule in achieving its purpose of deterring police misconduct.

**Read and brief each of the following cases relating to the Fourth Amendment and exclusionary rule and consider the questions following each case:**

1.   *Mapp v. Ohio*: the exclusionary rule in state criminal cases

2.   *Terry v. Ohio*: limited stop and frisk for weapons

3.   *Coolidge v. New Hampshire*: warrant requirements

4.   *Lange v. California*: warrantless hot pursuit

---

## MAPP V. OHIO

Supreme Court of the United States
Argued March 29, 1961
Decided June 19, 1961
Rehearing Denied Oct. 9, 1961
367 U.S. 643

### OPINION

### MR. JUSTICE CLARK delivered the opinion of the Court.

Appellant stands convicted of knowingly having had in her possession and under her control certain lewd and lascivious books, pictures, and photographs in violation of § 2905.34 of Ohio's Revised Code.[1] As officially stated in the syllabus to its opinion, the Supreme Court of Ohio found that her conviction was valid though "based primarily upon the introduction in evidence of lewd and lascivious books and pictures unlawfully seized during an unlawful search of defendant's home . . . ."

On May 23, 1957, three Cleveland police officers arrived at appellant's residence in that city pursuant to information that "a person [was] hiding out in the home, who was wanted for questioning in connection with a recent bombing, and that there was a large amount of policy paraphernalia being hidden in the home." Miss Mapp and her daughter by a former marriage lived on the top floor of the two-family dwelling. Upon their arrival at that house, the officers knocked on the door and demanded entrance but appellant, after telephoning her attorney, refused to admit them without a search warrant. They

---

[1]   The statute provides in pertinent part that

"No person shall knowingly . . . have in his possession or under his control an obscene, lewd, or lascivious book [or] . . . picture . . . .

"Whoever violates this section shall be fined not less than two hundred nor more than two thousand dollars or imprisoned not less than one nor more than seven years, or both."

advised their headquarters of the situation and undertook a surveillance of the house.

The officers again sought entrance some three hours later when four or more additional officers arrived on the scene. When Miss Mapp did not come to the door immediately, at least one of the several doors to the house was forcibly opened[2] and the policemen gained admittance. Meanwhile Miss Mapp's attorney arrived, but the officers, having secured their own entry, and continuing in their defiance of the law, would permit him neither to see Miss Mapp nor to enter the house. It appears that Miss Mapp was halfway down the stairs from the upper floor to the front door when the officers, in this highhanded manner, broke into the hall. She demanded to see the search warrant. A paper, claimed to be a warrant, was held up by one of the officers. She grabbed the "warrant" and placed it in her bosom. A struggle ensued in which the officers recovered the piece of paper and as a result of which they handcuffed appellant because she had been "belligerent" in resisting their official rescue of the "warrant" from her person. Running roughshod over appellant, a policeman "grabbed" her, "twisted [her] hand," and she "yelled [and] pleaded with him" because "it was hurting." Appellant, in handcuffs, was then forcibly taken upstairs to her bedroom where the officers searched a dresser, a chest of drawers, a closet and some suitcases. They also looked into a photo album and through personal papers belonging to the appellant. The search spread to the rest of the second floor including the child's bedroom, the living room, the kitchen and a dinette. The basement of the building and a trunk found therein were also searched. The obscene materials for possession of which she was ultimately convicted were discovered in the course of that widespread search.

At the trial no search warrant was produced by the prosecution, nor was the failure to produce one explained or accounted for. At best, "There is, in the record, considerable doubt as to whether there ever was any warrant for the search of defendant's home." The Ohio Supreme Court believed a "reasonable argument" could be made that the conviction should be reversed "because the 'methods' employed to obtain the [evidence] . . . were such as to 'offend "a sense of justice," ' '" but the court found determinative the fact that the evidence had not been taken "from defendant's person by the use of brutal or offensive physical force against defendant."

---

2    A police officer testified that "we did pry the screen door to gain entrance"; the attorney on the scene testified that a policeman "tried . . . to kick in the door" and then "broke the glass in the door and somebody reached in and opened the door and let them in"; the appellant testified that "The back door was broken."

The State says that even if the search were made without authority, or otherwise unreasonably, it is not prevented from using the unconstitutionally seized evidence at trial, citing *Wolf v. Colorado*, 338 U.S. 25 (1949), in which this Court did indeed hold "that in a prosecution in a State court for a State crime the Fourteenth Amendment does not forbid the admission of evidence obtained by an unreasonable search and seizure." At p. 33. On this appeal, of which we have noted probable jurisdiction, 364 U.S. 868, it is urged once again that we review that holding.[3]

## I.

Seventy-five years ago, in *Boyd v. United States*, 116 U.S. 616, 630 (1886), considering the Fourth[4] and Fifth Amendments as running "almost into each other" on the facts before it, this Court held that the doctrines of those Amendments

"apply to all invasions on the part of the government and its employees of the sanctity of a man's home and the privacies of life. It is not the breaking of his doors, and the rummaging of his drawers, that constitutes the essence of the offence; but it is the invasion of his indefeasible right of personal security, personal liberty and private property .... Breaking into a house and opening boxes and drawers are circumstances of aggravation; but any forcible and compulsory extortion of a man's own testimony or of his private papers to be used as evidence to convict him of crime or to forfeit his goods, is within the condemnation . . . [of those Amendments]."

The Court noted that

"constitutional provisions for the security of person and property should be liberally construed. . . . It is the duty of courts to be watchful for the constitutional rights of the citizen, and against any stealthy encroachments thereon." At p. 635.

In this jealous regard for maintaining the integrity of individual rights, the Court gave life to Madison's prediction that "independent tribunals of justice . . . will

---

3   Other issues have been raised on this appeal but, in the view we have taken of the case, they need not be decided. Although appellant chose to urge what may have appeared to be the surer ground for favorable disposition and did not insist that *Wolf* be overruled, the *amicus curiae*, who was also permitted to participate in the oral argument, did urge the Court to overrule *Wolf*.

4   "The right of the people to be secure in their persons, houses, papers, and effects, against unreasonable searches and seizures, shall not be violated, and no Warrants shall issue, but upon probable cause, supported by Oath or affirmation, and particularly describing the place to be searched, and the persons or things to be seized."

be naturally led to resist every encroachment upon rights expressly stipulated for in the Constitution by the declaration of rights." I Annals of Cong. 439 (1789). Concluding, the Court specifically referred to the use of the evidence there seized as "unconstitutional." At p. 638.

. . .

Less than 30 years after *Boyd*, this Court, in *Weeks v. United States*, 232 U.S. 383 (1914), stated that

> "the Fourth Amendment . . . put the courts of the United States and Federal officials, in the exercise of their power and authority, under limitations and restraints [and] . . . forever secure[d] the people, their persons, houses, papers and effects against all unreasonable searches and seizures under the guise of law . . . and the duty of giving to it force and effect is obligatory upon all entrusted under our Federal system with the enforcement of the laws." At pp. 391–392.

Specifically dealing with the use of the evidence unconstitutionally seized, the Court concluded:

> "If letters and private documents can thus be seized and held and used in evidence against a citizen accused of an offense, the protection of the Fourth Amendment declaring his right to be secure against such searches and seizures is of no value, and, so far as those thus placed are concerned, might as well be stricken from the Constitution. The efforts of the courts and their officials to bring the guilty to punishment, praiseworthy as they are, are not to be aided by the sacrifice of those great principles established by years of endeavor and suffering which have resulted in their embodiment in the fundamental law of the land." At p. 393.

Finally, the Court in that case clearly stated that use of the seized evidence involved "a denial of the constitutional rights of the accused." At p. 398. Thus, in the year 1914, in the *Weeks* case, this Court "for the first time" held that "in a federal prosecution the Fourth Amendment barred the use of evidence secured through an illegal search and seizure." . . .

## II.

In 1949, 35 years after *Weeks* was announced, this Court, in *Wolf v. Colorado, supra*, again for the first time, discussed the effect of the Fourth Amendment upon the States through the operation of the Due Process Clause of the Fourteenth Amendment. It said:

"We have no hesitation in saying that were a State affirmatively to sanction such police incursion into privacy it would run counter to the guaranty of the Fourteenth Amendment." At p. 28.

Nevertheless, after declaring that the "security of one's privacy against arbitrary intrusion by the police" is "implicit in 'the concept of ordered liberty' and as such enforceable against the States through the Due Process Clause," cf. *Palko v. Connecticut*, 302 U.S. 319 (1937), and announcing that it "stoutly adhere[d]" to the *Weeks* decision, the Court decided that the *Weeks* exclusionary rule would not then be imposed upon the States as "an essential ingredient of the right." 338 U.S., at 27–29. . . .

Significantly, among those now following the rule is California, which, according to its highest court, was "compelled to reach that conclusion because other remedies have completely failed to secure compliance with the constitutional provisions . . . ." *People v. Cahan*, 44 Cal. 2d 434, 445, 282 P. 2d 905, 911 (1955).

. . .Likewise, time has set its face against what *Wolf* called the "weighty testimony" of *People v. Defore*, 242 N. Y. 13 (1926). There Justice (then Judge) Cardozo, rejecting adoption of the *Weeks* exclusionary rule in New York, had said that "the Federal rule as it stands is either too strict or too lax."

However, the force of that reasoning has been largely vitiated by later decisions of this Court. These include the recent discarding of the "silver platter" doctrine which allowed federal judicial use of evidence seized in violation of the Constitution by state agents, *Elkins v. United States, supra*; the relaxation of the formerly strict requirements as to standing to challenge the use of evidence thus seized, so that now the procedure of exclusion, "ultimately referable to constitutional safeguards," is available to anyone even "legitimately on [the] premises" unlawfully searched, *Jones v. United States*, 362 U.S. 257, 266–267 (1960); and, finally, the formulation of a method to prevent state use of evidence unconstitutionally seized by federal agents, *Rea v. United States*, 350 U.S. 214 (1956). Because there can be no fixed formula, we are admittedly met with "recurring questions of the reasonableness of searches," but less is not to be expected when dealing with a Constitution, and, at any rate, "reasonableness is in the first instance for the [trial court] . . . to determine." *United States v. Rabinowitz*, 339 U.S. 56, 63 (1950).

It, therefore, plainly appears that the factual considerations supporting the failure of the *Wolf* Court to include the *Weeks* exclusionary rule when it recognized the enforceability of the right to privacy against the States in 1949, while not basically relevant to the constitutional consideration, could not, in any analysis, now be deemed controlling.

### III.

Some five years after *Wolf*, in answer to a plea made here Term after Term that we overturn its doctrine on applicability of the *Weeks* exclusionary rule, this Court indicated that such should not be done until the States had "adequate opportunity to adopt or reject the [*Weeks*] rule." *Irvine v. California, supra*, at 134. There again it was said:

> "Never until June of 1949 did this Court hold the basic search-and-seizure prohibition in any way applicable to the states under the Fourteenth Amendment." *Ibid.*

And only last Term, after again carefully re-examining the *Wolf* doctrine in *Elkins v. United States, supra*, the Court pointed out that "the controlling principles" as to search and seizure and the problem of admissibility "seemed clear" (at p. 212) until the announcement in *Wolf* "that the Due Process Clause of the Fourteenth Amendment does not itself require state courts to adopt the exclusionary rule" of the *Weeks* case. At p. 213. At the same time, the Court pointed out, "the underlying constitutional doctrine which *Wolf* established . . . that the Federal Constitution . . . prohibits unreasonable searches and seizures by state officers" had undermined the "foundation upon which the admissibility of state seized evidence in a federal trial originally rested . . . ." *Ibid.* The Court concluded that it was therefore obliged to hold, although it chose the narrower ground on which to do so, that all evidence obtained by an unconstitutional search and seizure was inadmissible in a federal court regardless of its source. Today we once again examine *Wolf's* constitutional documentation of the right to privacy free from unreasonable state intrusion, and, after its dozen years on our books, are led by it to close the only courtroom door remaining open to evidence secured by official lawlessness in flagrant abuse of that basic right, reserved to all persons as a specific guarantee against that very same unlawful conduct. We hold that all evidence obtained by searches and seizures in violation of the Constitution is, by that same authority, inadmissible in a state court.

### IV.

Since the Fourth Amendment's right of privacy has been declared enforceable against the States through the Due Process Clause of the Fourteenth, it is enforceable against them by the same sanction of exclusion as is used against the Federal Government. Were it otherwise, then just as without the *Weeks* rule the assurance against unreasonable federal searches and seizures would be "a form of words," valueless and undeserving of mention in a perpetual charter of inestimable human liberties, so too, without that rule the freedom from state invasions of privacy would be so ephemeral and so neatly severed from its conceptual nexus with the freedom from all brutish means of coercing evidence as not to merit this Court's high regard as a freedom "implicit in the concept of ordered liberty." At the time that the Court held in *Wolf* that the Amendment was applicable to the States through the Due Process Clause, the cases of this Court, as we have seen, had steadfastly held that as to federal officers the Fourth Amendment included the exclusion of the evidence seized in violation of its provisions. Even *Wolf* "stoutly adhered" to that proposition. The right to privacy, when conceded operatively enforceable against the States, was not susceptible of destruction by avulsion of the sanction upon which its protection and enjoyment had always been deemed dependent under the *Boyd*, *Weeks* and *Silverthorne* cases. Therefore, in extending the substantive protections of due process to all constitutionally unreasonable searches—state or federal—it was logically and constitutionally necessary that the exclusion doctrine—an essential part of the right to privacy—be also insisted upon as an essential ingredient of the right newly recognized by the *Wolf* case.

In short, the admission of the new constitutional right by *Wolf* could not consistently tolerate denial of its most important constitutional privilege, namely, the exclusion of the evidence which an accused had been forced to give by reason of the unlawful seizure. To hold otherwise is to grant the right but in reality to withhold its privilege and enjoyment. Only last year the Court itself recognized that the purpose of the exclusionary rule "is to deter—to compel respect for the constitutional guaranty in the only effectively available way—by removing the incentive to disregard it." *Elkins v. United States, supra*, at 217...

V.

Moreover, our holding that the exclusionary rule is an essential part of both the Fourth and Fourteenth Amendments is not only the logical dictate of prior cases, but it also makes very good sense. There is no war between the Constitution and common sense. Presently, a federal prosecutor may make no use of evidence illegally seized, but a State's attorney across the street may, although he supposedly is operating under the enforceable prohibitions of the same Amendment. Thus the State, by admitting evidence unlawfully seized, serves to encourage disobedience to the Federal Constitution which it is bound to uphold. Moreover, as was said in *Elkins*, "the very essence of a healthy federalism depends upon the avoidance of needless conflict between state and federal courts." 364 U.S., at 221. . . .

There are those who say, as did Justice (then Judge) Cardozo, that under our constitutional exclusionary doctrine "the criminal is to go free because the constable has blundered." *People v. Defore*, 242 N. Y., at 21. In some cases this will undoubtedly be the result. But, as was said in *Elkins*, "there is another consideration—the imperative of judicial integrity." 364 U.S., at 222. The criminal goes free, if he must, but it is the law that sets him free. Nothing can destroy a government more quickly than its failure to observe its own laws, or worse, its disregard of the charter of its own existence. As Mr. Justice Brandeis, dissenting, said in *Olmstead v. United States*, 277 U.S. 438, 485 (1928): "Our Government is the potent, the omnipresent teacher. For good or for ill, it teaches the whole people by its example. . . . If the Government becomes a lawbreaker, it breeds contempt for law; it invites every man to become a law unto himself; it invites anarchy." Nor can it lightly be assumed that, as a practical matter, adoption of the exclusionary rule fetters law enforcement. Only last year this Court expressly considered that contention and found that "pragmatic evidence of a sort" to the contrary was not wanting. *Elkins v. United States, supra*, at 218. The Court noted that

> "The federal courts themselves have operated under the exclusionary rule of *Weeks* for almost half a century; yet it has not been suggested either that the Federal Bureau of Investigation has thereby been rendered ineffective, or that the administration of criminal justice in the federal courts has thereby been disrupted. Moreover, the experience of the states is impressive. . . . The movement towards the rule of exclusion has been halting but seemingly inexorable."

*Id.*, at 218–219. . .

The ignoble shortcut to conviction left open to the State tends to destroy the entire system of constitutional restraints on which the liberties of the people rest. Having once recognized that the right to privacy embodied in the Fourth Amendment is enforceable against the States, and that the right to be secure against rude invasions of privacy by state officers is, therefore, constitutional in origin, we can no longer permit that right to remain an empty promise. Because it is enforceable in the same manner and to like effect as other basic rights secured by the Due Process Clause, we can no longer permit it to be revocable at the whim of any police officer who, in the name of law enforcement itself, chooses to suspend its enjoyment. Our decision, founded on reason and truth, gives to the individual no more than that which the Constitution guarantees him, to the police officer no less than that to which honest law enforcement is entitled, and, to the courts, that judicial integrity so necessary in the true administration of justice. . .

The judgment of the Supreme Court of Ohio is reversed and the cause remanded for further proceedings not inconsistent with this opinion.

**Reversed and remanded. . . .**

**After preparing the case brief, consider the answers to the following questions:**

1. This is clearly an unlawful search, why wasn't the evidence excluded at trial?

2. What was the "Silver Platter Doctrine" to which the Court refers?

3. What is the purpose of the exclusionary rule?

4. Do you believe the Court reached the right result in this case by excluding the evidence? Would your position change if the evidence had been critical evidence to a more serious charge, like murder?

# TERRY V. OHIO

Supreme Court of the United States
Argued Dec. 12, 1967
Decided June 10, 1968
392 U.S. 1

## OPINION

### MR. CHIEF JUSTICE WARREN delivered the opinion of the Court.

This case presents serious questions concerning the role of the Fourth Amendment in the confrontation on the street between the citizen and the policeman investigating suspicious circumstances.

Petitioner Terry was convicted of carrying a concealed weapon and sentenced to the statutorily prescribed term of one to three years in the penitentiary.[1] Following the denial of a pretrial motion to suppress, the prosecution introduced in evidence two revolvers and a number of bullets seized from Terry and a codefendant, Richard Chilton,[2] by Cleveland Police Detective Martin McFadden. At the hearing on the motion to suppress this evidence, Officer McFadden testified that while he was patrolling in plain clothes in downtown Cleveland at approximately 2:30 in the afternoon of October 31, 1963, his attention was attracted by two men, Chilton and Terry, standing on the corner of Huron Road and Euclid Avenue. He had never seen the two men before, and he was unable to say precisely what first drew his eye to them. However, he testified that he had been a policeman for 39 years and a detective for 35 and that he had been assigned to patrol this vicinity of downtown Cleveland for shoplifters and pickpockets for 30 years. He explained that he had developed routine habits of observation over the years and that he would "stand and watch people or walk and watch people at many intervals of the day." He added: "Now, in this case when I looked over they didn't look right to me at the time."

---

[1]    Ohio Rev. Code § 2923.01 (1953) provides in part that "no person shall carry a pistol, bowie knife, dirk, or other dangerous weapon concealed on or about his person." An exception is made for properly authorized law enforcement officers.

[2]    Terry and Chilton were arrested, indicted, tried, and convicted together. They were represented by the same attorney, and they made a joint motion to suppress the guns. After the motion was denied, evidence was taken in the case against Chilton. This evidence consisted of the testimony of the arresting officer and of Chilton. It was then stipulated that this testimony would be applied to the case against Terry, and no further evidence was introduced in that case. The trial judge considered the two cases together, rendered the decisions at the same time and sentenced the two men at the same time. They prosecuted their state court appeals together through the same attorney, and they petitioned this Court for certiorari together. Following the grant of the writ upon this joint petition, Chilton died. Thus, only Terry's conviction is here for review.

His interest aroused, Officer McFadden took up a post of observation in the entrance to a store 300 to 400 feet away from the two men. "I get more purpose to watch them when I seen their movements," he testified. He saw one of the men leave the other one and walk southwest on Huron Road, past some stores. The man paused for a moment and looked in a store window, then walked on a short distance, turned around and walked back toward the corner, pausing once again to look in the same store window. He rejoined his companion at the corner, and the two conferred briefly. Then the second man went through the same series of motions, strolling down Huron Road, looking in the same window, walking on a short distance, turning back, peering in the store window again, and returning to confer with the first man at the corner. The two men repeated this ritual alternately between five and six times apiece—in all, roughly a dozen trips. At one point, while the two were standing together on the corner, a third man approached them and engaged them briefly in conversation. This man then left the two others and walked west on Euclid Avenue. Chilton and Terry resumed their measured pacing, peering, and conferring. After this had gone on for 10 to 12 minutes, the two men walked off together, heading west on Euclid Avenue, following the path taken earlier by the third man.

By this time Officer McFadden had become thoroughly suspicious. He testified that after observing their elaborately casual and oft-repeated reconnaissance of the store window on Huron Road, he suspected the two men of "casing a job, a stick-up," and that he considered it his duty as a police officer to investigate further. He added that he feared "they may have a gun." Thus, Officer McFadden followed Chilton and Terry and saw them stop in front of Zucker's store to talk to the same man who had conferred with them earlier on the street corner. Deciding that the situation was ripe for direct action, Officer McFadden approached the three men, identified himself as a police officer and asked for their names. At this point his knowledge was confined to what he had observed. He was not acquainted with any of the three men by name or by sight, and he had received no information concerning them from any other source. When the men "mumbled something" in response to his inquiries, Officer McFadden grabbed petitioner Terry, spun him around so that they were facing the other two, with Terry between McFadden and the others, and patted down the outside of his clothing. In the left breast pocket of Terry's overcoat Officer McFadden felt a pistol. He reached inside the overcoat pocket, but was unable to remove the gun. At this point, keeping Terry between himself and the others, the officer ordered all three men to enter Zucker's store.

As they went in, he removed Terry's overcoat completely, removed a .38-caliber revolver from the pocket and ordered all three men to face the wall with their hands raised. Officer McFadden proceeded to pat down the outer clothing of Chilton and the third man, Katz. He discovered another revolver in the outer pocket of Chilton's overcoat, but no weapons were found on Katz. The officer testified that he only patted the men down to see whether they had weapons, and that he did not put his hands beneath the outer garments of either Terry or Chilton until he felt their guns. So far as appears from the record, he never placed his hands beneath Katz' outer garments. Officer McFadden seized Chilton's gun, asked the proprietor of the store to call a police wagon, and took all three men to the station, where Chilton and Terry were formally charged with carrying concealed weapons.

On the motion to suppress the guns the prosecution took the position that they had been seized following a search incident to a lawful arrest. The trial court rejected this theory, stating that it "would be stretching the facts beyond reasonable comprehension" to find that Officer McFadden had had probable cause to arrest the men before he patted them down for weapons. However, the court denied the defendants' motion on the ground that Officer McFadden, on the basis of his experience, "had reasonable cause to believe . . . that the defendants were conducting themselves suspiciously, and some interrogation should be made of their action." Purely for his own protection, the court held, the officer had the right to pat down the outer clothing of these men, who he had reasonable cause to believe might be armed. The court distinguished between an investigatory "stop" and an arrest, and between a "frisk" of the outer clothing for weapons and a full-blown search for evidence of crime. The frisk, it held, was essential to the proper performance of the officer's investigatory duties, for without it "the answer to the police officer may be a bullet, and a loaded pistol discovered during the frisk is admissible."

After the court denied their motion to suppress, Chilton and Terry waived jury trial and pleaded not guilty. The court adjudged them guilty, and the Court of Appeals for the Eighth Judicial District, Cuyahoga County, affirmed. *State v. Terry*, 5 Ohio App. 2d 122, 214 N. E. 2d 114 (1966). The Supreme Court of Ohio dismissed their appeal on the ground that no "substantial constitutional question" was involved. We granted certiorari, 387 U.S. 929 (1967), to determine whether the admission of the revolvers in evidence violated petitioner's rights under the Fourth Amendment, made applicable to the States by the Fourteenth. *Mapp v. Ohio*, 367 U.S. 643 (1961). We affirm the conviction.

### I.

The Fourth Amendment provides that "the right of the people to be secure in their persons, houses, papers, and effects, against unreasonable searches and seizures, shall not be violated . . . ." This inestimable right of personal security belongs as much to the citizen on the streets of our cities as to the homeowner closeted in his study to dispose of his secret affairs. For, as this Court has always recognized,

"No right is held more sacred, or is more carefully guarded, by the common law, than the right of every individual to the possession and control of his own person, free from all restraint or interference of others, unless by clear and unquestionable authority of law." *Union Pac. R. Co. v. Botsford*, 141 U.S. 250, 251(1891). We have recently held that "the Fourth Amendment protects people, not places," *Katz v. United States*, 389 U.S. 347, 351 (1967), and wherever an individual may harbor a reasonable "expectation of privacy," *id.*, at 361 (MR. JUSTICE HARLAN, concurring), he is entitled to be free from unreasonable governmental intrusion. Of course, the specific content and incidents of this right must be shaped by the context in which it is asserted. For "what the Constitution forbids is not all searches and seizures, but unreasonable searches and seizures." *Elkins v. United States*, 364 U.S. 206, 222 (1960). Unquestionably petitioner was entitled to the protection of the Fourth Amendment as he walked down the street in Cleveland. . .The question is whether in all the circumstances of this on-the-street encounter, his right to personal security was violated by an unreasonable search and seizure.

We would be less than candid if we did not acknowledge that this question thrusts to the fore difficult and troublesome issues regarding a sensitive area of police activity—issues which have never before been squarely presented to this Court. Reflective of the tensions involved are the practical and constitutional arguments pressed with great vigor on both sides of the public debate over the power of the police to "stop and frisk"—as it is sometimes euphemistically termed—suspicious persons. . .

On the other side the argument is made that the authority of the police must be strictly circumscribed by the law of arrest and search as it has developed to date in the traditional jurisprudence of the Fourth Amendment. . .

In this context we approach the issues in this case mindful of the limitations of the judicial function in controlling the myriad daily situations in which policemen and citizens confront each other on the street. . .

Thus in our system evidentiary rulings provide the context in which the judicial process of inclusion and exclusion approves some conduct as comporting with constitutional guarantees and disapproves other actions by state agents. A ruling admitting evidence in a criminal trial, we recognize, has the necessary effect of legitimizing the conduct which produced the evidence, while an application of the exclusionary rule withholds the constitutional imprimatur.

The exclusionary rule has its limitations, however, as a tool of judicial control. It cannot properly be invoked to exclude the products of legitimate police investigative techniques on the ground that much conduct which is closely similar involves unwarranted intrusions upon constitutional protections. Moreover, in some contexts the rule is ineffective as a deterrent. Street encounters between citizens and police officers are incredibly rich in diversity. They range from wholly friendly exchanges of pleasantries or mutually useful information to hostile confrontations of armed men involving arrests, or injuries, or loss of life. Moreover, hostile confrontations are not all of a piece. Some of them begin in a friendly enough manner, only to take a different turn upon the injection of some unexpected element into the conversation. . .Proper adjudication of cases in which the exclusionary rule is invoked demands a constant awareness of these limitations. The wholesale harassment by certain elements of the police community, of which minority groups, particularly Negroes, frequently complain, will not be stopped by the exclusion of any evidence from any criminal trial. . .Nothing we say today is to be taken as indicating approval of police conduct outside the legitimate investigative sphere. Under our decision, courts still retain their traditional responsibility to guard against police conduct which is overbearing or harassing, or which trenches upon personal security without the objective evidentiary justification which the Constitution requires. When such conduct is identified, it must be condemned by the judiciary and its fruits must be excluded from evidence in criminal trials. . .

Having thus roughly sketched the perimeters of the constitutional debate over the limits on police investigative conduct in general and the background against which this case presents itself, we turn our attention to the quite narrow question posed by the facts before us: whether it is always unreasonable for a policeman to seize a person and subject him to a limited search for weapons unless there is probable cause for an arrest. Given the narrowness of this question, we have no occasion to canvass in detail the constitutional limitations upon the scope of a policeman's power when he confronts a citizen without probable cause to arrest him.

## II.

Our first task is to establish at what point in this encounter the Fourth Amendment becomes relevant. That is, we must decide whether and when Officer McFadden "seized" Terry and whether and when he conducted a "search." There is some suggestion in the use of such terms as "stop" and "frisk" that such police conduct is outside the purview of the Fourth Amendment because neither action rises to the level of a "search" or "seizure" within the meaning of the Constitution. We emphatically reject this notion. It is quite plain that the Fourth Amendment governs "seizures" of the person which do not eventuate in a trip to the station house and prosecution for crime—"arrests" in traditional terminology. It must be recognized that whenever a police officer accosts an individual and restrains his freedom to walk away, he has "seized" that person. And it is nothing less than sheer torture of the English language to suggest that a careful exploration of the outer surfaces of a person's clothing all over his or her body in an attempt to find weapons is not a "search." Moreover, it is simply fantastic to urge that such a procedure performed in public by a policeman while the citizen stands helpless, perhaps facing a wall with his hands raised, is a "petty indignity." It is a serious intrusion upon the sanctity of the person, which may inflict great indignity and arouse strong resentment, and it is not to be undertaken lightly. . .

The distinctions of classical "stop-and-frisk" theory thus serve to divert attention from the central inquiry under the Fourth Amendment—the reasonableness in all the circumstances of the particular governmental invasion of a citizen's personal security. "Search" and "seizure" are not talismans. We therefore reject the notions that the Fourth Amendment does not come into play at all as a limitation upon police conduct if the officers stop short of something called a "technical arrest" or a "full-blown search."

In this case there can be no question, then, that Officer McFadden "seized" petitioner and subjected him to a "search" when he took hold of him and patted down the outer surfaces of his clothing. We must decide whether at that point it was reasonable for Officer McFadden to have interfered with petitioner's personal security as he did. And in determining whether the seizure and search were "unreasonable" our inquiry is a dual one—whether the officer's action was justified at its inception, and whether it was reasonably related in scope to the circumstances which justified the interference in the first place. . .

III.

If this case involved police conduct subject to the Warrant Clause of the Fourth Amendment, we would have to ascertain whether "probable cause" existed to justify the search and seizure which took place. However, that is not the case. We do not retreat from our holdings that the police must, whenever practicable, obtain advance judicial approval of searches and seizures through the warrant procedure, . . .or that in most instances failure to comply with the warrant requirement can only be excused by exigent circumstances, . . .But we deal here with an entire rubric of police conduct—necessarily swift action predicated upon the on-the-spot observations of the officer on the beat—which historically has not been, and as a practical matter could not be, subjected to the warrant procedure. Instead, the conduct involved in this case must be tested by the Fourth Amendment's general proscription against unreasonable searches and seizures. . .

Applying these principles to this case, we consider first the nature and extent of the governmental interests involved. One general interest is of course that of effective crime prevention and detection; it is this interest which underlies the recognition that a police officer may in appropriate circumstances and in an appropriate manner approach a person for purposes of investigating possibly criminal behavior even though there is no probable cause to make an arrest. It was this legitimate investigative function Officer McFadden was discharging when he decided to approach petitioner and his companions. He had observed Terry, Chilton, and Katz go through a series of acts, each of them perhaps innocent in itself, but which taken together warranted further investigation. There is nothing unusual in two men standing together on a street corner, perhaps waiting for someone. Nor is there anything suspicious about people in such circumstances strolling up and down the street, singly or in pairs. Store windows, moreover, are made to be looked in. But the story is quite different where, as here, two men hover about a street corner for an extended period of time, at the end of which it becomes apparent that they are not waiting for anyone or anything; where these men pace alternately along an identical route, pausing to stare in the same store window roughly 24 times; where each completion of this route is followed immediately by a conference between the two men on the corner; where they are joined in one of these conferences by a third man who leaves swiftly; and where the two men finally follow the third and rejoin him a couple of blocks away. It would have been poor police work indeed for an officer of 30 years' experience in the detection of thievery from stores in this same neighborhood to have failed to investigate this behavior further.

The crux of this case, however, is not the propriety of Officer McFadden's taking steps to investigate petitioner's suspicious behavior, but rather, whether there was justification for McFadden's invasion of Terry's personal security by searching him for weapons in the course of that investigation. We are now concerned with more than the governmental interest in investigating crime; in addition, there is the more immediate interest of the police officer in taking steps to assure himself that the person with whom he is dealing is not armed with a weapon that could unexpectedly and fatally be used against him. Certainly it would be unreasonable to require that police officers take unnecessary risks in the performance of their duties. American criminals have a long tradition of armed violence, and every year in this country many law enforcement officers are killed in the line of duty, and thousands more are wounded. Virtually all of these deaths and a substantial portion of the injuries are inflicted with guns and knives.[21]

In view of these facts, we cannot blind ourselves to the need for law enforcement officers to protect themselves and other prospective victims of violence in situations where they may lack probable cause for an arrest. When an officer is justified in believing that the individual whose suspicious behavior he is investigating at close range is armed and presently dangerous to the officer or to others, it would appear to be clearly unreasonable to deny the officer the power to take necessary measures to determine whether the person is in fact carrying a weapon and to neutralize the threat of physical harm.

We must still consider, however, the nature and quality of the intrusion on individual rights which must be accepted if police officers are to be conceded the right to search for weapons in situations where probable cause to arrest for crime is lacking. Even a limited search of the outer clothing for weapons constitutes a severe, though brief, intrusion upon cherished personal

---

[21] Fifty-seven law enforcement officers were killed in the line of duty in this country in 1966, bringing the total to 335 for the seven-year period beginning with 1960. Also in 1966, there were 23,851 assaults on police officers, 9,113 of which resulted in injuries to the policemen. Fifty-five of the 57 officers killed in 1966 died from gunshot wounds, 41 of them inflicted by handguns easily secreted about the person. The remaining two murders were perpetrated by knives. See Federal Bureau of Investigation, Uniform Crime Reports for the United States—1966, at 45–48, 152 and Table 51.

The easy availability of firearms to potential criminals in this country is well known and has provoked much debate. See, *e.g.*, President's Commission on Law Enforcement and Administration of Justice, The Challenge of Crime in a Free Society 239–243 (1967). Whatever the merits of gun-control proposals, this fact is relevant to an assessment of the need for some form of self-protective search power.

security, and it must surely be an annoying, frightening, and perhaps humiliating experience. Petitioner contends that such an intrusion is permissible only incident to a lawful arrest, either for a crime involving the possession of weapons or for a crime the commission of which led the officer to investigate in the first place. However, this argument must be closely examined.

Petitioner does not argue that a police officer should refrain from making any investigation of suspicious circumstances until such time as he has probable cause to make an arrest; nor does he deny that police officers in properly discharging their investigative function may find themselves confronting persons who might well be armed and dangerous. Moreover, he does not say that an officer is always unjustified in searching a suspect to discover weapons. Rather, he says it is unreasonable for the policeman to take that step until such time as the situation evolves to a point where there is probable cause to make an arrest. When that point has been reached, petitioner would concede the officer's right to conduct a search of the suspect for weapons, fruits or instrumentalities of the crime, or "mere" evidence, incident to the arrest. There are two weaknesses in this line of reasoning, however. First, it fails to take account of traditional limitations upon the scope of searches, and thus recognizes no distinction in purpose, character, and extent between a search incident to an arrest and a limited search for weapons. The former, although justified in part by the acknowledged necessity to protect the arresting officer from assault with a concealed weapon, *Preston v. United States*, 376 U.S. 364, 367 (1964), is also justified on other grounds, *ibid.*, and can therefore involve a relatively extensive exploration of the person. A search for weapons in the absence of probable cause to arrest, however, must, like any other search, be strictly circumscribed by the exigencies which justify its initiation. *Warden v. Hayden*, 387 U.S. 294, 310 (1967) (MR. JUSTICE FORTAS, concurring). Thus it must be limited to that which is necessary for the discovery of weapons which might be used to harm the officer or others nearby, and may realistically be characterized as something less than a "full" search, even though it remains a serious intrusion.

A second, and related, objection to petitioner's argument is that it assumes that the law of arrest has already worked out the balance between the particular interests involved here—the neutralization of danger to the policeman in the investigative circumstance and the sanctity of the individual. But this is not so. An arrest is a wholly different kind of intrusion upon individual freedom from a limited search for weapons, and the interests each is designed to serve are likewise quite different. An arrest is the initial stage of a criminal prosecution. . . .

Our evaluation of the proper balance that has to be struck in this type of case leads us to conclude that there must be a narrowly drawn authority to permit a reasonable search for weapons for the protection of the police officer, where he has reason to believe that he is dealing with an armed and dangerous individual, regardless of whether he has probable cause to arrest the individual for a crime. The officer need not be absolutely certain that the individual is armed; the issue is whether a reasonably prudent man in the circumstances would be warranted in the belief that his safety or that of others was in danger. . . . And in determining whether the officer acted reasonably in such circumstances, due weight must be given, not to his inchoate and unparticularized suspicion or "hunch," but to the specific reasonable inferences which he is entitled to draw from the facts in light of his experience. Cf. *Brinegar v. United States supra.* . .

IV.

We must now examine the conduct of Officer McFadden in this case to determine whether his search and seizure of petitioner were reasonable, both at their inception and as conducted. He had observed Terry, together with Chilton and another man, acting in a manner he took to be preface to a "stick-up." We think on the facts and circumstances Officer McFadden detailed before the trial judge a reasonably prudent man would have been warranted in believing petitioner was armed and thus presented a threat to the officer's safety while he was investigating his suspicious behavior. The actions of Terry and Chilton were consistent with McFadden's hypothesis that these men were contemplating a daylight robbery—which, it is reasonable to assume, would be likely to involve the use of weapons—and nothing in their conduct from the time he first noticed them until the time he confronted them and identified himself as a police officer gave him sufficient reason to negate that hypothesis. Although the trio had departed the original scene, there was nothing to indicate abandonment of an intent to commit a robbery at some point. Thus, when Officer McFadden approached the three men gathered before the display window at Zucker's store he had observed enough to make it quite reasonable to fear that they were armed; and nothing in their response to his hailing them, identifying himself as a police officer, and asking their names served to dispel that reasonable belief. We cannot say his decision at that point to seize Terry and pat his clothing for weapons was the product of a volatile or inventive imagination, or was undertaken simply as an act of harassment; the record evidences the tempered act of a policeman who in the course of an investigation had to make a quick decision as to how to protect himself and others from possible danger, and took limited steps to do so. The manner in which the seizure and search were conducted is, of course, as vital a part of the inquiry as whether they were warranted at all. The Fourth Amendment proceeds as much by limitations upon the scope of governmental action as by imposing preconditions upon its initiation. . . .

We need not develop at length in this case, however, the limitations which the Fourth Amendment places upon a protective seizure and search for weapons. These limitations will have to be developed in the concrete factual circumstances of individual cases. . . . The sole justification of the search in the present situation is the protection of the police officer and others nearby, and it must therefore be confined in scope to an intrusion reasonably designed to discover guns, knives, clubs, or other hidden instruments for the assault of the police officer.

The scope of the search in this case presents no serious problem in light of these standards. Officer McFadden patted down the outer clothing of petitioner and his two companions. He did not place his hands in their pockets or under the outer surface of their garments until he had felt weapons, and then he merely reached for and removed the guns. He never did invade Katz' person beyond the outer surfaces of his clothes, since he discovered nothing in his pat-down which might have been a weapon. Officer McFadden confined his search strictly to what was minimally necessary to learn whether the men were armed and to disarm them once he discovered the weapons. He did not conduct a general exploratory search for whatever evidence of criminal activity he might find.

## V.

We conclude that the revolver seized from Terry was properly admitted in evidence against him. At the time he seized petitioner and searched him for weapons, Officer McFadden had reasonable grounds to believe that petitioner was armed and dangerous, and it was necessary for the protection of himself and others to take swift measures to discover the true facts and neutralize the threat of harm if it materialized. The policeman carefully restricted his search to what was appropriate to the discovery of the particular items which he sought. Each case of this sort will, of course, have to be decided on its own facts. We merely hold today that where a police officer observes unusual conduct which leads him reasonably to conclude in light of his experience that criminal activity may be afoot and that the persons with whom he is dealing may be armed and presently dangerous, where in the course of investigating this behavior he identifies himself as a policeman and makes reasonable inquiries, and where nothing in the initial stages of the encounter serves to dispel his reasonable fear for his own or others' safety, he is entitled for the protection of himself and others in the area to conduct a carefully limited search of the outer clothing of such persons in an attempt to discover weapons which might be used to assault him. Such a search is a reasonable search under the Fourth Amendment, and any weapons seized may properly be introduced in evidence against the person from whom they were taken.

**Affirmed.** . . .

**After preparing the case brief, consider the answers to the following questions:**

1. What facts gave rise to the officer's suspicion in this case?

2. How significant is it that the officer was an experienced veteran?

3. According to the Court, what must be true in order for an officer to conduct a Terry Stop?

4. Do you agree with the Court that reasonable articulable suspicion is an appropriate amount of evidence to support the stop?

## COOLIDGE V. NEW HAMPSHIRE

Supreme Court of the United States
Argued Jan. 12, 1971
Decided June 21, 1971
Rehearing Denied Oct. 12, 1971
403 U.S. 443

### OPINION

### MR. JUSTICE STEWART delivered the opinion of the Court.

We are called upon in this case to decide issues under the Fourth and Fourteenth Amendments arising in the context of a state criminal trial for the commission of a particularly brutal murder. As in every case, our single duty is to determine the issues presented in accord with the Constitution and the law.

Pamela Mason, a 14-year-old girl, left her home in Manchester, New Hampshire, on the evening of January 13, 1964, during a heavy snowstorm, apparently in response to a man's telephone call for a babysitter. Eight days later, after a thaw, her body was found by the site of a major north-south highway several miles away. She had been murdered. The event created great alarm in the area, and the police immediately began a massive investigation.

On January 28, having learned from a neighbor that the petitioner, Edward Coolidge, had been away from home on the evening of the girl's disappearance, the police went to his house to question him. They asked him, among other things, if he owned any guns, and he produced three, two shotguns and a rifle. They also asked whether he would take a lie-detector test concerning his account of his activities on the night of the disappearance. He agreed to do so on the following Sunday, his day off. The police later described his attitude on the occasion of this visit as fully 'cooperative.' His wife was in the house throughout the interview.

On the following Sunday, a policeman called Coolidge early in the morning and asked him to come down to the police station for the trip to Concord, New Hampshire, where the lie-detector test was to be administered. That evening, two plainclothes policemen arrived at the Coolidge house, where Mrs. Coolidge was waiting with her mother-in-law for her husband's return. These two policemen were not the two who had visited the house earlier in the week, and they apparently did not know that Collidge had displayed three guns for inspection during the earlier visit. The plainclothesmen told Mrs. Coolidge that her husband was in 'serious trouble' and probably would not be home that night. They asked Coolidge's mother to leave, and proceeded to question Mrs.

Coolidge. During the course of the interview they obtained from her four guns belonging to Coolidge, and some clothes that Mrs. Coolidge thought her husband might have been wearing on the evening of Pamela Mason's disappearance.

Coolidge was held in jail on an unrelated charge that night, but he was released the next day. During the ensuing two and a half weeks, the State accumulated a quantity of evidence to support the theory that it was he who had killed Pamela Mason. On February 19, the results of the investigation were presented at a meeting between the police officers working on the case and the State Attorney General, who had personally taken charge of all police activities relating to the murder, and was later to serve as chief prosecutor at the trial. At this meeting, it was decided that there was enough evidence to justify the arrest of Coolidge on the murder charge and a search of his house and two cars. At the conclusion of the meeting, the Manchester police chief made formal application, under oath, for the arrest and search warrants. The complaint supporting the warrant for a search of Coolidge's Pontiac automobile, the only warrant that concerns us here, stated that the affiant 'has probable cause to suspect and believe, and does suspect and believe, and herewith offers satisfactory evidence, that there are certain objects and things used in the Commission of said offense, now kept, and concealed in or upon a certain vehicle, to wit: 1951 Pontiac two-door sedan * * *.' The warrants were then signed and issued by the Attorney General himself, acting as a justice of the peace. Under New Hampshire law in force at that time, all justices of the peace were authorized to issue search warrants. N.H.Rev.Stat.Ann. s 595:1 (repealed 1969).

The police arrested Coolidge in his house on the day the warrant issued. Mrs. Coolidge asked whether she might remain in the house with her small child, but was told that she must stay elsewhere, apparently in part because the police believed that she would be harassed by reporters if she were accessible to them. When she asked whether she might take her car, she was told that both cars had been 'impounded,' and that the police would provide transportation for her. Some time later, the police called a towing company, and about two and a half hours after Coolidge had been taken into custody the cars were towed to the police station. It appears that at the time of the arrest the cars were parked in the Coolidge driveway, and that although dark had fallen they were plainly visible both from the street and from inside the house where Coolidge was actually arrested. The 1951 Pontiac was searched and vacuumed on February 21, two days after it was seized, again a year later, in January 1965, and a third time in April 1965.

At Coolidge's subsequent jury trial on the charge of murder, vacuum sweepings, including particles of gun powder, taken from the Pontiac were introduced in evidence against him, as part of an attempt by the State to show by microscopic analysis that it was highly probable that Pamela Mason had been in Coolidge's car. Also introduced in evidence was one of the guns taken by the police on their Sunday evening visit to the Coolidge house—a 22-caliber Mossberg rifle, which the prosecution claimed was the murder weapon. Conflicting ballistics testimony was offered on the question whether the bullets found in Pamela Mason's body had been fired from this rifle. Finally, the prosecution introduced vacuum sweepings of the clothes taken from the Coolidge house that same Sunday evening, and attempted to show through microscopic analysis that there was a high probability that the clothes had been in contact with Pamela Mason's body. Pretrial motions to suppress all this evidence were referred by the trial judge to the New Hampshire Supreme Court, which ruled the evidence admissible. The jury found Coolidge guilty and he was sentenced to life imprisonment. The New Hampshire Supreme Court affirmed the judgment of conviction and we granted certiorari to consider the constitutional questions raised by the admission of this evidence against Coolidge at his trial.

I

The petitioner's first claim is that the warrant authorizing the seizure and subsequent search of his 1951 Pontiac automobile was invalid because not issued by a 'neutral and detached magistrate.' Since we agree with the petitioner that the warrant was invalid for this reason, we need not consider his further argument that the allegations under oath supporting the issuance of the warrant were so conclusory as to violate relevant constitutional standards. Cf. *Giordenello v. United States*, 357 U.S. 480, 78 S.Ct. 1245, 2 L.Ed.2d 1503; *Aguilar v. Texas*, 378 U.S. 108, 84 S.Ct. 1509, 12 L.Ed.2d 723.

The classic statement of the policy underlying the warrant requirement of the Fourth Amendment is that of Mr. Justice Jackson, writing for the Court in *Johnson v. United States*, 333 U.S. 10, 13–14, 68 S.Ct. 367, 369, 92 L.Ed. 436:

'The point of the Fourth Amendment, which often is not grasped by zealous officers, is not that it denies law enforcement the support of the usual inferences which reasonable men draw from evidence. Its protection consists in requiring that those inferences be drawn by a neutral and detached magistrate instead of being judged by the officer engaged in the often competitive enterprise of ferreting out crime. Any assumption that evidence sufficient to support a magistrate's disinterested determination to issue a search warrant will justify the officers in making a search without a warrant would reduce the Amendment to a nullity and leave the people's homes secure only in the discretion of police officers. * * * When the right of privacy must reasonably yield to the right of search is, as a rule, to be decided by a judicial officer, not by a policeman or Government enforcement agent.'. . .

In this case, the determination of probable cause was made by the chief 'government enforcement agent' of the State—the Attorney General—who was actively in charge of the investigation and later was to be chief prosecutor at the trial. To be sure, the determination was formalized here by a writing bearing the title 'Search Warrant,' whereas in Johnson there was no piece of paper involved, but the State has not attempted to uphold the warrant on any such artificial basis. Rather, the State argues that the Attorney General, who was unquestionably authorized as a justice of the peace to issue warrants under then existing state law, did in fact act as a 'neutral and detached magistrate.' Further, the State claims that any magistrate, confronted with the showing of probable cause made by the Manchester chief of police, would have issued the warrant in question. To the first proposition it is enough to answer that there could hardly be a more appropriate setting than this for a per se rule of disqualification rather than a case-by-case evaluation of all the circumstances. Without disrespect to the state law enforcement agent here involved, the whole point of the basic rule so well expressed by Mr. Justice Jackson is that prosecutors and policemen simply cannot be asked to maintain the requisite neutrality with regard to their own investigations—the 'competitive enterprise' that must rightly engage their single-minded attention. Cf. *Mancusi v. DeForte*, 392 U.S. 364.

As for the proposition that the existence of probable cause renders noncompliance with the warrant procedure an irrelevance, it is enough to cite *Agnello v. United States*, 269 U.S. 20, 33, decided in 1925: 'Belief, however well founded, that an article sought is concealed in a dwelling house, furnishes no justification for a search of that place without a warrant. And such searches are held unlawful notwithstanding facts unquestionably showing probable cause.'. . .

But the New Hampshire Supreme Court, in upholding the conviction, relied upon the theory that even if the warrant procedure here in issue would clearly violate the standards imposed on the Federal Government by the Fourth Amendment, it is not forbidden the States under the Fourteenth. . . . *Mapp*, however, established no assumption by this Court of supervisory authority over state courts * * * and, consequently, it implied no total obliteration of state laws relating to arrests and searches in favor of federal law. *Mapp* sounded no death knell for our federalism; rather, it echoed the sentiment of *Elkins v. United States*, supra, 364 U.S. (206), at 221, that 'a healthy federalism depends upon the avoidance of needless conflict between state and federal courts' by itself urging that '(f)ederal-state cooperation in the solution of crime under constitutional standards will be promoted, if only by recognition of their now mutual obligation to respect the same fundamental criteria in their approaches.' 367 U.S., at 658. (Emphasis in *Ker*.)

It is urged that the New Hampshire statutes which at the time of the searches here involved permitted a law enforcement officer himself to issue a warrant was one of those 'workable rules governing arrests, searches and seizures to meet 'the practical demands of effective criminal investigation and law enforcement' in the States,' authorized by Ker.

That such a procedure was indeed workable from the point of view of the police is evident from testimony at the trial in this case:

'The Court: You mean that another police officer issues these (search warrants)?

'The Witness: Yes. Captain Couture and Captain Shea and Captain Loveren are J.P.'s.

'The Court: Well, let me ask you, Chief, your answer is to the effect that you never go out of the department for the Justice of the Peace?

'The Witness: It hasn't been our—policy to go out of the department.

'Q. Right. Your policy and experience, is to have a fellow police officer take the warrant in the capacity of Justice of the Peace?

'A.   That has been our practice.'

But it is too plain for extensive discussion that this now abandoned New Hampshire method of issuing 'search warrants' violated a fundamental premise of both the Fourth and Fourteenth Amendments—a premise fully developed and articulated long before this Court's decisions in *Ker v. California*, supra, and

*Mapp v. Ohio*, 367 U.S. 643. As Mr. Justice Frankfurter put it in *Wolf v. Colorado*, 338 U.S. 25, 27–28:

> 'The security of one's privacy against arbitrary intrusion by the police—which is at the core of the Fourth Amendment—is basic to a free society. It is therefore implicit in 'the concept of ordered liberty' and as such enforceable against the States through the Due Process Clause. The knock at the door, whether by day or by night, as a prelude to a search, without authority of law but solely on the authority of the police, did not need the commentary of recent history to be condemned * * *.'

We find no escape from the conclusion that the seizure and search of the Pontiac automobile cannot constitutionally rest upon the warrant issued by the state official who was the chief investigator and prosecutor in this case. Since he was not the neutral and detached magistrate required by the Constitution, the search stands on no firmer ground than if there had been no warrant at all. If the seizure and search are to be justified, they must, therefore, be justified on some other theory. . .

The judgment is reversed and the case is remanded to the Supreme Court of New Hampshire for further proceedings not inconsistent with this opinion.

**It is so ordered.**

**Judgment reversed and case remanded. . .**

**MR. CHIEF JUSTICE BURGER, dissenting in part and concurring in part. . .**

On the merits of the case I find not the slightest basis in the record to reverse this conviction. Here again the Court reaches out, strains, and distorts rules that were showing some signs of stabilizing, and directs a new trial which will be held more than seven years after the criminal acts charged. Mr. Justice Stone, of the Minnesota Supreme Court, called the kind of judicial functioning in which the Court indulges today 'bifurcating elements too infinitesimal to be split.'

**MR. JUSTICE BLACK, concurring and dissenting.**

After a jury trial in a New Hampshire state court, petitioner was convicted of murder and sentenced to life imprisonment. Holding that certain evidence introduced by the State was seized during an 'unreasonable' search and that the evidence was inadmissible under the judicially created exclusionary rule of the Fourth Amendment, the majority reverses that conviction. Believing that the search and seizure here was reasonable and that the Fourth Amendment properly construed contains no such exclusionary rule, I dissent. . .evidence was presented to the state attorney general who was authorized under New Hampshire law to issue arrest and search warrants. The attorney general considered the evidence and issued a warrant for petitioner's arrest and four search warrants including a warrant for the seizure and search of petitioner's Pontiac automobile. . .

Petitioner challenges his conviction on the ground that the rifle obtained from his wife and the vacuum sweepings taken from his car were seized in violation of the Fourth Amendment and were improperly admitted at trial. With respect to the rifle voluntarily given to the police by petitioner's wife, the majority holds that it was properly received in evidence. I agree. But the Court reverses petitioner's conviction on the ground that the sweepings taken from his car were seized during an illegal search and for this reason the admission of the sweepings into evidence violated the Fourth Amendment. I dissent.

I

The Fourth Amendment prohibits unreasonable searches and seizures. The Amendment says nothing about consequences. It certainly nowhere provides for the exclusion of evidence as the remedy for violation. . . . Apparently the first suggestion that the Fourth Amendment somehow embodied a rule of evidence came in Justice Bradley's majority opinion in *Boyd v. United States*, 116 U.S. 616 (1886). The holding in that case was that ordinarily a person may not be compelled to produce his private books and papers for use against him as proof of crime. That decision was a sound application of accepted principles of common law and the command of the Fifth Amendment that no person shall be compelled to be a witness against himself. . . . It was not until 1914, some 28 years after Boyd and when no member of the Boyd Court remained, that the Court in *Weeks v. United States*, 232 U.S. 383, stated that the Fourth Amendment itself barred the admission of evidence seized in violation of the Fourth Amendment. The Weeks opinion made no express confession of a break with the past. But if it was merely a proper reading of the Fourth Amendment, it seems strange that it took this Court nearly 125 years to discover the true meaning of those words. The truth is that the source of the exclusionary rule simply cannot be found in the Fourth Amendment. That Amendment did not when adopted, and does not now, contain any constitutional rule barring the admission of illegally seized evidence. . .

The evidence seized by breaking into Mrs. Mapp's house and the search of all her possessions, was excluded from evidence, not by the Fourth

Amendment which contains no exclusionary rule, but by the Fifth Amendment which does. The introduction of such evidence compels a man to be a witness against himself, and evidence so compelled must be excluded under the Fifth Amendment, not because the Court says so, but because the Fifth Amendment commands it. . .

The majority holds that evidence it views as improperly seized in violation of its ever changing concept of the Fourth Amendment is inadmissible. The majority treats the exclusionary rule as a judge-made rule of evidence designed and utilized to enforce the majority's own notions of proper police conduct. The Court today announces its new rules of police procedure in the name of the Fourth Amendment, then holds that evidence seized in violation of the new 'guidelines' is automatically inadmissible at trial. The majority does not purport to rely on the Fifth Amendment to exclude the evidence in this case. Indeed it could not. The majority prefers instead to rely on 'changing times' and the Court's role as it sees it, as the administrator in charge of regulating the contacts of officials with citizens. The majority states that in the absence of a better means of regulation, it applies a court-created rule of evidence. . .

Our Government is founded upon a written Constitution. The draftsmen expressed themselves in careful and measured terms corresponding with the immense importance of the powers delegated to them. The Framers of the Constitution, and the people who adopted it, must be understood to have used words in their natural meaning, and to have intended what they said, the Constitution itself contains the standards by which the seizure of evidence challenged in the present case and the admissibility of that evidence at trial is to be measured in the absence of congressional legislation. It is my conclusion that both the seizure of the rifle offered by petitioner's wife and the seizure of the automobile at the time of petitioner's arrest were consistent with the Fourth Amendment and that the evidence so obtained under the circumstances shown in the record in this case could not be excluded under the Fifth Amendment.

## II

. . .Therefore, it is my conclusion that the warrant authorizing the seizure and search of petitioner's automobile was constitutional under the Fourth Amendment, and that the evidence obtained during that search cannot be excluded under the Fifth Amendment. Moreover, I am of the view that, even if the search warrant had not issued, the search in this case nonetheless would have been constitutional under all three of the principles considered and rejected by the majority. . .

**After preparing the case brief, consider the answers to the following questions:**

1.   Who issued the warrant in this case?

2.   Why is the Court convinced that the attorney general could not act as a neutral and detached magistrate?

3.   Do you agree with the Court's holding that the exclusionary rule demands reversal of the defendant's conviction and exclusion of the evidence from the vehicle?

4.   Read the dissenting opinions. What are their arguments that the exclusionary rule is not required in this case? Are they convincing?

## LANGE V. CALIFORNIA

Supreme Court of the United States
Argued Feb. 24, 2021
Decided June 23, 2021
141 S.Ct. 2011

KAGAN, J., delivered the opinion of the Court, in which BREYER, SOTOMAYOR, GORSUCH, KAVANAUGH, and BARRETT, JJ., joined, and in which THOMAS, J., joined as to all but Part II-A. KAVANAUGH, J., filed a concurring opinion. THOMAS, J., filed an opinion concurring in part and concurring in the judgment, in which KAVANAUGH, J., joined as to Part II. ROBERTS, C. J., filed an opinion concurring in the judgment, in which ALITO, J., joined. . . .

**JUSTICE KAGAN delivered the opinion of the Court.**

The Fourth Amendment ordinarily requires that police officers get a warrant before entering a home without permission. But an officer may make a warrantless entry when "the exigencies of the situation" create a compelling law enforcement need. *Kentucky v. King*, 563 U.S. 452, 460 (2011). The question presented here is whether the pursuit of a fleeing misdemeanor suspect always—or more legally put, categorically—qualifies as an exigent circumstance. We hold it does not. A great many misdemeanor pursuits involve exigencies allowing warrantless entry. But whether a given one does so turns on the particular facts of the case.

I

This case began when petitioner Arthur Lange drove past a California highway patrol officer in Sonoma. Lange, it is fair to say, was asking for attention: He was listening to loud music with his windows down and repeatedly honking his horn. The officer began to tail Lange, and soon afterward turned on his overhead lights to signal that Lange should pull over. By that time, though, Lange was only about a hundred feet (some four-seconds drive) from his home. Rather than stopping, Lange continued to his driveway and entered his attached garage. The officer followed Lange in and began questioning him. Observing signs of intoxication, the officer put Lange through field sobriety tests. Lange did not do well, and a later blood test showed that his blood-alcohol content was more than three times the legal limit.

The State charged Lange with the misdemeanor of driving under the influence of alcohol, plus a (lower-level) noise infraction. Lange moved to suppress all evidence obtained after the officer entered his garage, arguing that the warrantless entry had violated the Fourth Amendment. The State contested the motion. It contended that the officer had probable cause to arrest Lange for the misdemeanor of failing to comply with a police signal. See, *e.g.*, Cal. Veh. Code Ann. § 2800(a) (West 2015) (making it a misdemeanor to "willfully fail or refuse to comply with a lawful order, signal, or direction of a peace officer"). And it argued that the pursuit of a suspected misdemeanant always qualifies as an exigent circumstance authorizing a warrantless home entry. The Superior Court denied Lange's motion, and its appellate division affirmed.

The California Court of Appeal also affirmed, accepting the State's argument in full. 2019 WL 5654385, *1 (2019). In the court's view, Lange's "fail[ure] to immediately pull over" when the officer flashed his lights created probable cause to arrest him for a misdemeanor. *Id.*, at *7. And a misdemeanor suspect, the court stated, could "not defeat an arrest which has been set in motion in a public place" by "retreat[ing] into" a house or other "private place." See *id.*, at *6–*8 (internal quotation marks omitted). Rather, an "officer's 'hot pursuit' into the house to prevent the suspect from frustrating the arrest" is always permissible under the exigent-circumstances "exception to the warrant requirement." *Id.*, at *8 (some internal quotation marks omitted). That flat rule resolved the matter: "Because the officer was in hot pursuit" of a misdemeanor suspect, "the officer's warrantless entry into [the suspect's] driveway and garage [was] lawful." *Id.*, at *9. The California Supreme Court denied review.

Courts are divided over whether the Fourth Amendment always permits an officer to enter a home without a warrant in pursuit of a fleeing misdemeanor suspect. Some courts have adopted such a categorical rule, while others have required a case-specific showing of exigency. We granted certiorari to resolve the conflict. Because California abandoned its defense of the categorical rule applied below in its response to Lange's petition, we appointed Amanda Rice as *amicus curiae* to defend the Court of Appeal's judgment. She has ably discharged her responsibilities.

II

The Fourth Amendment provides that "[t]he right of the people to be secure in their persons, houses, papers, and effects, against unreasonable searches and seizures, shall not be violated." As that text makes clear, "the ultimate touchstone of the Fourth Amendment is 'reasonableness.'" *Brigham City v. Stuart*, 547 U.S. 398, 403 (2006). That standard "generally requires the obtaining of a judicial warrant" before a law enforcement officer can enter a home without permission. *Riley v. California*, 573 U.S. 373, 382 (2014) (internal quotation marks omitted). But not always: The "warrant requirement is subject to certain exceptions." *Brigham City*, 547 U.S., at 403, 126 S.Ct. 1943.

One important exception is for exigent circumstances. It applies when "the exigencies of the situation make the needs of law enforcement so compelling that [a] warrantless search is objectively reasonable." *King*, 563 U.S., at 460, 131 S.Ct. 1849. The exception enables law enforcement officers to handle "emergenc[ies]"—situations presenting a "compelling need for official action and no time to secure a warrant." *Riley*, 573 U.S., at 402, 134 S.Ct. 2473; *Missouri v. McNeely*, 569 U.S. 141 (2013). Over the years, this Court has identified several such exigencies. An officer, for example, may "enter a home without a warrant to render emergency assistance to an injured occupant[,] to protect an occupant from imminent injury," or to ensure his own safety. . .So too, the police may make a warrantless entry to "prevent the imminent destruction of evidence" or to "prevent a suspect's escape.". . .

Our cases have generally applied the exigent-circumstances exception on a "case-by-case basis." *Birchfield v. North Dakota*, 136 S.Ct. 2160, 2174 (2016). The exception "requires a court to examine whether an emergency justified a warrantless search in each particular case." . . . So the issue, we have thought, is most naturally considered by "look[ing] to the totality of circumstances" confronting the officer as he decides to make a warrantless entry. Id., at 149, 133 S.Ct. 1552.

The question here is whether to use that approach, or instead apply a categorical warrant exception, when a suspected misdemeanant flees from police into his home. Under the usual case-specific view, an officer can follow the misdemeanant when, but only when, an exigency—for example, the need to prevent destruction of evidence—allows insufficient time to get a warrant. The appointed *amicus* asks us to replace that case-by-case assessment with a flat (and sweeping) rule finding exigency in every case of misdemeanor pursuit. In her view, those "entries are categorically reasonable, regardless of whether" any risk of harm (like, again, destruction of evidence) "materializes in a particular case." Brief for Court-Appointed *Amicus Curiae* 31. The fact of flight from the officer, she says, is itself enough to justify a warrantless entry. (The principal concurrence agrees.) To assess that position, we look (as we often do in Fourth Amendment cases) both to this Court's precedents and to the common-law practices familiar to the Framers.

A

The place to start is with our often-stated view of the constitutional interest at stake: the sanctity of a person's living space. "[W]hen it comes to the Fourth Amendment, the home is first among equals." *Florida v. Jardines*, 569 U.S. 1, 6 (2013). At the Amendment's "very core," we have said, "stands the right of a man to retreat into his own home and there be free from unreasonable government intrusion." *Collins v. Virginia*, 584 U.S. ___, ___, 138 S.Ct. 1663, 1670 (2018). Or again: "Freedom" in one's own "dwelling is the archetype of the privacy protection secured by the Fourth Amendment"; conversely, "physical entry of the home is the chief evil against which [it] is directed." *Payton v. New York*, 445 U.S. 573 (1980). The Amendment thus "draw[s] a firm line at the entrance to the house." *Id.*, at 590, 100 S.Ct. 1371. What lies behind that line is of course not inviolable. An officer may always enter a home with a proper warrant. And as just described, exigent circumstances allow even warrantless intrusions. . . . ("[T]his Court has repeatedly declined to expand the scope" of "exceptions to the warrant requirement to permit warrantless entry into the home"). So we are not eager— more the reverse—to print a new permission slip for entering the home without a warrant.

The *amicus* argues, though, that we have already created the rule she advocates. In *United States v. Santana*, 427 U.S. 38 (1976), the main case she relies on, police officers drove to Dominga Santana's house with probable cause to think that Santana was dealing drugs, a felony under the applicable law. When the officers pulled up, they saw Santana standing in her home's open doorway, some 15 feet away. As they got out of the van and yelled "police," Santana "retreated into [the house's] vestibule." *Id.*, at 40, 96 S.Ct. 2406. The officers followed her in, and discovered heroin. We upheld the warrantless entry as one involving a police "hot pursuit," even though the chase "ended almost as soon as it began." *Id.*, at 43, 96 S.Ct. 2406. Citing "a realistic expectation that any delay would result in destruction of evidence," we recognized the officers' "need to act quickly." *Id.*, at 42–43, 96 S.Ct. 2406. But we framed our holding in broader terms: Santana's "act of retreating into her house," we stated, could "not defeat an arrest" that had "been set in motion in a public place." *Ibid.* The *amicus* takes that statement to support a flat rule permitting warrantless home entry when police officers (with probable cause) are pursuing any suspect— whether a felon or a misdemeanant. See Brief for *Amicus Curiae* 11, 26. For support, she points to a number of later decisions describing *Santana* in dicta as allowing warrantless home entries when police are "in 'hot pursuit' of a fugitive" or "a fleeing suspect." *E.g.*, *Steagald v. United States*, 451 U.S. 204, 221 (1981). The concurrence echoes her arguments.

We disagree with that broad understanding of *Santana*, as we have suggested before. In rejecting the *amicus*'s view, we see no need to consider Lange's counterargument that *Santana* did not establish *any* categorical rule— even one for fleeing felons. . . .

Key to resolving that issue are two facts about misdemeanors: They vary widely, but they may be (in a word) "minor." *Welsh*, 466 U.S., at 750, 104 S.Ct. 2091. In California and elsewhere, misdemeanors run the gamut of seriousness. As the *amicus* notes, some involve violence. California, for example, classifies as misdemeanors various forms of assault. See Cal. Penal Code Ann. § 241 (West Cum. Supp. 2021); Brief for *Amicus Curiae* 15a–16a. And across the country, "many perpetrators of domestic violence are charged with misdemeanors," despite "the harmfulness of their conduct." *Voisine v. United States*, 579 U.S. 686, ___, 136 S.Ct. 2272, 2276, 195 L.Ed.2d 736 (2016). So "a 'felon' is" not always "more dangerous than a misdemeanant." *Tennessee v. Garner*, 471 U.S. 1, 14 (1985). But calling an offense a misdemeanor usually limits prison time to one year. See 1 W. LaFave, J. Israel, N. King, & O. Kerr, Criminal Procedure § 1.8(c) (4th ed. Supp. 2020). States thus tend to apply that label to less violent and less dangerous crimes. In California, it is a misdemeanor to litter on a public beach. See Cal. Penal Code Ann. § 374.7(a) (2020). And to "negligently cut" a plant "growing upon public land." § 384a(a)(2), (f). And to "willfully disturb[] another person by loud and unreasonable noise." § 415(2). And (last one) to "artificially color[] any live chicks [or] rabbits." § 599(b). In forbidding such conduct, California is no outlier. Most States count as misdemeanors such offenses as traffic violations, public intoxication, and disorderly conduct. See, *e.g.*, Tex. Transp. Code Ann. § 545.413(a), (d) (West 2011) (driving without a seatbelt); Ill. Comp. Stat., ch. 610, § 90/1 (West 2018) (drinking alcohol in a railroad car); Ark. Code Ann. § 5–71–207(a)(3), (b) (2016) (using obscene language likely to promote disorder). So the *amicus*'s (and concurrence's) rule would cover lawbreakers of every type, including quite a few hard to think alarming.

This Court has held that when a minor offense alone is involved, police officers do not usually face the kind of emergency that can justify a warrantless home entry. In *Welsh*, officers responded to a call about a drunk driver only to discover he had abandoned his vehicle and walked home. See 466 U.S., at 742–743, 104 S.Ct. 2091. So no police pursuit was necessary, hot or otherwise. The officers just went to the driver's house, entered without a warrant, and arrested him for a "nonjailable" offense. *Ibid.* The State contended that exigent circumstances supported the entry because the driver's "blood-alcohol level might have dissipated while the police obtained a warrant." *Id.*, at 754, 104 S.Ct. 2091. We rejected that argument on the ground that the driver had been charged with only a minor offense. "[T]he gravity of the underlying offense," we reasoned, is "an important factor to be considered when determining whether any exigency exists." *Id.*, at 753, 104 S.Ct. 2091. "[W]hen only a minor offense has been committed" (again, without any flight), there is reason to question whether a compelling law enforcement need is present; so it is "particularly appropriate" to "hesitat[e] in finding exigent circumstances." *Id.*, at 750, 104 S.Ct. 2091. And we concluded: "[A]pplication of the exigent-circumstances exception in the context of a home entry should rarely be sanctioned when there is probable cause to believe that only a minor offense" is involved. *Id.*, at 753, 104 S.Ct. 2091.

Add a suspect's flight and the calculus changes—but not enough to justify the *amicus*'s categorical rule. We have no doubt that in a great many cases flight creates a need for police to act swiftly. A suspect may flee, for example, because he is intent on discarding evidence. Or his flight may show a willingness to flee yet again, while the police await a warrant. But no evidence suggests that every case of misdemeanor flight poses such dangers. . . . In misdemeanor cases, flight does not always supply the exigency that this Court has demanded for a warrantless home entry.

Our Fourth Amendment precedents thus point toward assessing case by case the exigencies arising from misdemeanants' flight. That approach will in many, if not most, cases allow a warrantless home entry. When the totality of circumstances shows an emergency—such as imminent harm to others, a threat to the officer himself, destruction of evidence, or escape from the home—the police may act without waiting. And those circumstances, as described just above, include the flight itself. But the need to pursue a misdemeanant does not trigger a categorical rule allowing home entry, even absent a law enforcement emergency. When the nature of the crime, the nature of the flight, and surrounding facts present no such exigency, officers must respect the sanctity of the home—which means that they must get a warrant.

B

. . .

Like our modern precedents, the common law afforded the home strong protection from government intrusion. As this Court once wrote: "The zealous and frequent repetition of the adage that a 'man's house is his castle' made it abundantly clear that both in England and in the Colonies 'the freedom of one's house' was one of the most vital elements of English liberty." *Id.*, at 596–597, 100 S.Ct. 1371 (footnote omitted); see *Semayne's Case*, 5 Co. Rep. 91a, 91b, 77 Eng. Rep. 194, 195 (K. B. 1604) ("[T]he house of every one is as to him as his castle and fortress, as well for his defen[s]e against injury and violence, as for his repose" (footnote omitted)); 3 W. Blackstone, Commentaries on the Laws of England 288 (1768) ("[E]very man's house is looked upon by the law to be his castle of defen[s]e and asylum"). . . .

The common law thus does not support a categorical rule allowing warrantless home entry when a misdemeanant flees. It had a rule of that kind for felonies. But much as in *Welsh* centuries later, the common law made distinctions based on "the gravity of the underlying offense." 466 U.S., at 753, 104 S.Ct. 2091. When it came to misdemeanors, flight alone was not enough. Whether a constable could make a warrantless entry depended as well on other circumstances suggesting a potential for harm and a need to act promptly. In that way, the common-law rules (even if sometimes hard to discern with precision) mostly mirror our modern caselaw. The former too demanded—and often found—a law enforcement exigency before an officer could "break open" a fleeing misdemeanant's doors. Blackstone 292.

III

The flight of a suspected misdemeanant does not always justify a warrantless entry into a home. An officer must consider all the circumstances in a pursuit case to determine whether there is a law enforcement emergency. On many occasions, the officer will have good reason to enter—to prevent imminent harms of violence, destruction of evidence, or escape from the home. But when the officer has time to get a warrant, he must do so—even though the misdemeanant fled.

Because the California Court of Appeal applied the categorical rule we reject today, we vacate its judgment and remand the case for further proceedings not inconsistent with this opinion.

*It is so ordered.* . . .

**After preparing the case brief, consider the answers to the following questions:**

1. What is the doctrine of hot pursuit in the context of the Fourth Amendment?

2.    What might justify an officer's entry to a suspect's home without a warrant based on hot pursuit?

3.    In *Lange* do you believe the officer was justified in entering Lange's garage based on the facts he observed?

## Chapter 8 Key Terms for Review

- **Search**: governmental intrusion upon a person's reasonable expectation of privacy.

- **Seizure**: governmental exercise of control over a person or thing.

- **Search warrant**: a document describing specific contraband or evidence, detailing the location to be searched by law enforcement.

- **Probable cause**: the reasonable basis for believing that a crime may have been committed (for arrest) or that evidence of a crime or contraband is in a specific location (for a search)

- **Arrest warrant**: describes a person suspected of a crime and authorizes law enforcement to take them into physical custody.

- **Particularity requirement**: warrants must specifically describe the places to be searched and persons or things to be seized.

- **Stale search warrant**: when too much time has passed between securing and executing a warrant or when the information provided to support the warrant was too old to provide "present" probable cause.

- **General warrant**: warrants that do not specify the places to be searched or the people or things to be seized. These are unlawful in the United States because of the Fourth Amendment's particularity requirement.

- **Exclusionary rule**: prevents the use of evidence collected in an unlawful manner in determining the guilt of the defendant; it is excluded from the case against him.

- **Derivative evidence**: evidence that is discovered indirectly as the result of other evidence.

- **Fruit of the poisonous tree doctrine**: when derivative evidence is discovered as the result of unlawful police misconduct, it is inadmissible at trial against the defendant because it is "tainted" fruit of the unlawful conduct.

- **Consent to search**: if a suspect consents to a search the evidence is admissible against him at trial.

- **Terry Stop**: a limited "stop and frisk" for weapons allowed without a warrant justified by the threat of potential weapons to officer and public safety. *Terry v. Ohio (1961)*.

- **Automobile exception**: allows for the search of automobiles upon probable cause without a warrant based on their mobility and the lesser expectation of privacy in vehicles. *Carroll v. United States (1925)*.

- **Hot pursuit**: The hot pursuit exception to the warrant requirement states that a suspect policy may enter private property to effect the arrest of a fleeing felon.

- **Plain view**: evidence that is left by a suspect in plain view for officers to see is admissible against them at trial.

- **Search incident to a lawful arrest**: officers may search a suspect's person and the area within his reach or "wingspan" incident to a lawful arrest for the officer's safety. *Chimel v. California (1969)*.

- **Attenuation**: where evidence is discovered illegally and would be excluded as fruit of the poisonous tree, it might be admitted over objection if the taint has become attenuated, or weakened. *Utah v. Strieff (2016)*.

# Self-Incrimination and the Admissibility of Confessions in Criminal Trials

The Fifth and Sixth Amendments provide the Constitutional foundation for the rules governing the admissibility of confessions. The Fifth Amendment privilege against self-incrimination and the Sixth Amendment right to counsel both impact the admissibility of a suspect's statements. **Self-incrimination** takes place when a suspect provides information that might help establish his guilt. Suspects have a right to remain silent. They are never compelled to answer questions or provide information that might incriminate them in a case—but many suspects do so willingly. At other times the information is obtained through coercion or other unlawful means by police against the suspect's will. In those cases the evidence is not admissible to prove the suspect's guilt at trial. The right to the assistance of counsel from the Sixth Amendment has been extended beyond the trial itself to apply to certain encounters with police.

## A. CONFESSIONS

A **confession** is an admission of guilt by a criminal suspect or defendant. A confession may be oral or written. It may be given spontaneously by a suspect prior to arrest or after many hours of investigation and interrogation by law enforcement. Whether a confession is admissible turns on the way it was secured from the suspect. A criminal defendant does not have to testify and has a right to remain silent throughout the criminal investigation and trial. The Fifth Amendment provides the privilege against self-incrimination.[1] This means that suspects are never required to provide incriminating evidence in a criminal case. This includes answering questions during an interrogation, giving testimony at a

---

[1] U.S. Const. amend. V, ". . . nor shall be compelled in any criminal case to be a witness against himself. . ."

trial, or could even involve physical evidence such as requiring a suspect to give a blood sample.

The core principle underlying the Supreme Court's decisions regarding confessions is voluntariness. For many years the Court employed a voluntariness standard evaluating the "totality of the circumstances" in order to determine whether a suspect had made a knowing and intelligent waiver of his constitutional rights.[2] Because the process of interrogating suspects involves officers exerting pressure on them to gain information, even when officers engage in this process in good faith there is an inherent risk of coercion. In other circumstances police may engage in the abuse of power, intentionally coercing suspects into confessing against their will.

## B. THE MIRANDA WARNING REQUIREMENT

The risk that innocent suspects may be coerced to confess led to the U.S. Supreme Court's decision in *Miranda v. Arizona (1966)*.[3] The Court's decision in Miranda gave rise to the well-known **Miranda warning** now employed by officers nationwide to advise suspects of their rights. The Miranda rule is a **bright line rule**, which means it must be followed whenever a suspect is subjected to custodial interrogation.

Custody on its own does not require that officers warn a suspect of their rights, nor does interrogation outside of custody. It is interrogation while in police custody that triggers the Miranda rule. For example, if a detective calls a suspect on the telephone and he answers the officer's questions about a crime, his answers are admissible even without a Miranda warning. It is the risk of coercion inherent in **custodial interrogation** that the Miranda warning seeks to prevent. Violations of suspect's Miranda rights are subject to the exclusionary rule.

The Court has held that any police discussion or comments directed at the accused with the intention of eliciting an incriminating response is questioning within the definition of Miranda and is inadmissible without a valid warning.[4] In *Rhode Island v. Innis (1980)* police officers talked among themselves about a school for handicapped children nearby in hopes that their suspect would offer information about the location of a gun they believed he had used in a robbery. The evidence was inadmissible against the defendant at trial because of the officer's failure to properly Mirandize the suspect. Even after a suspect has been

---

[2]  *Johnson v. Zerbst*, 304 U.S. 458 (1938).

[3]  384 U.S. 436 (1966).

[4]  *Rhode Island v. Innis*, 446 U.S. 291 (1980).

properly Mirandized and waived his rights, he may re-invoke his rights requiring officers to provide a new warning and secure a new waiver before engaging in any conversation or questioning in police custody.[5]

Incriminating evidence is inadmissible when obtained unlawfully. This is true whether it is **direct evidence**, which proves a fact without requiring the jurors to make any inference or presumptions, or it is **derivative evidence**. Derivative evidence may be inadmissible because of its connection with other unlawfully obtained evidence. When the original evidence was obtained unlawfully, the derivative evidence is tainted. It is referred to as the *fruit of the poisonous tree doctrine*. This was also discussed in the context of Fourth Amendment searches in Chapter 8 also applies where there are Fifth Amendment violations.

In *Wong Sun v. United States (1963)* the Court held that the incriminating statements made by an initial suspect were obtained unlawfully for lack of probable cause.[6] The initial suspect provided information that led to the arrest of others, and the Court held that the initial illegality tainted the confessions made by all of the suspects involved making them inadmissible fruit of the poisonous tree.

## C. EXCEPTIONS TO THE EXCLUSION OF EVIDENCE UNDER MIRANDA

**Voluntariness** is the most commonsense exception to the Miranda rule. If a suspect makes statements voluntarily, they are admissible against him at trial.[7] There are exceptions to application of the exclusionary rule for Miranda right violations. In *New York v. Quarles (1984)* the Supreme Court created an exception for **public safety**.[8] This is also referred to as an exigency, or emergency, exception to the Miranda rule.

In *Quarles* an armed suspect hid his firearm in a public place. When officers apprehended and handcuffed the suspect they asked him where he had thrown the gun before Mirandizing him. The suspect told them, without being warned of his Miranda rights, and the gun was used as evidence against him at trial. The Supreme Court held that where there is a risk to the safety of officers or the public, there is an exception to the Miranda warning requirement.

---

5    *Minnick v. Mississippi*, 498 U.S. 146 (1990).

6    *Wong Sun v. United States*, 371 U.S. 471 (1963).

7    *Id.*

8    467 U.S. 649 (1984).

**Inevitable discovery** is also an exception to the exclusionary rule for violations of *Miranda*. The Court adopted the rule in *Nix v. Williams (1984)* holding that evidence obtained in violation of Miranda was admissible because the body of the murder victim would have been inevitably discovered.[9] This case if often referred to as the "Christian burial" case because the officer pressed the suspect to reveal the location of his murder victim's body so that her family could have a Christian burial. The suspect, Williams, had not been read his Miranda warning. The Court held that the conversation in the car between the officer and the Williams violated his Miranda rights because he was in custody and the officer's comments, while not questions, were the functional equivalent of questioning. In the end, the Court allowed the use of the evidence even in violation of *Miranda,* because it would have been discovered inevitably.

The impact of the exclusionary rule is the same in the context of the Fourth, Fifth and Sixth Amendments—it prevents the use of illegally obtained evidence from criminal trials. While the practical application in the courts is the same (the defendant enjoys the benefit of exclusion) the foundation for exclusion, and the rules and exceptions governing exclusion differ depending upon the underlying constitutional principles.

---

[9]    467 U.S. 431 (1984).

**Read and brief each of the following cases relating to self-incrimination and the admissibility of confessions and consider the questions following each case:**

1. *Miranda v. Arizona*: Fifth and Sixth Amendment rights during custodial interrogation

2. *Orozco v. Texas*: *Miranda* outside of the police station

3. *New York v. Quarles*: public safety exception to *Miranda*

---

## MIRANDA V. ARIZONA

Supreme Court of the United States
Argued Feb. 28, March 1 and 2, 1966
Decided June 13, 1966
Rehearing Denied No. 584 Oct. 10, 1966
384 U.S. 436

[Note: *Miranda*'s appeal was brought together with No. 760, *Vignera v. New York*, on certiorari to the Court of Appeals of New York and No. 761, *Westover v. United States*, on certiorari to the United States Court of Appeals for the Ninth Circuit, both argued February 28–March 1, 1966; and No. 584, *California v. Stewart*, on certiorari to the Supreme Court of California, argued February 28–March 2, 1966.]

**MR. CHIEF JUSTICE WARREN delivered the opinion of the Court.**

The cases before us raise questions which go to the roots of our concepts of American criminal jurisprudence: the restraints society must observe consistent with the Federal Constitution in prosecuting individuals for crime. More specifically, we deal with the admissibility of statements obtained from an individual who is subjected to custodial police interrogation and the necessity for procedures which assure that the individual is accorded his privilege under the Fifth Amendment to the Constitution not to be compelled to incriminate himself.

We dealt with certain phases of this problem recently in *Escobedo v. Illinois*, 378 U.S. 478 (1964). There, as in the four cases before us, law enforcement officials took the defendant into custody and interrogated him in a police station for the purpose of obtaining a confession. The police did not effectively advise him of his right to remain silent or of his right to consult with his attorney. Rather, they confronted him with an alleged accomplice who accused him of having perpetrated a murder. When the defendant denied the accusation and said "I didn't shoot Manuel, you did it," they handcuffed him and took him to an interrogation room. There, while handcuffed and standing, he was questioned for four hours until he confessed. During this interrogation, the police denied his request to speak to his attorney, and they prevented his retained attorney, who had come to the police station, from consulting with him. At his trial, the State, over his objection, introduced the confession against him. We held that the statements thus made were constitutionally inadmissible.

This case has been the subject of judicial interpretation and spirited legal debate since it was decided two years ago. Both state and federal courts, in assessing its implications, have arrived at varying conclusions. A wealth of scholarly material has been written tracing its ramifications and underpinnings. Police and prosecutor have speculated on its range and desirability. We granted certiorari in these cases, in order further to explore some facets of the problems, thus exposed, of applying the privilege against self-incrimination to in-custody interrogation, and to give concrete constitutional guidelines for law enforcement agencies and courts to follow.

We start here, as we did in *Escobedo*, with the premise that our holding is not an innovation in our jurisprudence, but is an application of principles long recognized and applied in other settings. We have undertaken a thorough re-examination of the Escobedo decision and the principles it announced, and we reaffirm it. That case was but an explication of basic rights that are enshrined in our Constitution—that "No person . . . shall be compelled in any criminal case to be a witness against himself," and that "the accused shall . . . have the Assistance of Counsel"—rights which were put in jeopardy in that case through official overbearing. These precious rights were fixed in our Constitution only after centuries of persecution and struggle. And in the words of Chief Justice Marshall, they were secured "for ages to come, and . . . designed to approach immortality as nearly as human institutions can approach it," *Cohens v. Virginia*, 6 Wheat. 264, 387 (1821). . .

Our holding will be spelled out with some specificity in the pages which follow but briefly stated it is this: the prosecution may not use statements, whether exculpatory or inculpatory, stemming from custodial interrogation of the defendant unless it demonstrates the use of procedural safeguards effective to secure the privilege against self-incrimination. By custodial interrogation, we mean questioning initiated by law enforcement officers after a person has been taken into custody or otherwise deprived of his freedom of action in any significant way. As for the procedural safeguards to be employed, unless other fully effective means are devised to inform accused persons of their right of silence and to assure a continuous opportunity to exercise it, the following measures are required. Prior to any questioning, the person must be warned that he has a right to remain silent, that any statement he does make may be used as evidence against him, and that he has a right to the presence of an attorney, either retained or appointed. The defendant may waive effectuation of these rights, provided the waiver is made voluntarily, knowingly and intelligently. If, however, he indicates in any manner and at any stage of the process that he wishes to consult with an attorney before speaking there can be no questioning. Likewise, if the individual is alone and indicates in any manner that he does not wish to be interrogated, the police may not question him. The mere fact that he may have answered some questions or volunteered some statements on his own does not deprive him of the right to refrain from answering any further inquiries until he has consulted with an attorney and thereafter consents to be questioned.

## I.

The constitutional issue we decide in each of these cases is the admissibility of statements obtained from a defendant questioned while in custody or otherwise deprived of his freedom of action in any significant way. In each, the defendant was questioned by police officers, detectives, or a prosecuting attorney in a room in which he was cut off from the outside world. In none of these cases was the defendant given a full and effective warning of his rights at the outset of the interrogation process. In all the cases, the questioning elicited oral admissions, and in three of them, signed statements as well which were admitted at their trials. They all thus share salient features— incommunicado interrogation of individuals in a police-dominated atmosphere, resulting in self-incriminating statements without full warnings of constitutional rights.

An understanding of the nature and setting of this in-custody interrogation is essential to our decisions today. The difficulty in depicting what transpires at such interrogations stems from the fact that in this country they have largely taken place incommunicado. From extensive factual studies undertaken in the early 1930's, including the famous Wickersham Report to Congress by a Presidential Commission, it is clear that police violence and the "third degree" flourished at that time. In a series of cases decided by this Court long after these studies, the police resorted to physical brutality—beating, hanging, whipping—and to sustained and protracted questioning incommunicado in order to extort confessions. The Commission on Civil Rights in 1961 found much evidence to indicate that "some policemen still resort to physical force to obtain confessions," 1961 Comm'n on Civil Rights

Rep., Justice, pt. 5, 17. The use of physical brutality and violence is not, unfortunately, relegated to the past or to any part of the country. Only recently in Kings County, New York, the police brutally beat, kicked and placed lighted cigarette butts on the back of a potential witness under interrogation for the purpose of securing a statement incriminating a third party. *People v. Portelli*, 15 N. Y. 2d 235 (1965).

The examples given above are undoubtedly the exception now, but they are sufficiently widespread to be the object of concern. Unless a proper limitation upon custodial interrogation is achieved—such as these decisions will advance—there can be no assurance that practices of this nature will be eradicated in the foreseeable future. . . .

Again we stress that the modern practice of in-custody interrogation is psychologically rather than physically oriented. As we have stated before, "Since *Chambers v. Florida*, 309 U.S. 227, this Court has recognized that coercion can be mental as well as physical, and that the blood of the accused is not the only hallmark of an unconstitutional inquisition." *Blackburn v. Alabama*, 361 U.S. 199, 206 (1960). Interrogation still takes place in privacy. Privacy results in secrecy and this in turn results in a gap in our knowledge as to what in fact goes on in the interrogation rooms. A valuable source of information about present police practices, however, may be found in various police manuals and texts which document procedures employed with success in the past, and which recommend various other effective tactics. . .

The officers are told by the manuals that the "principal psychological factor contributing to a successful interrogation is privacy—being alone with the person under interrogation." The efficacy of this tactic has been explained as follows:

> "If at all practicable, the interrogation should take place in the investigator's office or at least in a room of his own choice. The subject should be deprived of every psychological advantage. In his own home he may be confident, indignant, or recalcitrant. He is more keenly aware of his rights and more reluctant to tell of his indiscretions or criminal behavior within the walls of his home. Moreover his family and other friends are nearby, their presence lending moral support. In his own office, the investigator possesses all the advantages. The atmosphere suggests the invincibility of the forces of the law.". . .

The texts thus stress that the major qualities an interrogator should possess are patience and perseverance. One writer describes the efficacy of these characteristics in this manner:

> "In the preceding paragraphs emphasis has been placed on kindness and stratagems. The investigator will, however, encounter many situations where the sheer weight of his personality will be the deciding factor. Where emotional appeals and tricks are employed to no avail, he must rely on an oppressive atmosphere of dogged persistence. He must interrogate steadily and without relent, leaving the subject no prospect of surcease. He must dominate his subject and overwhelm him with his inexorable will to obtain the truth. He should interrogate for a spell of several hours pausing only for the subject's necessities in acknowledgment of the need to avoid a charge of duress that can be technically substantiated. In a serious case, the interrogation may continue for days, with the required intervals for food and sleep, but with no respite from the atmosphere of domination. It is possible in this way to induce the subject to talk without resorting to duress or coercion. The method should be used only when the guilt of the subject appears highly probable.". . .

The interrogators sometimes are instructed to induce a confession out of trickery. The technique here is quite effective in crimes which require identification or which run in series. In the identification situation, the interrogator may take a break in his questioning to place the subject among a group of men in a line-up. "The witness or complainant (previously coached, if necessary) studies the line-up and confidently points out the subject as the guilty party." Then the questioning resumes "as though there were now no doubt about the guilt of the subject." A variation on this technique is called the "reverse line-up": "The accused is placed in a line-up, but this time he is identified by several fictitious witnesses or victims who associated him with different offenses. It is expected that the subject will become desperate and confess to the offense under investigation in order to escape from the false accusations."

The manuals also contain instructions for police on how to handle the individual who refuses to discuss the matter entirely, or who asks for an attorney or relatives. The examiner is to concede him the right to remain silent. "This usually has a very undermining effect. First of all, he is disappointed in his expectation of an unfavorable reaction on the part of the interrogator.

Secondly, a concession of this right to remain silent impresses the subject with the apparent fairness of his interrogator.". . .

In the event that the subject wishes to speak to a relative or an attorney, the following advice is tendered:

> "[T]he interrogator should respond by suggesting that the subject first tell the truth to the interrogator himself rather than get anyone else involved in the matter. If the request is for an attorney, the interrogator may suggest that the subject save himself or his family the expense of any such professional service, particularly if he is innocent of the offense under investigation. The interrogator may also add, 'Joe, I'm only looking for the truth, and if you're telling the truth, that's it. You can handle this by yourself.' "

From these representative samples of interrogation techniques, the setting prescribed by the manuals and observed in practice becomes clear. In essence, it is this: To be alone with the subject is essential to prevent distraction and to deprive him of any outside support. . . In the cases before us today, given this background, we concern ourselves primarily with this interrogation atmosphere and the evils it can bring. In No. 759, *Miranda v. Arizona*, the police arrested the defendant and took him to a special interrogation room where they secured a confession. In No. 760, *Vignera v. New York*, the defendant made oral admissions to the police after interrogation in the afternoon, and then signed an inculpatory statement upon being questioned by an assistant district attorney later the same evening. In No. 761, *Westover v. United States*, the defendant was handed over to the Federal Bureau of Investigation by local authorities after they had detained and interrogated him for a lengthy period, both at night and the following morning. After some two hours of questioning, the federal officers had obtained signed statements from the defendant. Lastly, in No. 584, *California v. Stewart*, the local police held the defendant five days in the station and interrogated him on nine separate occasions before they secured his inculpatory statement.

In these cases, we might not find the defendants' statements to have been involuntary in traditional terms. Our concern for adequate safeguards to protect precious Fifth Amendment rights is, of course, not lessened in the slightest. . .

Our decision in *Malloy v. Hogan*, 378 U.S. 1 (1964), necessitates an examination of the scope of the privilege in state cases as well. In *Malloy*, we squarely held the privilege applicable to the States, and held that the substantive standards underlying the privilege applied with full force to state court proceedings. . . .The implications of this proposition were elaborated in our decision in *Escobedo v. Illinois*, 378 U.S. 478, decided one week after *Malloy* applied the privilege to the States.

Our holding there stressed the fact that the police had not advised the defendant of his constitutional privilege to remain silent at the outset of the interrogation, and we drew attention to that fact at several points in the decision, 378 U.S., at 483, 485, 491. This was no isolated factor, but an essential ingredient in our decision. The entire thrust of police interrogation there, as in all the cases today, was to put the defendant in such an emotional state as to impair his capacity for rational judgment. The abdication of the constitutional privilege—the choice on his part to speak to the police—was not made knowingly or competently because of the failure to apprise him of his rights; the compelling atmosphere of the in-custody interrogation, and not an independent decision on his part, caused the defendant to speak. . .

Today, then, there can be no doubt that the Fifth Amendment privilege is available outside of criminal court proceedings and serves to protect persons in all settings in which their freedom of action is curtailed in any significant way from being compelled to incriminate themselves. We have concluded that without proper safeguards the process of in-custody interrogation of persons suspected or accused of crime contains inherently compelling pressures which work to undermine the individual's will to resist and to compel him to speak where he would not otherwise do so freely. In order to combat these pressures and to permit a full opportunity to exercise the privilege against self-incrimination, the accused must be adequately and effectively apprised of his rights and the exercise of those rights must be fully honored.

. . .At the outset, if a person in custody is to be subjected to interrogation, he must first be informed in clear and unequivocal terms that he has the right to remain silent. . . .

The warning of the right to remain silent must be accompanied by the explanation that anything said can and will be used against the individual in court. This warning is needed in order to make him aware not only of the privilege, but also of the consequences of forgoing it. . .

Thus, the need for counsel to protect the Fifth Amendment privilege comprehends not merely a right to consult with counsel prior to questioning, but also to have counsel present during any questioning if the defendant so desires.

The presence of counsel at the interrogation may serve several significant subsidiary functions as well. If the accused decides to talk to his interrogators, the assistance of counsel can mitigate the dangers of untrustworthiness. With a lawyer present the likelihood that the police will practice coercion is reduced, and if coercion is nevertheless exercised the lawyer can testify to it in court. The presence of a lawyer can also help to guarantee that the accused gives a fully accurate statement to the police and that the statement is rightly reported by the prosecution at trial. See *Crooker v. California*, 357 U.S. 433, 443–448 (1958) (DOUGLAS, J., dissenting).

An individual need not make a pre-interrogation request for a lawyer. While such request affirmatively secures his right to have one, his failure to ask for a lawyer does not constitute a waiver. No effective waiver of the right to counsel during interrogation can be recognized unless specifically made after the warnings we here delineate have been given. The accused who does not know his rights and therefore does not make a request may be the person who most needs counsel. . .

In order fully to apprise a person interrogated of the extent of his rights under this system then, it is necessary to warn him not only that he has the right to consult with an attorney, but also that if he is indigent a lawyer will be appointed to represent him. Without this additional warning, the admonition of the right to consult with counsel would often be understood as meaning only that he can consult with a lawyer if he has one or has the funds to obtain one. The warning of a right to counsel would be hollow if not couched in terms that would convey to the indigent—the person most often subjected to interrogation—the knowledge that he too has a right to have counsel present. As with the warnings of the right to remain silent and of the general right to counsel, only by effective and express explanation to the indigent of this right can there be assurance that he was truly in a position to exercise it.

Once warnings have been given, the subsequent procedure is clear. If the individual indicates in any manner, at any time prior to or during questioning, that he wishes to remain silent, the interrogation must cease. At this point he has shown that he intends to exercise his Fifth Amendment privilege; any statement taken after the person invokes his privilege cannot be other than the product of compulsion, subtle or otherwise. Without the right to cut off questioning, the setting of in-custody interrogation operates on the individual to overcome free choice in producing a statement after the privilege has been once invoked. If the individual states that he wants an attorney, the interrogation must cease until an attorney is present. At that time, the individual must have an opportunity to confer with the attorney and to have him present during any subsequent questioning. If the individual cannot obtain an attorney and he indicates that he wants one before speaking to police, they must respect his decision to remain silent.

This does not mean, as some have suggested, that each police station must have a "station house lawyer" present at all times to advise prisoners. It does mean, however, that if police propose to interrogate a person they must make known to him that he is entitled to a lawyer and that if he cannot afford one, a lawyer will be provided for him prior to any interrogation. If authorities conclude that they will not provide counsel during a reasonable period of time in which investigation in the field is carried out, they may refrain from doing so without violating the person's Fifth Amendment privilege so long as they do not question him during that time.

If the interrogation continues without the presence of an attorney and a statement is taken, a heavy burden rests on the government to demonstrate that the defendant knowingly and intelligently waived his privilege against self-incrimination and his right to retained or appointed counsel. . . .

An express statement that the individual is willing to make a statement and does not want an attorney followed closely by a statement could constitute a waiver. But a valid waiver will not be presumed simply from the silence of the accused after warnings are given or simply from the fact that a confession was in fact eventually obtained. A statement we made in *Carnley v. Cochran*, 369 U.S. 506, 516 (1962), is applicable here:

> "Presuming waiver from a silent record is impermissible. The record must show, or there must be an allegation and evidence which show, that an accused was offered counsel but intelligently and understandingly rejected the offer. Anything less is not waiver.". . .

The principles announced today deal with the protection which must be given to the privilege against self-incrimination when the individual is first subjected to police interrogation while in custody at the station or otherwise deprived of his freedom of action in any significant way. It is at this point that our adversary system of criminal proceedings commences, distinguishing itself at the outset from the inquisitorial system recognized in some countries. Under the system of warnings we delineate today or under any other system which may be devised and found effective, the safeguards to be erected about the privilege must come into play at this point.

Our decision is not intended to hamper the traditional function of police officers in investigating crime. . . .In dealing with statements obtained through interrogation, we do not purport to find all confessions inadmissible. Confessions remain a proper element in law enforcement. Any statement given freely and voluntarily without any compelling influences is, of course, admissible in evidence. . . .There is no requirement that police stop a person who enters a police station and states that he wishes to confess to a crime, or a person who calls the police to offer a confession or any other statement he desires to make. Volunteered statements of any kind are not barred by the Fifth Amendment and their admissibility is not affected by our holding today. . . .

## V.

Because of the nature of the problem and because of its recurrent significance in numerous cases, we have to this point discussed the relationship of the Fifth Amendment privilege to police interrogation without specific concentration on the facts of the cases before us. We turn now to these facts to consider the application to these cases of the constitutional principles discussed above. In each instance, we have concluded that statements were obtained from the defendant under circumstances that did not meet constitutional standards for protection of the privilege.

No. 759. *Miranda v. Arizona.*

On March 13, 1963, petitioner, Ernesto Miranda, was arrested at his home and taken in custody to a Phoenix police station. He was there identified by the complaining witness. The police then took him to "Interrogation Room No. 2" of the detective bureau. There he was questioned by two police officers. The officers admitted at trial that Miranda was not advised that he had a right to have an attorney present. 66 Two hours later, the officers emerged from the interrogation room with a written confession signed by Miranda. At the top of the statement was a typed paragraph stating that the confession was made voluntarily, without threats or promises of immunity and "with full knowledge of my legal rights, understanding any statement I make may be used against me."

At his trial before a jury, the written confession was admitted into evidence over the objection of defense counsel, and the officers testified to the prior oral confession made by Miranda during the interrogation. Miranda was found guilty of kidnapping and rape. He was sentenced to 20 to 30 years' imprisonment on each count, the sentences to run concurrently. On appeal, the Supreme Court of Arizona held that Miranda's constitutional rights were not violated in obtaining the confession and affirmed the conviction. 98 Ariz. 18, 401 P.2d 721. In reaching its decision, the court emphasized heavily the fact that Miranda did not specifically request counsel.

We reverse. From the testimony of the officers and by the admission of respondent, it is clear that Miranda was not in any way apprised of his right to consult with an attorney and to have one present during the interrogation, nor was his right not to be compelled to incriminate himself effectively protected in any other manner. Without these warnings the statements were inadmissible. The mere fact that he signed a statement which contained a typed-in clause stating that he had "full knowledge" of his "legal rights" does not approach the knowing and intelligent waiver required to relinquish constitutional rights. . . .

No. 760. *Vignera v. New York.*

Petitioner, Michael Vignera, was picked up by New York police on October 14, 1960, in connection with the robbery three days earlier of a Brooklyn dress shop. They took him to the 17th Detective Squad headquarters in Manhattan. Sometime thereafter he was taken to the 6Sixth Detective Squad. There a detective questioned Vignera with respect to the robbery. Vignera orally admitted the robbery to the detective. . . . We reverse. The foregoing indicates that Vignera was not warned of any of his rights before the questioning by the detective and by the assistant district attorney. No other steps were taken to protect these rights. Thus he was not effectively apprised of his Fifth Amendment privilege or of his right to have counsel present and his statements are inadmissible.

No. 761. *Westover v. United States.*

At approximately 9:45 p. m. on March 20, 1963, petitioner, Carl Calvin Westover, was arrested by local police in Kansas City as a suspect in two Kansas City robberies. A report was also received from the FBI that he was wanted on a felony charge in California. The local authorities took him to a police station and placed him in a line-up on the local charges, and at about 11:45 p. m. he was booked. Kansas City police interrogated Westover on the night of his arrest. He denied any knowledge of criminal activities. The next day local officers interrogated him again throughout the morning. Shortly before noon they informed the FBI that they were through interrogating Westover and that the FBI could proceed to interrogate him. There is nothing in the record to indicate that Westover was ever given any warning as to his rights by local police. At noon, three special agents of the FBI continued the interrogation in a private interview room of the Kansas City Police Department, this time with respect to the robbery of a savings and loan association and a bank in Sacramento, California. After two or two and one-half hours, Westover signed separate confessions to each of these two robberies which had been prepared by one of the agents during the interrogation. At trial one of the agents testified, and a paragraph on each of the statements states, that the agents advised Westover that he did not have to make a statement, that any statement he made could be used against him, and that he had the right to see an attorney.

Westover was tried by a jury in federal court and convicted of the California robberies. His statements were introduced at trial. He was sentenced to 15 years' imprisonment on each count, the sentences to run consecutively. On appeal, the conviction was affirmed by the Court of Appeals for the Ninth Circuit. 342 F.2d 684.

We reverse. On the facts of this case we cannot find that Westover knowingly and intelligently waived his right to remain silent and his right to consult with counsel prior to the time he made the statement. . . . In these circumstances an intelligent waiver of constitutional rights cannot be assumed. . .

No. 584. *California v. Stewart.*

In the course of investigating a series of purse-snatch robberies in which one of the victims had died of injuries inflicted by her assailant, respondent, Roy Allen Stewart, was pointed out to Los Angeles police as the endorser of dividend checks taken in one of the robberies. At about 7:15 p. m., January 31, 1963, police officers went to Stewart's house and arrested him. One of the officers asked Stewart if they could search the house, to which he replied, "Go ahead." The search turned up various items taken from the five robbery victims. . . . Stewart was taken to the University Station of the Los Angeles Police Department where he was placed in a cell. During the next five days, police interrogated Stewart on nine different occasions. Except during the first interrogation session, when he was confronted with an accusing witness, Stewart was isolated with his interrogators. During the ninth interrogation session, Stewart admitted that he had robbed the deceased and stated that he had not meant to hurt her. . . .Nothing in the record specifically indicates whether Stewart was or was not advised of his right to remain silent or his right to counsel. In a number of instances, however, the interrogating officers were asked to recount everything that was said during the interrogations. None indicated that Stewart was ever advised of his rights.

Stewart was charged with kidnapping to commit robbery, rape, and murder. . . . The jury found Stewart guilty of robbery and first degree murder and fixed the penalty as death. On appeal, the Supreme Court of California reversed. It held that under this Court's decision in Escobedo, Stewart should have been advised of his right to remain silent and of his right to counsel and that it would not presume in the face of a silent record that the police advised Stewart of his rights.

We affirm. . .

Therefore, in accordance with the foregoing, the judgments of the Supreme Court of Arizona in No. 759, of the New York Court of Appeals in No. 760, and of the Court of Appeals for the Ninth Circuit in No. 761 are reversed. The judgment of the Supreme Court of California in No. 584 is affirmed.

**It is so ordered. . . .**

**After preparing the case brief, consider the answers to the following questions:**

1.    What is the constitutional foundation for the rights at issue in the cases involved in *Miranda*?

2.    Why did the Court believe that custody and interrogation are circumstances of unique significance, requiring constitutional protection?

3.    Do you agree with the Court's holding that a bright-line rule is necessary, the warnings must all be given in every case? Why?

4.    Do you believe the Miranda warning requirement is too burdensome for police officers? Explain.

5.    Do you believe that the Miranda warning requirement is still meaningful—do suspects need to be told of these rights or are they now understood by the majority of citizens?

## OROZCO V. TEXAS

Supreme Court of the United States
Argued Feb. 26, 1969
Decided March 25, 1969
394 U.S. 324

### Opinion

**MR. JUSTICE BLACK delivered the opinion of the Court.**

The petitioner, Reyes Arias Orozco, was convicted in the Criminal District Court of Dallas County, Texas, of murder without malice and was sentenced to serve in the state prison not less than two nor more than 10 years. The Court of Criminal Appeals of Texas affirmed the conviction, rejecting petitioner's contention that a material part of the evidence against him was obtained in violation of the provision of the Fifth Amendment to the United States Constitution, made applicable to the States by the Fourteenth Amendment, that: 'No person * * * shall be compelled in any criminal case to be a witness against himself.'

The evidence introduced at trial showed that petitioner and the deceased had quarreled outside the El Farleto Cafe in Dallas shortly before midnight on the date of the shooting. The deceased had apparently spoken to petitioner's female companion inside the restaurant. In the heat of the quarrel outside, the deceased is said to have beaten petitioner about the face and called him 'Mexican Grease.' A shot was fired killing the deceased. Petitioner left the scene and returned to his boardinghouse to sleep. At about 4 a.m. four police officers arrived at petitioner's boardinghouse, were admitted by an unidentified woman, and were told that petitioner was asleep in the bedroom. All four officers entered the bedroom and began to question petitioner. From the moment he gave his name, according to the testimony of one of the officers, petitioner was not free to go where he pleased but was 'under arrest.' The officers asked him if he had been to the El Farleto restaurant that night and when he answered 'yes' he was asked if he owned a pistol. Petitioner admitted owning one. After being asked a second time where the pistol was located, he admitted that it was in the washing machine in a backroom of the boardinghouse. Ballistics tests indicated that the gun found in the washing machine was the gun that fired the fatal shot.

At petitioner's trial, held after the effective date of this Court's decision in Miranda v. Arizona, 384 U.S. 436 (1966), the trial court allowed one of the officers, over the objection of petitioner's lawyer, to relate the statements made by petitioner concerning the gun and petitioner's presence at the scene of the shooting. The trial testimony clearly shows that the officers questioned petitioner about incriminating facts without first informing him of his right to remain silent, his right to have the advice of a lawyer before making any statement, and his right to have a lawyer appointed to assist him if he could not afford to hire one. The Texas Court of Criminal Appeals held, with one judge dissenting, that the admission of testimony concerning the statements petitioner had made without the above warnings was not precluded by Miranda. We disagree and hold that the use of these admissions obtained in the absence of the required warnings was a flat violation of the Self-Incrimination Clause of the Fifth Amendment as construed in Miranda.

The State has argued here that since petitioner was interrogated on his own bed, in familiar surroundings, our Miranda holding should not apply. It is true that the Court did say in Miranda that 'compulsion to speak in the isolated setting of the police station may well be greater than in courts or other official investigations, where there are often impartial observers to guard against intimidation or trickery.' 384 U.S., at 461, 86 S.Ct., at 1621. But the opinion iterated and reiterated the absolute necessity for officers interrogating people 'in custody' to give the described warnings. See Mathis v. United States, 391 U.S. 1 (1968). According to the officer's testimony, petitioner was under arrest and not free to leave when he was questioned in his bedroom in the early hours of the morning. The Miranda opinion declared that the warnings were required when the person being interrogated was 'in custody at the station or otherwise deprived of his freedom of action in any significant way.' 384 U.S., at 477, 86 S.Ct., at 1629. (Emphasis supplied.) The decision of this Court in Miranda was reached after careful consideration and lengthy opinions were announced by both the majority and dissenting Justices. There is no need to canvass those arguments again. We do not, as the dissent implies, expand or extend to the slightest extent our Miranda decision. We do adhere to our well-considered holding in that case and therefore reverse the conviction below.

Reversed.

**MR. JUSTICE FORTAS took no part in the consideration or decision of this case.**

**MR. JUSTICE HARLAN, concurring.**

The passage of time has not made the Miranda case any more palatable to me than it was when the case was decided. See my dissenting opinion, and that of Mr. Justice White, in Miranda v. Arizona, 384 U.S. 436, 504, 526 (1966).

Yet, despite my strong inclination to join in the dissent of my Brother WHITE, I can find no acceptable avenue of escape from Miranda in judging this case, especially in light of Mathis v. United States, 391 U.S. 1 (1968), which has already extended the Miranda rules beyond the police station, over the protest of Justices Stewart, White, and myself. . .Therefore, and purely out of respect for stare decisis, I reluctantly feel compelled to acquiesce in today's decision of the Court, at the same time observing that the constitutional condemnation of this perfectly understandable, sensible, proper, and indeed commendable piece of police work highlights the unsoundness of Miranda.

**MR. JUSTICE WHITE, with whom MR. JUSTICE STEWART joins, dissenting.**

This decision carries the rule of Miranda v. Arizona, 384 U.S. 436 (1966), to a new and unwarranted extreme. I continue to believe that the original rule amounted to a 'constitutional straitjacket' on law enforcement which was justified neither by the words or history of the Constitution, nor by any reasonable view of the likely benefits of the rule as against its disadvantages. 384 U.S., at 526, 86 S.Ct. 1602. Even accepting Miranda, the Court extends the rule here and draws the straitjacket even tighter.

The opinion of the Court in Miranda was devoted in large part to an elaborate discussion of the subtle forms of psychological pressure which could be brought to bear when an accused person is interrogated at length in unfamiliar surroundings. The 'salient features' of the cases decided in Miranda were 'incommunicado interrogation of individuals in a police-dominated atmosphere.' 384 U.S., at 445, 86 S.Ct. at 1612. The danger was that in such circumstances the confidence of the prisoner could be eroded by techniques such as successive interrogations by police acting out friendly or unfriendly roles. These techniques are best developed in 'isolation and unfamiliar surroundings,' 384 U.S., at 450, 86 S.Ct. at 1615. And they take time: 'the major qualities an interrogator should possess are patience and perserverance.' *Ibid.* The techniques of an extended period of isolation, repeated interrogation, cajolery, and trickery often enough produced admissions which were actually coerced in the traditional sense so that new safeguards were deemed essential.

It is difficult to believe that the requirements there laid down were essential to prevent compulsion in every conceivable case of station house interrogation. Where the defendant himself as a lawyer, policeman, professional criminal, or otherwise has become aware of what his right to silence is, it is sheer fancy to assert that his answer to every question asked him is compelled unless he is advised of those rights with which he is already intimately familiar. If there is any warrant to Miranda at all, it rests on the likelihood that in a sufficient number of cases exposure to station house practices will result in compelled confessions and that additional safeguards should be imposed in all cases to prevent possible erosion of Fifth Amendment values. Hence, the detailed ritual which Miranda fashioned.

The Court now extends the same rules to all instances of in-custody questioning outside the station house. Once arrest occurs, the application of Miranda is automatic. The rule is simple but it ignores the purpose of Miranda to guard against what was thought to be the corrosive influence of practices which station house interrogation makes feasible. The Court wholly ignores the question whether similar hazards exist or even are possible when police arrest and interrogate on the spot, whether it be on the street corner or in the home, as in this case. No predicate is laid for believing that practices outside the station house are normally prolonged, carried out in isolation, or often productive of the physical or psychological coercion made so much of in Miranda. It is difficult to imagine the police duplicating in a person's home or on the street those conditions and practices which the Court found prevalent in the station house and which were thought so threatening to the right to silence. Without such a demonstration. Miranda hardly reaches this case or any cases similar to it.

Here, there was no prolonged interrogation, no unfamiliar surroundings, no opportunity for the police to invoke those procedures which moved the majority in Miranda. In fact, the conversation was by all accounts a very brief one. According to uncontradicted testimony, petitioner was awake when the officers entered his room, and they asked him four questions: his name, whether he had been at the El Farleto, whether he owned a pistol, and where it was. He gave his name, said he had been at the El Farleto, and admitted he owned a pistol without hesitation. He was slow in telling where the pistol was, and the question was repeated. He then took the police to the nearby washing machine where the gun was hidden.

It is unquestioned that this sequence of events in their totality would not constitute coercion in the traditional sense or lead any court to view the admissions as involuntary within the meaning of the rules by which we even now adjudicate claims of coercion relating to pre-Miranda trials. And, realistically, had Orozco refused to answer the questions asked of him, it seems most unlikely that prolonged interrogation would have followed in petitioner's own quarters; nothing similar to the station house model invoked by the court would have occurred here. The police had petitioner's name and description, had ample evidence that he had been at the night club and suspected that he had a gun. Surely had he refused to give his name or answer any other questions, they would have arrested him anyway, searched the house and found the gun, which would have been clearly admissible under all relevant authorities. But the Court insists that this case be reversed for failure to give Miranda warnings.

I cannot accept the dilution of the custody requirements of Miranda to this level, where the hazards to the right to silence are so equivocal and unsupported by experience in a recurring number of cases. Orozco was apprehended in the most familiar quarters, the questioning was brief, and no admissions were made which were not backed up by other evidence. This case does not involve the confession of an innocent man, or even of a guilty man from whom a confession has been wrung by physical abuse or the modern psychological methods discussed in Miranda. These are simply the terse remarks of a man who has been caught, almost in the act. Even if there were reason to encourage suspects to consult lawyers to tell them to be silent before quizzing at the station house, there is no reason why police in the field should have to preface every casual question of a suspect with the full panoply of Miranda warnings. The same danger of coercion is simply not present in such circumstances, and the answers to the questions may as often clear a suspect as help convict him. If the Miranda warnings have their intended effect, and the police are able to get no answers from suspects, innocent or guilty, without arresting them, then a great many more innocent men will be making unnecessary trips to the station house. Ultimately it may be necessary to arrest a man, bring him to the police station, and provide a lawyer, just to discover his name. Even if the man is innocent the process will be an unpleasant one.

Since the Court's extension of Miranda's rule takes it into territory where even what rationale there original was disappears, I dissent.

**Memorandum of MR. JUSTICE STEWART.**

Although there is much to be said for Mr. Justice HARLAN'S position, I join my Brother WHITE in dissent. It seems to me that those of us who dissented in Miranda v. Arizona, 384 U.S. 436, remain free not only to express our continuing disagreement with that decision, but also to oppose any broadening of its impact.

**After preparing the case brief, consider the answers to the following questions:**

1.   Does Orozco's interrogation share common characteristics with the cases discussed in *Miranda v. Arizona*? How is it different?

2.   What impact does the holding in *Orozco* have on future police interrogations taking place outside of the police station?

3.   Is the majority correct when it states that the decision in *Orozco* does not extend the reach of the Miranda requirement? Why?

# NEW YORK V. QUARLES

Supreme Court of the United States
Argued Jan. 18, 1984
Decided June 12, 1984
467 U.S. 649

**JUSTICE REHNQUIST delivered the opinion of the Court.**

Respondent Benjamin Quarles was charged in the New York trial court with criminal possession of a weapon. The trial court suppressed the gun in question, and a statement made by respondent, because the statement was obtained by police before they read respondent his "Miranda rights." That ruling was affirmed on appeal through the New York Court of Appeals. We granted certiorari and we now reverse. We conclude that under the circumstances involved in this case, overriding considerations of public safety justify the officer's failure to provide Miranda warnings before he asked questions devoted to locating the abandoned weapon.

On September 11, 1980, at approximately 12:30 a. m., Officer Frank Kraft and Officer Sal Scarring were on road patrol in Queens, N. Y., when a young woman approached their car. She told them that she had just been raped by a black male, approximately six feet tall, who was wearing a black jacket with the name "Big Ben" printed in yellow letters on the back. She told the officers that the man had just entered an A & P supermarket located nearby and that the man was carrying a gun.

The officers drove the woman to the supermarket, and Officer Kraft entered the store while Officer Scarring radioed for assistance. Officer Kraft quickly spotted respondent, who matched the description given by the woman, approaching a checkout counter. Apparently upon seeing the officer, respondent turned and ran toward the rear of the store, and Officer Kraft pursued him with a drawn gun. When respondent turned the corner at the end of an aisle, Officer Kraft lost sight of him for several seconds, and upon regaining sight of respondent, ordered him to stop and put his hands over his head.

Although more than three other officers had arrived on the scene by that time, Officer Kraft was the first to reach respondent. He frisked him and discovered that he was wearing a shoulder holster which was then empty. After handcuffing him, Officer Kraft asked him where the gun was. Respondent nodded in the direction of some empty cartons and responded, "the gun is over there." Officer Kraft thereafter retrieved a loaded .38-caliber revolver from one of the cartons, formally placed respondent under arrest, and read him his Miranda rights from a printed card. Respondent indicated that he would be willing to answer questions without an attorney present. Officer Kraft then asked respondent if he owned the gun and where he had purchased it. Respondent answered that he did own it and that he had purchased it in Miami, Fla.

In the subsequent prosecution of respondent for criminal possession of a weapon, the judge excluded the statement, "the gun is over there," and the gun because the officer had not given respondent the warnings required by our decision in *Miranda v. Arizona*, 384 U.S. 436 (1966), before asking him where the gun was located. The judge excluded the other statements about respondent's ownership of the gun and the place of purchase, as evidence tainted by the prior Miranda violation. The Appellate Division of the Supreme Court of New York affirmed without opinion.

The Court of Appeals granted leave to appeal and affirmed by a 4–3 vote. It concluded that respondent was in "custody" within the meaning of Miranda during all questioning and rejected the State's argument that the exigencies of the situation justified Officer Kraft's failure to read respondent his Miranda rights until after he had located the gun. The court declined to recognize an exigency exception to the usual requirements of Miranda because it found no indication from Officer Kraft's testimony at the suppression hearing that his subjective motivation in asking the question was to protect his own safety or the safety of the public. For the reasons which follow, we believe that this case presents a situation where concern for public safety must be paramount to adherence to the literal language of the prophylactic rules enunciated in Miranda.

The Fifth Amendment guarantees that "[n]o person . . . shall be compelled in any criminal case to be a witness against himself." In Miranda this Court for the first time extended the Fifth Amendment privilege against compulsory self-incrimination to individuals subjected to custodial interrogation by the police. The Fifth Amendment itself does not prohibit all incriminating admissions; "[a]bsent some officially coerced self-accusation, the Fifth Amendment privilege is not violated by even the most damning admissions." *United States v. Washington*, 431 U.S. 181, 187 (1977) (emphasis added). The Miranda Court, however, presumed that interrogation in certain custodial circumstances is inherently coercive and held that statements made under those circumstances are inadmissible unless the suspect is specifically informed of his Miranda rights and freely decides to forgo those rights. The prophylactic Miranda warnings therefore are "not themselves rights protected by the Constitution but [are] instead measures to insure that the right against compulsory self-incrimination [is] protected." *Michigan v. Tucker*, 417 U.S. 433, 444 (1974); see *Edwards v. Arizona*, 451 U.S. 477, 492 (1981) (POWELL, J., concurring). Requiring Miranda warnings before custodial interrogation provides "practical reinforcement" for the Fifth Amendment right. *Michigan v. Tucker*, supra, at 444.

In this case we have before us no claim that respondent's statements were actually compelled by police conduct which overcame his will to resist. Thus the only issue before us is whether Officer Kraft was justified in failing to make available to respondent the procedural safeguards associated with the privilege against compulsory self-incrimination since Miranda.

The New York Court of Appeals was undoubtedly correct in deciding that the facts of this case come within the ambit of the Miranda decision as we have subsequently interpreted it. We agree that respondent was in police custody because we have noted that "the ultimate inquiry is simply whether there is a 'formal arrest or restraint on freedom of movement' of the degree associated with a formal arrest," Here Quarles was surrounded by at least four police officers and was handcuffed when the questioning at issue took place. As the New York Court of Appeals observed, there was nothing to suggest that any of the officers were any longer concerned for their own physical safety. The New York Court of Appeals' majority declined to express an opinion as to whether there might be an exception to the Miranda rule if the police had been acting to protect the public, because the lower courts in New York had made no factual determination that the police had acted with that motive. *Ibid.*

We hold that on these facts there is a "public safety" exception to the requirement that Miranda warnings be given before a suspect's answers may be admitted into evidence, and that the availability of that exception does not depend upon the motivation of the individual officers involved. In a kaleidoscopic situation such as the one confronting these officers, where spontaneity rather than adherence to a police manual is necessarily the order of the day, the application of the exception which we recognize today should not be made to depend on post hoc findings at a suppression hearing concerning the subjective motivation of the arresting officer. Undoubtedly most police officers, if placed in Officer Kraft's position, would act out of a host of different, instinctive, and largely unverifiable motives—their own safety, the safety of others, and perhaps as well the desire to obtain incriminating evidence from the suspect.

Whatever the motivation of individual officers in such a situation, we do not believe that the doctrinal underpinnings of Miranda require that it be applied in all its rigor to a situation in which police officers ask questions reasonably prompted by a concern for the public safety. The Miranda decision was based in large part on this Court's view that the warnings which it required police to give to suspects in custody would reduce the likelihood that the suspects would fall victim to constitutionally impermissible practices of police interrogation in the presumptively coercive environment of the station house. The dissenters warned that the requirement of Miranda warnings would have the effect of decreasing the number of suspects who respond to police questioning. Id., at 504, 516–517 (Harlan, J., joined by Stewart and White, JJ., dissenting). The Miranda majority, however, apparently felt that whatever the cost to society in terms of fewer convictions of guilty suspects, that cost would simply have to be borne in the interest of enlarged protection for the Fifth Amendment privilege.

The police in this case, in the very act of apprehending a suspect, were confronted with the immediate necessity of ascertaining the whereabouts of a gun which they had every reason to believe the suspect had just removed from his empty holster and discarded in the supermarket. So long as the gun was concealed somewhere in the supermarket, with its actual whereabouts unknown, it obviously posed more than one danger to the public safety: an accomplice might make use of it, a customer or employee might later come upon it.

In such a situation, if the police are required to recite the familiar Miranda warnings before asking the whereabouts of the gun, suspects in Quarles' position might well be deterred from responding. Procedural safeguards which deter a suspect from responding were deemed acceptable in *Miranda* in order to protect the Fifth Amendment privilege; when the primary social cost of those added protections is the possibility of fewer convictions, the Miranda majority was willing to bear that cost. Here, had Miranda warnings deterred Quarles from responding to Officer Kraft's question about the whereabouts of the gun, the cost would have been something more than merely the failure to obtain evidence useful in convicting Quarles. Officer Kraft needed an answer to his question not simply to make his case against Quarles but to insure that further danger to the public did not result from the concealment of the gun in a public area.

We conclude that the need for answers to questions in a situation posing a threat to the public safety outweighs the need for the prophylactic rule protecting the Fifth Amendment's privilege against self-incrimination. We decline to place officers such as Officer Kraft in the untenable position of having to consider, often in a matter of seconds, whether it best serves society for them to ask the necessary questions without the Miranda warnings and render whatever probative evidence they uncover inadmissible, or for them to give the warnings in order to preserve the admissibility of evidence they might uncover but possibly damage or destroy their ability to obtain that evidence and neutralize the volatile situation confronting them.

In recognizing a narrow exception to the Miranda rule in this case, we acknowledge that to some degree we lessen the desirable clarity of that rule. At least in part in order to preserve its clarity, we have over the years refused to sanction attempts to expand our Miranda holding. See, e.g., *Minnesota v. Murphy*, 465 U.S. 420 (1984) (refusal to extend Miranda requirements to interviews with probation officers); *Fare v. Michael C.*, 442 U.S. 707 (1979) (refusal to equate request to see a probation officer with request to see a lawyer for Miranda purposes); *Beckwith v. United States*, 425 U.S. 341 (1976) (refusal to extend Miranda requirements to questioning in noncustodial circumstances). As we have in other contexts, we recognize here the importance of a workable rule "to guide police officers, who have only limited time and expertise to reflect on and balance the social and individual interests involved in the specific circumstances they confront." *Dunaway v. New York*, 442 U.S. 200, 213–214 (1979). But as we have pointed out, we believe that the exception which we recognize today lessens the necessity of that on-the-scene balancing process. The exception will not be difficult for police officers to apply because in each case it will be circumscribed by the exigency which justifies it. We think police officers can and will distinguish almost instinctively between questions necessary to secure their own safety or the safety of the public and questions designed solely to elicit testimonial evidence from a suspect.

The facts of this case clearly demonstrate that distinction and an officer's ability to recognize it. Officer Kraft asked only the question necessary to locate the missing gun before advising respondent of his rights. It was only after securing the loaded revolver and giving the warnings that he continued with investigatory questions about the ownership and place of purchase of the gun. The exception which we recognize today, far from complicating the thought processes and the on-the-scene judgments of police officers, will simply free them to follow their legitimate instincts when confronting situations presenting a danger to the public safety.

We hold that the Court of Appeals in this case erred in excluding the statement, "the gun is over there," and the gun because of the officer's failure to read respondent his Miranda rights before attempting to locate the weapon. Accordingly we hold that it also erred in excluding the subsequent statements as illegal fruits of a Miranda violation. We therefore reverse and remand for further proceedings not inconsistent with this opinion.

**It is so ordered. . .**

**JUSTICE O'CONNOR, concurring in the judgment in part and dissenting in part.**

In *Miranda v. Arizona*, 384 U.S. 436 (1966), the Court held unconstitutional, because inherently compelled, the admission of statements derived from in-custody questioning not preceded by an explanation of the privilege against self-incrimination and the consequences of forgoing it. Today, the Court concludes that overriding considerations of public safety justify the admission of evidence—oral statements and a gun—secured without the benefit of such warnings. Ante, at 657–658. In so holding, the Court acknowledges that it is departing from prior precedent, see ante, at 653, and that it is "lessen[ing] the desirable clarity of [the Miranda] rule," ante, at 658. Were the Court writing from a clean slate, I could agree with its holding. But Miranda is now the law and, in my view, the Court has not provided sufficient justification for departing from it or for blurring its now clear strictures. Accordingly, I would require suppression of the initial statement taken from respondent in this case. On the other hand, nothing in Miranda or the privilege itself requires exclusion of nontestimonial evidence derived from informal custodial interrogation, and I therefore agree with the Court that admission of the gun in evidence is proper. . .

**JUSTICE MARSHALL, with whom JUSTICE BRENNAN and JUSTICE STEVENS join, dissenting.**

The police in this case arrested a man suspected of possessing a firearm in violation of New York law. Once the suspect was in custody and found to be unarmed, the arresting officer initiated an interrogation. Without being advised of his right not to respond, the suspect incriminated himself by locating the gun. The majority concludes that the State may rely on this incriminating statement to convict the suspect of possessing a weapon. I disagree. The arresting officers had no legitimate reason to interrogate the suspect without advising him of his rights to remain silent and to obtain assistance of counsel. By finding on these facts justification for unconsented interrogation, the majority abandons the clear guidelines enunciated in *Miranda v. Arizona*, 384 U.S. 436 (1966), and condemns the American judiciary to a new era of post hoc inquiry into the propriety of custodial interrogations. More significantly and in direct conflict with this Court's longstanding interpretation of the Fifth Amendment, the majority has endorsed the introduction of coerced self-incriminating statements in criminal prosecutions. I dissent. . . .

**After preparing the case brief, consider the answers to the following questions:**

1.   What facts required asking the suspect where his weapon was before warning him of his rights?

2.   How important do you believe the location of this police/suspect encounter was? If this had been outside on the street would it have been different? Why?

3.   How long would it take for police to inform the suspect of his rights under *Miranda*?

4.   Do you agree with the Justice O'Connor that the Court should have excluded his statement, but admitted the gun into evidence? Why?

## Chapter 9 Key Terms for Review

- **Self-incrimination**: when a suspect provides statements or evidence that help establish his guilt.

- **Confession**: an admission of guilt by a suspect or defendant.

- **Miranda warning**: judicial rule requiring police officers to warn or inform suspects of their Fifth and Sixth Amendment rights. *Miranda v. Arizona (1966)*.

- **Bright line rule**: a per se legal rule that must be followed regardless of the circumstances. In relationship to Miranda, the warning must be given anytime a suspect is in police custody and officer's conduct interrogation.

- **Custodial interrogation**: any questioning of a suspect in police custody, including conversations or statements that are not direct questions but are intended to illicit an incriminating response from the suspect. *Rhode Island v. Innis (1980)*.

- **Direct evidence**: proves a fact without requiring jurors to make any inference or presumptions.

- **Derivative evidence**: is derived from or discovered as a result of other evidence and is inadmissible when the initial evidence was unlawfully obtained; it is "fruit of the poisonous tree."

- **Voluntariness of confessions**: if a suspect waives his rights and confesses voluntarily his statements are admissible against him at trial.

- **Public safety exception to Miranda**: where there is a threat to public safety officers may dispense with the Miranda warning and ask the suspect questions; also called the exigency or emergency exception. *New York v. Quarles (1984)*.

- **Inevitable discovery exception**: if the discovery of unlawfully obtained evidence would have occurred based on other facts or circumstances, the evidence is admissible against the defendant. *Nix v. Williams (1984)*.

# Criminal Trials

The majority of Americans have seen a criminal trial on television. In most cases, they have watched fictional television shows and movies depicting exciting criminal trials with plot twists and surprise endings. The reality is that these fictional trials typically could not be further from the truth. Trials often require weeks to conduct, with jurors listening to lengthy testimony from numerous witnesses. Jurors may have difficulty staying focused or even awake as they listen to hours of testimony. When expert witnesses testify jurors may be confused about the complex evidence they present. It is critically important to separate facts from fiction in order to understand and appreciate the experience of defendants and the other courtroom actors in criminal trials.

## A. THE RIGHT TO A TRIAL BY JURY

Article II, Section 2 of the U.S. Constitution guarantees the right to a **jury trial**. The right is also guaranteed by the Sixth Amendment: "In all criminal prosecutions, the accused shall enjoy the right to. . .trial, by an impartial jury." This right also applies to the states. In *Duncan v. Louisiana (1968)* the U.S. Supreme Court incorporated the right to a jury trial found in the Sixth Amendment, applying it to state criminal proceedings.[1]

A defendant can choose to waive the right to jury trial as long as the waiver is expressly and intelligently made. The government can require that the prosecution and the court approve the waiver.[2] In the event of a waiver the trial will be held before a judge alone serving as the fact-finder and is referred to as a **bench trial**. Members of the public have a right to attend criminal trials, and the media has the right to do so as representatives of the public.[3] Holding criminal trials open to the public is an important means of ensuring accountability on the

---

[1]   391 U.S. 145 (1968).

[2]   *Singer v. United States*, 380 U.S. 24 (1965).

[3]   *Richmond Newspapers, Inc. v. Virginia*, 448 U.S. 555 (1980).

part of the courts and instilling confidence in the criminal justice system in the public. A judge can order the **closure** of a case in unique situations. In order to do so, the judge must make specific findings that the closure is necessary and the extent of the closure is narrowly tailored and the *least restrictive alternative* under the circumstances.[4] There must be no other way to address the problem that closure of the case is intended to resolve.

## B. JURY SELECTION

A jury trial employs a group of unbiased members of the community to serve as fact-finders in a case. The purpose of a jury trial is to provide a check against arbitrary or vindictive law enforcement. Juries improve the fact-finding process helping to ensure a fair trial. Lastly, jury trials are important because they provide public participation in the criminal justice system. This is essential in a democratic society. The right to a jury trial attaches only to serious, not petty crimes. The Supreme Court held that an offense is serious when the accused faces imprisonment of more than six months as punishment for the crime charged.[5]

Potential jurors from the community where a court is located are sent a summons for jury duty periodically. This **summons** is a legal demand to appear at the court for jury service. Jurors are randomly selected from a **venire**, or pool of potential jurors. This pool is often drawn from voter registration and DMV records. The judge and attorneys in the case select individual jurors through a process called **voir dire**. In most jurisdictions, jurors begin by completing a questionnaire to provide basic background information. Later, they are called into the jury box individually and the prosecutor, defense attorney and judge in the case question them.

In federal cases 12-member juries are used and their decisions must be unanimous. The Supreme Court has declined to impose this requirement on the states, so the number of jurors for a criminal case varies between 6 and 12. In *Ballew v. Georgia (1978)* the Supreme Court held that juries of fewer than 6 members are unlawful because it could impair the accuracy of their fact-finding function.[6] For serious felony trials 12 are typically selected, along with two alternate jurors. In federal trials the attorneys may select as many as 6 alternate jurors. The alternates sit alongside the jury so that in the event a juror is unable to complete their service, an alternate can step in and no delay in the trial occurs as a result. In 2020 the Supreme Court held that jury verdicts in serious criminal cases

---

[4]   *Globe Newspaper v. Superior Court*, 457 U.S. 596 (1982).

[5]   *Baldwin v. New York*, 399 U.S. 66 (1970).

[6]   *Ballew v. Georgia*, 435 U.S. 223 (1978).

must be unanimous.[7] In that case, the defendant was convicted of murder and sentenced to life without the possibility of parole by a jury voting 10–2 in favor of guilt. The Court reversed his conviction on the basis that the Sixth Amendment right to a jury trial as incorporated by the Fourteenth Amendment requires a unanimous verdict.

During voir dire potential jurors are questioned about their background and knowledge of the case. This process ensures that jurors do not have preconceived biases about the guilt or innocence of the defendant. It also ensures against conflicts of interest resulting from personal relationships or connections to the defendant or witnesses in the case. In states where 12 member juries are used, the Supreme Court has not required unanimous verdicts;[8] but where 6 member juries are used unanimity is required.[9]

During the process of selecting jurors the attorneys may request that the judge **dismiss a juror for cause**. A challenge for cause asserts that the juror has a bias, prejudice or prior knowledge about the case, which should disqualify them from service. Attorneys may also use a **peremptory challenge** to remove them from the jury without offering a reason. In federal trials the attorneys may use as many as 20 peremptory challenges in a capital case or as few as 3 in a misdemeanor case. The number of challenges allowed to each attorney in a state case varies.

A peremptory challenge can be used to dismiss a juror without cause for any rational or irrational reason. Attorneys must not exclude jurors based on gender or race. A defendant is entitled to have the jury selected from a fair cross-section of the community.[10] In the landmark case of *Batson v. Kentucky (1989)* the Supreme Court held that the purposeful exclusion of black jurors was a violation of the Equal Protection Clause.[11] An equal protection-based attack on a peremptory challenge requires three steps:

1.  The defendant must show facts or circumstances that raise an inference that the exclusion of potential jurors was based on race or gender; *and if successful*

2.  the prosecutor must then come forward with a race-neutral explanation for the strike (it does not have to be reasonable, just race-neutral); *finally*

---

[7]  *Ramos v. Louisiana*, 140 S.Ct. 1390 (2020).

[8]  *Apodaca v. Oregon*, 406 U.S. 404 (1972); *Johnson v. Louisiana*, 406 U.S. 356 (1972).

[9]  *Burch v. Louisiana*, 441 U.S. 130 (1979).

[10]  *Carter v. Jury Commissioner*, 396 U.S. 320 (1970).

[11]  476 U.S. 79 (1989).

3.     the judge must determine whether the prosecutor's explanation was the genuine reason for the strike, or was merely a pretext for discrimination.[12]

# C.  PRE-TRIAL PUBLICITY

In some cases there is significant news coverage of the events surrounding a crime or the arrest of a suspect. This may turn on the identity of the accused. Where a celebrity or high-profile member of the local community is arrested, the news coverage can be significant. Examples of celebrity arrests include OJ Simpson for allegedly murdering his ex-wife and her boyfriend and Bill Cosby for numerous sexual assaults. These cases drew attention because of the fame and notoriety of the accused. The media might also cover a case extensively because of the nature of the crimes. In the Scott Peterson case there was extensive media coverage because of the nature of the crime. The horrific nature of the allegation that Scott had killed his wife and unborn son helped keep the case in the media throughout the trial. Pre-trial publicity creates a risk that potential juror's opinions be swayed by information they read or hear about the case prior to trial. Criminal defendant's have a Sixth Amendment right to a fair trial, and the Supreme Court held that this right is violated when pre-trial publicity unfairly taints the trial process.[13]

In the landmark case of *Sheppard v. Maxwell (1966)* the U.S. Supreme Court held that the defendant's Sixth Amendment right to a fair trial was violated. Sam Sheppard, arrested for the murder of his wife, was examined without counsel for three days in a televised inquest conducted before an audience in a local gymnasium. Prior to the trial, the local newspaper published the names of prospective jurors, causing them to receive letters and phone calls about the case. The trial coincided with a hotly contested election at which the chief prosecutor and trial judge were candidates for judgeships. Newsmen took over the courtroom after the judge assigned 20 of the reporters to seats inside the bar, normally reserved for court staff and attorneys. In an 8-to-1 decision the Supreme Court reversed his conviction and held that Sheppard's trial had been rendered unfair by the extensive pre-trial publicity.

---

[12]    *Purkett v. Elem*, 514 U.S. 765 (1995).

[13]    *Sheppard v. Maxwell*, 384 U.S. 333 (1966).

# D. TRIAL PROCEDURES

After the jury has been selected and sworn in for service, the prosecutor and defense attorney make **opening statements** to begin the trial. Opening statements are an introduction to the case and describe to the jury what each side believes the evidence will show. These are not arguments but instead are statements of the facts each attorney believes will be proved.

**Evidence** in a criminal trial is the information presented to the jury to prove or disprove specific facts. In order to introduce evidence in a trial the attorneys must be careful to follow the legal rules of evidence for the jurisdiction. The Federal Rules of Evidence govern the admissibility of evidence in federal trials. While not identical, many state evidence codes are modeled after the federal rules. The prosecutor bears the burden of proof in all criminal trials and must demonstrate through facts and evidence that the defendant is guilty, beyond a reasonable doubt. Because of this burden, the prosecutor is the first to put on evidence at trial. Defense counsel may attempt to have evidence excluded from the trial for a variety of reasons. Counsel might argue that the evidence was illegally obtained or violates another evidence rule. The judge must rule on the objection and decide whether the evidence is admissible or not. The prosecutor begins their case by calling witnesses for direct examination and offering facts and evidence to prove each element of the crime(s) charged.[14] There are four basic types of evidence:

1.   Real evidence—tangible things such as clothing or weapons.

2.   Demonstrative evidence—such as drawing or model to explain what took place.

3.   Documentary evidence—such as a letter or document.

4.   Testimonial evidence—witness testimony.

According to the Sixth Amendment, the defendant has a right to be present at the trial and to confront and cross-examine witnesses against him. Defense counsel has the opportunity to cross-examine the prosecutor's witnesses in order to raise doubts about the defendant's guilt and discredit their testimony.

---

[14]   *Taylor v. Kentucky*, 436 U.S. 478 (1978).

According to *California v. Green (1970)*[15] the confrontation requirement serves multiple purposes:

1.    It ensures reliability of the testimony given by requiring witnesses to take an oath of honesty.

2.    It exposes the witness to the probative effects of cross-examination.

3.    It permits the trier of fact (either the jury or judge) to weigh intangible factors such as the demeanor, body language, and expressions of the witness in determining their credibility.

Once the prosecution has finished presenting evidence, they rest their case, meaning it is complete. At that point the defendant may make a motion to dismiss the case for lack of evidence if she believes the prosecution has not met their burden of proof. If the judge denies the motion, the defendant will present any witnesses or evidence she believes support her theory of the case, including defenses or facts that will raise doubt about her guilt. The prosecution has a right to cross-examine defense witnesses in order to raise questions about their truthfulness or credibility.

Both parties have the right to call **expert witnesses** who can testify regarding facts and evidence that require specific knowledge or training. Experts must meet certain qualifications in order to testify as an expert witness in court. Requirements for expert witnesses in state courts vary, but in the federal courts a pre-trial hearing is conducted to qualify experts. At the hearing the expert presents a report summarizing their analysis and any findings their testimony will encompass.[16] Expert testimony is intended to help jurors understand complex information and experts may testify on any subject matter within their expertise so long as it will assist the jury.

The defendant may raise defenses to the crimes charged. Even if the prosecution has met the burden of proof for each element of the crime charged, they will be acquitted if they can prove a legal justification or excuse for their actions. Self-defense is an example of a legal *justification* and insanity is an example of a legal *excuse*. The specific rules governing these and other defenses vary among the states.

At the close of the defendant's case the attorneys make **closing arguments**. The prosecutor argues first, followed by the defense attorney and finally the

---

[15]    399 U.S. 149 (1970).

[16]    *Daubert v. Merrell Dow Pharmaceuticals*, 509 U.S. 570 (1993).

prosecutor has the opportunity for **rebuttal**, or a response to the defendant's argument. The prosecutor is given an opportunity for rebuttal because of the burden of proof beyond a reasonable doubt required to secure a guilty verdict. Closing arguments differ from opening statements in that they are persuasive arguments rather than an objective presentation of facts. The attorneys have the opportunity to argue to the jury what the outcome of the case should be based on the case they presented in the trial.

Finally, the judge gives the **jury instructions**. These jury instructions can be lengthy and jurors may find themselves bored by the tedious nature of this process. The judge explains to the jurors what rules of law govern the crimes in the case and what they must believe is true about the evidence in order to convict the defendant. In some cases the instructions are made at the request of the parties. In other situations the instructions are made by the judge **sua sponte**, because they are required even without a request. Erroneous jury instructions are a common reason for appeals in criminal cases.

## E. VICTIMS AND WITNESSES IN CRIMINAL TRIALS

Witness testimony is crucial in criminal trials. Witnesses testify to the facts and circumstances surrounding the alleged crimes committed by the defendant. The prosecution often calls police officers to testify at trials regarding the facts they observed or collected during the investigation of a crime. The prosecution may also call witnesses who can testify to other facts necessary to prove the elements of an offense. The defendant can testify on their behalf and can call additional witnesses to testify to facts that raise doubt about their guilt. Witnesses often experience fear, anxiety and frustration in association with their experience at trial.

Witnesses may have to take time off from work, losing wages, and must navigate the challenging atmosphere at the criminal courts. The courthouse can be very intimidating for unfamiliar witnesses. Courthouses are commonly located in urban areas, where navigating busy streets, public transportation and parking create frustration before even arriving in court. Long delays and rescheduled hearings may require witnesses to spend the day in relatively uncomfortable surroundings, with little to do, and anxiety about their participation in the trial growing. A rescheduled hearing may require them to return again another day only to face the same frustrations.

Victims of crime are a diverse group. People coming from all walks of life; rich and poor, young and old, and men or women can all be victims of crime. While victims do not have rights associated with the prosecution of the defendant there are growing trends recognizing the need to support victims during criminal trials.

### i.    Victims as Witnesses

Victims of crime often have a limited role in criminal trials. They are not a formal party to the case in the same way the defendant is, and as a result they do not have power to make decisions regarding how the case is prosecuted. In some cases the victim will be called to testify. The victim may welcome this opportunity or may be reluctant to participate with the prosecution. In cases where the victim and defendant are acquainted or have a prior relationship the matter of testifying is complicated. The victim might fear retribution for testifying and be unwilling to cooperate with the prosecution. Even in cases where victims testify willingly, they may experience extreme fear or anxiety associated with appearing at trial. The emotional difficulty of enduring the criminal trial can re-traumatize a victim who may already have suffered a great deal as a result of the crime.

### ii.    Victims of Domestic Violence

**Domestic violence** is violent or aggressive behavior within the home, typically between spouses or intimate partners. In domestic violence cases the victim may welcome the arrest and prosecution of their abuser, but in many cases they do not, and the victim and defendant remain in a relationship. The victim may be unwilling to testify because they do not want their partner to be convicted or jailed, or they fear retribution if they participate. According to the Bureau of Justice Statistics, between 2003 and 2012 domestic violence accounted for 21% of all violent crime. In those same years the majority of victims of domestic violence were female (76% compared to 24% male).[17]

Research indicates that the most common reason domestic violence charges are dropped is a lack of participation by victims. In a study performed in Chicago, prosecutors achieved a 73% conviction rate for domestic violence cases when the victim showed up in court, and significantly less (only 23%) when they did not testify.[18] Lack of cooperative or available victims is cited as the prime reason

---

[17]   Morgan, R., and Truman, J., Bureau of Justice Statistics, "Nonfatal Domestic Violence, 2003–2012"., BJS Statisticians. U.S. Dept. of Justice, Washington, DC: 2014.

[18]   Frohmann, L. and Hartley, C., "Cook County Target Abuser Call (TAC): An Evaluation of a Specialized Domestic Violence Court." Final report for National Institute of Justice, grant number 2000–WT–

prosecutors drop or dismiss domestic violence cases. In a Quincy, Mass. arrest study, a quarter of the arrested abusers were not prosecuted by the district attorney's office. The most common reasons given were "victim denies abuse" (18.8%), married victims invoked their marital privilege not to testify against their husband suspects (12.9%), or the victim could not be located (10.6%).[19] Studies show that the most successful prosecution of domestic violence cases occurs in specialized prosecutorial units that offer support services to victims.[20] Many states employ mandatory arrest statutes in an effort to protect victims of domestic violence. These statutes require that officers make an arrest when called to the scene of a domestic violence incident, even if the victim declines to press charges. Research in the area of battered women's syndrome by psychological experts has also resulted in changes to the rules of evidence in many states. State courts may allow juries to consider evidence of a victim's suffering from battered women's syndrome in cases where they attack their abusers.[21]

The right to a jury trial is foundational to the American system of justice and ensures fairness for defendants but poses challenges for victims and witnesses. Jurors may find themselves frustrated or annoyed at participating—failing to see the value in completing their civic duty. Victims and witnesses may experience significant emotional trauma as they endure testifying in or even attending criminal trials.

# F. THE COVID-19 PANDEMIC AND ACCESS TO JUSTICE

Since the onset of the Coronavirus Pandemic in March, 2020 courts across the country have been forced to find new ways to continue to conduct business. At the onset of the pandemic, courts across the nation closed, and immediately shifted many proceedings to remote/online platforms. While many courts have resumed in-person proceedings in part or in full, researchers are beginning to

---

VX–0003. Washington, DC: U.S. Department of Justice, National Institute of Justice, August 2003, NCJ 202944.

[19] Dawson, M. and Dinovitzer, R., "Victim Cooperation and the Prosecution of Domestic Violence in a Specialized Court." Justice Quarterly 18(3) (September 2001): 593–622, NCJ 190492. http://www.ncjrs.gov/App/Publications/abstract.aspx?ID=190492.

[20] Davies, H., Davis, R., Nickles, L., and Smith, B., "Evaluation of Efforts to Implement NoDrop Policies: Two Central Values in Conflict." Final report for National Institute of Justice, grant number 98–WT–VX–0029. Washington, DC: U.S. Department of Justice, National Institute of Justice, March 2001, NCJ 187772. http://www.ncjrs.gov/App/Publications/abstract.aspx?ID=187772.

[21] *People v. Humphrey*, 13 Cal.4th 1073 (1996).

study the impact of "remote justice." The *Brennan Center* has begun to gather data in this regard and reports the following:

- Video bail hearings resulted in higher bond amounts than their in-person counterparts.

- In immigration hearings, detainees were more likely to be deported when their hearings were conducted remotely.

- Remote witness testimony by children was perceived as less accurate, believable, consistent, and confident than those appearing in-person.

- Three out of six judges surveyed in immigration courts indicated that they had changed 'credibility assessments' made during a video hearing after holding an in-person hearing.

- Remote video hearings make attorney-client communication more difficult.

- Remote video hearings make it more difficult for self-represented litigants to obtain support from judicial services normally available at the physical courthouse.

- Video hearings might also benefit litigants by providing greater access to legal aid organizations by those in remote areas.

- The use of remote hearings for self-represented and low-income litigants in civil cases is a way to reduce costs (reducing the need for days off work; travelling to the courthouse).[22]

There is still a great deal of research to be done in evaluating the risks and benefits of remote/online access to the courts. There will likely be significant differences among various judicial proceedings, some enjoying a benefit from technology while others are negatively affected. It is likely courts will continue to employ technology post-pandemic. Lessons learned through the COVID-era will be drawn from local experience and permanent processes will be implemented that employ the technological tools that have proven effective during the crisis.

---

[22] See embedded studies referenced at: https://www.brennancenter.org/our-work/research-reports/impact-video-proceedings-fairness-and-access-justice-court.

**Read and brief each of the following cases relating to criminal trials and consider the questions following each case:**

1.  *Duncan v. Louisiana*: the right to a jury trial

2.  *Batson v. Kentucky*: racial discrimination in jury selection

3.  *Ramos v. Louisiana*: unanimous jury verdicts

4.  *Sheppard v. Maxwell*: pre-trial publicity

---

# DUNCAN V. LOUISIANA

Supreme Court of the United States
Argued Jan. 17, 1968
Decided May 20, 1968
Rehearing Denied June 17, 1968
391 U.S. 145

## OPINION

### MR. JUSTICE WHITE delivered the opinion of the Court.

Appellant, Gary Duncan, was convicted of simple battery in the Twenty-fifth Judicial District Court of Louisiana. Under Louisiana law simple battery is a misdemeanor, punishable by a maximum of two years' imprisonment and a $300 fine. Appellant sought trial by jury, but because the Louisiana Constitution grants jury trials only in cases in which capital punishment or imprisonment at hard labor may be imposed, the trial judge denied the request. Appellant was convicted and sentenced to serve 60 days in the parish prison and pay a fine of $150. Appellant sought review in the Supreme Court of Louisiana, asserting that the denial of jury trial violated rights guaranteed to him by the United States Constitution. The Supreme Court, finding '(n)o error of law in the ruling complained of,' denied appellant a writ of certiorari. Pursuant to 28 U.S.C. s 1257(2) appellant sought review in this Court, alleging that the Sixth and Fourteenth Amendments to the United States Constitution secure the right to jury trial in state criminal prosecutions where a sentence as long as two years may be imposed. We noted probable jurisdiction, and set the case for oral argument with No. 52, *Bloom v. State of Illinois*, 391 U.S. 194.

Appellant was 19 years of age when tried. While driving on Highway 23 in Plaquemines Parish on October 18, 1966, he saw two younger cousins engaged in a conversation by the side of the road with four white boys. Knowing his cousins, Negroes who had recently transferred to a formerly all-white high school, had reported the occurrence of racial incidents at the school, Duncan stopped the car, got out, and approached the six boys. At trial the white boys and a white onlooker testified, as did appellant and his cousins. The testimony was in dispute on many points, but the witnesses agreed that appellant and the white boys spoke to each other, that appellant encouraged his cousins to break off the encounter and enter his car, and that appellant was about to enter the car himself for the purpose of driving away with his cousins. The whites testified that just before getting in the car appellant slapped Herman Landry, one of the white boys, on the elbow. The Negroes testified that appellant had not slapped Landry, but had merely touched him. The trial judge concluded that the State had proved beyond a reasonable doubt that Duncan had committed simple battery, and found him guilty.

I.

The Fourteenth Amendment denies the States the power to 'deprive any person of life, liberty, or property, without due process of law.' In resolving conflicting claims concerning the meaning of this spacious language, the Court has looked increasingly to the Bill of Rights for guidance; many of the rights guaranteed by the first eight Amendments to the Constitution have been held to be protected against state action by the Due Process Clause of the Fourteenth Amendment. That clause now protects the right to compensation for property taken by the State; the rights of speech, press, and religion covered by the First Amendment; the Fourth Amendment rights to be free from unreasonable searches and seizures and to have excluded from criminal trials any evidence illegally seized; the right guaranteed by the Fifth Amendment to be free of compelled self-incrimination; and the Sixth Amendment rights to counsel, to a speedy and public trial, to confrontation of opposing witnesses, and to compulsory process for obtaining witnesses.

The test for determining whether a right extended by the Fifth and Sixth Amendments with respect to federal criminal proceedings is also protected against state action by the Fourteenth Amendment has been phrased in a variety of ways in the opinions of this Court. The question has been asked whether a right is among those "fundamental principles of liberty and justice which lie at the base of all our civil and political institutions," *Powell v. State of Alabama*, 287 U.S. 45, 67 (1932); whether it is 'basic in our system of jurisprudence. . .and whether it is 'a fundamental right, essential to a fair trial,' *Gideon v. Wainwright*, 372 U.S. 335, 343–344 (1963); . . .The claim before us is that the right to trial by jury guaranteed by the Sixth Amendment meets these tests. The position of Louisiana, on the other hand, is that the Constitution imposes upon the States no duty to give a jury trial in any criminal case, regardless of the seriousness of the crime or the size of the punishment which may be imposed. Because we believe that trial by jury in criminal cases is fundamental to the American scheme of justice, we hold that the Fourteenth Amendment guarantees a right of jury trial in all criminal cases which—were they to be tried in a federal court—would come within the Sixth Amendment's guarantee. Since we consider the appeal before us to be such a case, we hold that the Constitution was violated when appellant's demand for jury trial was refused.

The history of trial by jury in criminal cases has been frequently told. It is sufficient for present purposes to say that by the time our Constitution was written, jury trial in criminal cases had been in existence in England for several centuries and carried impressive credentials traced by many to Magna Carta. Its preservation and proper operation as a protection against arbitrary rule were among the major objectives of the revolutionary settlement which was expressed in the Declaration and Bill of Rights of 1689. In the Eighth century Blackstone could write:

'Our law has therefore wisely placed this strong and two-fold barrier, of a presentment and a trial by jury, between the liberties of the people and the prerogative of the crown. It was necessary, for preserving the admirable balance of our constitution, to vest the executive power of the laws in the prince: and yet this power might be dangerous and destructive to that very constitution, if exerted without check or control, by justices of oyer and terminer occasionally named by the crown; who might then, as in France or Turkey, imprison, dispatch, or exile any man that was obnoxious to the government, by an instant declaration that such is their will and pleasure. But the founders of the English law have, with excellent forecast, contrived that the truth of every accusation, whether preferred in the shape of indictment, information, or appeal, should afterwards be confirmed by the unanimous suffrage of twelve of his equals and neighbours, indifferently chosen and superior to all suspicion.'

Jury trial came to America with English colonists, and received strong support from them. Royal interference with the jury trial was deeply resented. Among the resolutions adopted by the First Congress of the American Colonies (the Stamp Act Congress) on October 19, 1765—resolutions deemed by their authors to state 'the most essential rights and liberties of the colonists'—was the declaration:

'That trial by jury is the inherent and invaluable right of every British subject in these colonies.'

The First Continental Congress, in the resolve of October 14, 1774, objected to trials before judges dependent upon the Crown alone for their salaries and to trials in England for alleged crimes committed in the colonies; the Congress therefore declared:

'That the respective colonies are entitled to the common law of England, and more especially to the great and inestimable privilege of being tried by their peers of the vicinage, according to the course of that law.'

The Declaration of Independence stated solemn objections to the King's making 'judges dependent on his will alone, for the tenure of their offices, and the amount and payment of their salaries,' to his 'depriving us in many cases, of the benefits of Trial by Jury,' and to his 'transporting us beyond Seas to be tried for pretended offenses.' The Constitution itself, in Art. III, s 2, commanded:

'The Trial of all Crimes, except in Cases of Impeachment, shall be by Jury; and such Trial shall be held in the State where the said Crimes shall have been committed.'

Objections to the Constitution because of the absence of a bill of rights were met by the immediate submission and adoption of the Bill of Rights. Included was the Sixth Amendment which, among other things, provided:

'In all criminal prosecutions, the accused shall enjoy the right to a speedy and public trial, by an impartial jury of the State and district wherein the crime shall have been committed.'

The constitutions adopted by the original States guaranteed jury trial. Also, the constitution of every State entering the Union thereafter in one form or another protected the right to jury trial in criminal cases.

Even such skeletal history is impressive support for considering the right to jury trial in criminal cases to be fundamental to our system of justice, . . .

The guarantees of jury trial in the Federal and State Constitutions reflect a profound judgment about the way in which law should be enforced and justice administered. A right to jury trial is granted to criminal defendants in order to prevent oppression by the Government. . . .Providing an accused with the right to be tried by a jury of his peers gave him an inestimable safeguard against the corrupt or overzealous prosecutor and against the compliant, biased, or eccentric judge. If the defendant preferred the common-sense judgment of a jury to the more tutored but perhaps less sympathetic reaction of the single judge, he was to have it. Beyond this, the jury trial provisions in the Federal and State Constitutions reflect a fundamental decision about the exercise of official power—a reluctance to entrust plenary powers over the life and liberty of the citizen to one judge or to a group of judges. Fear of unchecked power, so typical of our State and Federal Governments in other respects, found expression in the criminal law in this insistence upon community participation in the determination of guilt or innocence. The deep commitment of the Nation to the right of jury trial in serious criminal cases as a defense against arbitrary law enforcement qualifies for protection under the Due Process Clause of the Fourteenth Amendment, and must therefore be respected by the States. . .

Our conclusion is that in the American States, as in the federal judicial system, a general grant of jury trial for serious offenses is a fundamental right, essential for preventing miscarriages of justice and for assuring that fair trials are provided for all defendants. We would not assert, however, that every criminal trial—or any particular trial—held before a judge alone is unfair or that a defendant may never be as fairly treated by a judge as he would be by a jury. Thus we hold no constitutional doubts about the practices, common in both federal and state courts, of accepting waivers of jury trial and prosecuting petty crimes without extending a right to jury trial. However, the fact is that in most places more trials for serious crimes are to juries than to a court alone; a great many defendants prefer the judgment of a jury to that of a court. Even where defendants are satisfied with bench trials, the right to a jury trial very likely serves its intended purpose of making judicial or prosecutorial unfairness less likely.

II.

Louisiana's final contention is that even if it must grant jury trials in serious criminal cases, the conviction before us is valid and constitutional because here the petitioner was tried for simple battery and was sentenced to only 60 days in the parish prison. We are not persuaded. It is doubtless true that there is a category of petty crimes or offenses which is not subject to the Sixth Amendment jury trial provision and should not be subject to the Fourteenth Amendment jury trial requirement here applied to the States. Crimes carrying possible penalties up to six months do not require a jury trial if they otherwise qualify as petty offenses, *Cheff v. Schnackenberg*, 384 U.S. 373 (1966). But the penalty authorized for a particular crime is of major relevance in determining whether it is serious or not and may in itself, if severe enough, subject the trial to the mandates of the Sixth Amendment. *District of Columbia v. Clawans*, 300 U.S. 617 (1937). The penalty authorized by the law of the locality may be taken 'as a gauge of its social and ethical judgments. . . of the crime in question. In Clawans the defendant was jailed for 60 days, but it was the 90-day authorized punishment on which the Court focused in determining that the offense was not one for which the Constitution assured trial by jury. In the case before us the Legislature of Louisiana has made simple battery a criminal offense punishable by imprisonment for up to two years and a fine. The question, then, is whether a crime carrying such a penalty is an offense which Louisiana may insist on trying without a jury.

We think not. So-called petty offenses were tried without juries both in England and in the Colonies and have always been held to be exempt from the otherwise comprehensive language of the Sixth Amendment's jury trial provisions. There is no substantial evidence that the Framers intended to depart from this established common-law practice, and the possible consequences to defendants from convictions for petty offenses have been thought insufficient to outweigh the benefits to efficient law enforcement and simplified judicial administration resulting from the availability of speedy and inexpensive nonjury adjudications. These same considerations compel the same result under the Fourteenth Amendment. Of course the boundaries of the petty offense category have always been ill-defined, if not ambulatory. In the absence of an explicit constitutional provision, the definitional task necessarily falls on the courts, which must either pass upon the validity of legislative attempts to identify those petty offenses which are exempt from jury trial or, where the legislature has not addressed itself to the problem, themselves face the question in the first instance. In either case it is necessary to draw a line in the spectrum of crime, separating petty from serious infractions. This process, although essential, cannot be wholly satisfactory, for it requires attaching different consequences to events which, when they lie near the line, actually differ very little.

In determining whether the length of the authorized prison term or the seriousness of other punishment is enough in itself to require a jury trial, we are counseled by *District of Columbia v. Clawans*, supra, to refer to objective criteria, chiefly the existing laws and practices in the Nation. In the federal system, petty offenses are defined as those punishable by no more than six months in prison and a $500 fine. In 49 of the 50 States crimes subject to trial without a jury, which occasionally include simple battery, are punishable by no more than one year in jail. Moreover, in the late 18th century in America crimes triable without a jury were for the most part punishable by no more than a six-month prison term, although there appear to have been exceptions to this rule. We need not, however, settle in this case the exact location of the line between petty offenses and serious crimes. It is sufficient for our purposes to hold that a crime punishable by two years in prison is, based on past and contemporary standards in this country, a serious crime and not a petty offense. Consequently, appellant was entitled to a jury trial and it was error to deny it.

The judgment below is reversed and the case is remanded for proceedings not inconsistent with this opinion.

**Reversed and remanded.**

MR. JUSTICE BLACK, with whom MR. JUSTICE DOUGLAS joins, concurring.

The Court today holds that the right to trial by jury guaranteed defendants in criminal cases in federal courts by Art. III of the United States Constitution and by the Sixth Amendment is also guaranteed by the Fourteenth Amendment to defendants tried in state courts. With this holding I agree for reasons given by the Court. I also agree because of reasons given in my dissent in *Adamson v. People of State of California*, 332 U.S. 47. In that dissent, at 90, I took the position, contrary to the holding in *Twining v. State of New Jersey*, 211 U.S. 78, that the Fourteenth Amendment made all of the provisions of the Bill of Rights applicable to the States. This Court in *Palko v. State of Connecticut*, 302 U.S. 319, 323, decided in 1937, although saying '(t)here is no such general rule,' went on to add that the Fourteenth Amendment may make it unlawful for a State to abridge by its statutes the 'freedom of speech which the First Amendment safeguards against encroachment by the Congress * * * or the like freedom of the press * * * or the free exercise of religion * * * or the right of peaceable assembly * * * or the right of one accused of crime to the benefit of counsel * * *.

In these and other situations immunities that are valid as against the federal government by force of the specific pledges of particular amendments have been found to be implicit in the concept of ordered liberty, and thus, through the Fourteenth Amendment, become valid as against the states.' And the Palko opinion went on to explain, that certain Bill of Rights' provisions were made applicable to the States by bringing them 'within the Fourteenth Amendment by a process of absorption.' Thus *Twining v. State of New Jersey*, supra, refused to hold that any one of the Bill of Rights' provisions was made applicable to the States by the Fourteenth Amendment, but Palko, which must be read as overruling Twining on this point, concluded that the Bill of Rights Amendments that are 'implicit in the concept of ordered liberty' are 'absorbed' by the Fourteenth as protections against state invasion. . . . The historical appendix to my Adamson dissent leaves no doubt in my mind that both its sponsors and those who opposed it believed the Fourteenth Amendment made the first eight Amendments of the Constitution (the Bill of Rights) applicable to the States. . .

MR. JUSTICE HARLAN, whom MR. JUSTICE STEWART joins, dissenting.

Every American jurisdiction provides for trial by jury in criminal cases. The question before us is not whether jury trial is an ancient institution, which it is; nor whether it plays a significant role in the administration of criminal justice, which it does; nor whether it will endure, which it shall. The question in this case is whether the State of Louisiana, which provides trial by jury for all felonies, is prohibited by the Constitution from trying charges of simple battery to the court alone. In my view, the answer to that question, mandated alike by our constitutional history and by the longer history of trial by jury, is clearly 'no.'

The States have always borne primary responsibility for operating the machinery of criminal justice within their borders, and adapting it to their particular circumstances. In exercising this responsibility, each State is compelled to conform its procedures to the requirements of the Federal Constitution. The Due Process Clause of the Fourteenth Amendment requires that those procedures be fundamentally fair in all respects. It does not, in my view, impose or encourage nationwide uniformity for its own sake; it does not command adherence to forms that happen to be old; and it does not impose on the States the rules that may be in force in the federal courts except where such rules are also found to be essential to basic fairness. . .

I would affirm the judgment of the Supreme Court of Louisiana.

**After preparing the case brief, consider the answers to the following questions:**

1.    What are some of the reasons why the Court explains that jury trials are such an important part of the American criminal justice system?

2.   This case incorporates the right to a trial by jury, applying it to the states via the Fourteenth Amendment. Do you agree with the Court's decision to incorporate?

3.   The dissent argues that the states should have the power to decide how their criminal courts function, so long as they abide by the duty to be fundamentally fair. In this situation, do you think it would be possible for states to utilize different procedures and still achieve fairness?

4.   What challenges are presented by the majority's approach of uniform standards for jury trials?

## BATSON V. KENTUCKY

Supreme Court of the United States
Argued Dec. 12, 1985
Decided April 30, 1986
476 U.S. 79

### OPINION

### JUSTICE POWELL delivered the opinion of the Court.

This case requires us to reexamine that portion of *Swain v. Alabama,* 380 U.S. 202 (1965), concerning the evidentiary burden placed on a criminal defendant who claims that he has been denied equal protection through the State's use of peremptory challenges to exclude members of his race from the petit jury.

I

Petitioner, a black man, was indicted in Kentucky on charges of second-degree burglary and receipt of stolen goods. On the first day of trial in Jefferson Circuit Court, the judge conducted *voir dire* examination of the venire, excused certain jurors for cause, and permitted the parties to exercise peremptory challenges. The prosecutor used his peremptory challenges to strike all four black persons on the venire, and a jury composed only of white persons was selected. Defense counsel moved to discharge the jury before it was sworn on the ground that the prosecutor's removal of the black veniremen violated petitioner's rights under the Sixth and Fourteenth Amendments to a jury drawn from a cross section of the community, and under the Fourteenth Amendment to equal protection of the laws. Counsel requested a hearing on his motion. Without expressly ruling on the request for a hearing, the trial judge observed that the parties were entitled to use their peremptory challenges to "strike anybody they want to." The judge then denied petitioner's motion, reasoning that the cross-section requirement applies only to selection of the venire and not to selection of the petit jury itself.

The jury convicted petitioner on both counts. On appeal to the Supreme Court of Kentucky, petitioner pressed, among other claims, the argument concerning the prosecutor's use of peremptory challenges. Conceding that *Swain v. Alabama, supra,* apparently foreclosed an equal protection claim based solely on the prosecutor's conduct in this case, petitioner urged the court to follow decisions of other States, *People v. Wheeler,* 22 Cal.3d 258, 148 Cal.Rptr. 890 (1978); *Commonwealth v. Soares,* 377 Mass. 461, cert. denied, 444 U.S. 881 (1979), and to hold that such conduct violated his rights under the Sixth

Amendment and § 11 of the Kentucky Constitution to a jury drawn from a cross section of the community. Petitioner also contended that the facts showed that the prosecutor had engaged in a "pattern" of discriminatory challenges in this case and established an equal protection violation under *Swain.*

The Supreme Court of Kentucky affirmed. In a single paragraph, the court declined petitioner's invitation to adopt the reasoning of *People v. Wheeler, supra,* and *Commonwealth v. Soares, supra.* The court observed that it recently had reaffirmed its reliance on *Swain,* and had held that a defendant alleging lack of a fair cross section must demonstrate systematic exclusion of a group of jurors from the venire. We granted certiorari, and now reverse.

## II

In *Swain v. Alabama,* this Court recognized that a "State's purposeful or deliberate denial to Negroes on account of race of participation as jurors in the administration of justice violates the Equal Protection Clause." This principle has been "consistently and repeatedly" reaffirmed, in numerous decisions of this Court both preceding and following *Swain.* We reaffirm the principle today.

## A

More than a century ago, the Court decided that the State denies a black defendant equal protection of the laws when it puts him on trial before a jury from which members of his race have been purposefully excluded. *Strauder v. West Virginia,* 100 U.S. 303 (1880). That decision laid the foundation for the Court's unceasing efforts to eradicate racial discrimination in the procedures used to select the venire from which individual jurors are drawn. In *Strauder,* the Court explained that the central concern of the recently ratified Fourteenth Amendment was to put an end to governmental discrimination on account of race. Exclusion of black citizens from service as jurors constitutes a primary example of the evil the Fourteenth Amendment was designed to cure.

In holding that racial discrimination in jury selection offends the Equal Protection Clause, the Court in *Strauder* recognized, however, that a defendant has no right to a "petit jury composed in whole or in part of persons of his own race." . . .But the defendant does have the right to be tried by a jury whose members are selected pursuant to nondiscriminatory criteria. *Martin v. Texas,* 200 U.S. 316, 321(1906); *Ex parte Virginia,* 100 U.S. 339, 345 (1880). The Equal Protection Clause guarantees the defendant that the State will not exclude members of his race from the jury venire on account of race. . .Purposeful racial discrimination in selection of the venire violates a defendant's right to equal protection because it denies him the protection that a trial by jury is intended to secure. . . .

Racial discrimination in selection of jurors harms not only the accused whose life or liberty they are summoned to try. Competence to serve as a juror ultimately depends on an assessment of individual qualifications and ability impartially to consider evidence presented at a trial. . . .The harm from discriminatory jury selection extends beyond that inflicted on the defendant and the excluded juror to touch the entire community. Selection procedures that purposefully exclude black persons from juries undermine public confidence in the fairness of our system of justice. . . . Discrimination within the judicial system is most pernicious because it is "a stimulant to that race prejudice which is an impediment to securing to [black citizens] that equal justice which the law aims to secure to all others." . . .

### B

In *Strauder,* the Court invalidated a state statute that provided that only white men could serve as jurors. *Id.,* at 305. We can be confident that no State now has such a law. The Constitution requires, however, that we look beyond the face of the statute defining juror qualifications and also consider challenged selection practices to afford "protection against action of the State through its administrative officers in effecting the prohibited discrimination. . . Accordingly, the component of the jury selection process at issue here, the State's privilege to strike individual jurors through peremptory challenges, is subject to the commands of the Equal Protection Clause. Although a prosecutor ordinarily is entitled to exercise permitted peremptory challenges "for any reason at all, as long as that reason is related to his view concerning the outcome" of the case to be tried, . . .the Equal Protection Clause forbids the prosecutor to challenge potential jurors solely on account of their race or on the assumption that black jurors as a group will be unable impartially to consider the State's case against a black defendant.

### III

The principles announced in *Strauder* never have been questioned in any subsequent decision of this Court. Rather, the Court has been called upon repeatedly to review the application of those principles to particular facts. A recurring question in these cases, as in any case alleging a violation of the Equal Protection Clause, was whether the defendant had met his burden of proving purposeful discrimination on the part of the state. . . That question also was at the heart of the portion of *Swain v. Alabama* we reexamine today.

## A

*Swain* required the Court to decide, among other issues, whether a black defendant was denied equal protection by the State's exercise of peremptory challenges to exclude members of his race from the petit jury. 380 U.S., at 209–210, 85 S.Ct., at 830. The record in *Swain* showed that the prosecutor had used the State's peremptory challenges to strike the six black persons included on the petit jury venire. . .

Accordingly, a black defendant could make out a prima facie case of purposeful discrimination on proof that the peremptory challenge system was "being perverted" in that manner. *Ibid.* For example, an inference of purposeful discrimination would be raised on evidence that a prosecutor, "in case after case, whatever the circumstances, whatever the crime and whoever the defendant or the victim may be, is responsible for the removal of Negroes who have been selected as qualified jurors by the jury commissioners and who have survived challenges for cause, with the result that no Negroes ever serve on petit juries." Evidence offered by the defendant in *Swain* did not meet that standard. While the defendant showed that prosecutors in the jurisdiction had exercised their strikes to exclude blacks from the jury, he offered no proof of the circumstances under which prosecutors were responsible for striking black jurors beyond the facts of his own case.

A number of lower courts following the teaching of *Swain* reasoned that proof of repeated striking of blacks over a number of cases was necessary to establish a violation of the Equal Protection Clause. Since this interpretation of *Swain* has placed on defendants a crippling burden of proof, prosecutors' peremptory challenges are now largely immune from constitutional scrutiny. For reasons that follow, we reject this evidentiary formulation as inconsistent with standards that have been developed since *Swain* for assessing a prima facie case under the Equal Protection Clause.

## B

. . .As in any equal protection case, the "burden is, of course," on the defendant who alleges discriminatory selection of the venire "to prove the existence of purposeful discrimination." . . . Circumstantial evidence of invidious intent may include proof of disproportionate impact. . . .We have observed that under some circumstances proof of discriminatory impact "may for all practical purposes demonstrate unconstitutionality because in various circumstances the discrimination is very difficult to explain on nonracial grounds." *Ibid.* For example, "total or seriously disproportionate exclusion of

Negroes from jury venires," *ibid.,* "is itself such an 'unequal application of the law . . . as to show intentional discrimination,' " . . .Moreover, since *Swain,* we have recognized that a black defendant alleging that members of his race have been impermissibly excluded from the venire may make out a prima facie case of purposeful discrimination by showing that the totality of the relevant facts gives rise to an inference of discriminatory purpose. . . .

The showing necessary to establish a prima facie case of purposeful discrimination in selection of the venire may be discerned in this Court's decisions. . . .The defendant initially must show that he is a member of a racial group capable of being singled out for differential treatment. *Castaneda v. Partida, supra,* 430 U.S., at 494. In combination with that evidence, a defendant may then make a prima facie case by proving that in the particular jurisdiction members of his race have not been summoned for jury service over an extended period of time. *Id.,* at 494, 97 S.Ct., at 1280. Proof of systematic exclusion from the venire raises an inference of purposeful discrimination because the "result bespeaks discrimination." *Hernandez v. Texas,* 347 U.S., at 482, . . .

## C

The standards for assessing a prima facie case in the context of discriminatory selection of the venire have been fully articulated since *Swain.* . . .

In deciding whether the defendant has made the requisite showing, the trial court should consider all relevant circumstances. For example, a "pattern" of strikes against black jurors included in the particular venire might give rise to an inference of discrimination. Similarly, the prosecutor's questions and statements during *voir dire* examination and in exercising his challenges may support or refute an inference of discriminatory purpose. These examples are merely illustrative. We have confidence that trial judges, experienced in supervising *voir dire,* will be able to decide if the circumstances concerning the prosecutor's use of peremptory challenges creates a prima facie case of discrimination against black jurors.

Once the defendant makes a prima facie showing, the burden shifts to the State to come forward with a neutral explanation for challenging black jurors. Though this requirement imposes a limitation in some cases on the full peremptory character of the historic challenge, we emphasize that the prosecutor's explanation need not rise to the level justifying exercise of a challenge for cause. . . . But the prosecutor may not rebut the defendant's prima facie case of discrimination by stating merely that he challenged jurors of the defendant's race on the assumption-or his intuitive judgment-that they would be partial to the defendant because of their shared race. . . Just as the Equal Protection Clause forbids the States to exclude black persons from the venire on the assumption that blacks as a group are unqualified to serve as jurors. . . so it forbids the States to strike black veniremen on the assumption that they will be biased in a particular case simply because the defendant is black. . . . .

The prosecutor therefore must articulate a neutral explanation related to the particular case to be tried. The trial court then will have the duty to determine if the defendant has established purposeful discrimination. . .

V

In this case, petitioner made a timely objection to the prosecutor's removal of all black persons on the venire. Because the trial court flatly rejected the objection without requiring the prosecutor to give an explanation for his action, we remand this case for further proceedings. If the trial court decides that the facts establish, prima facie, purposeful discrimination and the prosecutor does not come forward with a neutral explanation for his action, our precedents require that petitioner's conviction be **reversed. . . .**

**It is so ordered. . .**

**JUSTICE MARSHALL, concurring.**

. . .I wholeheartedly concur in the Court's conclusion that use of the peremptory challenge to remove blacks from juries, on the basis of their race, violates the Equal Protection Clause. I would go further, however, in fashioning a remedy adequate to eliminate that discrimination. Merely allowing defendants the opportunity to challenge the racially discriminatory use of peremptory challenges in individual cases will not end the illegitimate use of the peremptory challenge. . . Any prosecutor can easily assert facially neutral reasons for striking a juror, and trial courts are ill equipped to second-guess those reasons. How is the court to treat a prosecutor's statement that he struck a juror because the juror had a son about the same age as defendant, see *People v. Hall*, 35 Cal.3d 161 (1983), or seemed "uncommunicative," *King, supra,* at 498, or "never cracked a smile" and, therefore "did not possess the sensitivities necessary to realistically look at the issues and decide the facts in this case," *Hall, supra,* at 165, 197? If such easily generated explanations are sufficient to discharge the prosecutor's obligation to justify his strikes on nonracial grounds, then the protection erected by the Court today may be illusory.

. . . A prosecutor's own conscious or unconscious racism may lead him easily to the conclusion that a prospective black juror is "sullen," or "distant," a characterization that would not have come to his mind if a white juror had acted identically. A judge's own conscious or unconscious racism may lead him to accept such an explanation as well supported. . . .

I applaud the Court's holding that the racially discriminatory use of peremptory challenges violates the Equal Protection Clause, and I join the Court's opinion. However, only by banning peremptories entirely can such discrimination be ended. . .

**CHIEF JUSTICE BURGER, joined by JUSTICE REHNQUIST, dissenting.**

Today the Court sets aside the peremptory challenge, a procedure which has been part of the common law for many centuries and part of our jury system for nearly 200 years. It does so on the basis of a constitutional argument that was rejected, without a single dissent, in *Swain v. Alabama,* 380 U.S. 202, 85 S.Ct. 824, 13 L.Ed.2d 759 (1965). Reversal of such settled principles would be unusual enough on its own terms, for only three years ago we said that "*stare decisis,* while perhaps never entirely persuasive on a constitutional question, is a doctrine that demands respect in a society governed by the rule of law." *Akron v. Akron Center for Reproductive Health, Inc.,* 462 U.S. 416, 420 (1983). What makes today's holding truly extraordinary is that it is based on a constitutional argument that the petitioner has *expressly* declined to raise, both in this Court and in the Supreme Court of Kentucky.

. . .During oral argument, counsel for petitioner was pointedly asked:

"QUESTION: Mr. Niehaus, Swain was an equal protection challenge, was it not?

"MR. NIEHAUS: Yes.

"QUESTION: Your claim here is based solely on the Sixth Amendment?

"MR. NIEHAUS: Yes.

"QUESTION: Is that correct?

"MR. NIEHAUS: That is what we are arguing, yes.

"QUESTION: You are not asking for a reconsideration of Swain, and you are making no equal protection claim here. Is that correct?

"MR. NIEHAUS: We have not made an equal protection claim.

. . . Even following oral argument, we could have-as we sometimes do-directed reargument on this particular question. . . .This step is particularly appropriate where reexamination of a prior decision is under consideration. . . .The Court today rejects these accepted courses of action, choosing instead to reverse a 21-year-old unanimous constitutional holding of this Court on the basis of constitutional arguments expressly disclaimed by petitioner. . . .Before contemplating such a holding, I would at least direct reargument and briefing on the issue of whether the equal protection holding in *Swain* should be reconsidered. . .

IV

An institution like the peremptory challenge that is part of the fabric of our jury system should not be casually cast aside, especially on a basis not raised or argued by the petitioner. As one commentator aptly observed:

> "The real question is whether to tinker with a system, be it of jury selection or anything else, that has done the job for centuries. We stand on the shoulders of our ancestors, as Burke said. It is not so much that the past is always worth preserving, he argued, but rather that 'it is with infinite caution that any man ought to venture upon pulling down an edifice, which has answered in any tolerable degree for ages the common purposes of society. . . .' " Younger, Unlawful Peremptory Challenges, 7 Litigation 23, 56 (Fall 1980).

At the very least, this important case reversing centuries of history and experience ought to be set for reargument next Term.

**JUSTICE REHNQUIST, with whom THE CHIEF JUSTICE joins, dissenting.**

The Court states, in the opening line of its opinion, that this case involves only a reexamination of that portion of *Swain v. Alabama*, 380 U.S. 202 (1965), . . . With little discussion and less analysis, the Court also overrules one of the fundamental substantive holdings of *Swain*, namely, that the State may use its peremptory challenges to remove from the jury, on a case-specific basis, prospective jurors of the same race as the defendant. Because I find the Court's rejection of this holding both ill considered and unjustifiable under established principles of equal protection, I dissent. . .

I cannot subscribe to the Court's unprecedented use of the Equal Protection Clause to restrict the historic scope of the peremptory challenge, which has been described as "a necessary part of trial by jury." *Swain*, 380 U.S., at 219, 85 S.Ct., at 835. In my view, there is simply nothing "unequal" about the State's using its peremptory challenges to strike blacks from the jury in cases involving black defendants, so long as such challenges are also used to exclude whites in cases involving white defendants, Hispanics in cases involving hispanic defendants, Asians in cases involving Asian defendants, and so on. This case-specific use of peremptory challenges by the State does not single out blacks, or members of any other race for that matter, for discriminatory treatment. Such use of peremptories is at best based upon seat-of-the-pants instincts, which are undoubtedly crudely stereotypical and may in many cases be hopelessly mistaken. But as long as they are applied across-the-board to jurors of all races and nationalities, I do not see-and the Court most certainly has not explained-how their use violates the Equal Protection Clause.

Nor does such use of peremptory challenges by the State infringe upon any other constitutional interests. The Court does not suggest that exclusion of blacks from the jury through the State's use of peremptory challenges results in a violation of either the fair-cross-section or impartiality component of the Sixth Amendment. See *ante,* at 1716, n. 4. And because the case-specific use of peremptory challenges by the State does not deny blacks the right to serve as jurors in cases involving nonblack defendants, it harms neither the excluded jurors nor the remainder of the community. See *ante,* at 1717–1718.

The use of group affiliations, such as age, race, or occupation, as a "proxy" for potential juror partiality, based on the assumption or belief that members of one group are more likely to favor defendants who belong to the same group, has long been accepted as a legitimate basis for the State's exercise of peremptory challenges. See *Swain,* . . . Indeed, given the need for reasonable limitations on the time devoted to *voir dire,* the use of such "proxies" by both the State and the defendant may be extremely useful in eliminating from the jury persons who might be biased in one way or another. The Court today holds that the State may not use its peremptory challenges to strike black prospective jurors on this basis without violating the Constitution. But I do not believe there is anything in the Equal Protection Clause, or any other constitutional provision, that justifies such a departure from the substantive holding contained in Part II of *Swain.* Petitioner in the instant case failed to make a sufficient showing to overcome the presumption announced in *Swain* that the State's use of peremptory challenges was related to the context of the case. I would therefore affirm the judgment of the court below. . .

**After preparing the case brief, consider the answers to the following questions:**

1. The Court announces a new rule, based on the Equal Protection Clause, in order to justify the peremptory challenge of a juror where there is a challenge racial discrimination. Explain the steps in this process.

2. What is a "prima facie" case of invidious discrimination?

3. What must the prosecutor who removed the jurors do in order to justify the use of the peremptory challenge?

4. Why is it important to prevent the exclusion of jurors based on race?

## RAMOS V. LOUISIANA

Supreme Court of the United States
Argued Oct. 7, 2019
Decided April 20, 2020
140 S.Ct. 1390

### Opinion

JUSTICE GORSUCH announced the judgment of the Court and delivered the opinion of the Court with respect to Parts I, II-A, III, and IV-B-1, an opinion with respect to Parts II-B, IV-B-2, and V, in which JUSTICE GINSBURG, JUSTICE BREYER, and JUSTICE SOTOMAYOR join, and an opinion with respect to Part IV-A, in which JUSTICE GINSBURG and JUSTICE BREYER join.

Accused of a serious crime, Evangelisto Ramos insisted on his innocence and invoked his right to a jury trial. Eventually, 10 jurors found the evidence against him persuasive. But a pair of jurors believed that the State of Louisiana had failed to prove Mr. Ramos's guilt beyond reasonable doubt; they voted to acquit.

In 48 States and federal court, a single juror's vote to acquit is enough to prevent a conviction. But not in Louisiana. Along with Oregon, Louisiana has long punished people based on 10-to-2 verdicts like the one here. So instead of the mistrial he would have received almost anywhere else, Mr. Ramos was sentenced to life in prison without the possibility of parole.

Why do Louisiana and Oregon allow nonunanimous convictions? Though it's hard to say why these laws persist, their origins are clear. Louisiana first endorsed nonunanimous verdicts for serious crimes at a constitutional convention in 1898. According to one committee chairman, the avowed purpose of that convention was to "establish the supremacy of the white race," and the resulting document included many of the trappings of the Jim Crow era: a poll tax, a combined literacy and property ownership test, and a grandfather clause that in practice exempted white residents from the most onerous of these requirements.

Nor was it only the prospect of African-Americans voting that concerned the delegates. Just a week before the convention, the U.S. Senate passed a resolution calling for an investigation into whether Louisiana was systemically excluding African-Americans from juries. Seeking to avoid unwanted national attention, and aware that this Court would strike down any policy of overt discrimination against African-American jurors as a violation of the Fourteenth

Amendment, the delegates sought to undermine African-American participation on juries in another way. With a careful eye on racial demographics, the convention delegates sculpted a "facially race-neutral" rule permitting 10-to-2 verdicts in order "to ensure that African-American juror service would be meaningless."

Adopted in the 1930s, Oregon's rule permitting nonunanimous verdicts can be similarly traced to the rise of the Ku Klux Klan and efforts to dilute "the influence of racial, ethnic, and religious minorities on Oregon juries." In fact, no one before us contests any of this; courts in both Louisiana and Oregon have frankly acknowledged that race was a motivating factor in the adoption of their States' respective nonunanimity rules.

We took this case to decide whether the Sixth Amendment right to a jury trial—as incorporated against the States by way of the Fourteenth Amendment—requires a unanimous verdict to convict a defendant of a serious offense. Louisiana insists that this Court has never definitively passed on the question and urges us to find its practice consistent with the Sixth Amendment. By contrast, the dissent doesn't try to defend Louisiana's law on Sixth or Fourteenth Amendment grounds; tacitly, it seems to admit that the Constitution forbids States from using nonunanimous juries. Yet, unprompted by Louisiana, the dissent suggests our precedent requires us to rule for the State anyway. What explains all this? To answer the puzzle, it's necessary to say a bit more about the merits of the question presented, the relevant precedent, and, at last, the consequences that follow from saying what we know to be true.

**I**

The Sixth Amendment promises that "[i]n all criminal prosecutions, the accused shall enjoy the right to a speedy and public trial, by an impartial jury of the State and district wherein the crime shall have been committed, which district shall have been previously ascertained by law." The Amendment goes on to preserve other rights for criminal defendants but says nothing else about what a "trial by an impartial jury" entails.

Still, the promise of a jury trial surely meant *something*—otherwise, there would have been no reason to write it down. Nor would it have made any sense to spell out the places from which jurors should be drawn if their powers as jurors could be freely abridged by statute. Imagine a constitution that allowed a "jury trial" to mean nothing but a single person rubberstamping convictions without hearing any evidence—but simultaneously insisting that the lone juror come from a specific judicial district "previously ascertained by law." And if that's not enough, imagine a constitution that included the same hollow guarantee *twice*—not only in the Sixth Amendment, but also in Article III. No: The text and structure of the Constitution clearly suggest that the term "trial by an impartial jury" carried with it *some* meaning about the content and requirements of a jury trial.

One of these requirements was unanimity. Wherever we might look to determine what the term "trial by an impartial jury trial" meant at the time of the Sixth Amendment's adoption—whether it's the common law, state practices in the founding era, or opinions and treatises written soon afterward—the answer is unmistakable. A jury must reach a unanimous verdict in order to convict.

The requirement of juror unanimity emerged in 14th century England and was soon accepted as a vital right protected by the common law. As Blackstone explained, no person could be found guilty of a serious crime unless "the truth of every accusation . . . should . . . be confirmed by the unanimous suffrage of twelve of his equals and neighbors, indifferently chosen, and superior to all suspicion." A " 'verdict, taken from eleven, was no verdict' " at all.

This same rule applied in the young American States. Six State Constitutions explicitly required unanimity. Another four preserved the right to a jury trial in more general terms. But the variations did not matter much; consistent with the common law, state courts appeared to regard unanimity as an essential feature of the jury trial. It was against this backdrop that James Madison drafted and the States ratified the Sixth Amendment in 1791. By that time, unanimous verdicts had been required for about 400 years. If the term "trial by an impartial jury" carried any meaning at all, it surely included a requirement as long and widely accepted as unanimity. Influential, postadoption treatises confirm this understanding. For example, in 1824, Nathan Dane reported as fact that the U.S. Constitution required unanimity in criminal jury trials for serious offenses. A few years later, Justice Story explained in his Commentaries on the Constitution that "in common cases, the law not only presumes every man innocent, until he is proved guilty; but unanimity in the verdict of the jury is indispensable." Similar statements can be found in American legal treatises throughout the 19th century.

Nor is this a case where the original public meaning was lost to time and only recently recovered. This Court has, repeatedly and over many years, recognized that the Sixth Amendment requires unanimity. As early as 1898, the Court said that a defendant enjoys a "constitutional right to demand that his liberty should not be taken from him except by the joint action of the court and the unanimous verdict of a jury of twelve persons." A few decades later, the Court elaborated that the Sixth Amendment affords a right to "a trial by jury as understood and applied at common law, . . . includ[ing] all the essential elements as they were recognized in this country and England when the Constitution was adopted." And, the Court observed, this includes a requirement "that the verdict should be unanimous." In all, this Court has commented on the Sixth Amendment's unanimity requirement no fewer than 13 times over more than 120 years.

There can be no question either that the Sixth Amendment's unanimity requirement applies to state and federal criminal trials equally. This Court has long explained that the Sixth Amendment right to a jury trial is "fundamental to the American scheme of justice" and incorporated against the States under the Fourteenth Amendment. This Court has long explained, too, that incorporated provisions of the Bill of Rights bear the same content when asserted against States as they do when asserted against the federal government. So if the Sixth Amendment's right to a jury trial requires a unanimous verdict to support a conviction in federal court, it requires no less in state court.

## II

### A

How, despite these seemingly straightforward principles, have Louisiana's and Oregon's laws managed to hang on for so long? It turns out that the Sixth Amendment's otherwise simple story took a strange turn in 1972. That year, the Court confronted these States' unconventional schemes for the first time— in *Apodaca v. Oregon* and a companion case, *Johnson v. Louisiana.* Ultimately, the Court could do no more than issue a badly fractured set of opinions. Four dissenting Justices would not have hesitated to strike down the States' laws, recognizing that the Sixth Amendment requires unanimity and that this guarantee is fully applicable against the States under the Fourteenth Amendment. But a four-Justice plurality took a very different view of the Sixth Amendment. These Justices declared that the real question before them was whether unanimity serves an important "function" in "contemporary society." Then, having reframed the question, the plurality wasted few words before concluding that unanimity's costs outweigh its benefits in the modern era, so the Sixth Amendment should not stand in the way of Louisiana or Oregon.

. . .

## III

Louisiana's approach may not be quite as tough as trying to defend Justice Powell's dual-track theory of incorporation, but it's pretty close. How does the State deal with the fact this Court has said 13 times over 120 years that the Sixth Amendment *does* require unanimity? Or the fact that five Justices in *Apodaca* said the same? The best the State can offer is to suggest that all these statements came in dicta. But even supposing (without granting) that Louisiana is right and it's dicta all the way down, why would the Court now walk away from many of its own statements about the Constitution's meaning? And what about the prior 400 years of English and American cases requiring unanimity—should we dismiss all those as dicta too?

Sensibly, Louisiana doesn't dispute that the common law required unanimity. Instead, it argues that the drafting history of the Sixth Amendment reveals an intent by the framers to leave this particular feature behind. The State points to the fact that Madison's proposal for the Sixth Amendment originally read: "The trial of all crimes . . . shall be by an impartial jury of freeholders of the vicinage, with the requisite of unanimity for conviction, of the right of challenge, and other accustomed requisites. . . ." Louisiana notes that the House of Representatives approved this text with minor modifications. Yet, the State stresses, the Senate replaced "impartial jury of freeholders of the vicinage" with "impartial jury of the State and district wherein the crime shall have been committed" and also removed the explicit references to unanimity, the right of challenge, and "other accustomed requisites." In light of these revisions, Louisiana would have us infer an intent to abandon the common law's traditional unanimity requirement.

But this snippet of drafting history could just as easily support the opposite inference. . . .

In the final accounting, the dissent's *stare decisis* arguments round to zero. We have an admittedly mistaken decision [*Apodaca*], on a constitutional issue, an outlier on the day it was decided, one that's become lonelier with time. In arguing otherwise, the dissent must elide the reliance the American people place in their constitutionally protected liberties, overplay the competing interests of two States, count some of those interests twice, and make no small amount of new precedent all its own.

## V

On what ground would anyone have us leave Mr. Ramos in prison for the rest of his life? Not a single Member of this Court is prepared to say Louisiana secured his conviction constitutionally under the Sixth Amendment. No one before us suggests that the error was harmless. Louisiana does not claim precedent commands an affirmance. In the end, the best anyone can seem to muster against Mr. Ramos is that, if we dared to admit in his case what we all know to be true about the Sixth Amendment, we might have to say the same in some others. But where is the justice in that? Every judge must learn to live with the fact he or she will make some mistakes; it comes with the territory. But it is something else entirely to perpetuate something we all know to be wrong only because we fear the consequences of being right. The judgment of the Court of Appeals is

*Reversed.* . . .

**After preparing the case brief, consider the answers to the following questions:**

1.   How did the states of Oregon and Louisiana differ from the rest of the nation with regard to criminal verdicts at the time Ramos filed his appeal?

2.   What did the Court decide was required in order to find a defendant guilty in a criminal case?

3.   What does it mean that the right to a jury trial was 'incorporated' (review chapter 3 re: fundamental rights and incorporation)?

4.   Do you agree with the Court's decision that guilty verdicts must be unanimous in order to be fair?

## SHEPPARD V. MAXWELL

Supreme Court of the United States
Argued Feb. 28, 1966
Decided June 6, 1966
384 U.S. 333

### OPINION

### MR. JUSTICE CLARK delivered the opinion of the Court.

This federal habeas corpus application involves the question whether Sheppard was deprived of a fair trial in his state conviction for the second-degree murder of his wife because of the trial judge's failure to protect Sheppard sufficiently from the massive, pervasive and prejudicial publicity that attended his prosecution.[1] The United States District Court held that he was not afforded a fair trial and granted the writ subject to the State's right to put Sheppard to trial again, 231 F.Supp. 37 (D.C.S.D.Ohio 1964). The Court of Appeals for the Sixth Circuit reversed by a divided vote, 346 F.2d 707 (1965). We granted certiorari. We have concluded that Sheppard did not receive a fair trial consistent with the Due Process Clause of the Fourteenth Amendment and, therefore, reverse the judgment.

I.

Marilyn Sheppard, petitioner's pregnant wife, was bludgeoned to death in the upstairs bedroom of their lakeshore home in Bay Village, Ohio, a suburb of Cleveland. On the day of the tragedy, July 4, 1954, Sheppard pieced together for several local officials the following story: He and his wife had entertained neighborhood friends, the Aherns, on the previous evening at their home. After dinner they watched television in the living room. Sheppard became drowsy and dozed off to sleep on a couch. Later, Marilyn partially awoke him saying that she was going to bed. The next thing he remembered was hearing his wife cry out in the early morning hours. He hurried upstairs and in the dim light from the hall saw a 'form' standing next to his wife's bed. As he struggled with the 'form' he was struck on the back of the neck and rendered unconscious. On regaining his senses he found himself on the floor next to his wife's bed. He rose, looked at her, took her pulse and 'felt that she was gone.' He then went to his son's room and found him unmolested. Hearing a noise he hurried downstairs. He saw a 'form' running out the door and pursued it to

---

[1]   Sheppard was convicted in 1954 in the Court of Common Pleas of Cuyahoga County, Ohio. His conviction was affirmed by the Court of Appeals for Cuyahoga County, *State v. Sheppard*, 100 Ohio App. 345, 128 N.E.2d 471 (1955), and the Ohio Supreme Court, 165 Ohio St. 293, 135 N.E.2d 340 (1956). We denied certiorari on the original application for review. 352 U.S. 910, 77 S.Ct. 118, 1 L.Ed.2d 119 (1956).

the lake shore. He grappled with it on the beach and again lost consciousness. Upon his recovery he was lying face down with the lower portion of his body in the water. He returned to his home, checked the pulse on his wife's neck, and 'determined or thought that she was gone.'[2] He then went downstairs and called a neighbor, Mayor Houk of Bay Village. The Mayor and his wife came over at once, found Sheppard slumped in an easy chair downstairs and asked, 'What happened?' Sheppard replied: 'I don't know but somebody ought to try to do something for Marilyn.' Mrs. Houk immediately went up to the bedroom. The Mayor told Sheppard, 'Get hold of yourself. Can you tell me what happened?' Sheppard then related the above-outlined events. After Mrs. Houk discovered the body, the Mayor called the local police, Dr. Richard Sheppard, petitioner's brother, and the Aherns. The local police were the first to arrive. They in turn notified the Coroner and Cleveland police. Richard Sheppard then arrived, determined that Marilyn was dead, examined his brother's injuries, and removed him to the nearby clinic operated by the Sheppardfamily.[3] When the Coroner, the Cleveland police and other officials arrived, the house and surrounding area were thoroughly searched, the rooms of the house were photographed, and many persons, including the Houks and the Aherns, were interrogated. The Sheppard home and premises were taken into 'protective custody' and remained so until after the trial.[4]

From the outset officials focused suspicion on Sheppard. After a search of the house and premises on the morning of the tragedy, Dr. Gerber, the Coroner, is reported—and it is undenied—to have told his men, 'Well, it is evident the doctor did this, so let's go get the confession out of him.' He proceeded to interrogate and examine Sheppard while the latter was under sedation in his hospital room. On the same occasion, the Coroner was given the clothes Sheppard wore at the time of the tragedy together with the personal items in them. Later that afternoon Chief Eaton and two Cleveland police officers interrogated Sheppard at some length, confronting him with evidence and demanding explanations. Asked by Officer Shotke to take a lie detector test, Sheppard said he would if it were reliable. Shotke replied that it was 'infallible' and 'you might as well tell us all about it now.' At the end of the interrogation Shotke told Sheppard: 'I think you killed your wife.' Still later in

---

[2]  The several witnesses to whom Sheppard narrated his experiences differ in their description of various details. Sheppard claimed the vagueness of his perception was caused by his sudden awakening, the dimness of the light, and his loss of consciousness.

[3]  Sheppard was suffering from severe pain in his neck, a swollen eye, and shock.

[4]  But newspaper photographers and reporters were permitted access to Sheppard's home from time to time and took pictures throughout the premises.

the same afternoon a physician sent by the Coroner was permitted to make a detailed examination of Sheppard. Until the Coroner's inquest on July 22, at which time he was subpoenaed, Sheppard made himself available for frequent and extended questioning without the presence of an attorney.

On July 7, the day of Marilyn Sheppard's funeral, a newspaper story appeared in which Assistant County Attorney Mahon—later the chief prosecutor of Sheppard—sharply criticized the refusal of the Sheppard family to permit his immediate questioning. From there on headline stories repeatedly stressed Sheppard's lack of cooperation with the police and other officials. Under the headline 'Testify Now In Death, Bay Doctor Is Ordered,' one story described a visit by Coroner Gerber and four police officers to the hospital on July 8. When Sheppard insisted that his lawyer be present, the Coroner wrote out a subpoena and served it on him. Sheppard then agreed to submit to questioning without counsel and the subpoena was torn up. The officers questioned him for several hours. On July 9, Sheppard, at the request of the Coroner, re-enacted the tragedy at his home before the Coroner, police officers, and a group of newsmen, who apparently were invited by the Coroner. The home was locked so that Sheppard was obliged to wait outside until the Coroner arrived. Sheppard's performance was reported in detail by the news media along with photographs. The newspapers also played up Sheppard's refusal to take a lie detector test and 'the protective ring' thrown up by his family. Front-page newspaper headlines announced on the same day that 'Doctor Balks At Lie Test; Retells Story.' A column opposite that story contained an 'exclusive' interview with Sheppard headlined: "Loved My Wife, She Loved Me," Sheppard Tells News Reporter.' The next day, another headline story disclosed that Sheppard had 'again late yesterday refused to take a lie detector test' and quoted an Assistant County Attorney as saying that 'at the end of a nin-hour questioning of Dr. Sheppard, I felt he was now ruling (a test) out completely.' But subsequent newspaper articles reported that the Coroner was still pushing Sheppard for a lie detector test. More stories appeared when Sheppard would not allow authorities to inject him with 'truth serum.'[5]

On the 20th, the 'editorial artillery' opened fire with a front-page charge that somebody is 'getting away with murder.' The editorial attributed the ineptness of the investigation to 'friendships, relationships, hired lawyers, a

---

[5]    At the same time, the newspapers reported that other possible suspects had been 'cleared' by lie detector tests. One of these persons was quoted as saying that he could not understand why an innocent man would refuse to take such a test.

husband who ought to have been subjected instantly to the same third-degree to which any other person under similar circumstances is subjected.' The following day, July 21, another page-one editorial was headed: 'Why No Inquest? Do It Now, Dr. Gerber.' The Coroner called an inquest the same day and subpoenaed Sheppard. It was staged the next day in a school gymnasium; the Coroner presided with the County Prosecutor as his advisor and two detectives as bailiffs. In the front of the room was a long table occupied by reporters, television and radio personnel, and broadcasting equipment. The hearing was broadcast with live microphones placed at the Coroner's seat and the witness stand. A swarm of reporters and photographers attended. Sheppard was brought into the room by police who searched him in full view of several hundred spectators. Sheppard's counsel were present during the three-day inquest but were not permitted to participate.

When Sheppard's chief counsel attempted to place some documents in the record, he was forcibly ejected from the room by the Coroner, who received cheers, hugs, and kisses from ladies in the audience. Sheppard was questioned for five and one-half hours about his actions on the night of the murder, his married life, and a love affair with Susan Hayes.[6] At the end of the hearing the Coroner announced that he 'could' order Sheppard held for the grand jury, but did not do so.

Throughout this period the newspapers emphasized evidence that tended to incriminate Sheppard and pointed out discrepancies in his statements to authorities. At the same time, Sheppard made many public statements to the press and wrote feature articles asserting his innocence.[7] During the inquest on July 26, a headline in large type stated: 'Kerr (Captain of the Cleveland Police) Urges Sheppard's Arrest.' In the story, Detective McArthur 'disclosed that scientific tests at the Sheppard home have definitely established that the killer washed off a trail of blood from the murder bedroom to the downstairs section,' a circumstance casting doubt on Sheppard's accounts of the murder. No such evidence was produced at trial. The newspapers also delved into Sheppard's personal life. Articles stressed his extramarital love affairs as a motive for the crime. The newspapers portrayed Sheppard as a Lothario, fully explored his relationship with Susan Hayes, and named a number of other women who were allegedly involved with him. The testimony at trial never

---

[6]   The newspapers had heavily emphasized Sheppard's illicit affair with Susan Hayes, and the fact that he had initially lied about it.

[7]   A number of articles calculated to evoke sympathy for Sheppard were printed, such as the letters Sheppard wrote to his son while in jail. These stories often appeared together with news coverage which was unfavorable to him.

showed that Sheppard had any illicit relationships besides the one with Susan Hayes.

On July 28, an editorial entitled 'Why Don't Police Quiz Top Suspect' demanded that Sheppard be taken to police headquarters. It described him in the following language: 'Now proved under oath to be a liar, still free to go about his business, shielded by his family, protected by a smart lawyer who has made monkeys of the police and authorities, carrying a gun part of the time, left free to do whatever he pleases.'

A front-page editorial on July 30 asked: 'Why Isn't Sam Sheppard in Jail?' It was later titled 'Quit Stalling—Bring Him In.' After calling Sheppard 'the most unusual murder suspect ever seen around these parts' the article said that '(e)xcept for some superficial questioning during Coroner Sam Gerber's inquest he has been scot-free of any official grilling.' It asserted that he was 'surrounded by an iron curtain of protection (and) concealment.' That night at 10 o'clock Sheppard was arrested at his father's home on a charge of murder. He was taken to the Bay Village City Hall where hundreds of people, newscasters, photographers and reporters were awaiting his arrival. He was immediately arraigned—having been denied a temporary delay to secure the presence of counsel—and bound over to the grand jury.

The publicity then grew in intensity until his indictment on August 17. Typical of the coverage during this period is a front-page interview entitled: 'DR. SAM: 'I Wish There Was Something I Could Get Off My Chest—but There Isn't.'' Unfavorable publicity included items such as a cartoon of the body of a sphinx with Sheppard's head and the legend below: "I Will Do Everything In My Power to Help Solve This Terrible Murder.'—Dr. Sam Sheppard.' Headlines announced, inter alia, that: 'Doctor Evidence is Ready for Jury,' 'Corrigan Tactics Stall Quizzing.' 'Sheppard 'Gay Set' Is Revealed By Houk,' 'Blood Is Found In Garage,' 'New Murder Evidence Is Found, Police Claim,' 'Dr. Sam Faces Quiz At Jail On Marilyn's Fear Of Him.' On August 18, an article appeared under the headline 'Dr. Sam Writes His Own Story.' And reproduced across the entire front page was a portion of the typed statement signed by Sheppard: 'I am not guilty of the murder of my wife, Marilyn. How could I, who have been trained to help people and devoted my life to saving life, commit such a terrible and revolting crime?' We do not detail the coverage further. There are five volumes filled with similar clippings from each of the three Cleveland newspapers covering the period from the murder until Sheppard's conviction in December 1954. The record includes no excerpts from newscasts on radio and television but since space was reserved in the courtroom for these media we assume that their coverage was equally large.

II.

With this background the case came on for trial two weeks before the November general election at which the chief prosecutor was a candidate for common pleas judge and the trial judge, Judge Blythin, was a candidate to succeed himself. Twenty-five days before the case was set, 75 veniremen were called as prospective jurors. All three Cleveland newspapers published the names and addresses of the veniremen. As a consequence, anonymous letters and telephone calls, as well as calls from friends, regarding the impending prosecution were received by all of the prospective jurors. The selection of the jury began on October 18, 1954.

The courtroom in which the trial was held measured 26 by 48 feet. A long temporary table was set up inside the bar, in back of the single counsel table. It ran the width of the courtroom, parallel to the bar railing, with one end less than three feet from the jury box. Approximately 20 representatives of newspapers and wire services were assigned seats at this table by the court. Behind the bar railing there were four rows of benches. These seats were likewise assigned by the court for the entire trial. The first row was occupied by representatives of television and radio stations, and the second and third rows by reporters from out-of-town newspapers and magazines.

One side of the last row, which accommodated 14 people, was assigned to Sheppard's family and the other to Marilyn's. The public was permitted to fill vacancies in this row on special passes only. Representatives of the news media also used all the rooms on the courtroom floor, including the room where cases were ordinarily called and assigned for trial Private telephone lines and telegraphic equipment were installed in these rooms so that reports from the trial could be speeded to the papers. Station WSRS was permitted to set up broadcasting facilities on the third floor of the courthouse next door to the jury room, where the jury rested during recesses in the trial and deliberated. Newscasts were made from this room throughout the trial, and while the jury reached its verdict.

On the sidewalk and steps in front of the courthouse, television and newsreel cameras were occasionally used to take motion pictures of the participants in the trial, including the jury and the judge. Indeed, one television broadcast carried a staged interview of the judge as he entered the courthouse. In the corridors outside the courtroom there was a host of photographers and television personnel with flash cameras, portable lights and motion picture cameras. This group photographed the prospective jurors during selection of the jury. After the trial opened, the witnesses, counsel, and jurors were photographed and televised whenever they entered or left the courtroom. Sheppard was brought to the courtroom about 10 minutes before each session began; he was surrounded by reporters and extensively photographed for the newspapers and television. A rule of court prohibited picture-taking in the courtroom during the actual sessions of the court, but no restraints were put on photographers during recesses, which were taken once each morning and afternoon, with a longer period for lunch.

All of these arrangements with the news media and their massive coverage of the trial continued during the entire nine weeks of the trial. The courtroom remained crowded to capacity with representatives of news media. Their movement in and out of the courtroom often caused so much confusion that, despite the loud-speaker system installed in the courtroom, it was difficult for the witnesses and counsel to be heard. Furthermore, the reporters clustered within the bar of the small courtroom made confidential talk among Sheppard and his counsel almost impossible during the proceedings. They frequently had to leave the courtroom to obtain privacy. And many times when counsel wished to raise a point with the judge out of the hearing of the jury it was necessary to move to the judge's chambers. Even then, news media representatives so packed the judge's anteroom that counsel could hardly return from the chambers to the courtroom. The reporters vied with each other to find out what counsel and the judge had discussed, and often these matters later appeared in newspapers accessible to the jury.

The daily record of the proceedings was made available to the newspapers and the testimony of each witness was printed verbatim in the local editions, along with objections of counsel, and rulings by the judge. Pictures of Sheppard, the judge, counsel, pertinent witnesses, and the jury often accompanied the daily newspaper and television accounts. At times the newspapers published photographs of exhibits introduced at the trial, and the rooms of Sheppard's house were featured along with relevant testimony.

The jurors themselves were constantly exposed to the news media. Every juror, except one, testified at voir dire to reading about the case in the Cleveland papers or to having heard broadcasts about it. Seven of the 12 jurors who rendered the verdict had one or more Cleveland papers delivered in their home; the remaining jurors were not interrogated on the point. Nor were there questions as to radios or television sets in the jurors' homes, but we must assume that most of them owned such conveniences. As the selection of the jury progressed, individual pictures of prospective members appeared daily. During the trial, pictures of the jury appeared over 40 times in the Cleveland papers alone. The court permitted photographers to take pictures of the jury in the box, and individual pictures of the members in the jury room. One newspaper ran pictures of the jurors at the Sheppard home when they went there to view the scene of the murder. Another paper featured the home life of an alternate juror. The day before the verdict was rendered—while the jurors were at lunch and sequestered by two bailiffs—the jury was separated into two groups to pose for photographs which appeared in the newspapers.

## III.

We now reach the conduct of the trial. While the intense publicity continued unabated, it is sufficient to relate only the more flagrant episodes:

1. On October 9, 1954, nine days before the case went to trial, an editorial in one of the newspapers criticized defense counsel's random poll of people on the streets as to their opinion of Sheppard's guilt or innocence in an effort to use the resulting statistics to show the necessity for change of venue. The article said the survey 'smacks of mass jury tampering,' called on defense counsel to drop it, and stated that the bar association should do something about it. It characterized the poll as 'non-judicial, non-legal, and nonsense.' The article was called to the attention of the court but no action was taken.

2. On the second day of voir dire examination a debate was staged and broadcast live over WHK radio. The participants, newspaper reporters, accused Sheppard's counsel of throwing roadblocks in the way of the prosecution and asserted that Sheppard conceded his guilt by hiring a prominent criminal lawyer. Sheppard's counsel objected to this broadcast and requested a continuance, but the judge denied the motion. When counsel asked the court to give some protection from such events, the judge replied that 'WHK doesn't have much coverage,' and that '(a)fter all, we are not trying this case by radio or in newspapers or any other means. We confine ourselves seriously to it in this courtroom and do the very best we can.'

3. While the jury was being selected, a two-inch headline asked: 'But Who Will Speak for Marilyn?' The frontpage story spoke of the 'perfect face' of the accused. 'Study that face as long as you want. Never will you get from it a hint of what might be the answer.' The two brothers of the accused were described as 'Prosperous, poised. His two sisters-in law. Smart, chic, well-groomed. His elderly father. Courtly, reserved. A perfect type for the patriarch

of a staunch clan.' The author then noted Marilyn Sheppard was 'still off stage,' and that she was an only child whose mother died when she was very young and whose father had no interest in the case. But the author—through quotes from Detective Chief James McArthur—assured readers that the prosecution's exhibits would speak for Marilyn. 'Her story,' McArthur stated, 'will come into this courtroom through our witnesses.' The article ends:

> 'Then you realize how what and who is missing from the perfect setting will be supplied.
>
> 'How in the Big Case justice will be done.
>
> 'Justice to Sam Sheppard.
>
> 'And to Marilyn Sheppard.'

4.    As has been mentioned, the jury viewed the scene of the murder on the first day of the trial. Hundreds of reporters, cameramen and onlookers were there, and one representative of the news media was permitted to accompany the jury while it inspected the Sheppard home. The time of the jury's visit was revealed so far in advance that one of the newspapers was able to rent a helicopter and fly over the house taking pictures of the jurors on their tour.

5.    On November 19, a Cleveland police officer gave testimony that tended to contradict details in the written statement Sheppard made to the Cleveland police. Two days later, in a broadcast heard over Station WHK in Cleveland, Robert Considine likened Sheppard to a perjurer and compared the episode to Alger Hiss' confrontation with Whittaker Chambers. Though defense counsel asked the judge to question the jury to ascertain how many heard the broadcast, the court refused to do so. The judge also overruled the motion for continuance based on the same ground, saying:

> 'Well, I don't know, we can't stop people, in any event, listening to it. It is a matter of free speech, and the court can't control everybody. * * * We are not going to harass the jury every morning. * * * It is getting to the point where if we do it every morning, we are suspecting the jury. I have confidence in this jury * * *.'

6.    On November 24, a story appeared under an eight-column headline: 'Sam Called A 'Jekyll-Hyde' By Marilyn, Cousin To Testify.' It related that Marilyn had recently told friends that Sheppard was a 'Dr. Jekyll and Mr. Hyde' character. No such testimony was ever produced at the trial. The story went on to announce: 'The prosecution has a 'bombshell witness' on tap who will testify to Dr. Sam's display of fiery temper—countering the defense claim that the defendant is a gently physician with an even disposition.' Defense counsel

made motions for change of venue, continuance and mistrial, but they were denied. No action was taken by the court.

7.   When the trial was in its seventh week, Walter Winchell broadcast over WXEL television and WJW radio that Carole Beasley, who was under arrest in New York City for robbery, had stated that, as Sheppard's mistress, she had borne him a child. The defense asked that the jury be queried on the broadcast. Two jurors admitted in open court that they had heard it. The judge asked each: 'Would that have any effect upon your judgment?' Both replied, 'No.' This was accepted by the judge as sufficient; he merely asked the jury to 'pay no attention whatever to that type of scavenging. Let's confine ourselves to this courtroom, if you please.' In answer to the motion for mistrial, the judge said:

> 'Well, even, so, Mr. Corrigan, how are you ever going to prevent those things, in any event? I don't justify them at all. I think it is outrageous, but in a sense, it is outrageous even if there were no trial here. The trial has nothing to do with it in the Court's mind, as far as its outrage is concerned, but—
>
> 'Mr. CORRIGAN: I don't know what effect it had on the mind of any of these jurors, and I can't find out unless inquiry is made.
>
> 'The COURT: How would you ever, in any jury, avoid that kind of a thing?'

8.   On December 9, while Sheppard was on the witness stand he testified that he had been mistreated by Cleveland detectives after his arrest. Although he was not at the trial, Captain Kerr of the Homicide Bureau issued a press statement denying Sheppard's allegations which appeared under the headline: " 'Bare-faced Liar,' Kerr Says of Sam." Captain Kerr never appeared as a witness at the trial.

9.   After the case was submitted to the jury, it was sequestered for its deliberations, which took five days and four nights. After the verdict, defense counsel ascertained that the jurors had been allowed to make telephone calls to their homes every day while they were sequestered at the hotel. Although the telephones had been removed from the jurors' rooms, the jurors were permitted to use the phones in the bailiffs' rooms. The calls were placed by the jurors themselves; no record was kept of the jurors who made calls, the telephone numbers or the parties called. The bailiffs sat in the room where they could hear only the jurors' end of the conversation. The court had not instructed the bailiffs to prevent such calls. By a subsequent motion, defense

counsel urged that this ground alone warranted a new trial, but the motion was overruled and no evidence was taken on the question.

## IV.

The principle that justice cannot survive behind walls of silence has long been reflected in the 'Anglo-American distrust for secret trials.' *In re Oliver*, 333 U.S. 257, 268 (1948). A responsible press has always been regarded as the handmaiden of effective judicial administration, especially in the criminal field. Its function in this regard is documented by an impressive record of service over several centuries. The press does not simply publish information about trials but guards against the miscarriage of justice by subjecting the police, prosecutors, and judicial processes to extensive public scrutiny and criticism. This Court has, therefore, been unwilling to place any direct limitations on the freedom traditionally exercised by the news media for '(w)hat transpires in the court room is public property.' *Craig v. Harney*, 331 U.S. 367, 374 (1947). The 'unqualified prohibitions laid down by the framers were intended to give to liberty of the press the broadest scope that could be countenanced in an orderly society.'. . . And where there was 'no threat or menace to the integrity of the trial. . . we have consistently required that the press have a free hand, even though we sometimes deplored its sensationalism.

But the Court has also pointed out that '(l)egal trials are not like elections, to be won through the use of the meeting-hall, the radio, and the newspaper.' . . . And the Court has insisted that no one be punished for a crime without 'a charge fairly made and fairly tried in a public tribunal free of prejudice, passion, excitement, and tyrannical power.' *Chambers v. State of Florida*, 309 U.S. 227, 236–237 (1940). 'Freedom of discussion should be given the widest range compatible with the essential requirement of the fair and orderly administration of justice.' *Pennekamp v. State of Florida*, 328 U.S. 331, 347 (1946). But it must not be allowed to divert the trial from the 'very purpose of a court system to adjudicate controversies, both criminal and civil, in the calmness and solemnity of the courtroom according to legal procedures.' *Cox v. State of Louisiana*, 379 U.S. 559, 583 (1965) (Black, J., dissenting). Among these 'legal procedures' is the requirement that the jury's verdict be based on evidence received in open court, not from outside sources. Thus, in *Marshall v. United States*, 360 U.S. 310 (1959), we set aside a federal conviction where the jurors were exposed 'through news accounts' to information that was not admitted at trial. We held that the prejudice from such material 'may indeed be greater' than when it is part of the prosecution's evidence 'for it is then not tempered by protective procedures.' At 313, 79 S.Ct. at 1173. . . .

The undeviating rule of this Court was expressed by Mr. Justice Holmes over half a century ago in *Patterson v. State of Colorado ex rel. Attorney General*, 205 U.S. 454, 462 (1907): 'The theory of our system is that the conclusions to be reached in a case will be induced only by evidence and argument in open court, and not by any outside influence, whether of private talk or public print.'. . .

## V.

It is clear that the totality of circumstances in this case also warrants such an approach. Unlike Estes, Sheppard was not granted a change of venue to a locale away from where the publicity originated; nor was his jury sequestered. The Estes jury saw none of the television broadcasts from the courtroom. On the contrary, the Sheppard jurors were subjected to newspaper, radio and television coverage of the trial while not taking part in the proceedings. They were allowed to go their separate ways outside of the courtroom, without adequate directions not to read or listen to anything concerning the case. The judge's 'admonitions' at the beginning of the trial are representative:

'I would suggest to you and caution you that you do not read any newspapers during the progress of this trial, that you do not listen to radio comments nor watch or listen to television comments, insofar as this case is concerned. You will feel very much better as the trial proceeds. I am sure that we shall all feel very much better if we do not indulge in any newspaper reading or listening to any comments whatever about the matter while the case is in progress. After it is all over, you can read it all to your heart's content.'

At intervals during the trial, the judge simply repeated his 'suggestions' and 'requests' that the jurors not expose themselves to comment upon the case. Moreover, the jurors were thrust into the role of celebrities by the judge's failure to insulate them from reporters and photographers. . . . The numerous pictures of the jurors, with their addresses, which appeared in the newspapers before and during the trial itself exposed them to expressions of opinion from both cranks and friends. The fact that anonymous letters had been received by prospective jurors should have made the judge aware that this publicity seriously threatened the jurors' privacy.

The press coverage of the Estes trial was not nearly as massive and pervasive as the attention given by the Cleveland newspapers and broadcasting stations to Sheppard's prosecution.[8] Sheppard stood indicted for the murder of his wife; the State was demanding the death penalty. For months the virulent

---

[8] Many more reporters and photographers attended the Sheppard trial. And it attracted several nationally famous commentators as well.

publicity about Sheppard and the murder had made the case notorious. Charges and countercharges were aired in the news media besides those for which Sheppard was called to trial. In addition, only three months before trial, Sheppard was examined for more than five hours without counsel during a three-day inquest which ended in a public brawl. The inquest was televised live from a high school gymnasium seating hundreds of people. Furthermore, the trial began two weeks before a hotly contested election at which both Chief Prosecutor Mahon and Judge Blythin were candidates for judgeships.[9]

While we cannot say that Sheppard was denied due process by the judge's refusal to take precautions against the influence of pretrial publicity alone, the court's later rulings must be considered against the setting in which the trial was held. In light of this background, we believe that the arrangements made by the judge with the news media caused Sheppard to be deprived of that 'judicial serenity and calm to which (he) was entitled.' *Estes v. State of Texas*, supra, 381 U.S., at 536, 85 S.Ct., at 1629. The fact is that bedlam reigned at the courthouse during the trial and newsmen took over practically the entire courtroom, hounding most of the participants in the trial, especially Sheppard. At a temporary table within a few feet of the jury box and counsel table sat some 20 reporters staring at Sheppard and taking notes. The erection of a press table for reporters inside the bar is unprecedented. The bar of the court is reserved for counsel, providing them a safe place in which to keep papers and exhibits, and to confer privately with client and co-counsel. It is designed to protect the witness and the jury from any distractions, intrusions or influences, and to permit bench discussions of the judge's rulings away from the hearing of the public and the jury. Having assigned almost all of the available seats in the courtroom to the news media the judge lost his ability to supervise that environment. The movement of the reporters in and out of the courtroom caused frequent confusion and disruption of the trial. And the record reveals constant commotion within the bar. Moreover, the judge gave the throng of newsmen gathered in the corridors of the courthouse absolute free rein. Participants in the trial, including the jury, were forced to run a gantlet of

---

[9]  At the commencement of trial, defense counsel made motions for continuance and change of venue. The judge postponed ruling on these motions until he determined whether an impartial jury could be impaneled. Voir dire examination showed that with one exception all members selected for jury service had read something about the case in the newspapers. Since, however, all of the jurors stated that they would not be influenced by what they had read or seen, the judge overruled both of the motions. Without regard to whether the judge's actions in this respect reach dimensions that would justify issuance of the habeas writ, it should be noted that a short continuance would have alleviated any problem with regard to the judicial elections. The court in *Delaney v. United States*, 199 F.2d 107, 115 (C.A.1st. Cir. 1952), recognized such a duty under similar circumstances, holding that 'if assurance of a fair trial would necessitate that the trial of the case be postponed until after the election, then we think the law required no less than that.'

reporters and photographers each time they entered or left the courtroom. The total lack of consideration for the privacy of the jury was demonstrated by the assignment to a broadcasting station of space next to the jury room on the floor above the courtroom, as well as the fact that jurors were allowed to make telephone calls during their five-day deliberation.

## VI.

There can be no question about the nature of the publicity which surrounded Sheppard's trial. We agree, as did the Court of Appeals, with the findings in Judge Bell's opinion for the Ohio Supreme Court:

'Murder and mystery, society, sex and suspense were combined in this case in such a manner as to intrigue and captivate the public fancy to a degree perhaps unparalleled in recent annals. Throughout the preindictment investigation, the subsequent legal skirmishes and the nine-week trial, circulation-conscious editors catered to the insatiable interest of the American public in the bizarre. In this atmosphere of a 'Roman holiday' for the news media, Sam Sheppard stood trial for his life.' 165 Ohio St., at 294, 135 N.E.2d, at 342.

Indeed, every court that has considered this case, save the court that tried it, has deplored the manner in which the news media inflamed and prejudiced the public.[10]

Much of the material printed or broadcast during the trial was never heard from the witness stand, such as the charges that Sheppard had purposely impeded the murder investigation and must be guilty since he had hired a prominent criminal lawyer; that Sheppard was a perjurer; that he had sexual relations with numerous women; that his slain wife had characterized him as a 'Jekyll-Hyde'; that he was 'a bare-faced liar' because of his testimony as to police treatment; and finally, that a woman convict claimed Sheppard to be the father of her illegitimate child. As the trial progressed, the newspapers summarized and interpreted the evidence, devoting particular attention to the material that incriminated Sheppard, and often drew unwarranted inferences from

---

[10]   Typical comments on the trial by the press itself include:

'The question of Dr. Sheppard's guilt or innocence still is before the courts. Those who have examined the trial record carefully are divided as to the propriety of the verdict. But almost everyone who watched the performance of the Cleveland press agrees that a fair hearing for the defendant, in that area, would be a modern miracle.' Harrison, 'The press vs. the Courts,' The Saturday Review (Oct. 15, 1955).

'At this distance, some 100 miles from Cleveland, it looks to us as though the Sheppard murder case was sensationalized to the point at which the press must ask itself if its freedom, carried to excess, doesn't interfere with the conduct of fair trials.' Editorial, The Toledo Blade (Dec. 22, 1954).

testimony. At one point, a front-page picture of Mrs. Sheppard's blood-stained pillow was published after being 'doctored' to show more clearly an alleged imprint of a surgical instrument.

Nor is there doubt that this deluge of publicity reached at least some of the jury. On the only occasion that the jury was queried, two jurors admitted in open court to hearing the highly inflammatory charge that a prison inmate claimed Sheppard as the father of her illegitimate child. Despite the extent and nature of the publicity to which the jury was exposed during trial, the judge refused defense counsel's other requests that the jurors be asked whether they had read or heard specific prejudicial comment about the case, including the incidents we have previously summarized. In these circumstances, we can assume that some of this material reached members of the jury. See *Commonwealth v. Crehan*, 345 Mass. 609, 188 N.E.2d 923 (1963).

## VII.

The court's fundamental error is compounded by the holding that it lacked power to control the publicity about the trial. From the very inception of the proceedings the judge announced that neither he nor anyone else could restrict prejudicial news accounts. And he reiterated this view on numerous occasions. Since he viewed the news media as his target, the judge never considered other means that are often utilized to reduce the appearance of prejudicial material and to protect the jury from outside influence. We conclude that these procedures would have been sufficient to guarantee Sheppard a fair trial and so do not consider what sanctions might be available against a recalcitrant press nor the charges of bias now made against the state trial judge.[11]

The carnival atmosphere at trial could easily have been avoided since the courtroom and courthouse premises are subject to the control of the court. As we stressed in Estes, the presence of the press at judicial proceedings must be limited when it is apparent that the accused might otherwise be prejudiced or disadvantaged.[12] Bearing in mind the massive pretrial publicity, the judge should have adopted stricter rules governing the use of the courtroom by newsmen, as Sheppard's counsel requested. The number of reporters in the

---

[11] In an unsworn statement, which the parties agreed would have the status of a deposition, made 10 years after Sheppard's conviction and six years after Judge Blythin's death, Dorothy Kilgallen asserted that Judge Blythin had told her: 'It's an open and shut case * * * he is guilty as hell.' It is thus urged that Sheppard be released on the ground that the judge's bias infected the entire trial. But we need not reach this argument, since the judge's failure to insulate the proceedings from prejudicial publicity and disruptive influences deprived Sheppard of the chance to receive a fair hearing.

[12] The judge's awareness of his power in this respect is manifest from his assignment of seats to the press.

courtroom itself could have been limited at the first sign that their presence would disrupt the trial. They certainly should not have been placed inside the bar. Furthermore, the judge should have more closely regulated the conduct of newsmen in the courtroom. For instance, the judge belatedly asked them not to handle and photograph trial exhibits lying on the counsel table during recesses.

Secondly, the court should have insulated the witnesses. All of the newspapers and radio stations apparently interviewed prospective witnesses at will, and in many instances disclosed their testimony. A typical example was the publication of numerous statements by Susan Hayes, before her appearance in court, regarding her love affair with Sheppard. Although the witnesses were barred from the courtroom during the trial the full verbatim testimony was available to them in the press. This completely nullified the judge's imposition of the rule. See *Estes v. State of Texas*, supra, 381 U.S., at 547, 85 S.Ct., at 1635.

Thirdly, the court should have made some effort to control the release of leads, information, and gossip to the press by police officers, witnesses, and the counsel for both sides. Much of the information thus disclosed was inaccurate, leading to groundless rumors and confusion.[13] That the judge was aware of his responsibility in this respect may be seen from his warning to Steve Sheppard, the accused's brother, who had apparently made public statements in an attempt to discredit testimony for the prosecution. The judge made this statement in the presence of the jury:

> 'Now, the Court wants to say a word. That he was told—he has not read anything about it at all—but he was informed that Dr. Steve Sheppard, who has been granted the privilege of remaining in the court room during the trial, has been trying the case in the newspapers and making rather uncomplimentary comments about the testimony of the witnesses for the State.
>
> 'Let it be now understood that if Dr. Steve Sheppard wishes to use the newspapers to try his case while we are trying it here, he will be

---

[13] The problem here was further complicated by the independent action of the newspapers in reporting 'evidence' and gossip which they uncovered. The press not only inferred that Sheppard was guilty because he 'stalled' the investigation, hid behind his family, and hired a prominent criminal lawyer, but denounced as 'mass jury tampering' his efforts to gather evidence of community prejudice caused by such publications. Sheppard's counterattacks added some fuel but, in these circumstances, cannot preclude him from asserting his right to a fair trial. Putting to one side news stories attributed to police officials, prospective witnesses, the Sheppards, and the lawyers, it is possible that the other publicity 'would itself have had a prejudicial effect.' Cf. Report of the President's Commission on the Assassination of President Kennedy, at 239.

barred from remaining in the court room during the progress of the trial if he is to be a witness in the case.

'The Court appreciates he cannot deny Steve Sheppard the right of free speech, but he can deny him the privilege of being in the courtroom, if he wants to avail himself of that method during the progress of the trial.'

Defense counsel immediately brought to the court's attention the tremendous amount of publicity in the Cleveland press that 'misrepresented entirely the testimony' in the case. Under such circumstances, the judge should have at least warned the newspapers to check the accuracy of their accounts. And it is obvious that the judge should have further sought to alleviate this problem by imposing control over the statements made to the news media by counsel, witnesses, and especially the Coroner and police officers. The prosecution repeatedly made evidence available to the news media which was never offered in the trial. Much of the 'evidence' disseminated in this fashion was clearly inadmissible. The exclusion of such evidence in court is rendered meaningless when news media make it available to the public. For example, the publicity about Sheppard's refusal to take a lie detector test came directly from police officers and the Coroner.[14] The story that Sheppard had been called a 'Jekyll-Hyde' personality by his wife was attributed to a prosecution witness. No such testimony was given. The further report that there was 'a 'bombshell witness' on tap' who would testify as to Sheppard's 'fiery temper' could only have emanated from the prosecution. Moreover, the newspapers described in detail clues that had been found by the police, but not put into the record.[15]

The fact that many of the prejudicial news items can be traced to the prosecution, as well as the defense, aggravates the judge's failure to take any action. See *Stroble v. State of California*, 343 U.S. 181, 201, 72 S.Ct. 599, 609, 96 L.Ed. 872 (1952) (Frankfurter, J., dissenting). Effective control of these sources—concededly within the court's power—might well have prevented the divulgence of inaccurate information, rumors, and accusations that made up much of the inflammatory publicity, at least after Sheppard's indictment.

---

[14] When two police officers testified at trial that Sheppard refused to take a lie detector test, the judge declined to give a requested instruction that the results of such a test would be inadmissible in any event. He simply told the jury that no person has an obligation 'to take any lie detector test.'

[15] Such 'premature disclosure and weighing of the evidence' may seriously jeopardize a defendant's right to an impartial jury. '(N)either the press nor the public had a right to be contemporaneously informed by the police or prosecuting authorities of the details of the evidence being accumulated against (Sheppard).' Cf. Report of the President's Commission, supra, at 239, 240.

More specifically, the trial court might well have proscribed extrajudicial statements by any lawyer, party, witness, or court official which divulged prejudicial matters, such as the refusal of Sheppard to submit to interrogation or take any lie detector tests; any statement made by Sheppard to officials; the identity of prospective witnesses or their probable testimony; any belief in guilt or innocence; or like statements concerning the merits of the case. See *State v. Van Duyne*, 43 N.J., 369, 389 (1964), in which the court interpreted Canon 20 of the American Bar Association's Canons of Professional Ethics to prohibit such statements. Being advised of the great public interest in the case, the mass coverage of the press, and the potential prejudicial impact of publicity, the court could also have requested the appropriate city and county officials to promulgate a regulation with respect to dissemination of information about the case by their employees.[16] In addition, reporters who wrote or broadcast prejudicial stories, could have been warned as to the impropriety of publishing material not introduced in the proceedings. The judge was put on notice of such events by defense counsel's complaint about the WHK broadcast on the second day of trial. See p. 1513, supra. In this manner, Sheppard's right to a trial free from outside interference would have been given added protection without corresponding curtailment of the news media. Had the judge, the other officers of the court, and the police placed the interest of justice first, the news media would have soon learned to be content with the task of reporting the case as it unfolded in the courtroom—not pieced together from extrajudicial statements.

From the cases coming here we note that unfair and prejudicial news comment on pending trials has become increasingly prevalent. Due process requires that the accused receive a trial by an impartial jury free from outside influences. Given the pervasiveness of modern communications and the difficulty of effacing prejudicial publicity from the minds of the jurors, the trial courts must take strong measures to ensure that the balance is never weighed against the accused. And appellate tribunals have the duty to make an independent evaluation of the circumstances. Of course, there is nothing that proscribes the press from reporting events that transpire in the courtroom. But where there is a reasonable likelihood that prejudicial news prior to trial will prevent a fair trial, the judge should continue the case until the threat abates, or transfer it to another county not so permeated with publicity. In addition,

---

[16]   The Department of Justice, the City of New York, and other governmental agencies have issued such regulations. E.g., 28 CFR s 50.2 (1966). For general information on this topic see periodic publications (e.g., Nos. 71, 124, and 158) by the Freedom of Information Center, School of Journalism, University of Missouri.

sequestration of the jury was something the judge should have raised sua sponte with counsel. If publicity during the proceedings threatens the fairness of the trial, a new trial should be ordered. But we must remember that reversals are but palliatives; the cure lies in those remedial measures that will prevent the prejudice at its inception. The courts must take such steps by rule and regulation that will protect their processes from prejudicial outside interferences. Neither prosecutors, counsel for defense, the accused, witnesses, court staff nor enforcement officers coming under the jurisdiction of the court should be permitted to frustrate its function. Collaboration between counsel and the press as to information affecting the fairness of a criminal trial is not only subject to regulation, but is highly censurable and worthy of disciplinary measures.

Since the state trial judge did not fulfill his duty to protect Sheppard from the inherently prejudicial publicity which saturated the community and to control disruptive influences in the courtroom, we must reverse the denial of the habeas petition. The case is remanded to the District Court with instructions to issue the writ and order that Sheppard be released from custody unless the State puts him to its charges again within a reasonable time.

It is so ordered.

**MR. JUSTICE BLACK dissents.**

## After preparing the case brief, consider the answers to the following questions:

1.    The Court begins by discussing the importance of a free press. What are some of the reasons they cite?

2.    What specific information that was shared in the press stands out as particularly damaging to Sheppard's fair trial?

3.    The Court states: "Due process requires that the accused receive a trial by an impartial jury free from outside influences. Given the pervasiveness of modern communications and the difficulty of effacing prejudicial publicity from the minds of the jurors, the trial courts must take strong measures to ensure that the balance is never weighed against the accused." Consider that this decision was written in 1966, is it possible for courts to achieve this in the age of digital media?

## Chapter 10 Key Terms for Review

- **Jury trial**: a trial where the fact-finders, or decision makers, are members of the community "a jury of your peers." Guaranteed by Article II, Sec. 2 of the Constitution, and the Sixth Amendment.

- **Bench trial**: a trial where the fact-finder is the judge rather than a jury.

- **Closure of a case**: in certain circumstances the judge can close proceedings in a trial to the public but must do so in the least restrictive way possible.

- **Summons**: a legal order sent to potential jurors to appear for jury service.

- **Venire**: the pool of people from which potential jurors are selected.

- **Voir dire**: the process of questioning and selecting jurors for a case.

- **Dismissal for cause**: when a juror demonstrates bias or prejudice, or has a conflict of interest such as a relationship to a party in the case, they will be dismissed for cause.

- **Peremptory challenge**: allows for removal of jurors without cause, so long as there is no unlawful reason for their exclusion.

- **Opening statements**: signal the start of the trial and are offered by attorneys for each side. Opening statements should point to what the evidence will show in an objective way.

- **Evidence**: information presented to the jury in a criminal trial. Four basic categories of evidence are real (tangible things), demonstrative (models/examples), documentary (papers or documents) and testimonial (witness testimony).

- **Expert witness**: a person whose knowledge or training qualifies them to offer testimony about or analysis of facts presented at trial.

- **Closing argument**: made by the prosecution and defense and are intended to persuade the jury to agree with their position.

- **Rebuttal**: the prosecutor's response to the defendant's closing argument before the case is given to the jury for deliberation.

- **Jury instructions**: basic rules provided by the judge to the jury governing their deliberations and very specific rules about the law and what is required to make a finding of guilt.

- **Sua sponte jury instructions**: must be given by the judge even without a request by one of the parties.

- **Domestic violence**: violent or aggressive behavior within the home, typically between spouses or intimate partners.

# Sentencing

Much of the attention in the criminal justice system is on the dramatic aspects of a case—like the arrest and the trial—but the sentencing phase of the process is vital to understanding the American judicial system. In fact, the question of what should be done with people who have been convicted of crimes is an ancient one.

In 2015, the United States had approximately 2.2 million people in jails or prisons, in the state and federal systems.[1] About 93% of federal criminal cases end in a conviction. Because of the fragmented nature of our criminal justice system, statistics for state court conviction rates are more difficult to track. A study of the largest 75 counties in the nation has shown that about 66% of criminal cases filed resulted in a conviction[2] (just over half of the cases charged resulted in a felony conviction, and 12% of those arrested were convicted of a misdemeanor). In most cases where a defendant was not convicted, it was because the charges were dismissed. About 9% of cases resolved with a diversion program.

## A. PURPOSE OF SENTENCING

There are five major justifications for sentencing: retribution, deterrence, rehabilitation, incapacitation, and restoration. Each of these has different goals, yet each is reflected to some extent in our sentencing law and practice.

**Retribution** as punishment seeks to settle the score with the offender, to ensure he or she get her "just deserts." The defendant has done something wrong, and therefore, deserves to be punished. Retributive sentencing seeks to match the severity of the wrong with the punishment—a proportional response to the crime. A different model of sentencing looks at punishment as a **deterrence**. A sentence will send a message to the defendant (specific deterrence) and to the public

---

[1]   *Prisoners in 2015*, Bureau of Justice Statistics, December 2016.

[2]   Reaves, B., *Felony Defendants in Large Urban Counties*, 2009, Bureau of Justice Statistics (2013).

(general deterrence) that crime does not pay. This is a forward-looking theory of punishment that aims to prevent future crimes.

**Rehabilitation** attempts to diagnose and address the underlying reasons for the defendant's criminal conduct. This theory supports the principle that society benefits by treating the defendant's mental illness, addiction, or other disorder, rather than merely cycling him through the criminal justice system unchanged— or worse, more likely to commit another crime.

The **incapacitation** justification also attempts to prevent future crimes, but does so by banishing the defendant from society for a period of time. Physically removing the person from the community keeps the public safe from that individual's future crimes. Unlike deterrence, which also seeks to prevent future crimes, incapacitation does not attempt to change the defendant.

**Restoration** or **restorative justice** focuses on the victims and the community affected by the crime, as much as it does on the offender. This theory rejects the idea of retribution, which provides no healing for victims. The aim of restoration is to repair the damage caused by the crime through reconciliation.

## B. TYPES OF SENTENCING SCHEMES

Sentencing laws are passed by legislatures. These lawmakers are responsible for setting the minimum and maximum sentencing ranges for all crimes. Some sentencing laws restrict judges' discretion more than others, such as mandatory minimum sentences. There are two types of sentencing schemes: determinate and indeterminate sentencing.

In a court system with a **determinate sentencing** scheme, the legislature sets a presumptive range for a criminal conviction, and the judge can impose a definite term of incarceration within that range. The offender can earn time off that sentence with good behavior or by demonstrating rehabilitation. In some systems, this is called "good time credits."

In the federal criminal system, a defendant can earn up to 54 days per year off a sentence. For example, if a defendant were sentenced to a term of 60 months, he could expect to spend approximately 51 months in prison. This amounts to just fewer than 15% off.

**Indeterminate sentencing** laws give judges a range of years, such as zero to 20 years, that may be imposed for certain convictions. When the judge imposes a sentence that has a low and high-end, that means the offender will serve at least the minimum term, but no more than the high-end of the sentencing range of the imposed term. The idea behind this structure is that an offender can earn his or her way out of prison with proof of rehabilitation. After the offender has served the minimum term, a **parole board** can allow the offender to be released.

## C. MANDATORY MINIMUM SENTENCES

**Mandatory minimum sentences** take the discretion in sentencing away from the judges—which was the purpose behind such sentencing laws. These laws set by statute the lowest term of incarceration that a judge may impose for a conviction. These statutes often come about because the legislature or the public do not trust that judges will sentence offenders to prison for a length of time that fits the crime. In cases where a person is convicted of violating a law that specifies a mandatory sentence, the judge has no choice but to impose that term, even if there are good reasons to impose a lower sentence on a particular defendant. Three-strikes sentencing laws are an example of mandatory minimum sentencing statutes. They require a specific minimum sentence for offenders who have a prior criminal history and commit certain specified offenses.

## D. INCARCERATION

All felonies and most misdemeanor criminal convictions carry a potential sentence of **incarceration**. Incarceration is confinement or imprisonment in a correctional institution such as a jail or prison. Misdemeanor crimes can be punished by up to one year in jail. Felony convictions can carry far longer terms, usually served in prisons, not county jails.

## E. ALTERNATIVES TO INCARCERATION

Some crimes do not merit being locked up in prison and for these offenses, judges have other options available. The most common of these is **probation**, a period of time during which the offender is under the supervision of a probation officer. This type of sentence allows the offender to live at home and keep his or her job, but still be accountable to the court. Probation terms typically include travel restrictions, curfews, or drug testing. The terms can be tailored to the individual. If a defendant has a history of drug abuse, the court can order regular drug testing or counseling. A defendant who has been ordered to pay a fine or to reimburse a victim (see *restitution*, below) can be ordered to make a monthly payment toward that debt.

If a defendant violates a term of probation, the court can increase the supervision or alter the probation terms to address the underlying issue, such as ordering an offender to attend a rehabilitation program if he fails a drug test. Or the judge can impose a short jail term. **Home confinement** is similar to probation, and sometimes is a condition of probation that is more intensive. The offender is restricted to their home, with the exception of pre-authorized windows of time when they can go to work, school, to medical appointments, or attend religious services. The restrictions are monitored either by unannounced visits by a probation officer, or by electronic monitoring, typically via an electronic ankle monitor.

Some sentences will also require that the offender spend a specified number of hours performing **community service**. The service can include volunteer work at a local nonprofit agency, or can include work detail directed by law enforcement, such as removing litter in parks or on roadways. **Diversion programs** are slightly different than these other sentencing options. With a diversion program, the defendant agrees to participate in a treatment program—usually drug rehabilitation or counseling—and upon completion, if the defendant has stayed out of trouble, the charge will be dismissed.

## F. FINES AND RESTITUTION

Another type of sanction that defendants can face is monetary penalties—a **fine** that is paid to the government as part of a sentence.[3] The amount of a fine is based on the defendant's ability to pay, and on the severity of the conviction.[4] Because most defendants qualify for appointed counsel, fines do not get imposed as often as other penalties. In those cases, judges often find the defendant lacks the ability to pay a fine and will waive it.

For some criminal defendants, however, a fine is the only real punishment that is available. In cases where the government has brought criminal charges against a **corporate defendant**, often the only way to punish is by imposing a large financial penalty. Sentencing guidelines in federal cases against corporations do not consider whether the defendant has the ability to pay the fine, only that it not interfere with any restitution order that directs money to victims.

Where a criminal act has caused a victim to incur a financial loss, the defendant may also face **restitution**—a court order to repay the victims for their actual loss. The goal of restitution is to make the victim whole. In some cases, this

---

[3]    *See*, e.g., 18 U.S.C. § 3571 ("A defendant who has been found guilty of an offense may be sentenced to pay a fine.").

[4]    Goodwin, C., *Federal Criminal Restitution* (2012), § 12:3, p. 591.

is easy to calculate. A defendant steals a car. The court can order the defendant to repay the victim the value of the car.

In other situations, losses claimed by a victim are harder to calculate, or to trace directly to the crime. Restitution can be ordered when the loss was a reasonably foreseeable harm of the offense—like clean up costs for a criminal violation of the Clean Water Act that led to pollution of a waterway.[5] But it would not include routine costs that would be incurred regardless of the defendant's criminal conduct.

Take a hypothetical case of an employer who uncovers embezzlement by a bookkeeper. The employee is immediately fired and escorted off the premises. The business has to conduct an audit to determine the loss. This audit is not routine, but is directly a result of the theft, so the victim could ask for that cost to be reimbursed. However, the business would not be able to get restitution for routine costs associated with any employee termination, such as the cost to have the office keys replaced.

## G. SENTENCING HEARINGS

After a defendant has been found guilty at trial or has pleaded guilty to criminal charges, the sentencing phase begins. At this point, the attention shifts from determining what happened on one specific occasion to an examination of the defendant's life as a whole. The purpose of putting the criminal conduct into a larger context is to aid the judge in deciding a proper sanction that will achieve the sentencing goals set out in the law. In misdemeanor cases, this will sometimes follow a guilty plea immediately. But when the judge needs more information before imposing a sentence, and in the case of felony convictions, the case will get referred to the probation department.

A probation officer will conduct a **pre-sentence investigation (PSI)** into the defendant's history and the facts of the case. This will include an interview to learn about the defendant's family background, employment history, mental and physical health, finances, and any prior criminal record. The final report by the probation officer will also include a review of the evidence in the criminal case, in particular, the defendant's role in the offense. The PSI is a vital tool that provides the judge more personal information about the person who is being sentenced. With the vast majority of cases settling without a trial—about 94% resolve with a plea agreement. The PSI is how the judge learns about the details of the case, as well as the defendant's role in it. Often the PSI will include an analysis of the

---

[5]  *United States v. Phillips*, 356 F.3d 1086 (9th Cir. 2004).

available sentencing options, and in some cases, a recommendation of what sentence the judge should impose. The report, called a **pre-sentence report** (PSR), contains such detailed personal information that it is kept confidential. It is released only to the prosecutor, defense attorney, and judge, and is not filed in the public record. After both sides have had a chance to review the PSR and file any objections to it, the judge conducts the sentencing hearing, at which time the defendant will learn his or her fate.

Sentencing hearings can be routine in cases where the facts are not in dispute and all parties are in relative agreement as to the appropriate sentence. They can also be contentious, with both sides presenting additional evidence to the judge to influence the length of the sentence. Prosecutors may bring in **aggravating evidence** that shows the defendant deserves a longer sentence—such as proof that the defendant was a ringleader in the criminal conduct, lacks remorse for his crime, abused a position of trust, or attempted to obstruct justice by lying on the stand or by intimidating witnesses. Conversely, the defense may introduce **mitigating evidence** that lessens the defendant's culpability, such as a history of addiction, mental illness, or other circumstances that might explain (though not excuse) the criminal conduct. It could also include information about the defendant's limited role in the case, such as a drug courier who did not know the larger scope of the drug-trafficking operation. And it could also address the defendant's successful addiction treatment since the offense, his marital or family situation, or current employment, all of which might convince the judge that a long prison sentence is not necessary to rehabilitate this individual.

Judges also sometimes hear from the victims, who are permitted to make a **victim impact statement** at the sentencing hearing. These statements can be letters submitted to the court, possibly read out loud by a prosecutor during the hearing, or in-person testimony during the court hearing. This allows the judge to hear about the emotional, physical, or financial toll that the defendant's criminal conduct caused. In *Payne v. Tennessee (1991)* the U.S. Supreme Court held that victim impact testimony at sentencing does not violate the Eighth Amendment.[6]

The judge has the final word in determining the sentence imposed and must consider all that evidence before applying the law and announcing his or her decision. In most criminal convictions, the law will give the judge discretion in fashioning a sentence, though some convictions carry a **mandatory minimum sentence** which sets the lowest possible prison term a judge can impose.

---

[6]   501 U.S. 808.

Sentencing laws incorporate the goals of the various theories discussed previously. For example, the federal sentencing statute 18 U.S.C. § 3553(a) directs the judge to impose a sentence "sufficient, but not greater than necessary" to meet the goals of the sentencing law. That includes the need to promote respect for the law, provide just punishment and reflect the seriousness of the crime (retribution), deter the defendant and others from future criminal conduct (deterrence), and address treatment or educational needs of the defendant (rehabilitation).

After weighing all of the factors and the facts of the case, the judge then imposes the sentence. The defendant is advised of the entire sentence, whether it is imprisonment or probation, as well as any fees, fines, restitution orders, forfeiture orders, and any term of supervised release that may follow a prison sentence. If the judge imposes a prison sentence and the defendant is not yet in custody, he or she may be taken to jail at that point to await transfer to prison. If the judge determines there is little risk that the defendant will flee, the defendant could be allowed to self-surrender to prison at a date set by the judge.

The end of the sentencing hearing also marks the end of the case in the trial court. Any future challenges to the criminal conviction or the sentence would be at the appellate court.

# H. FEDERAL SENTENCING REFORMS 1980s TO PRESENT

Traditionally, federal judges had broad discretion when it came to imposing sentences.[7] Each statute had a sentencing range, such as zero to 20 years and the judge could sentence a defendant to a term of imprisonment within that range with nearly unfettered authority.

This sentencing system led to a public perception that judges had too much leeway in determining sentences, that the system was too lenient on criminals, and that parole was too easily granted. It also resulted in an unpredictable sentencing structure, and created vast disparities among defendants with similar criminal convictions and backgrounds.[8] This dissatisfaction and a prevailing "tough on crime" sentiment led to the Sentencing Reform Act of 1984 (SRA). This vast change to federal sentencing law limited judicial discretion in sentencing and the sentencing process became controlled by a mandatory set of guidelines.

---

[7] Koh, S. and Stith, K., *A Decade of Sentencing Guidelines: Revisiting the Role of the Legislatures*, 28 Wake Forest L. Rev. 223, 225 (Summer 1993).

[8] See generally *id.* at 225–230.

The SRA made several major changes to federal sentencing law. First, it abolished parole in the federal system. Federal inmates now must serve approximately 85% of the prison sentence imposed. Inmates can earn a reduction of up to 54 days per year of incarceration, which amounts to a little less than 15% of their sentence, if they stay out of trouble while incarcerated. The SRA also created the U.S. Sentencing Commission, a nonpartisan panel of legal scholars and practitioners who were directed to draft the sentencing guidelines that would overhaul sentencing law in federal court. The law also permitted appellate review of sentences for the first time.

The sentencing guidelines were enacted in 1987. The goal was to establish a uniform sentencing structure so that courts would impose sentences that were blind to defendants' race, gender, or socio-economic status.[9] Because the guidelines were mandatory, judges had little discretion to alter sentences from what the guidelines calculated.

The sentencing guidelines were designed to capture a wide variety of data on all aspects of the crime that was committed. For example, in a financial fraud case, the guidelines consider the amount of money lost by the victims, the numbers of victims, whether the defendant was in a position of trust when the fraud happened or if he or she was a ringleader in a fraud scheme, and whether the scheme targeted a vulnerable population, such as the elderly.[10]

In addition, the guidelines pull information from the defendant's background into the calculations. This includes whether or not the defendant has prior convictions, how many and what sorts of convictions, and the length of any prior sentences.[11] The guidelines also factor in if the defendant "obstructed justice" by attempting to destroy evidence or by testifying falsely at trial, and if so, additional punishment may be imposed.[12] In fact, federal sentencing law says there is no limit on the information the court can consider in determining the sentence for a defendant.[13]

The sentencing guidelines allow for consideration of "relevant conduct" or acquitted conduct. **Relevant conduct** is a determination of the "real" conduct that may go beyond what the jury determined at trial. It may include "all acts and omissions committed, aided, abetted, counseled, commanded, induced, procured,

[9]   United States Sentencing Commission, *Guidelines Manual*, § 5H1.10 (Nov. 2016).

[10]   USSG § 2B1.1(b)(1) (loss amount); § 2B1.1(b)(2) (number of victims); § 3B1.1 (aggravating role); § 3B1.2 (mitigating role); § 3A1.1(b)(1)(vulnerable victims).

[11]   USSG § 4A1.1.

[12]   USSG § 3C1.1.

[13]   18 U.S.C. § 3661.

or willfully caused" by the defendant, regardless of whether those acts "occurred during the commission of the offense of conviction, in preparation for that offense, or in the course of attempting to avoid detection or responsibility for that offense."[14] In some cases, particularly drug and fraud crimes, relevant conduct extends even further, to acts and omissions that were not part of the offense of conviction but were "part of the same course of conduct or common scheme or plan as the offense of conviction."[15]

Relevant conduct can even include conduct underlying dismissed, acquitted, or even uncharged counts, provided the sentencing judge finds the conduct was reliably established by a preponderance of the evidence.[16] Because the guidelines allowed increased punishment based on facts determined by a judge and not a jury, the mandatory relevant conduct sentencing was challenged on constitutional grounds in a 2006 case, *United States v. Booker*.[17]

Freddie J. Booker was charged with possessing more than 50 grams of crack with the intent to distribute. The jury heard testimony that he had 92.5 grams in a duffel bag and convicted him of the charge. After a post-trial sentencing hearing, the judge concluded by a preponderance of the evidence that Booker actually had possessed an additional 566 grams of crack, and which mandated a sentenced under the guidelines of 360 months to life imprisonment. Booker appealed and in 2005, the Supreme Court held that the mandatory guidelines violated the Sixth Amendment right to a jury trial. The Supreme Court did not bar the use of relevant conduct and instead made the guidelines advisory rather than mandatory. Once again, judges would have discretion in how they sentenced defendants.

In the decade since, the U.S. Supreme Court has repeatedly held that trial courts are not bound by the sentencing guidelines. In 2016, 48.6 sentences imposed in federal court fell with the advisory guideline range, and 49% of all federal sentences were below what the sentencing guidelines recommended.[18]

The guidelines are not the only factor in sentencing, and Congress has authority to legislate mandatory minimum sentences. In those cases, a judge is bound by law to impose no less than the mandatory minimum sentence that Congress has put in statute.

---

[14] USSG § 1B1.3(a)(1).

[15] USSG § 1B1.3(a)(2).

[16] See *United States v. Watts*, 519 US 148, 153–54 (1997) (per curiam) (discussing acquitted conduct).

[17] *United States v. Booker*, 543 U.S. 220 (2005).

[18] United States Sentencing Commission, *Fiscal Year 2016 Federal Sentencing Statistics*, Table 8. (April 2017).

The guidelines are just one factor among a broad variety of guidance provided in federal the federal sentencing statute, 18 USC § 3553(a). Under the statute judges are directed to consider the nature and circumstances of the offense, the history and characteristics of the defendant, the purposes of sentencing, the kinds of sentences available, the need to avoid unwarranted sentencing disparities, and the need to provide restitution. The law requires the sentencing court to impose a sentence "sufficient, but not greater than necessary," to achieve a specific set of sentencing purposes:

1.   To reflect the seriousness of the offense, to promote respect for the law, and to provide just punishment for the offense;

2.   To afford adequate deterrence to criminal conduct;

3.   To protect the public from further crimes of the defendant; and

4.   To provide the defendant with needed education or vocational training, medical care, or other correctional treatment in the most effective manner.[19]

Beyond this statute and a requirement that the judge give a reason for the sentence imposed, the SRA as modified by *Booker* guides the sentence, but no longer requires strict adherence to the sentencing guidelines.

In 2018, the **First Step Act**[20] was signed into law—enacting several reforms to federal mandatory minimum sentencing laws and changes to the federal prison system. Among the changes to sentencing laws, the new legislation shortened mandatory minimum sentences for nonviolent drug offenses, and it gave judges more discretion to deviate from those mandatory minimum sentences for certain defendants.

The First Step Act also made retroactive a prior criminal justice reform effort, the 2010 Fair Sentencing Act. The Fair Sentencing Act had reduced the sentencing disparity between crack and powder cocaine offenses. That earlier reform had not applied to about 2,660 people who were convicted of crack cocaine offenses prior to when that law went into effect. The First Step Act extended that earlier law to those individuals and allows them to have their sentences reduced.

Another mandatory minimum sentence that the First Step Act addressed was to clarify sentencing in cases where a defendant was charged with multiple violations of 18 U.S.C. § 924(c)—using, carrying, or possessing a firearm in furtherance of a crime of violence or drug trafficking offense. The statute

---

[19]   18 U.S.C. § 3553(a)(2).
[20]   First Step Act of 2018, Pub. L. No. 115-391 (2018).

triggered a higher mandatory minimum sentence for a second or subsequent conviction of this law. The Supreme Court held in 1993 that even when multiple counts were in the same indictment, the first count did not have to be final before the mandatory increases applied.[21] That meant a defendant with two or more counts in one indictment was subject to a five-year mandatory minimum on the first count, and 25 years on each additional count. Under the new law, in a case where the defendant has not previously been convicted of that violation, each 924(c) count in a single indictment would carry a five-year mandatory minimum.

The reforms to prison conditions included allowing some federal inmates can earn time off their sentence through participation in rehabilitative programs, such as substance abuse treatment. The act also changed how the Bureau of Prisons calculates "good time" credit—time off a sentence for good conduct. The First Step Act increased the credit from 47 days to 54 days per year. It also allows those credits to be redeemed for early transfer to pre-release custody, such as home confinement or a half-way house, for certain low-risk inmates.

Another important change to prison conditions is that inmates who apply to the Bureau of Prisons for compassionate release and were rejected, are now able to appeal to a court. Prior to the First Step Act, the director of the Bureau of Prisons had to file a motion to the court in support of an inmate's early release, and rarely granted requests to do so. Those decisions were not appealable. But under the First Step Act, inmates themselves can file a motion for early release due to "extraordinary and compelling reasons"[22] if they have exhausted all administrative options with the Bureau of Prisons.

That change to the law took effect just months before the COVID-19 pandemic. The United States Sentencing Commission calculated that courts received thousands of compassionate release motions filed by inmates in 2020 and 2021 due to the COVID-19.[23] Of the 21,150 compassionate motions filed with federal courts between January 2020 and June 2021, courts granted early release to 3,608 inmates. The vast majority of those motions—approximately 96%—were filed by defendants.

---

[21] *Deal v. United States*, 508 U.S. 129 (1993).

[22] 18 USC § 3582(c)(1)(A)(i).

[23] U.S. Sentencing Commission Compassionate Release Data Report, Calendar Years 2020 to 2021 (September 2021).

# I.  THE DEATH PENALTY

Death as a criminal sanction has been an option in legal codes throughout history, dating at least as far back as the 18th century B.C., when it was memorialized in the Hammurabi Code as the sanction proscribed for 20 different crimes.[24] In the 7th century B.C., the Draconian Code of Athens mandated the death penalty as punishment for all crimes. The Roman Law of the Twelve Tablets in the 5th century B.C. even proscribed the methods of carrying out a death sentence—including beheading, drowning, hanging, impalement, strangling, being thrown to wild animals, and other unpleasant means.

William the Conqueror, who ruled England in the 11th century A.D., did not allow the death penalty, except in times of war. That did not last, however, and during Henry VIII's reign in the 16th Century, it is estimated that over 72,000 people were put to death for their crimes. The use of the death penalty in America traces back to 1608, when the first execution was recorded—George Kendall, a colonist hanged for "spying for the Spanish."[25]

Opposition to the death penalty also has a long history. Italian philosopher Cesare Beccaria, influenced by the writings of John Locke, advocated for the abolition of the death penalty in his work, *An Essay on Crimes and Punishment* (1764).[26] Early in the United States' history, states allowed, and in some cases, mandated the **death penalty** for a wide assortment of crimes—including murder, rape, and robbery. A few states limited the death penalty to only murder or treason. In 1852, Rhode Island became the first state to outlaw capital punishment for all crimes, followed by Wisconsin. Religious leaders, particularly the Quakers, led the anti-death penalty movement. In the early 1900s, six states (Kansas, Minnesota, Washington, Oregon, South Dakota, and Missouri) abolished the death penalty. But there was a resurgence in capital punishment laws starting around the time of World War I and during the 1930s the United States put to death more offenders than in any other decade—averaging approximately 167 executions per year.

## i.  Constitutional Issues

The first constitutional challenge to the death penalty to reach the U.S. Supreme Court was in 1878, when Wallace Wilkerson argued that Utah's plan to execute him by firing squad violated the Eighth Amendment as cruel and unusual

---

[24]  Death Penalty Information Center (2017).

[25]  Bedau, H. and Cassell, P., eds., *Debating the Death Penalty* (Oxford: Oxford University Press, Inc., 2004).

[26]  Vollum, S., et al., *The Death Penalty: Constitutional Issues, Commentaries, and Case Briefs* (3rd ed., 2015).

punishment.[27] The Court stated that Utah's law did not provide any other means of execution, and noted that executions by firing squads were common practice.

Other challenges to capital punishment followed, usually challenging the method of execution. In 1890, William Kemmler appealed to the Supreme Court, arguing that use of the electric chair—at that point, an untried method—was cruel and unusual and in violation of the Eighth Amendment.[28] The Supreme Court held that the Eighth Amendment did not apply to states, and upheld Kemmler's sentence.

The death sentences imposed on the "Scottsboro Boys" in *Powell v. Alabama (1932)* were overturned, but on the grounds that the defendants were denied due process because they were not assisted by counsel at trial.[29] It was not until 1972 that the Supreme Court heard a case challenging capital punishment as unconstitutional, rather than the method of execution or the trial procedures that led to a death sentence. William Henry Furman tried to break into a home at night and shot the homeowner through a closed door.[30] Though he was in his mid-20s, he had a sixth grade education and had been diagnosed with "mental deficiency, mild to moderate, with psychotic episodes associated with convulsive disorder." His appeal challenged the imposition and method of the death penalty as cruel and unusual punishment, violating the Eighth and Fourteenth amendments.

In a one-page decision, the Supreme Court declared the death penalty unconstitutional on a 5–4 vote. But the majority did not come to a conclusion on the basis of their finding. In the 200 pages that followed the brief decision, the justices laid out nine different concurring and dissenting opinions. Two justices based their opinions on Eighth Amendment grounds. Justice William J. Brennan said that the prohibition against cruel and unusual punishment "must draw its meaning from the evolving standards of decency that mark the progress of a maturing society."[31]

Justice Thurgood Marshall's exhaustive concurrence noted that "American citizens know almost nothing about capital punishment" but if they did, they would surely consider it cruel and unusual.[32] Three justices felt it violated the equal protection clause because of how the death penalty discriminated against the poor, minorities, and the disadvantaged. Justice Potter Stewart summed up his objection

---

[27]  *Wilkerson v. Utah*, 99 U.S. 130 (1878).

[28]  *In re Kemmler*, 136 U.S. 436 (1890).

[29]  *Powell v. Alabama*, 287 U.S. 45 (1932).

[30]  *Furman v. Georgia*, 408 U.S. 238 (1972).

[31]  *Id.* at 409.

[32]  *Id.* at 363. This became known as the "Marshall hypothesis."

to the death penalty as one that is "so wantonly and so freakishly imposed."[33] He based his argument in the equal protection clause, saying:

> *These death sentences are cruel and unusual in the same way that being struck by lightning is cruel and unusual. For, of all the people convicted of [death-eligible crimes], many just as reprehensible as these, the petitioners are among a capriciously selected random handful upon which the sentence of death has in fact been imposed.*

Four justices dissented from the majority opinion, arguing that the Constitution did not bar capital punishment. Justice Harry Blackmun said that he personally abhorred the death penalty and felt it served "no useful purpose that can be demonstrated."[34] If he were a legislator, Blackmun said, he would vote against capital punishment as a policy for the reasons stated in the majority concurring opinions.

> *Although personally I may rejoice at the Court's result, I find it difficult to accept or to justify as a matter of history, of law, or of constitutional pronouncement. I fear the Court has overstepped. It has sought and has achieved an end.*

Justice William Rehnquist's dissent discussed at length the nation's history and the relationship between the judicial and legislative branches.[35] The majority, he argued, went beyond the limits of judicial review by invalidating a penalty that the legislators have "thought necessary since our country was founded."

Because five justices had a slim majority, Furman's case resulted in ending capital punishment. But because there was no consensus as to *why* Georgia's death penalty was unconstitutional, it was a weak decision. That is why four years later, *Furman v. Georgia (1972)* was overturned. In 1976, the Supreme Court's decision in *Gregg v. Georgia* ended the short moratorium on capital punishment in the United States.

Troy Gregg was charged with murdering two men he had met while hitchhiking.[36] Gregg claimed he shot the men in self-defense, but a jury convicted him and sentenced him to death under Georgia's new death penalty statute, which had been revised after the *Furman* decision. Gregg appealed, challenging the constitutionality of the new statute. The issue was two-fold: 1) Is the death penalty constitutional as a form of punishment? and 2) if so, does Georgia's revised death

---

[33]   *Id.* at 310.

[34]   *Id.* at 405.

[35]   *Id.* at 466.

[36]   *Gregg v. Georgia*, 428 U.S. 153 (1976).

penalty law contain sufficient safeguards against arbitrary and capricious application?

In a 7–2 decision, the Supreme Court held that the death penalty is constitutional, if states have proper safeguards to prevent the equal protection problems seen in *Furman*. Justice Stewart, who four years earlier in Furman had found that the death penalty violated the equal protection clause, wrote the majority opinion. This time, he came to a different conclusion based on the changes to the statute.

> *No longer can a Georgia jury do as Furman's jury did: reach a finding of the defendant's guilt and then, without guidance or direction, decide whether he should live or die. Instead, the jury's attention is directed to the specific circumstances of the crime: Was it committed in the course of another capital felony? Was it committed for money? Was it committed upon a peace officer or judicial officer? Was it committed in a particularly heinous way or in a manner that endangered the lives of many persons? In addition, the jury's attention is focused on the characteristics of the person who committed the crime: Does he have a record of prior convictions for capital offenses? Are there any special facts about this defendant that mitigate against imposing capital punishment (E.g., his youth, the extent of his cooperation with the police, his emotional state at the time of the crime). As a result, while some jury discretion still exists, "the discretion to be exercised is controlled by clear and objective standards so as to produce non-discriminatory application."[37]*

The Court held that this guidance minimizes "the risk of wholly arbitrary and capricious action."

Justices Brennan and Marshall dissented, holding to their opinions in *Furman* that the death penalty itself is unconstitutional and no number of procedural safeguards could make it otherwise. Justice Marshall reiterated his objections to the death penalty that he had made in *Furman*, that it is excessive and serves no purpose as a deterrent nor as retribution.[38]

Justice Brennan's strident dissent stressed that the Court had a duty to hold that "the law has progressed to the point where we should declare that the punishment of death, like punishments on the rack, the screw, and the wheel, is no longer morally tolerable in our civilized society."[39] The death penalty's fatal flaw is that "it treats members of the human race as nonhumans, as objects to be toyed with and discarded. (It is) thus inconsistent with the fundamental premise

---

[37] *Id.* at 198.

[38] *Id.* at 232.

[39] *Id.* at 229.

of the Clause that even the vilest criminal remains a human being possessed of common human dignity."

Since *Gregg,* the Supreme Court has addressed the death penalty's imposition in many different situations. In 2002, the Court held that the execution of mentally disabled defendants is a violation of the Eighth Amendment's prohibition against cruel and unusual punishment.[40] Other holdings restricting capital punishment required a jury to impose the death penalty, not a judge,[41] and barred the death penalty for juveniles who committed crimes at 16 or 17 years old.[42] More recently, the Supreme Court has taken up challenges on the methods of executions, finding that Oklahoma's three-drug protocol for lethal injections did not constitute cruel and unusual punishment, despite expert testimony that the drugs may not render the inmate unable to feel pain.[43]

Today, there are 31 states with the death penalty.[44] The number of death sentences imposed each year has dropped dramatically since its post-*Gregg* peak in 1998, when 295 defendants were sentenced to die. In 2016, 30 defendants were given a death sentence. Though it is not imposed as often, the death penalty remains as controversial as ever. Driving that is the increasing number of exonerations, many through DNA technology that was not available at the time of trial. Since 1973, 159 defendants have been exonerated and released from death row.[45]

## ii.   Role of the Jury in Capital Cases

When a prosecutor chooses to charge a defendant with a capital crime, and thus seek the death penalty instead of another punishment, this sets in motion a different type of criminal trial. In most states, the defendant's lawyer must be **death-qualified**, meaning he or she has experience in a capital case. Because the stakes are so high, these cases are not rushed to trial, and courts will generally permit more time to investigate and prepare a defense strategy. It can also take longer to seat a jury, as the jurors are screened for their views on capital punishment. Jurors who express opposition to the death penalty can be excused

---

[40]   *Atkins v. Virginia,* 536 U.S. 304 (2002).

[41]   *Ring v. Arizona,* 536 U.S. 584 (2002).

[42]   *Roper v. Simmons,* 543 U.S. 551 (2005).

[43]   *Glossip v. Gross,* 576 U.S. 863 (2015).

[44]   Fact Sheet 2017, Death Penalty Information Center.

[45]   https://deathpenaltyinfo.org/innocence-list-those-freed-death-row.

if they say they cannot follow the law.[46] This leads to criticism of death-qualified juries as being more prone to impose capital punishment.

Death penalty trials are **bifurcated**—with the jury first determining the verdict, guilty or not guilty. If the defendant is found guilty, then the penalty phase starts. During this part of the trial, the jury hears mitigating and aggravating evidence on the issue of whether to impose the death penalty or a term of imprisonment, usually a life sentence. As all criminal defendants who are convicted, those sentenced to death have a right to appeal. In death penalty cases, there are some special procedures. Most states have automatic appeals for death penalty defendants. Most states also require review of the conviction by the state's highest appellate court, or an intermediate appellate court. If the conviction is upheld, the prisoner can file a writ of certiorari at the U.S. Supreme Court.

If this direct appeal is upheld, then the defendant can start the *habeas corpus* process—filing a writ in state and federal courts to challenge the constitutionality of his or her detention. These collateral attacks have been limited since 1996, when Congress passed the Antiterrorism and Effective Death Penalty Act, which imposed a strict deadline for filing a *habeas* appeal, restricted review to issues heard by state courts, and required one petition rather than permitting successive filings. Defendants can waive their rights to appeal and ask to have an execution date set. Defendants who do this are called "volunteers." A court will review that decision to ensure that the prisoner has made a knowing, voluntary, and intelligent waiver of his or her right to appeal, and that the inmate is mentally competent.[47]

---

[46] *Uttecht v. Brown*, 551 U.S. 1 (2007).

[47] Roundtree, M., *Volunteers for Execution: Directions for Further Research into Grief, Culpability, and Legal Structures*, 82 Univ. Missouri-Kansas City L.R. 295 (2014).

Read and brief each of the following cases relating to sentencing and consider the questions following each case:

1.  *Gregg v. Georgia*: the death penalty

2.  *Payne v. Tennessee*: victim impact statements at sentencing

---

## GREGG V. GEORGIA

Supreme Court of the United States
Argued March 31, 1976
Decided July 2, 1976
Stay Granted July 22, 1976
Rehearing Denied Oct. 4, 1976
428 U.S. 153

### Opinion

**Judgment of the Court, and opinion of MR. JUSTICE STEWART, MR. JUSTICE POWELL, and MR. JUSTICE STEVENS, announced by MR. JUSTICE STEWART.**

The issue in this case is whether the imposition of the sentence of death for the crime of murder under the law of Georgia violates the Eighth and Fourteenth Amendments.

I

The petitioner, Troy Gregg, was charged with committing armed robbery and murder. In accordance with Georgia procedure in capital cases, the trial was in two stages, a guilt stage and a sentencing stage. The evidence at the guilt trial established that on November 21, 1973, the petitioner and a traveling companion, Floyd Allen, while hitchhiking north in Florida were picked up by Fred Simmons and Bob Moore. . . While still in Florida, they picked up another hitchhiker, Dennis Weaver, who rode with them to Atlanta, where he was let out about 11 p. m. A short time later the four men interrupted their journey for a rest stop along the highway. The next morning the bodies of Simmons and Moore were discovered in a ditch nearby.

On November 23, after reading about the shootings in an Atlanta newspaper, Weaver communicated with the Gwinnett County police and related information concerning the journey with the victims, including a description of the car. The next afternoon, the petitioner and Allen, while in Simmons' car, were arrested in Asheville, N. C. In the search incident to the arrest a .25-caliber pistol, later shown to be that used to kill Simmons and Moore, was found in the petitioner's pocket. After receiving the warnings required by *Miranda v. Arizona*, and signing a written waiver of his rights, the petitioner signed a statement in which he admitted shooting, then robbing Simmons and Moore. He justified the slayings on grounds of self-defense. The next day, while being transferred to Lawrenceville, Ga., the petitioner and Allen were taken to the scene of the shootings. Upon arriving there, Allen recounted the events leading to the slayings. His version of these events was as follows: After Simmons and Moore left the car, the petitioner stated that he intended to rob them. The petitioner then took his pistol in hand and positioned himself on the car to improve his aim. As Simmons and Moore came up an embankment toward the car, the petitioner fired three shots and the two men fell near a ditch. The petitioner, at close range, then fired a shot into the head of each. He robbed them of valuables and drove away with Allen.

A medical examiner testified that Simmons died from a bullet wound in the eye and that Moore died from bullet wounds in the cheek and in the back of the head. He further testified that both men had several bruises and abrasions about the face and head which probably were sustained either from the fall into the ditch or from being dragged or pushed along the embankment. Although Allen did not testify, a police detective recounted the substance of Allen's statements about the slayings and indicated that directly after Allen had made these statements the petitioner had admitted that Allen's account was accurate. The petitioner testified in his own defense. He confirmed that Allen had made the statements described by the detective, but denied their truth or ever having admitted to their accuracy. He indicated that he had shot Simmons and Moore because of fear and in self-defense, testifying they had attacked Allen and him, one wielding a pipe and the other a knife.

. . .The jury found the petitioner guilty of two counts of armed robbery and two counts of murder.

At the penalty stage, which took place before the same jury, neither the prosecutor nor the petitioner's lawyer offered any additional evidence. Both counsel, however, made lengthy arguments dealing generally with the propriety of capital punishment under the circumstances and with the weight of the evidence of guilt. The trial judge instructed the jury that it could recommend either a death sentence or a life prison sentence on each count. The judge further charged the jury that in determining what sentence was appropriate the jury was free to consider the facts and circumstances, if any, presented by the parties in mitigation or aggravation.

Finally, the judge instructed the jury that it "would not be authorized to consider (imposing) the penalty of death" unless it first found beyond a reasonable doubt one of these aggravating circumstances:

"One That the offense of murder was committed while the offender was engaged in the commission of two other capital felonies, to-wit the armed robbery of (Simmons and Moore).

"Two That the offender committed the offense of murder for the purpose of receiving money and the automobile described in the indictment.

"Three The offense of murder was outrageously and wantonly vile, horrible and inhuman, in that they. . . involved the depravity of (the) mind of the defendant."

Finding the first and second of these circumstances, the jury returned verdicts of death on each count.

The Supreme Court of Georgia affirmed the convictions and the imposition of the death sentences for murder. . . .

We granted the petitioner's application for a writ of certiorari limited to his challenge to the imposition of the death sentences in this case as "cruel and unusual" punishment in violation of the Eighth and the Fourteenth Amendments.

## II

Before considering the issues presented it is necessary to understand the Georgia statutory scheme for the imposition of the death penalty. The Georgia statute, as amended after our decision in *Furman v. Georgia*, 408 U.S. 238 (1972), retains the death penalty for six categories of crime: murder, kidnaping for ransom or where the victim is harmed, armed robbery rape, treason, and aircraft hijacking. The capital defendant's guilt or innocence is determined in the traditional manner, either by a trial judge or a jury, in the first stage of a bifurcated trial.

If trial is by jury, the trial judge is required to charge lesser-included offenses when they are supported by any view of the evidence. After a verdict, finding, or plea of guilty to a capital crime, a presentence hearing is conducted before whoever made the determination of guilt. The sentencing procedures are essentially the same in both bench and jury trials. At the hearing:

"(T)he judge (or jury) shall hear additional evidence in extenuation, mitigation, and aggravation of punishment, including the record of any prior criminal convictions . . . of the defendant, or the absence of any prior conviction. . . . The judge (or jury) shall also hear argument by the defendant or his counsel and the prosecuting attorney . . . regarding the punishment to be imposed."

. . . Before a convicted defendant may be sentenced to death, however, . . .the jury, or the trial judge in cases tried without a jury, must find beyond a reasonable doubt one of the 10 aggravating circumstances specified in the statute. The sentence of death may be imposed only if the jury (or judge) finds one of the statutory aggravating circumstances and then elects to impose that sentence. If the verdict is death, the jury or judge must specify the aggravating circumstance(s) found. In jury cases, the trial judge is bound by the jury's recommended sentence.

The statute provides in part:

". . .(b)   In all cases of other offenses for which the death penalty may be authorized, the judge shall consider, or he shall include in his instructions to the jury for it to consider, any mitigating circumstances or aggravating circumstances otherwise authorized by law and any of the following statutory aggravating circumstances which may be supported by the evidence:

"(1) The offense of murder, rape, armed robbery, or kidnapping was committed by a person with a prior record of conviction for a capital felony, or the offense of murder was committed by a person who has a substantial history of serious assaultive criminal convictions.

"(2) The offense of murder, rape, armed robbery, or kidnapping was committed while the offender was engaged in the commission of another capital felony, or aggravated battery, or the offense of murder was committed while the offender was engaged in the commission of burglary or arson in the first degree.

"(3) The offender by his act of murder, armed robbery, or kidnapping knowingly created a great risk of death to more than one person in a public place by means of a weapon or device which would normally be hazardous to the lives of more than one person.

"(4) The offender committed the offense of murder for himself or another, for the purpose of receiving money or any other thing of monetary value.

"(5) The murder of a judicial officer, former judicial officer, district attorney or solicitor or former district attorney or solicitor during or because of the exercise of his official duty.

"(6) The offender caused or directed another to commit murder or committed murder as an agent or employee of another person.

"(7) The offense of murder, rape, armed robbery, or kidnapping was outrageously or wantonly vile, horrible or inhuman in that it involved torture, depravity of mind, or an aggravated battery to the victim.

"(8) The offense of murder was committed against any peace officer, corrections employee or fireman while engaged in the performance of his official duties.

"(9) The offense of murder was committed by a person in, or who has escaped from, the lawful custody of a peace officer or place of lawful confinement.

"(10)     The murder was committed for the purpose of avoiding, interfering with, or preventing a lawful arrest or custody in a place of lawful confinement, of himself or another.

"(c) The statutory instructions as determined by the trial judge to be warranted by the evidence shall be given in charge and in writing to the jury for its deliberation. The jury, if its verdict be a recommendation of death, shall designate in writing, signed by the foreman of the jury, the aggravating circumstance or circumstances which it found beyond a reasonable doubt. In non-jury cases the judge shall make such designation. Except in cases of treason or aircraft hijacking, unless at least one of the statutory aggravating circumstances enumerated in section 27–2534.1(b) is so found, the death penalty shall not be imposed."

The Supreme Court of Georgia recently. . .held unconstitutional the portion of the first circumstance encompassing persons who have a "substantial history of serious assaultive criminal convictions" because it did not set "sufficiently 'clear and objective standards.' "

### III

We address initially the basic contention that the punishment of death for the crime of murder is, under all circumstances, "cruel and unusual" in violation of the Eighth and Fourteenth Amendments of the Constitution. In Part IV of this opinion, we will consider the sentence of death imposed under the Georgia statutes at issue in this case.

The Court on a number of occasions has both assumed and asserted the constitutionality of capital punishment. In several cases that assumption provided a necessary foundation for the decision, as the Court was asked to decide whether a particular method of carrying out a capital sentence would be allowed to stand under the Eighth Amendment. But until *Furman v. Georgia*, the Court never confronted squarely the fundamental claim that the punishment of death always, regardless of the enormity of the offense or the procedure followed in imposing the sentence, is cruel and unusual punishment in violation of the Constitution. Although this issue was presented and addressed in *Furman*, it was not resolved by the Court. Four Justices would have held that capital punishment is not unconstitutional *per se*; two Justices would have reached the opposite conclusion; and three Justices, while agreeing that the statutes then before the Court were invalid as applied, left open the question whether such punishment may ever be imposed. We now hold that the punishment of death does not invariably violate the Constitution.

A

The history of the prohibition of "cruel and unusual" punishment already has been reviewed at length. The phrase first appeared in the English Bill of Rights of 1689, which was drafted by Parliament at the accession of William and Mary. The English version appears to have been directed against punishments unauthorized by statute and beyond the jurisdiction of the sentencing court, as well as those disproportionate to the offense involved. The American draftsmen, who adopted the English phrasing in drafting the Eighth Amendment, were primarily concerned, however, with proscribing "tortures" and other "barbarous" methods of punishment."

In the earliest cases raising Eighth Amendment claims, the Court focused on particular methods of execution to determine whether they were too cruel to pass constitutional muster. The constitutionality of the sentence of death itself was not at issue, and the criterion used to evaluate the mode of execution was its similarity to "torture" and other "barbarous" methods. See *Wilkerson v. Utah* (1879) ("(I)t is safe to affirm that punishments of torture . . . and all others in the same line of unnecessary cruelty, are forbidden by that amendment . . ."); *In re Kemmler* (1890) ("Punishments are cruel when they involve torture or a lingering death . . ."). See also *Louisiana ex rel. Francis v. Resweber* (1947) (second attempt at electrocution found not to violate Eighth Amendment, since failure of initial execution attempt was "an unforeseeable accident" and "(t)here (was no purpose to inflict unnecessary pain nor any unnecessary pain involved in the proposed execution").

But the Court has not confined the prohibition embodied in the Eighth Amendment to "barbarous" methods that were generally outlawed in the 18th century. Instead, the Amendment has been interpreted in a flexible and dynamic manner. The Court early recognized that "a principle to be vital, must be capable of wider application than the mischief which gave it birth." Thus the Clause forbidding "cruel and unusual" punishments "is not fastened to the obsolete but may acquire meaning as public opinion becomes enlightened by a humane justice.". . .

The substantive limits imposed by the Eighth Amendment on what can be made criminal and punished were discussed in *Robinson v. California* (1962). The Court found unconstitutional a state statute that made the status of being addicted to a narcotic drug a criminal offense. It held, in effect, that it is "cruel and unusual" to impose any punishment at all for the mere status of addiction. The cruelty in the abstract of the actual sentence imposed was irrelevant: "Even one day in prison would be a cruel and unusual punishment for the 'crime' of having a common cold." Most recently, in *Furman v. Georgia*, three Justices in separate concurring opinions found the Eighth Amendment applicable to procedures employed to select convicted defendants for the sentence of death.

It is clear from the foregoing precedents that the Eighth Amendment has not been regarded as a static concern. As Mr. Chief Justice Warren said, in an oft-quoted phrase, "(t)he Amendment must draw its meaning from the evolving standards of decency that mark the progress of a maturing society." Thus, an assessment of contemporary values concerning the infliction of a challenged sanction is relevant to the application of the Eighth Amendment. As we develop below more fully, this assessment does not call for a subjective judgment. It requires, rather, that we look to objective indicia that reflect the public attitude toward a given sanction.

But our cases also make clear that public perceptions of standards of decency with respect to criminal sanctions are not conclusive. A penalty also must accord with "the dignity of man," which is the "basic concept underlying the Eighth Amendment." This means, at least, that the punishment not be "excessive." When a form of punishment in the abstract (in this case, whether capital punishment may ever be imposed as a sanction for murder) rather than in the particular (the propriety of death as a penalty to be applied to a specific defendant for a specific crime) is under consideration, the inquiry into "excessiveness" has two aspects. First, the punishment must not involve the unnecessary and wanton infliction of pain. Second, the punishment must not be grossly out of proportion to the severity of the crime.

B

Of course, the requirements of the Eighth Amendment must be applied with an awareness of the limited role to be played by the courts. This does not mean that judges have no role to play, for the Eighth Amendment is a restraint upon the exercise of legislative power.

> "Judicial review by definition, often involves a conflict between judicial and legislative judgment as to what the Constitution means or requires. In this respect, Eighth Amendment cases come to us in no different posture. It seems conceded by all that the Amendment imposes some obligations on the judiciary to judge the constitutionality of punishment and that there are punishments that the Amendment would bar whether legislatively approved or not."

But, while we have an obligation to insure that constitutional bounds are not overreached, we may not act as judges as we might as legislators.

> "Courts are not representative bodies. They are not designed to be a good reflex of a democratic society. Their judgment is best informed, and therefore most dependable, within narrow limits. Their essential quality is detachment, founded on independence. History teaches that the independence of the judiciary is jeopardized when courts become embroiled in the passions of the day and assume primary responsibility in choosing between competing political, economic and social pressures."

Therefore, in assessing a punishment selected by a democratically elected legislature against the constitutional measure, we presume its validity. We may not require the legislature to select the least severe penalty possible so long as the penalty selected is not cruelly inhumane or disproportionate to the crime involved. And a heavy burden rests on those who would attack the judgment of the representatives of the people.

This is true in part because the constitutional test is intertwined with an assessment of contemporary standards and the legislative judgment weighs heavily in ascertaining such standards. "(I)n a democratic society legislatures, not courts, are constituted to respond to the will and consequently the moral values of the people." The deference we owe to the decisions of the state legislatures under our federal system is enhanced where the specification of punishments is concerned, for "these are peculiarly questions of legislative policy." . . . A decision that a given punishment is impermissible under the Eighth Amendment cannot be reversed short of a constitutional amendment. . . .

## C

. . . We now consider specifically whether the sentence of death for the crime of murder is a *per se* violation of the Eighth and Fourteenth Amendments to the Constitution. We note first that history and precedent strongly support a negative answer to this question.

The imposition of the death penalty for the crime of murder has a long history of acceptance both in the United States and in England. . . .

It is apparent from the text of the Constitution itself that the existence of capital punishment was accepted by the Framers. At the time the Eighth Amendment was ratified, capital punishment was a common sanction in every State. Indeed, the First Congress of the United States enacted legislation providing death as the penalty for specified crimes. The Fifth Amendment, adopted at the same time as the Eighth, contemplated the continued existence of the capital sanction by imposing certain limits on the prosecution of capital cases:

> "No person shall be held to answer for a capital, or otherwise infamous crime, unless on a presentment or indictment of a Grand Jury. . .; nor shall any person be subject for the same offense to be twice put in jeopardy of life or limb; . . . nor be deprived of life, liberty, or property, without due process of law. . . ."

And the Fourteenth Amendment, adopted over three-quarters of a century later, similarly contemplates the existence of the capital sanction in providing that no State shall deprive any person of "life, liberty, or property" without due process of law.

For nearly two centuries, this Court, repeatedly and often expressly, has recognized that capital punishment is not invalid *per se*. In *Wilkerson v. Utah*, where the Court found no constitutional violation in inflicting death by public shooting, it said:

> "Cruel and unusual punishments are forbidden by the Constitution, but the authorities referred to are quite sufficient to show that the punishment of shooting as a mode of executing the death penalty for the crime of murder in the first degree is not included in that category, within the meaning of the eighth amendment."

Rejecting the contention that death by electrocution was "cruel and unusual," the Court in *In re Kemmler*, reiterated:

> "(T)he punishment of death is not cruel, within the meaning of that word as used in the Constitution. It implies there something inhuman and barbarous, something more than the mere extinguishment of life."

Again, in *Louisiana ex rel. Francis v. Resweber*, the Court remarked: "The cruelty against which the Constitution protects a convicted man is cruelty inherent in the method of punishment, not the necessary suffering involved in any method employed to extinguish life humanely." And in *Trop v. Dulles*, Mr. Chief Justice Warren, for himself and three other Justices, wrote:

> "Whatever the arguments may be against capital punishment, both on moral grounds and in terms of accomplishing the purposes of punishment . . . the death penalty has been employed throughout our history, and, in a day when it is still widely accepted, it cannot be said to violate the constitutional concept of cruelty."

Four years ago, the petitioners in Furman and its companion cases predicated their argument primarily upon the asserted proposition that standards of decency had evolved to the point where capital punishment no longer could be tolerated. The petitioners in those cases said, in effect, that the evolutionary process had come to an end, and that standards of decency required that the Eighth Amendment be construed finally as prohibiting capital punishment for any crime regardless of its depravity and impact on society. This view was accepted by two Justices. Three other Justices were unwilling to go so far; focusing on the procedures by which convicted defendants were selected for the death penalty rather than on the actual punishment inflicted, they joined in the conclusion that the statutes before the Court were constitutionally invalid.

The petitioners in the capital cases before the Court today renew the "standards of decency" argument, but developments during the four years since Furman have undercut substantially the assumptions upon which their argument rested. Despite the continuing debate, dating back to the 19th century, over the morality and utility of capital punishment, it is now evident that a large proportion of American society continues to regard it as an appropriate and necessary criminal sanction.

The most marked indication of society's endorsement of the death penalty for murder is the legislative response to Furman. The legislatures of at least 35

States have enacted new statutes that provide for the death penalty for at least some crimes that result in the death of another person. And the Congress of the United States, in 1974, enacted a statute providing the death penalty for aircraft piracy that results in death. These recently adopted statutes have attempted to address the concerns expressed by the Court in *Furman* Primarily (i) by specifying the factors to be weighed and the procedures to be followed in deciding when to impose a capital sentence, or (ii) by making the death penalty mandatory for specified crimes. But all of the post-*Furman* Statutes make clear that capital punishment itself has not been rejected by the elected representatives of the people.

In the only statewide referendum occurring since *Furman* And brought to our attention, the people of California adopted a constitutional amendment that authorized capital punishment, in effect negating a prior ruling by the Supreme Court of California in *People v. Anderson*, that the death penalty violated the California Constitution.

The jury also is a significant and reliable objective index of contemporary values because it is so directly involved. The Court has said that "one of the most important functions any jury can perform in making . . . a selection (between life imprisonment and death for a defendant convicted in a capital case) is to maintain a link between contemporary community values and the penal system." It may be true that evolving standards have influenced juries in recent decades to be more discriminating in imposing the sentence of death. But the relative infrequency of jury verdicts imposing the death sentence does not indicate rejection of capital punishment Per se. Rather, the reluctance of juries in many cases to impose the sentence may well reflect the humane feeling that this most irrevocable of sanctions should be reserved for a small number of extreme cases. Indeed, the actions of juries in many States since Furman are fully compatible with the legislative judgments, reflected in the new statutes, as to the continued utility and necessity of capital punishment in appropriate cases. At the close of 1974 at least 254 persons had been sentenced to death since Furman, and by the end of March 1976, more than 460 persons were subject to death sentences.

As we have seen, however, the Eighth Amendment demands more than that a challenged punishment be acceptable to contemporary society. The Court also must ask whether it comports with the basic concept of human dignity at the core of the Amendment. . . .

The death penalty is said to serve two principal social purposes: retribution and deterrence of capital crimes by prospective offenders.

In part, capital punishment is an expression of society's moral outrage at particularly offensive conduct. This function may be unappealing to many, but it is essential in an ordered society that asks its citizens to rely on legal processes rather than self-help to vindicate their wrongs.

"The instinct for retribution is part of the nature of man, and channeling that instinct in the administration of criminal justice serves an important purpose in promoting the stability of a society governed by law. When people begin to believe that organized society is unwilling or unable to impose upon criminal offenders the punishment they 'deserve,' then there are sown the seeds of anarchy of self-help, vigilante justice, and lynch law."

"Retribution is no longer the dominant objective of the criminal law," but neither is it a forbidden objective nor one inconsistent with our respect for the dignity of men. Indeed, the decision that capital punishment may be the appropriate sanction in extreme cases is an expression of the community's belief that certain crimes are themselves so grievous an affront to humanity that the only adequate response may be the penalty of death.

Statistical attempts to evaluate the worth of the death penalty as a deterrent to crimes by potential offenders have occasioned a great deal of debate. The results simply have been inconclusive. . . .

The value of capital punishment as a deterrent of crime is a complex factual issue the resolution of which properly rests with the legislatures, which can evaluate the results of statistical studies in terms of their own local conditions and with a flexibility of approach that is not available to the courts. Indeed, many of the post-*Furman* statutes reflect just such a responsible effort to define those crimes and those criminals for which capital punishment is most probably an effective deterrent.

In sum, we cannot say that the judgment of the Georgia Legislature that capital punishment may be necessary in some cases is clearly wrong. Considerations of federalism, as well as respect for the ability of a legislature to evaluate, in terms of its particular State, the moral consensus concerning the death penalty and its social utility as a sanction, require us to conclude, in the absence of more convincing evidence, that the infliction of death as a punishment for murder is not without justification and thus is not unconstitutionally severe.

Finally, we must consider whether the punishment of death is disproportionate in relation to the crime for which it is imposed. There is no question that death as a punishment is unique in its severity and irrevocability. When a defendant's life is at stake, the Court has been particularly sensitive to insure that every safeguard is observed. But we are concerned here only with the imposition of capital punishment for the crime of murder, and when a life has been taken deliberately by the offender, we cannot say that the punishment is invariably disproportionate to the crime. It is an extreme sanction, suitable to the most extreme of crimes.

We hold that the death penalty is not a form of punishment that may never be imposed, regardless of the circumstances of the offense, regardless of the character of the offender, and regardless of the procedure followed in reaching the decision to impose it.

## IV

We now consider whether Georgia may impose the death penalty on the petitioner in this case.

### A

While *Furman* did not hold that the infliction of the death penalty Per se violates the Constitution's ban on cruel and unusual punishments, it did recognize that the penalty of death is different in kind from any other punishment imposed under our system of criminal justice. Because of the uniqueness of the death penalty, *Furman* held that it could not be imposed under sentencing procedures that created a substantial risk that it would be inflicted in an arbitrary and capricious manner. . . . ". . .(T)he Eighth and Fourteenth Amendments cannot tolerate the infliction of a sentence of death under legal systems that permit this unique penalty to be so wantonly and so freakishly imposed."

*Furman* mandates that where discretion is afforded a sentencing body on a matter so grave as the determination of whether a human life should be taken or spared, that discretion must be suitably directed and limited so as to minimize the risk of wholly arbitrary and capricious action.

It is certainly not a novel proposition that discretion in the area of sentencing be exercised in an informed manner. We have long recognized that "(f)or the determination of sentences, justice generally requires . . . that there be taken into account the circumstances of the offense together with the character and propensities of the offender." Otherwise, "the system cannot function in a consistent and a rational manner.". . .

Jury sentencing has been considered desirable in capital cases in order "to maintain a link between contemporary community values and the penal system a link without which the determination of punishment could hardly reflect 'the evolving standards of decency that mark the progress of a maturing society.' " But it creates special problems. Much of the information that is relevant to the sentencing decision may have no relevance to the question of guilt, or may even be extremely prejudicial to a fair determination of that question. This problem, however, is scarcely insurmountable. Those who have studied the question suggest that a bifurcated procedure one in which the question of sentence is not considered until the determination of guilt has been made is the best answer. . .

When a human life is at stake and when the jury must have information prejudicial to the question of guilt but relevant to the question of penalty in order to impose a rational sentence, a bifurcated system is more likely to ensure elimination of the constitutional deficiencies identified in *Furman*.

But the provision of relevant information under fair procedural rules is not alone sufficient to guarantee that the information will be properly used in the imposition of punishment, especially if sentencing is performed by a jury. Since the members of a jury will have had little, if any, previous experience in sentencing, they are unlikely to be skilled in dealing with the information they are given. To the extent that this problem is inherent in jury sentencing, it may not be totally correctible. It seems clear, however, that the problem will be alleviated if the jury is given guidance regarding the factors about the crime and the defendant that the State, representing organized society, deems particularly relevant to the sentencing decision.

The idea that a jury should be given guidance in its decision-making is also hardly a novel proposition. Juries are invariably given careful instructions on the law and how to apply it before they are authorized to decide the merits of a lawsuit. . . . It is quite simply a hallmark of our legal system that juries be carefully and adequately guided in their deliberations.

While some have suggested that standards to guide a capital jury's sentencing deliberations are impossible to formulate, the fact is that such standards have been developed. When the drafters of the Model Penal Code faced this problem, they concluded "that it is within the realm of possibility to point to the main circumstances of aggravation and of mitigation that should be weighed *and weighed against each other* when they are presented in a concrete case." While such standards are by necessity somewhat general, they do provide guidance to the sentencing authority and thereby reduce the likelihood that it will impose a sentence that fairly can be called capricious or arbitrary. Where the sentencing authority is required to specify the factors it relied upon in reaching its decision, the further safeguard of meaningful appellate review is available to ensure that death sentences are not imposed capriciously or in a freakish manner.

In summary, the concerns expressed in *Furman* that the penalty of death not be imposed in an arbitrary or capricious manner can be met by a carefully drafted statute that ensures that the sentencing authority is given adequate information and guidance. . . .

We do not intend to suggest that only the above-described procedures would be permissible under *Furman* or that any sentencing system constructed along these general lines would inevitably satisfy the concerns of *Furman*, for each distinct system must be examined on an individual basis. Rather, we have embarked upon this general exposition to make clear that it is possible to construct capital-sentencing systems capable of meeting *Furman's* constitutional concerns.

B

We now turn to consideration of the constitutionality of Georgia's capital-sentencing procedures. In the wake of *Furman*, Georgia amended its capital punishment statute, but chose not to narrow the scope of its murder provisions. Thus, now as before *Furman*, in Georgia "(a) person commits murder when he unlawfully and with malice aforethought, either express or implied, causes the death of another human being." All persons convicted of murder "shall be punished by death or by imprisonment for life."

Georgia did act, however, to narrow the class of murderers subject to capital punishment by specifying 10 statutory aggravating circumstances, one of which must be found by the jury to exist beyond a reasonable doubt before a death sentence can ever be imposed. In addition, the jury is authorized to consider any other appropriate aggravating or mitigating circumstances. The jury is not required to find any mitigating circumstance in order to make a recommendation of mercy that is binding on the trial court, but it must find a *statutory* aggravating circumstance before recommending a sentence of death.

These procedures require the jury to consider the circumstances of the crime and the criminal before it recommends sentence. No longer can a Georgia jury do as *Furman's* jury did: reach a finding of the defendant's guilt and then, without guidance or direction, decide whether he should live or die.

Instead, the jury's attention is directed to the specific circumstances of the crime: Was it committed in the course of another capital felony? Was it committed for money? Was it committed upon a peace officer or judicial officer? Was it committed in a particularly heinous way or in a manner that endangered the lives of many persons? In addition, the jury's attention is focused on the characteristics of the person who committed the crime: Does he have a record of prior convictions for capital offenses? Are there any special facts about this defendant that mitigate against imposing capital punishment (E.g., his youth, the extent of his cooperation with the police, his emotional state at the time of the crime). As a result, while some jury discretion till exists, "the discretion to be exercised is controlled by clear and objective standards so as to produce non-discriminatory application."

As an important additional safeguard against arbitrariness and caprice, the Georgia statutory scheme provides for automatic appeal of all death sentences to the State's Supreme Court. That court is required by statute to review each sentence of death and determine whether it was imposed under the influence of passion or prejudice, whether the evidence supports the jury's finding of a statutory aggravating circumstance, and whether the sentence is disproportionate compared to those sentences imposed in similar cases.

. . . On their face these procedures seem to satisfy the concerns of Furman. No longer should there be "no meaningful basis for distinguishing the few cases in which (the death penalty) is imposed from the many cases in which it is not."

The petitioner contends, however, that the changes in the Georgia sentencing procedures are only cosmetic, that the arbitrariness and capriciousness condemned by Furman continue to exist in Georgia both in traditional practices that still remain and in the new sentencing procedures adopted in response to *Furman*.

1

First, the petitioner focuses on the opportunities for discretionary action that are inherent in the processing of any murder case under Georgia law. He notes that the state prosecutor has unfettered authority to select those persons whom he wishes to prosecute for a capital offense and to plea bargain with them. Further, at the trial the jury may choose to convict a defendant of a lesser-included offense rather than find him guilty of a crime punishable by death, even if the evidence would support a capital verdict. And finally, a defendant who is convicted and sentenced to die may have his sentence commuted by the Governor of the State and the Georgia Board of Pardons and Paroles.

The existence of these discretionary stages is not determinative of the issues before us. At each of these stages an actor in the criminal justice system makes a decision which may remove a defendant from consideration as a candidate for the death penalty. *Furman*, in contrast, dealt with the decision to impose the death sentence on a specific individual who had been convicted of a capital offense. Nothing in any of our cases suggests that the decision to afford an individual defendant mercy violates the Constitution. *Furman* held only that, in order to minimize the risk that the death penalty would be imposed on a capriciously selected group of offenders, the decision to impose it had to be guided by standards so that the sentencing authority would focus on the particularized circumstances of the crime and the defendant.

2

The petitioner further contends that the capital-sentencing procedures adopted by Georgia in response to *Furman* do not eliminate the dangers of arbitrariness and caprice in jury sentencing that were held in *Furman* to be violative of the Eighth and Fourteenth Amendments. He claims that the statute is so broad and vague as to leave juries free to act as arbitrarily and capriciously as they wish in deciding whether to impose the death penalty. While there is no claim that the jury in this case relied upon a vague or overbroad provision to establish the existence of a statutory aggravating circumstance, the petitioner looks to the sentencing system as a whole (as the Court did in *Furman* and we do today) and argues that it fails to reduce sufficiently the risk of arbitrary infliction of death sentences. Specifically, Gregg urges that the statutory aggravating circumstances are too broad and too vague, that the sentencing procedure allows for arbitrary grants of mercy, and that the scope of the evidence and argument that can be considered at the presentence hearing is too wide.

The petitioner attacks the seventh statutory aggravating circumstance, which authorizes imposition of the death penalty if the murder was "outrageously or wantonly vile, horrible or inhuman in that it involved torture, depravity of mind, or an aggravated battery to the victim," contending that it is so broad that capital punishment could be imposed in any murder case. It is, of course, arguable that any murder involves depravity of mind or an aggravated battery. But this language need not be construed in this way, and there is no reason to assume that the Supreme Court of Georgia will adopt such an open-ended construction. . . .

The petitioner also argues that two of the statutory aggravating circumstances are vague and therefore susceptible of widely differing interpretations, thus creating a substantial risk that the death penalty will be arbitrarily inflicted by Georgia juries. In light of the decisions of the Supreme Court of Georgia we must disagree. . . .

The petitioner next argues that the requirements of *Furman* are not met here because the jury has the power to decline to impose the death penalty even if it finds that one or more statutory aggravating circumstances are present in the case. This contention misinterprets *Furman*. Moreover, it ignores the role of the Supreme Court of Georgia which reviews each death sentence to determine whether it is proportional to other sentences imposed for similar crimes. Since the proportionality requirement on review is intended to prevent caprice in the decision to inflict the penalty, the isolated decision of a jury to afford mercy does not render unconstitutional death sentences imposed on defendants who were sentenced under a system that does not create a substantial risk of arbitrariness or caprice.

The petitioner objects, finally, to the wide scope of evidence and argument allowed at presentence hearings. We think that the Georgia court wisely has chosen not to impose unnecessary restrictions on the evidence that can be offered at such a hearing and to approve open and far-ranging argument. So long as the evidence introduced and the arguments made at the presentence hearing do not prejudice a defendant, it is preferable not to impose restrictions. We think it desirable for the jury to have as much information before it as possible when it makes the sentencing decision.

### 3

Finally, the Georgia statute has an additional provision designed to assure that the death penalty will not be imposed on a capriciously selected group of convicted defendants. The new sentencing procedures require that the State Supreme Court review every death sentence to determine whether it was imposed under the influence of passion, prejudice, or any other arbitrary factor, whether the evidence supports the findings of a statutory aggravating circumstance, and "(w)hether the sentence of death is excessive or disproportionate to the penalty imposed in similar cases, considering both the crime and the defendant." In performing a sentence-review function, the Georgia court has held that "if the death penalty is only rarely imposed for an act or it is substantially out of line with sentences imposed for other acts it will be set aside as excessive." The court on another occasion stated that "we view it to be our duty under the similarity standard to assure that no death sentence is affirmed unless in similar cases throughout the state the death penalty has been imposed generally. . . ."

It is apparent that the Supreme Court of Georgia has taken its review responsibilities seriously. In *Coley*, it held that "(t)he prior cases indicate that the past practice among juries faced with similar factual situations and like aggravating circumstances has been to impose only the sentence of life imprisonment for the offense of rape, rather than death." It thereupon reduced Coley's sentence from death to life imprisonment. Similarly, although armed robbery is a capital offense under Georgia law, the Georgia court concluded that the death sentences imposed in this case for that crime were "unusual in that they are rarely imposed for (armed robbery). Thus, under the test provided by statute, . . . they must be considered to be excessive or disproportionate to the penalties imposed in similar cases." The court therefore vacated Gregg's death sentences for armed robbery and has followed a similar course in every other armed robbery death penalty case to come before it.

The provision for appellate review in the Georgia capital-sentencing system serves as a check against the random or arbitrary imposition of the death penalty. In particular, the proportionality review substantially eliminates the possibility that a person will be sentenced to die by the action of an aberrant jury. If a time comes when juries generally do not impose the death sentence in a certain kind of murder case, the appellate review procedures assure that no defendant convicted under such circumstances will suffer a sentence of death.

V

The basic concern of *Furman* centered on those defendants who were being condemned to death capriciously and arbitrarily. Under the procedures before the Court in that case, sentencing authorities were not directed to give attention to the nature or circumstances of the crime committed or to the character or record of the defendant. Left unguided, juries imposed the death sentence in a way that could only be called freakish. The new Georgia sentencing procedures, by contrast, focus the jury's attention on the particularized nature of the crime and the particularized characteristics of the individual defendant. While the jury is permitted to consider any aggravating or mitigating circumstances, it must find and identify at least one statutory aggravating factor before it may impose a penalty of death. In this way the jury's discretion is channeled. No longer can a jury wantonly and freakishly impose the death sentence; it is always circumscribed by the legislative guidelines. In addition, the review function of the Supreme Court of Georgia affords additional assurance that the concerns that prompted our decision in *Furman* are not present to any significant degree in the Georgia procedure applied here.

For the reasons expressed in this opinion, we hold that the statutory system under which Gregg was sentenced to death does not violate the Constitution. Accordingly, the judgment of the Georgia Supreme Court is affirmed.

**It is so ordered. . . .**

**After preparing the case brief, consider the answers to the following questions:**

1.   What does the Eighth Amendment require for fines and punishment?

2.   Which branch of government is responsible for sentencing law?

3.   What kinds of evidence should assist the Court in evaluating the "evolving standards of decency" in American society?

4.   Do you believe Georgia's new approach for capital sentencing less arbitrary?

5.   Do you believe societal views on the death penalty changed since 1976?

# PAYNE V. TENNESSEE

Supreme Court of the United States
Argued April 24, 1991
Decided June 27, 1991
Rehearing Denied Sept. 13, 1991
501 U.S. 808

## OPINION

### CHIEF JUSTICE REHNQUIST delivered the opinion of the Court.

In this case we reconsider our holdings in *Booth v. Maryland* (1987), and *South Carolina v. Gathers* (1989), that the Eighth Amendment bars the admission of victim impact evidence during the penalty phase of a capital trial.

Petitioner, Pervis Tyrone Payne, was convicted by a jury on two counts of first-degree murder and one count of assault with intent to commit murder in the first degree. He was sentenced to death for each of the murders and to 30 years in prison for the assault.

The victims of Payne's offenses were 28-year-old Charisse Christopher, her 2-year-old daughter Lacie, and her 3-year-old son Nicholas. The three lived together in an apartment in Millington, Tennessee, across the hall from Payne's girlfriend, Bobbie Thomas. On Saturday, June 27, 1987, Payne visited Thomas' apartment several times in expectation of her return from her mother's house in Arkansas, but found no one at home. On one visit, he left his overnight bag, containing clothes and other items for his weekend stay, in the hallway outside Thomas' apartment. With the bag were three cans of malt liquor.

Payne passed the morning and early afternoon injecting cocaine and drinking beer. . . . Sometime around 3 p.m., Payne returned to the apartment complex, entered the Christophers' apartment, and began making sexual advances towards Charisse. Charisse resisted and Payne became violent. A neighbor who resided in the apartment directly beneath the Christophers heard Charisse screaming, " 'Get out, get out,' as if she were telling the children to leave." The noise briefly subsided and then began, " 'horribly loud.' ". The neighbor called the police after she heard a "blood curdling scream" from the Christopher's apartment.

When the first police officer arrived at the scene, he immediately encountered Payne, who was leaving the apartment building, so covered with blood that he appeared to be " 'sweating blood.' " The officer confronted Payne, who responded, " 'I'm the complainant.' " When the officer asked,

" 'What's going on up there?' " Payne struck the officer with the overnight bag, dropped his tennis shoes, and fled.

Inside the apartment, the police encountered a horrifying scene. Blood covered the walls and floor throughout the unit. Charisse and her children were lying on the floor in the kitchen. Nicholas, despite several wounds inflicted by a butcher knife that completely penetrated through his body from front to back, was still breathing. Miraculously, he survived, but not until after undergoing seven hours of surgery. . . . Charisse and Lacie were dead.

Charisse's body was found on the kitchen floor on her back, her legs fully extended. She had sustained 42 direct knife wounds and 42 defensive wounds on her arms and hands. The wounds were caused by 41 separate thrusts of a butcher knife. None of the 84 wounds inflicted by Payne were individually fatal; rather, the cause of death was most likely bleeding from all of the wounds.

Lacie's body was on the kitchen floor near her mother. She had suffered stab wounds to the chest, abdomen, back, and head. The murder weapon, a butcher knife, was found at her feet. Payne's baseball cap was snapped on her arm near her elbow. Three cans of malt liquor bearing Payne's fingerprints were found on a table near her body, and a fourth empty one was on the landing outside the apartment door.

Payne was apprehended later that day hiding in the attic of the home of a former girlfriend. As he descended the stairs of the attic, he stated to the arresting officers, " 'Man, I ain't killed no woman.' " . . . He had blood on his body and clothes and several scratches across his chest. It was later determined that the blood stains matched the victims' blood types. A search of his pockets revealed a packet containing cocaine residue, a hypodermic syringe wrapper, and a cap from a hypodermic syringe. His overnight bag, containing a bloody white shirt, was found in a nearby dumpster.

At trial, Payne took the stand and, despite the overwhelming and relatively uncontroverted evidence against him, testified that he had not harmed any of the Christophers. Rather, he asserted that another man had raced by him as he was walking up the stairs to the floor where the Christophers lived. He stated that he had gotten blood on himself when, after hearing moans from the Christophers' apartment, he had tried to help the victims. According to his testimony, he panicked and fled when he heard police sirens and noticed the blood on his clothes. The jury returned guilty verdicts against Payne on all counts.

During the sentencing phase of the trial, Payne presented the testimony of four witnesses: his mother and father, Bobbie Thomas, and Dr. John T. Hutson, a clinical psychologist specializing in criminal court evaluation work. Bobbie Thomas testified that she met Payne at church, during a time when she was being abused by her husband. She stated that Payne was a very caring person, and that he devoted much time and attention to her three children, who were being affected by her marital difficulties. She said that the children had come to love him very much and would miss him, and that he "behaved just like a father that loved his kids." She asserted that he did not drink, nor did he use drugs, and that it was generally inconsistent with Payne's character to have committed these crimes.

Dr. Hutson testified that based on Payne's low score on an IQ test, Payne was "mentally handicapped." Hutson also said that Payne was neither psychotic nor schizophrenic, and that Payne was the most polite prisoner he had ever met. Payne's parents testified that their son had no prior criminal record and had never been arrested. They also stated that Payne had no history of alcohol or drug abuse, he worked with his father as a painter, he was good with children, and he was a good son.

The State presented the testimony of Charisse's mother, Mary Zvolanek. When asked how Nicholas had been affected by the murders of his mother and sister, she responded:

> "He cries for his mom. He doesn't seem to understand why she doesn't come home. And he cries for his sister Lacie. He comes to me many times during the week and asks me, Grandmama, do you miss my Lacie. And I tell him yes. He says, I'm worried about my Lacie."

In arguing for the death penalty during closing argument, the prosecutor commented on the continuing effects of Nicholas' experience, stating:

> "But we do know that Nicholas was alive. And Nicholas was in the same room. Nicholas was still conscious. His eyes were open. He responded to the paramedics. He was able to follow their directions. He was able to hold his intestines in as he was carried to the ambulance. So he knew what happened to his mother and baby sister."

> "There is nothing you can do to ease the pain of any of the families involved in this case. There is nothing you can do to ease the pain of Bernice or Carl Payne, and that's a tragedy. There is nothing you can

do basically to ease the pain of Mr. and Mrs. Zvolanek, and that's a tragedy. They will have to live with it the rest of their lives. There is obviously nothing you can do for Charisse and Lacie Jo. But there is something that you can do for Nicholas.

"Somewhere down the road Nicholas is going to grow up, hopefully. He's going to want to know what happened. And he is going to know what happened to his baby sister and his mother. He is going to want to know what type of justice was done. He is going to want to know what happened. With your verdict, you will provide the answer."

In the rebuttal to Payne's closing argument, the prosecutor stated:

"You saw the videotape this morning. You saw what Nicholas Christopher will carry in his mind forever. When you talk about cruel, when you talk about atrocious, and when you talk about heinous, that picture will always come into your mind, probably throughout the rest of your lives. . .

". . . No one will ever know about Lacie Jo because she never had the chance to grow up. Her life was taken from her at the age of two years old. So, no there won't be a high school principal to talk about Lacie Jo Christopher, and there won't be anybody to take her to her high school prom. And there won't be anybody there—there won't be her mother there or Nicholas' mother there to kiss him at night. His mother will never kiss him good night or pat him as he goes off to bed, or hold him and sing him a lullaby.

"[Petitioner's attorney] wants you to think about a good reputation, people who love the defendant and things about him. He doesn't want you to think about the people who love Charisse Christopher, her mother and daddy who loved her. The people who loved little Lacie Jo, the grandparents who are still here. The brother who mourns for her every single day and wants to know where his best little playmate is. He doesn't have anybody to watch cartoons with him, a little one. These are the things that go into why it is especially cruel, heinous, and atrocious, the burden that that child will carry forever."

The jury sentenced Payne to death on each of the murder counts.

The Supreme Court of Tennessee affirmed the conviction and sentence. The court rejected Payne's contention that the admission of the grandmother's testimony and the State's closing argument constituted prejudicial violations of his rights under the Eighth Amendment. . . The court characterized the grandmother's testimony as "technically irrelevant," but concluded that it "did not create a constitutionally unacceptable risk of an arbitrary imposition of the death penalty and was harmless beyond a reasonable doubt."

The court determined that the prosecutor's comments during closing argument were "relevant to [Payne's] personal responsibility and moral guilt." The court explained that "[w]hen a person deliberately picks a butcher knife out of a kitchen drawer and proceeds to stab to death a twenty-eight-year-old mother, her two and one-half year old daughter and her three and one-half year old son, in the same room, the physical and mental condition of the boy he left for dead is surely relevant in determining his 'blameworthiness.' " The court concluded that any violation of Payne's rights under *Booth* and *Gathers* "was harmless beyond a reasonable doubt."

We granted certiorari to reconsider our holdings in *Booth* and *Gathers* that the Eighth Amendment prohibits a capital sentencing jury from considering "victim impact" evidence relating to the personal characteristics of the victim and the emotional impact of the crimes on the victim's family.

In *Booth,* the defendant robbed and murdered an elderly couple. As required by a state statute, a victim impact statement was prepared based on interviews with the victims' son, daughter, son-in-law, and granddaughter. The statement, which described the personal characteristics of the victims, the emotional impact of the crimes on the family, and set forth the family members' opinions and characterizations of the crimes and the defendant, was submitted to the jury at sentencing. The jury imposed the death penalty. The conviction and sentence were affirmed on appeal by the State's highest court.

This Court held by a 5-to-4 vote that the Eighth Amendment prohibits a jury from considering a victim impact statement at the sentencing phase of a capital trial. The Court made clear that the admissibility of victim impact evidence was not to be determined on a case-by-case basis, but that such evidence was *per se* inadmissible in the sentencing phase of a capital case except to the extent that it "relate[d] directly to the circumstances of the crime." In *Gathers,* decided two years later, the Court extended the rule announced in *Booth* to statements made by a prosecutor to the sentencing jury regarding the personal qualities of the victim.

The *Booth* Court began its analysis with the observation that the capital defendant must be treated as a " 'uniquely individual human bein[g],' " and therefore the Constitution requires the jury to make an individualized determination as to whether the defendant should be executed based on the " 'character of the individual and the circumstances of the crime.' " The Court concluded that while no prior decision of this Court had mandated that only the defendant's character and immediate characteristics of the crime may constitutionally be considered, other factors are irrelevant to the capital sentencing decision unless they have "some bearing on the defendant's 'personal responsibility and moral guilt.' " To the extent that victim impact evidence presents "factors about which the defendant was unaware, and that were irrelevant to the decision to kill," the Court concluded, it has nothing to do with the "blameworthiness of a particular defendant." Evidence of the victim's character, the Court observed, "could well distract the sentencing jury from its constitutionally required task [of] determining whether the death penalty is appropriate in light of the background and record of the accused and the particular circumstances of the crime." The Court concluded that, except to the extent that victim impact evidence relates "directly to the circumstances of the crime," the prosecution may not introduce such evidence at a capital sentencing hearing because "it creates an impermissible risk that the capital sentencing decision will be made in an arbitrary manner."

*Booth* and *Gathers* were based on two premises: that evidence relating to a particular victim or to the harm that a capital defendant causes a victim's family do not in general reflect on the defendant's "blameworthiness," and that only evidence relating to "blameworthiness" is relevant to the capital sentencing decision. However, the assessment of harm caused by the defendant as a result of the crime charged has understandably been an important concern of the criminal law, both in determining the elements of the offense and in determining the appropriate punishment. Thus, two equally blameworthy criminal defendants may be guilty of different offenses solely because their acts cause differing amounts of harm. "If a bank robber aims his gun at a guard, pulls the trigger, and kills his target, he may be put to death. If the gun unexpectedly misfires, he may not. His moral guilt in both cases is identical, but his responsibility in the former is greater." The same is true with respect to two defendants, each of whom participates in a robbery, and each of whom acts with reckless disregard for human life; if the robbery in which the first defendant participated results in the death of a victim, he may be subjected to the death penalty, but if the robbery in which the second defendant participates does not result in the death of a victim, the death penalty may not be imposed.

The principles which have guided criminal sentencing—as opposed to criminal liability—have varied with the times. The book of Exodus prescribes the *Lex talionis,* "An eye for an eye, a tooth for a tooth." Exodus 21:22–23. In England and on the continent of Europe, as recently as the 18th century, crimes which would be regarded as quite minor today were capital offenses. Writing in the 18th century, the Italian criminologist Cesare Beccaria advocated the idea that "the punishment should fit the crime." He said that "[w]e have seen that the true measure of crimes is the injury done to society."

Gradually the list of crimes punishable by death diminished, and legislatures began grading the severity of crimes in accordance with the harm done by the criminal. The sentence for a given offense, rather than being precisely fixed by the legislature, was prescribed in terms of a minimum and a maximum, with the actual sentence to be decided by the judge. . . .

Wherever judges in recent years have had discretion to impose sentence, the consideration of the harm caused by the crime has been an important factor in the exercise of that discretion:

> "The first significance of harm in Anglo-American jurisprudence is, then, as a prerequisite to the criminal sanction. The second significance of harm—one no less important to judges—is as a measure of the seriousness of the offense and therefore as a standard for determining the severity of the sentence that will be meted out."

Whatever the prevailing sentencing philosophy, the sentencing authority has always been free to consider a wide range of relevant material. In the federal system, we observed that "a judge may appropriately conduct an inquiry broad in scope, largely unlimited either as to the kind of information he may consider, or the source from which it may come." Even in the context of capital sentencing, prior to *Booth* the joint opinion of Justices Stewart, Powell, and STEVENS in *Gregg v. Georgia* (1976), had rejected petitioner's attack on the Georgia statute because of the "wide scope of evidence and argument allowed at presentence hearings." The joint opinion stated:

> "We think that the Georgia court wisely has chosen not to impose unnecessary restrictions on the evidence that can be offered at such a hearing and to approve open and far-ranging argument. . . . So long as the evidence introduced and the arguments made at the presentence hearing do not prejudice a defendant, it is preferable not to impose restrictions. We think it desirable for the jury to have as much information before it as possible when it makes the sentencing decision."

The Maryland statute involved in *Booth* required that the presentence report in all felony cases include a "victim impact statement" which would describe the effect of the crime on the victim and his family. Congress and most of the States have, in recent years, enacted similar legislation to enable the sentencing authority to consider information about the harm caused by the crime committed by the defendant. . . . While the admission of this particular kind of evidence—designed to portray for the sentencing authority the actual harm caused by a particular crime—is of recent origin, this fact hardly renders it unconstitutional.

We have held that a State cannot preclude the sentencer from considering "any relevant mitigating evidence" that the defendant proffers in support of a sentence less than death. Thus we have, as the Court observed in *Booth*, required that the capital defendant be treated as a " 'uniquely individual human bein[g],' " But it was never held or even suggested in any of our cases preceding *Booth* that the defendant, entitled as he was to individualized consideration, was to receive that consideration wholly apart from the crime which he had committed. . . . This misreading of precedent in *Booth* has, we think, unfairly weighted the scales in a capital trial; while virtually no limits are placed on the relevant mitigating evidence a capital defendant may introduce concerning his own circumstances, the State is barred from either offering "a quick glimpse of the life" which a defendant "chose to extinguish," or demonstrating the loss to the victim's family and to society which has resulted from the defendant's homicide.

The *Booth* Court reasoned that victim impact evidence must be excluded because it would be difficult, if not impossible, for the defendant to rebut such evidence without shifting the focus of the sentencing hearing away from the defendant, thus creating a " 'mini-trial' on the victim's character." In many cases the evidence relating to the victim is already before the jury at least in part because of its relevance at the guilt phase of the trial. But even as to additional evidence admitted at the sentencing phase, the mere fact that for tactical reasons it might not be prudent for the defense to rebut victim impact evidence makes the case no different than others in which a party is faced with this sort of a dilemma. As we explained in rejecting the contention that expert testimony on future dangerousness should be excluded from capital trials, "the rules of evidence generally extant at the federal and state levels anticipate that relevant, unprivileged evidence should be admitted and its weight left to the factfinder, who would have the benefit of cross-examination and contrary evidence by the opposing party."

Payne echoes the concern voiced in *Booth*'s case that the admission of victim impact evidence permits a jury to find that defendants whose victims were assets to their community are more deserving of punishment than those whose victims are perceived to be less worthy. As a general matter, however, victim impact evidence is not offered to encourage comparative judgments of this kind—for instance, that the killer of a hardworking, devoted parent deserves the death penalty, but that the murderer of a reprobate does not. It is designed to show instead *each* victim's "uniqueness as an individual human being," whatever the jury might think the loss to the community resulting from his death might be. The facts of *Gathers* are an excellent illustration of this: The evidence showed that the victim was an out of work, mentally handicapped individual, perhaps not, in the eyes of most, a significant contributor to society, but nonetheless a murdered human being.

Under our constitutional system, the primary responsibility for defining crimes against state law, fixing punishments for the commission of these crimes, and establishing procedures for criminal trials rests with the States. The state laws respecting crimes, punishments, and criminal procedure are, of course, subject to the overriding provisions of the United States Constitution. Where the State imposes the death penalty for a particular crime, we have held that the Eighth Amendment imposes special limitations upon that process.

> "First, there is a required threshold below which the death penalty cannot be imposed. In this context, the State must establish rational criteria that narrow the decisionmaker's judgment as to whether the circumstances of a particular defendant's case meet the threshold. . . . Second, States cannot limit the sentencer's consideration of any relevant circumstance that could cause it to decline to impose the penalty. In this respect, the State cannot challenge the sentencer's discretion, but must allow it to consider any relevant information offered by the defendant."

But, as we noted in *California v. Ramos* (1983), "[b]eyond these limitations . . . the Court has deferred to the State's choice of substantive factors relevant to the penalty determination."

. . . The States remain free, in capital cases, as well as others, to devise new procedures and new remedies to meet felt needs. Victim impact evidence is simply another form or method of informing the sentencing authority about the specific harm caused by the crime in question, evidence of a general type long considered by sentencing authorities. We think the *Booth* Court was wrong in stating that this kind of evidence leads to the arbitrary imposition of the death penalty. In the majority of cases, and in this case, victim impact evidence serves entirely legitimate purposes. In the event that evidence is introduced that is so unduly prejudicial that it renders the trial fundamentally unfair, the Due Process Clause of the Fourteenth Amendment provides a mechanism for relief. Courts have always taken into consideration the harm done by the defendant in imposing sentence, and the evidence adduced in this case was illustrative of the harm caused by Payne's double murder.

We are now of the view that a State may properly conclude that for the jury to assess meaningfully the defendant's moral culpability and blameworthiness, it should have before it at the sentencing phase evidence of the specific harm caused by the defendant. "[T]he State has a legitimate interest in counteracting the mitigating evidence which the defendant is entitled to put in, by reminding the sentencer that just as the murderer should be considered as an individual, so too the victim is an individual whose death represents a unique loss to society and in particular to his family." By turning the victim into a "faceless stranger at the penalty phase of a capital trial," *Booth* deprives the State of the full moral force of its evidence and may prevent the jury from having before it all the information necessary to determine the proper punishment for a first-degree murder.

The present case is an example of the potential for such unfairness. The capital sentencing jury heard testimony from Payne's girlfriend that they met at church; that he was affectionate, caring, and kind to her children; that he was not an abuser of drugs or alcohol; and that it was inconsistent with his character to have committed the murders. Payne's parents testified that he was a good son, and a clinical psychologist testified that Payne was an extremely polite prisoner and suffered from a low IQ. None of this testimony was related to the circumstances of Payne's brutal crimes. In contrast, the only evidence of the impact of Payne's offenses during the sentencing phase was Nicholas' grandmother's description—in response to a single question—that the child misses his mother and baby sister. Payne argues that the Eighth Amendment commands that the jury's death sentence must be set aside because the jury heard this testimony. But the testimony illustrated quite poignantly some of the harm that Payne's killing had caused; there is nothing unfair about allowing the jury to bear in mind that harm at the same time as it considers the mitigating evidence introduced by the defendant. . . .

In *Gathers,* as indicated above, we extended the holding of *Booth* barring victim impact evidence to the prosecutor's argument to the jury. Human nature being what it is, capable lawyers trying cases to juries try to convey to the jurors that the people involved in the underlying events are, or were, living human beings, with something to be gained or lost from the jury's verdict. Under the aegis of the Eighth Amendment, we have given the broadest latitude to the defendant to introduce relevant mitigating evidence reflecting on his individual personality, and the defendant's attorney may argue that evidence to the jury. Petitioner's attorney in this case did just that. For the reasons discussed above, we now reject the view—expressed in *Gathers*—that a State may not permit the prosecutor to similarly argue to the jury the human cost of the crime of which the defendant stands convicted. We reaffirm the view expressed by Justice Cardozo in *Snyder v. Massachusetts,* 291 U.S. 97 (1934): "[J]ustice, though due to the accused, is due to the accuser also. The concept of fairness must not be strained till it is narrowed to a filament. We are to keep the balance true."

We thus hold that if the State chooses to permit the admission of victim impact evidence and prosecutorial argument on that subject, the Eighth Amendment erects no *per se* bar. A State may legitimately conclude that evidence about the victim and about the impact of the murder on the victim's family is relevant to the jury's decision as to whether or not the death penalty should be imposed. There is no reason to treat such evidence differently than other relevant evidence is treated.

Payne and his *amicus* argue that despite these numerous infirmities in the rule created by *Booth* and *Gathers,* we should adhere to the doctrine of *stare decisis* and stop short of overruling those cases. *Stare decisis* is the preferred course because it promotes the evenhanded, predictable, and consistent development of legal principles, fosters reliance on judicial decisions, and contributes to the actual and perceived integrity of the judicial process. Adhering to precedent "is usually the wise policy, because in most matters it is more important that the applicable rule of law be settled than it be settled right." Nevertheless, when governing decisions are unworkable or are badly reasoned, "this Court has never felt constrained to follow precedent." *Stare decisis* is not an inexorable command; rather, it "is a principle of policy and not a mechanical formula of adherence to the latest decision." This is particularly true in constitutional cases, because in such cases "correction through legislative action is practically impossible." . . .

Applying these general principles, the Court has during the past 20 Terms overruled in whole or in part 33 of its previous constitutional decisions. *Booth* and *Gathers* were decided by the narrowest of margins, over spirited dissents challenging the basic underpinnings of those decisions. They have been questioned by Members of the Court in later decisions, and have defied consistent application by the lower courts. Reconsidering these decisions now, we conclude, for the reasons heretofore stated, that they were wrongly decided and should be, and now are, overruled.

We accordingly affirm the judgment of the Supreme Court of Tennessee.

*It is so ordered.*

**JUSTICE MARSHALL, with whom JUSTICE BLACKMUN joins, dissenting.**

Power, not reason, is the new currency of this Court's decision-making. Four Terms ago, a five-Justice majority of this Court held that "victim impact" evidence of the type at issue in this case could not constitutionally be introduced during the penalty phase of a capital trial. By another 5–4 vote, a majority of this Court rebuffed an attack upon this ruling just two Terms ago. Nevertheless, having expressly invited respondent to renew the attack, today's majority overrules *Booth* and *Gathers* and credits the dissenting views expressed in those cases. Neither the law nor the facts supporting *Booth* and *Gathers* underwent any change in the last four years. Only the personnel of this Court did.

In dispatching *Booth* and *Gathers* to their graves, today's majority ominously suggests that an even more extensive upheaval of this Court's precedents may be in store. Renouncing this Court's historical commitment to a conception of "the judiciary as a source of impersonal and reasoned judgments," the majority declares itself free to discard any principle of constitutional liberty which was recognized or reaffirmed over the dissenting votes of four Justices and with which five or more Justices *now* disagree. The implications of this radical new exception to the doctrine of *stare decisis* are staggering. The majority today sends a clear signal that scores of established constitutional liberties are now ripe for reconsideration, thereby inviting the very type of open defiance of our precedents that the majority rewards in this case. Because I believe that this Court owes more to its constitutional precedents in general and to *Booth* and *Gathers* in particular, I dissent.

I

Speaking for the Court as then constituted, Justice Powell and Justice Brennan set out the rationale for excluding victim-impact evidence from the sentencing proceedings in a capital case. As the majorities in *Booth* and *Gathers* recognized, the core principle of this Court's capital jurisprudence is that the sentence of death must reflect an " '*individualized* determination' " of the defendant's " 'personal responsibility and moral guilt' " and must be based upon factors that channel the jury's discretion " 'so as to minimize the risk of wholly arbitrary and capricious action.' " The State's introduction of victim-impact evidence, Justice Powell and Justice Brennan explained, violates this fundamental principle. Where, as is ordinarily the case, the defendant was unaware of the personal circumstances of his victim, admitting evidence of the victim's character and the impact of the murder upon the victim's family predicates the sentencing determination on "factors . . . wholly unrelated to the blameworthiness of [the] particular defendant." And even where the defendant *was* in a position to foresee the likely impact of his conduct, admission of victim-impact evidence creates an unacceptable risk of sentencing arbitrariness. As Justice Powell explained in *Booth,* the probative value of such evidence is always outweighed by its prejudicial effect because of its inherent capacity to draw the jury's attention away from the character of the defendant and the circumstances of the crime to such illicit considerations as the eloquence with which family members express their grief and the status of the victim in the community. I continue to find these considerations wholly persuasive, and I see no purpose in trying to improve upon Justice Powell's and Justice Brennan's exposition of them.

There is nothing new in the majority's discussion of the supposed deficiencies in *Booth* and *Gathers.* Every one of the arguments made by the majority can be found in the dissenting opinions filed in those two cases, and, as I show in the margin, each argument was convincingly answered by Justice Powell and Justice Brennan.

But contrary to the impression that one might receive from reading the majority's lengthy rehearsing of the issues addressed in *Booth* and *Gathers,* the outcome of this case does not turn simply on who—the *Booth* and *Gathers* majorities or the *Booth* and *Gathers* dissenters—had the better of the argument. Justice Powell and Justice Brennan's position carried the day in those cases and became the law of the land. The real question, then, is whether today's majority has come forward with the type of extraordinary showing that this Court has historically demanded before overruling one of its precedents. In my view, the majority clearly has not made any such showing. Indeed, the striking feature of the majority's opinion is its radical assertion that it need not even try.

II

The overruling of one of this Court's precedents ought to be a matter of great moment and consequence. Although the doctrine of *stare decisis* is not an "inexorable command," this Court has repeatedly stressed that fidelity to precedent is fundamental to "a society governed by the rule of law."

Consequently, this Court has never departed from precedent without "special justification." Such justifications include the advent of "subsequent changes or development in the law" that undermine a decision's rationale; and a showing that a particular precedent has become a "detriment to coherence and consistency in the law."

The majority cannot seriously claim that *any* of these traditional bases for overruling a precedent applies to *Booth* or *Gathers*. The majority does not suggest that the legal rationale of these decisions has been undercut by changes or developments in doctrine during the last two years. Nor does the majority claim that experience over that period of time has discredited the principle that "any decision to impose the death sentence be, and appear to be, based on reason rather than caprice or emotion," the larger postulate of political morality on which *Booth* and *Gathers* rest. . .

This truncation of the Court's duty to stand by its own precedents is astonishing. . .In my view, this impoverished conception of *stare decisis* cannot possibly be reconciled with the values that inform the proper judicial function. Contrary to what the majority suggests, *stare decisis* is important not merely because individuals rely on precedent to structure their commercial activity but because fidelity to precedent is part and parcel of a conception of "the judiciary as a source of impersonal and reasoned judgments." Indeed, this function of *stare decisis* is in many respects even *more* critical in adjudication involving constitutional liberties than in adjudication involving commercial entitlements. Because enforcement of the Bill of Rights and the Fourteenth Amendment frequently requires this Court to rein in the forces of democratic politics, this Court can legitimately lay claim to compliance with its directives only if the public understands the Court to be implementing "principles . . . founded in the law rather than in the proclivities of individuals." Thus, as Justice STEVENS has explained, the "stron[g] presumption of validity" to which "recently decided cases" are entitled "is an essential thread in the mantle of protection that the law affords the individual. . . . It is the unpopular or beleaguered individual—not the man in power—who has the greatest stake in the integrity of the law."

Carried to its logical conclusion, the majority's debilitated conception of *stare decisis* would destroy the Court's very capacity to resolve authoritatively the abiding conflicts between those with power and those without. If this Court shows so little respect for its own precedents, it can hardly expect them to be treated more respectfully by the state actors whom these decisions are supposed to bind. By signaling its willingness to give fresh consideration to any constitutional liberty recognized by a 5–4 vote "over spirited dissen[t]," the majority invites state actors to renew the very policies deemed unconstitutional in the hope that this Court may now reverse course, even if it has only recently reaffirmed the constitutional liberty in question.

. . . It is hard to imagine a more complete abdication of this Court's historic commitment to defending the supremacy of its own pronouncements on issues of constitutional liberty. In light of the cost that such abdication exacts on the authoritativeness of *all* of this Court's pronouncements, it is also hard to imagine a more short-sighted strategy for effecting change in our constitutional order.

III

Today's decision charts an unmistakable course. If the majority's radical reconstruction of the rules for overturning this Court's decisions is to be taken at face value—and the majority offers us no reason why it should not—then the overruling of *Booth* and *Gathers* is but a preview of an even broader and more far-reaching assault upon this Court's precedents. Cast aside today are those condemned to face society's ultimate penalty. Tomorrow's victims may be minorities, women, or the indigent. Inevitably, this campaign to resurrect yesterday's "spirited dissents" will squander the authority and the legitimacy of this Court as a protector of the powerless.

I dissent.

**JUSTICE STEVENS, with whom JUSTICE BLACKMUN joins, dissenting.**

The novel rule that the Court announces today represents a dramatic departure from the principles that have governed our capital sentencing jurisprudence for decades. Justice MARSHALL is properly concerned about the majority's trivialization of the doctrine of *stare decisis*. But even if *Booth v. Maryland,* 482 U.S. 496 (1987), and *South Carolina v. Gathers,* 490 U.S. 805 (1989), had not been decided, today's decision would represent a sharp break with past decisions. Our cases provide no support whatsoever for the majority's conclusion that the prosecutor may introduce evidence that sheds no light on the defendant's guilt or moral culpability, and thus serves no purpose other than to encourage jurors to decide in favor of death rather than life on the basis of their emotions rather than their reason.

Until today our capital punishment jurisprudence has required that any decision to impose the death penalty be based solely on evidence that tends to inform the jury about the character of the offense and the character of the defendant. Evidence that serves no purpose other than to appeal to the sympathies or emotions of the jurors has never been considered admissible. Thus, if a defendant, who had murdered a convenience store clerk in cold blood in the course of an armed robbery, offered evidence unknown to him at the time of the crime about the immoral character of his victim, all would recognize immediately that the evidence was irrelevant and inadmissible. Evenhanded justice requires that the same constraint be imposed on the advocate of the death penalty.

I

In *Williams v. New York,* 337 U.S. 241 (1949), this Court considered the scope of the inquiry that should precede the imposition of a death sentence. Relying on practices that had developed "both before and since the American colonies became a nation," Justice Black described the wide latitude that had been accorded judges in considering the source and type of evidence that is relevant to the sentencing determination. Notably, that opinion refers not only to the relevance of evidence establishing the defendant's guilt, but also to the relevance of "the fullest information possible concerning the defendant's life and characteristics." "Victim impact" evidence, however, was unheard of when *Williams* was decided. The relevant evidence of harm to society consisted of proof that the defendant was guilty of the offense charged in the indictment.

Almost 30 years after our decision in *Williams,* the Court reviewed the scope of evidence relevant in capital sentencing. In his plurality opinion, Chief Justice Burger concluded that in a capital case, the sentencer must not be prevented "from considering, as a mitigating factor, any aspect of a defendant's character or record and any of the circumstances of the offense that the defendant proffers as a basis for a sentence less than death." As in *Williams,* the character of the offense and the character of the offender constituted the entire category of relevant evidence. "Victim impact" evidence was still unheard of when *Lockett* was decided.

As the Court acknowledges today, the use of victim impact evidence "is of recent origin." Insofar as the Court's jurisprudence is concerned, this type of evidence made its first appearance in 1987 in *Booth v. Maryland.* In his opinion for the Court, Justice Powell noted that our prior cases had stated that the question whether an individual defendant should be executed is to be determined on the basis of " 'the character of the individual and the circumstances of the crime.' Relying on those cases. . . the Court concluded that unless evidence has some bearing on the defendant's personal responsibility and moral guilt, its admission would create a risk that a death sentence might be based on considerations that are constitutionally impermissible or totally irrelevant to the sentencing process. Evidence that served no purpose except to describe the personal characteristics of the victim and the emotional impact of the crime on the victim's family was therefore constitutionally irrelevant.

Our decision in *Booth* was entirely consistent with the practices that had been followed "both before and since the American colonies became a nation." Our holding was mandated by our capital punishment jurisprudence, which requires any decision to impose the death penalty to be based on reason rather than caprice or emotion. The dissenting opinions in *Booth* and in *Gathers* can be searched in vain for any judicial precedent sanctioning the use of evidence unrelated to the character of the offense or the character of the offender in the sentencing process. Today, however, relying on nothing more than those dissenting opinions, the Court abandons rules of relevance that are older than the Nation itself and ventures into uncharted seas of irrelevance.

II

Today's majority has obviously been moved by an argument that has strong political appeal but no proper place in a reasoned judicial opinion. Because our decision in *Lockett,* recognizes the defendant's right to introduce all mitigating evidence that may inform the jury about his character, the Court suggests that fairness requires that the State be allowed to respond with similar evidence about the *victim.* This argument is a classic *non sequitur.* The victim is not on trial; her character, whether good or bad, cannot therefore constitute either an aggravating or a mitigating circumstance.

Even if introduction of evidence about the victim could be equated with introduction of evidence about the defendant, the argument would remain flawed in both its premise and its conclusion. The conclusion that exclusion of victim impact evidence results in a significantly imbalanced sentencing procedure is simply inaccurate. . . .

The premise that a criminal prosecution requires an even-handed balance between the State and the defendant is also incorrect. The Constitution grants certain rights to the criminal defendant and imposes special limitations on the State designed to protect the individual from overreaching by the disproportionately powerful State. Thus, the State must prove a defendant's guilt beyond a reasonable doubt. Rules of evidence are also weighted in the defendant's favor. . . . Even if balance were required or desirable, today's decision, by permitting both the defendant and the State to introduce irrelevant evidence for the sentencer's consideration without any guidance, surely does nothing to enhance parity in the sentencing process.

III

Victim impact evidence, as used in this case, has two flaws, both related to the Eighth Amendment's command that the punishment of death may not be meted out arbitrarily or capriciously. First, aspects of the character of the victim unforeseeable to the defendant at the time of his crime are irrelevant the defendant's "personal responsibility and moral guilt" and therefore cannot justify a death sentence.

Second, the quantity and quality of victim impact evidence sufficient to turn a verdict of life in prison into a verdict of death is not defined until after the crime has been committed and therefore cannot possibly be applied consistently in different cases. The sentencer's unguided consideration of victim impact evidence thus conflicts with the principle central to our capital punishment jurisprudence that, "where discretion is afforded a sentencing body on a matter so grave as the determination of whether a human life should be taken or spared, that discretion must be suitably directed and limited so as to minimize the risk of wholly arbitrary and capricious action." . . .

The majority attempts to justify the admission of victim impact evidence by arguing that "consideration of the harm caused by the crime has been an important factor in the exercise of [sentencing] discretion." This statement is misleading and inaccurate. It is misleading because it is not limited to harm that is foreseeable. It is inaccurate because it fails to differentiate between legislative determinations and judicial sentencing. It is true that an evaluation of the harm caused by different kinds of wrongful conduct is a critical aspect in legislative definitions of offenses and determinations concerning sentencing guidelines. There is a rational correlation between moral culpability and the foreseeable harm caused by criminal conduct. Moreover, in the capital sentencing area, legislative identification of the special aggravating factors that may justify the imposition of the death penalty is entirely appropriate. But the majority cites no authority for the suggestion that unforeseeable and indirect harms to a victim's family are properly considered as aggravating evidence on a case-by-case basis. . . .

V

. . .

Given the current popularity of capital punishment in a crime-ridden society, the political appeal of arguments that assume that increasing the severity of sentences is the best cure for the cancer of crime, and the political strength of the "victims' rights" movement, I recognize that today's decision will be greeted with enthusiasm by a large number of concerned and thoughtful citizens. The great tragedy of the decision, however, is the danger that the "hydraulic pressure" of public opinion that Justice Holmes once described— and that properly influences the deliberations of democratic legislatures—has played a role not only in the Court's decision to hear this case, and in its decision to reach the constitutional question without pausing to consider affirming on the basis of the Tennessee Supreme Court's rationale, but even in its resolution of the constitutional issue involved. Today is a sad day for a great institution.

**After preparing the case brief, consider the answers to the following questions:**

1.  What is victim impact testimony?

2.  What purpose does the government argue this testimony serves?

3.  What are the risks or problems posed by victim impact evidence?

4.  Did the Court reach the right result—if mitigating evidence is admissible, should victim impact evidence also be considered?

# Chapter 11 Key Terms for Review

- **Retribution**: a theory of punishment that seeks to match the severity of the wrong committed with the severity of the punishment the offender receives.

- **Deterrence**: a theory of punishment that utilizes punishment to send a message to the defendant and the public that discourages future criminality.

- **Rehabilitation**: a theory of punishment that seeks to diagnose and address the underlying reasons for the defendant's criminal conduct.

- **Incapacitation**: a theory of punishment that attempts to prevent future crimes, like deterrence, but does so by banishing the defendant from society for a period of time, physically removing them rendering them incapable of future criminality.

- **Restorative Justice**: a theory of punishment which focuses on victims and the community affected by the crime as much as it does the offender by seeking to repair the damage caused by the crime through reconciliation.

- **Determinate sentencing**: the legislature determines the appropriate range for a sentence for each crime and judges can impose a definite term of incarceration within that range; the sentence is not subject to review by a parole board or other agency.

- **Indeterminate sentencing**: provides judges with a range of years that may be imposed for certain convictions, such as 1 to 5 years. In most states the offender can request parole or early release after a set portion of the sentence is complete (typically at least half).

- **Parole board**: a group of individuals who evaluate prisoner petitions for early release. Typically composed of experts working in the field of corrections, each state has its own parole board and may also take the board with reviewing pardons.

- **Mandatory minimum sentence**: sentencing laws which take discretion from judges and impose pre-determined sentences for specific convictions.

- **Relevant conduct**: in the context of federal sentencing is a determination of the "real" conduct that may go beyond what the jury determined at trial.

- **First Step Act (2018)**: enacted several reforms to federal mandatory minimum sentencing laws and changes to the federal prison system, including reducing the length of some mandatory minimum sentences.

- **Incarceration**: all felonies and most misdemeanor convictions carry a potential sentence of incarceration, confinement or imprisonment in a correctional institution such as a jail or prison.

- **Probation**: an alternative punishment to incarceration that allows the convicted offender to live at home while under supervision by a correctional agency.

- **Home-confinement**: similar to probation this allows the offender to live at home but under more restricted supervision and monitoring.

- **Community service**: volunteer work performed by offenders in exchange for work credits or as a condition of release on probation.

- **Diversion programs**: permit diversion to a treatment program—completion of which results in dismissal of the pending charges; the most common are drug treatment and counseling programs.

- **Fine**: a monetary penalty paid to the government for certain convictions.

- **Corporate defendant**: when a corporation rather than an individual is the defendant fines are the only real punishment available to the court.

- **Restitution**: when a criminal act has caused a victim to incur a financial loss, the defendant may have to repay the victims for their actual loss.

- **Pre-sentence investigation (PSI)**: probation officers conduct a PSI to provide the court with sentencing recommendations based on the defendant's family background, employment, mental and physical health, finances and prior criminal history.

- **Pre-sentence report (PSR)**: contains detailed, confidential information, and is not made public. This report provides the court with a recommendation for sentencing the defendant.

- **Aggravating evidence**: evidence that demonstrates that the defendant deserves a longer or harsher sentence or punishment.

- **Mitigating evidence**: evidence that reduces the defendant's culpability—such as a history of addiction, mental illness, or other circumstances that may explain (but not excuse) their criminal conduct.

- **Victim impact statement**: victims are permitted to speak or have statements read before the judge at sentencing hearings. They are allowed to explain the emotional, physical, or financial toll that the defendant's conduct caused.

- **Death penalty**: execution as punishment for a crime.

- **Death-qualified attorney**: many states an attorney appointed to represent a defendant in a death penalty case must have experience in a capital case.

- **Bifurcated trials**: death penalty trials are divided into two phases—first, the guilt phase where a jury determines the verdict (guilty or innocent); and second, the penalty phase, where the jury hears mitigating and aggravating evidence to guide their sentencing decision.

# Criminal Appeals and Post-Conviction Relief

## A. CRIMINAL APPEALS

Once a defendant has been convicted at trial they have a right to challenge their conviction through an **appeal**. An appeal is a request made to a higher court to review some aspect of the trial below. Criminal defendants, unhappy with the result, may appeal their case asserting that errors were made which require reversal of their conviction. The party filing the appeal is referred to as the **appellant or petitioner,** and the responding party is referred to the **appellee or respondent**.

The basic process of an appeal varies among jurisdictions, but typically involves first filing a notice of appeal with the trial court. The specific rules in each jurisdiction dictate the time frame within which a defendant must file notice of appeal. Once notice is filed, the trial court prepares the **appellate record** for transmittal to the appellate court. This record includes all of the materials and transcript of the trial. The parties then prepare and submit **appellate briefs** arguing their positions advocating for a favorable outcome.

After the briefs have been submitted, the case may be scheduled for **oral argument**. Oral argument is not a right and some jurisdictions have eliminated them altogether for routine cases. When they are used, the lawyers for both parties are allotted a specific amount of time for oral argument.

Once the appellate court has reached a decision, they issue a written **opinion**. The opinion explains the court's reasoning and the outcome of the case. A **per curium opinion** is written by the court without naming a specific author. Judges who agree with the majority of the court but wish to write separately to further explain their reasoning author **concurring opinions**. Judges who disagree with the result may choose to write a **dissenting opinion**. In some cases the judges may be able to agree in the result, but not in the reasoning for it, so there is no majority opinion. These are called **plurality opinions**.

The Supreme Court has never held that there is a federal constitutional right to appeal.[1] Appeals are authorized by state and federal statutes and are either mandatory or discretionary. In a **mandatory or automatic appeal** the defendant has a right to the appeal. The Supreme Court held in *Douglas v. California (1963)* that defendants have a right to the assistance of counsel for mandatory appeals.[2] This right encompasses the constitutional right to the effective assistance of counsel, but the attorney need not raise every frivolous issue asserted by the defendant in order to meet that requirement.[3]

For a **discretionary appeal** the defendant may request review but the appellate court is not required to grant it. According to the Supreme Court's holding in *Ross v. Moffitt (1974)*[4] states are not required to grant defendants a right to appeal, but when they do, they must do so in a way that does not discriminate against the poor. In *Griffin v. Illinois (1956)*[5] the Supreme Court held that the Equal Protection Clause is violated if appellate review is more difficult to access for the poor than the rich. The defendant has no right to the assistance of counsel for discretionary appeals.[6]

Even when an error is made during a defendant's trial the mistake may not require reversal of the conviction. Appellate courts must determine whether the error was harmless or reversible. **Harmless error** results when there is no reasonable probability that the error contributed to the defendant's conviction and is should be affirmed.[7] The Court has considered a wide variety of errors under this harmless error standard, such as prosecutorial comments on the right to remain silent, illegally obtained confessions or evidence used at trial, and the right to counsel at non-trial stages. In all of these examples, so long as there was a reasonable probability that the errors had not contributed to the defendant's conviction, they were deemed harmless.

**Reversible error** is one so significant that there is a reasonable probability that the court's error contributed to the defendant's conviction. One situation where the error is always a reversible error is the failure to provide counsel at trial.

---

[1]   *Ross v. Moffitt*, 417 U.S. 600 (1974).

[2]   *Douglas v. California*, 372 U.S. 353 (1963).

[3]   *Evitts v. Lucey*, 469 U.S. 387 (1985).

[4]   417 U.S. 600 (1974).

[5]   351 U.S. 12 (1956).

[6]   417 U.S. 600 (1974).

[7]   *Chapman v. California*, 386 U.S. 18 (1967).

A defendant's right to counsel at trial is absolute and failure to provide counsel would result in automatic reversal on appeal.[8] Indigent defendants must also be provided with a free copy of the full transcript for any appeal where it is required for review. In *Mayer v. City of Chicago (1971)* the Supreme Court held that this is true even in misdemeanor cases.[9]

## B. POST-CONVICTION RELIEF THROUGH THE WRIT OF HABEAS CORPUS

Article I, Section 9 of the U.S. Constitution provides that "the **Writ of Habeas Corpus** shall not be suspended, unless when in cases of rebellion or invasion the public safety may require it." The Judiciary Act of 1789 gave federal judges the power to grant the writ of habeas corpus to federal prisoners and in 1867 this authority was extended to granting the writ to state prisoners as well. A **habeas petition** is a civil action brought by an inmate requesting that the court direct their release because their confinement violates the Constitution or fundamental law.[10]

A habeas corpus proceeding is a **collateral attack**, or indirect challenge alleging unlawful confinement, not a direct attack on the defendant's conviction.[11] The defendant, not the state, bears the **burden of proof** in a habeas proceeding. The standard of proof is a **preponderance of the evidence**, which means that it is more likely than not that the detention is unlawful. The defendant must be released if the constitutional error alleged, ". . .had a substantial and injurious effect or influence in determining the jury's verdict" in light of the entire context of the case.[12] The *preponderance* standard is applied because of the civil nature of habeas proceedings.

The standard of review in habeas cases is de novo. **De novo review** means that the appellate court gives deference to the interpretation of the facts from the trial record and reviews primarily whether the law was correctly interpreted and applied by the lower court. The defendant has no right to counsel in habeas proceedings except for defendants in capital cases under a federal statute.[13]

For a state prisoner to gain access to the federal courts for habeas relief, they must allege a violation of federal constitutional rights. The inmate may petition

---

[8]  *Sullivan v. Louisiana,* 508 U.S. 275 (1993).

[9]  404 U.S. 189 (1971).

[10]  *Preiser v. Rodriguez,* 411 U.S. 475 (1973).

[11]  *Wall v. Kholi,* 562 U.S. 545 (2011).

[12]  *Calderon v. Coleman,* 525 U.S. 141 (1993).

[13]  18 U.S.C. § 3599.

the U.S. Supreme Court for review, but **exhaustion of their state-based rights and remedies** must take place first. This means that they have navigated the entire appellate process provided by the state courts before petitioning the Supreme Court for review. They can also petition the federal district court directly asking them to issue the writ of habeas corpus.

The Due Process Revolution under the Warren Court resulted in greatly expanded Constitutional rights for defendants, and as a result access to the federal courts for habeas relief expanded dramatically as well. Under the Berger and Rehnquist courts access to habeas review contracted somewhat as limitations were placed on its use. In *Stone v. Powell (1976)* the Supreme Court held that Fourth Amendment claims were not within the scope of habeas review.[14] In 1989 the Supreme Court held that petitioner's are not allowed habeas review based on new rules of law announced after their conviction.[15]

---

[14]   428 U.S. 465 (1976).

[15]   *Teague v. Lane*, 489 U.S. 288 (1989).

**Read and brief each of the following cases relating to criminal appeals and post-conviction relief and consider the questions following each case:**

1.  *Douglas v. California*: the right to counsel for mandatory appeals

2.  *Ross v. Moffit*: the right to counsel for discretionary appeals

3.  *Teague v. Lane*: retroactivity of constitutional rights, the writ of habeas corpus

---

## DOUGLAS V. CALIFORNIA

Supreme Court of the United States
Reargued Jan. 16, 1963
Decided March 18, 1963
Rehearing Denied April 29, 1963
372 U.S. 353

### OPINION

### MR. JUSTICE DOUGLAS delivered the opinion of the Court.

Petitioners, Bennie Will Meyes and William Douglas, were jointly tried and convicted in a California court on an information charging them with 13 felonies. A single public defender was appointed to represent them. At the commencement of the trial, the defender moved for a continuance, stating that the case was very complicated, that he was not as prepared as he felt he should be because he was handling a different defense every day, and that there was a conflict of interest between the petitioners requiring the appointment of separate counsel for each of them. This motion was denied. Thereafter, petitioners dismissed the defender, claiming he was unprepared, and again renewed motions for separate counsel and for a continuance. These motions also were denied, and petitioners were ultimately convicted by a jury of all 13 felonies, which included robbery, assault with a deadly weapon, and assault with intent to commit murder. Both were given prison terms. Both appealed as of right to the California District Court of Appeal. That court affirmed their convictions. Both Meyes and Douglas then petitioned for further discretionary review in the California Supreme Court, but their petitions were denied without a hearing. We granted certiorari.

Although several questions are presented in the petition for certiorari, we address ourselves to only one of them. The record shows that petitioners requested, and were denied, the assistance of counsel on appeal, even though it plainly appeared they were indigents. In denying petitioners' requests, the California District Court of Appeal stated that it had 'gone through' the record and had come to the conclusion that 'no good whatever could be served by appointment of counsel.' The District Court of Appeal was acting in accordance with a California rule of criminal procedure which provides that state appellate courts, upon the request of an indigent for counsel, may make 'an independent investigation of the record and determine whether it would be of advantage to the defendant or helpful to the appellate court to have counsel appointed. \* \* \* After such investigation, appellate courts should appoint counsel if in their opinion it would be helpful to the defendant or the court, and should deny the appointment of counsel only if in their judgment such appointment would be of no value to either the defendant or the court.'

We agree, however, with Justice Traynor of the California Supreme Court, who said that the '(d)enial of counsel on appeal (to an indigent) would seem to be a discrimination at least as invidious as that condemned in *Griffin v. People of State of Illinois* . . .we held that a State may not grant appellate review in such a way as to discriminate against some convicted defendants on account of their poverty. There. . .the right to a free transcript on appeal was in issue. Here the issue is whether or not an indigent shall be denied the assistance of counsel on appeal. In either case the evil is the same: discrimination against the indigent. For there can be no equal justice where the kind of an appeal a man enjoys 'depends on the amount of money he has.' *Griffin v. Illinois*, supra, at p. 19, 76 S.Ct., at p. 591.

In spite of California's forward treatment of indigents, under its present practice the type of an appeal a person is afforded in the District Court of Appeal hinges upon whether or not he can pay for the assistance of counsel. If he can the appellate court passes on the merits of his case only after having the full benefit of written briefs and oral argument by counsel. If he cannot the appellate court is forced to prejudge the merits before it can even determine whether counsel should be provided. At this stage in the proceedings only the barren record speaks for the indigent, and, unless the printed pages show that an injustice has been committed, he is forced to go without a champion on appeal. Any real chance he may have had of showing that his appeal has hidden merit is deprived him when the court decides on an ex parte examination of the record that the assistance of counsel is not required.

We are not here concerned with problems that might arise from the denial of counsel for the preparation of a petition for discretionary or mandatory review beyond the stage in the appellate process at which the claims have once been presented by a lawyer and passed upon by an appellate court. We are dealing only with the first appeal, granted as a matter of right to rich and poor alike (Cal.Penal Code §§ 1235, 1237), from a criminal conviction.

We need not now decide whether California would have to provide counsel for an indigent seeking a discretionary hearing from the California Supreme Court after the District Court of Appeal had sustained his conviction (see Cal.Const., Art. VI, s 4c; Cal.Rules on Appeal, Rules 28, 29), or whether counsel must be appointed for an indigent seeking review of an appellate affirmance of his conviction in this Court by appeal as of right or by petition for a writ of certiorari which lies within the Court's discretion. But it is appropriate to observe that a State can, consistently with the Fourteenth Amendment, provide for differences so long as the result does not amount to a denial of due process or an 'invidious discrimination.' . . .But where the merits of the one and only appeal an indigent has as of right are decided without benefit of counsel, we think an unconstitutional line has been drawn between rich and poor.

When an indigent is forced to run this gantlet of a preliminary showing of merit, the right to appeal does not comport with fair procedure. In the federal courts, on the other hand, an indigent must be afforded counsel on appeal whenever he challenges a certification that the appeal is not taken in good faith. *Johnson v. United States*, 352 U.S. 565. The federal courts must honor his request for counsel regardless of what they think the merits of the case may be; and 'representation in the role of an advocate is required.' *Ellis v. United States*, 356 U.S. 674, 675. In California, however, once the court has 'gone through' the record and denied counsel, the indigent has no recourse but to prosecute his appeal on his own, as best he can, no matter how meritorious his case may turn out to be. The present case, where counsel was denied petitioners on appeal, shows that the discrimination is not between 'possibly good and obviously bad cases,' but between cases where the rich man can require the court to listen to argument of counsel before deciding on the merits, but a poor man cannot. There is lacking that equality demanded by the Fourteenth Amendment where the rich man, who appeals as of right, enjoys the benefit of counsel's examination into the record, research of the law, and marshalling of arguments on his behalf, while the indigent, already burdened by a preliminary determination that his case is without merit, is forced to shift for himself. The indigent, where the record is unclear or the errors are hidden, has only the right to a meaningless ritual, while the rich man has a meaningful appeal.

We vacate the judgment of the District Court of Appeal and remand the case to that court for further proceedings not inconsistent with this opinion.

**It is so ordered.**

**Judgment of the District Court of Appeal vacated and case remanded.**

MR. JUSTICE CLARK, dissenting.

I adhere to my vote in *Griffin v. Illinois*, 351 U.S. 12 (1956), but, as I have always understood that case, it does not control here. It had to do with the State's obligation to furnish a record to an indigent on appeal. There we took pains to point out that the State was free to 'find other means of affording adequate and effective appellate review to indigent defendants.' Id., at 20, 76 S.Ct., at 591. Here California has done just that in its procedure for furnishing attorneys for indigents on appeal. We all know that the overwhelming percentage of in forma pauperis appeals are frivolous. Statistics of this Court show that over 96% of the petitions filed here are of this variety. California, in the light of a like experience, has provided that upon the filing of an application for the appointment of counsel the District Court of Appeal shall make 'an independent investigation of the record and determine whether it would be of advantage to the defendant or helpful to the appellate court to have counsel appointed.' *People v. Hyde*, 51 Cal.2d 152, 154 (1958).

California's courts did that here and after examining the record certified that such an appointment would be neither advantageous to the petitioners nor helpful to the court. It, therefore, refused to go through the useless gesture of appointing an attorney. In my view neither the Equal Protection Clause nor the Due Process Clause requires more. I cannot understand why the Court says that this procedure afforded petitioners 'a meaningless ritual.' To appoint an attorney would not only have been utter extravagance and a waste of the State's funds but as surely 'meaningless' to petitioners.

. . . California furnishes the indigent a complete record and if counsel is requested requires its appellate courts either to (1) appoint counsel or (2) make an independent investigation of that record and determine whether it would be of advantage to the defendant or helpful to the court to have counsel appointed. . . .

California's concern for the rights of indigents is clearly revealed in *People v. Hyde*, supra. There, although the Public Defender had not undertaken the prosecution of the appeal, the District Court of Appeal nevertheless referred the application for counsel and the record to the Los Angeles Bar Association. One of its members reviewed these papers, after which he certified that no meritorious ground for appeal was disclosed. Despite this the California District Court of Appeal made its own independent examination of the record.

There is an old adage which my good Mother used to quote to me, i.e., 'People who live in glass houses had best not throw stones.' I dissent.

**MR. JUSTICE HARLAN, whom MR. JUSTICE STEWART joins, dissenting.**

In holding that an indigent has an absolute right to appointed counsel on appeal of a state criminal conviction, the Court appears to rely both on the Equal Protection Clause and on the guarantees of fair procedure inherent in the Due Process Clause of the Fourteenth Amendment, with obvious emphasis on 'equal protection.' In my view the Equal Protection Clause is not apposite, and its application to cases like the present one can lead only to mischievous results. This case should be judged solely under the Due Process Clause, and I do not believe that the California procedure violates that provision. . .

**After preparing the case brief, consider the answers to the following questions:**

1.  What is the constitutional basis for the Court's decision regarding whether California's procedure for indigent defense was fair?

2.  Do you agree that the Constitution requires appointment of counsel to indigent defendants in the first appeal? Why?

3.  Based on the Court's opinion what is it that the Equal Protection Clause was intended to prevent or provide?

4.  Review the dissenting opinions. Why did the dissenters believe that California's procedures were already constitutionally appropriate? Are their arguments compelling?

## ROSS V. MOFFITT

Supreme Court of the United States
Argued April 22, 1974
Decided June 17, 1974
417 U.S. 600

### OPINION

### MR. JUSTICE REHNQUIST delivered the opinion of the Court.

We are asked in this case to decide whether *Douglas v. California*, 372 U.S. 353 (1963), which requires appointment of counsel for indigent state defendants on their first appeal as of right, should be extended to require counsel for discretionary state appeals and for applications for review in this Court. The Court of Appeals for the Fourth Circuit held that such appointment was required by the Due Process and Equal Protection Clauses of the Fourteenth Amendment.

I

The case now before us has resulted from consolidation of two separate cases, North Carolina criminal prosecutions brought in the respective Superior Courts for the counties of Mecklenburg and Guilford. In both cases respondent pleaded not guilty to charges of forgery and uttering a forged instrument, and because of his indigency was represented at trial by court-appointed counsel. He was convicted and then took separate appeals to the North Carolina Court of Appeals, where he was again represented by court-appointed counsel, and his convictions were affirmed. At this point the procedural histories of the two cases diverge.

Following affirmance of his Mecklenburg County conviction, respondent sought to invoke the discretionary review procedures of the North Carolina Supreme Court. His court-appointed counsel approached the Mecklenburg County Superior Court about possible appointment to represent respondent on this appeal, but counsel was informed that the State was not required to furnish counsel for that petition. Respondent sought collateral relief in both the state and federal courts, first raising his right-to-counsel contention in a habeas corpus petition filed in the United States District Court for the Western District of North Carolina in February 1971. Relief was denied at that time, and respondent's appeal to the Court of Appeals for the Fourth Circuit was dismissed by stipulation in order to allow respondent to first exhaust state remedies on this issue. After exhausting state remedies, he reapplied for habeas relief, which was again denied. Respondent appealed that denial to the Court of Appeals for the Fourth Circuit.

Following affirmance of his conviction on the Guilford County charges, respondent also sought discretionary review in the North Carolina Supreme Court. On this appeal, however, respondent was not denied counsel but rather was represented by the public defender who had been appointed for the trial and respondent's first appeal. The North Carolina Supreme Court denied certiorari. Respondent then unsuccessfully petitioned the Superior Court for Guilford County for court-appointed counsel to prepare a petition for a writ of certiorari to this Court, and also sought post-conviction relief throughout the state courts. After these motions were denied, respondent again sought federal habeas relief, this time in the United States District Court for the Middle District of North Carolina, 341 F.Supp. 853. That court denied relief, and respondent took an appeal to the Court of Appeals for the Fourth Circuit.

The Court of Appeals reversed the two District Court judgments, holding that respondent was entitled to the assistance of counsel at state expense both on his petition for review in the North Carolina Supreme Court and on his petition for certiorari to this Court. Reviewing the procedures of the North Carolina appellate system and the possible benefits that counsel would provide for indigents seeking review in that system, the court stated:

> 'As long as the state provides such procedures and allows other convicted felons to seek access to the higher court with the help of retained counsel, there is a marked absence of fairness in denying an indigent the assistance of counsel as he seeks access to the same court.'

This principle was held equally applicable to petitions for certiorari to this Court. For, said the Court of Appeals, '(t)he same concepts of fairness and equality, which require counsel in a first appeal of right, require counsel in other and subsequent discretionary appeals.'

We granted certiorari, to consider the Court of Appeals' decision in light of *Douglas v. California*, and apparently conflicting decisions of the Courts of Appeals for the Seventh and Tenth Circuits. For the reasons hereafter stated we reverse the Court of Appeals.

II

This Court, in the past 20 years, has given extensive consideration to the rights of indigent persons on appeal. In *Griffin v. Illinois*, 351 U.S. 12 (1956), the first of the pertinent cases, the Court had before it an Illinois rule allowing a convicted criminal defendant to present claims of trial error to the Supreme Court of Illinois only if he procured a transcript of the testimony adduced at his trial. No exception was made for the indigent defendant, and thus one who was unable to pay the cost of obtaining such a transcript was precluded from obtaining appellate review of asserted trial error. Mr. Justice Frankfurter, who cast the deciding vote, said in his concurring opinion:

> '. . . Illinois has decreed that only defendants who can afford to pay for the stenographic minutes of a trial may have trial errors reviewed on appeal by the Illinois Supreme Court.' . . .

The Court in *Griffin* held that this discrimination violated the Fourteenth Amendment.

Succeeding cases invalidated similar financial barriers to the appellate process, at the same time reaffirming the traditional principle that a State is not obliged to provide any appeal at all for criminal defendants. . . . For example, *Lane v. Brown*, 372 U.S. 477 (1963), involved an Indiana provision declaring that only a public defender could obtain a free transcript of a hearing on a coram nobis application. If the public defender declined to request one, the indigent prisoner seeking to appeal had no recourse. In *Draper v. Washington*, 372 U.S. 487 (1963), the State permitted an indigent to obtain a free transcript of the trial at which he was convicted only if he satisfied the trial judge that his contentions on appeal would not be frivolous. The appealing defendant was in effect bound by the trial court's conclusions in seeking to review the determination of frivolousness, since no transcript or its equivalent was made available to him. . . The decisions discussed above stand for the proposition that a State cannot arbitrarily cut off appeal rights for indigents while leaving open avenues of appeal for more affluent persons. In *Douglas v. California*, 372 U.S. 353 (1963), however, a case decided the same day as *Lane*, and *Draper*, the Court departed somewhat from the limited doctrine of the transcript and fee cases and undertook an examination of whether an indigent's access to the appellate system was adequate. The Court in *Douglas* concluded that a State does not fulfill its responsibility toward indigent defendants merely by waiving its own requirements that a convicted defendant procure a transcript or pay a fee in order to appeal, and held that the State must go further and provide counsel for the indigent on his first appeal as of right. It is this decision we are asked to extend today.

Petitioners in *Douglas*, each of whom had been convicted by a jury on 13 felony counts, took appeals as of right to the California District Court of Appeal. No filing fee was exacted of them, no transcript was required in order to present their arguments to the Court of Appeal, and the appellate process was therefore open to them. Petitioners, however, claimed that they not only had the right to make use of the appellate process, but were also entitled to court-appointed and state-compensated counsel because they were indigent. . . .This Court held unconstitutional California's requirement that counsel on appeal would be appointed for an indigent only if the appellate court determined that such appointment would be helpful to the defendant or to the court itself. The Court noted that under this system an indigent's case was initially reviewed on the merits without the benefit of any organization or argument by counsel. By contrast, persons of greater means were not faced with the preliminary 'ex parte examination of the record,' . . . but had their arguments presented to the court in fully briefed form.

The Court noted, however, that its decision extended only to initial appeals as of right, and went on to say:

> 'We need not now decide whether California would have to provide counsel for an indigent seeking a discretionary hearing from the California Supreme Court after the District Court of Appeal had sustained his conviction . . . or whether counsel must be appointed for an indigent seeking review of an appellate affirmance of his conviction in this Court by appeal as of right or by petition for a writ of certiorari which lies within the Court's discretion. But it is appropriate to observe that a State can, consistently with the Fourteenth Amendment, provide for differences so long as the result does not amount to a denial of due process or an 'invidious discrimination.' . . .Absolute equality is not required; lines can be and are drawn and we often sustain them.' . . .

The precise rationale for the *Griffin* and *Douglas* lines of cases has never been explicitly stated, some support being derived from the Equal Protection Clause of the Fourteenth Amendment, and some from the Due Process Clause of that Amendment. Neither Clause by itself provides an entirely satisfactory basis for the result reached, each depending on a different inquiry which emphasizes different factors. 'Due process' emphasizes fairness between the State and the individual dealing with the State, regardless of how other individuals in the same situation may be treated. 'Equal protection,' on the other hand, emphasizes disparity in treatment by a State between classes of individuals whose situations are arguably indistinguishable. We will address these issues separately in the succeeding sections.

### III

Recognition of the due process rationale in *Douglas* is found both in the Court's opinion and in the dissenting opinion of Mr. Justice Harlan. The Court in *Douglas* stated that '(w)hen an indigent is forced to run this gantlet of a preliminary showing of merit, the right to appeal does not comport with fair procedure.' . . . Mr. Justice Harlan thought that the due process issue in *Douglas* was the only one worthy of extended consideration, remarking: 'The real question in this case, I submit, and the only one that permits of satisfactory analysis, is whether or not the state rule, as applied in this case, is consistent with the requirements of fair procedure guaranteed by the Due Process Clause.' . . .

We do not believe that the Due Process Clause requires North Carolina to provide respondent with counsel on his discretionary appeal to the State Supreme Court. At the trial stage of a criminal proceeding, the right of an indigent defendant to counsel is fundamental and binding upon the States by virtue of the Sixth and Fourteenth Amendments. *Gideon v. Wainwright*, 372 U.S. 335 (1963). But there are significant differences between the trial and appellate stages of a criminal proceeding. The purpose of the trial stage from the State's point of view is to convert a criminal defendant from a person presumed innocent to one found guilty beyond a reasonable doubt. To accomplish this purpose, the State employs a prosecuting attorney who presents evidence to the court, challenges any witnesses offered by the defendant, argues rulings of the court, and makes direct arguments to the court and jury seeking to persuade them of the defendant's guilt. Under these circumstances 'reason and reflection require us to recognize that in our adversary system of criminal justice, any person haled into court, who is too poor to hire a lawyer, cannot be assured a fair trial unless counsel is provided for him.' . . .

By contrast, it is ordinarily the defendant, rather than the State, who initiates the appellate process, seeking not to fend off the efforts of the State's prosecutor but rather to overturn a finding of guilt made by a judge or a jury below. The defendant needs an attorney on appeal not as a shield to protect him against being 'haled into court' by the State and stripped of his presumption of innocence, but rather as a sword to upset the prior determination of guilt. This difference is significant for, while no one would agree that the State may simply dispense with the trial stage of proceedings without a criminal defendant's consent, it is clear that the State need not provide any appeal at all. *McKane v. Durston*, 153 U.S. 684 (1894). The fact that an appeal has been provided does not automatically mean that a State then acts unfairly by refusing to provide counsel to indigent defendants at every stage of the way. *Douglas v. California.* Unfairness results only if indigents are singled out by the State and denied meaningful access to the appellate system because of their poverty. That question is more profitably considered under an equal protection analysis.

IV

Language invoking equal protection notions is prominent both in *Douglas* and in other cases treating the rights of indigents on appeal. The Court in *Douglas* for example, stated: '(W)here the merits of the one and only appeal an indigent has as of right are decided without benefit of counsel, we think an unconstitutional line has been drawn between rich and poor.'. . . Despite the tendency of all rights 'to declare themselves absolute to their logical extreme,' there are obviously limits beyond which the equal protection analysis may not be pressed without doing violence to principles recognized in other decisions of this Court. The Fourteenth Amendment 'does not require absolute equality or precisely equal advantages,' . . .The question is not one of absolutes, but one of degrees. In this case we do not believe that the Equal Protection Clause, when interpreted in the context of these cases, requires North Carolina to provide free counsel for indigent defendants seeking to take discretionary appeals to the North Carolina Supreme Court, or to file petitions for certiorari in this Court.

A.   . . .These provisions, although perhaps on their face broad enough to cover appointments such as those respondent sought here, have generally been construed to limit the right to appointed counsel in criminal cases to direct appeals taken as of right. Thus North Carolina has followed the mandate of *Douglas v. California*, . . .and authorized appointment of counsel for a convicted defendant appealing to the intermediate Court of Appeals, but has not gone beyond Douglas to provide for appointment of counsel for a defendant who seeks either discretionary review in the Supreme Court of North Carolina or a writ of certiorari here.

B.   The facts show that respondent, in connection with his Mecklenburg County conviction, received the benefit of counsel in examining the record of his trial and in preparing an appellate brief on his behalf for the state Court of Appeals. Thus, prior to his seeking discretionary review in the State Supreme Court, his claims had 'once been presented by a lawyer and passed upon by an appellate court.' . . .We do not believe that it can be said, therefore, that a defendant in respondent's circumstances is denied meaningful access to the North Carolina Supreme Court simply because the State does not appoint counsel to aid him in seeking review in that court. At that stage he will have, at the very least, a transcript or other record of trial proceedings, a brief on his behalf in the Court of Appeals setting forth his claims of error, and in many cases an opinion by the Court of Appeals disposing of his case. These materials, supplemented by whatever submission respondent may make pro se, would appear to provide the Supreme Court of North Carolina with an adequate basis for its decision to grant or deny review. . .

This is not to say, of course, that a skilled lawyer, particularly one trained in the somewhat arcane art of preparing petitions for discretionary review, would not prove helpful to any litigant able to employ him. An indigent defendant seeking review in the Supreme Court of North Carolina is therefore somewhat handicapped in comparison with a wealthy defendant who has counsel assisting him in every conceivable manner at every stage in the proceeding. But both the opportunity to have counsel prepare an initial brief in the Court of Appeals and the nature of discretionary review in the Supreme Court of North Carolina make this relative handicap far less than the handicap borne by the indigent defendant denied counsel on his initial appeal as of right in *Douglas*. And the fact that a particular service might be of benefit to an indigent defendant does not mean that the service is constitutionally required. The duty of the State under our cases is not to duplicate the legal arsenal that may be privately retained by a criminal defendant in a continuing effort to reverse his conviction, but only to assure the indigent defendant an adequate opportunity to present his claims fairly in the context of the State's appellate process. We think respondent was given that opportunity under the existing North Carolina system.

V

Much of the discussion in the preceding section is equally relevant to the question of whether a State must provide counsel for a defendant seeking review of his conviction in this Court. North Carolina will have provided counsel for a convicted defendant's only appeal as of right, and the brief prepared by that counsel together with one and perhaps two North Carolina appellate opinions will be available to this Court in order that it may decide whether or not to grant certiorari. This Court's review, much like that of the Supreme Court of North Carolina, is discretionary and depends on numerous factors other than the perceived correctness of the judgment we are asked to review.

There is also a significant difference between the source of the right to seek discretionary review in the Supreme Court of North Carolina and the source of the right to seek discretionary review in this Court. The former is conferred by the statutes of the State of North Carolina, but the latter is granted by statute enacted by Congress. Thus the argument relied upon in the Griffin and *Douglas* cases, that the State having once created a right of appeal must give all persons an equal opportunity to enjoy the right, is by its terms inapplicable. The right to seek certiorari in this Court is not granted by any State, and exists by virtue of federal statute with or without the consent of the State whose judgment is sought to be reviewed.

The suggestion that a State is responsible for providing counsel to one petitioning this Court simply because it initiated the prosecution which led to the judgment sought to be reviewed is unsupported by either reason or authority. . .

## VI

We do not mean by this opinion to in any way discourage those States which have, as a matter of legislative choice, made counsel available to convicted defendants at all stages of judicial review. Some States which might well choose to do so as a matter of legislative policy may conceivably find that other claims for public funds within or without the criminal justice system preclude the implementation of such a policy at the present time. North Carolina, for example, while it does not provide counsel to indigent defendants seeking discretionary review on appeal, does provide counsel for indigent prisoners in several situations where such appointments are not required by any constitutional decision of this Court. Our reading of the Fourteenth Amendment leaves these choices to the State, and respondent was denied no rights secured by the Federal Constitution when North Carolina refused to provide counsel to aid him in obtaining discretionary appellate review.

The judgment of the Court of Appeals' holding to the contrary is reversed.

**Reversed.**

**MR. JUSTICE DOUGLAS, with whom MR. JUSTICE BRENNAN and MR. JUSTICE MARSHALL concur, dissenting.**

I would affirm the judgment below because I am in agreement with the opinion of Chief Judge Haynsworth for a unanimous panel in the Court of Appeals. . . . we considered the necessity for appointed counsel on the first appeal as of right, the only issue before us. We did not deal with the appointment of counsel for later levels of discretionary review, either to the higher state courts or to this Court, but we noted that 'there can be no equal justice where the kind of an appeal a man enjoys 'depends on the amount of money he has." . . .

Chief Judge Haynsworth could find 'no logical basis for differentiation between appeals of right and permissive review procedures in the context of the Constitution and the right to counsel.' . . . More familiar with the functioning of the North Carolina criminal justice system than are we, he concluded that 'in the context of constitutional questions arising in criminal prosecutions, permissive review in the state's highest court may be predictably the most meaningful review the conviction will receive.' *Ibid.* The North Carolina Court of Appeals, for example, will be constrained in diverging from an earlier opinion of the State Supreme Court, even if subsequent developments have rendered the earlier Supreme Court decision suspect. '(T)he state's highest court remains the ultimate arbiter of the rights of its citizens.'

Chief Judge Haynsworth also correctly observed that the indigent defendant proceeding without counsel is at a substantial disadvantage relative to wealthy defendants represented by counsel when he is forced to fend for himself in seeking discretionary review from the State Supreme Court or from this Court. It may well not be enough to allege error in the courts below in layman's terms; a more sophisticated approach may be demanded: 'An indigent defendant is as much in need of the assistance of a lawyer in preparing and filing a petition for certiorari as he is in the handling of an appeal as of right. In many appeals, an articulate defendant could file an effective brief by telling his story in simple language without legalisms, but the technical requirements for applications for writs of certiorari are hazards which one untrained in the law could hardly be expected to negotiate. "Certiorari proceedings constitute a highly specialized aspect of appellate work. The factors which (a court) deems important in connection with deciding whether to grant certiorari are certainly not within the normal knowledge of an indigent appellant. . . .

Furthermore, the lawyer who handled the first appeal in a case would be familiar with the facts and legal issues involved in the case. It would be a relatively easy matter for the attorney to apply his expertise in filing a petition for discretionary review to a higher court, or to advise his client that such a petition would have no chance of succeeding. *Douglas v. California* was grounded on concepts of fairness and equality. The right to seek discretionary review is a substantial one, and one where a lawyer can be of significant assistance to an indigent defendant. It was correctly perceived below that the 'same concepts of fairness and equality, which require counsel in a first appeal of right, require counsel in other and subsequent discretionary appeals.' . . .

**After preparing the case brief, consider the answers to the following questions:**

1.     What rights does the Court say the Due Process and Equal Protection clauses seek to protect? How are those rights different?

2.     The Court holds that appointed counsel is not required by the Constitution for discretionary appeals. What reasons do they point to for the difference between these appeals and the ones discussed in *Douglas v. California*?

3.     Are you convinced by the Court's argument that the assistance of counsel on the direct appeal has adequately assisted the indigent defendant in presenting future appeals? Why?

# TEAGUE V. LANE

Supreme Court of the United States
Argued Oct. 4, 1988
Decided Feb. 22, 1989
Rehearing Denied April 17, 1989
489 U.S. 288

## OPINION

JUSTICE O'CONNOR announced the judgment of the Court and delivered the opinion of the Court with respect to Parts I, II, and III, and an opinion with respect to Parts IV and V, in which THE CHIEF JUSTICE, JUSTICE SCALIA, and JUSTICE KENNEDY join.

In *Taylor v. Louisiana*, 419 U.S. 522, 95 S.Ct. 692, 42 L.Ed.2d 690 (1975), this Court held that the Sixth Amendment required that the jury venire be drawn from a fair cross section of the community. The Court stated, however, that "in holding that petit juries must be drawn from a source fairly representative of the community we impose no requirement that petit juries actually chosen must mirror the community and reflect the various distinctive groups in the population. Defendants are not entitled to a jury of any particular composition." *Id.,* at 538, 95 S.Ct., at 702. The principal question presented in this case is whether the Sixth Amendment's fair cross section requirement should now be extended to the petit jury. Because we adopt Justice Harlan's approach to retroactivity for cases on collateral review, we leave the resolution of that question for another day.

I

Petitioner, a black man, was convicted by an all-white Illinois jury of three counts of attempted murder, two counts of armed robbery, and one count of aggravated battery. During jury selection for petitioner's trial, the prosecutor used all 10 of his peremptory challenges to exclude blacks. Petitioner's counsel used one of his 10 peremptory challenges to exclude a black woman who was married to a police officer. After the prosecutor had struck six blacks, petitioner's counsel moved for a mistrial. The trial court denied the motion. When the prosecutor struck four more blacks, petitioner's counsel again moved for a mistrial, arguing that petitioner was "entitled to a jury of his peers." The prosecutor defended the challenges by stating that he was trying to achieve a balance of men and women on the jury. The trial court denied the motion, reasoning that the jury "appear[ed] to be a fair [one]."

On appeal, petitioner argued that the prosecutor's use of peremptory challenges denied him the right to be tried by a jury that was representative of the community. The Illinois Appellate Court rejected petitioner's fair cross section claim. . . .Petitioner then filed a petition for a writ of habeas corpus in the United States District Court for the Northern District of Illinois. Petitioner repeated his fair cross section claim, . . .He also argued, for the first time, that under *Swain* a prosecutor could be questioned about his use of peremptory challenges once he volunteered an explanation. The District Court, though sympathetic to petitioner's arguments, held that it was bound by *Swain* and Circuit precedent.

On appeal, petitioner repeated his fair cross section claim and his *McCray* argument. A panel of the Court of Appeals agreed with petitioner that the Sixth Amendment's fair cross section requirement applied to the petit jury and held that petitioner had made out a prima facie case of discrimination. A majority of the judges on the Court of Appeals voted to rehear the case en banc, and the panel opinion was vacated. . . Rehearing was postponed until after our decision in *Batson v. Kentucky,* 476 U.S. 79 (1986), which overruled a portion of *Swain.* After *Batson* was decided, the Court of Appeals held that petitioner could not benefit from the rule in that case because *Allen v. Hardy,* 478 U.S. 255 (1986) (*per curiam*), had held that *Batson* would not be applied retroactively to cases on collateral review. 820 F.2d 832, 834, n. 4 (CA7 1987) (en banc). The Court of Appeals also held that petitioner's *Swain* claim was procedurally barred and in any event meritless. . .

## II

Petitioner's first contention is that he should receive the benefit of our decision in *Batson* even though his conviction became final before *Batson* was decided. . . .

In *Batson,* the Court overruled that portion of *Swain* setting forth the evidentiary showing necessary to make out a prima facie case of racial discrimination under the Equal Protection Clause. The Court held that a defendant can establish a prima facie case by showing that he is a "member of a cognizable racial group," that the prosecutor exercised "peremptory challenges to remove from the venire members of the defendant's race," and that those "facts and any other relevant circumstances raise an inference that the prosecutor used that practice to exclude the veniremen from the petit jury on account of their race." . . .the defendant makes out a prima facie case of discrimination, the burden shifts to the prosecutor "to come forward with a neutral explanation for challenging black jurors." . . .

In *Allen v. Hardy,* the Court held that *Batson* constituted an "explicit and substantial break with prior precedent" because it overruled a portion of *Swain.* 478 U.S., at 258, 106 S.Ct., at 2880. Employing the retroactivity standard of *Linkletter v. Walker,* 381 U.S. 618, 636, 85 S.Ct. 1731, 1741, 14 L.Ed.2d 601 (1965), the Court concluded that the rule announced in *Batson* should not be applied retroactively on collateral review of convictions that became final before *Batson* was announced. The Court defined final to mean a case " 'where the judgment of conviction was rendered, the availability of appeal exhausted, and the time for petition for certiorari had elapsed before our decision in' *Batson.* . . ." 478 U.S., at 258, n. 1, 106 S.Ct., at 2880, n. 1 (citation omitted).

Petitioner's conviction became final 2½ years prior to *Batson,* thus depriving petitioner of any benefit from the rule announced in that case. . .We find that *Allen v. Hardy* is dispositive, and that petitioner cannot benefit from the rule announced in *Batson.*

### III

Petitioner's second contention is that he has established a violation of the Equal Protection Clause under *Swain.* Recognizing that he has not shown any systematic exclusion of blacks from petit juries in case after case, petitioner contends that when the prosecutor volunteers an explanation for the use of his peremptory challenges, *Swain* does not preclude an examination of the stated reasons to determine the legitimacy of the prosecutor's motive. . . .Petitioner candidly admits that he did not raise the *Swain* claim at trial or on direct appeal. . . . Because of this failure, petitioner has forfeited review of the claim in the Illinois courts. "It is well established that 'where an appeal was taken from a conviction, the judgment of the reviewing court is *res judicata* as to all issues actually raised, and those that could have been presented but were not are deemed waived.' " *People v. Gaines,* 105 Ill.2d 79, 87–88 (1984) The default prevents petitioner from raising the *Swain* claim in collateral proceedings under the Illinois Post-Conviction Act, Ill.Rev.Stat., ch. 38, ¶ 122–1 *et seq.* (1987), unless fundamental fairness requires that the default be overlooked. *People v. Brown,* 52 Ill.2d 227 (1972). . .

Under *Wainwright v. Sykes,* 433 U.S. 72 (1977), petitioner is barred from raising the *Swain* claim in a federal habeas corpus proceeding unless he can show cause for the default and prejudice resulting therefrom. . . Petitioner does not attempt to show cause for his default. Instead, he argues that the claim is not barred because it was addressed by the Illinois Appellate Court. . .We cannot agree with petitioner's argument. The Illinois Appellate Court rejected petitioner's Sixth Amendment fair cross section claim *without* mentioning the Equal Protection Clause on which *Swain* was based or discussing whether *Swain* allows a prosecutor to be questioned about his use of peremptory challenges once he volunteers an explanation. . . Accordingly, we hold that petitioner's *Swain* claim is procedurally barred, and do not address its merits. . .

B

Justice Harlan believed that new rules generally should not be applied retroactively to cases on collateral review. . .The relevant frame of reference, in other words, is "not the purpose of the new rule whose benefit the [defendant] seeks, but instead the purposes for which the writ of habeas corpus is made available." *Mackey,* 401 U.S., at 682, 91 S.Ct., at 1175 (opinion concurring in judgments in part and dissenting in part). . .

Justice Harlan identified only two exceptions to his general rule of nonretroactivity for cases on collateral review. First, a new rule should be applied retroactively if it places "certain kinds of primary, private individual conduct beyond the power of the criminal law-making authority to proscribe." *Mackey,* 401 U.S., at 692, 91 S.Ct., at 1180. Second, a new rule should be applied retroactively if it requires the observance of "those procedures that . . . are 'implicit in the concept of ordered liberty.' " *Id.,* at 693, 91 S.Ct., at 1180 (quoting *Palko v. Connecticut,* 302 U.S. 319, 325 (1937) (Cardozo, J.)).

. . .We agree with Justice Harlan's description of the function of habeas corpus. "[T]he Court never has defined the scope of the writ simply by reference to a perceived need to assure that an individual accused of crime is afforded a trial free of constitutional error." *Kuhlmann v. Wilson,* 477 U.S. 436, 447 (1986) (plurality opinion). Rather, we have recognized that interests of comity and finality must also be considered in determining the proper scope of habeas review. Thus, if a defendant fails to comply with state procedural rules and is barred from litigating a particular constitutional claim in state court, the claim can be considered on federal habeas only if the defendant shows cause for the default and actual prejudice resulting therefrom. . .

This Court has not "always followed an unwavering line in its conclusions as to the availability of the Great Writ. Our development of the law of federal habeas corpus has been attended, seemingly, with some backing and filling." *Fay v. Noia,* 372 U.S. 391, 411–412 (1963). . . . In *Chicot County Drainage Dist. v. Baxter,* 308 U.S. 371 (1940), the Court held that a judgment based on a jurisdictional statute later found to be unconstitutional could have res judicata effect. The Court based its decision in large part on finality concerns. "The actual existence of a statute, prior to such a determination [of unconstitutionality], is an operative fact and may have consequences which cannot justly be ignored. The past cannot always be erased by a new judicial declaration. . . . Questions of. . . prior determinations deemed to have finality and acted upon accordingly . . . demand examination." . . .

These underlying considerations of finality find significant and compelling parallels in the criminal context. Application of constitutional rules not in existence at the time a conviction became final seriously undermines the principle of finality which is essential to the operation of our criminal justice system. Without finality, the criminal law is deprived of much of its deterrent effect. . . .

As explained by Professor Mishkin:

"From this aspect, the *Linkletter* problem becomes not so much one of prospectivity or retroactivity of the rule but rather of the availability of collateral attack—in [that] case federal habeas corpus—to go behind the otherwise final judgment of conviction. . . . For the potential availability of collateral attack is what created the 'retroactivity' problem of *Linkletter* in the first place; there seems little doubt that without that possibility the Court would have given short shrift to any arguments for 'prospective limitation' of the *Mapp* rule."

. . .

The "costs imposed upon the State[s] by retroactive application of new rules of constitutional law on habeas corpus . . . generally far outweigh the benefits of this application." *Stumes*, 465 U.S., at 654 (Powell, J., concurring in judgment). In many ways the application of new rules to cases on collateral review may be more intrusive than the enjoining of criminal prosecutions. . . for it *continually* forces the States to marshal resources in order to keep in prison defendants whose trials and appeals conformed to then-existing constitutional standards. Furthermore, as we recognized in *Engle v. Isaac*, "[s]tate courts are understandably frustrated when they faithfully apply existing constitutional law only to have a federal court discover, during a [habeas] proceeding, new constitutional commands. . .

We find these criticisms to be persuasive, and we now adopt Justice Harlan's view of retroactivity for cases on collateral review. Unless they fall within an exception to the general rule, new constitutional rules of criminal procedure will not be applicable to those cases which have become final before the new rules are announced.

V

Petitioner's conviction became final in 1983. As a result, the rule petitioner urges would not be applicable to this case, which is on collateral review, unless it would fall within an exception.

The first exception suggested by Justice Harlan—that a new rule should be applied retroactively if it places "certain kinds of primary, private individual conduct beyond the power of the criminal law-making authority to proscribe," . . . .is not relevant here. Application of the fair cross section requirement to the petit jury would not accord constitutional protection to any primary activity whatsoever.

The second exception suggested by Justice Harlan—that a new rule should be applied retroactively if it requires the observance of "those procedures that . . . are 'implicit in the concept of ordered liberty,' " *id.,* at 693, 91 S.Ct., at 1180 (quoting *Palko,* 302 U.S., at 325, 58 S.Ct., at 152)—we apply with a modification. The language used by Justice Harlan in *Mackey* leaves no doubt that he meant the second exception to be reserved for watershed rules of criminal procedure:

> "Typically, it should be the case that any conviction free from federal constitutional error at the time it became final, will be found, upon reflection, to have been fundamentally fair and conducted under those procedures essential to the substance of a full hearing. However, in some situations it might be that time and growth in social capacity, as well as judicial perceptions of what we can rightly demand of the adjudicatory process, will properly alter our understanding of the *bedrock procedural elements* that must be found to vitiate the fairness of a particular conviction. For example, such, in my view, is the case with the right to counsel at trial now held a necessary condition precedent to any conviction for a serious crime." . . .

In *Desist,* Justice Harlan had reasoned that one of the two principal functions of habeas corpus was "to assure that no man has been incarcerated under a procedure which creates an impermissibly large risk that the innocent will be convicted," and concluded "from this that all 'new' constitutional rules which significantly improve the pre-existing fact-finding procedures are to be retroactively applied on habeas." . . .

Because we operate from the premise that such procedures would be so central to an accurate determination of innocence or guilt, we believe it unlikely that many such components of basic due process have yet to emerge. We are also of the view that such rules are "best illustrated by recalling the classic grounds for the issuance of a writ of habeas corpus—that the proceeding was dominated by mob violence; that the prosecutor knowingly made use of perjured testimony; or that the conviction was based on a confession extorted from the defendant by brutal methods. . .

An examination of our decision in *Taylor* applying the fair cross section requirement to the jury venire leads inexorably to the conclusion that adoption of the rule petitioner urges would be a far cry from the kind of absolute prerequisite to fundamental fairness that is "implicit in the concept of ordered liberty." The requirement that the jury venire be composed of a fair cross section of the community is based on the role of the jury in our system. Because the purpose of the jury is to guard against arbitrary abuses of power by interposing the commonsense judgment of the community between the State and the defendant, the jury venire cannot be composed only of special segments of the population. "Community participation in the administration of the criminal law . . . is not only consistent with our democratic heritage but is also critical to public confidence in the fairness of the criminal justice system." *Taylor,* 419 U.S., at 530, 95 S.Ct., at 698. But as we stated in *Daniel v. Louisiana,* 420 U.S. 31, 32, 95 S.Ct. 704, 705, 42 L.Ed.2d 790 (1975), which held that *Taylor* was not to be given retroactive effect, the fair cross section requirement "[does] not rest on the premise that every criminal trial, or any particular trial, [is] necessarily unfair because it [is] not conducted in accordance with what we determined to be the requirements of the Sixth Amendment." Because the absence of a fair cross section on the jury venire does not undermine the fundamental fairness that must underlie a conviction or seriously diminish the likelihood of obtaining an accurate conviction, we conclude that a rule requiring that petit juries be composed of a fair cross section of the community would not be a "bedrock procedural element" that would be retroactively applied under the second exception we have articulated.

. . . Because a decision extending the fair cross section requirement to the petit jury would not be applied retroactively to cases on collateral review under the approach we adopt today, we do not address petitioner's claim.

For the reasons set forth above, the judgment of the Court of Appeals is affirmed.

*It is so ordered.*

**JUSTICE WHITE, concurring in part and concurring in the judgment.**

I join Parts I, II, and III of Justice O'CONNOR's opinion. Otherwise, I concur only in the judgment.

Our opinion in *Stovall v. Denno,* 388 U.S. 293, 297 (1967), authored by Justice BRENNAN, articulated a three-factor formula for determining the retroactivity of decisions changing the constitutional rules of criminal procedure. The formula, which applied whether a case was on direct review or arose in collateral proceedings, involved consideration of the purpose of the new rule, the extent of reliance on the old rule, and the effect on the administration of justice of retroactive application of the new rule. n a series of cases, however, the Court has departed from *Stovall* and has held that decisions changing the governing rules in criminal cases will be applied retroactively to all cases then pending on direct review, . . . I dissented in those cases, believing that *Stovall* was the sounder approach. Other Justices, including THE CHIEF JUSTICE and Justice O'CONNOR, joined my dissents in those cases. THE CHIEF JUSTICE indicated in *Shea* and *Griffith,* and Justice O'CONNOR has now concluded, that the *Stovall* formula should also be abandoned in cases where convictions have become final and the issue of retroactivity arises in collateral proceedings.

I regret the course the Court has taken to this point, but cases like *Johnson, Shea,* and *Griffith* have been decided, and I have insufficient reason to continue to object to them. In light of those decisions, the result reached in Parts IV and V of Justice O'CONNOR's opinion is an acceptable application in collateral proceedings of the theories embraced by the Court in cases dealing with direct review, and I concur in that result. If we are wrong in construing the reach of the habeas corpus statutes, Congress can of course correct us; but because the Court's recent decisions dealing with direct review appear to have constitutional underpinnings, see *e.g., Griffith v. Kentucky, supra,* 479 U.S., at 322–323, 107 S.Ct. at 713, correction of our error, if error there is, perhaps lies with us, not Congress. . .

**JUSTICE STEVENS, with whom JUSTICE BLACKMUN joins as to Part I, concurring in part and concurring in the judgment.**

I

For the reasons stated in Part III of Justice BRENNAN's dissent, *post,* at 1092, I am persuaded this petitioner has alleged a violation of the Sixth

Amendment. I also believe the Court should decide that question in his favor. . .

## After preparing the case brief, consider the answers to the following questions:

1. What is a writ of habeas corpus intended to do? What is a collateral attack on a conviction?

2. The Court adopts Justice Harlan's view of retroactivity. Describe the basic premise of his view.

3. What are the two exceptions Justice Harlan identified to the general rule of non-retroactivity?

4. What was the "fair cross-section" requirement from *Batson* the defendant sought to have retroactively applied?

5. Do you agree with the Court's holding that the lack of a fair cross-section does not undermine the fundamental fairness of the trial? Why?

# Chapter 12 Key Terms for Review

- **Appeal**: a request made to have a higher court review the decision of a lower court.

- **Appellant or petitioner**: the party who applies to the higher court for reversal of the lower court's decision.

- **Appellee or respondent**: the party responding to the appeal requested by the appellant.

- **Appellate record**: all of the materials from the trial including a transcript of the proceedings from the trial court.

- **Appellate brief**: written arguments in support of the party's claims on appeal.

- **Oral argument**: litigants do not always have a right to oral argument before the appeals court, but in cases where it is offered, it is an opportunity to present the case in person before a panel of judges and answer their questions about the issues before them on appeal.

- **Opinion**: the written decision of the court of appeals.

- **Per curium opinion**: a written opinion which does not identify a specific author.

- **Concurring opinion**: opinions written by judges who agree with the majority vote but who write separately to articulate additional or different reasons for their position.

- **Dissenting opinion**: written opinion by a judge who voted against the majority of the court. Dissenting opinions are not law.

- **Plurality opinion**: where the judges on an appellate panel vote in agreement for the result, but do not agree in the reasoning for it, and write separately to explain their position.

- **Mandatory appeal**: where the defendant has a right to appeal to a higher court.

- **Automatic appeal**: where an appeal is brought even against the wishes of the defendant. Common in death penalty cases.

- **Discretionary appeal**: where a defendant can request an appeal but the appellate court is not bound to grant it.

- **Harmless error**: when there is no reasonable probability that the error in a trial contributed to the conviction.

- **Reversible error**: error so significant that it warrants reversal of the defendant's conviction because of reasonable probability that it contributed to his conviction.

- **Writ of habeas corpus**: a civil action brought by an inmate alleging unlawful confinement; it is a collateral attack on his conviction rather than a direct claim that his conviction should be reversed. The defendant bears the burden of proof in habeas proceedings.

- **Preponderance of the evidence**: the standard of proof in habeas proceedings; the defendant must show that it is "more likely than not" that his detention is unlawful and must be released if the error had a substantial effect or influence on the jury's verdict.

- **De novo review**: the appellate court gives deference to the interpretation of the facts from the trial record and reviews primarily whether the law was correctly interpreted and applied.

- **Exhaustion of state-based right and remedies**: a state prisoner must exhaust, or seek all of his state-based rights and remedies before seeking habeas relief in federal court.

# Specialized Courts

The United States is home to a diverse population and this diversity gives rise to unique challenges in each state and local jurisdiction. Congress and the states have developed unique specialized courts in an effort to respond to the specific kind of problems each community faces. Examples of specialized courts include local treatment courts, the courts of military justice, juvenile courts, and tribal courts.

Many jurisdictions have established **collaborative courts** to work in partnership with public health agencies. They connect defendants who present specific social problems with the services they need. The ability to divert these cases out of the caseload of the criminal courts is both efficient and effective. Examples of collaborative courts include drug treatment courts, homeless courts, domestic violence courts, re-entry court and veteran's services courts. This attention to the social problems presented by individual defendants represents a marked shift in the approach to court process.

Communities across the nation are facing crises in providing mental health services. Often, law enforcement is the first point of contact with individuals suffering from mental illness, and many jurisdictions are evaluating whether there are better ways to respond to calls that involve the mentally ill. Many communities have established mental health courts. Much like drug treatment courts, these courts would divert defendants from criminal court and connect them with mental health services. Another way communities can divert cases away from criminal courts and direct them to appropriate service providers are 911 Dispatch Diversion Programs. This model embeds mental health clinicians into the 911 call center and those clinicians can evaluate calls before police are dispatched. Early data from pilot projects indicates success. In Tucson, Arizona 80% of calls diverted to their 'Crisis Line' were resolved over the phone.[1] The benefit of this diversion is felt by both the individuals making the calls and the community whose law enforcement resources are preserved.

Over the past few decades Congress has authorized specialized federal courts to address unique problems such as international trade, patent law and bankruptcy matters, appeals for veteran's claims, and appeals for the Armed Forces. Each of these specialized courts serves an important purpose and their development reflects the willingness of policy-makers to "think outside the box" regarding judicial process. Across the country in specialized courts individuals are receiving specialized treatment, often where assembly line justice would have prevailed in the past.

## A. DRUG TREATMENT COURTS

**Drug treatment courts** are collaborative courts that create a partnership between local criminal courts and drug treatment facilities or programs. The first drug treatment court was established in Dade County, Florida, in 1989. The vision of drug treatment courts is to effect lasting change in the lives of drug offenders by addressing a root cause of their criminal activity: drug dependency and abuse. According to the National Association of Drug Court Professionals (NADCP) there are now drug treatment courts operating in every state and U.S. territory. At the end of 2015 there were nearly 3,000 drug courts operating nationwide.[2] The NADCP points to the success of drug treatment court programs to explain their rapid expansion. Their research indicates that 75% of drug court graduates remain arrest-free for at least two years after completing the program. In addition to successfully treating offenders, drug courts save taxpayer money by diverting participants out of the jail or prison system, as well as reduced healthcare costs due to reduced victimization and utilization.[3]

## B. JUVENILE COURTS

### i.    History of the Juvenile Courts

**Juvenile courts** are the most common of the specialized courts at the state level. In the juvenile courts, juvenile offenders are not subject to the same criminal

---

[1]    National Association of State Mental Health Program Directors, Cops, Clinicians, or Both? Collaborative Approaches to Responding to Behavioral Health Emergencies (Alexandria, VA: National Association of State Mental Health Program Directors, 2020), 10.

[2]    http://www.nadcp.org.

[3]    *Id.*

judicial process as adults. The evolution of the juvenile courts began with the simple proposition that children are different than adults. This was a departure from the common law principles which treated age as a defense to criminal conduct. At common law children under 7 years old were *presumed incapable* of forming the mens rea necessary for committing crime. If a child was between 7 and 14 years old, there was a **rebuttable presumption** that they could *not* form the requisite mens rea for criminal conduct. A rebuttable presumption assumes that the presumed fact is true, but allows for the presumption to be overcome by evidence to the contrary. Finally, at common law if children were over 14 years of age, there was a rebuttable presumption that they *could* form the requisite mens rea for crimes. If they engaged in a criminal act they were treated as adults for the purposes of punishment.

The legal doctrine of **parens patriae** (state as parent) began gaining prominence by the end of the 19th century and completely changed the way children were viewed under the law. Now, rather than parents alone having responsibility for children and their welfare, the state could intervene and even terminate the rights of parents over their children under extreme circumstances.

The plight of children subjected to child labor and those orphans subjected to horrible conditions in "reform schools" was shocking and offended the moral values of **progressives**. Beginning around 1890 progressives began to advocate for children accused of delinquent behavior and those without parents. These early advocates for the juvenile courts believed that children were more amenable to rehabilitation and treatment than adults and sought to develop a juvenile justice system with that focus. The **Illinois Juvenile Court Act** established the first juvenile court in Illinois in 1899. Soon after, every state and the District of Columbia established juvenile courts for the disposition of cases involving youthful offenders.

## ii. Juvenile Court Organization and Process

Juvenile courts are based on civil, not criminal law. This highlights the underlying principles and values at the foundation of the juvenile court system. While it may seem like semantics, there are very important distinctions between adult and juvenile court processes. When a juvenile commits an act that would be a crime for an adult, they are brought to juvenile court for **adjudication** not a trial. Adjudication of a juvenile as delinquent is not deemed a conviction, but rather a determination of status. Through adjudication a determination is made whether the juvenile has engaged in an act of **delinquency**, and if appropriate, they may be subject to **residential placement** (not jail or prison).

Delinquency proceedings are:

1.    Focused on helping the child.

2.    Secret to protect the child's identity.

3.    Seek to rehabilitate and reintegrate the juvenile into community without stigma.

4.    Typically informal when compared against adult criminal judicial process.

Early advocates for the juvenile courts envisioned the judge serving as a paternal figure to wayward youth whose guiding hand would put them back on the right path. While much has changed in the way juvenile courts function, they are still guided by the foundational belief in rehabilitation—that children are more amenable to treatment than adults and that the justice system should treat them differently.

The juvenile court may be its own separate court in some jurisdictions, or it may be organized as part of the family court or a unit of the local trial court. Juvenile courts have jurisdiction over juvenile delinquency proceedings as well as status offense cases such as truancy, violation of curfew and possession of alcohol. In addition to handling cases involving violations of the law by youthful offenders, juvenile courts also have jurisdiction over **juvenile dependency** cases in which children are victims in need of court supervision. This may be the result of child neglect, abuse or abandonment.

Depending upon the jurisdiction there are age limits for original jurisdiction regarding juvenile delinquency matters. In some states there are both minimum and maximum ages for juvenile courts jurisdiction. In other states there is a maximum but no minimum age established by statute. Instead, these states often follow the common law rule that children under 7 years old are incapable of forming the mens rea necessary for criminal culpability or blameworthiness. In two states the maximum age for juvenile court jurisdiction is 15 years old,[4] in seven other states the maximum age is 16 years old[5] and in the remaining forty-two states children up to age 17 are within the juvenile court's jurisdiction.[6]

The first step in a juvenile case is the commission of a delinquent act. A **summons** is issued authorizing the arrest of the juvenile and requiring them to

---

[4]    New York and North Carolina.

[5]    Georgia, Louisiana, Michigan, Missouri, South Carolina, Texas and Wisconsin.

[6]    OJJDP, Juvenile Justice System Structure & Process, https://www.ojjdp.gov/ojstatbb/structure_process/qa04101.asp.

appear in court. The initial hearing in a juvenile case is informal and often an intake decision is made. The juvenile court may keep the youth in custody before case disposition. The intake decision results in either non-filing or a **petition** is filed alleging delinquency or status offenses and asking the juvenile court to assume jurisdiction. Juveniles do not have a right to indictment by a grand jury.

There is a **conference** after the petition is filed which provides the suspect with information about his rights and a disposition decision may be reached. In the vast majority of cases, the juvenile admits guilt at the conference. There are plea negotiations much like those which take place in adult court and cases are resolved this way even more often in the juvenile court. Prior to adjudication many juvenile cases are diverted out of the juvenile courts through the efforts of probation and other agency personnel who are able to suggest effective alternatives to delinquency proceedings.

If the case moves forward and the juvenile does not admit guilt, an **adjudicatory hearing** is held so that the judge can evaluate whether the offender is guilty or not guilty. Juveniles do not have a right to a jury trial, although they are not without due process protections.[7] According to the landmark case of *In re Gault (1967)* juveniles have the right to proper notice of hearings and the assistance of counsel at the adjudication.[8] While present, the role of defense attorneys in juvenile proceedings differs significantly from adult court. This is largely because of the informal nature of juvenile proceedings as well as the reality that the caseload of the juvenile courts is made up primarily of minor offenses.

If the juvenile is found guilty of the conduct, they are adjudicated delinquent and a **disposition** is entered explaining the court's decision about what will happen to the youth. This is the equivalent of sentencing in the adult court. State statutes require that judges make a written record of their dispositional findings.[9] Juveniles have the right to appeal in the majority of states but appeals in juvenile cases are extremely rare.

At the disposition hearing judges have broad discretion to choose from a wide array of sentencing alternatives for youth such as paying restitution, formal or informal probation, out-of-home placement or institutional confinement. Juvenile court judges work closely with social workers and probation staff in making this determination. The juvenile court judge's primary focus is the best interest of the child.

---

[7] *McKeiver v. Pennsylvania*, 403 U.S. 528 (1971).

[8] 387 U.S. 1 (1967).

[9] E.g., Minn. Stat. § 260B.185 (2000).

### iii.  Children in Adult Court

Children up to 17 years old are typically within the jurisdiction of the juvenile court although it is possible for the juvenile court to **waive jurisdiction** and transfer juvenile offenders to adult court. If a juvenile offender is transferred, they are tried and punished according to the law applicable to adult offenders. While transfer to adult court is possible, it is very rare.[10] In 2013 only 4,000 out of just over one million delinquency cases were tried in adult courts.

**Waiver hearings** are held to allow juvenile court judges to determine whether the juvenile offender is fit for treatment by the juvenile court. Juvenile offenders have a right to be represented by counsel in waiver hearings.[11] The Supreme Court held in *Kent v. United States (1966)* that the nature of the transfer decision is critical and representation by counsel is imperative to ensure that juveniles enjoy fair process.[12] In other situations when specific crimes are alleged statutes may require that a juvenile be in adult court.

In addition to the 45 states which utilize waiver hearings, there are 30 others who also have statutory or legislative waivers. These statutes *require* certain serious offenses (most commonly murder or violent felonies) to be handled by the criminal courts entirely. Some state statutes authorize prosecutors to exercise discretion and file criminal charges against juveniles accused of certain serious and violent crimes directly in adult court. This is referred to as a **prosecutorial waiver** or a district attorney direct-file provision.

Even where harsh statutes requiring waiver to adult court exist there are often statutes that allow a reverse waiver permitting a juvenile to petition to be returned to the juvenile courts. Judges may also have the option of **blended sentencing** for juveniles convicted in adult court. This allows them to impose a combination of adult and juvenile sentencing options focused on rehabilitation.

## C.  OTHER SPECIALIZED COURTS

### i.   Courts of Military Justice

The U.S. Constitution is the foundation for military law in the same way it is for civilian law. Under the Constitution, Congress has the power to make rules to regulate the military and the Constitution establishes the president as commander

---

[10]   Kang, W., Sickmund, M. and Sladky, A., (2015) "Easy Access to Juvenile Court Statistics: 1985–2013." Online. Available: http://www.ojjdp.gov/ojstatbb/ezajcs.

[11]   *Kent v. United States*, 383 U.S. 541 (1966).

[12]   *Id.*

in chief of the Armed Forces. The **Courts of Military Justice** enforce the Uniform Code of Military Justice applicable to members of the Armed Forces.

In early American history the standing army of the United States was small and there was little need for military courts. After World War I, that changed with the large number of citizen-soldiers employed by the Armed Forces. Still, because the post-war membership of the military shrunk back to normal after the end of the war, there was no perceived need for change or growth in the military courts. It was not until after World War II that this changed. World War II saw 16 million Americans serve in the Armed Forces and 2 million **courts martial** occurred during the war years. This rapid and dramatic growth led for calls to reorganize the military courts.[13] A court martial is the equivalent of a civilian criminal trial.

After the consolidation of all branches of the Armed Forces under the Department of Defense in 1947, Congress enacted the Uniform Code of Military Justice (UCMJ). Title 10 of the United States Code, Sections 801 through 946 is the military's criminal code. Enacted in 1950, it was a major revision of then-existing military criminal law. As enacted, the UCMJ provided significant guarantees for fair judicial process. It was amended significantly in 1968 and 1983 with periodic minor changes at other times.

Some of the primary changes enhanced the role of trial judges. The need for qualified military judges, who were experienced attorneys, to be in charge of the judicial process and all courts-martial was made clear. Also, the requirement to have a licensed attorney as defense counsel in courts-martial was established.

According to the U.S. Marine Corps' Military Justice Fact Sheets:

*The UCMJ is implemented through Executive Orders of the President of the United States pursuant to his authority under Article 36, UCMJ (10 USC § 836). Those Executive Orders form a comprehensive volume of law known as the Manual for Courts-Martial ("MCM"). The Preamble to the MCM explains that:*

> *"The purpose of military law is to promote justice, to assist in maintaining good order and discipline in the armed forces, to promote efficiency and effectiveness in the military establishment, and thereby to strengthen the national security of the United States."[14]*

---

[13]  According to the United States Marine Corps' Military Justice Overview, available at: https://www.hqmc.marines.mil/sja/Branches/Military-Justice-Branch-JMJ/Military-Justice/.

[14]  *Id.*

In 1984, there was another substantial revision to the MCM and the military rules of evidence became substantially the same as the Federal Rules of Evidence. The procedural requirements were also changed into Rules for Courts-Martial.

If a member of the Armed Forces commits a crime in violation of the UCMJ, and is brought up for court martial they are entitled to a licensed attorney under the MCM. This defense attorney is called a **judge advocate general (JAG)**. The military prosecutor is referred to as **trial counsel**. If a service member is tried in a civilian criminal court, whether a state or foreign court, they may also be tried in a military court martial for the same incident. This is true regardless of whether they were acquitted in the civilian case. This is the result of the **doctrine of separate or dual sovereigns**. Under this doctrine, the double jeopardy rule the state is seen as an independent entity with a right to enforce its own laws.

Some differences between military courts martial and civilian criminal trials are:

- Court martial members (jurors) are summoned from the military community from which the accused is a member,

- Courts martial are open to the military community,

- Members of the military may be tried in both civilian court and a military court martial for the same offense,

- Jury verdicts must only be by a 2/3 vote to convict the accused of the crime and less than 2/3 requires acquittal (there are no "hung juries" in military trials),

- In non-death penalty cases military defendants have the right to choose whether to be sentenced by the judge or the jury,

- Any court-martial member may suggest a sentence for the accused,

- Military judges have a wider range of sentencing options including death, confinement, separation from the service, reduction in pay grade, forfeiture of pay and allowances, fine, and reprimand,

- Convicted defendants are given a single sentence regardless of the number of counts or various offenses charged, and

- Convictions are automatically appealed unless the defendant waives review (death sentences must be reviewed).

## ii.  Tribal Courts

There are 562 federally recognized Indian tribes in the United States. These tribes are "distinct, independent political communities, retaining their original natural rights."[15] And although tribes lack "the full attributes of sovereignty," they retain the power of self-government.[16] Nevertheless, Congress has "plenary and exclusive" control over Indian tribes, which includes the power to limit or eliminate tribal sovereignty.[17]

The role of **tribal courts** is critical to maintaining and promoting tribal sovereignty, and Congress has long supported the development of these courts in Indian country. Tribal courts range from highly sophisticated systems with robust rules and procedures overseen by law-trained judges to small, one-room courts operating under tribal customs and traditions, with the judge often a well-respected tribal member or tribal elder. Regardless of their composition and level of sophistication, tribal courts fulfill an important role in dispensing justice on reservations that are often remote and underserved by state and federal courts.

There is no federal statute that requires a tribe to establish a tribal court or regulates the way a tribe creates one. Tribal courts are generally created by a grant contained in a tribe's constitution or by a tribal legislative enactment. Even though tribal courts created by way of a legislative ordinance or resolution lack the "permanence and independence" of constitutionally created courts, they "typically function in much the same way."[18]

Whether created by a constitutional grant or by legislative enactment, a key issue for all tribal courts is the scope of their jurisdiction. That jurisdiction can either be general, meaning it covers all matters, places and individuals within the exterior boundaries of the reservation, or, limited, meaning it is confined to specific issues and controversies.[19]

Tribal court jurisdiction, whether civil or criminal, is a complicated patchwork of federal laws and Supreme Court precedents, especially when a party to the case is a not a member of an Indian tribe. In general, tribal courts have civil jurisdiction over non-Indians who voluntarily come onto tribal property or enter into a consensual relationship with the tribe through a contract, lease or other

---

[15]  *Worcester v. Georgia*, 31 U.S. (6 Pet.) 515, 559 (1832).

[16]  *United States v. Kagama*, 118 U.S. 375, 381–82 (1886).

[17]  *Washington v. Confederated Bands and Tribes of Yakima Nation*, 439 U.S. 463, 470–71 (1979).

[18]  *Cohen's Handbook of Federal Indian Law*, § 4.04[3][c] p. 265 (ed. 2012).

[19]  One example is the issue of election disputes. Some tribes allow those disputes to be heard by tribal courts, but others do not allow for judicial review of disputed election results.

legal agreement.[20] The rules affecting tribal court criminal jurisdiction are far more restrictive. Except for the special jurisdiction provided to tribes under the Violence Against Women Act, tribal courts do not have the power to prosecute non-Indians who commit crimes on the reservation, regardless of the severity of the crime.[21]

On the other hand, tribal members who live on the reservation are subject to the jurisdiction of the tribal court, including criminal jurisdiction if the tribe has adopted a criminal code. And unless the reservation is located in a state subject to **Public Law 280**, state courts have no civil jurisdiction over a case that involves an Indian defendant sued for activities that occurred on the reservation.[22]

In those states subject to Public Law 280, the state has jurisdiction over crimes occurring on the reservation, and the state's general civil jurisdiction applies as well. Public Law 280 does not, however, supplant tribal court jurisdiction; rather the state's jurisdiction is concurrent with that of the tribal court. Criminal jurisdiction for tribal courts is an important and evolving area of law. A landmark decision in tribal criminal law was handed down by the Supreme Court in *McGirt v. Oklahoma (2020)*.[23] In *McGirt*, the Court affirmed the right of Indian nations to govern criminal trials on their land. The Court's landmark opinion speaks to the right of the tribes as sovereign governments:

> *On the far end of the Trail of Tears was a promise. Forced to leave their ancestral lands in Georgia and Alabama, the Creek Nation received assurances that their new lands in the West would be secure forever. In exchange for ceding "all their land, East of the Mississippi river," the U.S. government agreed by treaty that "[t]he Creek country west of the Mississippi shall be solemnly guarantied to the Creek Indians." Treaty With the Creeks, Arts. I, XIV, Mar. 24, 1832, 7 Stat. 366, 368 (1832 Treaty). Both parties settled on boundary lines for a new and "permanent home to the whole Creek nation," located in what is now Oklahoma. Treaty With the Creeks, preamble, Feb. 14, 1833, 7 Stat. 418 (1833 Treaty).*
>
> *The government further promised that "[no] State or Territory [shall] ever have a right to pass laws for the government of such Indians, but they shall be allowed to govern themselves." 1832 Treaty, Art. XIV, 7 Stat. 368. Today we are asked whether the land these treaties promised remains an Indian reservation for purposes*

---

[20]   *Montana v. United States*, 450 U.S. 544 (1981).

[21]   *Oliphant v. Suquamish Indian Tribe*, 435 U.S. 191 (1978).

[22]   *Williams v. Lee*, 358 U.S. 217 (1959).

[23]   *McGirt v. Oklahoma*, 140 S.Ct. 2452 (2020).

*of federal criminal law. Because Congress has not said otherwise, we hold the government to its word.*

Significantly, because Indian tribes have sovereignty that predates the U.S. Constitution, they are not subject to the same constitutional restraints that bind the federal government and the states.[24] In other words, a party over which a tribal court has jurisdiction does not have the same constitutional protections afforded to a person appearing in federal or state court. Congress has acted, however, to provide certain protections to individuals appearing in tribal court. The **Indian Civil Rights Act** ("ICRA")[25] requires tribal courts to adhere to most but not all the constitutional protections of the Bill of Rights. For example, under the ICRA a tribal court is not required to provide an indigent criminal defendant with court-appointed counsel.

The importance of this distinction cannot be overstated. A violation of the federal Bill of Rights can be vindicated by the appropriate federal court action; however, a violation of the ICRA can only be challenged in federal court by way of a habeas corpus petition, which only applies to challenges to illegal detentions. Consequently, many alleged violations of the ICRA cannot be challenged outside of the tribal court.

Whenever a party challenges the jurisdiction of a tribal court in a civil matter, that court must first be given the opportunity to rule on the issue before a party can appeal to another court. This is known as the "exhaust tribal remedies," doctrine, which requires the challenging party to exhaust all their potential remedies in the tribal court system before challenging the tribal court's jurisdiction in federal or state court.[26]

**Tribal sovereign immunity** has a significant impact on the operation of tribal courts. Tribal sovereign immunity protects a tribe and tribal entities from being sued in any court, unless the tribe has waived the immunity. Without a waiver, tribes cannot be sued even in their own tribal courts. A waiver of tribal sovereign immunity must be clear and unequivocal for it to be effective.[27]

The judgments and orders of tribal courts are entitled to be respected and honored by sister courts, whether state or federal. Some types of tribal court orders, such as domestic violence restraining orders are given "full faith and

---

[24] *Talton v. Mayes*, 163 U.S. 376 (1896).

[25] 25 U.S.C.A. § 1301 et seq.

[26] *National Farmers Union Ins. Co. v. Crow Tribe of Indians*, 471 U.S. 845 (1985).

[27] With the advent of tribal gaming facilities, whose clientele often is made up of non-Indians, the issue of tribal sovereign immunity has come under scrutiny, particularly in situations where casino patrons who have been injured on tribal property come to learn that their remedies against the tribe are limited.

credit," whereas others are respected under the notion of "comity." With "full faith and credit" the receiving court automatically honors the order, while a court exercising "comity" has more discretion to reject the order under certain circumstances.

Tribal courts are deeply ingrained and form an essential part of the American court system. The cases and controversies tribal courts routinely address are as challenging, complex and relevant as those heard in any other court in the land. And although often far different from their state and federal counterparts, tribal courts deserve no less respect than those more familiar tribunals.[28]

---

[28]  *Special thanks to Joseph J. Wiseman, Esq. for contributing this section on Tribal Courts.*

**Read and brief each of the following cases relating to specialized courts and consider the questions following each case:**

1. *In re Gault*: Due Process rights in juvenile court

2. *Roper v. Simmons*: capital punishment for juveniles

3. *McKeiver v. Pennsylvania*: right to a jury trial in juvenile court

4. *McGirt v. Oklahoma*: criminal jurisdiction for tribal courts

---

### IN RE GAULT

Supreme Court of the United States
Argued Dec. 6, 1966
Decided May 15, 1967
387 U.S. 1

#### OPINION

**MR. JUSTICE FORTAS delivered the opinion of the Court.**

This is an appeal under from a judgment of the Supreme Court of Arizona affirming the dismissal of a petition for a writ of habeas corpus. The petition sought the release of Gerald Francis Gault, appellants' 15-year-old son, who had been committed as a juvenile delinquent to the State Industrial School by the Juvenile Court of Gila County, Arizona. The Supreme Court of Arizona affirmed dismissal of the writ against various arguments . . . The court agreed that the constitutional guarantee of due process of law is applicable in such proceedings. . . . It concluded that the proceedings ending in commitment of Gerald Gault did not offend those requirements. We do not agree, and we reverse. We begin with a statement of the facts.

I.

On Monday, June 8, 1964, at about 10 a.m., Gerald Francis Gault and a friend, Ronald Lewis, were taken into custody by the Sheriff of Gila County. Gerald was then still subject to a six months' probation order which had been entered on February 25, 1964, as a result of his having been in the company of another boy who had stolen a wallet from a lady's purse. The police action on June 8 was taken as the result of a verbal complaint by a neighbor of the boys, Mrs. Cook, about a telephone call made to her in which the caller or callers made lewd or indecent remarks. It will suffice for purposes of this opinion to say that the remarks or questions put to her were of the irritatingly offensive, adolescent, sex variety. At the time Gerald was picked up, his mother and father were both at work. No notice that Gerald was being taken into custody was left at the home. No other steps were taken to advise them that their son had, in effect, been arrested. Gerald was taken to the Children's Detention Home. When his mother arrived home at about 6 o'clock, Gerald was not there. Gerald's older brother was sent to look for him at the trailer home of the Lewis family. He apparently learned then that Gerald was in custody. He so informed his mother. The two of them went to the Detention Home. The deputy probation officer, Flagg, who was also superintendent of the Detention Home, told Mrs. Gault 'why Jerry was there' and said that a hearing would be held in Juvenile Court at 3 o'clock the following day, June 9.

Officer Flagg filed a petition with the court on the hearing day, June 9, 1964. It was not served on the Gaults. Indeed, none of them saw this petition until the habeas corpus hearing on August 17, 1964. The petition was entirely formal. It made no reference to any factual basis for the judicial action which it initiated. It recited only that 'said minor is under the age of eighteen years, and is in need of the protection of this Honorable Court; (and that) said minor is a delinquent minor.' It prayed for a hearing and an order regarding 'the care and custody of said minor.' Officer Flagg executed a formal affidavit in support of the petition.

On June 9, Gerald, his mother, his older brother, and Probation Officers Flagg and Henderson appeared before the Juvenile Judge in chambers. Gerald's father was not there. He was at work out of the city. Mrs. Cook, the complainant, was not there. No one was sworn at this hearing. No transcript or recording was made. No memorandum or record of the substance of the proceedings was prepared. Our information about the proceedings and the subsequent hearing on June 15, derives entirely from the testimony of the Juvenile Court Judge, Mr. and Mrs. Gault and Officer Flagg at the habeas corpus proceeding conducted two months later. From this, it appears that at the June 9 hearing Gerald was questioned by the judge about the telephone call. There was conflict as to what he said. His mother recalled that Gerald said he only dialed Mrs. Cook's number and handed the telephone to his friend, Ronald. Officer Flagg recalled that Gerald had admitted making the lewd remarks. Judge McGhee testified that Gerald 'admitted making one of these (lewd) statements.' At the conclusion of the hearing, the judge said he would 'think about it.' Gerald was taken back to the Detention Home. He was not sent to his own home with his parents. On June 11 or 12, after having been detained since June 8, Gerald was released and driven home. There is no explanation in the record as to why he was kept in the Detention Home or why he was released. At 5 p.m. on the day of Gerald's release, Mrs. Gault received a note signed by Officer Flagg. It was on plain paper, not letterhead. Its entire text was as follows:

'Mrs. Gault:

'Judge McGHEE has set Monday June 15, 1964 at 11:00 A.M. as the date and time for further Hearings on Gerald's delinquency

'/s/ Flagg'

At the appointed time on Monday, June 15, Gerald, his father and mother, Ronald Lewis and his father, and Officers Flagg and Henderson were present before Judge McGhee. Witnesses at the habeas corpus proceeding differed in their recollections of Gerald's testimony at the June 15 hearing. Mr. and Mrs. Gault recalled that Gerald again testified that he had only dialed the number and that the other boy had made the remarks. Officer Flagg agreed that at this hearing Gerald did not admit making the lewd remarks. But Judge McGhee recalled that 'there was some admission again of some of the lewd statements. He—he didn't admit any of the more serious lewd statements.' Again, the complainant, Mrs. Cook, was not present. Mrs. Gault asked that Mrs. Cook be present 'so she could see which boy that done the talking, the dirty talking over the phone.' The Juvenile Judge said 'she didn't have to be present at that hearing.' The judge did not speak to Mrs. Cook or communicate with her at any time. Probation Officer Flagg had talked to her once—over the telephone on June 9.

At this June 15 hearing a 'referral report' made by the probation officers was filed with the court, although not disclosed to Gerald or his parents. This listed the charge as 'Lewd Phone Calls.' At the conclusion of the hearing, the judge committed Gerald as a juvenile delinquent to the State Industrial School 'for the period of his minority (that is, until 21), unless sooner discharged by due process of law.' An order to that effect was entered. It recites that 'after a full hearing and due deliberation the Court finds that said minor is a delinquent child, and that said minor is of the age of 15 years.'

No appeal is permitted by Arizona law in juvenile cases. On August 3, 1964, a petition for a writ of habeas corpus was filed with the Supreme Court of Arizona and referred by it to the Superior Court for hearing. At the habeas corpus hearing on August 17, Judge McGhee was vigorously cross-examined as to the basis for his actions. He testified that he had taken into account the fact that Gerald was on probation. He was asked 'under what section of * * * the code you found the boy delinquent?'

. . .he concluded that Gerald came within ARS s 8–201, subsec. 6(a), which specifies that a 'delinquent child' includes one 'who has violated a law of the state or an ordinance or regulation of a political subdivision thereof.' The law which Gerald was found to have violated is ARS s 13–377. This section of the Arizona Criminal Code provides that a person who 'in the presence or hearing of any woman or child * * * uses vulgar, abusive or obscene language, is guilty of a misdemeanor * * *.' The penalty specified in the Criminal Code, which would apply to an adult, is $5 to $50, or imprisonment for not more than two months. The judge also testified that he acted under ARS s 8–201, subsec. 6(d) which includes in the definition of a 'delinquent child' one who, as the judge phrased it, is 'habitually involved in immoral matters.'

Asked about the basis for his conclusion that Gerald was 'habitually involved in immoral matters,' the judge testified, somewhat vaguely, that two years earlier, on July 2, 1962, a 'referral' was made concerning Gerald, 'where the boy had stolen a baseball glove from another boy and lied to the Police Department about it.' The judge said there was 'no hearing,' and 'no accusation' relating to this incident, 'because of lack of material foundation.' But it seems to have remained in his mind as a relevant factor. The judge also testified that Gerald had admitted making other nuisance phone calls in the past which, as the judge recalled the boy's testimony, were 'silly calls, or funny calls, or something like that.'

The Superior Court dismissed the writ, and appellants sought review in the Arizona Supreme Court. . . .

The Supreme Court handed down an elaborate and wide-ranging opinion affirming dismissal of the writ and stating the court's conclusions as to the issues raised by appellants and other aspects of the juvenile process. In their jurisdictional statement and brief in this Court, appellants do not urge upon us all of the points passed upon by the Supreme Court of Arizona. They urge that we hold the Juvenile Code of Arizona invalid on its face or as applied in this case because, contrary to the Due Process Clause of the Fourteenth Amendment, the juvenile is taken from the custody of his parents and committed to a state institution pursuant to proceedings in which the Juvenile Court has virtually unlimited discretion, and in which the following basic rights are denied:

1.   Notice of the charges;

2.   Right to counsel;

3.   Right to confrontation and cross-examination;

4.    Privilege against self-incrimination;

5.    Right to a transcript of the proceedings; and

6.    Right to appellate review.

We shall not consider other issues which were passed upon by the Supreme Court of Arizona. We emphasize that we indicate no opinion as to whether the decision of that court with respect to such other issues does or does not conflict with requirements of the Federal Constitution.

II.

The Supreme Court of Arizona held that due process of law is requisite to the constitutional validity of proceedings in which a court reaches the conclusion that a juvenile has been at fault, has engaged in conduct prohibited by law, or has otherwise misbehaved with the consequence that he is committed to an institution in which his freedom is curtailed. This conclusion is in accord with the decisions of a number of courts under both federal and state constitutions.

. . . We consider only the problems presented to us by this case. These relate to the proceedings by which a determination is made as to whether a juvenile is a 'delinquent' as a result of alleged misconduct on his part, with the consequence that he may be committed to a state institution. As to these proceedings, there appears to be little current dissent from the proposition that the Due Process Clause has a role to play. The problem is to ascertain the precise impact of the due process requirement upon such proceedings.

From the inception of the juvenile court system, wide differences have been tolerated—indeed insisted upon—between the procedural rights accorded to adults and those of juveniles. In practically all jurisdictions, there are rights granted to adults which are withheld from juveniles. In addition to the specific problems involved in the present case, for example, it has been held that the juvenile is not entitled to bail, to indictment by grand jury, to a public trial or to trial by jury. It is frequent practice that rules governing the arrest and interrogation of adults by the police are not observed in the case of juveniles.

The history and theory underlying this development are well-known, but a recapitulation is necessary for purposes of this opinion. The Juvenile Court movement began in this country at the end of the last century. From the juvenile court statute adopted in Illinois in 1899, the system has spread to every State in the Union, the District of Columbia, and Puerto Rico. The constitutionality of juvenile court laws has been sustained in over 40 jurisdictions against a variety of attacks.

The early reformers were appalled by adult procedures and penalties, and by the fact that children could be given long prison sentences and mixed in jails with hardened criminals. They were profoundly convinced that society's duty to the child could not be confined by the concept of justice alone. They believed that society's role was not to ascertain whether the child was 'guilty' or 'innocent,' but 'What is he, how has he become what he is, and what had best be done in his interest and in the interest of the state to save him from a downward career.' The child—essentially good, as they saw it—was to be made 'to feel that he is the object of (the state's) care and solicitude,' not that he was under arrest or on trial. The rules of criminal procedure were therefore altogether inapplicable. . . .

The right of the state, as parens patriae, to deny to the child procedural rights available to his elders was elaborated by the assertion that a child, unlike an adult, has a right 'not to liberty but to custody.' He can be made to attorn to his parents, to go to school, etc. If his parents default in effectively performing their custodial functions—that is, if the child is 'delinquent'—the state may intervene. In doing so, it does not deprive the child of any rights, because he has none. It merely provides the 'custody' to which the child is entitled. On this basis, proceedings involving juveniles were described as 'civil' not 'criminal' and therefore not subject to the requirements which restrict the state when it seeks to deprive a person of his liberty.

Accordingly, the highest motives and most enlightened impulses led to a peculiar system for juveniles, unknown to our law in any comparable context. The constitutional and theoretical basis for this peculiar system is—to say the least—debatable. And in practice, as we remarked in the *Kent* case, supra, the results have not been entirely satisfactory. Juvenile Court history has again demonstrated that unbridled discretion, however benevolently motivated, is frequently a poor substitute for principle and procedure. . . .The absence of procedural rules based upon constitutional principle has not always produced fair, efficient, and effective procedures. Departures from established principles of due process have frequently resulted not in enlightened procedure, but in arbitrariness. The Chairman of the Pennsylvania Council of Juvenile Court Judges has recently observed: 'Unfortunately, loose procedures, high-handed methods and crowded court calendars, either singly or in combination, all too often, have resulted in depriving some juveniles of fundamental rights that have resulted in a denial of due process.'

Failure to observe the fundamental requirements of due process has resulted in instances, which might have been avoided, of unfairness to individuals and inadequate or inaccurate findings of fact and unfortunate prescriptions of remedy. Due process of law is the primary and indispensable foundation of individual freedom. It is the basic and essential term in the social compact which defines the rights of the individual and delimits the powers which the state may exercise. As Mr. Justice Frankfurter has said: 'The history of American freedom is, in no small measure, the history of procedure.' . . . 'Procedure is to law what 'scientific method' is to science. . .

Ultimately, however, we confront the reality of that portion of the Juvenile Court process with which we deal in this case. A boy is charged with misconduct. The boy is committed to an institution where he may be restrained of liberty for years. It is of no constitutional consequence—and of limited practical meaning—that the institution to which he is committed is called an Industrial School. The fact of the matter is that, however euphemistic the title, a 'receiving home' or an 'industrial school' for juveniles is an institution of confinement in which the child is incarcerated for a greater or lesser time. His world becomes 'a building with whitewashed walls, regimented routine and institutional hours' Instead of mother and father and sisters and brothers and friends and classmates, his world is peopled by guards, custodians, state employees, and 'delinquents' confined with him for anything from waywardness to rape and homicide.

In view of this, it would be extraordinary if our Constitution did not require the procedural regularity and the exercise of care implied in the phrase 'due process.' Under our Constitution, the condition of being a boy does not justify a kangaroo court. The traditional ideas of Juvenile Court procedure, indeed, contemplated that time would be available and care would be used to establish precisely what the juvenile did and why he did it—was it a prank of adolescence or a brutal act threatening serious consequences to himself or society unless corrected? Under traditional notions, one would assume that in a case like that of Gerald Gault, where the juvenile appears to have a home, a working mother and father, and an older brother, the Juvenile Judge would have made a careful inquiry and judgment as to the possibility that the boy could be disciplined and dealt with at home, despite his previous transgressions. Indeed, so far as appears in the record before us, except for some conversation with Gerald about his school work and his 'wanting to go to * * * Grand Canyon with his father,' the points to which the judge directed his attention were little different from those that would be involved in determining any charge of violation of a penal statute. The essential difference between Gerald's case and a normal criminal case is that safeguards available to adults were discarded in Gerald's case. The summary procedure as well as the long commitment was possible because Gerald was 15 years of age instead of over 18.

If Gerald had been over 18, he would not have been subject to Juvenile Court proceedings. For the particular offense immediately involved, the maximum punishment would have been a fine of $5 to $50, or imprisonment in jail for not more than two months. Instead, he was committed to custody for a maximum of six years. If he had been over 18 and had committed an offense to which such a sentence might apply, he would have been entitled to substantial rights under the Constitution of the United States as well as under Arizona's laws and constitution. The United States Constitution would guarantee him rights and protections with respect to arrest, search, and seizure, and pretrial interrogation. It would assure him of specific notice of the charges and adequate time to decide his course of action and to prepare his defense. He would be entitled to clear advice that he could be represented by counsel, and, at least if a felony were involved, the State would be required to provide counsel if his parents were unable to afford it. If the court acted on the basis of his confession, careful procedures would be required to assure its voluntariness. If the case went to trial, confrontation and opportunity for cross-examination would be guaranteed. So wide a gulf between the State's treatment of the adult and of the child requires a bridge sturdier than mere verbiage, and reasons more persuasive than cliche can provide. As Wheeler and Cottrell have put it, 'The rhetoric of the juvenile court movement has developed without any necessarily close correspondence to the realities of court and institutional routines.'

In *Kent v. United States*, supra, we stated that the Juvenile Court Judge's exercise of the power of the state as parens patriae was not unlimited. We said that 'the admonition to function in a 'parental' relationship is not an invitation to procedural arbitrariness.' With respect to the waiver by the Juvenile Court to the adult court of jurisdiction over an offense committed by a youth, we said that 'there is no place in our system of law for reaching a result of such tremendous consequences without ceremony—without hearing, without effective assistance of counsel, without a statement of reasons.' We announced with respect to such waiver proceedings that while 'We do not mean to indicate that the hearing to be held must conform with all of the requirements of a criminal trial or even of the usual administrative hearing; but we do hold that the hearing must measure up to the essentials of due process and fair treatment.' We reiterate this view, here in connection with a juvenile court adjudication of 'delinquency,' as a requirement which is part of the Due Process Clause of the Fourteenth Amendment of our Constitution.

We now turn to the specific issues which are presented to us in the present case.

### III. NOTICE OF CHARGES.

Appellants allege that the Arizona Juvenile Code is unconstitutional or alternatively that the proceedings before the Juvenile Court were constitutionally defective because of failure to provide adequate notice of the hearings. No notice was given to Gerald's parents when he was taken into custody on Monday, June 8. On that night, when Mrs. Gault went to the Detention Home, she was orally informed that there would be a hearing the next afternoon and was told the reason why Gerald was in custody. The only written notice Gerald's parents received at any time was a note on plain paper from Officer Flagg delivered on Thursday or Friday, June 11 or 12, to the effect that the judge had set Monday, June 15, 'for further Hearings on Gerald's delinquency.'

A 'petition' was filed with the court on June 9 by Officer Flagg, reciting only that he was informed and believed that 'said minor is a delinquent minor and that it is necessary that some order be made by the Honorable Court for said minor's welfare.' The applicable Arizona statute provides for a petition to be filed in Juvenile Court, alleging in general terms that the child is 'neglected, dependent or delinquent.' The statute explicitly states that such a general allegation is sufficient, 'without alleging the facts.' There is no requirement that the petition be served and it was not served upon, given to, or shown to Gerald or his parents.

The Supreme Court of Arizona rejected appellants' claim that due process was denied because of inadequate notice. It stated that 'Mrs. Gault knew the exact nature of the charge against Gerald from the day he was taken to the detention home.' The court also pointed out that the Gaults appeared at the two hearings 'without objection.' . . .

We cannot agree with the court's conclusion that adequate notice was given in this case. Notice, to comply with due process requirements, must be given sufficiently in advance of scheduled court proceedings so that reasonable opportunity to prepare will be afforded, and it must 'set forth the alleged misconduct with particularity.' . . . The 'initial hearing' in the present case was a hearing on the merits. Notice at that time is not timely; and even if there were a conceivable purpose served by the deferral proposed by the court below, it would have to yield to the requirements that the child and his parents or guardian be notified, in writing, of the specific charge or factual allegations to be considered at the hearing, and that such written notice be given at the earliest practicable time, and in any event sufficiently in advance of the hearing to permit preparation. Due process of law requires notice of the sort we have described—that is, notice which would be deemed constitutionally adequate in a civil or criminal proceeding. It does not allow a hearing to be held in which a youth's freedom and his parents' right to his custody are at stake without giving them timely notice, in advance of the hearing, of the specific issues that they must meet. Nor, in the circumstances of this case, can it reasonably be said that the requirement of notice was waived.

## IV.  RIGHT TO COUNSEL

Appellants charge that the Juvenile Court proceedings were fatally defective because the court did not advise Gerald or his parents of their right to counsel, and proceeded with the hearing, the adjudication of delinquency and the order of commitment in the absence of counsel for the child and his parents or an express waiver of the right thereto. . . .

A proceeding where the issue is whether the child will be found to be 'delinquent' and subjected to the loss of his liberty for years is comparable in seriousness to a felony prosecution. The juvenile needs the assistance of counsel to cope with problems of law, to make skilled inquiry into the facts, to insist upon regularity of the proceedings, and to ascertain whether he has a defense and to prepare and submit it. The child 'requires the guiding hand of counsel at every step in the proceedings against him.' Just as in *Kent v. United States*, supra, 383 U.S., at 561–562, we indicated our agreement with the United States Court of Appeals for the District of Columbia Circuit that the assistance of counsel is essential for purposes of waiver proceedings, so we hold now that it is equally essential for the determination of delinquency, carrying with it the awesome prospect of incarceration in a state institution until the juvenile reaches the age of 21.

. . .

We conclude that the Due Process Clause of the Fourteenth Amendment requires that in respect of proceedings to determine delinquency which may result in commitment to an institution in which the juvenile's freedom is curtailed, the child and his parents must be notified of the child's right to be represented by counsel retained by them, or if they are unable to afford counsel, that counsel will be appointed to represent the child.

At the habeas corpus proceeding, Mrs. Gault testified that she knew that she could have appeared with counsel at the juvenile hearing. This knowledge is not a waiver of the right to counsel which she and her juvenile son had, as we have defined it. They had a right expressly to be advised that they might retain counsel and to be confronted with the need for specific consideration of whether they did or did not choose to waive the right. If they were unable to afford to employ counsel, they were entitled in view of the seriousness of the charge and the potential commitment, to appointed counsel, unless they chose waiver. Mrs. Gault's knowledge that she could employ counsel was not an 'intentional relinquishment or abandonment' of a fully known right.

## V. CONFRONTATION, SELF-INCRIMINATION, CROSS-EXAMINATION

Appellants urge that the writ of habeas corpus should have been granted because of the denial of the rights of confrontation and cross-examination in the Juvenile Court hearings, and because the privilege against self-incrimination was not observed. The Juvenile Court Judge testified at the habeas corpus hearing that he had proceeded on the basis of Gerald's admissions at the two hearings. Appellants attack this on the ground that the admissions were obtained in disregard of the privilege against self-incrimination. If the confession is disregarded, appellants argue that the delinquency conclusion, since it was fundamentally based on a finding that Gerald had made lewd remarks during the phone call to Mrs. Cook, is fatally defective for failure to accord the rights of confrontation and cross-examination which the Due Process Clause of the Fourteenth Amendment of the Federal Constitution guarantees in state proceedings generally.

Our first question, then, is whether Gerald's admission was improperly obtained and relied on as the basis of decision, in conflict with the Federal Constitution. For this purpose, it is necessary briefly to recall the relevant facts.

Mrs. Cook, the complainant, and the recipient of the alleged telephone call, was not called as a witness. Gerald's mother asked the Juvenile Court Judge why Mrs. Cook was not present and the judge replied that 'she didn't have to be present.' So far as appears, Mrs. Cook was spoken to only once, by Officer Flagg, and this was by telephone. The judge did not speak with her on any occasion.

Gerald had been questioned by the probation officer after having been taken into custody. The exact circumstances of this questioning do not appear but any admissions Gerald may have made at this time do not appear in the record. Gerald was also questioned by the Juvenile Court Judge at each of the two hearings. The judge testified in the habeas corpus proceeding that Gerald admitted making 'some of the lewd statements * * * (but not) any of the more serious lewd statements.' There was conflict and uncertainty among the witnesses at the habeas corpus proceeding—the Juvenile Court Judge, Mr. and Mrs. Gault, and the probation officer—as to what Gerald did or did not admit.

We shall assume that Gerald made admissions of the sort described by the Juvenile Court Judge, as quoted above. Neither Gerald nor his parents were advised that he did not have to testify or make a statement, or that an incriminating statement might result in his commitment as a 'delinquent.'

The Arizona Supreme Court rejected appellants' contention that Gerald had a right to be advised that he need not incriminate himself. It said: 'We think the necessary flexibility for individualized treatment will be enhanced by a rule which does not require the judge to advise the infant of a privilege against self-incrimination.'

In reviewing this conclusion of Arizona's Supreme Court, we emphasize again that we are here concerned only with a proceeding to determine whether a minor is a 'delinquent' and which may result in commitment to a state institution. Specifically, the question is whether, in such a proceeding, an admission by the juvenile may be used against him in the absence of clear and unequivocal evidence that the admission was made with knowledge that he was not obliged to speak and would not be penalized for remaining silent. In light of *Miranda v. State of Arizona*, 384 U.S. 436 (1966), we must also consider whether, if the privilege against self-incrimination is available, it can effectively be waived unless counsel is present or the right to counsel has been waived. . .

This Court has emphasized that admissions and confessions of juveniles require special caution. In *Haley v. State of Ohio*, 332 U.S. 596, where this Court reversed the conviction of a 15-year-old boy for murder, Mr. Justice Douglas said:

> 'What transpired would make us pause for careful inquiry if a mature man were involved. And when, as here, a mere child—an easy victim of the law—is before us, special care in scrutinizing the record must be used. Age 15 is a tender and difficult age for a boy of any race. He cannot be judged by the more exacting standards of maturity. That

which would leave a man could and unimpressed can overawe and overwhelm a lad in his early teens. This is the period of great instability which the crisis of adolescence produces. A 15-year-old lad, questioned through the dead of night by relays of police, is a ready victim of the inquisition. Mature men possibly might stand the ordeal from midnight to 5 a.m. But we cannot believe that a lad of tender years is a match for the police in such a contest. He needs counsel and support if he is not to become the victim first of fear, then of panic. He needs someone on whom to lean lest the overpowering presence of the law, as he knows it, crush him. No friend stood at the side of this 15-year-old boy as the police, working in relays, questioned him hour after hour, from midnight until dawn. No lawyer stood guard to make sure that the police went so far and no farther, to see to it that they stopped short of the point where he became the victim of coercion. No counsel or friend was called during the critical hours of questioning.'. . .

It would indeed be surprising if the privilege against self-incrimination were available to hardened criminals but not to children. The language of the Fifth Amendment, applicable to the States by operation of the Fourteenth Amendment, is unequivocal and without exception. And the scope of the privilege is comprehensive. As Mr. Justice White, concurring, stated in *Murphy v. Waterfront Commission*, 378 U.S. 52, 94 (1964): 'The privilege can be claimed in any proceeding, be it criminal or civil, administrative or judicial, investigatory or adjudicatory. * * * it protects any disclosures which the witness may reasonably apprehend could be used in a criminal prosecution or which could lead to other evidence that might be so used.' (Emphasis added.)

With respect to juveniles, both common observation and expert opinion emphasize that the 'distrust of confessions made in certain situations' to which Dean Wigmore referred in the passage quoted supra, at 1453, is imperative in the case of children from an early age through adolescence. . .It would be entirely unrealistic to carve out of the Fifth Amendment all statements by juveniles on the ground that these cannot lead to 'criminal' involvement. In the first place, juvenile proceedings to determine 'delinquency,' which may lead to commitment to a state institution, must be regarded as 'criminal' for purposes of the privilege against self-incrimination.

. . . In Arizona, as in other States, provision is made for Juvenile Courts to relinquish or waive jurisdiction to the ordinary criminal courts. In the present case, when Gerald Gault was interrogated concerning violation of a section of the Arizona Criminal Code, it could not be certain that the Juvenile Court Judge would decide to 'suspend' criminal prosecution in court for adults by proceeding to an adjudication in Juvenile Court. . .

We conclude that the constitutional privilege against self-incrimination is applicable in the case of juveniles as it is with respect to adults. We appreciate that special problems may arise with respect to waiver of the privilege by or on behalf of children, and that there may well be some differences in technique—but not in principle—depending upon the age of the child and the presence and competence of parents. The participation of counsel will, of course, assist the police, Juvenile Courts and appellate tribunals in administering the privilege. If counsel was not present for some permissible reason when an admission was obtained, the greatest care must be taken to assure that the admission was voluntary, in the sense not only that it was not coerced or suggested, but also that it was not the product of ignorance of rights or of adolescent fantasy, fright or despair.

The 'confession' of Gerald Gault was first obtained by Officer Flagg, out of the presence of Gerald's parents, without counsel and without advising him of his right to silence, as far as appears. The judgment of the Juvenile Court was stated by the judge to be based on Gerald's admissions in court. Neither 'admission' was reduced to writing, and, to say the least, the process by which the 'admissions,' were obtained and received must be characterized as lacking the certainty and order which are required of proceedings of such formidable consequences. Apart from the 'admission,' there was nothing upon which a judgment or finding might be based. There was no sworn testimony. Mrs. Cook, the complainant, was not present. The Arizona Supreme Court held that 'sworn testimony must be required of all witnesses including police officers, probation officers and others who are part of or officially related to the juvenile court structure.' We hold that this is not enough. No reason is suggested or appears for a different rule in respect of sworn testimony in juvenile courts than in adult tribunals. Absent a valid confession adequate to support the determination of the Juvenile Court, confrontation and sworn testimony by witnesses available for cross-examination were essential for a finding of 'delinquency' and an order committing Gerald to a state institution for a maximum of six years. . .

As we said in *Kent v. United States*, 383 U.S. 541, 554 (1966) with respect to waiver proceedings, 'there is no place in our system of law of reaching a result of such tremendous consequences without ceremony * * *.' We now hold that, absent a valid confession, a determination of delinquency and an order of commitment to a state institution cannot be sustained in the absence of sworn testimony subjected to the opportunity for cross-examination in accordance with our law and constitutional requirements.

VI.  APPELLATE REVIEW AND TRANSCRIPT OF PROCEEDINGS.

. . .In view of the fact that we must reverse the Supreme Court of Arizona's affirmance of the dismissal of the writ of habeas corpus for other reasons, we need not rule on this question in the present case or upon the failure to provide a transcript or recording of the hearings—or, indeed, the failure of the Juvenile Judge to state the grounds for his conclusion. . . .

For the reasons stated, the judgment of the Supreme Court of Arizona is reversed and the cause remanded for further proceedings not inconsistent with this opinion. It is so ordered.

**Judgment reversed and cause remanded with directions. . . .**

**After preparing the case brief, consider the answers to the following questions:**

1.    What are some of the important reasons for the establishment of the juvenile courts? Are those reasons still valid today, over 100 years later?

2.    Consider each of the rights the Court applied to juveniles: the right to notice of charges, the right to counsel, and confrontation/self-incrimination/cross-examination. How do you believe the application of these rights to juveniles may have changed the dynamic in juvenile proceedings? Are these changes positive or negative? Why?

## ROPER V. SIMMONS

Supreme Court of the United States
Argued Oct. 13, 2004
Decided March 1, 2005
543 U.S. 551

### OPINION

### JUSTICE KENNEDY delivered the opinion of the Court.

This case requires us to address, for the second time in a decade and a half, whether it is permissible under the Eighth and Fourteenth Amendments to the Constitution of the United States to execute a juvenile offender who was older than 15 but younger than 18 when he committed a capital crime. In *Stanford v. Kentucky,* 492 U.S. 361 (1989), a divided Court rejected the proposition that the Constitution bars capital punishment for juvenile offenders in this age group. We reconsider the question.

I

At the age of 17, when he was still a junior in high school, Christopher Simmons, the respondent here, committed murder. About nine months later, after he had turned 18, he was tried and sentenced to death. There is little doubt that Simmons was the instigator of the crime. Before its commission Simmons said he wanted to murder someone. In chilling, callous terms he talked about his plan, discussing it for the most part with two friends, Charles Benjamin and John Tessmer, then aged 15 and 16 respectively. Simmons proposed to commit burglary and murder by breaking and entering, tying up a victim, and throwing the victim off a bridge. Simmons assured his friends they could "get away with it" because they were minors.

The three met at about 2 a.m. on the night of the murder, but Tessmer left before the other two set out. (The State later charged Tessmer with conspiracy, but dropped the charge in exchange for his testimony against Simmons.) Simmons and Benjamin entered the home of the victim, Shirley Crook, after reaching through an open window and unlocking the back door. Simmons turned on a hallway light. Awakened, Mrs. Crook called out, "Who's there?" In response Simmons entered Mrs. Crook's bedroom, where he recognized her from a previous car accident involving them both. Simmons later admitted this confirmed his resolve to murder her.

Using duct tape to cover her eyes and mouth and bind her hands, the two perpetrators put Mrs. Crook in her minivan and drove to a state park. They reinforced the bindings, covered her head with a towel, and walked her to a railroad trestle spanning the Meramec River. There they tied her hands and feet together with electrical wire, wrapped her whole face in duct tape and threw her from the bridge, drowning her in the waters below.

By the afternoon of September 9, Steven Crook had returned home from an overnight trip, found his bedroom in disarray, and reported his wife missing. On the same afternoon fishermen recovered the victim's body from the river. Simmons, meanwhile, was bragging about the killing, telling friends he had killed a woman "because the bitch seen my face."

The next day, after receiving information of Simmons' involvement, police arrested him at his high school and took him to the police station in Fenton, Missouri. They read him his *Miranda* rights. Simmons waived his right to an attorney and agreed to answer questions. After less than two hours of interrogation, Simmons confessed to the murder and agreed to perform a videotaped reenactment at the crime scene.

The State charged Simmons with burglary, kidnaping, stealing, and murder in the first degree. As Simmons was 17 at the time of the crime, he was outside the criminal jurisdiction of Missouri's juvenile court system. See Mo.Rev.Stat. §§ 211.021 (2000) and 211.031 (Supp.2003). He was tried as an adult. At trial the State introduced Simmons' confession and the videotaped reenactment of the crime, along with testimony that Simmons discussed the crime in advance and bragged about it later. The defense called no witnesses in the guilt phase. The jury having returned a verdict of murder, the trial proceeded to the penalty phase.

The State sought the death penalty. As aggravating factors, the State submitted that the murder was committed for the purpose of receiving money; was committed for the purpose of avoiding, interfering with, or preventing lawful arrest of the defendant; and involved depravity of mind and was outrageously and wantonly vile, horrible, and inhuman. The State called Shirley Crook's husband, daughter, and two sisters, who presented moving evidence of the devastation her death had brought to their lives.

In mitigation Simmons' attorneys first called an officer of the Missouri juvenile justice system, who testified that Simmons had no prior convictions and that no previous charges had been filed against him. Simmons' mother, father, two younger half brothers, a neighbor, and a friend took the stand to tell the jurors of the close relationships they had formed with Simmons and to plead for mercy on his behalf. Simmons' mother, in particular, testified to the responsibility Simmons demonstrated in taking care of his two younger half brothers and of his grandmother and to his capacity to show love for them.

During closing arguments, both the prosecutor and defense counsel addressed Simmons' age, which the trial judge had instructed the jurors they could consider as a mitigating factor. Defense counsel reminded the jurors that juveniles of Simmons' age cannot drink, serve on juries, or even see certain movies, because "the legislatures have wisely decided that individuals of a certain age aren't responsible enough." Defense counsel argued that Simmons' age should make "a huge difference to [the jurors] in deciding just exactly what sort of punishment to make." In rebuttal, the prosecutor gave the following response: "Age, he says. Think about age. Seventeen years old. Isn't that scary? Doesn't that scare you? Mitigating? Quite the contrary I submit. Quite the contrary."

The jury recommended the death penalty after finding the State had proved each of the three aggravating factors submitted to it. Accepting the jury's recommendation, the trial judge imposed the death penalty.

Simmons obtained new counsel, who moved in the trial court to set aside the conviction and sentence. One argument was that Simmons had received ineffective assistance at trial. To support this contention, the new counsel called as witnesses Simmons' trial attorney, Simmons' friends and neighbors, and clinical psychologists who had evaluated him.

Part of the submission was that Simmons was "very immature," "very impulsive," and "very susceptible to being manipulated or influenced." The experts testified about Simmons' background including a difficult home environment and dramatic changes in behavior, accompanied by poor school performance in adolescence. Simmons was absent from home for long periods, spending time using alcohol and drugs with other teenagers or young adults. The contention by Simmons' postconviction counsel was that these matters should have been established in the sentencing proceeding.

The trial court found no constitutional violation by reason of ineffective assistance of counsel and denied the motion for postconviction relief. In a consolidated appeal from Simmons' conviction and sentence, and from the denial of postconviction relief, the Missouri Supreme Court affirmed. . .

After these proceedings in Simmons' case had run their course, this Court held that the Eighth and Fourteenth Amendments prohibit the execution of a mentally retarded person. *Atkins v. Virginia,* 536 U.S. 304 (2002). Simmons filed a new petition for state postconviction relief, arguing that the reasoning of

*Atkins* established that the Constitution prohibits the execution of a juvenile who was under 18 when the crime was committed. The Missouri Supreme Court agreed. . . . It held that since *Stanford,* "a national consensus has developed against the execution of juvenile offenders, as demonstrated by the fact that eighteen states now bar such executions for juveniles, that twelve other states bar executions altogether, that no state has lowered its age of execution below 18 since *Stanford,* that five states have legislatively or by case law raised or established the minimum age at 18, and that the imposition of the juvenile death penalty has become truly unusual over the last decade."

On this reasoning it set aside Simmons' death sentence and resentenced him to "life imprisonment without eligibility for probation, parole, or release except by act of the Governor."

We granted certiorari, and now affirm.

## II

The Eighth Amendment provides: "Excessive bail shall not be required, nor excessive fines imposed, nor cruel and unusual punishments inflicted." The provision is applicable to the States through the Fourteenth Amendment. *Furman v. Georgia,* 408 U.S. 238, 239 (1972) *(per curiam);* . . . As the Court explained in *Atkins,* the Eighth Amendment guarantees individuals the right not to be subjected to excessive sanctions. The right flows from the basic " 'precept of justice that punishment for crime should be graduated and proportioned to [the] offense.' " . . . By protecting even those convicted of heinous crimes, the Eighth Amendment reaffirms the duty of the government to respect the dignity of all persons.

The prohibition against "cruel and unusual punishments," like other expansive language in the Constitution, must be interpreted according to its text, by considering history, tradition, and precedent, and with due regard for its purpose and function in the constitutional design. To implement this framework we have established the propriety and affirmed the necessity of referring to "the evolving standards of decency that mark the progress of a maturing society" to determine which punishments are so disproportionate as to be cruel and unusual. *Trop v. Dulles,* 356 U.S. 86, 100–101 (1958).

In *Thompson v. Oklahoma,* 487 U.S. 815 (1988), a plurality of the Court determined that our standards of decency do not permit the execution of any offender under the age of 16 at the time of the crime. . . . The plurality opinion explained that no death penalty State that had given express consideration to a minimum age for the death penalty had set the age lower than 16. . . . The plurality also observed that "[t]he conclusion that it would offend civilized standards of decency to execute a person who was less than 16 years old at the time of his or her offense is consistent with the views that have been expressed by respected professional organizations, by other nations that share our Anglo-American heritage, and by the leading members of the Western European community." The opinion further noted that juries imposed the death penalty on offenders under 16 with exceeding rarity; the last execution of an offender for a crime committed under the age of 16 had been carried out in 1948, 40 years prior.

Bringing its independent judgment to bear on the permissibility of the death penalty for a 15-year-old offender, the *Thompson* plurality stressed that "[t]he reasons why juveniles are not trusted with the privileges and responsibilities of an adult also explain why their irresponsible conduct is not as morally reprehensible as that of an adult." . . . According to the plurality, the lesser culpability of offenders under 16 made the death penalty inappropriate as a form of retribution, while the low likelihood that offenders under 16 engaged in "the kind of cost-benefit analysis that attaches any weight to the possibility of execution" made the death penalty ineffective as a means of deterrence. . . .

The next year, in *Stanford v. Kentucky*, 492 U.S. 361 (1989), the Court, over a dissenting opinion joined by four Justices, referred to contemporary standards of decency in this country and concluded the Eighth and Fourteenth Amendments did not proscribe the execution of juvenile offenders over 15 but under 18. The Court noted that 22 of the 37 death penalty States permitted the death penalty for 16-year-old offenders, and, among these 37 States, 25 permitted it for 17-year-old offenders. These numbers, in the Court's view, indicated there was no national consensus "sufficient to label a particular punishment cruel and unusual." A plurality of the Court also "emphatically reject [ed]" the suggestion that the Court should bring its own judgment to bear on the acceptability of the juvenile death penalty. . . .

The same day the Court decided *Stanford*, it held that the Eighth Amendment did not mandate a categorical exemption from the death penalty for the mentally retarded. *Penry v. Lynaugh*, 492 U.S. 302 (1989). In reaching this conclusion it stressed that only two States had enacted laws banning the imposition of the death penalty on a mentally retarded person convicted of a capital offense. . . . According to the Court, "the two state statutes prohibiting execution of the mentally retarded, even when added to the 14 States that have rejected capital punishment completely, [did] not provide sufficient evidence at present of a national consensus." *Ibid.*

Three Terms ago the subject was reconsidered in *Atkins*. We held that standards of decency have evolved since *Penry* and now demonstrate that the execution of the mentally retarded is cruel and unusual punishment. The Court noted objective indicia of society's standards, as expressed in legislative enactments and state practice with respect to executions of the mentally retarded. When *Atkins* was decided only a minority of States permitted the practice, and even in those States it was rare. . . . On the basis of these indicia the Court determined that executing mentally retarded offenders "has become truly unusual, and it is fair to say that a national consensus has developed against it."

. . .

Just as the *Atkins* Court reconsidered the issue decided in *Penry,* we now reconsider the issue decided in *Stanford*. The beginning point is a review of objective indicia of consensus, as expressed in particular by the enactments of legislatures that have addressed the question. These data give us essential instruction. We then must determine, in the exercise of our own independent judgment, whether the death penalty is a disproportionate punishment for juveniles.

### III

### A

The evidence of national consensus against the death penalty for juveniles is similar, and in some respects parallel, to the evidence *Atkins* held sufficient to demonstrate a national consensus against the death penalty for the mentally retarded. When *Atkins* was decided, 30 States prohibited the death penalty for the mentally retarded. This number comprised 12 that had abandoned the death penalty altogether, and 18 that maintained it but excluded the mentally retarded from its reach. 536 U.S., at 313–315, 122 S.Ct. 2242. By a similar calculation in this case, 30 States prohibit the juvenile death penalty, comprising 12 that have rejected the death penalty altogether and 18 that maintain it but, by express provision or judicial interpretation, exclude juveniles from its reach. . . . Since *Stanford,* six States have executed prisoners for crimes committed as juveniles. In the past 10 years, only three have done so: Oklahoma, Texas, and Virginia. . . . In December 2003 the Governor of Kentucky decided to spare the life of Kevin Stanford, and commuted his sentence to one of life imprisonment without parole, with the declaration that

" '[w]e ought not be executing people who, legally, were children.' . . .By this act the Governor ensured Kentucky would not add itself to the list of States that have executed juveniles within the last 10 years even by the execution of the very defendant whose death sentence the Court had upheld in *Stanford v. Kentucky.*

There is, to be sure, at least one difference between the evidence of consensus in *Atkins* and in this case. Impressive in *Atkins* was the rate of abolition of the death penalty for the mentally retarded. . . .The number of States that have abandoned capital punishment for juvenile offenders since *Stanford* is smaller than the number of States that abandoned capital punishment for the mentally retarded after *Penry;* yet we think the same consistency of direction of change has been demonstrated. Since *Stanford,* no State that previously prohibited capital punishment for juveniles has reinstated it. This fact, coupled with the trend toward abolition of the juvenile death penalty, carries special force in light of the general popularity of anticrime legislation, and in light of the particular trend in recent years toward cracking down on juvenile crime in other respects. . . Any difference between this case and *Atkins* with respect to the pace of abolition is thus counterbalanced by the consistent direction of the change.

The slower pace of abolition of the juvenile death penalty over the past 15 years, moreover, may have a simple explanation. When we heard *Penry,* only two death penalty States had already prohibited the execution of the mentally retarded. When we heard *Stanford,* by contrast, 12 death penalty States had already prohibited the execution of any juvenile under 18, and 15 had prohibited the execution of any juvenile under 17. If anything, this shows that the impropriety of executing juveniles between 16 and 18 years of age gained wide recognition earlier than the impropriety of executing the mentally retarded. In the words of the Missouri Supreme Court: "It would be the ultimate in irony if the very fact that the inappropriateness of the death penalty for juveniles was broadly recognized sooner than it was recognized for the mentally retarded were to become a reason to continue the execution of juveniles now that the execution of the mentally retarded has been barred.". . .

As in *Atkins,* the objective indicia of consensus in this case—the rejection of the juvenile death penalty in the majority of States; the infrequency of its use even where it remains on the books; and the consistency in the trend toward abolition of the practice—provide sufficient evidence that today our society views juveniles, in the words *Atkins* used respecting the mentally retarded, as "categorically less culpable than the average criminal."

## B

A majority of States have rejected the imposition of the death penalty on juvenile offenders under 18, and we now hold this is required by the Eighth Amendment. Because the death penalty is the most severe punishment, the Eighth Amendment applies to it with special force. *Thompson*, 487 U.S., at 856 Capital punishment must be limited to those offenders who commit "a narrow category of the most serious crimes" and whose extreme culpability makes them "the most deserving of execution." This principle is implemented throughout the capital sentencing process. States must give narrow and precise definition to the aggravating factors that can result in a capital sentence. *Godfrey v. Georgia*, 446 U.S. 420, 428–429 (1980). In any capital case a defendant has wide latitude to raise as a mitigating factor "any aspect of [his or her] character or record and any of the circumstances of the offense that the defendant proffers as a basis for a sentence less than death." . . . There are a number of crimes that beyond question are severe in absolute terms, yet the death penalty may not be imposed for their commission. *Coker v. Georgia*, 433 U.S. 584 (1977) (rape of an adult woman); *Enmund v. Florida*, 458 U.S. 782 (1982) (felony murder where defendant did not kill, attempt to kill, or intend to kill). The death penalty may not be imposed on certain classes of offenders, such as juveniles under 16, the insane, and the mentally retarded, no matter how heinous the crime. . . These rules vindicate the underlying principle that the death penalty is reserved for a narrow category of crimes and offenders.

Three general differences between juveniles under 18 and adults demonstrate that juvenile offenders cannot with reliability be classified among the worst offenders. First, as any parent knows and as the scientific and sociological studies respondent and his *amici* cite tend to confirm, "[a] lack of maturity and an underdeveloped sense of responsibility are found in youth more often than in adults and are more understandable among the young. These qualities often result in impetuous and ill-considered actions and decisions." *Johnson, supra,* at 367, 113 S.Ct. 2658; see also *Eddings, supra,* at 115–116, 102 S.Ct. 869 ("Even the normal 16-year-old customarily lacks the maturity of an adult"). It has been noted that "adolescents are overrepresented statistically in virtually every category of reckless behavior." . . .

The second area of difference is that juveniles are more vulnerable or susceptible to negative influences and outside pressures, including peer pressure. *Eddings, supra,* at 115, 102 S.Ct. 869 ("[Y]outh is more than a chronological fact. It is a time and condition of life when a person may be most susceptible to influence and to psychological damage"). This is explained in part by the prevailing circumstance that juveniles have less control, or less experience with control, over their own environment. . . .

The third broad difference is that the character of a juvenile is not as well formed as that of an adult. The personality traits of juveniles are more transitory, less fixed. . . .

These differences render suspect any conclusion that a juvenile falls among the worst offenders. The susceptibility of juveniles to immature and irresponsible behavior means "their irresponsible conduct is not as morally reprehensible as that of an adult." Their own vulnerability and comparative lack of control over their immediate surroundings mean juveniles have a greater claim than adults to be forgiven for failing to escape negative influences in their whole environment. The reality that juveniles still struggle to define their identity means it is less supportable to conclude that even a heinous crime committed by a juvenile is evidence of irretrievably depraved character. From a moral standpoint it would be misguided to equate the failings of a minor with those of an adult, for a greater possibility exists that a minor's character deficiencies will be reformed. Indeed, "[t]he relevance of youth as a mitigating factor derives from the fact that the signature qualities of youth are transient; as individuals mature, the impetuousness and recklessness that may dominate in younger years can subside." . . .

In *Thompson*, a plurality of the Court recognized the import of these characteristics with respect to juveniles under 16, and relied on them to hold that the Eighth Amendment prohibited the imposition of the death penalty on juveniles below that age. 487 U.S., at 833–838, 108 S.Ct. 2687. We conclude the same reasoning applies to all juvenile offenders under 18.

Once the diminished culpability of juveniles is recognized, it is evident that the penological justifications for the death penalty apply to them with lesser force than to adults. We have held there are two distinct social purposes served by the death penalty: " 'retribution and deterrence of capital crimes by prospective offenders.' " *Atkins*, 536 U.S., at 319, 122 S.Ct. 2242 (quoting *Gregg v. Georgia*, 428 U.S. 153, 183, 96 S.Ct. 2909, 49 L.Ed.2d 859 (1976) (joint opinion of Stewart, Powell, and STEVENS, JJ.)). . . .

Here, however, the absence of evidence of deterrent effect is of special concern because the same characteristics that render juveniles less culpable than adults suggest as well that juveniles will be less susceptible to deterrence. In particular, as the plurality observed in *Thompson*, "[t]he likelihood that the teenage offender has made the kind of cost-benefit analysis that attaches any weight to the possibility of execution is so remote as to be virtually nonexistent." 487 U.S., at 837, 108 S.Ct. 2687. To the extent the juvenile death penalty might have residual deterrent effect, it is worth noting that the punishment of life imprisonment without the possibility of parole is itself a severe sanction, in particular for a young person.

In concluding that neither retribution nor deterrence provides adequate justification for imposing the death penalty on juvenile offenders, we cannot deny or overlook the brutal crimes too many juvenile offenders have committed. See Brief for Alabama et al. as *Amici Curiae*. Certainly it can be argued, although we by no means concede the point, that a rare case might arise in which a juvenile offender has sufficient psychological maturity, and at the same time demonstrates sufficient depravity, to merit a sentence of death. Indeed, this possibility is the linchpin of one contention pressed by petitioner and his *amici*. They assert that even assuming the truth of the observations we have made about juveniles' diminished culpability in general, jurors nonetheless should be allowed to consider mitigating arguments related to youth on a case-by-case basis, and in some cases to impose the death penalty if justified. A central feature of death penalty sentencing is a particular assessment of the circumstances of the crime and the characteristics of the offender. The system is designed to consider both aggravating and mitigating circumstances, including youth, in every case. Given this Court's own insistence on individualized consideration, petitioner maintains that it is both arbitrary and unnecessary to adopt a categorical rule barring imposition of the death penalty on any offender under 18 years of age.

We disagree. The differences between juvenile and adult offenders are too marked and well understood to risk allowing a youthful person to receive the death penalty despite insufficient culpability. An unacceptable likelihood exists that the brutality or cold-blooded nature of any particular crime would overpower mitigating arguments based on youth as a matter of course, even where the juvenile offender's objective immaturity, vulnerability, and lack of true depravity should require a sentence less severe than death. In some cases a defendant's youth may even be counted against him. In this very case, as we noted above, the prosecutor argued Simmons' youth was aggravating rather than mitigating. . . .

Drawing the line at 18 years of age is subject, of course, to the objections always raised against categorical rules. The qualities that distinguish juveniles from adults do not disappear when an individual turns 18. By the same token, some under 18 have already attained a level of maturity some adults will never reach. For the reasons we have discussed, however, a line must be drawn. The plurality opinion in *Thompson* drew the line at 16. In the intervening years the *Thompson* plurality's conclusion that offenders under 16 may not be executed has not been challenged. The logic of *Thompson* extends to those who are under 18. The age of 18 is the point where society draws the line for many purposes between childhood and adulthood. It is, we conclude, the age at which the line for death eligibility ought to rest.

These considerations mean *Stanford v. Kentucky* should be deemed no longer controlling on this issue. To the extent *Stanford* was based on review of the objective indicia of consensus that obtained in 1989, 492 U.S., at 370–371, 109 S.Ct. 2969, it suffices to note that those indicia have changed. . . . Last, to the extent *Stanford* was based on a rejection of the idea that this Court is required to bring its independent judgment to bear on the proportionality of the death penalty for a particular class of crimes or offenders, it suffices to note that this rejection was inconsistent with prior Eighth Amendment decisions. . . It is also inconsistent with the premises of our recent decision in *Atkins*.

In holding that the death penalty cannot be imposed upon juvenile offenders, we take into account the circumstance that some States have relied on *Stanford* in seeking the death penalty against juvenile offenders. This consideration, however, does not outweigh our conclusion that *Stanford* should no longer control in those few pending cases or in those yet to arise.

IV

Our determination that the death penalty is disproportionate punishment for offenders under 18 finds confirmation in the stark reality that the United States is the only country in the world that continues to give official sanction to the juvenile death penalty. This reality does not become controlling, for the task of interpreting the Eighth Amendment remains our responsibility. . .

Respondent and his *amici* have submitted, and petitioner does not contest, that only seven countries other than the United States have executed juvenile offenders since 1990: Iran, Pakistan, Saudi Arabia, Yemen, Nigeria, the Democratic Republic of Congo, and China. Since then each of these countries has either abolished capital punishment for juveniles or made public disavowal of the practice. In sum, it is fair to say that the United States now stands alone in a world that has turned its face against the juvenile death penalty.

. . . In the 56 years that have passed since the United Kingdom abolished the juvenile death penalty, the weight of authority against it there, and in the international community, has become well established.

It is proper that we acknowledge the overwhelming weight of international opinion against the juvenile death penalty, resting in large part on the understanding that the instability and emotional imbalance of young people may often be a factor in the crime. See Brief for Human Rights Committee of the Bar of England and Wales et al. as *Amici Curiae* 10–11. The opinion of the world community, while not controlling our outcome, does provide respected and significant confirmation for our own conclusions.

Over time, from one generation to the next, the Constitution has come to earn the high respect and even, as Madison dared to hope, the veneration of the American people. See The Federalist No. 49, p. 314 (C. Rossiter ed.1961). . . .Not the least of the reasons we honor the Constitution, then, is because we know it to be our own. It does not lessen our fidelity to the Constitution or our pride in its origins to acknowledge that the express affirmation of certain fundamental rights by other nations and peoples simply underscores the centrality of those same rights within our own heritage of freedom.

* * *

The Eighth and Fourteenth Amendments forbid imposition of the death penalty on offenders who were under the age of 18 when their crimes were committed. The judgment of the Missouri Supreme Court setting aside the sentence of death imposed upon Christopher Simmons is affirmed.

### *It is so ordered*

. . .

### JUSTICE STEVENS, with whom JUSTICE GINSBURG joins, concurring.

Perhaps even more important than our specific holding today is our reaffirmation of the basic principle that informs the Court's interpretation of the Eighth Amendment. If the meaning of that Amendment had been frozen when it was originally drafted, it would impose no impediment to the execution of 7-year-old children today. See *Stanford v. Kentucky,* 492 U.S. 361, 368 (1989) (describing the common law at the time of the Amendment's adoption). The evolving standards of decency that have driven our construction of this critically important part of the Bill of Rights foreclose any such reading of the Amendment. In the best tradition of the common law, the pace of that evolution is a matter for continuing debate; but that our understanding of the Constitution does change from time to time has been settled since John Marshall breathed life into its text. If great lawyers of his day—Alexander Hamilton, for example—were sitting with us today, I would expect them to join Justice KENNEDY's opinion for the Court. In all events, I do so without hesitation.

**JUSTICE O'CONNOR, dissenting.**

The Court's decision today establishes a categorical rule forbidding the execution of any offender for any crime committed before his 18th birthday, no matter how deliberate, wanton, or cruel the offense. Neither the objective evidence of contemporary societal values, nor the Court's moral proportionality analysis, nor the two in tandem suffice to justify this ruling.

Although the Court finds support for its decision in the fact that a majority of the States now disallow capital punishment of 17-year-old offenders, it refrains from asserting that its holding is compelled by a genuine national consensus. Indeed, the evidence before us fails to demonstrate conclusively that any such consensus has emerged in the brief period since we upheld the constitutionality of this practice in *Stanford v. Kentucky,* 492 U.S. 361, 109 S.Ct. 2969, 106 L.Ed.2d 306 (1989).

Instead, the rule decreed by the Court rests, ultimately, on its independent moral judgment that death is a disproportionately severe punishment for any 17-year-old offender. I do not subscribe to this judgment. Adolescents *as a class* are undoubtedly less mature, and therefore less culpable for their misconduct, than adults. But the Court has adduced no evidence impeaching the seemingly reasonable conclusion reached by many state legislatures: that at least *some* 17-year-old murderers are sufficiently mature to deserve the death penalty in an appropriate case. Nor has it been shown that capital sentencing juries are incapable of accurately assessing a youthful defendant's maturity or of giving due weight to the mitigating characteristics associated with youth.

On this record—and especially in light of the fact that so little has changed since our recent decision in *Stanford*—I would not substitute our judgment about the moral propriety of capital punishment for 17-year-old murderers for the judgments of the Nation's legislatures. Rather, I would demand a clearer showing that our society truly has set its face against this practice before reading the Eighth Amendment categorically to forbid it.

. . .

C

Seventeen-year-old murderers must be categorically exempted from capital punishment, the Court says, because they "cannot with reliability be classified among the worst offenders." *Ante,* at 1195. That conclusion is premised on three perceived differences between "adults," who have already reached their 18th birthdays, and "juveniles," who have not. See *ante,* at 1195–1196. First, juveniles lack maturity and responsibility and are more reckless than adults. Second, juveniles are more vulnerable to outside influences because they have less control over their surroundings. And third, a juvenile's character is not as fully formed as that of an adult. Based on these characteristics, the Court determines that 17-year-old capital murderers are not as blameworthy as adults guilty of similar crimes; that 17-year-olds are less likely than adults to be deterred by the prospect of a death sentence; and that it is difficult to conclude that a 17-year-old who commits even the most heinous of crimes is "irretrievably depraved." *Ante,* at 1195–1197. The Court suggests that "a rare case might arise in which a juvenile offender has sufficient psychological maturity, and at the same time demonstrates sufficient depravity, to merit a sentence of death." *Ante,* at 1197. However, the Court argues that a categorical age-based prohibition is justified as a prophylactic rule because "[t]he differences between juvenile and adult offenders are too marked and well understood to risk allowing a youthful person to receive the death penalty despite insufficient culpability." *Ante,* at 1197.

It is beyond cavil that juveniles as a class are generally less mature, less responsible, and less fully formed than adults, and that these differences bear on juveniles' comparative moral culpability. See, *e.g., Johnson v. Texas,* 509 U.S. 350, 367, 113 S.Ct. 2658, 125 L.Ed.2d 290 (1993) ("There is no dispute that a defendant's youth is a relevant mitigating circumstance"); . . .

. . .that it is only in "rare" cases, if ever, that 17-year-old murderers are sufficiently mature and act with sufficient depravity to warrant the death penalty. The fact that juveniles are generally *less* culpable for their misconduct than adults does not necessarily mean that a 17-year-old murderer cannot be *sufficiently* culpable to merit the death penalty. At most, the Court's argument suggests that the average 17-year-old murderer is not as culpable as the average adult murderer. But an especially depraved juvenile offender may nevertheless be just as culpable as many adult offenders considered bad enough to deserve the death penalty. Similarly, the fact that the availability of the death penalty may be *less* likely to deter a juvenile from committing a capital crime does not imply that this threat cannot *effectively* deter some 17-year-olds from such an act. Surely there is an age below which no offender, no matter what his crime, can be deemed to have the cognitive or emotional maturity necessary to warrant the death penalty. But at least at the margins between adolescence and adulthood—and especially for 17-year-olds such as respondent—the relevant differences between "adults" and "juveniles" appear to be a matter of degree, rather than of kind. It follows that a legislature may reasonably conclude that at least *some* 17-year-olds can act with sufficient moral culpability, and can be sufficiently deterred by the threat of execution, that capital punishment may be warranted in an appropriate case.

Indeed, this appears to be just such a case. Christopher Simmons' murder of Shirley Crook was premeditated, wanton, and cruel in the extreme. Well before he committed this crime, Simmons declared that he wanted to kill someone. On several occasions, he discussed with two friends (ages 15 and 16) his plan to burglarize a house and to murder the victim by tying the victim up and pushing him from a bridge. Simmons said they could " 'get away with it' " because they were minors. In accord with this plan, Simmons and his 15-year-old accomplice broke into Mrs. Crook's home in the middle of the night, forced her from her bed, bound her, and drove her to a state park. There, they walked her to a railroad trestle spanning a river, "hog-tied" her with electrical cable, bound her face completely with duct tape, and pushed her, still alive, from the trestle. She drowned in the water below. *Id.,* at 4. One can scarcely imagine the terror that this woman must have suffered throughout the ordeal leading to her death. Whatever can be said about the comparative moral culpability of 17-year-olds as a general matter, Simmons' actions unquestionably reflect " 'a consciousness materially more "depraved" than that of' . . . the average murderer." *Atkins,* 536 U.S., at 319, 122 S.Ct. 2242 (quoting *Godfrey v. Georgia,* 446 U.S. 420, 433, 100 S.Ct. 1759, 64 L.Ed.2d 398 (1980)). And Simmons' prediction that he could murder with impunity because he had not yet turned 18—though inaccurate—suggests that he *did* take into account the perceived risk of punishment in deciding whether to commit the crime. Based on this evidence, the sentencing jury certainly had reasonable grounds for concluding that, despite Simmons' youth, he "ha[d] sufficient psychological maturity" when he committed this horrific murder, and "at the same time demonstrate[d] sufficient depravity, to merit a sentence of death." . . .

Although the prosecutor's apparent attempt to use respondent's youth as an aggravating circumstance in this case is troubling, that conduct was never challenged with specificity in the lower courts and is not directly at issue here. As the Court itself suggests, such "overreaching" would best be addressed, if at all, through a more narrowly tailored remedy. See *ante,* at 1197. . .

Many jurisdictions have abolished capital punishment altogether, while many others have determined that even the most heinous crime, if committed before the age of 18, should not be punishable by death. Indeed, were my office that of a legislator, rather than a judge, then I, too, would be inclined to support legislation setting a minimum age of 18 in this context. But a significant number of States, including Missouri, have decided to make the death penalty potentially available for 17-year-old capital murderers such as respondent. Without a clearer showing that a genuine national consensus forbids the execution of such offenders, this Court should not substitute its own "inevitably subjective judgment" on how best to resolve this difficult moral question for the judgments of the Nation's democratically elected legislatures. See *Thompson*, 487 U.S., at 854, 108 S.Ct. 2687 (O'CONNOR, J., concurring in judgment). I respectfully dissent.

**JUSTICE SCALIA, with whom THE CHIEF JUSTICE and JUSTICE THOMAS join, dissenting.**

In urging approval of a constitution that gave life-tenured judges the power to nullify laws enacted by the people's representatives, Alexander Hamilton assured the citizens of New York that there was little risk in this, since "[t]he judiciary . . . ha[s] neither FORCE nor WILL but merely judgment." The Federalist No. 78, p. 465 (C. Rossiter ed.1961). But Hamilton had in mind a traditional judiciary, "bound down by strict rules and precedents which serve to define and point out their duty in every particular case that comes before them." *Id.,* at 471. Bound down, indeed. What a mockery today's opinion makes of Hamilton's expectation, announcing the Court's conclusion that the meaning of our Constitution has changed over the past 15 years—not, mind you, that this Court's decision 15 years ago was *wrong,* but that the Constitution *has changed.* The Court reaches this implausible result by purporting to advert, not to the original meaning of the Eighth Amendment, but to "the evolving standards of decency," *ante,* at 1190 (internal quotation marks omitted), of our national society. It then finds, on the flimsiest of grounds, that a national consensus which could not be perceived in our people's laws barely 15 years ago now solidly exists. Worse still, the Court says in so many words that what our people's laws say about the issue does not, in the last analysis, matter: "[I]n the end our own judgment will be brought to bear on the question of the acceptability of the death penalty under the Eighth Amendment." *Ante,* at 1191–1192 (internal quotation marks omitted). The Court thus proclaims itself sole arbiter of our Nation's moral standards—and in the course of discharging that awesome responsibility purports to take guidance from the views of foreign courts and legislatures. Because I do not believe that the meaning of our Eighth Amendment, any more than the meaning of other provisions of our Constitution, should be determined by the subjective views of five Members of this Court and like-minded foreigners, I dissent. . .

Moreover, the cited studies describe only adolescents who engage in risky or antisocial behavior, as many young people do. Murder, however, is more than just risky or antisocial behavior. It is entirely consistent to believe that young people often act impetuously and lack judgment, but, at the same time, to believe that those who commit premeditated murder are—at least sometimes—just as culpable as adults. Christopher Simmons, who was only seven months shy of his 18th birthday when he murdered Shirley Crook, described to his friends *beforehand*—"[i]n chilling, callous terms," as the Court puts it, *ante,* at 1187—the murder he planned to commit. He then broke into the home of an innocent woman, bound her with duct tape and electrical wire, and threw her off a bridge alive and conscious. *Ante,* at 1188. In their *amici* brief, the States of Alabama, Delaware, Oklahoma, Texas, Utah, and Virginia offer additional examples of murders committed by individuals under 18 that involve truly monstrous acts. In Alabama, two 17-year-olds, one 16-year-old, and one 19-year-old picked up a female hitchhiker, threw bottles at her, and kicked and stomped her for approximately 30 minutes until she died. They then sexually assaulted her lifeless body and, when they were finished, threw her body off a cliff. They later returned to the crime scene to mutilate her corpse. . . Though these cases are assuredly the exception rather than the rule, the studies the Court cites in no way justify a constitutional imperative that prevents legislatures and juries from treating exceptional cases in an exceptional way— by determining that some murders are not just the acts of happy-go-lucky teenagers, but heinous crimes deserving of death. . .

The Court's contention that the goals of retribution and deterrence are not served by executing murderers under 18 is also transparently false. The argument that "[r]etribution is not proportional if the law's most severe penalty is imposed on one whose culpability or blameworthiness is diminished," *ante,* at 1196, is simply an extension of the earlier, false generalization that youth *always* defeats culpability. The Court claims that "juveniles will be less susceptible to deterrence," *ibid.,* because " '[t]he likelihood that the teenage offender has made the kind of cost-benefit analysis that attaches any weight to the possibility of execution is so remote as to be virtually nonexistent,' " *ibid.* (quoting *Thompson,* 487 U.S., at 837, 108 S.Ct. 2687). The Court unsurprisingly finds no support for this astounding proposition, save its own case law. The facts of this very case show the proposition to be false. Before committing the crime, Simmons encouraged his friends to join him by assuring them that they could "get away with it" because they were minors. *State ex rel. Simmons v. Roper,* 112 S.W.3d 397, 419 (Mo.2003) (Price, J., dissenting). This fact may have influenced the jury's decision to impose capital punishment despite Simmons' age. Because the Court refuses to entertain the possibility that its own unsubstantiated generalization about juveniles could be wrong, it ignores this evidence entirely.

### III

. . .More fundamentally, however, the basic premise of the Court's argument—that American law should conform to the laws of the rest of the world—ought to be rejected out of hand. In fact the Court itself does not believe it. In many significant respects the laws of most other countries differ from our law—including not only such explicit provisions of our Constitution as the right to jury trial and grand jury indictment, but even many interpretations of the Constitution prescribed by this Court itself. The Court-pronounced exclusionary rule, for example, is distinctively American. When we adopted that rule in *Mapp v. Ohio,* 367 U.S. 643 (1961), it was "unique to American jurisprudence." Since then a categorical exclusionary rule has been "universally rejected" by other countries, including those with rules prohibiting illegal searches and police misconduct. . .

And let us not forget the Court's abortion jurisprudence, which makes us one of only six countries that allow abortion on demand until the point of viability. See Larsen, Importing Constitutional Norms from a "Wider Civilization": *Lawrence* and the Rehnquist Court's Use of Foreign and International Law in Domestic Constitutional Interpretation, 65 Ohio St. L.J. 1283, 1320 (2004); Center for Reproductive Rights, The World's Abortion Laws (June 2004), http://www.reproductiverights.org/pub_fac_abortion_laws.html. Though the Government and *amici* in cases following *Roe v. Wade,* 410 U.S. 113, 93 S.Ct. 705, 35 L.Ed.2d 147 (1973), urged the Court to follow the international community's lead, these arguments fell on deaf ears. See McCrudden, A Part of the Main? The Physician-Assisted Suicide Cases and Comparative Law Methodology in the United States Supreme Court, in Law at the End of Life: The Supreme Court and Assisted Suicide 125, 129–130 (C. Schneider ed.2000). The Court's special reliance on the laws of the United Kingdom is perhaps the most indefensible part of its opinion. It is of course true that we share a common history with the United Kingdom, and that we often consult English sources when asked to discern the meaning of a constitutional text written against the backdrop of 18th-century English law and legal thought. If we applied that approach today, our task would be an easy one. As we explained in *Harmelin v. Michigan,* 501 U.S. 957, 973–974, 111 S.Ct. 2680, 115 L.Ed.2d 836 (1991), the "Cruell and Unusuall Punishments" provision of the English Declaration of Rights was originally meant to describe those punishments " 'out of [the Judges'] Power' "—that is, those punishments that were not authorized by common law or statute, but that were nonetheless administered by the Crown or the Crown's judges. Under that reasoning, the death penalty for under-18 offenders would easily survive this challenge. The Court has, however—I think wrongly—long rejected a purely originalist approach to our Eighth Amendment, and that is certainly not the approach the Court takes today. Instead, the Court undertakes the majestic task of determining (and thereby prescribing) *our* Nation's *current* standards of decency. It is beyond comprehension why we should look, for that purpose, to a country that has developed, in the centuries since the Revolutionary War—and with increasing speed since the United Kingdom's recent submission to the jurisprudence of European courts dominated by continental jurists—a legal, political, and social culture quite different from our own. If we took the Court's directive seriously, we would also consider relaxing our double jeopardy prohibition, since the British Law Commission recently published a report that would significantly extend the rights of the prosecution to appeal cases where an acquittal was the result of a judge's ruling that was legally incorrect. . . .

The Court should either profess its willingness to reconsider all these matters in light of the views of foreigners, or else it should cease putting forth foreigners' views as part of the *reasoned basis* of its decisions. To invoke alien law when it agrees with one's own thinking, and ignore it otherwise, is not reasoned decisionmaking, but sophistry.

. . .

## IV

To add insult to injury, the Court affirms the Missouri Supreme Court without even admonishing that court for its flagrant disregard of our precedent in *Stanford*. Until today, we have always held that "it is this Court's prerogative alone to overrule one of its precedents." *State Oil Co. v. Khan,* 522 U.S. 3, 20, 118 S.Ct. 275, 139 L.Ed.2d 199 (1997). . . .Today, however, the Court silently approves a state-court decision that blatantly rejected controlling precedent.

. . .We must disregard the new reality that, to the extent our Eighth Amendment decisions constitute something more than a show of hands on the current Justices' current personal views about penology, they purport to be nothing more than a snapshot of American public opinion at a particular point in time (with the timeframes now shortened to a mere 15 years). We must treat these decisions just as though they represented real law, real prescriptions democratically adopted by the American people, as conclusively (rather than sequentially) construed by this Court. Allowing lower courts to reinterpret the Eighth Amendment whenever they decide enough time has passed for a new snapshot leaves this Court's decisions without any force—especially since the "evolution" of our Eighth Amendment is no longer determined by objective criteria. To allow lower courts to behave as we do, "updating" the Eighth Amendment as needed, destroys stability and makes our case law an unreliable basis for the designing of laws by citizens and their representatives, and for action by public officials. The result will be to crown arbitrariness with chaos.

**After preparing the case brief, consider the answers to the following questions:**

1.  What is the standard for determining when a criminal punishment is cruel and unusual within the meaning of the Eighth Amendment?

2.  What reasons does the Court cite to justify reversing *Stanford*? Do you agree with the Court's analysis?

3.  Do you agree that juvenile offenders under the age of 18 lack the psychological maturity to be responsible for capital murder?

4.  Are you swayed by the dissenting justice's arguments? If so, which seem the most compelling?

## McKeiver v. Pennsylvania

Supreme Court of the United States
Argued Dec. 9 and 10, 1970
Decided June 21, 1971
403 U.S. 528

### Opinion

**MR. JUSTICE BLACKMUN announced the judgments of the Court and an opinion in which THE CHIEF JUSTICE, MR. JUSTICE STEWART, and MR. JUSTICE WHITE join.**

These cases present the narrow but precise issue whether the Due Process Clause of the Fourteenth Amendment assures the right to trial by jury in the adjudicative phase of a state juvenile court delinquency proceeding.

I

The issue arises understandably, for the Court in a series of cases already has emphasized due process factors protective of the juvenile:

1. *Haley v. Ohio*, 332 U.S. 596 (1948), concerned the admissibility of a confession taken from a 15-year-old boy on trial for first-degree murder. It was held that upon the facts there developed, the Due Process Clause barred the use of the confession. Mr. Justice Douglas, in an opinion in which three other Justices joined, said, 'Neither man nor child can be allowed to stand condemned by methods which flout constitutional requirements of due process of law.' 332 U.S., at 601, 68 S.Ct., at 304.

2. *Gallegos v. Colorado*, 370 U.S. 49 (1962) where a 14-year-old was on trial, is to the same effect.

3. *Kent v. United States*, 383 U.S. 541 (1966), concerned a 16-year-old charged with housebreaking, robbery, and rape in the District of Columbia. The issue was the propriety of the juvenile court's waiver of jurisdiction 'after full investigation,' as permitted by the applicable statute. It was emphasized that the latitude the court possessed within which to determine whether it should retain or waive jurisdiction 'assumes procedural regularity sufficient in the particular circumstances to satisfy the basic requirements of due process and fairness, as well as compliance with the statutory requirement of a 'full investigation.'' 383 U.S., at 553, 86 S.Ct., at 1053.

4. *In re Gault*, 387 U.S. 1 (1967), concerned a 15-year-old, already on probation, committed in Arizona as a delinquent after being apprehended upon

a complaint of lewd remarks by telephone. Mr. Justice Fortas, in writing for the Court, reviewed the cases just cited and observed.

'Accordingly, while these cases relate only to restricted aspects of the subject, they unmistakably indicate that, whatever may be their precise impact, neither the Fourteenth Amendment nor the Bill of Rights is for adults alone.' 387 U.S., at 13, 87 S.Ct., at 1436. The Court focused on 'the proceedings by which a determination is made as to whether a juvenile is a 'delinquent' as a result of alleged misconduct on his part, with the consequence that he may be committed to a state institution' and, as to this, said that 'there appears to be little current dissent from the proposition that the Due Process Clause has a role to play.' *Ibid.* Kent was adhered to: We reiterate this view, here in connection with a juvenile court adjudication of 'delinquency,' as a requirement which is part of the Due Process Clause of the Fourteenth Amendment of our Constitution.' Id., at 30–31, 87 S.Ct., at 1445. Due process, in that proceeding, was held to embrace adequate written notice; advice as to the right to counsel, retained or appointed; confrontation; and cross-examination. The privilege against self-incrimination was also held available to the juvenile. The Court refrained from deciding whether a State must provide appellate review in juvenile cases or a transcript or recording of the hearings.

5. *DeBacker v. Brainard,* 396 U.S. 28 (1969), presented, by state habeas corpus, a challenge to a Nebraska statute providing that juvenile court hearings 'shall be conducted by the judge without a jury in an informal manner.' However, because that appellant's hearing had antedated the decisions in *Duncan v. Louisiana* (1968), and *Bloom v. Illinois* (1968), and because Duncan and Bloom had been given only prospective application by *DeStefano v. Woods* (1968), DeBacker's case was deemed an inappropriate one for resolution of the jury trial issue. His appeal was therefore dismissed. . . .

6. *In re Winship,* 397 U.S. 358 (1970), concerned a 12-year-old charged with delinquency for having taken money from a woman's purse. The Court held that 'the Due Process Clause protects the accused against conviction except upon proof beyond a reasonable doubt of every fact necessary to constitute the crime with which he is charged, and then went on to hold, that this standard was applicable, too, 'during the adjudicatory stage of a delinquency proceeding.'

From these six cases—*Haley, Gallegos, Kent, Gault, DeBacker,* and *Winship*—it is apparent that:

1.    Some of the constitutional requirements attendant upon the state criminal trial have equal application to that part of the state juvenile proceeding that is adjudicative in nature. Among these are the rights to appropriate notice, to counsel, to confrontation and to cross-examination, and the privilege against self-incrimination. Included, also, is the standard of proof beyond a reasonable doubt.

2.    The Court, however, has not yet said that all rights constitutionally assured to an adult accused of crime also are to be enforced or made available to the juvenile in his delinquency proceeding. Indeed, the Court specifically has refrained from going that far: 'We do not mean by this to indicate that the hearing to be held must conform with all of the requirements of a criminal trial or even of the usual administrative hearing; but we do hold that the hearing must measure up to the essentials of due process and fair treatment.' . . .

3.    The Court, although recognizing the high hopes and aspirations of Judge Julian Mack, the leaders of the Jane Addams School and the other supporters of the juvenile court concept, has also noted the disappointments of the system's performance and experience and the resulting widespread disaffection. . . . There have been, at one and the same time, both an appreciation for the juvenile court judge who is devoted, sympathetic, and conscientious, and a disturbed concern about the judge who is untrained and less than fully imbued with an understanding approach to the complex problems of childhood and adolescence. There has been praise for the system and its purposes, and there has been alarm over its defects.

4.    The Court has insisted that these successive decisions do not spell the doom of the juvenile court system or even deprive it of its 'informality, flexibility, or speed.' . . .On the other hand, a concern precisely to the opposite effect was expressed by two dissenters in (*In re Winship*).

II

With this substantial background already developed, we turn to the facts of the present cases:

No. 322. Joseph McKeiver, then age 16, in May 1968 was charged with robbery, larceny, and receiving stolen goods (felonies under Pennsylvania law, Pa.Stat.Ann., Tit. 18, ss 4704, 4807, and 4817 (1963)) as acts of juvenile delinquency. At the time of the adjudication hearing he was represented by counsel. His request for a jury trial was denied . . .[he] was adjudged a delinquent upon findings that he had violated a law of the Commonwealth. . . . On appeal, the Superior Court affirmed without opinion.

Edward Terry, then age 15, in January 1969 was charged with assault and battery on a police officer and conspiracy (misdemeanors under Pennsylvania law, Pa.Stat.Ann., Tit. 18, ss 4708 and 4302 (1963)) as acts of juvenile delinquency. His counsel's request for a jury trial was denied . . .Terry was adjudged a delinquent on the charges. This followed an adjudication and commitment in the preceding week for an assault on a teacher. . . . On appeal, the Superior Court affirmed without opinion.

The Supreme Court of Pennsylvania granted leave to appeal in both cases and consolidated them. The single question considered, as phrased by the court, was 'whether there is a constitutional right to a jury trial in juvenile court.' The answer, one justice dissenting, was in the negative. . . .

The details of the McKeiver and Terry offenses are set forth in Justice Roberts' opinion for the Pennsylvania court. . .and need not be repeated at any length here. It suffices to say that McKeiver's offense was his participating with 20 or 30 youths who pursued three young teenagers and took 25 cents from them; that McKeiver never before had been arrested and had a record of gainful employment; that the testimony of two of the victims was described by the court as somewhat inconsistent and as 'weak'; and that Terry's offense consisted of hitting a police officer with his fists and with a stick when the officer broke up a boys' fight Terry and others were watching.

Barbara Burrus and approximately 45 other black children, ranging in age from 11 to 15 years, were the subjects of juvenile court summonses issued in Hyde County, North Carolina, in January 1969.

The charges arose out of a series of demonstrations in the county in late 1968 by black adults and children protesting school assignments and a school consolidation plan. Petitions were filed by North Carolina state highway patrolmen. Except for one relating to James Lambert Howard, the petitions charged the respective juveniles with wilfully impeding traffic. The charge against Howard was that he wilfully made riotous noise and was disorderly in the O. A. Peay School in Swan Quarter; interrupted and disturbed the school during its regular sessions; and defaced school furniture. The acts so charged are misdemeanors under North Carolina law. . . .A request for a jury trial in each case was denied.

The evidence as to the juveniles other than Howard consisted solely of testimony of highway patrolmen. No juvenile took the stand or offered any witness. The testimony was to the effect that on various occasions the juveniles and adults were observed walking along Highway 64 singing, shouting, clapping, and playing basketball. As a result, there was interference with traffic. The marchers were asked to leave the paved portion of the highway and they were warned that they were committing a statutory offense. They either refused or left the roadway and immediately returned. The juveniles and participating adults were taken into custody. Juvenile petitions were then filed with respect to those under the age of 16.

The evidence as to Howard was that on the morning of December 5, he was in the office of the principal of the O. A. Peay School with 15 other persons while school was in session and was moving furniture around; that the office was in disarray; that as a result the school closed before noon; and that neither he nor any of the others was a student at the school or authorized to enter the principal's office.

In each case the court found that the juvenile had committed 'an act for which an adult may be punished by law.' . . . None of the juveniles has been confined on these charges.

On appeal, the cases were consolidated into two groups. The North Carolina Court of Appeals affirmed. . . . In its turn the Supreme Court of North Carolina deleted that portion of the order in each case relating to commitment, but otherwise affirmed. . . . Two justices dissented without opinion. We granted certiorari.

. . .

IV

The right to an impartial jury '(i)n all criminal prosecutions' under federal law is guaranteed by the Sixth Amendment. Through the Fourteenth Amendment that requirement has now been imposed upon the States 'in all criminal cases which—were they to be tried in a federal court—would come within the Sixth Amendment's guarantee.' This is because the Court has said it believes 'that trial by jury in criminal cases is fundamental to the American scheme of justice.' . . .

This, of course, does not automatically provide the answer to the present jury trial issue, if for no other reason than that the juvenile court proceeding has not yet been held to be a 'criminal prosecution,' within the meaning and reach of the Sixth Amendment, and also has not yet been regarded as devoid of criminal aspects merely because it usually has been given the civil label.

. . .

Thus, accepting 'the proposition that the Due Process Clause has a role to play,' our task here with respect to trial by jury, as it was in *Gault* with respect to other claimed rights, 'is to ascertain the precise impact of the due process requirement.'

### V

The Pennsylvania juveniles' basic argument is that they were tried in proceedings 'substantially similar to a criminal trial.' They say that a delinquency proceeding in their State is initiated by a petition charging a penal code violation in the conclusory language of an indictment; that a juvenile detained prior to trial is held in a building substantially similar to an adult prison; that in Philadelphia juveniles over 16 are, in fact, held in the cells of a prison; that counsel and the prosecution engage in plea bargaining; that motions to suppress are routinely heard and decided; that the usual rules of evidence are applied; that the customary common-law defenses are available; that the press is generally admitted in the Philadelphia juvenile courtrooms; that members of the public enter the room; that arrest and prior record may be reported by the press (from police sources, however, rather than from the juvenile court records); that, once adjudged delinquent, a juvenile may be confined until his majority in what amounts to a prison (see *In re Bethea*, 215 Pa.Super. 75, 76, 257 A.2d 368, 369 (1969), describing the state correctional institution at Camp Hill as a 'maximum security prison for adjudged delinquents and youthful criminal offenders'); and that the stigma attached upon delinquency adjudication approximates that resulting from conviction in an adult criminal proceeding.

The North Carolina juveniles particularly urge . . .jury trials in juvenile courts are manageable; that no reason exists why protection traditionally accorded in criminal proceedings should be denied young people subject to involuntary incarceration for lengthy periods; and that the juvenile courts deserve healthy public scrutiny.

### VI

All the litigants here agree that the applicable due process standard in juvenile proceedings, as developed by *Gault* and *Winship*, is fundamental fairness. . . . we conclude that trial by jury in the juvenile court's adjudicative stage is not a constitutional requirement. We so conclude for a number of reasons:

1.   The Court has refrained, in the cases heretofore decided, from taking the easy way with a flat holding that all rights constitutionally assured for the adult accused are to be imposed upon the state juvenile proceeding. . . .

2.     There is a possibility, at least, that the jury trial, if required as a matter of constitutional precept, will remake the juvenile proceeding into a fully adversary process and will put an effective end to what has been the idealistic prospect of an intimate, informal protective proceeding.

. . .

4.     The Court specifically has recognized by dictum that a jury is not a necessary part even of every criminal process that is fair and equitable. . . .

5.     The imposition of the jury trial on the juvenile court system would not strengthen greatly, if at all, the fact-finding function, and would, contrarily, provide an attrition of the juvenile court's assumed ability to function in a unique manner. . . .

8.     There is, of course, nothing to prevent a juvenile court judge, in a particular case where he feels the need, or when the need is demonstrated, from using an advisory jury.

. . .

10.   Since *Gault* and since *Duncan* the great majority of States, in addition to Pennsylvania and North Carolina, that have faced the issue have concluded that the considerations that led to the result in those two cases do not compel trial by jury in the juvenile court. . . .

. . .

12.   If the jury trial were to be injected into the juvenile court system as a matter of right, it would bring with it into that system the traditional delay, the formality, and the clamor of the adversary system and, possibly, the public trial. . . .

**Affirmed. . . .**

**After preparing the case brief, consider the answers to the following questions:**

1.     Describe some of Due Process rights that the Court has applied to juvenile adjudications over the years.

2.     How is the right to a jury trial different than those earlier applied rights?

3.     Do you agree with the Court that to afford juveniles the right to a jury trial might put an end to the juvenile adjudication process by making it too similar to adult criminal trials?

# McGirt v. Oklahoma

Supreme Court of the United States
Argued May 11, 2020
Decided July 9, 2020
140 S.Ct. 2452

**JUSTICE GORSUCH delivered the opinion of the Court.**

On the far end of the Trail of Tears was a promise. Forced to leave their ancestral lands in Georgia and Alabama, the Creek Nation received assurances that their new lands in the West would be secure forever. In exchange for ceding "all their land, East of the Mississippi river," the U.S. government agreed by treaty that "[t]he Creek country west of the Mississippi shall be solemnly guarantied to the Creek Indians." Treaty With the Creeks (1832 Treaty). Both parties settled on boundary lines for a new and "permanent home to the whole Creek nation," located in what is now Oklahoma. Treaty With the Creeks (1833 Treaty). The government further promised that "[no] State or Territory [shall] ever have a right to pass laws for the government of such Indians, but they shall be allowed to govern themselves."

Today we are asked whether the land these treaties promised remains an Indian reservation for purposes of federal criminal law. Because Congress has not said otherwise, we hold the government to its word.

I

At one level, the question before us concerns Jimcy McGirt. Years ago, an Oklahoma state court convicted him of three serious sexual offenses. Since then, he has argued in postconviction proceedings that the State lacked jurisdiction to prosecute him because he is an enrolled member of the Seminole Nation of Oklahoma and his crimes took place on the Creek Reservation. A new trial for his conduct, he has contended, must take place in federal court. The Oklahoma state courts hearing Mr. McGirt's arguments rejected them, so he now brings them here.

Mr. McGirt's appeal rests on the federal Major Crimes Act (MCA). The statute provides that, within "the Indian country," "[a]ny Indian who commits" certain enumerated offenses "against the person or property of another Indian or any other person" "shall be subject to the same law and penalties as all other persons committing any of the above offenses, within the exclusive jurisdiction of the United States." By subjecting Indians to federal trials for crimes committed on tribal lands, Congress may have breached its promises to tribes like the Creek that they would be free to govern themselves. But this particular incursion has its limits—applying only to certain enumerated crimes and allowing only the federal government to try Indians. State courts generally have no jurisdiction to try Indians for conduct committed in "Indian country."

The key question Mr. McGirt faces concerns that last qualification: Did he commit his crimes in Indian country? A neighboring provision of the MCA defines the term to include, among other things, "all land within the limits of any Indian reservation under the jurisdiction of the United States Government, notwithstanding the issuance of any patent, and, including rights-of-way running through the reservation." Mr. McGirt submits he can satisfy this condition because he committed his crimes on land reserved for the Creek since the 19th century.

The Creek Nation has joined Mr. McGirt as *amicus curiae*. Not because the Tribe is interested in shielding Mr. McGirt from responsibility for his crimes. Instead, the Creek Nation participates because Mr. McGirt's personal interests wind up implicating the Tribe's. No one disputes that Mr. McGirt's crimes were committed on lands described as the Creek Reservation in an 1866 treaty and federal statute. But, in seeking to defend the state-court judgment below, Oklahoma has put aside whatever procedural defenses it might have and asked us to confirm that the land once given to the Creeks is no longer a reservation today.

At another level, then, Mr. McGirt's case winds up as a contest between State and Tribe. The scope of their dispute is limited; nothing we might say today could unsettle Oklahoma's authority to try non-Indians for crimes against non-Indians on the lands in question. Still, the stakes are not insignificant. If Mr. McGirt and the Tribe are right, the State has no right to prosecute Indians for crimes committed in a portion of Northeastern Oklahoma that includes most of the city of Tulsa. Responsibility to try these matters would fall instead to the federal government and Tribe. Recently, the question has taken on more salience too. While Oklahoma state courts have rejected any suggestion that the lands in question remain a reservation, the Tenth Circuit has reached the opposite conclusion. We granted certiorari to settle the question.

II

Start with what should be obvious: Congress established a reservation for the Creeks. In a series of treaties, Congress not only "solemnly guarantied" the land but also "establish[ed] boundary lines which will secure a country and permanent home to the whole Creek Nation of Indians." The government's promises weren't made gratuitously. Rather, the 1832 Treaty acknowledged that "[t]he United States are desirous that the Creeks should remove to the country west of the Mississippi" and, in service of that goal, required the Creeks to cede all lands in the East. Nor were the government's promises meant to be delusory. Congress twice assured the Creeks that "[the] Treaty shall be obligatory on the contracting parties, as soon as the same shall be ratified by the United States." Both treaties were duly ratified and enacted as law.

Because the Tribe's move west was ostensibly voluntary, Congress held out another assurance as well. In the statute that precipitated these negotiations, Congress authorized the President "to assure the tribe . . . that the United States will forever secure and guaranty to them . . . the country so exchanged with them." Indian Removal Act of 1830, § 3, 4 Stat. 412. "[A]nd if they prefer it," the bill continued, "the United States will cause a patent or grant to be made and executed to them for the same; *Provided always*, that such lands shall revert to the United States, if the Indians become extinct, or abandon the same." If agreeable to all sides, a tribe would not only enjoy the government's solemn treaty promises; it would hold legal title to its lands.

It was an offer the Creek accepted. The 1833 Treaty fixed borders for what was to be a "permanent home to the whole Creek nation of Indians." It also established that the "United States will grant a patent, in fee simple, to the Creek nation of Indians for the land assigned said nation by this treaty." That grant came with the caveat that "the right thus guaranteed by the United States shall be continued to said tribe of Indians, so long as they shall exist as a nation, and continue to occupy the country hereby assigned to them." The promised patent formally issued in 1852.

These early treaties did not refer to the Creek lands as a "reservation"— perhaps because that word had not yet acquired such distinctive significance in federal Indian law. But we have found similar language in treaties from the same era sufficient to create a reservation. And later Acts of Congress left no room for doubt. . . .

There is a final set of assurances that bear mention, too. In the Treaty of 1856, Congress promised that "no portion" of the Creek Reservation "shall ever be embraced or included within, or annexed to, any Territory or State." And within their lands, with exceptions, the Creeks were to be "secured in the unrestricted right of self-government," with "full jurisdiction" over enrolled Tribe members and their property. So the Creek were promised not only a "permanent home" that would be "forever set apart"; they were also assured a right to self-government on lands that would lie outside both the legal jurisdiction and geographic boundaries of any State. Under any definition, this was a reservation.

III

A

While there can be no question that Congress established a reservation for the Creek Nation, it's equally clear that Congress has since broken more than a few of its promises to the Tribe. Not least, the land described in the parties' treaties, once undivided and held by the Tribe, is now fractured into pieces. While these pieces were initially distributed to Tribe members, many were sold and now belong to persons unaffiliated with the Nation. So in what sense, if any, can we say that the Creek Reservation persists today?

To determine whether a tribe continues to hold a reservation, there is only one place we may look: the Acts of Congress. This Court long ago held that the Legislature wields significant constitutional authority when it comes to tribal relations, possessing even the authority to breach its own promises and treaties. But that power, this Court has cautioned, belongs to Congress alone. Nor will this Court lightly infer such a breach once Congress has established a reservation.

Under our Constitution, States have no authority to reduce federal reservations lying within their borders. Just imagine if they did. A State could encroach on the tribal boundaries or legal rights Congress provided, and, with enough time and patience, nullify the promises made in the name of the United States. That would be at odds with the Constitution, which entrusts Congress with the authority to regulate commerce with Native Americans, and directs that federal treaties and statutes are the "supreme Law of the Land." It would also leave tribal rights in the hands of the very neighbors who might be least inclined to respect them.

Likewise, courts have no proper role in the adjustment of reservation borders. Mustering the broad social consensus required to pass new legislation is a deliberately hard business under our Constitution. Faced with this daunting task, Congress sometimes might wish an inconvenient reservation would simply disappear. Short of that, legislators might seek to pass laws that tiptoe to the edge of disestablishment and hope that judges—facing no possibility of electoral consequences themselves—will deliver the final push. But wishes don't make for laws, and saving the political branches the embarrassment of disestablishing a reservation is not one of our constitutionally assigned prerogatives. "[O]nly Congress can divest a reservation of its land and diminish its boundaries." So it's no matter how many other promises to a tribe the federal government has already broken. If Congress wishes to break the promise of a reservation, it must say so. . . .

B

In an effort to show Congress has done just that with the Creek Reservation, Oklahoma points to events during the so-called "allotment era." Starting in the 1880s, Congress sought to pressure many tribes to abandon their communal lifestyles and parcel their lands into smaller lots owned by individual tribe members. Some allotment advocates hoped that the policy would create a class of assimilated, landowning, agrarian Native Americans. Others may have hoped that, with lands in individual hands and (eventually) freely alienable, white settlers would have more space of their own.

. . .

The Commission's work culminated in an allotment agreement with the Tribe in 1901. With exceptions for certain pre-existing town sites and other special matters, the Agreement established procedures for allotting 160-acre parcels to individual Tribe members who could not sell, transfer, or otherwise encumber their allotments for a number of years. Tribe members were given deeds for their parcels that "convey[ed] to [them] all right, title, and interest of the Creek Nation." . . . One way or the other, individual Tribe members were eventually free to sell their land to Indians and non-Indians alike.

Missing in all this, however, is a statute evincing anything like the "present and total surrender of all tribal interests" in the affected lands. . . .

Oklahoma reminds us that allotment was often the first step in a plan ultimately aimed at disestablishment. As this Court explained in *Mattz*, Congress's expressed policy at the time "was to continue the reservation system and the trust status of Indian lands, but to allot tracts to individual Indians for agriculture and grazing." Then, "[w]hen all the lands had been allotted and the trust expired, the reservation could be abolished." This plan was set in motion nationally in the General Allotment Act of 1887, and for the Creek specifically in 1901. No doubt, this is why Congress at the turn of the 20th century "believed to a man" that "the reservation system would cease" "within a generation at most." Still, just as wishes are not laws, future plans aren't either. Congress may have passed allotment laws to create the conditions for disestablishment. But to equate allotment with disestablishment would confuse the first step of a march with arrival at its destination. . . .

C

If allotment by itself won't work, Oklahoma seeks to prove disestablishment by pointing to other ways Congress intruded on the Creek's promised right to self-governance during the allotment era. It turns out there were many. For example, just a few years before the 1901 Creek Allotment Agreement, and perhaps in an effort to pressure the Tribe to the negotiating table, Congress abolished the Creeks' tribal courts and transferred all pending civil and criminal cases to the U.S. Courts of the Indian Territory. Separately, the Creek Allotment Agreement provided that tribal ordinances "affecting the lands of the Tribe, or of individuals after allotment, or the moneys or other property of the Tribe, or of the citizens thereof " would not be valid until approved by the President of the United States.

Plainly, these laws represented serious blows to the Creek. But, just as plainly, they left the Tribe with significant sovereign functions over the lands in question. For example, the Creek Nation retained the power to collect taxes, operate schools, legislate through tribal ordinances, and, soon, oversee the federally mandated allotment process. And, in its own way, the congressional incursion on tribal legislative processes only served to prove the power: Congress would have had no need to subject tribal legislation to Presidential review if the Tribe lacked any authority to legislate. Grave though they were, these congressional intrusions on pre-existing treaty rights fell short of eliminating all tribal interests in the land.

Much more ominously, the 1901 allotment agreement ended by announcing that the Creek tribal government "shall not continue" past 1906, although the agreement quickly qualified that statement, adding the proviso "subject to such further legislation as Congress may deem proper." Thus, while suggesting that the tribal government *might* end in 1906, Congress also necessarily understood it had not ended in 1901. All of which was consistent with the Legislature's general practice of taking allotment as a first, not final, step toward disestablishment and dissolution.

When 1906 finally arrived, Congress adopted the Five Civilized Tribes Act. But instead of dissolving the tribal government as some may have expected, Congress "deem[ed] proper" a different course, simply cutting away further at the Tribe's autonomy. Congress empowered the President to remove and replace the principal chief of the Creek, prohibited the tribal council from meeting more than 30 days a year, and directed the Secretary of the Interior to assume control of tribal schools. The Act also provided for the handling of the

Tribe's funds, land, and legal liabilities in the event of dissolution. Despite these additional incursions on tribal authority, however, Congress expressly recognized the Creek's "tribal existence and present tribal governmen[t]" and "continued [them] in full force and effect for all purposes authorized by law."

In the years that followed, Congress continued to adjust its arrangements with the Tribe. . . . But Congress never withdrew its recognition of the tribal government, and none of its adjustments would have made any sense if Congress thought it had already completed that job.

Indeed, with time, Congress changed course completely. Beginning in the 1920s, the federal outlook toward Native Americans shifted "away from assimilation policies and toward more tolerance and respect for traditional aspects of Indian culture." . . . Pursuant to this new national policy, in 1936, Congress authorized the Creek to adopt a constitution and bylaws, enabling the Creek government to resume many of its previously suspended functions.

The Creek Nation has done exactly that. In the intervening years, it has ratified a new constitution and established three separate branches of government. Today the Nation is led by a democratically elected Principal Chief, Second Chief, and National Council; operates a police force and three hospitals; commands an annual budget of more than $350 million; and employs over 2,000 people. In 1982, the Nation passed an ordinance reestablishing the criminal and civil jurisdiction of its courts. The territorial jurisdiction of these courts extends to any Indian country within the Tribe's territory as defined by the Treaty of 1866. And the State of Oklahoma has afforded full faith and credit to its judgments since at least 1994.

Maybe some of these changes happened for altruistic reasons, maybe some for other reasons. It seems, for example, that at least certain Members of Congress hesitated about disestablishment in 1906 because they feared any reversion of the Creek lands to the public domain would trigger a statutory commitment to hand over portions of these lands to already powerful railroad interests. Many of those who advanced the reorganization efforts of the 1930s may have done so more out of frustration with efforts to assimilate Native Americans than any disaffection with assimilation as the ultimate goal. But whatever the confluence of reasons, in all this history there simply arrived no moment when any Act of Congress dissolved the Creek Tribe or disestablished its reservation. In the end, Congress moved in the opposite direction. . . .

The dissent charges that we have failed to take account of the "compelling reasons" for considering extratextual evidence as a matter of course. But

Oklahoma and the dissent have cited no case in which this Court has found a reservation disestablished without first concluding that a statute required that result. Perhaps they wish this case to be the first. To follow Oklahoma and the dissent down that path, though, would only serve to allow States and courts to finish work Congress has left undone, usurp the legislative function in the process, and treat Native American claims of statutory right as less valuable than others. None of that can be reconciled with our normal interpretive rules, let alone our rule that disestablishment may not be lightly inferred and treaty rights are to be construed in favor, not against, tribal rights.

. . .

In the end, only one message rings true. Even the carefully selected history Oklahoma and the dissent recite is not nearly as tidy as they suggest. It supplies us with little help in discerning the law's meaning and much potential for mischief. If anything, the persistent if unspoken message here seems to be that we should be taken by the "practical advantages" of ignoring the written law. How much easier it would be, after all, to let the State proceed as it has always assumed it might. But just imagine what it would mean to indulge that path. A State exercises jurisdiction over Native Americans with such persistence that the practice seems normal. Indian landowners lose their titles by fraud or otherwise in sufficient volume that no one remembers whose land it once was. All this continues for long enough that a reservation that was once beyond doubt becomes questionable, and then even farfetched. Sprinkle in a few predictions here, some contestable commentary there, and the job is done, a reservation is disestablished. None of these moves would be permitted in any other area of statutory interpretation, and there is no reason why they should be permitted here. That would be the rule of the strong, not the rule of law.

. . .

## V

That leaves Oklahoma to attempt yet another argument in the alternative. . . .Now, the State accepts for argument's sake that the Creek land is a reservation and thus "Indian country" for purposes of the Major Crimes Act. It accepts, too, that this would normally mean serious crimes by Indians on the Creek Reservation would have to be tried in federal court. But, the State tells us, none of that matters; everything the parties have briefed and argued so far is beside the point. It's all irrelevant because it turns out the MCA just doesn't apply to the eastern half of Oklahoma, and it never has. That federal law may apply to other States, even to the western half of Oklahoma itself. But eastern Oklahoma is and has always been exempt. So whether or not the Creek have a reservation, the State's historic practices have always been correct and it remains free to try individuals like Mr. McGirt in its own courts.

. . . In support of its argument, Oklahoma points to statutory artifacts from its territorial history. The State of Oklahoma was formed from two territories: the Oklahoma Territory in the west and Indian Territory in the east. Originally, it seems criminal prosecutions in the Indian Territory were split between tribal and federal courts. But, in 1897, Congress abolished that scheme, granting the U.S. Courts of the Indian Territory "exclusive jurisdiction" to try "all criminal causes for the punishment of any offense." These federal territorial courts applied federal law and state law borrowed from Arkansas "to all persons . . . irrespective of race." A year later, Congress abolished tribal courts and transferred all pending criminal cases to U.S. courts of the Indian Territory. And, Oklahoma says, sending Indians to federal court and all others to state court would be inconsistent with this established and enlightened policy of applying the same law in the same courts to everyone.

Here again, however, arguments along these and similar lines have been "frequently raised" but rarely "accepted." "The policy of leaving Indians free from state jurisdiction and control is deeply rooted in this Nation's history." Chief Justice Marshall, for example, held that Indian Tribes were "distinct political communities, having territorial boundaries, within which their authority is exclusive . . . which is not only acknowledged, but guarantied by the United States," a power dependent on and subject to no state authority. And in many treaties, like those now before us, the federal government promised Indian Tribes the right to continue to govern themselves. For all these reasons, this Court has long "require[d] a clear expression of the intention of Congress" before the state or federal government may try Indians for conduct on their lands.

Oklahoma cannot come close to satisfying this standard. In fact, the only law that speaks expressly here speaks *against* the State. When Oklahoma won statehood in 1907, the MCA applied immediately according to its plain terms. That statute, as phrased at the time, provided exclusive federal jurisdiction over qualifying crimes by Indians in *"any Indian reservation"* located within "the boundaries of *any State*." By contrast, every one of the statutes the State directs us to merely discusses the assignment of cases among courts in the *Indian Territory*. They say nothing about the division of responsibilities between federal and state authorities after Oklahoma entered the Union. And however enlightened the State may think it was for territorial law to apply to all persons irrespective of race, some Tribe members may see things differently, given that the same policy entailed the forcible closure of tribal courts in defiance of treaty terms.

. . .

With time, too, Congress has filled many of the gaps Oklahoma worries about. One way Congress has done so is by reauthorizing tribal courts to hear minor crimes in Indian country. Congress chose exactly this course for the Creeks and others in 1936. Another option Congress has employed is to allow affected Indian tribes to consent to state criminal jurisdiction. Finally, Congress has sometimes expressly expanded state criminal jurisdiction in targeted bills addressing specific States. But Oklahoma doesn't claim to have complied with the requirements to assume jurisdiction voluntarily over Creek lands. Nor has Congress ever passed a law conferring jurisdiction on Oklahoma. As a result, the MCA applies to Oklahoma according to its usual terms: Only the federal government, not the State, may prosecute Indians for major crimes committed in Indian country.

VI

In the end, Oklahoma abandons any pretense of law and speaks openly about the potentially "transform[ative]" effects of a loss today. Here, at least, the State is finally rejoined by the dissent. If we dared to recognize that the Creek Reservation was never disestablished, Oklahoma and dissent warn, our holding might be used by other tribes to vindicate similar treaty promises. Ultimately, Oklahoma fears that perhaps as much as half its land and roughly 1.8 million of its residents could wind up within Indian country.

It's hard to know what to make of this self-defeating argument. Each tribe's treaties must be considered on their own terms, and the only question before us concerns the Creek. Of course, the Creek Reservation alone is hardly insignificant, taking in most of Tulsa and certain neighboring communities in Northeastern Oklahoma. But neither is it unheard of for significant non-Indian populations to live successfully in or near reservations today. Oklahoma replies that its situation is different because the affected population here is large and many of its residents will be surprised to find out they have been living in Indian country this whole time. But we imagine some members of the 1832 Creek Tribe would be just as surprised to find them there.

What are the consequences the State and dissent worry might follow from an adverse ruling anyway? Primarily, they argue that recognizing the continued existence of the Creek Reservation could unsettle an untold number of convictions and frustrate the State's ability to prosecute crimes in the future. But the MCA applies only to certain crimes committed in Indian country by Indian defendants. A neighboring statute provides that federal law applies to a broader range of crimes by or against Indians in Indian country. States are otherwise free to apply their criminal laws in cases of non-Indian victims and defendants, including within Indian country. And Oklahoma tells us that somewhere between 10% and 15% of its citizens identify as Native American. Given all this, even Oklahoma admits that the vast majority of its prosecutions will be unaffected whatever we decide today.

Still, Oklahoma and the dissent fear, "[t]housands" of Native Americans like Mr. McGirt "wait in the wings" to challenge the jurisdictional basis of their state-court convictions. But this number is admittedly speculative, because many defendants may choose to finish their state sentences rather than risk reprosecution in federal court where sentences can be graver. Other defendants who do try to challenge their state convictions may face significant procedural obstacles, thanks to well-known state and federal limitations on postconviction review in criminal proceedings.

In any event, the magnitude of a legal wrong is no reason to perpetuate it. When Congress adopted the MCA, it broke many treaty promises that had once allowed tribes like the Creek to try their own members. But, in return, Congress allowed only the federal government, not the States, to try tribal members for major crimes. All our decision today does is vindicate that replacement promise. And if the threat of unsettling convictions cannot save a precedent of this Court, it certainly cannot force us to ignore a statutory promise when no precedent stands before us at all.

What's more, a decision for *either* party today risks upsetting some convictions. Accepting the State's argument that the MCA never applied in Oklahoma would preserve the state-court convictions of people like Mr. McGirt, but simultaneously call into question every *federal* conviction obtained for crimes committed on trust lands and restricted Indian allotments since Oklahoma recognized its jurisdictional error more than 30 years ago. It's a consequence of their own arguments that Oklahoma and the dissent choose to ignore, but one which cannot help but illustrate the difficulty of trying to guess how a ruling one way or the other might affect past cases rather than simply proceeding to apply the law as written.

Looking to the future, Oklahoma warns of the burdens federal and tribal courts will experience with a wider jurisdiction and increased caseload. But, again, for every jurisdictional reaction there seems to be an opposite reaction:

recognizing that cases like Mr. McGirt's belong in federal court simultaneously takes them out of state court. So while the federal prosecutors might be initially understaffed and Oklahoma prosecutors initially overstaffed, it doesn't take a lot of imagination to see how things could work out in the end.

Finally, the State worries that our decision will have significant consequences for civil and regulatory law. The only question before us, however, concerns the statutory definition of "Indian country" as it applies in federal criminal law under the MCA, and often nothing requires other civil statutes or regulations to rely on definitions found in the criminal law.

. . . More importantly, dire warnings are just that, and not a license for us to disregard the law. By suggesting that our interpretation of Acts of Congress adopted a century ago should be inflected based on the costs of enforcing them today, the dissent tips its hand. Yet again, the point of looking at subsequent developments seems not to be determining the meaning of the laws Congress wrote in 1901 or 1906, but emphasizing the costs of taking them at their word.

. . . In reaching our conclusion about what the law demands of us today, we do not pretend to foretell the future and we proceed well aware of the potential for cost and conflict around jurisdictional boundaries, especially ones that have gone unappreciated for so long. But it is unclear why pessimism should rule the day. With the passage of time, Oklahoma and its Tribes have proven they can work successfully together as partners. Already, the State has negotiated hundreds of intergovernmental agreements with tribes, including many with the Creek. These agreements relate to taxation, law enforcement, vehicle registration, hunting and fishing, and countless other fine regulatory questions. No one before us claims that the spirit of good faith, "comity and cooperative sovereignty" behind these agreements will be imperiled by an adverse decision for the State today any more than it might be by a favorable one. And, of course, should agreement prove elusive, Congress remains free to supplement its statutory directions about the lands in question at any time. It has no shortage of tools at its disposal.

*

The federal government promised the Creek a reservation in perpetuity. Over time, Congress has diminished that reservation. It has sometimes restricted and other times expanded the Tribe's authority. But Congress has never withdrawn the promised reservation. As a result, many of the arguments before us today follow a sadly familiar pattern. Yes, promises were made, but the price of keeping them has become too great, so now we should just cast a blind eye. We reject that thinking. If Congress wishes to withdraw its promises, it must say so. Unlawful acts, performed long enough and with sufficient vigor, are never enough to amend the law. To hold otherwise would be to elevate the most brazen and longstanding injustices over the law, both rewarding wrong and failing those in the right.

The judgment of the Court of Criminal Appeals of Oklahoma is

*Reversed.*

CHIEF JUSTICE ROBERTS, with whom JUSTICE ALITO and JUSTICE KAVANAUGH join, and with whom JUSTICE THOMAS joins except as to footnote 9, dissenting.

In 1997, the State of Oklahoma convicted petitioner Jimcy McGirt of molesting, raping, and forcibly sodomizing a four-year-old girl, his wife's granddaughter. McGirt was sentenced to 1,000 years plus life in prison. Today, the Court holds that Oklahoma lacked jurisdiction to prosecute McGirt—on the improbable ground that, unbeknownst to anyone for the past century, a huge swathe of Oklahoma is actually a Creek Indian reservation, on which the State may not prosecute serious crimes committed by Indians like McGirt. Not only does the Court discover a Creek reservation that spans three million acres and includes most of the city of Tulsa, but the Court's reasoning portends that there are four more such reservations in Oklahoma. The rediscovered reservations encompass the entire eastern half of the State—19 million acres that are home to 1.8 million people, only 10%–15% of whom are Indians.

Across this vast area, the State's ability to prosecute serious crimes will be hobbled and decades of past convictions could well be thrown out. On top of that, the Court has profoundly destabilized the governance of eastern Oklahoma. The decision today creates significant uncertainty for the State's continuing authority over any area that touches Indian affairs, ranging from zoning and taxation to family and environmental law.

None of this is warranted. What has gone unquestioned for a century remains true today: A huge portion of Oklahoma is not a Creek Indian reservation. Congress disestablished any reservation in a series of statutes leading up to Oklahoma statehood at the turn of the 19th century. The Court reaches the opposite conclusion only by disregarding the "well settled" approach required by our precedents.

Under those precedents, we determine whether Congress intended to disestablish a reservation by examining the relevant Acts of Congress and "all the [surrounding] circumstances," including the "contemporaneous and subsequent understanding of the status of the reservation." Yet the Court declines to consider such understandings here, preferring to examine only individual statutes in isolation.

Applying the broader inquiry our precedents require, a reservation did not exist when McGirt committed his crimes, so Oklahoma had jurisdiction to prosecute him. I respectfully dissent. . . .

**After preparing the case brief, consider the answers to the following questions:**

1. Why was McGirt appealing his conviction in Oklahoma state court?

2. Do you agree that crimes committed in Indian Territory or on tribal land should fall under the jurisdiction of the tribes and the federal government?

3. What are some of the potential pitfalls of eliminating state court jurisdiction for crimes that take place on tribal land?

4. Do you agree with the Court's decision? How should Indian tribes—which are sovereign nations—exist within the legal framework of American states?

## Chapter 13 Key Terms for Review

- **Collaborative courts**: specialized courts working in partnership with other agencies and organizations to achieve solutions to social problems such as drug use and homelessness.

- **Drug treatment courts**: collaborative courts tasked with assisting drug offenders in successfully completing drug-treatment programs in lieu of serving jail or prison sentences.

- **Juvenile courts**: the forum for adjudication of acts by minor children for offenses which would be criminal if committed by adults.

- **Rebuttable presumption**: children under the age of seven years are presumed incapable of forming the mens rea necessary for conviction of a crime.

- **Parens patriae**: Latin translated literally "the state as parent" is the doctrine which laid the foundation for the establishment of juvenile courts.

- **Progressives**: reformers in the late 1800's who advocated for children who were subjected to child labor and horrible conditions in "reform schools" prior to the existence of the juvenile courts.

- **Illinois Juvenile Court Act**: the first state legislation establishing a juvenile court in the United States.

- **Adjudication**: the determination of delinquency by the juvenile court.

- **Delinquency**: analogous to an adult conviction, a juvenile who is found guilty of violating a criminal law is adjudicated delinquent.

- **Residential placement**: juveniles are not sentenced to prison; rather they are subject to residential placement.

- **Juvenile dependency**: cases where the child is a victim in need of court supervision and support as a result of child neglect, abuse or abandonment.

- **Summons**: authorizes the arrest of a juvenile and requires them to appear in court.

- **Petition**: the allegation that a juvenile is delinquent for violation of the law.

- **Conference**: after the petition is filed, the conference provides the juvenile with information about his rights and a disposition decision may be reached.

- **Adjudicatory hearing**: if the juvenile does not admit guilt and the case progresses, an adjudicatory hearing is held where the judge will determine whether the juvenile is guilty or not of the delinquent acts alleged.

- *In re Gault (1967)*: landmark U.S. Supreme Court decision providing juvenile offenders with substantial rights in delinquency proceedings such as the right to notice of charges, the right to counsel, confrontation and cross-examination of witnesses, and the privilege against self-incrimination.

- **Disposition**: formal findings regarding the court's decision about what will happen to the juvenile offender.

- **Waive jurisdiction**: the juvenile court may waive jurisdiction and transfer a juvenile offender to adult court for criminal proceedings under certain circumstances in some states.

- **Waiver hearing**: a juvenile court judge hears evidence about the juvenile to determine whether he is fit for adjudication in the juvenile courts; if not, he will be transferred to adult court.

- **Prosecutorial waiver**: in some jurisdictions the prosecutor can "direct-file" certain very serious criminal charges in adult court against juvenile offenders without a waiver hearing.

- **Blended sentencing**: even when a juvenile is waived to adult court some jurisdictions allow judges to impose a blend of juvenile and adult sanctions for juvenile offenders.

- **Courts of Military Justice**: under the Department of Defense, the Courts of Military Justice enforce the Uniform Code of Military Justice (UCMJ).

- **Court martial**: a criminal case against a member of the United States Military.

- **Judge advocate general**: attorney member of Armed Forces who serves as defense counsel in courts of military justice.

- **Trial counsel**: a military prosecutor.

- **Doctrine of separate or dual sovereigns**: allows a service member who is tried in a civilian criminal court, whether a state or foreign court, to also be tried in a military court martial for the same incident.

- **Tribal courts**: maintain and promote tribal sovereignty for the 562 federally recognized Indian tribes in the United States.

- **Public Law 280**: gives the state concurrent jurisdiction with the tribal court over crimes occurring on Indian reservations in states subject to the law.

- **Indian Civil Rights Act**: requires tribal courts to adhere to most, but not all, of the provisions of the Bill of Rights enjoyed by defendants in American courts. Violations of the ICRA can only be challenged in habeas proceedings.

- **Tribal sovereign immunity**: protects tribes and tribal entities from being sued in any court (even their own tribal courts) unless the tribe has waived immunity.

# Index